THE ULTIMATE SHIPWRECK GUIDE

THE ULTIMATE SHIPWRECK GUIDE

WHITBY TO BERWICK

Ron Young

Whittles Publishing

Published by
Whittles Publishing,
Dunbeath,
Caithness KW6 6EG,
Scotland, UK

www.whittlespublishing.com

ISBN 978-1904445-89-0

Printed by 4edge Limited, UK

CONTENTS

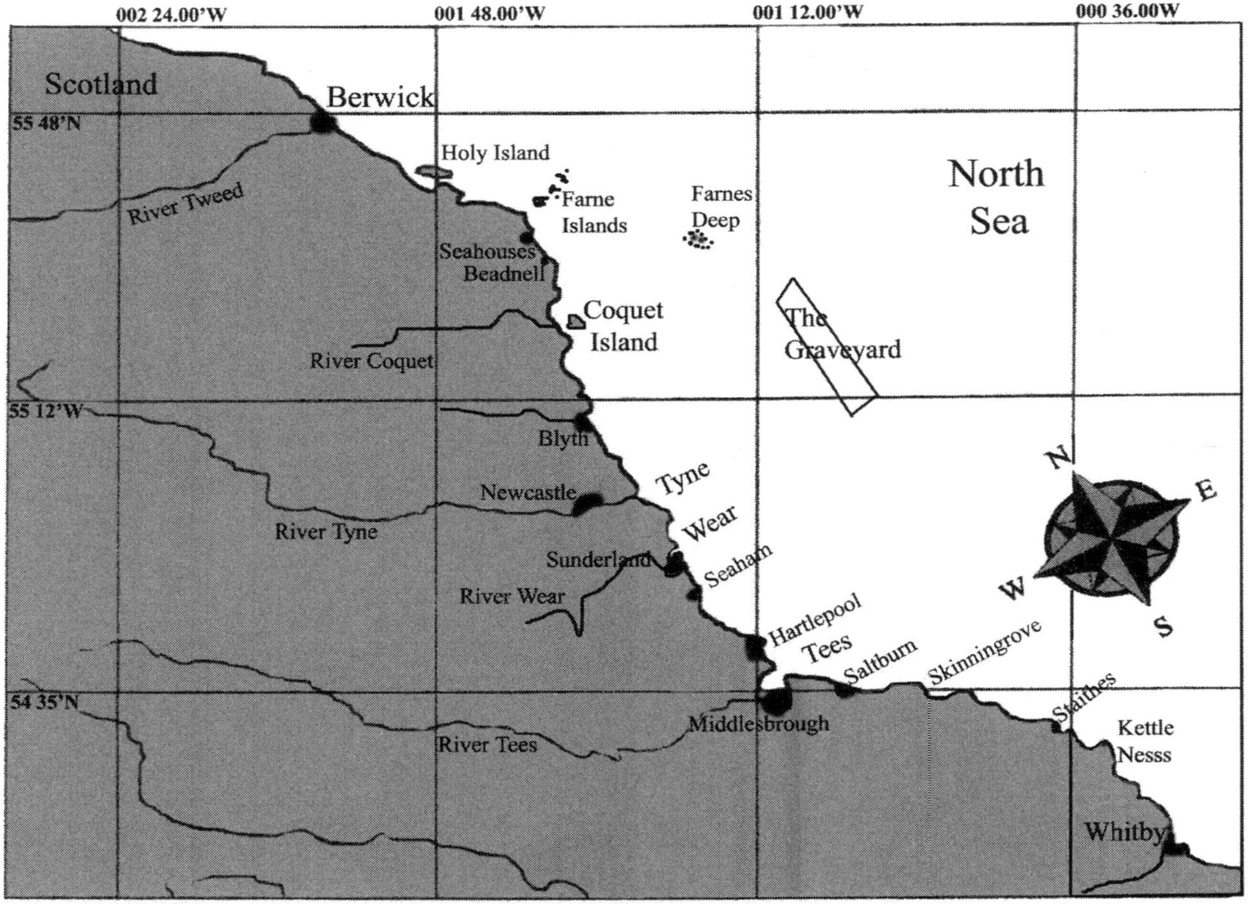
002 24.00'W
001 48.00'W
001 12.00'W
000 36.00W
55 48'N
55 12'W
54 35'N
Scotland
Berwick
River Tweed
Holy Island
Farne Islands
Farnes Deep
North Sea
Seahouses
Beadnell
Coquet Island
The Graveyard
River Coquet
Blyth
Tyne
Newcastle
River Tyne
Wear
Sunderland
Seaham
River Wear
Hartlepool
Tees
Saltburn
Skinningrove
Middlesbrough
River Tees
Staithes
Kettle Nesss
Whitby
N
E
W
S

PREFACE

About ten years ago I had two books published on shipwrecks along the north-east coast from Whitby to Berwick. Both of these were written just using a font-writer, as I had no computer or access to the Internet. To gather the information I required, I wrote letters to museums, libraries, archive holders and individuals trying to acquire data about certain vessels. I frequently had to wait weeks, or even months for replies, but very often none were forthcoming which was very frustrating. The books were aimed mainly at the diving fraternity and boat-anglers and, thankfully, I know that many divers and fishermen have found them useful. However, much to my amazement, lots of other folk had purchased the books, with some individuals even contacting me personally in the hope of finding out about family friends and relatives who had sailed on the ships, or were drowned or killed.

Up to about the turn of the 21st century, the majority of sport divers were visiting wrecks up to the 50-metres range, so those two wreck books served their purpose and there seemed little point in including wrecks in much deeper water. However, times have now changed dramatically.

Ten years is really just a blip in time, but over the last decade, digital technology has advanced in leaps and bounds, and so much so that most people have difficulty in keeping up with it. What is top-of-the-range today is sometimes old-dated within a matter of months. These days, with the help of re-breathers and mixed gasses, divers are reaching depths undreamed of a few years ago, and both fishermen and divers are willing to travel much further out to sea than ever before – their quest being those large and untouched wrecks that teem with marine life.

Since I wrote those first two volumes I have been unable to do very much other than write and read. Travel has been difficult due to immobility caused by health problems, so my PC has become a way of life for me and keeps me sane. The world wide web and new found friends have helped me to amass a huge database about ships and wrecks.

I never forgot about all those queries from those asking about friends and relatives, so I made a point of collecting records from various sources and in doing so, have been able to acquire lists of all of the crewmen in the Merchant and Royal Navy, who were lost, especially those during the Great War and thus formed what has become *The Ultimate Shipwreck Guide*. No other single publication has ever been written with so much information about the shipwrecks and crews that were lost, over this huge region of the North Sea, between Whitby and Berwick and up to about 40 miles offshore; making this a cut-above the others. There are 286 wrecks in total, including 22, located in an area known ominously as the "*Graveyard*", about 30 miles off the River Tyne that nobody has ever written about, plus dozens of almost certainly virgin wrecks, just waiting to be explored.

Precise WGS84 GPS positions are supplied for each wreck and the correct distance from the wreck to a recognisable point on the shore, i.e., harbour, hill or point, etc., have been provided. All distances in the book are measured in nautical miles; (one-nautical mile equalling: 1.150 miles).

I have spent several years, with help from some very knowledgeable maritime historians, analysing and reassessing the ships and wreck positions, taking into consideration all of the relevant facts, tides, where and how it was sunk, the size of the wreck compared to the ship, the age and condition of the wreck, articles recovered, the U-boat KTBs where appropriate and Board of Trade Reports, etc., etc., to ensure the wreck is the correct one, or as near as is humanly possible. Of course the only sure way to identify a ship/wreck is with the help from divers. Obviously the easiest way, is to recover the ship's bell or name plate, but that is much easier said than done, so in this book I have also included as much technical details of the ship as possible, by supplying the cylinder measurements, type of steam engine and number of boilers, etc., etc. It also details, the ship's builders, yard number, dates of launching, any previous names and owners and in many cases, even their captains. Where possible, the ship's previous service history has been supplied, followed by a detailed explanation of its last voyage/patrol and its final demise. Some of the Board of Trade Wreck reports, survivor and witnesses statements tell of harrowing and shocking anecdotes, enough to make your blood run cold.

At the end of the chapter on the 'Final voyage', the names of all the crewmen that perished, has also been included. The last chapter for each ship, gives a brief description of what the wreck-site appears to looks like, according to divers or/and side-scan sonar surveys.

The same 'star-rating' system that I have used in previous books is used in this one, to help when planning to visit a wreck, whether it is for fishing or diving and to save what could have been a wasted journey. Five stars is a fantastic wreck while one star is a rubbish one.

Ron Young

THE *GRAVEYARD*

Left: SMS Albatross *took part in a battle with Russian cruisers off the island of Gotland on 2nd July 1915, where the ship was severely damaged, and forced to beach herself in neutral Swedish waters. The ship was salvaged after the war and broken up in 1921.*

Right: The 3,470-ton light cruiser SMS Stuttgart, *which was capable of carrying 108 mines and assisted SMS* Albatross *in laying mines off the Tyne in 1914.*

The area ominously known as the *Graveyard*, is a 'close' concentration of 22 wrecks about 2–3 miles across that begin 27-nautical miles ENE from Tynemouth lighthouse, at position 55 09'N 000 40'W and run in a NNW direction for about 11 nautical miles, to position 55 19.N 000 46'W.

The reason the majority of the wrecks are there, is because of a barrier of mines that were laid by the German warships SMS *Albatross* which carried up to 600 mines and the SMS *Stuttgart*, which was capable of carrying 108 mines. Between 0130hrs & 0152hrs on August 26th 1914 (continental time), the 2,200-ton *Kaiserlichen Marine minenkreuzer* SMS *Albatross*, commanded by Korvettenkapitänleutnant West, with the 3,470-ton light cruiser SMS *Stuttgart*, laid a barrier of 200 mines between them, 11-miles in length on a SSE course, from 5-miles NE to 5-miles SE of the Tyne estuary at approximately: 55° 07'N 01° 18'W to 54° 58'N 01° 10'W; the distance between the mines was 100-metres and at a depth setting of two metres, under middle-low ebb tide. However the ships had misjudged the distance, placing them further seaward. Over the following months many ships were lost as a result of these mines: HM Trawler *Crathie*, HM Trawler *Thomas W. Irvin*, the Swedish SS *Andrea*, the British steamer *Runo*, the Norwegian *Gottried*, the Swedish steamer *St. Paul*, the Norwegian SS *Tromø*, probably the Russian steamer *Paul Spoliansky* and possibly the Norwegian steamer *Gjesø*.

However there are at least a further fourteen vessels that sank after detonating mines in that area and from which, many crewmen perished. All of those other vessels still need to be identified. There are a few other wrecks in this area that were probably not sunk by the *Albatross* mines, the RN destroyer HMS *Cupar*, the 50 ton MFV *Constellation*, the 34-ton MFV *Kirsty Jane*, MFV *Cutty II* and the old 892-ton German barque-rigged paddle steamer *Ajax* that sank in 1895, although she has never been positively identified to date. The other wrecks, which are mostly fairly small, lie at the following coordinates:

(1) 55 21'.653 N 000 52'.069 W; it lies in 91m (LAT), is upright and intact, 33m in length, 6m across & 2.5m shadow height.

(2) 55 20'.687 N 000 53'.735 W; it lies in 92m (LAT), is partially buried, but intact, 30m in length, 6m across and 3.8m shadow height

(3) 55 20'.620 N 000 57'.635 W; it lies in 93m (LAT), is intact but very old and decayed, 42m in length, 8m across and nearly 7m shadow height.

(4) 55 19'.137 N 000 46'.170 W; it lies in 90m (LAT), is on its side, is intact, but partially buried, with dimensions of 32m in length, 7m across and over 5.5m shadow height.

(5) 55 18'.947 N 001 02'.812 W; it lies in 91m (LAT), is intact with floating nets, 25m in length, 12m across and 5.6m shadow height.

(6) 55 18'.137 N 000 44'.770 W; it lies in 85m (LAT), is on its side, but intact, 38m in length, 8m across and 4.5m shadow height.

(7) 55 17'.887 N 000 44'.653 W; it lies in 84m (LAT), is very broken up, with dimensions of 26m in length, 8m across and 7.5m shadow height.

(8) 55 16'.171 N 000 46'.686 W; it lies in 85m (LAT), is very old and decayed, with dimensions of 42m in length, 8m across and 3.5m shadow height.

(9) 55 15'.454 N 001 00'.151 W; it lies in 90m, is quite broken up, with dimensions of 30m in length, 10m across and 3.2m shadow height.

(10) 55 15'.137 N 000 44'.603 W; it lies in 79m (LAT), is intact and upright, with dimensions of 30m in length, 7m across and 5m shadow height.

(11) 55 15'.121 N 000 55'.035 W; it lies in 88m (LAT), is partially buried, well broken up and decayed, with dimensions of 22m in length, 8m across and 4.7m shadow height.

(12) 55 14'.404 N 000 42'.570 W; it lies in 76m, appears intact, with dimensions of 48m in length, 7m across and 5.6m shadow height.

(13) 55 13'.638 N 000 41'.953 W; it lies in 72m (LAT), is broken in twp parts, with dimensions of 40m in length, 6m across and 6.8m shadow height.

(13) 55 13'.154 N 000 42'.636 W; it lies in 73m (LAT), is partially broken up and decayed, with dimensions of 60m in length, 10m across and nearly 8m shadow height.

(14) 55 12'.105 N 000 38'.354 W; it lies in 72m (LAT), is well decayed, with dimensions of 58m in length, 25m across and 7m shadow height.

(15) 55 11'.505 N 000 42'.136 W; it lies in 70, is well decayed and partially buried, with dimensions of 38m in length, 8m across and 6.8m shadow height.

1

WHITBY TO TEES BAY AND HARTLEPOOL

LONDON

Date of loss: 23 June 1918
Wreck: ★★★★★
Depth: 47 m
Reference: 54 30'.494 N 000 29'.886 W
Location: 2.82 nm NE from North Cheek (Ness Point) at Robin Hood's Bay

The Dundee, Perth & London Shipping Company, 1737-ton steamer London, *c.1912 (Author's collection)*

The *London* (Official No. 99213) was a 1737-ton steel-hulled British steam passenger/cargo ship measuring 85.34 m in length, with an 11.12-m beam and a draught of 5.1 m. Gourlay Brothers and Company built and completed her as Yard No. 153 in May 1892 at Dundee for The Dundee, Perth and London Shipping Company, Dundee which owned her at the time of loss.

Left: Engine makers plate from SS London *(Courtesy Carl Racey)*

Right: Scarborough divers in 2007 with recovered marine artefacts, including the bell from SS London *(centre). From left to right, Scarborough Diving Club members: Tony Herbert; Anne Polkey; Caroline Pinder; Rob Broadhead; Ian Hamp; Karen Herbert; and Chris Baker (long-standing chairman of Filey Sub Aqua Association (SSA) dive centre). Artefacts from the Seaham Sub Aqua Club, from left to right: (top row)* John Miles's *engine maker's plate; (middle row)* John Miles's *bell;* London *bell;* Elfrida *bell; (bottom row)* Empress *Crew's portholes and* London's *portholes (Courtesy Carl Racey)*

The single steel screw was powered by a 425-nhp three-cylinder triple expansion steam engine that used two double-ended boilers, 12 ribbed furnaces (six in each boiler with three at each end) and gave 15 knots. The cylinders measured 76.20 cm, 119.38 cm and 195.58 cm (30 in., 47 in., and 77 in.). Gourlay Brothers and Company also manufactured the machinery. She had two decks and an 18.59-m poop deck, a 22.56-m bridge deck and an 18.90-m forecastle.

In April 1901 a fire broke out in a hold, while the *London* was on passage for London with 13 passengers and a general cargo. Her crew fought the blaze for 11 hours, as the vessel steamed back to Dundee.

At 1900 hrs on the evening of 13 February 1913, the *London* was on passage from Dundee for London when 2 nm west of Haisborough lightvessel, the *Norfolk*, she collided with the 1645-ton steamship *Edinburgh* (1884 – Edinburgh S.S. Co., Ltd., Dundee) that was on passage from Methil for Oran, Algeria with coal. The *Edinburgh* foundered and was lost with four of her crew. The *London* was holed in the port bow about 3 ft above the water, but proceeded to London and arrived at Gravesend. The crew lost were: Beare, the master MM; Woods, second mate MM; Martin, lamp trimmer MM; and Hammond, fireman MM.

During the First World War the *London* was armed for defence with a stern-mounted 13-pounder deck gun.

Final voyage

On 23 June 1918 the unseen SMU *UB-88*, a submarine of the KDM commanded by Reinhard von Rabenau, torpedoed the *London*. The steamer was on passage from Methil for London with a cargo of coal and jute, with Captain W. Chapman in charge. The torpedo struck at 2215 hrs, detonating about 3 metres forward of the stern, which completely blew the stern end off, but left her upper deck still intact. The 28-man crew abandoned ship in the lifeboats, with one man slightly injured. They had no sooner cleared away from her, when, as the crew looked on, the ship reared up at the bows and plunged down to the bottom. Soon after a patrol vessel arrived and picked up the crew who were then landed at Immingham.

Starke Schell Registers; ADM 137/2964; LCWLR 1914–1918, p. 222; BVLS 1914–1918, p. 92.

Wrecksite

The wreck of the *London* – identified by the maker's plate – is orientated in a NNE to SSW direction. It lies on a seabed of dirty sand, mud, shells and gravel in a general depth of 47 m (LAT). A Scarborough diver reported it as a very large wreck, standing some 7 m proud of the seabed, but from amidships to the bows it is inverted and split open. One of her boilers with two furnaces is visible and exposed, along with a donkey boiler. The stern end, having been completely blown off in the explosion, lies over on its port side and an iron screw, plus the spare one, lie close by on the seabed along with some toilets and a sink. One report says that the auxiliary steering wheel, complete with a steel boss, is still in position. In 2001 there were still rows of portholes in several places and a number of lifeboat davits were visible, as well as large green copper boxes possibly containing ammunition. The stern end is very broken up, but amongst it is the gun pedestal. The hull is also intact around the engine room, but is well over on its side.

This site is a good boat-angling venue when conditions permit, as a number of large fish have been observed. Much of the upper and most exposed structures of the wreck are covered in soft corals, which are a sure sign of the brisk tidal streams.

BRENTWOOD

Date of loss: 12 January 1917
Wreck: ★★★★
Depth: 48 m
Reference: 54 30'.539 N 000 32'.491 W
Location: 2.67 nm NE from Whitby piers

The *Brentwood* (Official No. 118470) was a steel-hulled 1192-ton British steam cargo ship that measured 68.5 m in length, with an 11.04-m beam and a 4.36-m draught. S.P. Austin and Son built and completed her as Yard No. 225 in August 1904 at Wear Dock, Sunderland. On 29 June 1904 she was launched as the *Brentwood* for Cory Colliers & Son, Ltd. London, the owner at the time of loss. The single steel screw was powered by a 180-hp (800-ihp), three-cylinder triple expansion steam engine that used one single-ended boiler. G. Clark Ltd. Sunderland manufactured the amidships-positioned machinery. She had one main deck, a well deck, a 6.7-m poop deck, a 17-m quarterdeck, and a 14.6-m bridge deck plus a 7.6-m forecastle.

Final voyage

At 0155 hrs on 12 January 1917 the *Brentwood* detonated a mine laid on 11 January 1917 by SMU *UC 43*, a KDM submarine commanded by Oblt.z.S. Erwin Sebelin. The steamer was in ballast and *en route* from London to North Shields. The explosion took place at the forepart of the vessel, instantly killing the second mate and a fireman, both of whom were on watch duty at the time. With her bows almost blown off, she filled up rapidly and went down in just four minutes, taking confidential papers with her. Captain R. Hunter and the 13 surviving crew managed to get safely away in the ship's boat. Just over an hour and twenty minutes later the 1057-ton steamer *Togston* (1909: South Metropolitan Gas Company, London) picked up the men and took them to Sunderland. Two of the crew were killed:

Nathan Bie, 40 yrs, second mate MM
Otto Severin, 36 yrs of age, Fireman (Swedish) MM.

On 18 October 1917 the SS *Togston* also detonated a mine and sank 20 miles S by E ½ E of Flamborough Head; she was voyaging from Newcastle to London, with a cargo of coal. *UB 47* had laid the mine.

ADM 137/2961; BVLS 1914–1918, p. 30; LCWLR 1914–1918, p. 85; CWGC; Starke Schell Registers; Jarvis (2000).

Wrecksite

The wreck is orientated in a NE to SW (045/225°) direction and lies on a seabed of sand and mud in a general depth of 48 m (LAT). It is very substantial and upright, but lies in two sections. From the amidships to the stern is intact, but forward of the bridge and up to the bows is collapsed and broken up. The wreck stands 8 m high and covers an area 80 m long by about 12 m across. There are two holds aft and the accommodation area is at the stern and amidships. Soft corals are well established on the upper and most exposed parts of the wreck, evidence of the strong tidal streams that sweep over it. Fair numbers of large cod, ling and conger have been observed. In 2007 the bell was recovered from inside the stern end. (Wreck position courtesy of Carl Racey.)

FERVENT (… or Crimdon?)

Date of loss: 5 March 1883
Wreck: ★★
Depth: 43 m
Reference: 54 30'.161 N 000 33'.286 W
Location: 2.14 nm ENE of Whitby light

The *Fervent* (Official No. 68943) was an iron-hulled 901-ton steam cargo ship that measured 65.22 m in length and had a beam of 8.94 m. In June 1876, she was completed as Yard No. 75 by Short Brothers, at Pallion, Sunderland for shipowner/manager James Westoll of John Street, Sunderland. The iron screw was powered by a 98-nhp two-cylinder compound steam engine that used one boiler. Lloyds classed her 90A1. She was a well deck ship with a long raised quarterdeck, connected with a short bridge house. The whole was protected in front by the iron bulkhead which formed the forepart of the engine room compartment, and which was carried up to the top of the quarterdeck. Forward of the iron bulkhead were the galley and some storerooms, which were also protected in front by another iron bulkhead, ensuring that the most vulnerable part of the vessel was protected. Forward of the galley and store-rooms was the well, extending to the topgallant forecastle. The hatchways, of which she had four – two on the quarterdeck and two in the well – were particularly strong, having three hatchways fore and aft measuring: 20.32 cm (8 in.) by 17.78 cm (7 in.), 20.32 cm (8 in.) by 17.78 cm (7 in.), with crosspieces and four tiers of hatch coverings 7.62 cm (3 in.) thick. The iron coamings were 89.82 cm (2 ft 9 in.) high on the quarterdeck, and 99.06 cm (3 ft 3 in.) in the well. In January 1883 the ship was put into Wallsend Slipway where her butts were cemented.

At 0230 hrs on Friday, 11 November 1881 the *Fervent* was returning from London when she was involved in a collision with the 239-ton Hull-registered steamer *Fairy*, 20 miles off Flamborough Head. The *Fairy* (1876) was laden with a general cargo and passengers, travelling from the Tyne to Yarmouth and was struck a violent blow amidships, sending her to the bottom within ten minutes. All of her crew and passengers were saved by the *Fervent* and returned to North Shields; however, the *Fervent* had her bows stove in.

The Board of Trade wreck report for the *Fervent* describes the vessel also having had permanent wingboards in the holds to facilitate 'the trimming of the cargo', preventing it shifting into the wings if the vessel list. The report goes on to confirm 'two temporary wooden bulkheads, one forward in the way of No.1 hatch, and the other aft in the way of No.4 hatch, which were secured above to the beams and extended downwards to about the hold beams, and were intended to keep the coals in the centre of the ship, and to prevent their going either forward or aft' when the vessel pitched. An empty space sufficient to contain 40–50 tons of coal was left both in the fore as well as the after part of the hold, so as to make the ends of the ship light. On the whole the report concluded that the vessel, so far as her hull, equipment and machinery were concerned, appeared to be in a good and seaworthy condition.

Final voyage

The *Fervent* left Tyne docks at about midnight on 5 March 1883 for a voyage to London. She carried a crew of 17 hands and a 993-ton cargo of coal: 300 tons of coal from the East Pontop Colliery, 300 tons from East Castle Colliery, 261 tons from Boldon Colliery and 132 tons from Red Heugh Colliery, as well as 81 tons of coal in the bunkers. The pilot left her off the bar of the Tyne and she was never seen again.

Accordingly, the Board of Trade directed an inquiry into the loss of the *Fervent*. The hearing was told that within one and a half hours of leaving the Tyne, a severe gale sprang up. The extreme violence of the gale caused the loss of some 60–70 fishing boats belonging to the English east coast ports, as well as a large number from the coast of Friesland, in the Netherlands. Altogether no fewer than six steamers were lost. Witnesses who had had 40 years' experience of the coast, as well as the Whitby pilot, Mr Cass, reported that they had never seen one worse.

It is probable, therefore, that the *Fervent* had foundered with all her crew. That same day the 564-ton SS *Marie Stuart* sank and wreckage from both vessels was washed ashore not far apart. Unsurprisingly, it has been suggested that the *Fervent* and the *Marie Stewart* may have collided (see section on the *Marie Stewart* (page 30)).

Board of Trade wreck report: Fervent, 1883; Miramar Ship Index; Starke Schell Registers; *The Times:* Thursday, 8 March 1883, p. 12, issue 30762.

Wrecksite

The wreck, which is possibly that of the *Fervent*, is orientated in a SSE to NNW direction. It lies on a seabed of dirty sand, stones and mud in a general depth of 43 m (LAT). The wreck is partially buried, collapsed, very broken up and decayed. It lies in two separate sections: one about 35 m long and the other about 20 m long, and both are scattered about. The stern with the propeller shaft to amidships is the most recognisable section, where the compound stem engine and single boiler can be found, but most of it is rather flat. The highest part stands no more than 3.8 m high.

The question of the wreck's identity is still open to debate. Although there has been no positive identification, many Yorkshire divers are of the firm belief that this wreck is that of the iron-hulled 1710-ton schooner-rigged Swedish steam cargo ship *Crimdon* that was sunk on 27 July 1918. She was transporting 2050 tons of coal from the Tyne to Rouen in France and was the twelfth ship in the starboard column of a convoy. At 1750 hrs, about 2.5 nm west of Whitby, she was shaken by a violent explosion amidships on the starboard side and began to sink immediately. The crew launched the port lifeboat, which capsized, drowning the mate and ship's cook; two stokers were also killed in the engine room. The surviving 16 members of the crew and a British pilot were picked up by other ships and landed at Grimsby and Scarborough.

The *Crimdon* was completed in March 1878 by William Gray and Company, West Hartlepool as Yard No. 181 for Sir R. Ropner and Company, West Hartlepool and launched that same month. The single screw was powered by a 140-nhp two-cylinder compound steam engine that used two boilers.

POLRUAN, ex POLNAY, ex POLLACSEK

Date of loss: 25 October 1916
Wreck: ★★★
Depth: 24 m
Reference: 54 30'.277 N 00 36'.102 W
Location: 0.75 nm N by E of Whitby's West Pier

The *Polruan* (Official No. 136785) was a steel-hulled 3692-ton British steam cargo ship that measured 100.89 m in length, with a 14.7-m beam and a 6.7-m draught. William Gray and Company, West Hartlepool built and completed her in April 1907 as Yard No. 744. She was launched on 28 March 1907 as the *Pollacsek* for Atlantica Sea Navigation Co., Ltd., at, Fiume (Darum). The single screw was powered by a 292-nhp three-cylinder triple expansion steam engine that used two single-ended boilers and gave 10 knots service speed. Central Marine Engineering Works, West Hartlepool manufactured the machinery. She had one deck, five cemented bulkheads, a 7.3-m poop deck, 37.7-m bridge deck and an 8.8-m forecastle.

Eugen Jenö Pollacsek, who lived in Budapest, was director of Atlantica Trust and in 1910 became the Hungarian Adel, as Eugen Polnay of Tiszasüly in Hungary; the ship was renamed *Polnay* by the same owner in 1912.

In August 1914 the *Polnay* was seized at Falmouth and requisitioned by the Admiralty, London.

From 1916 the Admiralty was the registered owner and renamed her *Polruan*. Hall Brothers, Cairns, Noble and Company, Newcastle upon Tyne was listed as the Crown nominee manager.

Final voyage

On 25 October 1916 the *Polruan* was on passage from the Tyne docks for Dunkerque, with a cargo of coal and a crew of 26, when she was reported to have struck a German-laid mine. However, a Board of Trade inquiry later suggested that it was more likely that the vessel had struck Whitby Rock. At the inquiry the ship's master, Captain Jeffrey, was censured and ordered to pay £50 towards the court costs.

LR 1915/16, Issue no. 768; Board of Trade: World War I Wreck Return 1916, Part II, p. 23; Starke Schell Registers.

Wrecksite

The *Polruan* is orientated in a NE to SW direction and lies on a dirty seabed in a general depth of 24 m (LAT). It is upright and intact but collapsed and well broken up, covering an area 75 m long and 15 m across. The highest part is midships where the engine and boilers are positioned and stands about 4.2 m high from the seabed. Shoals of pout whiting have been reported over and around the wrecksite. It lies just to the east of the Whitby bell buoy and is fairly easy to locate using an echo sounder. It takes only 7–8 minutes to reach by RHIB from Whitby harbour. Local Whitby divers own both the wreck of the *Polruan* and *Rohilla*.

LANTHORN, EX MAGNUS MAIL

Date of loss: 22 May 1917
Wreck: ★★★
Depth: 27 m
Reference: 54 30'.779 N 00 37'.146 W
Location: 1.24 nm N by W of Whitby piers

The *Lanthorn* (Official No. 95287) was a steel-hulled 2317-ton British steam cargo ship that measured 88.52 m in length, with an 11.91-m beam and a 6.55-m draught. Short Brothers at Pallion, Sunderland built and completed her as Yard No. 184 in April 1889. On 19 February 1889 she was launched and registered as the *Magnus Mail* for James Westoll in Sunderland. The single steel screw was powered by a 202-nhp three-cylinder triple expansion steam engine that used one boiler. T. Richardson and Sons manufactured the engine and ancillary machinery at Hartlepool. She had one deck and an amidships-positioned superstructure consisting of a 9.7-m poop deck, a 23.8-m bridge deck and a 10.3-m forecastle.

In 1917 she was renamed *Lanthorn* by the Gas Light & Coke Co., London. S. Clarke & Co., London was the manager at the time of loss.

Final voyage

On 22 May 1917 an Imperial German (KDM) submarine, about one and a half miles astern of the *Lanthorn*, shelled her with its deck gun. The steamer was in ballast and *en route* from London to the Tyne. The master, Captain Shewan, altered course and increased speed to bring his vessel inshore, but the submarine kept on firing. It scored at least five direct hits over the next half hour. To save the lives of his men, the master stopped the engines and, at 0900 hrs, ordered 'abandon ship'. The 18 crewmen got away in the lifeboats and motor fishing boats rescued them soon after, putting them ashore at Whitby. Some of the crew from the U-boat boarded the *Lanthorn* and placed explosive scuttling charges below her decks. At 1120 hrs the ship exploded and went to the bottom. Records later showed the submarine to be SMU *UB 41*, commanded by Oblt.z.S. Günther Krause.

ADM 137/2962; BVLS 1914–1918, p. 51; LCWLR 1914–1918, p. 136; Starke Schell Registers.

Wrecksite

The wreck is often referred to locally, as the 'Sparrow' or 'Steeple-in-Street wreck', because of the easy transit marks – which include a church steeple. The remains, which cover an area 105 m long and 20 m across, are very decayed and broken, and at the northern end stand about 4 m high. The wreck is orientated in a NNE to SSW direction and lies on a seabed of dirty sand and mud in a general depth of 27 m (LAT). The sternpost is still standing high with a section of the stern, but the steering quadrant has fallen on the seabed. The prop shaft is still in place and runs along to the large upright triple expansion engine. The large double boiler has three ribbed furnaces on both sides, and has moved over and rolled a little to port. The donkey boiler has fallen over backwards and is lying on its side almost touching the main boiler. There is more wreckage on the port side where two brass-backed port holes where recovered. The bow section has fallen back and lies a little over to port but can be clearly made out. There are a lot of winches all along the vessel.

This is quite a silty wreck and best dived in the summer months when the visibility is good. Large cod often hide amongst the wreckage and shoals of pout whiting are a common sight.

The wreck has frequently been confused with the iron-hulled 871-ton British steam cargo vessel *Spero* that sank on 11 August 1899. (Wreck report and position courtesy of Carl Racey.)

UC 70, Seiner Majestät Unterseeboot

Date of Loss: 28 August 1918
Depth: 25 m
Reference: 54 31'.599 N 000 40'.033 W
Location: 1.5 nm N of Sandsend and 2.78 nm NW of Whitby

UC 70 was a Type UCII coastal mine-laying submarine. She was ordered on 12 January 1916 as part of a batch of boats – SMU *UC 65–UC 73*. Blohm & Voss, Hamburg laid the keel as yard number 286 and launched her for the KDM on 7 August 1916. Oblt.z.S. Werner Fürbringer commissioned her on 20 November 1916.

The Type UCII boats had an outer hull and a thicker inner pressure hull, a surface displacement of 427 tons and an underwater displacement of 508 tons. They measured 50.35 m in length, 5.22 m across the beam and had a draught of 3.68 m. The tallest part, at 7.46 m, was the conning tower. The machinery consisted of two 250-hp diesel oil engines manufactured by Maschinenfabrik Augsburg Nürnberg (MAN) and powered by two bronze screws that gave a surface speed of 12 knots. The surface operational range was 10 420 nm at 7 knots carrying and using 41 tons of diesel oil in the fuel tanks, plus 15 tons of spare fuel in the ballast tanks. For underwater, the boats were equipped with two 230-hp electric motors using lead-acid batteries and gave a submerged speed of 7.5 knots. Armament consisted of a maximum of seven 50.04-cm (19.7-in.) torpedoes, with two external 50.04-cm torpedo tubes at the bow – one on either side of the mine chutes and one stern internal tube. They were also armed with one 88-mm deck gun at the fore and carried 133 rounds of ammunition for the gun. Other weapons on board were 18 Type UC200 mines with six mine chutes for laying the mines. The boats were capable of diving to a maximum operational depth of 50 m (164 ft), accomplished in 33 seconds on a crash dive, and usually manned by three officers and 23 ratings.

Final patrol

The *UC 70*, a KDM submarine commanded by Oblt.z.S. Karl Dobberstein, left Zeebrugge on 21 August 1918 on her tenth patrol and mine-laying operation in the Hoofden, and with the mission of attacking allied shipping off the English east coast. At 1530 hrs on 28 August 1918, however, a Blackburn Kangaroo bomber (Serial No. B9983) of 246 Squadron (at the time based at Seaton Carew near Hartlepool), on anti-submarine patrol and piloted by Pilot Officer Waring RAF, spotted an oil slick apparently emanating from an elongated shape beneath the surface.

Suspecting that a U-boat might be lurking below, Pilot Officer Waring followed the oil slick and dropped a single 250-pound (113.39-kilo) bomb over the top of the boat. Waring noted that large quantities of oil and air bubbled to the surface. The destroyer HMS *Ouse* witnessed the explosion and made full speed for the scene, guided by Waring's pistol flares.

SMS UC 71, *sister boat to SMU* UC 70 *(Author's collection)*

Above: Sketch of the wreck of UC 70 *(Courtesy Pamela Armstrong)*

Ouse made several runs and dropped ten depth charges set at 50 ft (15.24 m), aimed in the centre of a big oil patch bubbling to the surface. More oil and bits of debris came up in the maelstrom. It is not clear whether the aircraft, the destroyer or a combination of both destroyed the submarine. It is possible that the U-boat had been damaged previously in the new British minefield off the Yorkshire coast and was lying on the bottom effecting repairs when the slick was spotted.

On 14 September Lt.Cdr. Damant's 'Tin Openers' arrived and the celebrated Dusty Miller was sent down. He confirmed the wreck of a U-boat and entered her through a massive hole in the hull. Pushing his way through the devastation and dead inside, Dusty entered the control room and very quickly located the waterproof metal box containing the logs and codebooks. Thus the boat was identified as *UC 70*. Contained in the box were some papers, charting the minefields she had laid since leaving Flanders.

As for Pilot Officer Waring, he survived the war only to die in a crash in 1919. The crewmen that died were:

Baethke, Ernst, U-Maschinistenmaat
Bau, Paul, U-Matrose
Bürger, Martin, U-F.T.Ober Gast
Baalmann, Johann, U-Obermatrose
Christensen, H., U-Obermatrose
Dames, Hans, T-Maschinistenmaat
Dienst, Friedrich, U-Obermaschinistenmaat
Dobberstein, Karl, Oberleutnant zur See
Drees, Heinrich, U-Heizer
Eckert, Alfred, U-Obermaschinist
Engelhard, W., U-Maschinistenmaat
Fischer, Ludwig, U-Oberheizer
Hartmann, Paul, U-Obermatrose
Heinrich, Kurt, Leutnant zur.See.d.Reserve
Michelsen, G., U-Matrose
Paffen, Wilhelm, U-Heizer
Peters, Heinrich, U-Heizer
Rabe, Wilhelm, U-Maschinistenmaat
Rochna, Emil, U-Obermaschinist
Rosenbaum, H., U-Matrose
Schaller, Johann, U-Oberheizer
Schattschneider, Bootsmannsmaat
Scheibner, Felix, Obermaschinistenmaat
Schmidt, Andreas, U-Matrose
Schröter, P., U-Heizer
Seidel, Paul, U-Matrose
Siedhoff, Heinrich, U-Heizer
Stolze, Erich, U-Steuermann
Thomale, Johann, U-F.T.Gast
Tillmann, Anton, Obermaschinistenmaat
Wörmann, W., U-Heizer

NARA: Series T-1022, Roll 109, PG61991; Möltenort U-boat Memorial Foundation; ADM 137/2963.

Wrecksite

The wreck is intact, with some areas of plate where the seams have blown and stands 3 m high – although it has a slight list to starboard and sits in a small scour – on a flat sand and gravel seabed in a general depth of 25 m (LAT). The wreck shows up well on an echo sounder. Don Foster asserts that the two deck hatches are open, as are five of the mine chutes that can clearly be seen. The deck gun is still mounted and intact. The conning tower has collapsed and lies to port. The hatch is open, but the inside is festooned with cables and is very silted – just waiting to claim its first careless diver. The screws and torpedo tubes have been removed. Diving is permitted but only on a look-but-don't-touch basis and the wreck should be treated with due respect as a war grave.

CETO (?)

Date of loss: 20 August 1886
Wreck: ✯✯✯
Depth: 55 m
Reference: 54 32'.027 N 000 25'.753 W
Location: 6.91 nm ENE from Whitby piers

The *Ceto* (Official No. 77074) was an iron-hulled 970-ton schooner-rigged cargo vessel that measured 65.58 m in length with a 6.42-m beam. M. Pearse & Co., Stockton built and completed her as Yard No. 159. On 26 January 1878 she was launched as the *Ceto* for Henry Cloake, London (Cardiff), the owners until the time of loss. The single iron screw was powered by an amidships-positioned, two-cylinder inverted compound steam engine that used one boiler. The cylinders measured 67.31 cm and 124.46 cm, with a 83.82-cm stroke (26½ in. by 49 in. with 33-in. stroke). Blair and Company manufactured the engine and ancillary machinery at Stockton. She had one deck.

Final voyage

On 20 August 1886 the *Ballater*, a 741-ton steamer owned by Davidson Steam Ship Company, Aberdeen, was voyaging from the Tyne to Malta with a cargo of coal when she was struck by the *Ceto* six miles south of Whitby. The *Ballater* was almost cut in two and sank within minutes, but her crew of 15 managed to scramble onto the deck of the *Ceto*, which then continued with her journey. The *Ceto* was in ballast and carrying a crew of 17 and six passengers from Rouen to the Tyne. However, the vessel had only travelled a short distance when it was involved in another collision off Whitby. This time it was with the 767-ton Sunderland-registered SS *Lebanon* (1870 – W. J. Pope & Co., London) and it was the *Ceto* that foundered. The crews and passengers of both the *Ballater* and *Ceto*, 36 in all, were taken on board the *Lebanon* and landed at Sunderland later that day. Though weather conditions were calm at the time of the incidents, there was a dense fog shrouding all of the Yorkshire coast and well out to sea.

The Times: Saturday, 21 August 1886, p. 8, Starke Schell Registers; Board of Trade Wreck Return 1886, p. 145.

Wrecksite

The wreck, which is probably that of the *Ceto*, is orientated in a SSE to NNW direction. It lies on a reasonably firm seabed of sand, shell, mud and gravel in a general depth of 55 m (LAT).

The wreck is now collapsed, very decayed and well broken up. It covers an area 65 m long and 10 m across, with the highest point being about 4.7 m from the seabed.

COUNTESS OF STRATHMORE

Date of loss: 14 July 1853
Wreck: ★★
Depth: 44 m
Reference: 54 32'.694 N 000 35'.752 W
Location: 3.20 nm N by E of Whitby's West Pier

The *Countess of Strathmore* was an iron-hulled 527-ton cargo steamship that measured 48.8 m in length. Palmer Bros. & Co., at Jarrow built and completed her as Yard No. 4. She was launched on 12 March 1853 for General Iron Screw Collier Company, London which also owned her at the time of loss. The single basic iron screw was powered by a simple two-cylinder expansion steam engine that used two small square boilers with ferrous tubes and cylinders of equal dimensions.

Final voyage

On Thursday, 14 July 1853 the *Countess of Strathmore* was on passage from Newcastle for London when she foundered off Whitby during a NE force 10 gale and three men were lost. The new vessel had left the Tyne heavily laden on the Wednesday afternoon, carrying three passengers and a crew of fifteen. The huge sea was washing over her decks and large quantities of water flooded the engine room. The master, Captain Nicholson, kept her before the wind until the fore part blew away. He then tried to get back to Hartlepool, but the ship was flooded by a wave, which disabled the rudder, extinguished the furnace fires and threw the ship into a trough of big waves, thoroughly disabling her. A Billyboy rescued ten of the crew and two of the passengers using a rope. The lifeboats had been washed away.

A Whitby brig, the *Bounty*, also came to help and saved others from the ill-fated vessel. However, there were casualties. The mate, William Harrison, having lashed himself to a ladder, was being drawn towards the brig when a large wave caught the ladder and knocked him off, drowning him. The master, who was a rather heavy figure, secured himself to a rope and the people on the *Bounty* had almost dragged him into the brig when the rope snapped. He fell under the stern and was never seen again. One of the crewmen, a young man who lived in Boston, had been hauled aboard the *Bounty* in an extremely exhausted state and, although every effort was made to revive him, he died soon afterwards. The surviving crew and passengers were landed at Hartlepool that same evening.

Board of Trade Wreck Return 1853; Miramar Ship Index.

Wrecksite

The wreck, believed to be that of the old steamer, is orientated in an E to W direction and lies on a seabed of sand, mud and shells in a general depth of 44 m (LAT). The remains are very decayed, and it is collapsed and well broken up, covering an area 44 m long and 5.7 m across, with the highest part being around the engine which stands about 3 m from the seabed. The hull also appears partially buried and the gunwhales, or ribs of the vessel, protrude about one metre from the seabed. Many of the pieces of metal on the wreck are concreted together.

DROMIO, M Trawler

Date of loss: 22 December 1939
Wreck: ✯✯✯✯
Depth: 46 m
Reference: 54 32'.027 N 000 35'.786 W
Location: 2.56 nm N by E of Whitby

The 380-ton steam trawler Dromio *before requisition, c.1935 (Author's collection)*

The *Dromio* (Official No. 160859) was a steel-hulled 380-ton British steam trawler measuring 42.4 m in length with a 7.77-m beam. Cook, Welton and Gemmell built and completed her as Yard No. 528 at Beverley on 2 November 1929 registering her at Hull. On 23 September 1929 she was launched as the *Dromio* for Northern Fishing Company, Hull. Hellyer Brothers. was the manager. The single steel screw was powered by a 111-nhp three-cylinder triple expansion steam engine that used one single-ended boiler working at a 210-psi pressure, with three plain furnaces, 4.73 sq.m (51 sq.ft) of grate surface and 184.50 sq.m (1986 sq.ft) of heating surface which gave 10.8 knots. The cylinders measured 34.28 cm, 59.69 cm and 97.79 cm with a 66.04-cm stroke (13.5 in., 23.5 in. and 38.5 in. with a 26-in. stroke). Amos and Smith Ltd. at Hull manufactured the machinery. She had one deck, four bulkheads cemented, a 23.46-m quarterdeck and 7.31-m forecastle. Lloyds classed her as 100 A1. Her designated wartime code recognition letters were: LFBR.

On 27 August 1939, the Admiralty requisitioned the trawler and converted her to a minesweeper. Based at Sheerness, she was equipped with one 12-pounder deck gun, an echo-sounding device, a wireless and a direction finder.

The Luftwaffe attempted to bomb the *Dromio* on Sunday, 17 December 1939, but no damage was caused.

Final patrol

HMT *Dromio*, bound for the Arctic fishing grounds, left harbour on Thursday, 22 December 1939, with Lt. Cdr. George Dibley RNR in command. However she sank north of Whitby that same night following a collision with the 5714-ton Italian steamship *Valdarno* (1919: Società Anonima di Navigazione Ltd.). All of the crew of 17 were rescued by the *Valdarno* and taken on board the trawler *Colonio*, which put them ashore at a north-east port. The *Valdarno* was only slightly damaged and continued on her voyage.

Toghill (2004); Thompson (1999); SRN, Vol. 2, p. 108; LR.

Wrecksite

This wreck is orientated in a SE to NW direction. It lies on a seabed of dirty sand and shell in a general depth of 46 m (LAT). The wreck stands 7.9 m high and is listing about 60° to the port side. It is generally intact with nets attached, particularly at the bows. From the bows to amidships the decking is fully intact, but the starboard side at the stern is holed and open. The front hold on the starboard side is open and there is a large winch in front of the wheelhouse. The wheelhouse also has a toilet in it. The deck gun, which was located on the port side behind the wheelhouse, is no longer in position. It may have fallen onto the seabed or have been recovered in recent times. In 2003 two navigation lights were recovered from the stern area with the maker's plates inscribed: 'Hellyer Bros Ltd. St Andrew's Dock Hull'. There is no mention of her bell being located. Large numbers of cod and pout whiting have been observed around the wreck which is fished regularly by boats from Whitby.

MARCHIONESS OF LONDONDERRY

Date of loss: 16 May 1889
Wreck: ✯✯
Depth: 39 m
Reference: 54 32'.527 N 000 39'.135 W
Location: 3.27 nm NW of Whitby's West Pier

The *Marchioness of Londonderry* (Official No. 68966) was an iron-hulled 708-ton steam cargo vessel that measured 54.86 m in length and 8.68 m across the beam. Edward Withy and Company built and completed her as Yard No. 71 at the Middleton Yard, Hartlepool in February 1878. She was launched on 3 January 1878 for Charles Stewart Vane-Tempest-Stewart, 6th Marquess of Londonderry at Sunderland. The single iron screw was powered by a 90-shp, two-cylinder compound steam engine that used one boiler. T. Richardson and Sons Ltd. manufactured the engine and ancillary machinery.

Final voyage

At 0830 hrs on 16 May 1889 the *Marchioness of Londonderry*, while on passage from Sunderland for Amsterdam with a general cargo, sank three miles off Sandsend near Whitby following a collision with the Middlesbrough passenger/cargo steamer *Forth* (1887: Carron Company,

SS Marchioness *of Londonderry in port, c.1880 (Author's collection)*

Grangemouth). The *Forth*, which had her bows stove in and stem bent in the collision, rescued the crew of the *Marchioness of Londonderry* and landed them at Middlesbrough.

Starke Schell Registers; Miramar Ship Index; Board of Trade Wreck Return 1889; *The Times*: Friday, 17 May 1889, p. 11, Issue no. 32701.

Wrecksite

This wreck is orientated in a SE to NW direction. It lies on a seabed of mud, sand, gravel and shell in a general depth of 39 m (LAT). The wreck is very broken up and decayed with the highest point being around a fairly intact section of the bows at 4 m high. A number of portholes and brass shuttering have been observed and on the starboard side there is an area where bottles are cemented together. A wheel can also be found on the starboard side, aft. The old compound engine, single boiler and size of the wreckage are very similar to that of the *Marquess of Londonderry*. Numerous fish have been sighted all around the wreck, which is often visited by local angling boats.

ATHOS

Date of loss: 26 January 1918
Wreck: ✯✯
Depth: 23 m
Reference: 54 32'.220 N 000 41'.300 W
Location: 1 nm E of Kettleness Point

Athos *(Courtesy Norwegian Maritime Museum)*

The *Athos* was a steel-hulled 1708-ton Norwegian steam cargo ship that measured 80.69 m in length with a 12.24-m beam and a 5.63-m draught. Nylands Verksted, Kristiania (Oslo), Norway completed her as Yard No. 236 on 1 December 1913. She was launched as *Athos* on 4 November 1913 for Dampskipsselskapet Aktieselskapet Concordia, Flekkefjord, Norway, and registered at Flekkefjord. Bernhard Hanssen was the manager. The single steel screw was powered by a 189-nhp three-cylinder triple expansion steam engine that used one boiler. She had one deck and an amidships superstructure, consisting of a 14.9-m poop deck, an 18.5-m bridge deck and 9.1-m forecastle. The designated code recognition signal letters were: MJVL.

In 1916 the ship was sold to Aktieselskapet Romulus, Kristiania and A.O. Lindvig was the manager. In 1917 Aktieselskapet Martens and Company Skibs and Assuranceforretning, Bergen purchased her. From late 1917 onwards Torp and Weise of Bergen was the registered owner.

Final voyage

On 26 January 1918 the *Athos*, commanded by 37-year old Captain Jens Hansen, was torpedoed and sunk by Oblt.z.S. Helmuth von Rucktescell's KDM submarine the SMU *UB 34*. The steamer was in ballast and on passage from Rouen in France for Middlesbrough when she was hit in the engine room at approximately 1645 hrs. Two of her crew of 21 were lost: Ludvig Dahl, third engineer from Bergen and Sverre Kristiansen, 18 years of age, boy mechanic from Trondheim. After 20 minutes in the lifeboat, the survivors were picked up by a patrol vessel and after five hours disembarked in Middlesbrough.

Maritime Accident Statements for Norwegian Ships Sunk in Wartime: 1814–1918; LCWLR 1914–1918, p. 197; ANCL 1914–1918, p. 197; Starke Schell Registers.

Wrecksite

The wreck lies on a seabed of sand and mud in a general depth of 23 m (LAT). It is totally collapsed, well broken up and covers a large area of seabed. However, quite large sections of the wreck remain. Piles of steel debris, twisted plates, ribs, pieces of hollow mast and broken machinery surround the boiler and engine. Two screws lie at the stern end. The deck winches are still there as well as a fair number of battered pipes, some of them made of copper. During the summer months good-sized plaice can be found close to the wreck and large pollack hover around the wreckage.

UB 30, Seiner Majestät Unterseeboot

Date of Loss: 13 August 1918
Depth: 45 m
Reference: 54 32'.344 N 00 35'.686 W
Location: 2.92 nm NNE of Whitby's West Pier

UB 30 was a Type UBII coastal torpedo-attack submarine built and completed by Blohm & Voss at Hamburg. She was ordered on 22 July 1915 as part of a batch of boats: UB 30–UB 41. The keel was laid as Yard No. 254 and she was launched on 16 November 1916 and delivered to the KDM on 16 March 1916 when she was commissioned by Oblt.z.S. Kurt Schapler.

Type UBII boats had a single steel hull and displaced 274 tons on the surface and 303 tons under water. Overall they measured 36.90 m in length, had a 4.37-m beam, a 3.70-m draught and stood 7.34 m tall at the conning tower. The machinery consisted of two 142-hp Benz diesel oil engines which powered two bronze screws, giving a surface speed of 9.06 knots. The operational range was 7030 nm at 5 knots; while travelling submerged they had a range of 45 nm at 5 knots. Underwater, the U-boat used two 140-hp electric motors that gave a maximum 5.71 knots. Power for the motors came from rows of Accumlatoren-Fabrik-Aktiengesellshcaft (AFA) lead-acid batteries. Armament consisted of four 50.04-cm (19.7 in.) torpedoes which were fired through two 50.04-cm bow torpedo tubes. UBII boats were fitted with one 88-mm (3.46 in.) forward deck gun and carried 120 rounds of 88-mm ammunition. No mines were carried as these boats were not mine layers. The maximum operational diving depth was 50 m (164 ft) and it took 30 seconds to crash dive. Two officers and 21 ratings was the normal complement.

Final patrol

On 6 August 1918 *UB 30* departed Zeebrugge with Oblt.z.S. Rudolf Stier in command for her 20th patrol. Area-8, which was the designated Auxiliary Patrol Zone *c*.1917, anti-submarine patrols first became aware that there was a U-boat heading their way at 0410 hrs when Rudolf Stier transmitted the following message: 'Have started journey to the north.'

Room 40 – a top secret office within the Admiralty building at Whitehall – was thus able to warn Immingham, the base from which several patrols operated, that a U-boat could be arriving off Flamborough Head that night. Confirmation came on the 10th when *UB 30* destroyed the 509-ton coaster SS *Madame Renée* (1904 – T. G. Beatley & Son) which was travelling from London to the Tyne with copper pyrites. The torpedo detonated amidships on the ship's port side at 0837 hrs and she sank almost instantly. The crew were forced to jump into the sea where ten of them drowned, including three DAMS gunners. Local boats from

Scarborough picked up seven survivors found clinging to floating wreckage. The crew from the *Madam Renee* who lost their lives were:

Austwick, Charles Robert, 33 yrs, 2nd Engineer MM
Balmain, Robert Dunn, 32 yrs, 1st Mate MM
Douglas, Robert, 22 yrs, Able Seaman and Lamps MM
House, John Evans Peel, 22 yrs, Able Seaman MM
MacKenzie, John, Leading Seaman RNR (DAMS)
Manley, William, 56 yrs, Steward MM
Oldershaw, Francis Richard, AB RNVR (DAMS)
Osborne, John, AB RNVR (DAMS)
Sutoe, Iwai, 26 yrs, Donkeyman MM
Woodward, Harold, 24 yrs, 2nd Officer MM

At 1208 hrs on the 13th, Oblt.z.S. Stier was observing a distant Methil–Thames (southbound) convoy at periscope depth when the armed trawler *John Gillman* (Admiralty No. 3502) spotted the reflection of the periscope mirror from a range of 300 yards. The trawler made full speed and attempted to ram the U-boat, but Stier saw it coming and commenced an emergency dive. The *John Gillman* scraped noisily over the casing of *UB 30*. Two depth charges set at 100 ft were dropped and another two at 80 ft, bringing an oil slick and air to the surface. A DAN buoy was placed over the spot while the trawler called for reinforcements and waited in anticipation.

Two hours later *UB 30* attempted to surface, but the Tyne-based requisitioned anti-submarine trawlers *John Brooker* (Admiralty No. 3605) and *Viola II* (Admiralty No. 6) were listening in on the U-boat's motors with hydrophones. When the submarine broke surface they were ready and fired two shells each before *UB 30* dived again. The two boats then dropped five depth charges between them, set at 100 ft. It seems likely that this barrage of depth charges caused the fatal damage as the trawler crews could see oil pouring out of the submarine's pressure hull – UBII boats were fitted with external saddle tanks which carried water ballast amidships and oil fuel toward the ends.

Ten minutes later Stier made another attempt to surface but the RN yacht *Miranda II* together with requisitioned minesweeping trawler *Florio* (Admiralty No.1653) and HMT *Sparrow* (Admiralty No.58) joined in the attack, dropping four more depth charges set at 100 ft and two more at 150 ft.

UB 30 did not move again. Readily equipped, the auxiliary patrol had carried out a highly efficient attack. The evidence of such efficiency came to light at 2030 hrs when wire sweeps revealed an obstruction. Four days later Royal Navy divers under the charge of Cdr. Wheeler inspected the wreck. A telegram sent by Admiralty Salvage states: 'Submarine sunk on 13th August near L Buoy was today, Saturday, located by divers in 27½ fathoms LWOS. Unable to obtain boat number.' Salvage work on *UB 30* was called off in favour of lifting the all-important *UB 110*, which sank on 9 July off Saltburn, North Yorkshire. *UB 30* carried a crew of 26 at the time of her loss – her normal complement should have been 22.

NARA: T-1022. Roll 56, PG61777; Möltenort U-boat Memorial Foundation; CWGC; ADM 137/2964; Starke Schell Registers.

UB 110 was one of the larger 519-ton UBIII torpedo-attack submarines commanded by Kptlt Werner Fürbringer. It was sunk by warships 4.5 nm NE from Huntcliff, Saltburn on 19 July 1918. The wreck was raised to the surface and the long tow to Swan Hunter's shipyard on the Tyne began. On arrival at Swan Hunter shipyards on 4 October, the Admiralty wasted no time in opening her up. A valuable haul of code books, ciphers, documents and radio logs was recovered on 9 October. However, one of the most important finds was the General Message/Radio Book, (or *Allgemeines Funkspruchbuch*) with the substitution tables for Gamma Alpha ciphers. A journalist was later to claim that material found during the salvage of *UB 110* was responsible for the capture or destruction of about six more U-boats, in particular charts giving the location of safe bottoming-out zones off Flamborough Head in Yorkshire and Souter Point, just south of the Tyne.

The *UB30* crew killed were:

Beuckert, Alfred, U-Matrose
Biller, Peter, U-Matrose
Boesen, Heinrich, U-Maschinist
Breitfeld, Max, U-Oberheizer
Daut, Johann, U-Heizer
Dieterich, Will, U-Heizer
Feit, Wilhelm, U-Obermaschinistenmaat
Franke, Karl, U-Matrose
Kirchhoff, August, U-Matrose
Kraest, Willy, U-Oberbootsmannsmaat
Kruczeck, Al, U-Oberheizer
Kusche, Adolf, U-F.T.Ober Gast
Lettau, Robert, U-Maschinistenmaat
Möller, Robert, U-Maschinistenmaat
Müller, Gottfried, U-Oberheizer
Pohl, Adolf, U-Maschinistenmaat
Prescher, Joseph, U-Maschinistenmaat
Prinz, Heinrich, Leutnant zur See
Schneider, Fritz, U-Matrose
Schreiber, E., U-Heizer
Schwartz, Paul, U-Obermatrose
Stier, Rudolf, Oberleutnant zur See
Tielke, Fritz, T-Maschinistenmaat
Voget, Hans, U-Matrose
Wiatzka, Josef, U-Matrose
Wohlers, Martin, U-Oberbootsmannsmaat

Wrecksite

The wreck leans over to port at about 45-degrees and lies on a dirty seabed of sand and mud, just outside the Whitby spoil-ground, in a general depth of 45 m. Sport divers from Scarborough Sub Aqua Club – Carl Racey, Andrew Jackson and a comparatively novice diver – first located the wreck in June 1993. Carl reported:

> [T]he conning tower hatch, which must have been blown off by Royal Navy divers soon after it sank, was the first thing we found. It was alone on the seabed, well off on the port side, the dive boat's anchor having slipped off the wreck before we got down. All I saw was the hatch then, as my eyes adjusted in the gloom, I could make out the bow area of my first submarine. There was some damage and decay in places, mostly in the bow area, but the pressure hull was largely intact. One of the torpedo tubes was in place with the remains of a torpedo still inside. The other tube, which was badly damaged and had broken off, was found on the seabed shrouded in lost fishing nets. The twin screws, which have thick encased prop shafts attached, were still in place. The small conning tower was still intact, but the hatch cover was missing. This was found on the seabed well clear of the wreck. The forward and rear hatches were also both open, with high levels of silt inside them. Both periscopes were mostly retracted with the rear one bent forward. One of the exhausts was laid on the seabed aft of the conning tower on the port side, along with some other wreckage. The deck gun that used to be in place on the fore deck has now fallen onto the seabed on the port side and is also entwined with lost nets. When the wreck was first located it was absolutely enveloped with gill and trawl

> nets, plus numerous lost crab/lobster pots that had accumulated and these were tangled up with the wreckage and nets. However, divers have patiently removed many of these since it was found.

The find has been reported to the German Embassy and the Archives at Cuxhaven and no attempt should be made to try and enter the wreck because it is a war grave.

On 25 August 1994 a Whitby diver died after his air ran out while diving the wreck.

HURSTWOOD

Date of loss: 5 February 1917
Wreck: ★★★
Depth: 52 m
Reference: 54 32'.293 N 000 31'.369 W
Location: 4.17 nm NE from Whitby

The *Hurstwood* (Official No. 120651) was a steel-hulled 1209-ton British steam cargo ship that measured 68.58 m in length, with an 11.04-m beam and a 4.34-m draught.

S.P. Austin and Son built and completed her as Yard No. 234 at Wear Dock, Sunderland in January 1906. She was launched on 8 November 1905 for W. Cory & Son, London.

The single screw was powered by a 179-nhp three-cylinder triple expansion steam engine that used one single-ended boiler working at 160–90 psi with four corrugated furnaces, 7.71 m (83 sq.ft) of grate surface and 253.81 m (2732 sq.ft) of heating surface. George Clark Ltd. manufactured the engine and ancillary machinery at Sunderland. She had one deck, a 6.7-m poop deck, a 17-m quarterdeck, a 14.3-m bridge deck and a 7.6-m forecastle.

From 1916 Cory Colliers Ltd. London was the registered owner.

Final voyage

On 5 February 1917 the *Hurstwood* was in ballast and carrying a crew of 15 on a voyage from London to pick up a cargo of coal at Newcastle. She was making 9 knots when the periscope of a KDM submarine was seen about 140 metres off her port beam at 1150 hrs. At almost that same instant and without time to put out a warning, a torpedo detonated on her port side, abreast of the engine room. The submarine was later identified as the KDM U-boat SMU *UB 34*, commanded by Oblt.z.S. Theodor Schultz. The ship was settling fast as the engine room area was half full of oil and water, therefore Captain Carlson ordered the engine stopped and instructed the crew to take to the boats and abandon ship. Three of the men had been injured in the massive explosion and the master had to attend to their wounds before helping them into the boat. After a roll call it was discovered that a fireman, the chief and the second engineer – who had all been in the engine room when she was hit – were missing. There was no response to the crew's shouts and with the vessel sinking they had to leave to save themselves. An armed escort trawler picked up the survivors almost immediately and took them to Whitby, where the injured received further treatment for their wounds, although a donkeyman, one of the three men badly injured, died in the boat. The *Hurstwood* remained afloat for one hour and twenty five minutes after being torpedoed and sank at 1315 hrs. The men that died were:

Bidmead, Edward James, 52 yrs, Donkeyman MM
Sibbald, Frederick Matthew, 38 yrs, 2nd Engineer MM
Udall, Robert, 43 yrs, 1st Engineer MM
Wrathmall, Richard, 40 yrs, Fireman MM.

ADM 137/2961; LCWLR 1914–1918, p. 90; BVLS 1914–1918, p. 31; Starke Schell Registers; CWGC; Jarvis (2000).

Wrecksite

The wreck is orientated in an almost E to W (085/265-degrees) direction and lies on a seabed of sand, shell and mud in a general depth of 52 m (LAT). It is well broken up, with the highest section being around 5.2 m high. A lot of broken machinery and steel debris are scattered around in an area measuring about 75 m by 15 m. The wreck attracts a variety of large fish, especially at the western end which has the two highest points and should make a good boat-angling venue.

AFRICAN TRANSPORT

Date of Loss: 25 June 1918
Wreck: ✯✯✯
Depth: 28 m
Reference: 54 32'.906 N 000 42'.447 W
Location: 1.66 nm NE from Runswick Village and 0.87 nm N by E of Kettleness

The *African Transport* (Official No. 135886) was a steel-hulled 4482-ton British steam cargo ship that measured 117.34 m in length, with a 15.84-m beam and an 8.25-m draught. Northumberland Shipbuilding Company at Howdon near North Shields built and completed her as Yard No. 206 in July 1913. She was launched on 21 April 1913 for Empire Transport Company Ltd. at West Hartlepool, who also owned her at the time of loss. The manager was Houlder Bros and Company. The single screw was powered by a 320-nhp three-cylinder triple expansion steam engine that used three single-ended boilers. The cylinders measured 63.5 cm, 101.6 cm and 172.72 cm with a 121.92-cm stroke (25 in., 40 in. and 68 in. with a 48-in. stroke). Richardsons, Westgarth and Company at Sunderland manufactured the engine and ancillary machinery. She had one deck, a 14.3-m poop deck, a 36.2-m bridge deck and 12.2-m forecastle. In 1915/16, the ship was armed for defence with a stern-mounted 4.7-inch Q.F. gun.

Final voyage

On 25 June 1918 two armed trawlers were escorting the *African Transport* (Captain T.H. Tamblyn) when the submerged KDM submarine SMU *UB 88*, commanded by Oblt.z.S Reinhard von Rabenau, torpedoed her without warning. The ship was transporting coal from the Tyne to Gibraltar via Falmouth. The torpedo detonated next to the ship's engine room, instantly killing the fourth engineer and two firemen. The ship was taken in tow by the two escorts, but was badly damaged below the waterline and abandoned soon after. Twenty five minutes later the ship heeled up – the bows coming up in the air – and went down to the bottom. The surviving crew were landed at ports in the Tees and Humber later that day. The three crewmen killed were:

Gibson, John, 25 yrs, Fireman and Trimmer MM
McCormack, Dennis ,52 yrs, Fireman and Trimmer MM
Parker, John George, 20 yrs, 4th Engineer Officer MM.

ADM 137/2964; CWGC; LCWLR 1914–1918, p. 223; BVLS 1914–1918, p. 92; Starke Schell Registers; Jarvis & Jarvis (1993) Vol. 2.

Wrecksite

The remains of *African Transport* lie on a rather dirty seabed of sand, stone and rocks in a general depth of 28 m (LAT). It is very substantial, standing about 5 m high amidships and covers a large area of seabed. The boilers, condenser and the battered engine are surrounded by masses of broken pieces of winch and machinery, bollards, twisted steel plates, pipes and valves – many of them non-ferrous. Nets are very often draped over the top of the wreck.

The owner of the wreck was alleged to have removed the vessel's stern gun and had it mounted on a memorial plinth at Whitby West Cliff, however, some divers say that the gun in question came from a different wreck.

LAMPADA, ex SNILESWORTH

Date of loss: 8 December 1917
Wreck: ★★★
Depth: 41 m
Reference: 54 33'.126 N 000 37'.518 W
Location: 3.65 nm N of Whitby

The *Lampada* (Official No. 95280) was a steel-hulled 2220-ton British steam cargo ship that measured 85.64 m in length, with a 12.19-m beam and a 5.99-m draught. Short Brothers at Pallion, Sunderland built and completed her as Yard No. 180 in January 1889. She was launched as the schooner-rigged *Snilesworth* on 15 November 1888 for J. Tully of Sunderland with Captain G. Matthews the master until 1887. The single steel screw was powered by a 180-nhp three-cylinder triple expansion steam engine that used two single-ended boilers. The cylinders measured 53.34 cm, 88.9 cm and 154.32 cm with a 106.68-cm stroke (21 in., 35 in. and 53 in. with a 42-in. stroke). J. Dickinson at Sunderland

Steering gear from the steamer Lampada *recovered by Rob Broadhead and Anne Polkey of Scarborough Sub Aqua Club in June 2006 (Courtesy Carl Racey)*

manufactured the machinery. She had water ballast, one deck, four watertight bulkheads and a 9.7-m poop deck, a 23.1-m bridge deck and 9.7-m forecastle.

In 1906 Tully Steam Ship Company at Sunderland was the registered owner and J. Tully and Sons was the manager. From 1915 Gas Light and Coke Company, London was the registered owner and Stephenson Clarke & Co was manager. The ship was renamed *Lampada*. The *Lampada* was equipped with a stern-mounted, 6-pounder deck gun in 1916.

Final voyage

At 1515 hrs on 8 December 1917 and in heavy seas, SMU *UB 75*, a KDM submarine commanded by Oblt.z.S Franz Walther, torpedoed and sunk the *Lampada* without any warning. The steamer was on passage from the Tyne for London with a cargo of coal and carrying a crew of 22. All of the crew escaped in the ship's two boats, but the boat carrying the master Captain Wigham capsized when a huge wave suddenly swamped it and two of the men were drowned. Three others were picked up, either dead or dying. A steamship rescued all remaining survivors and later transferred them to a Royal Navy motorboat which landed at Whitby harbour. The five crewmen that died were:

Johansen, Gustave, Fireman MM, born in Sweden
McColl, Michael, 27 yrs, Steward MM
Pazzal, Ralph Nathaniel, 14 yrs, Mess Room Steward MM
Ringholdsten, A., Fireman MM, born in Norway
Smith, John Edward, 40 yrs, Fireman MM.

ADM 137/2963; LCWLR 1914–1918, p. 188; CWGC; BVLS 1914–1918, p. 75; Starke Schell Registers; Jarvis & Jarvis (1993), Vol. 2.

Wrecksite

The wreck is orientated in a SW to NE direction and lies on a seabed of sand, gravel and broken shells in a general depth of 41 m (LAT). It covers an area 95 m in length, 20 m across and stands 4.4 m high. It is well broken up with the stern section inverted and the bow is lying alongside it. The triple expansion steam engine is over on its side and the wreck is well covered in nets floating up about 10 m. Artefacts recovered from the site suggest that this is the *Lampada*. There are two single boilers but the furnaces are not fully visible, being somewhat silted up. The bow section has collapsed back and over a little but is still standing about 4 m. The two large winches are down at the lower hold level. The remains of a compass was found by a diver in August 2003 and a brass steering pedestal top and wheel boss, inscribed: 'John Lynn and Company Ltd. - Makers - Sunderland', recovered in June 2006. The bows face towards the northwest and the wreck has no sign of any cargo.

ELLIDA

Date of loss: 19 April 1917
Wreck: ☆☆☆
Depth: 42 m
Reference: 54 33'.094 N 000 37'.235 W
Location: 3.60 nm N by W of Whitby

Ellida *(Courtesy Norwegian Maritime Museum)*

The *Ellida* was a steel-hulled 1124-ton Norwegian steam cargo ship that measured 69.62 m in length, with a 10.76-m beam and a 4.8-m draught. Bergens Mekaniske Verksteder (BMV), Bergen built and completed her as Yard No. 112 in June 1901. She was launched on 20 September 1901 for Adolph Halvorsen, Bergen. The single steel screw was powered by a 101-nhp three-cylinder triple expansion steam engine that used one single-ended boiler. The cylinders measured 40.64 cm, 63.5 cm and 109.22 cm with a 76.2-cm stroke (16 in., 25 in. and 43 in. with a 30-in. stroke). BMV, Bergen manufactured the machinery. She had one deck.

Her designated code recognition signal letters were: JPQD.

From 1915 until the time of loss Aktieselskapet Dampskipsselskapet 'Ellida', Bergen was the registered owner and A. Halvorsen was the manager.

Final voyage

On 19 April 1917 the *Ellida* was in ballast and *en route* from Caen to the Tyne, when Oblt.z.S Günther Krause's KDM submarine SMU *UB 41* torpedoed her without warning. She was hit on the port side and in the aft part of the ship at 1115 hrs, 2.5 miles east-by-north of Whitby. The crew of 16 including Captain Jens Torgersen took to the boats and were rescued 20 minutes later by a steam trawler.

LCWLR 1914–1918, p. 120; ANCL 1914–1918, p. 81; Starke Schell Registers; Miramar Ship Index; *Maritime Accident Statements for Norwegian Ships Sunk in Wartime: 1814–1918.*

Wrecksite

The wreck is orientated in an E to W direction and lies on a dirty seabed of mud, sand, gravel and broken shells in a general depth of 42 m (LAT). It is very substantial and intact, but completely inverted with the bows burst open and a large hole amidships where the boiler is visible. Lots of debris and a large tank lie over to the starboard side. Interestingly, a cast-iron four-bladed screw is in place – very unusual for a vessel built in 1901. This wreck should make a good boat-angling venue as numerous fish have been observed around the wrecksite.

HERKULES

Date of loss: 30 December 1917
Wreck: ✯✯✯✯
Depth: 39 m
Reference: N 54 33'.655 W 000 39'.948
Location: 4.46 nm NNW of Whitby light

The *Herkules* (Official No. 140440) was a steel-hulled 1295-ton Norwegian steam cargo ship that measured 71.67 m in length, with a 10.41-m beam and a 4.39-m draught. Bergens Mekaniske Verksteder (BMV), Bergen built and completed her as Yard No. 156 in April 1909. She was launched on 20 February 1909 for Det Bergenske Dampskibsselskab, Bergen. The single screw was powered by a 144-nhp three-cylinder triple expansion steam engine that used one boiler. The cylinders measured 46.99 cm, 76.2 cm and 127 cm with an 83.82-cm stroke (18.5 in., 30 in. and 50 in. with a 33-in. stroke). BMV also manufactured the engine and ancillary machinery. She had one deck and a 25.2-m quarterdeck.

In 1917 the ship was requisitioned by the Admiralty and placed under the management of The Shipping Controller, London to use as a collier, with W. Coupland and Co of London the managers. The vessel was then fitted with one 610-kilo (12-cwt) stern-mounted 12-pounder deck gun.

Final voyage

At 1550 hrs on 30 December 1917, Oblt.z.S. Walter Scheffler, commander of the KDM submarine SMU *UB 21*, torpedoed the *Herkules* without warning. The steamer was on passage from the Tyne for Newhaven and carrying a crew of 20 and a cargo of coal. When the torpedo detonated amidships on the port side, panic broke out as the crew tried to abandon ship. The second officer had to take charge when the master, Captain Alfred Longstaff, and nine of his crewmen were drowned after their lifeboat capsized. He ordered the dinghy to be carefully lowered into the sea and the remaining ten men clambered into it. Unfortunately, the weather was poor and in the freezing conditions two of the men died from exposure before they were rescued by a fishing vessel and landed at Whitby. Twelve crewmen died, including one DAMS gunner:

Griffith, Charles, 47 yrs, Steward MM
Hamid, A.,Fireman MM (buried in Whitby Cemetery).
Kayopolos, J., Able Seaman MM
Kylimbas, C., Able Seaman MM
Longstaff, Alfred, 50 yrs, Master/Captain MM
Richardson, Albert, 17 yrs, 2nd Engineer MM
Said, M., Fireman MM (buried in Whitby Cemetery)
Stevenson, Hector MacDonald, 17 yrs, Mess Room Boy
Symon, William Pyper, 68 yrs, 1st Mate MM
Abdul Ali, Fireman MM
Salim, A., Fireman MM
Battye, Joseph Ingham, Leading Seaman RNVR

CWGC; Starke Schell Registers; ADM 137/2963; LCWLR 1914–1918, p. 92; BVLS 1914–1918, p. 77; *Maritime Accident Statements for Norwegian Ships Sunk in Wartime: 1814–1918*; Jarvis & Jarvis (1993), Vol. 2; Jarvis & Jarvis (1996), Vol. 4.

Wrecksite

The wreck lies on a dirty seabed of mud, sand, gravel and broken shells in a general depth of 39 m (LAT). It is very substantial, but collapsed and broken and standing about 5 m high with the boiler and engine exposed. A donkey engine also lies close by, surrounded by collapsed hull plates, broken machinery and debris. The bows and stern section are covered in soft corals and her iron screw is still in place. At least one trawl net hangs over the bow section like a curtain. There are numerous large copper pipes, massive brass valves and a large pump amidships, which is the highest part of the wreck. A lot of big fish have also been spotted including cod and ling at least ten kilos in size, so it should make an excellent boat-angling venue.

GWALIA (?)

Date of loss: 24 April 1907
Wreck: ★★
Depth: 49 m
Reference: 54 33'.909 N 000 35'.768 W
Location: 4.37 nm N of Whitby light

The *Gwalia* (Official No. 84990) was an iron-hulled 1354-ton British steam cargo ship that measured 73.15 m in length, with a 10.05-m beam and a 5.05-m draught. William Pickersgill and Sons at Southwick, Sunderland built and completed her as Yard No. 51 in 1881. She was launched on 11 August 1881 for Hurley, Mathews and Company, Cardiff. The single iron screw was powered by a 120-nhp two-cylinder compound steam engine that used two Scotch boilers. The cylinders measured 73.66 cm and 142.24 cm with a 91.44-cm stroke (29 in. and 56 in. with a 36-in. stroke). She had one deck, four bulkheads and water ballast.

In 1884 Gwalia Steam Ship Company Cardiff was the registered owner, Captain D. Hughes was the master and Hurley, Matthews and Company the manager. Captain J.R. Mead was master from 1885 to 1895, followed by Captain W.H. Cornish who served up until at least 1900. From 1888 F.J. Broomfield was the registered owner. By 1900 *Gwalia* had the same owner, but E.C. Hurley and Company was the manager until 1905 when F.J. Broomfield took over. The designated code recognition signals letters were: WCFM.

Final voyage

At about midnight on 24 April 1907 the *Gwalia* sank following a collision six miles NE of Whitby, with the 919-ton Polish steamer *Theodor* (1890 – Renate Dampfschiff Ges. Th. Gribel, Stettin). The *Theodor* rescued the *Gwalia*'s crew and landed them at Blyth, Northumberland. The *Gwalia* had been on passage from the Tyne for Bordeaux with a cargo of coal.

Starke Schell Registers; American Lloyd's Register of American and Foreign Shipping 1857–1900; Miramar Ship Index; *The Times*: Friday, 26 April 1907, p. 12, Issue no. 38317.

Wrecksite

The wreck, which is possibly that of the *Gwalia*, is orientated in a N to S direction, with the bows to the south. It lies on a seabed of dirty sand, shell and stones in a general depth of 49 m (LAT). The bow section is quite high, but leans at a 45 –degrees angle to port and has fallen backwards. The forward holds have collapsed onto the seabed, but the midships area stands about 5.2 m high where the two boilers and engine are located. The engine is also leaning over to starboard next to the starboard boiler. The wreck is fairly broken up and well decayed. A number of decent-sized fish were observed close to the engine and a pout whiting shoal over the wreck.

PANDORA, EX ICEWHALE

Date of Loss: 22 October 1951
Wreck: ✯✯✯✯
Depth: 34 m
Reference: 54 34'.259 N 000 41'.401 W
Location: 3.34 nm NE from Runswick

Above: Pandora, *ex*-Icewhale, *c.1910 (Author's collection)*

Left: Polished bell from the Pandora *(Courtesy Carl Racey)*

The *Pandora* (Official No. 90948) was an iron-hulled 203-ton British steam coaster that measured 35.35 m in length, with a 7.03-m beam and a 2.36-m draught. Schlisinger, Davies and Company at Wallsend built and completed her as Yard No. 165 in January 1893. She was launched as *Pandora*, on 30 August 1892, for Leith and Montrose Shipping Company, Montrose. J. McKenzie and Sons of Liverpool was the manager. The single iron screw was powered by a 35-rhp two-cylinder compound steam engine that used one single-ended boiler, two plain furnaces, 2.32 sq.m (25 sq.ft) of grate surface and 51.56 sq.m (555 sq.ft) of heating surface, which gave 8 knots in reasonable weather. The cylinders measured 33.02 cm and 66.04 cm with a 40.63-cm stroke (13 in. and 26 in. with a 16-in. stroke). Messrs Hedley and Boyd at North Shields manufactured the machinery. She had one deck, three transverse steel bulkheads cemented and a 14-m quarterdeck, a 2.1-m bridge deck and a 4.2-m forecastle. The cargo was carried in one long hold between the forecastle and the bridge structure, with a single hatchway that was fitted with transverse hatch beams, wooden hatchboards and covered with tarpaulins – which were secured at the hatch coamings by battens and wooden wedges that were hammered into cleats. She also had a forepeak tank of 16 tons. A light derrick was rigged on the foremast and a steam winch provided for cargo handling. In her early years the *Pandora* carried fore and aft sails.

In 1903 she was owned by the Anglesey Shipping Company and began a long association with Port Penrhyn and the slate trade. In 1917 the Rt. Hon. Baron Penrhyn owned her and O.J. Jones was the manager. She was re-boilered with a single Scotch-type boiler in the 1930. Her coal consumption was 3–4 tons per day and her steaming speed was 7–8 knots.

On 28 February 1941 the Admiralty requisitioned her and she was renamed *Icewhale* because the Royal Navy already had a submarine called *Pandora*. She was used as an air target. Her designated code recognition signal letters were: MQTD.

The vessel was sold in October 1947 to Anglesey Shipping at Beaumaris, where she was registered and renamed *Pandora*. R.J. Lewis was the manager. Soon after, the vessel was registered to John D. Ormiston of Edinburgh. From November 1948 Merchiston Steam Ship Company, Edinburgh was the registered owner and George A. Morrison and Company of Leith was the manager.

The *Pandora* spent most of her career with this owner plying the northeast coast and called in at the Tees fairly regularly, often discharging grain at the Cleveland flourmill at Thornaby on Tees.

Final voyage

The *Pandora* was *en route* from Newburgh, Fife to Hull with a 180-ton and 4-cwt (203.20-kilo) cargo of half-inch whinstone chippings, and carrying a crew of six when she got into difficulties. On the morning of 22 October 1951 the weather, which had been moderate, rapidly deteriorated, resulting in a bad weather watch being set at the local coastguard stations. At 0430 hrs the wind increased to force 8 with a heavy sea, continuing till about noon when it rapidly improved. At about 0630 hrs distress rockets throwing red stars were fired from the *Pandora* and observed by nearby coastguard stations and the 2852-ton steam collier *Gripfast* (1941: Newbiggin Steam Shipping Company, Newcastle). The *Gripfast* was to the northward of Whitby, in ballast and *en route* to the Tyne. She proceeded towards the *Pandora* and closed within 60 feet (18.28 m). With no response to the hailing to the crew of the *Pandora* to jump, *Gripfast* was manoeuvred alongside to windward, with her port side alongside the starboard side of the *Pandora*, and was in close contact for a few minutes. Lines and ladders were over the side ready for the *Pandora*'s crew to board whilst the ships were in contact, but none of the *Pandora*'s crew took advantage of this opportunity, even though the bulwarks of the *Gripfast* were at times in close contact with the rails of the stricken steamer with the *Gripfast*'s crew lined along her rail waiting to assist. About 20 minutes later, after the ships had drifted about 150 yards apart, the *Pandora* foundered. The *Gripfast* attempted to pick up survivors, but was unable to do so on account of having suffered damage to her screw in the rescue attempt. She was forced to anchor off the leeward shore and receive tugboat assistance. The *Pandora* sank with all hands at 0744 hrs on 22 October 1951. The position given was approximately: latitude 54 degrees 36¼ minutes N and Longitude 0 degrees 41 minutes W.

The nearest lifeboats at Whitby, Runswick and Redcar were unable to respond to the call due to the horrendous weather conditions. The only boat able to put out to sea was the

Teesmouth lifeboat, but when she arrived at the scene the crew were unable to manoeuvre close enough to render assistance.

Back at Hartlepool the master of the *Gripfast*, Captain W. Norman Bainbridge, said:

> At about 0600 hrs the second mate saw star shells ahead and, on closing, we found the *Pandora*. She had already tried to launch a boat and it was upside down. Her crew were trying to launch their other boat, but it was impossible because of the state of the sea and the ship was pitching and rolling. I took my ship alongside *Pandora* and my crew was standing by with heaving lines, but they were reluctant to do so. The ships were in danger of crashing together in the big seas. I had to back away and in doing so damaged my screw and then a few minutes later *Pandora* sank. We could see men floating amongst the wreckage. I tried to pick them up but with my screw damaged and the state of the sea, it was too difficult, then they were carried away out of sight.

Captain Bainbridge said his own ship was drifting towards the lee shore, but a tug from the Tees, after a radio message, towed them back.

Three bodies were later recovered and during the afternoon, the body of one man, who was believed to have been a crewman on the *Pandora*, was washed ashore along with a ship's boat at Saltwick, a mile east of Whitby. The men that died were:

Allison, J., Master from Aberdeen
Morris, G.A., Mate from Aberdeen
Thom, A.R., Chief Engineer from Peterhead
Crawford, A., 2nd engineer from Fraserburgh
Dyker, William, Cook A.B. from Aberdeen
Ramsay, R., Able Seaman from Edinburgh

The loss of this vessel and her crew drew a great deal of criticism, anger and bitterness from the press and local fishing communities of North Yorkshire, with questions being asked as to the whereabouts of so many local lifeboats. The lifeboat management was criticised and even though the RNLI supported them, the entire crew of the Whitby boat resigned. At Runswick there was so much resentment that it was impossible to get enough crew members to man the boat and as a result the station was forced to close.

In 1995 an ex-crewman on the *Gripfast*, Bert G. Spaldin of Hartlepool, said that he recalled Captain Bainbridge as being a superb seaman and his chief officer, Jimmy Reed, as being another good seaman. Both men lived in Tyneside.

LCR 1951, p. 29; LR 1949/50 No. 21440 (P); Starke Schell Register; Miramar Ship Index; Board of Trade Wreck Return 1951; *The Times*: Tuesday, 23 October 1951, p. 4, Issue no. 52139; *The Times*: Friday, 9 November 1951, p. 2, Issue no. 52154; *The Times*: Saturday, 24 November 1951, p. 4, Issue no. 52167.

Wrecksite

The wreck is lying on a seabed of dirty sand, gravel, shells and mud in a general depth of 37 m (LAT). It is upright and reported to be still largely intact, standing about 6 m high, but collapsed in on itself amidships, where much of the bridge superstructure was located. The hull stands up 2 m or so from the seabed, with the screw in place and half buried. Soft corals have now taken hold on the hull plates and surrounds, and large cod and a shoal of pout whiting were observed.

MARIE STUART

Date of loss: 7 March 1883
Wreck: ★★★
Depth: 53 m
Reference: 54 34'.759 N 000 33'.652 W
Location: 5.55 nm NNE from Whitby's West Pier

The *Marie Stuart* was an iron-hulled 564-ton steam cargo vessel that measured 60 m in length, with an 8-m beam. Messrs Andrew Leslie and Company at Hebburn on Tyne built and completed her as Yard No. 59 in August 1864. She was launched on 20 August 1864 for George Gibson and Co of Leith. The single iron screw was powered by a 120-nhp two-cylinder compound steam engine that used one simple boiler. The bulkhead on the fore part of the deck house was made of iron, while that on the after part was of wood, as was also the bulkhead at the fore part of the poop. A wooden bulkhead, it was said, may be made capable of resisting almost any pressure and no doubt that is so; still experience has shown that an iron bulkhead is generally safer. The vessel had a midships steering wheel and two wells, one forward the other aft, with two hatchways in each. In bad weather they would be liable to take in and retain large quantities of water.

At the time of her loss she was the property of Messrs Gibson & Somerville, while Mr Mungo Campbell Gibson of Leith was the manager.

Final voyage

At 2200 hrs on 5 March 1883 the *Marie Stuart* sailed from Burntisland for passage to Dunkerque with a crew of 18 and a cargo of 464 tons, comprised mainly of coal, plus about 60 tons in her bunkers. The ship disappeared off Whitby in mountainous seas and gale force N to NNE winds. The pilot from Burntisland left her about a mile outside the harbour and continued to see her lights as she passed Inch Keith, but that was the last sighting. She never arrived at her destination and there was every reason to believe that she was been lost with all hands. George Gibson gave the vessel up as lost and published a crew list on 16 March.

At the official court of inquiry Mr. Lewis, the Board of Trade surveyor at Leith, said it was owing to her tunnel not being watertight that he had refused to give her a certificate for more than six months and that he should not have given her a certificate at all if she had not already had a passenger certificate granted to her.

It seems that early in the morning of 7 March, a man named Robinson, a jet worker at Whitby, went down to the beach a little south of the harbour to see if he could pick up anything on the shore, there having been a very severe gale on the previous day. He found wreckage that included part of the stern board of one of the *Marie Stuart*'s boats and a lifebuoy. Her name was painted on both. Other articles were also found, including a cushion, a lifejacket, and a wooden pump-break broken away from the bolt hole and branded 'E, V.S.H.' (What these initials refer to, we are yet to elicit.) There was also a ladder, identified as having belonged to the 901-ton *Fervent* (1876 – James Westoll, Sunderland). In fact it was suggested at the inquiry that the two vessels were in all probability involved in a collision and both foundered with all hands. Other suggestions put forward were that it was possibly one of the boats, which were stowed abreast of the engine room casing, which might have been struck by a beam sea, and thrown against the funnel thus disabling her, but this, again, is pure conjecture. Another suggestion was that the rods connecting the midships wheel with the rudder might have been carried along the sides above the rail and could have been damaged by something striking against the rods, in which case the *Marie Stuart* would have been at once disabled, and might then have fallen into the trough of the sea and sunk.

Board of Trade Wreck Report: Marie Stuart, 1883; Miramar Ship Index; *The Times*, Thursday, 8 March 1883, p. 12, Issue no. 30762.

Wrecksite

The wreck – identified by Scarborough divers Andrew Jackson and Carl Racey by the engine maker's plate – is orientated in a NE to SW direction. It lies on a seabed of sand, mud, pebbles and shells in a general depth of 53 m (LAT). The wreck stands 5.1 m high and covers an area 60 m long and 8 m across, with the NW section intact but the SE part well broken up. Lots of soft corals adorn the highest parts and numerous fish have been observed, all around the northwestern section.

DISPERSER, EX HMS BONETTA

Date of loss: 8 February 1934
Wreck: ✯✯✯
Depth: 49 m
Reference: 54 34'.025 N 000 32'.185 W
Location: 5.24 nm NNE of Whitby light

The *Disperser* (Official No. 127450) was an iron-hulled 139-ton British steam vessel measuring 25.9 m in length, with a 7.95-m beam and a 2.66-m draught. J. and G. Rennie, Greenwich completed her in 1871. She was launched on 20 May 1871 as the *Bonetta*, an Ant class gunboat for the Royal Navy. The twin bronze screws were powered by a 100-rhp two-cylinder horizontal compound steam engine that used one boiler and gave 8 knots. The cylinders measured 40.64 cm and 38.1 cm (16 in. and 15 in.). She had one deck. In 1908 a new boiler was fitted.

After decommissioning in 1909 William H. Loveridge of West Hartlepool purchased the boat. From 12 January 1919 the North East Salvage and Shipbroking Company, West Hartlepool was the registered owner and converted the *Bonetta* to a salvage vessel renamed *Disperser*.

Final voyage

At 0400 hrs on 8 February 1934 the *Disperser* was in ballast and being towed from Whitby to Ramsgate by a tug. During the voyage a fierce WNW gale developed. In heavy seas, about 5 miles NNE of Staithes in North Yorkshire, the vessel sprang a serious leak. Her skipper therefore fired off a number of distress flares. The coastguard observed the flares and notified the RNLI. The new Runswick lifeboat, *The Always Ready* was launched in torrential rain at 0420 hrs. The lifeboat had just arrived at the station in October 1933 and was one of the 10.85-metre non self-righting Liverpool class boats, fitted with a single 35-nhp Weyburn AE6 petrol engine that gave a top speed of 7.33 knots. She also carried a full set of sails.

Coxswain Robert Patton was at the helm of the lifeboat, but when they arrived at the scene – the journey having taken one hour – they discovered eight of the vessel's crew had been rescued by a tug which was already towing the *Disperser* with one injured man still on board. Realising the vessel was sinking rapidly, Coxswain Patton skilfully manoeuvred the lifeboat alongside and the lifeboatmen shouted for the man to jump. Being quite badly injured, he was only able to lower himself over the side and cling on. Coxswain Patton grabbed hold of the man and shouted for him to let go, but the injured man panicked and tightened his grip. Just at that moment a huge wave smashed into the steamer's side, pushing the lifeboat away. Coxswain Patton had a split second to react and instinctively grabbed the man. The lifeboat was pushed further away from the *Disperser* by the incoming wave and both men fell into the sea, with the Coxswain still holding the man. The next surge of water picked up the lifeboat and smashed her back into the side of the *Disperser*, crushing Coxswain Patton. This happened twice more before the lifeboatmen could pull the two men on board. With Coxswain Patton seriously injured, Second Coxswain George Taylor took the *The Always Ready* back to Runswick at high speed, landing the Coxswain at 0615 hrs when he was rushed to Whitby hospital. His injuries included several broken ribs, a pelvis fractured in three places, a fractured vertebra and numerous other injuries.

He was able to tell a member of the RNLI's headquarter staff, who visited him two days later, what happened and said: "I could not let the poor lad go, as he might have drowned." Sadly, Robert Patton died of his injuries on 17 February. The *Disperser* went down to the bottom just as the lifeboat was leaving the scene.

LCR 1934, p. 5; LR 1931/2, No. 19209 (D); Morris (1987); *The Times*: Friday, 9 February 1934, pp. 16, 24, Issue no. 46674.

Wrecksite

The wreck lies in a general depth of 49 m (LAT). From the gunwhales to the seabed is about 3 m high, with the bow intact and the stern reasonably intact. However, the wheelhouse is no longer prominent and the decking is mostly gone, exposing a lot of the air pipes that were used for the standard diving suits. A number of divers have visited the wrecksite and at least one standard diving helmet has been recovered, along with lead boots.

POLANNA, ex ANNA WOERMANN, ex ANTONINA

Date of loss: 6 August 1917
Wreck: ★★★★★
Depth 52 m
Reference: 54 34'.793 N 000 32'.336 W
Location: 5.88 nm NNE of Whitby harbour

The *Polanna* (Official No. 139452) was a steel-hulled 2335-ton steam cargo ship measuring 85.95 m in length, with an 11.58-m beam. Blohm & Voss, Hamburg built and completed her as Yard No. 96 on 9 September 1893. She was launched as the *Antonina* for Hamburg-Südamerik, Dampfschifffahrts Gesellschaft, Hamburg on 29 July 1893 and registered in

Hamburg. The single screw was powered by a 1000-ihp three-cylinder triple expansion steam engine that used two boilers and gave 9.5 knots. Blohm & Voss manufactured the engine and ancillary machinery. In 1897 Woermann Line (Woermann Linie KG), Hamburg purchased and renamed her *Anna Woermann.*

With the outbreak of the First World War the ship was scuttled at Douala, Cameroon in September 1914 in order to obstruct the harbour, but was raised and repaired by the British.

In 1916 the Admiralty appointed Pardoe-Thomas and Company, Newport the Crown nominee mangers and renamed her *Polanna.* The ship was equipped with a stern-mounted 15-pounder (6.80-kilo shells) deck gun. From 1917 the owner was The Shipping Controller and Clyde Shipping Company, Glasgow was the Crown nominee manager.

Final voyage

On 6 August 1917 the *Polanna* was torpedoed and sunk without warning by the KDM mine-laying submarine SMU *UC 40*, commanded by Oblt.z.S. Gustav Deuerlich. The ship was on passage from the Tyne for Dunkerque with a 3000-ton cargo of coal and a crew of 26. While proceeding at 8 knots and taking a zig-zag course, one of the crew observed the track of an approaching torpedo about 50 yards away on the starboard quarter. The helm was thrown hard to port, but they were too late. The missile detonated on the port side in the number two hold at 1530 hrs. The ship went down within one and a half minutes, but not before the crew had scrambled to launch one of the boats and got away with 15 men in it. The other men went into the sea where two of them drowned, however, the other nine were rescued. The survivors in the boat made their way to shore and landed two miles south of Whitby. The two crewmen who died were:

Moriates, 21 yrs, Fireman and Trimmer from Greece
Peterson, August, 43 yrs Able Seaman from Denmark.

BVLS 1914–1918, p. 62; LCWLR 1914–1918, p. 161; CWGC; Starke Schell Registers; Jarvis (2000).

Wrecksite

The wreck is orientated in a SE to NW direction with the highest part standing almost 8 m high at the southeastern end. It lies on a seabed of dirty sand, mud and shells, in a general depth of 52 m (LAT). It is upright and intact, covering an area 90 m long and about 20 m across, with a lot of marine life. Andrew Jackson and Carl Racey identified the wreck from a steam whistle – manufactured in Hamburg – and some deck fittings, plus the engine and boiler details matched with the *Polanna.* This is a huge wreck and should make an excellent boat-angling venue.

DEPTFORD

Date of loss: 13 March 1862
Wreck: ★★★
Depth: 29 m
Reference: 54 34'.800 N 000 47'.509 W
Location: 1.23 nm N of Staithes harbour

The *Deptford* was an iron-hulled 606-ton schooner-rigged British steam cargo vessel that was registered in North Shields. James Laing at Deptford, Sunderland completed her as Yard No. 27 in 1861. She was launched on 27 October 1860. The single iron screw was powered by a two-cylinder compound steam engine that used two boilers. George Clark Ltd. manufactured the engine and ancillary machinery at Sunderland. She had one deck and four bulkheads.

Final voyage

On 13 March 1862 the steamer ran aground on Whitby Rock during a dense fog and Whitby's two lifeboats – the *Lucy* and *Fisherman's Friend* – were launched. It was the first time in service for the *Lucy*, but the faster and lighter of the two boats, the private lifeboat *Fisherman's Friend*, reached the stricken steamer first. The crew of the *Fisherman's Friend* shared the monetary salvage award for saving the ship with the steam tugs that were also involved in the rescue. She was successfully re-floated on the high tide and taken in tow, but the hull was badly damaged and even though frantic efforts were made to stem the flood of water rushing into her engine room, she was abandoned and foundered 2.25 miles off Boulby near Staithes.

SYC, p. 153; Miramar Ship Index; American Lloyd's Register of American and Foreign Shipping 1857–1900; *The Times*: Monday, 17 March 1862, p. 11, Issue no. 24195.

Wrecksite

For some reason, local fishermen and boat-anglers refer to this wreck as The Navigator while local divers have christened it The Toilet Wreck, because a bronze toilet was recovered from it.

The remains of the *Deptford* lie on a dirty sand and mud seabed in a general depth of 29 m (LAT). The remains are surprisingly large for such an old wreck, with the majority largely collapsed, except for the bow section which is reportedly still intact. The two boilers and large engine are surrounded by a mass of twisted iron plates, copper pipes, a donkey engine with a hole through it and broken machinery, though sections of it stand almost 4 m high around amidships. At the stern end are two screws – one attached to a shaft and the other probably a spare – while the ribs and plates making up the outline of the ship can plainly be seen. Occasionally shoals of small fish mainly pout whiting can be seen hovering over the wreck, but it is hardly worth spending much time angling over. Visibility is never very good because of the fallout from Boulby potash mine.

MOORWOOD

Date of Loss: 11 June 1941
Wreck: ★★★
Depth: 40 m
Reference: 54 34'.859 N 000 44'.217 W
Location: 2.23 nm NE of Staithes harbour

The *Moorwood* (Official No. 167413) was a steel-hulled 2056-ton British steam cargo ship that measured 83.28 m in length, with a 12.47-m beam and a 5.28-m draught. S.P. Austin and Son, Wear Dock, Sunderland built and completed her as Yard No. 352 in March 1940. She was launched on 24 February 1940 for France Fenwick and Company, London that owned the *Moorwood* at the time of loss. The single steel screw was powered by a 205-nhp three-cylinder triple expansion steam engine that used two single-ended boilers working at 220 psi, with six corrugated furnaces, 4.64 sq.m (50 sq.ft) of grate surface and 269.79 sq.m (2904 sq.m) of heating surface. The cylinders measured 43.18 cm, 68.58 cm and 121.92 cm with a 91.44-cm stroke (17 in., 27 in. and 48 in. with a 36-in. stroke). North Eastern Marine Engineering Company manufactured the aft-positioned machinery. She had one deck, five bulkheads part-cemented, a cruiser stern, and a 48.7-m quarterdeck and 9.7-m forecastle. She also had some cellular double bottom and an aft peak and fore peak tank. Lloyd's classed her 100 A1. Her designated code recognition signal letters were: GDWW.

Final voyage

On 11 June 1941 the *Moorwood* was bombed by the Luftwaffe and sank abeam of the 19C Buoy north of Whitby. She had sailed without a convoy from London in ballast for Blyth and was armed for defence. Her crew of 22, including three DEMS gunners, were rescued by escort vessels.

LCWLR 1939–1945, p. 266; BVLS 1939–1945, p. 24; Starke Schell Registers; LR 1940/1, No. 7980.

Wrecksite

The wreck is orientated in an ENE to WSW direction and lies on a seabed of sand, gravel, pebbles and mud in a general depth of 40 m (LAT). The remains are broken up and split amidships, with a cargo hold forward, now collapsed, towards the bows. The engine and two boilers are located aft at the eastern end, the tallest section. It is alleged that a telegraph has also been recovered from this area. The wreck attracts a variety of marine life, including large cod and ling, so it should make a good boat-angling venue.

COMMERCIAL

Date of loss: 16 January 1904
Wreck: ★★★
Depth: 44 m
Reference: 54 34'.876 N 000 40'.451 W
Location: 3.84 nm NE of Runswick

The *Commercial* (Official No. 115931) was an iron-hulled 496-ton British steam collier that measured 50.36 m in length, with an 8.75-m beam and a 4.03-m draught. John Fullerton and Company Paisley built and completed her as Yard No. 166 in November 1902. She was launched in October 1902 for the Commercial Gas Company London, which was also the owner at the time of loss. The single steel screw was powered by a 75-rhp two-cylinder compound steam engine that used one single-ended boiler working at 160 psi pressure, three corrugated furnaces, 5.66 sq.m (61 sq.ft) of grate surface and 161.16 sq.m (1950 sq.ft) of heating surface. McKie and Baxter Ltd. manufactured the machinery at Glasgow. She had one deck, four bulkheads cemented, and a 5.8-m poop deck and 5.8-m forecastle.

Final voyage

On Saturday, 16 January 1904, during force 5 WNW wind conditions, the *Commercial* – captained by George Skelton – foundered off Whitby. The steamer had left Tyne Dock near South Shields at 0200 hrs for passage to London, with a cargo of coal and 21 crewmen. All of the crew perished with the exception of the first mate, Gerald O'Brien of London, who was picked up by the 679-ton steamer *Garthdee* (1890: Aberdeen and Glasgow Steam Ship Company, Aberdeen) and taken to Hartlepool. The mate later stated that the ship was north of Whitby and got broadside to the waves, capsized and sank almost immediately. He said he was in his bunk when the alarm was raised at 0400 hrs on Saturday morning. He rushed on deck and finding the vessel sinking, jumped over board and made for an upturned boat that he had noticed in the water some distance away. With considerable difficulty due to the heavy sea, he scrambled onto it and was joined by the chief mate, Mr Durie. The two men remained on the upturned boat for about five hours until Durie, in an exhausted state and benumbed by the cold, couldn't hang on any longer. He released his hold and sank from sight. About three quarters of an hour later the steamer *Garthdee* arrived on the scene. Nothing could be seen of the *Commercial* or the other crewmen, but the end of the small upturned boat was spotted intermittently bobbing above the surface. The men who died were:

Skelton, George, Master, from London
Durie, Chief Mate from Montrose
Smith, Chief Engineer from Middlesbrough
Edmonds, 2nd Engineer from Camden Town
Corker, Steward from Wapping;
Two men called Reynolds from Dover.

The other 13 men killed were Scandinavian.

> On 22 October 1908 the *Garthdee* was wrecked near Peterhead, while in ballast and on a voyage from Aberdeen to Fraserburgh.

Board of Trade Wreck Return 1904; LR 1903/4, Issue no. 1172 (C); Starke Schell Registers; MOD Hydro. Wreck No. 6363; *The Times*: Monday, 18 January 1904, p. 6, Issue no. 37293.

Wrecksite

The wreck is orientated in an ESE to WNW direction and lies on a seabed of sand, gravel and mud in a general depth of 44 m (LAT). The remains are partially buried, well broken up and decayed, especially the bow section where there is a large pile of anchor chain. The single boiler and three furnaces are visible and the engine is lying over on its side. A number of portholes were located along with a steel telegraph and a steering pedestal manufactured by and inscribed with: Thomas Reid and Sons, Paisley 1902. From the reference number on the steering pedestal, divers Andrew Jackson and Carl Racey identified the wreck as being that of the *Commercial*.

HETTY (?)

Date of loss: 26 July 1894
Wreck: ✯✯✯
Depth: 53 m
Reference: 54 35'.059 N 000 34'.535 W
Location: 5.68 nm NNE from Whitby pier

The *Hetty* (Official No. 70433) was an iron-hulled 532-ton steam schooner-rigged cargo vessel measuring 50.47 m in length, with a 7.59-m beam. Raylton Dixon and Company, Middlesbrough built and completed her as Yard No. 118 in April 1875. She was launched on 7 April 1875 for J.P. Hornung of Middlesbrough. A 65-rhp two-cylinder compound steam engine that used one single-ended boiler powered the single iron screw. The cylinders measured 55.88 cm and 104.14 cm with a 66.04-cm stroke (22 in. and 41 in. with a 26-in. stroke). Blair and Company, Stockton-on-Tees manufactured the engine and ancillary machinery. She had one deck.

In 1887 J.F. Wilson, Middlesbrough was the registered owner, with Paterson Fox and Co. the manager Hetty Steam Ship Company, Middlesbrough became the registered owner in 1888 and Jervelund and Clephan manager. In 1889 she was sold to T.F. Bell and Co at Hull. Thomas Wilson Sons and Company at Hull was the registered owner in 1894 at the time of loss.

Final voyage

On the evening of Thursday 26 July 1894 the *Hetty* sank about five miles NE by N of Whitby following a collision with the 554-ton British steamer *John Johnasson* (1870 – John Sinclair, West Hartlepool). She was on voyage from Hull to Newcastle with a general cargo. The *John Johnasson*, which was slightly damaged in the collision, rescued all of the *Hetty*'s crew.

The Times: Monday, 30 July 1894, p. 10, Issue no. 34329; Starke Schell Registers; American Lloyd's Register of American and Foreign Shipping, 1857–1900.

Wrecksite

The wreck – which is probably that of the *Hetty* – is orientated in a SSE to NNW direction. It lies on a seabed of sand, mud, gravel and shells in a general depth of 53 m (LAT). The remains are well broken up, with the highest part standing 4 m from the seabed and the whole wreck covering an area 50 m long and 15 m across. This site is reported as being an interesting rummage dive, with a few crustaceans about.

LOCHIEL, HMS

Date of Loss: 24 July 1918
Wreck: ✯✯✯
Depth: 44 m
Reference: 54 35'.159 N 000 41'.418 W
Location: 3.7 nm NNE from the village of Runswick

The 241-ton well-decked steam passenger/cargo ferry Lochiel, *c.1910 (Author's collection)*

The *Lochiel* (Official No. 128207) was steel-hulled 241-ton well-decked steam passenger/cargo vessel measuring 41.16 m in length, with a 6.78-m beam, a 2.80-m draught and a 3.01-m moulded depth. Scott and Sons at Bowling completed her as Yard No. 207 in 1908. She was launched on 30 May 1908 for David MacBrayne Ltd. The single steel screw was powered by a 74-rhp compound two-cylinder steam engine that used one boiler. The cylinders measured 43.18 cm and 91.44 cm with a 60.96-cm stroke (17 in. and 36 in. with a 24-in. stroke). She had one deck, a well deck, a 17.67-m quarterdeck, a 7.92-m bridge deck and a 12.49-m forecastle.

The Admiralty, who owned her at the time of loss, requisitioned her in 1917 as Minesweeper No. 14 and armed her with two deck guns – one 12-pounder positioned amidships and one 6-pounder positioned aft.

Final patrol

At 1615 hrs on Wednesday, 24 July 1918 *Lochiel* (Skipper D. Macdougall) was escorting the 'UT' – Humber to Tyne – convoy at position 54° 36 30'N 00° 04'W, when she foundered and was lost. No mines were laid around that area, but the KDM submarine SMU *UB 34*, commanded by Oblt.z.S. Erich Förste, fired a single torpedo at a '2000 ton steamer' in a large convoy. The U-boat then dived, probably to avoid being rammed by another vessel in the path of the U-boat. Förste reportedly heard an explosion and presumed he had sunk the vessel he had fired at. The location of the sinking given by *UB 34* was: 54° 38'N, 0° 54'W. Oblt.z.S. Förste did note, however, that the convoy's escorts included trawlers, which can manoeuvre easily. Escort vessels counter attacked and 30 depth charges were noted as going off, but the submarine got away safely. It is certainly possible that *Lochiel* was inadvertently torpedoed by

UB 34 although not the intended target, if it got in the way of the U-boat and the vessel that the *UB 34* fired the torpedo at. The crewmen who died were:

Brannon, Thomas, Fireman MM
Cook, Robert Duff, Engineer Sub-Lt RNR
Crockford, George Henry, Greaser MM
Hall, Richard Hugh, Seaman RNR
Inman, Robert Hardwick, Ordinary Seaman RN
Langley, Walter, Deck Hand MM
Lovejoy, Alfred Leonard, Deck Hand MM
Maynard, Thomas James, Deck Hand MM
Mitchell, Herbert James, Fireman MM
Morrison, Angus, Seaman RNR
Robertsons, Alexander, Seaman RNR
Sandercock, Courtenay Lyne, Sub-Lt RNVR

The Admiralty replaced the vessel for David MacBrayne at the end of the First World War.

CWGC; Toghill (2004); DY, p. 28; SRN Vol. 2, p. 213; Jarvis & Jarvis (1993); Jarvis & Jarvis (1996); Jarvis (2000); LR 1918/19.

Wrecksite

The wreck is orientated in a SSE to NNW direction. It lies in a general depth of 44 m (LAT). The wreck is on an even keel, well decayed but mostly intact, with the stern the most intact section. The bows have collapsed to starboard and are rather scattered from what appears to have been a mine detonation. There was a trawl net on the stern and a bigger net over the port gunwales, about level with the boiler. Both guns are visible – a 12-pounder amidships and a 6-pounder fitted aft. Shoals of fish can be seen all over the wreck.

RUTIL

Date of loss: missing since 13 September 1916
Wreck: ★★
Depth: 45 m
Reference: 54 35'.992 N 000 41'.285 W
Location: 4.15 nm NE of Staithes Harbour

The *Rutil* was a 706-ton Norwegian steam cargo vessel that measured 56.08 m in length, with a 9.17-m beam and a 4.05-m draught. Akers Mekaniske Verksted, Kristiania (Oslo) built and completed her as Yard No. 359 in September 1913 for A/S Rutil, Kristiania and registered at Kristiania. A.O. Lindvig was the manager. The single screw was powered by a 600-ihp three-cylinder triple expansion steam engine that used one single-ended boiler. Akers Mekaniske Verksted manufactured the engine and ancillary machinery at Kristiania. The designated code letters were: MJSK. From 1916 Skibs A/S Adelante, Kristiania was the registered owner and Aug. F. Christensen was the manager until loss.

Final voyage

On 13 September 1916 the SS *Rutil* sailed from the Tyne with a cargo of coke for Le Tréport. Nothing was heard about the SS *Rutil* or her crew of 14 until a lifeboat from the ship was found at Leith in January 1917. The Admiralty concluded that she had detonated a mine and was lost with all hands, however, records show that there was a terrible storm raging in the North Sea at the time, with winds reaching force 12.

Lloyd's War Losses: World War I, p. 307; Starke Schell Registers; *Maritime Accident Statements for Norwegian Ships Sunk in Wartime: 1814–1918.*

Wrecksite

The wreck is orientated in a SSE to NNW direction and lies on a seabed of sand, gravel and mud in a general depth of 45 m (LAT). It is well decayed and broken up covering an area of 60 m in length by 12 m across, with the highest part standing just over 3 m. The cargo of iron ore is standing upright in square heaps. Scarborough sport divers Andrew Jackson and Carl Racey identified the wreck by the engine manufacturer's plate in 1995.

ATHELSTANE

Date of loss: 16 December 1892
Wreck: ★★★
Depth: 37 m
Reference: 54 35'.133 N 000 47'.060 W
Location: 1.55 nm N from Staithes Harbour

The *Athelstane* (Official No. 65436) was an iron-hulled 1123-ton schooner-rigged steam passenger/cargo vessel that measured 68.58 m in length, with a 9.14-m beam and 5.18-m draught. Andrew Leslie and Company, Hebburn on Tyne built and completed her as Yard No. 145. She was launched on 23 April 1872 for Adamson and Company at North Shields.

The single iron screw was powered by an amidships 99-nhp two-cylinder compound inverted steam engine that used two single-ended boilers and four plain furnaces. The cylinders measured 66.04 cm and 132.06 cm with a 76.2-cm stroke (26 in. and 52 in. with a 30-in. stroke). Thompson Boyd and Company manufactured the engine and ancillary machinery at Newcastle. She had one deck, four bulkheads, a 6.70-m poop deck and 12.49-m deck house. Captain W. Barwes was the master until 1877. In 1878 the registered owner was Adamson and Short of Tyne Street, North Shields and Captain W. Garrick was the master. From 1880 Captain Blacklock was the master until at least 1882. In 1883 new boilers were fitted. In 1887 the registered owner became H.E.P. Adamson of North Shields, the owner at the time of loss.

At about 2200 hrs on 9 March 1883 the *Athelstane* was coming into the Tyne when she struck the bar in passing through The Narrows and remained fast for about one hour until she came off with the flow of the tide. She then proceeded up river to Elswick where she discharged her cargo of iron ore at Sir William Armstrong's works. Shortly after, the Norwegian brig *Loven*, commanded by Captain Toft from Arendal, was entering the Tyne and grounded close to where the steamer had struck. Neither vessel was damaged.

Final voyage

At around 1830 hrs on the evening of Friday, 16 December 1892 a collision occurred between

The Athelstane's *bell after recovery (left) and polished (right) (Courtesy Carl Racey)*

the steamer *Athelstane* (Captain J. Foreman) and the 178-ton three-masted wooden schooner *Psyche* (1875 - Captain Barden) allegedly off Whitby High Light.

The steamer was transporting coal from North Shields to Rotterdam, while the *Psyche* was laden with bulk cement from Rochester to Leith. Conditions were squally and dark, with the wind WSW force-four at the time. According to the Norwegian seaman who was at the helm of the schooner, the mate also being on deck, the *Psyche* was sailing along beautifully under all sail when the steamer struck their vessel on the port bow, critically damaging the head (bows). Both vessels sustained serious damage.

After doing their utmost to keep the vessels afloat, the crews found it impossible to keep pace with the in-rush of water. After managing to keep the schooner above water for almost 18 hours she sank by the head at 1400 hrs on Saturday afternoon. A few minutes prior to that, the skipper, Captain D. Wright of the Scarborough trawler *Hero*, observed that both vessels were labouring heavily and appeared to be sinking. He quickly made towards them and got some of his crew into a small boat. His intention was to go to the assistance of the schooner to take the men off, but just as they were about to leave, he noticed that the crew of the *Psyche* - six in all, including the master - had already taken to their boat and were making towards the *Athelstane*, on which they eventually boarded.

The crew of the *Psyche* had just got clear of their vessel when it sank. The men had rowed in the boats until they were picked up by the steamer *Kronos* of Seaham Harbour. The *Kronos* remained by the stricken vessel all night, taking her in tow at daybreak. When the *Hero*, which was owned by Mr F. Goodwill of Scarborough, arrived on the scene, it was found that the *Athelstane* was in tow of the *Kronos*. The two ships had not proceeded very far however, before the master of the *Athelstane* ordered his crew to take to the boats and quickly the men from both the *Psyche* and the *Athelstane* were taken on board the *Hero*. The tow line between the steamers was then severed. The skipper of the *Hero* had decided to get clear away from the sinking ship and at 1420 hrs on Saturday afternoon, when they had travelled a quarter of a mile, the *Athelstane* was seen to founder.

All of the 23 crewmen, six from the *Psyche* and 17 from the steamer, were landed at Whitby by the *Hero* at about 1600 hrs on Saturday 23 December. The crew of both vessels lost everything they had on board, the steward of the steamer losing about £18 of provisions of which he was supplying the crew with; all he saved was his poorest set of clothes. The bright-faced cabin boy from the schooner left the ship in his bare feet and was provided with a half worn pair of shoes on board the rescuing boat. Immediately on their arrival at Whitby, Mr J.N. Lawson, the representative of the Shipwrecked Mariners' Society, was sent for and he provided all the seamen with a good meal at the Seamen's Institute. The men were able to leave the town by the six o'clock train that same night. All of the crew from the *Athelstane* came from North Shields.

The Times: Monday, 19 December 1892, p. 6, Issue no. 33825; LR 1890/1, No. 1028 (P); LRoS 1874–1882; American Lloyd's Register of American and Foreign Shipping 1857–1900; Starke Schell Registers; Board of Trade Wreck Report 1892 Appendix C Table 1, p. 139; *Shields Daily News*: 10 March 1883; *Whitby Gazette*: 23 December 1892.

Wrecksite

The wreck is orientated in a SE to NW (140/320°) direction and lies on a seabed of sand, pebble and shells in a general depth of 37 m (LAT). It is collapsed and very decayed, covering an area of 75 m in length, 20 m across and stands 5 m high. The wreck was identified when Scarborough diver Julia Racey located the ship's bell, which was hooked onto a winch in the area where the bows would have been. Julia was assisted in recovering the bell by her husband, Carl Racey and Joyce Jesson and Andy Dowsland. Brian Smith and Gordon Wadsworth found and recovered a bronze signal cannon from this wrecksite in 1986.

Most of the wreck is collapsed to the seabed, but two small boilers can be seen with one of them twisted and pushed back towards the big compound steam engine positioned amidships. A small donkey engine sits between the boilers and a large propeller shaft leads to the steel screw that stands upright. There is very little else forward of the engine. Underwater visibility is often poor.

AFRIQUE

Date of Loss: 12 June 1918
Wreck: ★★★
Depth: 47 m
Reference: 54 36'.909 N 000 42'.451 W
Location: 4.35 nm NE of Staithes Harbour

The *Afrique* was a steel-hulled 2457-ton French steam cargo ship that measured 89.94 m in length, with a 12.59-m beam and a 6.09-m draught. Ateliers et Chantiers de France, Dunkerque built and completed her as Yard No. 80 in November 1911 for the Compagnie des Bateaux à Vapeur du Nord, Dunkirk, which was also the owner at the time of loss. The single screw was powered by a 223-nhp (1100-ihp) three-cylinder triple expansion steam engine that used two single-ended boilers and 10.12 sq.m (109 sq.ft) of grate surface and 343.36 sq.m (3696 sq.ft) of heating surface. The cylinders measured 53.34 cm, 83.82 cm and 142.24 cm, with a 91.44-cm stroke (21 in., 33 in. and 56 in. with a 36-in. stroke). Ateliers et Chantiers de France also manufactured the engine and ancillary machinery. She had one deck, a second steel deck in the holds, five cemented bulkheads as well as a 6.70-m poop deck, a 28.65-m bridge deck and 9.14-m forecastle. In 1916 she was equipped with a deck gun.

Final voyage

The *Afrique* (Captain Chandler) foundered and was lost on 12 June 1918 when the KDM mine-laying submarine SMU *UC 40*, commanded by Oblt.z.S. Hermann Menzel, torpedoed her without warning, 6 miles NW of Whitby. The ship was in ballast and on passage from Bilbao for Middlesbrough.

LCWLR 1914–1918, p. 222; ANCL 1914–1918, p. 14; LR 1917/18, No. 299; Starke Schell Registers.

Wrecksite

The wreck is orientated in a SE to NW direction and lies on a dirty seabed of mud, sand, gravel and broken shells in a general depth of 47 m (LAT). The wreck, which is very broken up and decayed, covers an area 100 m long and 25 m wide, with the highest section standing about 5 m. The engine has swung over to the port side and leans towards the starboard side amidships. The wreck was previously thought to be that of the *Audax* until the bell was located along with a steering pedestal. The large deck gun can be found at the stern end. This wreck should make a decent boat-angling venue.

AUDAX, EX HAARDRAADE

Date of Loss: 6 September 1918
Wreck: ✯✯✯
Depth: 47 m
Reference: 54 36'.542 N 000 41'.418 W
Location: 4.96 nm NNE of Runswick Harbour

The *Audax* (Official No. 140356) was a steel-hulled 928-ton British steam cargo vessel that measured 64.18 m in length, with a 10.59-m beam and a 3.88-m draught. Koninklijke Maatschappij "De Schelde", Vlissingen (Flushing) in the Netherlands built and completed her as Yard No. 105 in September 1903, and launched her as the *Haardraade* for D/S A/S Haardraade, Skien, Norway. The manager was Blakstad, Holt and Company. The single steel screw was powered by an aft-positioned 123-nhp three-cylinder triple expansion steam engine that used one boiler. Schelde manufactured the machinery. She had three masts, one deck, an 11.8-m poop deck and 12.8-m forecastle.

In 1915 she was renamed *Audax* by Dampskipsselskapet Aktieselskapet, Fredrikstad which purchased her. C. Homann-Mürer bacame manager. Fredrikstad Shipping Company A/S became the registered owner in 1917 and continued to use the same manager.

Left: Carl Racey and fellow divers after recovering the bell of the Audax

Right: Polished Audax *bell (Courtesy Carl Racey)*

In 1917 the vessel was requisitioned by the Admiralty and placed under The Shipping Controller, London. L.S. Carr and Co was appointed as the Crown nominee manager. The *Audax* was then armed for defence with one 7.6-cm (3-in) BL stern-mounted gun.

Final voyage

At 0430 hrs on 6 September 1918 the *Audax* (Captain S. Soronsen), sailing under the British flag, was steaming at 9 knots when a massive explosion rocked the aft starboard side of the ship 6.5 miles east by north from North Cheek, Robin Hood Bay at 54° 29'N 00° 21'W. The ship was in ballast and *en route* from Rouen, France to the Tyne. The 26-year old second engineer Gustav Johansson from Sweden and a fireman died instantly. The vessel was seriously damaged, but the remaining 17 crewmen stayed on board until 1325 hrs when the patrol vessel *Richard Jewel* arrived. The crew then abandoned ship leaving the captain, chief officer, chief engineer, a steward and a donkeyman on board. The *Richard Jewel* towed the *Audax* about 14 miles before one of the bulkheads collapsed. Ten minutes later she went down. Fifteen of the crew were landed at Scarborough and the other two at Whitby. German records reveal that the KDM submarine SMU *UB 80*, commanded by Kptlt Max Viebeg, torpedoed the ship without warning.

ADM 137/2964; LCWLR 1914–1918, p. 233; BVLS 1914–1918, p. 96; Starke Schell Registers.

Wrecksite

The wreck is orientated in an approximately E to W direction, lying on a seabed of sand, shell and gravel in a general depth of 42 m (LAT). The wreck is partially buried and well broken up, with the bridge at the stern end collapsed and rather decayed. The triple expansion steam engine has fallen over to starboard, while the bow section has collapsed to port. The two forward holds are virtually level with the seabed, but the single boiler and two furnaces are still visible. In 1995 divers observed a large trawl net floating menacingly upwards. Lots of pout whiting were spotted around the engine area and a few cod could be seen. The wreck was identified in 1995 by Scarborough divers Andrew Jackson and Carl Racey when they recovered the bell on the seabed at the port side of the bows.

MERRIE ISLINGTON

Date of loss: 6 May 1915
Wreck: ✭✭
Depth: 51 m
Reference: 54 36'.043 N 000 37'.168 W
Location: 6.47 nm N of Whitby light

The *Merrie Islington* (Official No. 99551) was an iron-hulled 147-ton steam trawler that measured 30.58 m in length, with a 6.27-m beam and a 3.35-m draught. Cook, Welton and Gemmell built and completed her at Hull as Yard No. 81 on 17 December 1891. She was launched on 19 November 1891 for Humber Steam Trawling Company, Hull that had registered her as Hull trawler number H183 on completion. Her single iron screw was powered by a 45-nhp two-cylinder compound steam engine that used one boiler and gave 10 knots. Bailey and Leetham manufactured the machinery at Hull. She had one deck, three bulkheads and a 6.1-m quarterdeck.

Final voyage

On 6 May 1915, the *Merrie Islington* was on a return fishing trip from her port of Hull and was about 7.5 miles north of Whitby when she was captured by the KDM U-boat SMU *U 9*, commanded by Kptlt Johannes Spiess. The *Merrie Islington*'s crew was forced to abandon ship in the boat. The *SM U 9*'s crew sank the vessel using explosive scuttling charges.

BVLS 1914–1918, p. 102; LCWLR 1914–1918, p. 12; LR 1913/14, No. 1029 (M); Thompson (1999).

Wrecksite

The wreck is orientated in a SSE to NNW direction and lies on a seabed of sand, gravel and mud in a general depth of 51 m (LAT). It is collapsed in places with the bows lying over to the starboard side, while the amidships section is upright and the port side at the stern is down. The tallest section stands 3.9 m high. Large nets float upwards off the port side at amidships and at the stern end. The site is very gloomy with a lot of silt. Andrew Jackson and Carl Racey identified the wreck after they located the ship's bell.

MIRANDA

Date of loss: 14 March 1899
Wreck: ✭✭
Depth: 43 m
Reference: 54 36'.042 N 000 43'.118 W
Location: 3.5 nm NE from Staithes

The *Miranda* (Official No. 52702) was an iron-hulled 996-ton steam powered barquentine, though the Bureau Veritas records from 1886/7 state that she was a three-masted schooner.

(A barquentine (or barkenteen) was a sailing vessel with three or more masts, and with a square-rigged foremast and only fore-and-aft rigged sails on the main, mizzen and any other masts. A schooner was a sailing ship rigged with fore-and-aft sails on its two or more masts.) It measured 71.93 m in length, with an 8.55-m beam and a 4.74-m draught. Palmer Bros. and Company, Jarrow built and completed her as Yard No. 170 in 1865. She was launched on 28 March 1865 for the London Steam Ship Company and registered in London. A single iron screw was powered by a 140-nhp two-cylinder compound steam engine that used two single-ended boilers. The cylinders measured 63.5 cm and 121.92 cm with a 76.2-cm stroke (25 in. and 48 in., with a 30-in. stroke). She had one deck, a well deck, four bulkheads, water ballast, an amidships-positioned 20.7-m quarterdeck and 10.4-m bridge deck. Her designated code recognition signal letters were: HGRC.

Captain E. Dilley was the master in 1867. In 1875 she was registered to John Finnegan in London and Edward Dilley was the master. In 1893 the master was Captain A. Keys and at the time weighed 948 tons gross. From 1897 the registered owner was Miranda S.S. Company, London with Captain R.T. Humble as master. That same year her tonnage was increased to 954 tons.

Final voyage

In the early hours of 14 March 1899 the *Miranda*, commanded by Captain R.T. Humble, foundered 3.5 miles NE from Staithes, for reasons unknown. The vessel was on passage from Hartlepool for London, carrying a cargo of coal, 16 crewmen and two passengers – both of whom were stowaways – however everyone was saved. The wind at the time was a moderate westerly force 4 and weather conditions were very reasonable.

LR 1898/9, No. 797 (M); Board of Trade Wreck Return 1899, p. 115 (687); American Lloyd's Register of American and Foreign Shipping, 1857–1900; Miramar Ship Index; *The Times*: Wednesday, 15 March 1899, p. 13, Issue no. 35777.

Wrecksite

The wreck is orientated in an E to W direction and lies on a seabed of dirty sand, shell, gravel and pebbles in a general depth of 43 m (LAT). The remains are totally collapsed, badly decayed and well broken up, with the highest point of 4.5 m being at the western end, which is aft. A few flattened and bent piping, cogs, an iron wheel, and broken iron machinery are protruding out of the pile of iron plates, ribs and girders. What appear to be a large square boiler and a two-cylinder compound engine are visible and the remnants of a bow winch. Lobsters and several big cod and a large anglerfish have been observed in the wreck debris, so the site may be worth investigating as a boat-angling venue.

RUTHIN CASTLE, HM Trawler

Date of Loss: 21 April 1917
Wreck: ★★★
Depth: 30 m
Reference: 54 36'.708 N 000 52'.529 W
Location: 2.37 nm NNE of Skinningrove

The *Ruthin Castle* was a steel-hulled 275-ton steam trawler that measured 38.22 m in length, with a 7.08-m beam and 3.35-m draught. Smith's Dock Company at South Bank, Middlesbrough built and completed her as Yard No. 656 in December 1916. She was launched on 26 October 1916 for Castle Steam Trawlers, Swansea with C. Heron as the manager. Port Registration No. SA.67. The single steel propeller was powered by an aft-positioned 87-rhp, three-cylinder triple expansion steam engine that used one single-ended boiler working at 180 psi pressure and three plain furnaces. The cylinders measured 31.75 cm, 53.34 cm and 88.9 cm (12½ in 21 in. and 35 in.). She had one deck and two steel bulkheads.

The Admiralty requisitioned her on completion in December 1916 as Minesweeper No. 3317 and equipped her with one 6-pounder deck gun.

Final Patrol

On 21 April 1917 the *Ruthin Castle* sank after detonating a mine laid off Skinningrove by the KDM submarine SMU *UC 50*, commanded by Kptlt Rudolf Seuffer. The following crewmen were killed:

Bambrough, Robert, Deckhand RNR
Clark, Charles Turnbull, Trimmer RNR
Cole, R., Deckhand RNR
Foster, Stanley, Trimmer Engineman RNR
Galbraith, James, Leading Deckhand RNR
Lauvaux, Leon, Deckhand RNR
Wilson, Isaac, Trimmer Cook RNR
Wood, James, 2nd Hand RNR

BVLS 1914–1918, p. 21; SRN Vol. 2, p. 311; SYC, p. 161; LCWLR 1914–1918, p. 121.

Wrecksite

The wreck lies on a hard seabed, on top of several large boulders and next to a long rocky reef in a general depth of 30 m (LAT). It is well decayed and broken up and lies over on its port side. The most obvious damage is to the area forward of the single boiler, which is very collapsed, broken up and spread about the seabed. The steam engine is in place, but is also over on its port side. The deck gun is at the stern end lying on its side on the seabed. On 21 June 2003 the ship's bell – inscribed *Ruthin Castle* – was found almost buried on the seabed, about 20 metres off the port side by Carl Racey. Andrew Jackson recovered the maker's plate just forward and on the port side of the boiler inscribed: *Smith's Dock Company Ltd. Engine No 141, Shipbuilders & Engineers, Middlesbrough-on-Tees.* A small maker's plate from the deck gun was also recovered and inscribed: *HIGH ANGLE MTG. MARK IV made by R. Hoe & Company Ltd. 1916. WT. Slide 550lbs, Carriage 644lbs, Total 1204lbs. ADMY No.567.* (Information courtesy of Carl Racey).

HARTLEY

Date of Loss: 26 January 1918
Wreck: ✯✯✯
Depth: 36 m
Reference: 54 37'.009 N 000 52'.133 W
Location: 2.85 nm NNE of Skinningrove

The *Hartley* (Official No. 118616) was a steel-hulled 1150-ton British steam cargo ship measuring 69.79 m in length, with a 10.18-m beam, a 4.44-m draught and a 5.13-m moulded depth. Wood, Skinner and Company at Bill Quay, near Gateshead built and completed her as Yard No. 114 in August 1903. She was launched on 23 July 1903 for Burnett Steamship Company, Newcastle. Burnett and Company was the manager. The single steel screw was powered by a 151-nhp three-cylinder triple expansion steam engine that used one single-ended boiler, four furnaces, 6.03 sq.m (65 sq.ft) of grate surface and 228.26 sq.m (2457 sq.ft) of heating surface. The cylinders measured 46.99 cm, 76.2 cm and 124.46 cm with an 83.82 cm stroke (18.5 in., 30 in. and 49 in. with a 33-in. stroke). North Eastern Marine Engineering Company, Wallsend-on-Tyne manufactured the engine and ancillary machinery. She had one deck, a well deck, a 36.5-m quarterdeck, a 7.6-m forecastle and a 3-m bridge deck.

From 1910 the Liverpool-based British and African Steam Navigation Company was the registered owner and Elder Dempster and Company the manager.

On 9 June 1917 a German seaplane attacked the ship with a torpedo, but it missed.

Final voyage

On 26 January 1918 the submerged KDM submarine SMU *UB 34*, commanded by Oblt.z.S. Helmuth von Rucktescell torpedoed without any warning and sunk the *Hartley* off Staithes. The steamer, which was armed for defence and under the command of Captain F. Inskip, was in ballast and *en route* from Boulogne to the Tyne. Escort vessels rescued the crew.

LCWLR 1914–1918, p. 197; BVLS 1914–1918; p. 79; Starke Schell Registers; Miramar Ship Index.

Wrecksite

The wreck is orientated in a NNE to SSW direction with the bows to the NNE. It lies in a general depth of 36 m (LAT) and is generally intact, but the stern has collapsed to starboard. The boiler and engine are upright and positioned amidships. Yorkshire diver Gordon Wadsworth identified the wreck when he located the ship's bell in 1993. Numerous fish can be observed around the wreck, so this should make an interesting boat-angling venue.

SERENITY (?)

Date of loss: 17 December 1939
Wreck ✯✯✯✯
Depth 55 m
Reference: 54 37'.059 N 000 29'.803 W
Location: 8.53 nm NNE from Whitby pier

The *Serenity* (Official No. 165499) was a steel-hulled 487-ton British cargo motor vessel that measured 48 m by length, with an 84-m beam and a 2.9-m draught. George Brown and Company (Marine) Ltd. built and completed her at Greenock as Yard No. 201 in June 1937. She was launched on 14 June 1937 for Fred T. Everard and Sons, London which owned her at the time of loss. An aft-positioned 139-nhp five-cylinder two-stroke single acting diesel oil engine, manufactured by Newbury Diesel Company at Newbury, powered her single, possibly bronze, screw. She had a cruiser stern, one deck, three bulkheads part cemented, a 29.87-m quarterdeck and 5.18-m forecastle. The wartime designated code letters were: MMKP.

Final voyage

On 17 December 1939 the *Serenity* was sailing independently on passage from Methil for London with a 587-ton cargo of coal when the Luftwaffe bombed and sank her off Whitby. The crew safely abandoned ship without loss of life.

Wrecksite

The wreck – most likely that of the *Serenity* – is orientated in a NNE to SSW direction. It lies on a seabed of sand, shell and pebbles in a general depth of 55 m (LAT). The wreck is upright, appears to be intact and stands 5.3 m high, covering an area 40 m long and 6 m across.

ARDGANTOCK

Date of Loss: 18 February 1918
Wreck: ✯✯✯
Depth: 53 m
Reference: 54 37'.792 N 000 32'.486 W
Location: 8.6 nm NNE of Whitby's West Pier

On 18 February 1918 the newly-built Ardgantock *foundered following a collision with the RN* destroyer Tartar *(Author's collection)*

The *Ardgantock* (Official No. 137057) was a steel-hulled 841-ton British steam cargo vessel that measured 61.03 m in length, with a 9.19-m beam, a 3.86-m registered depth, a 4.57-m moulded depth and 4.29-m draught. Ferguson Brothers, Port Glasgow built and completed her as Yard No. 223 in December 1917 for Ard Coasters Ltd. Greenock, with Lang and Fulton Ltd. the manager. The single steel screw was powered by an aft-positioned 90-rhp, three-cylinder triple expansion steam engine that used one single-ended boiler. The cylinders measured 40.64 cm, 66.04 cm and 100.68 cm with a 68.58 cm stroke (16 in., 26 in. and 42 in., with a 27 in. stroke). Ferguson Brothers also manufactured the engine and ancillary machinery. She had one steel deck, a well deck and web frames, a 33.83-m quarterdeck and 7.92-m forecastle.

A photo of the ship in the book *Collisions at Sea – How?* by Cdr M.D. Dewar shows the fore well deck is lower than the deck abaft the central island, raised forecastle. There is also one mast well forward, another mast in front and one mast behind the bridge structure, the island and practically touching it; she has a tall smoke stack/funnel at the stern with a strange-looking deckhouse at the very stern.

Final voyage

On 18 February 1918 this newly-built vessel was transporting a cargo of navigation buoys from Purfleet on the river Thames to Inverness when she foundered following a collision with the 870-ton Tribal class destroyer HMS *Tartar* (built 1907 by J.I. Thornycroft, Woolston) off West Hartlepool. None of her crew of 15 was lost.

Starke Schell Registers; Board of Trade Wreck Return World War I, 1915 vol. Pt. 2, p. 38 (3); JANE'S Fighting Ships of WWI.

Wrecksite

The wreck is orientated in a SSE to NNW direction and lies on a seabed of sand, mud, shells and pebbles in a general depth of 53 m (LAT). The two holds have completely collapsed as has most of the rest of the wreck, which is generally flat. At the stern the single boiler can be seen standing upright. The bow is intact and lies over to the port side, but the stern is all smashed and twisted, with a few boulders close by. The bell is still unaccounted for, but Scarborough divers Andrew Jackson and Carl Racey identified the wreck from the maker's number on the steering pedestal in 1998. The wrecksite covers an area of 52 m in length by 13 m across and stands 3.4 m high. A large trawl net was found on the port side near the bow area and a number of shell casings were observed at the stern, although there was no sign of a deck gun.

EARL PERCY

Date of loss: 15 September 1888
Wreck: ★★★
Depth: 47 m
Reference: 54 37'.459 N 000 44'.351 W
Location: 4.20 nm NNE of Staithes Harbour and 9.04 nm NNW of Whitby's West Pier

The *Earl Percy* (Official No. 51362) was an iron-hulled 951-ton three-masted schooner-rigged steam cargo vessel. It measured 72.10 m in length, with an 8.58-m beam and a 4.92-m draught. Registered in Newcastle the *Earl Percy* was built by Palmer Brothers and Company Jarrow and completed as Yard No. 176. She was launched on 29 April 1865 for Tyne Steam Shipping Company Newcastle, which owned her at the time of loss.

The single four-blade iron screw was powered by an aft-positioned 130-hp two-cylinder inverted compound steam engine that that used two boilers. The cylinders measured 71.12 cm and 142.24 cm with a 91.44 cm stroke (28 in and 56 in. with a 36-in. stroke). Her designated code signal letters were: HKCN. In 1879 R. and W. Hawthorn and Company fitted a new 130-hp engine that used two Scotch boilers.

On 23 December 1880 the *Earl Percy* ran aground on Haisborough Sands, whilst on a voyage from Newcastle to London. The master thought the Haisborough shore lights were those of the lightship. He accordingly gave orders to port the helm, with the view of bringing the vessel back into the proper channel to the west of Haisborough Sands. She had come round several points when she was found to be trailing the ground. After striking two or three times the ship became fast and although every effort was made to get her off, they were not able to move her as the tide began to fall. She was grounded at the north-east point of Haisborough Sands. At about 0500 hrs the tide had fallen considerably and the vessel began to bump heavily, so rockets were set off. After some time two lifeboats came to their assistance. While waiting for assistance, the master had ordered the after hatch to be opened, and about 20–30 tons of the cargo to be jettisoned. As the tide rose the engines were set to work and at 0900 hrs she was afloat again. It was found, however, that the rudder was gone, but the captain, by a series of skilful manoeuvres, got her clear of the sand, and by backing and going ahead managed to get her along the east side of the Haisborough Sands, until a steam tug arrived. For an agreed price the tug assisted in steering her to London.

Final voyage

The *Earl Percy* – commanded by Captain Cay since 1882 – left Newcastle upon Tyne for a voyage to Rotterdam with passengers and general cargo, including clay pipes and large copper slabs. On the evening of Saturday, 15 September 1888 she was 9.04 nm NNE of Whitby and enduring foggy weather when the 699 ton Sunderland-registered cargo steamer *Wear* (1865) ran into her. The *Earl Percy* sank, but the Sunderland steamer rescued her crew and passengers, many of whom were women. The *Wear*, which had her bows badly damaged in the collision, later arrived at the Tyne with the survivors. (Steve Tunstall originally supplied the author with a report of the *Earl Percy* wrecksite).

MOD Hydro Wreck No. 6018; Miramar Ship Index; Board of Trade Wreck Return 1881; *The Times*: Monday, 17 September 1888, p. 5, Issue no. 32493.

Wrecksite

The wreck is orientated in a SSE to NNW direction and lies on a seabed of sand, mud and gravel in a general depth of 47 m (LAT). It is collapsed and well broken up, covering an area 70 m long and 20 m wide. Only the frames are left of the two forward holds which have both collapsed. Part of the bows section is still intact. Some steering gear was observed well forward near the bows area and a telegraph has been recovered from the port side of the engine. The engine, six furnaces and two boilers are now all exposed. The ship carried a mixed cargo and some of it – clay pipes and large pavingstone-sized slabs of copper ingots – can be found in the forward hold. A shoal of bib has been reported swimming around the engine area, but very few cod have been observed.

STEPHANOTIS

Date of loss: 30 April 1901
Wreck: ★★★
Depth: 48 m
Reference: 54 37'.809 N 000 42'.968 W
Location: 4.93 nm NNE of Staithes

The *Stephanotis* (Official No. 65382) was an iron-hulled 1042-ton British brigantine-rigged steam cargo vessel that measured 67.18 m in length, with a 9.29-m beam and a 5.84-m draught. Iliff Mounsey and Co at South Dock, Sunderland built and completed her as Yard No. 49 in March 1871. She was launched on 22 February 1871 for J. Robinson and Sons and registered in North Shields. The single iron screw was powered by a 98-nhp two-cylinder compound steam engine that used one boiler. The cylinders measured 68.58 cm and 119.38 cm with a 76.2-cm stroke (27 in. and 47 in. with a 30-in. stroke). R. and W. Hawthorn manufactured the engine and ancillary machinery at Newcastle. She had one deck, two tiers of beams, four bulkheads cemented and an amidships-positioned 13.7-m raised quarterdeck as well as a 48-ton (135.92 cubic metres) bridge deck. The designated code recognition signal letters were: KBLT.

A new boiler was fitted in 1977 and the shipbuilders made repairs to damages in the years 1875, 1877, 1879 and 1886. In 1883 the registered owner became J. Robinson & Sons at North Sheilds. Stag Line Ltd., purchased her in 1895 and J. Robinson & Sons became the managers. From 1898 the registered owner became R. Brown & Sons, Ltd., at North Sheilds. Robson, Brown and Sons at Sunderland was the registered owner at the time of loss.

Final voyage

The *Stephanotis*, with Captain R. Thompson in charge, foundered and was lost on 30 April 1901 following a collision with the 522-ton steamship *Guyers* (1864: P.S. Haggie, Newcastle) six miles north-east of Staithes. The *Stephanotis* was on a voyage from Bilbao to Middlesbrough with a cargo of iron ore and a crew of 16. Sea and wind conditions – SSE force two – were quite good at the time, although it was foggy and dark. The smaller *Guyers* had her bows stove in, but managed to beach one mile north of Black Halls coastguard station. It was a total loss. Both crews were saved and later landed at Yarmouth.

LR 1900/1, No. 1220 (S); Board of Trade Wreck Return 1901; SYC, p. 162; Hydro Wk. No. 6398; Miramar Ship Index; *The Times*: Thursday, 2 May 1901, p. 6, Issue no. 36444.

Wrecksite

The wreck – which is probably that of the *Stephanotis* – is orientated in an almost S to N direction. It lies on a dirty seabed of sand, mud, gravel and shells in a general depth of 48 m (LAT). The wreck has totally collapsed, is well broken up and badly decayed, with her amidships boiler and engine visibly exposed. A large broken mast lies across the wreckage. There are three taller parts of the wreck, with the tallest standing some 5.2 m at the southern end which is part of the stern. The remains of the wreck cover an area 70 m long and 20 m across. At the bows there is a large pile of wreckage, two anchors and two winches. The remains of the cargo of iron ore is also largely in evidence. The stern end stands just over 2 m high.

STORA KORSNAS LINK I, EX NERLANDIA, EX JOLLY ORO, EX TOR NERLANDIA

Date of loss: 5 November 1991
Wreck: ✶✶✶✶✶
Depth: 38 m
Reference: 54 37'.600 N 000 53'.358 W
Location: 5.99 nm E of Redcar

Stora Korsnas Link I (Official No. 7230680) was a steel roll-on/roll-off (RO/RO) motor container ship of 4128 tons that was registered in Nacka, Sweden. She measured 163.50 m in length, with a 21-m beam and a 7.10-m draught. A/S Framnæs Mekaniske Verksted, Sandefjord, Norway built and completed her as Yard No. 180 in November 1972. She was launched as the *Tor Nerlandia* on 12 July 1972. The ship was delivered to Triport Shipping Company, London in November 1972. Her two steel screws and two bow thrust screws were powered by 12 000-hp 12-cylinder diesel oil engines that were installed aft and manufactured by Lindholmen Motor AB (Lindholmen–Pielstick) of Gothenburg. They gave a speed of 18.5 knots. She had two decks and stern door ramps.

In 1970 she was chartered by Foss Shipping, London for service on the Rotterdam—Antwerpen—Bremen—Felixstowe—Jeddah—Damman—Dubai—Hodeidah—Port Sudan—Kuwait—Aqaba—Yenbu route. In November 1972 the ship was chartered to Tor Line and was in service to and from Gothenburg and central Europe. In March 1976 she was in service on Middle Eastern routes. In August of that year the ship was lengthened in Flushing, the Netherlands by 26.7 m.

In 1979 she was renamed *Nerlandia* by new owners Intermodel Shipping Services, Panama. The new manager was Orconsult Shipping Company, Zurich, Switzerland. In the May of 1979 she was chartered to Ignazio Messina and Cie. Naples, Italy. In 1980 her Panamanian owners renamed her *Jolly Oro*. In 1986 the Panamanian owners renamed her *Nerlandia*. The ship was laid-up at Genoa, Italy in January 1986.

From January 1987 A/B Sea-Link at Nacka, Sweden was the registered owner. On 28 January 1987 she arrived at engine manufacturers Wärtsilä Oy Ab's plant in Åbo (present-day Turku in Finland) for a rebuild, and was subsequently renamed *Stora Korsnäs Link I.*

Final voyage

While off Teesbay on 5 November 1991 the engine room of the *Stora Korsnas Link I* caught fire. The vessel was *en route* from Gävle to Chatham with a cargo of timber, large rolls of news printing paper and sodium chlorate. The fire soon became intense and quickly spread out of control through the cargo holds. After a series of violent explosions, the crew abandoned ship, three miles off Skinningrove. She burned for five days with her cargo of wood and paper. Then, on 10 November, there was a huge explosion and the vessel foundered, but with no loss of life.

The wreck lies in navigable waters and when divers surveyed her, she was found to be above the required clearance depth and thus declared a shipping hazard. Following a restriction order in August 1991 the wreck was reduced in height.

The following is a report from the *Daily Mirror* on Wednesday, 8 July 1992:

> On Wednesday, 8 July 1992 the *Daily Mirror* newspaper printed a story headlined: 'SHIP SCOTCH SPIRITED OFF BY PIRATES' and claiming that 'underwater pirates (local divers) had plundered the wreck by stealing hundreds of bottles of bonded scotch whisky, a consignment of cigarettes and anything else that could be removed. Eight months later, an exclusion zone was placed around the wreck to prevent any further looting, however John Noble, the salvage firm manager stated that there was now just a skeleton of the vessel left, although his divers did recover the ship's bell. The bonded booze and baccy had been put on board for the captain and his crew'.

LCR 1991, p. 34; LR, Seadata 04 November 1996; LR 1988/9, No. 7230680; *Daily Mirror*: 8 July 1992; Miramar Ship Index.

Wrecksite

Don Foster of Teesside first dived the *Stora Korsnas Link I* on 1 December 1991. It was found to be a complete ship, still with the immaculate blue and white paintwork and lying on her port side, stern towards the shore. It is orientated at NE to SW direction, in a general depth of 38 m (LAT). The wreck is so large it can quite easily be found using only an echo sounder. Great care should be taken when descending the shot line because sections of the hull have been cut away, leaving jagged steel holes. The stern suffered massive explosions and large areas of steel plates are peeled back, as if cut by a giant tin opener. The stern section, with the huge cargo deck doors and screws, are reported as being very impressive. Some of the containers are still to be found and at least one still remains locked.

The wreck has become a haven for small shoals of cod, and soft corals are beginning to colonise the hull. The surrounding seabed is firm sand and gravel. The most up-to-date information about the *Stora Korsnas Link I* is that it would appear explosives have been used on the wreck. It is also reported to be lying on one side and somewhat collapsed.

JOHN MILES

Date of loss: 22 February 1917
Wreck: ★★★
Depth: 33 m
Reference: 54 38'.092 N 000 53'.333 W
Location: 3.64 nm N of Skinningrove

The *John Miles* (Official No. 125659) was a steel-hulled 687-ton British steam cargo vessel that measured 49.98 m in length, with a 9.14-m beam and 3.58-m draught. S.P. Austin and Son built and completed her at Wear Dock, Sunderland in 1908 as Yard No. 245. She was

Clockwise from left: Rob Broadhead holding the engine manufacturer's plate he recovered from the John Miles *wreck, while Tony Herbert proudly displays the bell he found*

SS John Miles, *c.1910 (Author's collection)*

Bell recovered from the steamer John Miles *(Courtesy Carl Racey)*

launched on 17 December 1907 for Stephenson Clarke and Company London, also the owner at the time of loss. The single steel screw was powered by an aft-positioned 113-nhp three-cylinder triple expansion steam engine that used one single-ended boiler working at 180 psi pressure with three plain furnaces, 4.73 sq.m (51 sq.ft) of grate surface and 177.81 sq.m (1914 sq.ft) of heating surface. She also had a well deck. North Eastern Marine Engineering Company manufactured the machinery at Sunderland.

Final voyage

Oblt.z.S. Franz Walther, commander of the KDM submarine SMU *UB 21*, torpedoed the *John Miles* without any warning on 22 February 1917, 11 miles SE of Hartlepool. The ship was travelling at 8.25 knots and on passage from Newcastle for Shoreham-by-Sea, carrying 870 tons of coal and a crew of 14. The chief engineer, being the senior surviving officer, stated in his report that a violent explosion took place on the port side, abaft of the main hatch at 1235 hrs. The ship sank by the stern within two minutes. Those of the crew who were on deck at the time were washed overboard. The chief said that he and four others clung onto floating wreckage for about 30 minutes before they were picked up by a Royal Navy minesweeper and taken to Hartlepool. Nine men – including the master – died in the sea and the second engineer, who was one of the five rescued, died on board the minesweeper. The men that perished were:

Atkinson, Andrew, 61 yrs, Fireman MM
Brazier, Thomas Daniel, 50 yrs, Chief Mate MM
Eggen, Magnus, 35 yrs, Fireman MM
Johnson, Victor, 51 yrs, Able Seaman MM

Sharman, Henry, 61 yrs, 2nd Mate MM
Tester, Emanuel, 61 yrs, Steward MM
Uwins, George, 35 yrs, Able Seaman MM
Vallint, Thomas, 65 yrs, Master MM
Welfare, Horace George, 65 yrs, Lamps MM
Wilkinson, Robert Slater, 54 yrs, 2nd Engineer MM

CWGC; LCWLR 1914–1918, p. 97; LR 1915/16, No. 375 (J); Tennent (1990), p. 34; Jarvis (2000).

Wrecksite

The wreck is orientated in a near N to S direction and lies on a seabed of sand and stone in a general depth of 33 m (LAT). It has a slight list to starboard, is still fairly intact and stands almost 4 m high. The hull sides have somewhat collapsed on both sides, while the bows are smashed up, with a bow winch inverted. The two masts are also lying on the seabed close by. Its superstructure is now partially collapsed down around the engine, boiler and machinery, and the surrounds towards the stern end, which is the highest half of the wreck. Little remains in the way of interesting artefacts, because the brass pedestal mounted steering helm – stamped: *Davis and Company Ltd. Patentees, Oulton Broad Lowestoft, England* – and a box full of engine tools, copper pipes and lots of portholes were removed in the mid-1990s. Lobsters are often spotted amongst the wreckage and a few large cod have been observed. Photographs taken of the ship identified it incorrectly but in August 2007 the ship's bell – inscribed: *John Miles 1908* – was found in the bow area by Tony Herbert. On the same dive the engine maker's plate – marked *NEME Sunderland* – was recovered from the side of the engine by Rob Broadhead. (Wreck location courtesy of Carl Racey.)

ANBOTO MENDI

Date of Loss: 10 May 1918
Wreck: ✯✯✯✯
Depth: 48 m
Reference: 54 38'.392 N 000 43'.418 W
Location: 5.31 nm NNE of Staithes Harbour

The *Anboto Mendi* was a steel-hulled 2114-ton Spanish steam cargo ship measuring 83.87 m in length, with a 12.62-m beam and a 5.3-m draught. Cia Euskalduna de Construccion y Reparacion de Buq, Bilbao built and completed her as Yard No. 13 in February 1907 for Cia. Naviera Sota y Aznar, Bilbao, which owned her at the time of loss. Sota y Aznar was the manager. The single steel screw was powered by a 220-hp three-cylinder triple expansion steam engine that used two single-ended boilers. Wallsend Slipway and Engineering Company at Newcastle upon Tyne manufactured the machinery. She had one deck, four bulkheads cemented, a well deck, 32.2-m quarterdeck and 22.5-m bridge deck.

Final voyage

On 10 May 1918 the *Anboto Mendi* (Captain W. Iturrospe) was torpedoed and sunk without warning by SMU *UB 21*, a KDM U-boat commanded by Oblt.z.S. Bruno Mahn. The steamer was *en route* from Sagunto to Middlesbrough with a cargo of iron ore. The author is unaware as to what happened to the crew.

ANCL 1914–18, p. 108; LCWLR 1914–1918, p. 215; Starke Schell Registers.

Wrecksite

The wreck is orientated in a SSE to NNW direction. It lies on a seabed of gravel, sand, mud and shells in a general depth of 48 m (LAT). The wreck is broken into two sections with the largest part sitting with a slight list to starboard. The engine is upright with the two boilers partially exposed and a large donkey boiler standing in front of them. The bow is intact and leaning over to starboard. Most of the wreck has partially collapsed, with ribs and frames showing, especially in the forward cargo hold. The main section lies to the south and covers an area 60 m in length by about 12 m across, with the highest parts over 8 m from the seabed. The northern part is about 2 m long. A trawl net is suspended over the wreck, but the major hazards are the monofilament fishing lines with hooks and lures attached, which are extremely difficult to see in the murky waters. Large cod are fairly commonplace around the wreck, which is an excellent boat-angling venue.

CORSHAM

Date of loss: 8 March 1918
Wreck: ✯✯✯✯
Depth: 45 m
Reference: 54 39'.975 N 000 57'.699 W
Location: 6.20 nm ENE of South Gare light

The *Corsham* (Official No. 142295) was a steel-hulled 2797-ton British steam cargo ship that measured 95.22 m in length, with a 13.79-m beam and a 6.29-m draught. S.P. Austin and Son built and completed her as Yard No. 288 at Wear Dock, Sunderland in January 1918. She was launched on 29 November 1917 for Cory Colliers, London, which was also the owner at the time of loss. The single steel screw was powered by a 270-nhp three-cylinder triple expansion steam engine that used two single-ended boilers. The cylinders measured 57.15 cm, 93.98 cm and 154.94 cm, with a 106.68-cm stroke (22.5 in., 37 in. and 61 in. with a 42-in. stroke). Richardsons, Westgarth and Company manufactured the machinery at the Scotia Engine Works, Sunderland. She had one deck, a 7.62-m poop deck, 20.11-m bridge deck and 8.53-m forecastle. The ship was armed for defence after launching.

Final voyage

On 8 March 1918 SMU *UC 40* – a KDM minelaying submarine commanded by Oblt. Hermann Menzel – torpedoed the *Corsham* without any warning. The ship was in ballast and *en route* from London to the river Tyne and foundered in minutes, taking the master and eight crewmen down with it. The crewmen who died were:

Adamson, William, 22 yrs, 3rd Engineer MM
Cheyne, Arthur, 59 yrs, Boatswain (Bosun) MM

Fridd, Ernest Pearson, 18 yrs, Mess Room Boy MM
Grant, Albert Edward, 35 yrs, 1st Engineer MM
Hutchinson, Frederick Martin, 42 yrs, 2nd Engineer MM
Jensen, Carsten William Christian, 57 yrs, 1st Mate MM
Kristiansen, Oskar, 40 yrs, Carpenter MM
Niedolin, Jekab, Able Seaman MM

CWGC; Starke Schell Registers; BVLS 1914–1918, p. 83; LCWLR 1914–1918, p. 205.

Wrecksite

The wreck is orientated in an ENE to WSW direction and lies on a seabed of sand in a general depth of 39 m (LAT). It leans over on its side and is broken into four large pieces with the deck facing south. It covers an area of 105 m in length by 12 m across. The highest section stands 3.4 m high and is festooned in monofilament fishing lines and trawl nets. The uppermost exposed sections are covered in soft corals and shoals of pout whiting swarm over them. Large cod, conger and ling have also been observed around the wreck.

HÉLÉNE

Date of loss: 28 May 1904
Wreck: ✯✯
Depth: 47 m
Reference: 54 39'.908 N 000 50'.300 W
Location: 5.68 nm NE from Huntcliff, Saltburn

The 464-ton Rouen-registered steamer Helene *sank following a collision during thick fog on 28 May 1904; photo (Courtesy Theodor Dorgeist, Germany)*

The *Héléne* was a 464-ton steam cargo vessel that measured 45.7 m in length, with a 7.7-m beam. Wood, Skinner and Co at Bill Quay, near Hebburn on Tyne built and completed her as Yard No. 36 in April 1892. She was launched on 12 March 1892 for X. Kneider at Rouen, in France. A. Bissee at Rouen was the manager. The single screw was powered by a 71-nhp three-cylinder triple expansion steam engine that used one single-ended boiler working at 160 psi pressure, with two plain furnaces and 113.15 sq.m (1218 sq.ft) of heating surface. The cylinders measured 33.02 m, 54.61 cm and 60.96 cm with a 68.57-cm stroke (13 in., 21½ in. and 24 in. with a 27-in. stroke). North Eastern Marine Engineering Company manufactured the machinery at Sunderland. She also had a well deck.

Final voyage

On 28 May 1894 the *Héléne* (Captain Teste) was transporting a cargo of iron ore on a regular voyage from Rouen to West Hartlepool when she collided with the 634-ton British steamer *General Havelock* (1884: R.M. Hudson and Sons, Sunderland) during thick fog. The *General Havelock* had left the river Wear on Saturday night on her usual voyage to London, with cargo and passengers. The collision happened near Saltburn and about two or three hours after leaving Sunderland. It is understood that the foreign vessel was damaged to such an extent that she went down immediately. The Sunderland steamer stood by and picked up several of the sailors belonging to the French vessel, but seven others, all Frenchmen, are reported to have drowned. The *General Havelock* seems to have sustained no serious damage, as her skipper, Captain Stock, continued his voyage to the Thames.

Miramar Ship Index; *The Times*: Wednesday, 1 June 1904, p. 11, Issue no. 37409; *Scarborough Evening News*: 30 May 1904; *Scarborough Evening News*: 31 May 1904.

Wrecksite

The wreck is orientated in an E to W direction and lies on a firm seabed of sand, gravel and shells in a general depth of 47 m (LAT). It is collapsed, decayed and well broken up, and covers an area 50 m long and 12 m across with the highest section of 3.5 m being amidships. The bell inscribed *Héléne* was recovered from the wreck by sport divers Carl Racey and Andrew Jackson, and thus identified the vessel. Very little marine life is to be found, but tidal streams are quite strong.

BURNHOPE

Date of loss: 14 December 1916
Wreck: ✯✯
Depth: 11 m
Reference: 54 40'.975 N 0001 09'.048 W
Location: 1.6 nm SE from The Heugh, Hartlepool

The *Burnhope* (Official No. 125430) was a steel-hulled 1941-ton British steam cargo ship measuring 82.9 m in length, with a 12.19-m beam and a 5.35-m draught. Wood Skinner and Company, at Bill Quay near Hebburn on Tyne built and completed her as Yard No. 145 in September 1907. She was launched on 14 August 1907 for the Burnett Steamship Company, Newcastle, which was also the owner at the time of loss. Burnett and Co. was the manager. The single steel screw was powered by a 200-nhp three-cylinder triple expansion steam engine that used two single-ended boilers working at 180 psi pressure, with six corrugated furnaces and 131.36 sq.m (3246 sq.ft) of heating surface, which gave 10 knots. The cylinders measured 50.8 cm, 83.82 cm and 137.16 cm with a 91.44-cm stroke (20 in., 33 in. and 54 in. with a 36-in. stroke). North Eastern Marine Engineering Company manufactured the machinery at Newcastle. She had one deck and a well deck.

Final voyage

On 14 December 1916 the SS *Burnhope* (Captain William C. Saddler) detonated a mine laid that same day by the KDM submarine SMU *UC 32*, commanded by Oblt.z.S. Herbert Breyer. The steamer had just set out on a voyage from Hartlepool to London with a 2600-ton cargo of coal and was swinging to starboard before altering course in Hartlepool Bay. The pressure and blast from the enormous explosion that followed smashed the ships wheelhouse windows and even the glass in the compass binnacles. A second explosion beneath the port bow followed seconds later, which so seriously damaged the vessel that she began to sink by the bows. The captain immediately ordered the starboard lifeboat made ready and swung the ship to portside in order to reach shallow water. After 20 minutes her bows touched ground and a minesweeper towed her stern end round into the shallower water. However, at 0900 hrs the steamer took on a big list to port and her crew, except for the master, abandoned ship. Gradually the list became so bad that by 1015 hrs she went over on her side and Captain Saddler had to be picked up out of the sea by the crew of the minesweeper, unfortunately, only to suffer a heart attack and die soon afterwards.

ADM 137/2960; Starke Schell Registers; BVLS 1914–1918, p. 28; LCWLR 1914–1918, p. 77.

Wrecksite

The wreck of the *Burnhope* was dispersed using explosives and what is left lies in a general depth of 11 m (LAT). The surrounding seabed consists of dirty sand and the majority of the wreck is now covered over by a few metres of sand. There is a deep scour around the wreck where steel plating, ribs, frames and broken machinery protrude. Other debris lies scattered around the top of the wreck. Winter storms often expose much of the ships remains.

EMPIRE BAY

Date of Loss: 15 January 1942
Wreck: ★★
Depth: 13 m
Reference: 54 41'.141 N 001 08'.698 W
Location: 1.27 nm SE from The Heugh, Hartlepool

The *Empire Bay* (Official No. 160786) was a steel-hulled 2824-ton British steam cargo ship measuring 94.64 m in length, with a 13.51-m beam and a 5.89-m draught. William Gray and Company built and completed her as Yard No. 1107 in November 1940 at West Hartlepool. She was launched on 20 August 1940 for the Ministry of Shipping – which later became part of the Ministry of War Transport in 1941 – which also owned her at the time of loss. Joseph Constantine Steamship Line Ltd. was the manager. The single screw was powered by a 255-hp three-cylinder triple expansion steam engine that used two single-ended boilers working at 200 psi pressure, with six corrugated furnaces, two 37 sq.m (84 sq.ft) of grate surface and 99.95 sq.m (3530 sq.ft) of heating surface. The cylinders measured 50.8 cm, 78.74 cm and 139.7 cm, with a 99.06-cm stroke (20 in., 31 in. and 55 in., with a 39-in. stroke). Central Marine Engineering Works, West Hartlepool manufactured the aft-positioned engine and ancillary machinery. She had a cruiser stern, one deck, four bulkheads cemented, a 53.2-m quarterdeck and 11.3-m forecastle. She also had some cellular double bottom and aft and fore peak tanks.

Final voyage

Just after she left Hartlepool as part of the 11-ship convoy FS.700 (Methil–Southend) on 14 January 1942, German bombers attacked the *Empire Bay*. She was on passage for London, carrying a crew of 28, including three DEMS gunners and a 3800-ton cargo of coal. The ship was badly damaged, caught fire and was in danger of sinking, so the crew abandoned her. But the *Empire Bay* stayed afloat and drifted for almost 24 hours before finally sinking in Hartlepool Bay the following night. All of the crew and DEMS gunners were saved.

The story of her sinking has a strange twist to it. In 1998 a water pipeline was being excavated near to South Bank railway station, near Middlesbrough. Approximately six miles inland and 4.5-metres down, part of an aeroplane was found. The matter was reported to the authorities as a matter of course – a legal requirement. An RAF crash team arrived at the scene to investigate and found markings on the wreckage that showed it to be a Second World War German aeroplane. The full site needed to be excavated in case of unexploded bombs. As work progressed, the remains of a crewmember were found. The man was identified by a ring and the remains of his paybook. All of this was reported in the local press, radio and television, and a number of people came forward to say that they remembered the incident.

One man had worked at the local steelworks overlooking the river estuary and said he could remember the aircraft that had bombed the *Empire Bay* flying into a burst of gunfire and then diving to the ground with a great crash. Another man who was a boy at the time lived near to the site and remembered going to the crash site the next morning to look for souvenirs. A Home Guard soldier told him that the plane had just bombed and sank a ship before she was shot down.

When the plane came down it left a large crater, which was quickly backfilled because the adjacent railway line was needed for urgent war supplies to the local docks and steelworks.

A further twist developed. The rest of the crew of the aircraft had been killed instantly, but thrown clear of the bomber on impact. All of them had been accounted for and buried with full military honours in Thornaby on Tees cemetery, ten miles away. It was found that a gravestone with the airman's name on it had already been erected. The German embassy in London carried out an investigation, the aircraft records were traced and all of the crew identified. A new headstone was provided and the remains of the crewman – now identified as the plane's radio operator – found at the site were laid to rest with his fellow crewmen, 56 years after they crashed.

Starke Schell Registers; BVLS 1939–1945, p. 32; LCWLR 1939–1945, p. 336; Miramar Ship Index; Lloyd's Register of Steamers and Motor Ships 1940/1.

Wrecksite

In 1946 the Admiralty dispersed most of the wreck because it was considered a hazard to shipping. The wreck is not dived very often as it is close to the main shipping channel and visibility tends to be very poor. Local transit marks are not very good, therefore a little time is needed to locate the wreck and because not many divers visit her, who knows what may turn up. The wreck is now well smashed up and scattered around, with the anchor and chain lying at the bow section and one of the boilers is lying intact but on its side, next to the broken remains of the engine. Scattered parts of machinery, steel plating and framework lie in small jumbled heaps. A fair number of portholes have been recovered over the years, but now it is just a good second rummage dive. The seabed is hard sand with small rocks and some slag balls from the local steelworks.

BENEFICENT (?)

Date of loss: 24 February 1917
Wreck: ★★★★★
Depth: 40 m
Reference: 54 41'.875 N 000 58'.499 W
Location: 7.02 nm E from The Heugh, Hartlepool

The *Beneficent* (Official No. 84996) was an iron-hulled 1963-ton British steam cargo ship that measuring 83.82 m in length, with an 11.3-m beam and a 6.24-m draught. Short Brothers Ltd. at Pallion shipyard, Sunderland built and completed her as Yard No. 120 in December 1881. She was launched on 6 December 1881 for James Westoll, Sunderland, who was also the owner at the time of loss. The single iron screw was powered by a 224-hp two-cylinder compound steam engine that used two boilers. The cylinders measured 91.44 cm and 170.18 cm with a 91.44-cm stroke (36 in. and 67 in. with a 36-in. stroke). T. Richardson and Sons manufactured the machinery at Hartlepool. She had one iron deck, a well deck, a 69-ton (195.38 m) poop deck, a 90-ton (254.85 m) quarterdeck and 160-ton (453.06 m) bridge deck.

Final voyage

At 0800 hrs on 24 February 1917 a huge explosion on her starboard side rocked the *Beneficent* (Captain F.C. Munroe) when she was 4½–5 miles ENE from The Heugh, Hartlepool, at position 54° 44½ N 01° 04'W. The ship was armed for defence and *en route* from Newcastle upon Tyne to Le Havre with a cargo of coal. The blast took place abreast of the engine room, instantly killing the donkeyman and two firemen. At 0818 hrs orders were issued to abandon ship and the 19 survivors left in the boats. Two minutes later the ship sank taking confidential papers down with it. The surviving crew was picked up by a passing patrol vessel shortly afterwards and landed at the Tees. The three crewmen that died were:

Ali, Abde, Donkeyman MM
Hasan, Ali, Fireman MM
Sulman, H., Fireman MM

The KDM submarine SMU *UC 31*, commanded by Kptlt Otto von Schrader, had laid mine barriers between Whitby and Hartlepool before Kptlt Schrader torpedoed and sank the *Beneficent* without warning. He continued to lay nine more mines in Tees Bay, before sinking two more British steamers further south: the 521-ton *Kathleen Lily* (1872: Bargate Steamship Company) and the 993-ton *Quaggy* (1904: The South Metropolitan Gas Company).

ADM 137/2961; LCWLR 1914–1918, p. 98; BVLS 1914–1918, p. 34; LR 1915/16, No. 551 (B); CWGC; Jarvis & Jarvis (1993), Vol. 1; Jarvis & Jarvis (1993) Vol. 2.

Wrecksite

The wreck – which is probably that of the *Beneficent* – is orientated in a NNE to SSW direction. It lies on a seabed of mud, gravel and coarse sand in a general depth of 40 m (LAT), very close to, or in the Teesmouth spoil ground. The wreck is quite substantial and lies in three sections, with the largest amidships part standing about 6 m high. It stands upright, but the stern end has partially collapsed and is around 40 m by 6 m, lying orientated in a NE to SW direction. The amidships-positioned bridge section, which is about 10 m by 4 m, faces ENE to WSW. The third section is rather smaller than the latter two. The boilers and engine are visibly exposed. Copper piping, brass valves and even a couple of portholes can be seen protruding out of the twisted wreckage, which has collected a fair amount of muddy-looking sediment. Cod and a number of large pollack were observed on this wreck, making her well worth visiting for boat angling.

REMA, EX FIVEL, EX PERGO

Date of loss: 25 April 1998
Wreck: ★★★★★
Depth: 63 m
Reference: 54 41'.951 N 000 08'.856 W
Location: 20.35 nm NE of Whitby

The *Rema* (Official No. 01961755) was a steel-hulled 748-ton Honduran motor cargo vessel that measured 63 m in length and had a 9.5-m beam. Van Goor's S & M Monnickendam, the Netherlands, built and completed her as Yard No. 660 in May 1976. She was launched as the *Pergo* for Venootschap G. de Vries & Zn, the Netherlands. The manager was Scheepvaart-en Expertisekantoor E. Wagenborg, Delfzijl, the Netherlands. The single four-blade fixed-pitch steel screw was powered by a 750-hp six-cylinder diesel engine that gave 10 knots. The accommodation and engine room were located aft and she had a single hold fitted with MacGregor single pull-hatch covers.

From 1985 to March 1987, the owners were Wagenborg Scheepvaert BV, Markstraat 10, Postbus 14, 9930 AA Delfzyl, Netherlands. After the 1st January 1987, the registered owner was V.O.F. Vega & Zonen, Delfzijl and the manager was Wagenborg Shipping BV, Delfzijl (until 1 January 1993). In September 1987 she renamed *Fivel*. Amasus Scheepvaert BV., AG Delfzyl, Netherlands was the commercial operator from the 1st January 1987 to 26 December 1991. Wagenborg Scheepvaert B.V. was the commercial operator from 27 December 1991 until 1st September 1995. In 1992 she was sold to J V Ten Hoor, Delfzijl and the manager was Wagenborg Scheepvaert BV, Delfzijl. The *Fivel* was at Delfzijl for most of 1995 'for repairs'. Delfzijl is a city in northeast Netherlands, on the bank of the river Ems estuary. Lamar Shipping Ltd. was the registered owner from 2 September 1995 to 17 December 1995. After September 2nd, 1995, Seatrend Scheepvaert N.V., Essen was the commercial operator until 17 December 1995. From 18 December 1995 to 23 June 1996, the registered owner was Herbert Trading Ltd. Honduras and the commercial operator was Halcyon Shipping Ltd. Captain Mike Clayton, Torpoint was the registered owner from 24

June 1996 to the 27th April 1997 and he was also the commercial operator that period. On April 28th 1997 the ship was renamed *Rema* by new registered owner Herbert Trading Ltd. of 50, Shirley Street, Nassau, Bahamas, but she operated under the Belize flag. The commercial operator was Halcyon Shipping Ltd. Great Yarmouth, Norfolk, UK, over the same period. The management company's involvement was primarily for cargo broking and business management. Crewing, maintenance and repairs were the responsibility of the owner, who was also the master.

During her time afloat the vessel had a very chequered safety history. On 14 March 1997 an inspection in a German port showed that there were major problems with:

- hull damage impairing seaworthiness
- decks cracking
- railing cat walks
- ventilator air pipe
- anchoring devices
- musters and drills
- minimum safe manning certificates
- charts
- auxiliary engines
- steering gear
- certificates of competency

The last time the *Rema* had trouble was on 9 February 1998 when an inspection was carried out and the vessel was placed in detention in a UK port for the following detainable deficiency concerns:

- captain unable to produce certificate of competency;
- no personnel on board who were able to produce a radio certificate;
- various navigation charts out of date;
- various nautical publications out of date;
- no fire fighting system in paint locker;
- fire hose leaking;
- no lifeboats or equivalent on board as required by SOLAS 60; and
- radio batteries found dry and in need of replacement.

The vessel was released on the 13 February 1998 after the problems had been rectified. The *Rema* arrived at Berwick on Tweed in ballast on 22 April 1998 and the following day she was fully loaded with 930 tons of redstone chippings.

Final voyage

At about 1230 hrs on Friday, 24 April 1998 the *Rema* sailed for Terneuzen in the Netherlands with a crew of four and all of her water ballast tanks empty. The weather on departure was good; the wind south-west force 3–4, with a slight to moderate swell. On Saturday the 25th the *Rema* was 22 miles NE from Whitby when she transmitted a mayday on a very high frequency (VHF) channel 16 giving her location. The Humber coastguard immediately mobilised local RNLI lifeboats, RAF helicopters and a number of merchant vessels. There was little to be found of the *Rema*, though a helicopter did locate an upturned dingy and oil on the surface, confirming that she had sunk at position 54° 41'.95N 00° 08'.86W with all four hands. The men who died in the tragedy were:

skipper Michael Clayton, 41 yrs, from Castleford
Robert Clayton, 40 yrs, from Southampton
Shaun Norton, 26 yrs, from Glass Houghton
Andrew James, 34 yrs, from Allerton Bywater.

Their bodies have never been recovered.

During 24–27 June 1998 an underwater survey was carried out and the wreck was found to be upright and intact, but there was evidence of damage at the bows where it had struck the seabed with some force. When it sank the cargo had actually shifted forward and forced its way out through the hatches, which imploded on impact. The cargo spilled onto the seabed. The forecastle head, wheelhouse and a screw blade were also damaged. The conclusion was that the vessel had suddenly plunged vertically, by the head, to the seabed and then dropped down onto an even keel. It seems she sank so quickly her four British crewmen had no chance of survival. It was never officially established how water had entered the hull, but calculations later showed that she would have foundered if an additional 769 tons of water had entered the hull.

LR; Lloyd's Confidential Index; Lloyd's Shipping Index 1976/7–1998; Marine Accident Report 1/00 - Report of the Inspector's Inquiry into the loss of mv *Rema* - February 2000.

Wrecksite

The wreck is orientated in a SE to NW direction and lies on a seabed of sand and shell in a general depth of 63 m (LAT). It is upright and intact and stands over 10 m high at the stern end. A lot of fish occupy the wreck, so it should make an excellent boat-angling venue. The bell, if located, will almost certainly be inscribed: *Pergo 1976*.

OCEAN

Date of loss: 23 November 1917
Wreck: ✯✯✯✯
Depth: 36 m
Reference: 54 41'.991 N 001 01'.432 W
Location: 5.04 nm NE of South Gare light

The *Ocean* (Official No. 102856) was a steel-hulled 1442-ton British steam cargo ship that measured 75.28 m in length, with a 10.74-m beam and a 4.72-m draught. S.P. Austin and Son at Wear Dock, Sunderland built and completed her as Yard No. 183 in April 1894. She was launched on 8 March 1894 for Lambert Brothers Ltd. London and registered in London. The single screw was powered by a 155-hp three-cylinder triple expansion steam engine that used one boiler. North Eastern Marine Engineering Company in Sunderland manufactured the engine and ancillary machinery. She had one deck, four bulkheads cemented, an 8.5-m poop deck, a 19.1-m quarterdeck, 13.85-m bridge deck and an 8.2-m forecastle.

William Cory & Son, London was the registered owner in 1896. From 1916 Cory Colliers Ltd. London was the registered owner. In 1916 the ship was armed for defence.

Final voyage

On 23 November 1917 Oblt.z.S. Walter Scheffler in the KDM submarine SMU *UB 21*, torpedoed the *Ocean* (Captain H. Norman) without any warning. The ship was sunk while *en route* from Granton to London with a cargo of coal.

BVLS 1914–1916, p. 73; LCWLR 1914–1918, p. 184; LR 1915/16, No. 42 (O); Starke Schell Register.

Wrecksite

The wreck is orientated in a NE to SW direction. It is upright and in two substantial sections with both the stern and bow sections standing proud of the seabed. The midships section where the bridge and forecastle were, has collapsed and is inverted onto the engines and boiler. The depth to the top of the stern section is about 25 m, with the top of the bows at around 28 m. Peter Hale reports that the wreck is very impressive and a top quality dive site, but very often monofilament nets and trawl nets shroud the wreck. Large cod and ling have been seen on numerous occasions and it is not unusual to observe large crustaceans under the wreckage.

WINGA

Date of loss: 2 June 1940
Wreck: ★★★★★
Depth: 33 m
Reference: 54 41'.691 N 001 02'.399 W
Location: 4.41 nm NE of South Gare light

The *Winga* (Official No. 147927) was an iron-hulled 1748-ton British steam cargo ship that measured 76.2 m in length, with an 11.3-m beam and a 4.95-m draught. New Waterway Ship Building Co at Schiedam built and completed her as Yard No. 123 in August 1924. She was launched on 12 July 1924 for Scandinavian Shipping Company, Glasgow, with Glen and Company as the manager. The single iron screw was powered by a 144-nhp three-cylinder triple expansion steam engine that used one single-ended boiler and gave 9 knots. The cylinders measured 45.72 cm, 76.2 cm and 124.46 cm with a 91.44-cm stroke (18 in., 30 in. and 49 in. with a 36-in. stroke). New Waterway Ship Building Company manufactured the engine and ancillary machinery. She had one deck, water ballast, a 4.2-m poop deck, 19.1-m quarterdeck, 25.5-m bridge deck and an 8.5-m forecastle. She was also fitted with electric lights and a wireless. Her designated signal code letters were: MNBK.

From 1929 Clydesdale Shipowners Company, Glasgow was the registered owner. Her designated signal code letters became: KRMF.

Final voyage

On the morning of Sunday, 2 June 1940 the *Winga* collided with the 1289-ton Norwegian steamer *Jernland* (1905: Halvorsen Shipping Co., A/S, Bergen). The *Winga* sank almost immediately, five miles east of West Hartlepool. The *Winga* was sailing independently and carrying a cargo of iron ore from Santander, Spain for the Tyne. The *Jernland* picked up eight survivors and landed them at the Tees. It was badly damaged and had to be dry-docked. Fourteen crewmen, including the master, were lost when the *Winga* went down:

Allsop, Henry St Clair, 65 yrs, Steward MM
Bell, Thomas, 51 yrs, Sailor MM
Botha, Thomas Ernest, 44 yrs, 2nd Engineer Officer MM
Harrison, Thomas Whitewat, 60 yrs, Sailor MM
Hill, Edward Reilly, 20 yrs, Cabin Boy MM
Hogan, Thomas, 29 yrs, Sailor MM
Keenan, John, 27 yrs, Fireman and Trimmer MM
Macleod, Farquhar, 28 yrs, Able Seaman MM
McAulay, Duncan, 28 yrs, Able Seaman MM
McPhail, Thomas Lovat, 28 yrs, Fireman and Trimmer MM
Preshur, John, 60 yrs, Junior Engineer Officer MM
Prior, John, 60 yrs, Fireman and Trimmer MM
Scotland, John, 35 yrs, Master MM
Shaw, Percival Merlin, 34 yrs, Cook MM

CWGC; LCR 1940, p. 8 (f); LR 1940/1, No. 86391 (W); Starke Schell Registers.

Wrecksite

This wreck is orientated in a NE to SW direction and sits in a half-metre scour. It lies on a dirty seabed of sand, mud and stones in a general depth of 33 m (LAT) and is very substantial. In 1988 the wreck was reported to be almost upright, standing 6 m high and reasonably intact at both ends, with the bows lying to the WNW – the tallest part being to the north. The superstructure amidships had collapsed to the deck level and the iron screw was still in place. The wreck was identified by Gordon Wadsworth when he recovered the bell. A fairly large number of fish and crustaceans can be seen around the wreck.

BEN ADEN (?)

Date of loss: 14 July 1916
Wreck: ★★
Depth: 55 m
Reference: 54 41'.075 N 000 39'.235 W
Location: 18.24 nm E from The Heugh, Hartlepool and 11.65 nm NNW from Whitby

The *Ben Aden* (Official No. 12935) was a steel-hulled 176-ton British steam trawler measuring 32.35 m by length, with a 6.42-m beam and 3.5-m draught. Hall Russell and Company, Aberdeen built and completed her as Yard No. 338. She was launched on 26 September 1900 for the North British Steam Fishing Company, Aberdeen, which registered her in Aberdeen. A 62-hp three-cylinder triple expansion steam engine that used one single-ended boiler powered the single steel screw. In 1908 she was registered to R. Irvin and Sons Ltd. at Aberdeen. From 1915 until the time of loss, R.H. Davidson at Hartlepool was the registered owner.

Final voyage

On 14 July 1916 the *Ben Aden* was fishing 15–21 miles east of Hartlepool when Oblt.z.S. Heinrich Küstner, in the KDM submarine SMU *UB 39*, stopped her. The crew was forced to abandon ship in a boat and it was sunk by the Germans using explosive scuttling charges.

LCWLR 1914–1918, p. 47; BVOS 1914–1918; Aberdeen Built Ships Project.

Wrecksite

The wreck, possibly that of the *Ben Aden*, is orientated in an E to W direction. It lies on a seabed of sand, mud, gravel and shells in a general depth of 55 m (LAT). The remains are collapsed and well broken up, with the highest part standing just over 3 m from the seabed. It is broken into two (or possibly three) sections, with the largest part being about 18 m in length and 5 m across. Quite a lot of the wreck appears to be well buried, but a lot of various-sized pieces of debris lie close by.

PATRIA

Date of loss: 29 December 1917
Wreck: ****
Depth: 35 m
Reference: 54 42'.008 N 001 02'.349 W
Location: 4.66 nm NNE of South Gare light

SS Patria *in port, c.1910 (Norwegian Collection)*

The *Patria* (Official No. 19) was an iron-hulled 837-ton Russian steam cargo vessel measuring 62.69 m in length, with an 8.88-m beam and 4.63-m draught. Murdock and Murry at

Port Glasgow built and completed her as Yard No. 61 in May 1882. She was launched on 22 April 1882 for Wasa Nordsjö Ångbåts A/B, at Wasa, Russia (Vaasa, in present-day Finland) which owned her at the time of loss. A. Schauman was the manager. The single iron screw was powered by a 93-hp two-cylinder compound steam engine that used one boiler. Kincaid and Company at Greenock manufactured the engine and auxiliary machinery. She had one deck, four bulkheads, a 20.7-m quarterdeck, 17-m bridge deck and an 8.5-m forecastle.

The *Patria* was built mainly to operate between Finland and Hull. From 1907 until the time of loss, K. Kurten was the manager.

Final voyage

On 29 December 1917 the *Patria* was torpedoed without warning by the KDM submarine SMU *UB 21*, commanded by Oblt.z.S. Walter Scheffler. The vessel, with a cargo of coal and making 8 knots, was proceeding south from Dunston in Tyne and Wear to Caen, France as part of a convoy. Scheffler fired two torpedoes. The first one struck the *Patria* on the port side in the area of the bulkhead between the stokehold and forehold, two firemen, one sailor and a cabin girl were killed in the explosion. The second torpedo, fired shortly afterwards, damaged the 3734-ton turret-hulled steamer *Inverness* (1902: Sutherland Steam Ship Company, Newcastle), which put in to Middlesbrough. The *Inverness* had been on passage from the Tyne to Genoa, also with coal, and was north of the river Tees when she was hit. At no time was the submarine spotted. The surviving crew of the *Patria* took to the lifeboats. They were picked up by an armed trawler and landed at Middlesbrough.

ADM 137/4007; Starke Schell Registers; Lloyd's Register 1915/16, p. 219 (P); LCWLR 1914–1918, p. 192; ANCL 1914–1918, p. 52.

Wrecksite

The wreck is orientated in an ENE to WSW direction, with the bows to the ENE. It lies in a general depth of 35 m (LAT) within one mile of five other wrecks. Unfortunately, the site is also rather close to the spoil ground, an area of 5–6 square miles used by the river Tees' dredgers for dumping sludge and such like. As a result visibility is usually very poor.

The hull is still intact and sitting upright on the seabed. The bridge and quarterdeck of the ship are missing as they were deemed a navigation hazard to large vessels and so dispersed by explosives. All that is left is a large hole and broken framework. The wreck stands around 4 m high, and other than the missing bridge and quarterdeck is largely complete. It has, however, collected a number of nets including monofilament ones. There is also a 1.5-m scour around the wrecksite caused by the strong tidal streams which sweep over and around it.

KILKIS, EX NICHOLAOS EX REPUBLIC

Date of loss: 24 July 1918
Wreck: ✭✭✭✭
Depth: 36 m
Reference: 54 42'.008 N 001 02'.915 W
Location: 4.42 nm N by E of South Gare light

The *Kilkis* (Official No. 123269) was a steel-hulled 4281-ton Greek steam cargo ship measuring 111.25 m in length, with a 15.39-m beam and 5.71-m draught. Sunderland Ship Builders Company at South Dock, Sunderland built and completed her as Yard No. 238 in August 1906. She was launched as the *Republic* on 5 July 1906 for W.H. Cockerline and Company at Hull, where she was registered. The single screw was powered by a 353-hp three-cylinder triple expansion steam engine which used three boilers. North Eastern Marine Engineering Company at Sunderland manufactured the engine and ancillary machinery. She had one deck, six bulkheads, a 9.1-m poop deck, a 32.6-m bridge deck and 10.7-m forecastle.

In 1915 E.E. Ambatielos, in Argostoli Greece purchased her and renamed her *Nicholaos*. Ambatielo Brothers was the manager. In 1916 she was renamed *Kilkis* by Bistis & Hadzikyriakos, Argostoli the new registered owner.

Final voyage

On 24 July 1918 SMU *UC 70*, a KDM minelaying submarine commanded by Oblt.z.S. Karl Dobberstein, torpedoed the *Kilkis* off West Hartlepool. The ship, with Captain A. Lucus in charge, was transporting a 6800-ton cargo of iron ore on a voyage from Almeria to Newcastle and was sunk without warning.

LCWLR 1914–1918, p. 226; ANCL 1914–1918, p. 28; LR 1915/16, No. 41 (K); Starke Schell Registers.

Wrecksite

The wreck of the *Kilkis* is standing upright, 6 m high and fairly intact on a seabed of hard sand and small rocks. It lies in a general depth of 33 m (LAT) and is surrounded by a 1.5-metre scour. It is orientated in a SSE to NNW direction.

When observed from the seabed for the first time, the bows are impressive. Finning up and over the bows, the forecastle deck is almost intact, with the anchor windlass dropping down onto the deck. Large winches can be viewed as you swim along towards the bridge deck and come to a black hole. This presumably is where it was hit by the torpedo because the hull has collapsed along this area. From this position dive times do not allow further inspection – even if you add another two minutes of decompression time – so the stern section must wait for another dive. If you drop a shot onto the rear section of the wreck, it ought to be mostly intact but the poop deck bulkheads have collapsed, making access easy and reasonably safe. By continuing along the deck, you can cross over the deck beams. All of the timber decking has long since gone, though it is easy to make out where the holds begin. They are very dark and eerie but the *Kilkis*'s cargo of iron ingots can still be seen, along with more deck winches. On approach to the bridge deck there are jagged steel plates protruding from the superstructure so extra care is needed. From the bridge deck the engine room can be accessed, though it is not recommended. The wreck is festooned with dead-man's fingers and is very colourful in the dim light. Shoals of pout whiting and large cod can often be seen. In August large shoals of mackerel can also be seen swimming round the wreck in pursuit of sprats and sand eels that come in their millions. (Original dive report courtesy of Don Foster from Norton, Stockton-on-Tees.)

MILE END

Date of loss: 19 January 1940
Wreck: ✯✯✯✯
Depth: 28 m
Reference: 54 42'.691 N 001 06'.848 W
Location: 2.34 nm ENE from The Heugh, Hartlepool

The *Mile End* (Official No. 132561) was a steel-hulled 859-ton British steam cargo vessel measuring 50.44 m in length, with an 11.58-m beam and a 4.39-m draught. William Dobson and Company at Low Walker, Newcastle upon Tyne built and completed her as Yard No. 170 in July 1911. She was launched on 25 May 1911 for the Commercial Gas Company, London, which registered her in London and owned her at the time of loss. The single screw was powered by a 16-nhp three-cylinder triple expansion steam engine that used one single-ended boiler, working at 180 psi pressure, with four corrugated furnaces, 7.52 sq.m (81 sq. ft) of grate surface and 264.86 sq.m (2851 sq.ft) of heating surface. The cylinders measured 44.45 cm, 73.66 cm and 121.92 cm with an 83.82-cm stroke (17.5 in., 29 in. and 48 in. with a 33-in. stroke). MacColl and Pollack Ltd. at Sunderland manufactured the machinery. She had one steel deck, four bulkheads cemented, a 13.4-m bridge deck and a 5.5-m forecastle. She also had some cellular double bottom and a fore peak tank, an aft peak tank, plus a deep tank in the engine room on both the starboard and port sides. Lloyd's classed her as 100 A1.

Final voyage

During the early hours of 19 January 1940 the *Mile End*, in ballast and *en route* from London to Sunderland, sank at the mouth of the river Tees following a collision with HM Trawler *Faraday* (Admiralty No. 3312). The *Mile End* was lost along with four of her crew of 16. Three of the 11 survivors were trapped in the forecastle by a jammed door; they tried to smash their way out using chairs but failed. Their colleagues were able to beak the door open using crowbars. The survivors abandoned ship in two lifeboats but as they were pulling away from the ship one of them capsized. Those in the other boat pulled the capsized crew out of the water. A messroom boy was also rescued having been found struggling in the water. The *Mile End* sank within minutes. A trawler picked up the survivors. They were taken on board a destroyer that landed them at a north-east port. The crewman lost were:

Gillbertson, Peter, 42 yrs, Able Seaman
Lecomber, Arthur Benjamin, 57 yrs, Donkeyman
Petersen, Carl Andreas, 31 yrs, Chief Officer
Robson, Andrew, 58 yrs, Master.

LCR 1940, p. 9 (f); LR 1939/40, No. 79639 (M); Starke Schell Registers; CWGC.

Wrecksite

The wreck – most likely that of the *Mile End* – is orientated in a NNE to SSW direction. It lies on a bottom of hard sand in a general depth of 28 m (LAT). The wreck is partially broken up and covers an area 60 m by 8 m, with the tallest structure standing 4 m proud of the seabed. Soft corals are taking hold on the most exposed parts of the wreck. Large cod and pollack are a fairly common sight.

LOCH NAVER, EX SIR JOHN HOTHAM, EX EDWARD CATTELLY

Date of loss: 6 May 1940
Wreck: ✯✯✯✯
Depth: 35 m
Reference: 54 42'.675'N 001 04'.165'W
Location: 3.77 nm E from The Heugh, Hartlepool

The *Loch Naver* (Official No. 141947) was a steel-hulled 278-ton British steam trawler measuring 38.22 m in length, with a 7.11-m beam and a 3.86-m draught. Ailsa Shipbuilding Company at Ayr, Scotland built and completed her as Yard No. 350A in 1919. She was launched as the *Edward Cattelly* (Fleetwood Port registration number FD.204) on 17 March 1919. The single steel screw was powered by an 83-rhp, three-cylinder triple expansion steam engine that used one single-ended boiler working at 180 pressure psi, with three plain furnaces, 4.64 sq.m (50 sq.ft) of grate surface and 152.36 sq.m (1640 sq.ft) of heating surface. Smith's Dock Company, Middlesbrough manufactured the machinery. She had one deck, three bulkheads cemented, a 21.94-m quarterdeck and a 6.4-m forecastle. Lloyd's classed her as 100 A1. The designated code recognition signal letters were: GMFT.

In 1930–1, H. Blackburn was the registered owner. In 1932 Blackburn Trawlers Ltd. became registered owner and she was renamed *Sir John Hotham* (Hull Port registration number H.432). H. Blackburn was the manager. In 1935 the registered owner was Empire Steam Fishing Company of Aberdeen who renamed her *Loch Naver*. Harry Wight Ltd. was the manager. In 1939 the *Loch Naver* was acquired by Malcolm Smith Ltd. of Aberdeen and Malcolm Smith was also the manager. In August 1939 the trawler was requisitioned and converted to Admiralty minesweeper *Loch Naver*, No. 4459 and equipped with wireless direction finder and an echo-sounding device.

Final patrol

On 6 May 1940 the *Loch Naver*, with Skipper George Robert Burwood RNR in charge, was on patrol off Hartlepool when she foundered following a collision with an unknown vessel 260° from No. 20 Buoy, 4.5 miles east of Hartlepool. The crew was picked up by HMS *Breda*.

Toghill (2003), pp. 51–2; SRN Vol. 2, p. 213; LR 1939.

Wrecksite

The wreck is orientated in an E to W (090/270) direction and lies on a dirty seabed of sand, stone and pebbles in a general depth of 35 m (LAT). It stands about 4 m high, is intact and upright with nets snagging much of the wreck. Soft corals are established on the upper structures and hundreds of pout whiting shoal over the top of it.

BERWICK

Date of loss: 14 August 1884
Wreck: ☆☆
Depth: 56 m
Reference: 54 42'.342 N 000 37'.119 W
Location: 13.10 nm NE from F 12.9 nm N from Whitby

The *Berwick* (Official No. 6131) was an iron-hulled 537-ton cargo/passenger steamer measuring 55.77 m in length, with an 8.22-m beam and 4.57-m depth of hold. Scott and Company at Greenock built and completed her as Yard No. 29 by in 1855. She was launched on 22 October 1855 and registered in London. The iron four-bladed propeller was powered by a 90-nhp two-cylinder compound inverted steam engine that used one boiler. The designated code recognition signal letters were: JMNR.

George Elliot, London was the registered owner from 1857 until 1884 and the master was J.G. Elliot. In 1884 Isaac Whitfield, London took over as registered owner.

Final voyage

On 14 August 1884 the *Berwick* was transporting a cargo of coal from Sunderland to Portsmouth when she foundered about ten miles NE of Hunt Cliff, near Saltburn. Wind conditions at the time were variable force 2. The crew of 16 was saved.

The Times: Friday, 15 August 1884, p. 4, Issue no. 31213; ULR; Board of Trade Wreck Return 1884, p.99 (375).

Wrecksite

The wreck – most likely that of the *Berwick* – is orientated in an ESE to WNW direction. It lies on a seabed of sand and shells in a general depth of 56 m (LAT). The wreck is broken into two main sections lying about 20 m apart with a small surrounding scour. The bow section is 25 m long while the main body of the wreck, which is 30 m long, lies 20 m to the north of the bows. The highest part is at the eastern end, standing just over 3 m from the seabed. The remains are collapsed and fairly decayed with a fair bit of debris spread about.

ROSELLA, EX FEDERAL (?)

Date of loss: 29 October 1914
Wreck: ☆☆
Depth: 45 m
Reference: 54 42'.925 N 000 57'.083 W
Location: 7.86 nm E by N from The Heugh, Hartlepool

The *Rosella* (Official No. 125058) was a steel-hulled 243-ton British steam trawler measuring 36.72 m in length, with a 6.7-m beam and a 3.58-m draught. Cook, Welton and Gemmell at Beverley built and completed her as Yard No. 136 on 8 May 1907. She was launched as the *Federal* on 14 February 1907 for Pelham Steam Fishing Company who had registered her as GY.272 (Grimsby Port/Fishing registration number) on 8 May 1907. The single screw was powered by a 63-nhp three-cylinder triple expansion steam engine that used one boiler and gave 10.5 knots. C.D. Holmes and Company, Hull manufactured the machinery. She had one deck, four bulkheads and a 22.7-m quarterdeck.

From 14 January 1911 to the time of loss Thomas Baskcomb at Grimsby was the registered owner and renamed her *Rosella.*

Final voyage

On 29 October 1914 the *Rosella*, commanded by Skipper William Sperring, was on passage from the Faroe Islands for Grimsby when she detonated a German-laid mine and foundered with two of her crew – William Sperring, 42 yrs, Skipper and P. Petersen, 29 yrs, Mate – about 25 miles SE of Tynemouth.

LCWLR 1914–1918, p. 4; LR 1913/14, No. 821 (R); CWGC; Jarvis (1993) Vol. 2; Thompson (1999); Groos (1922).

Wrecksite

The wreck – possibly that of the *Rosella* – is orientated in an ESE to WNW direction. It lies in a general depth of 45 m (LAT) and very close to another wreck. It is intact, with the bows to the ESE, but beginning to break up. There are also at least two trawl nets fouling the stern end of the wreck. A number of soft corals have taken hold on the upper structures, but few other kinds of marine life are to be seen.

TALISMAN (?)

Date of loss: 6 August 1917
Wreck: ✯✯
Depth: 47 m
Reference: 54 43'.325 N 000 57'.200 W
Location: 7.87 nm miles E by N from The Heugh, Hartlepool

The *Talisman* was an iron-hulled 153-ton British steam vessel that was registered in Glasgow and measured 34.13 m in length, with a 5.51-m beam and a 2.54-m draught. William Watson at Greenock built her in 1882 for W. McLachlan and Company in Glasgow who owned her at the time of loss. The single iron screw was powered by a 50-nhp two-cylinder compound steam engine that used one single-ended-boiler. The cylinders measured 30.48 cm and 50.8 cm, with a 35.56-cm stroke (12 in. and 20 in. with a 14-in. stroke). She had one deck and wheelhouse amidships.

Final voyage

On 6 August 1917 the *Talisman*, with her skipper N. Hyndman in charge, was in ballast and *en route* from Greenock to Grimsby when the KDM submarine SMU *UB 41*, commanded by Oblt.z.S. Gunther Krause, captured her. The crew was forced to abandon ship in the lifeboat. The *Talisman* was sunk by German explosive scuttling charges.

LCWLR 1914–1918, p. 162; BVLS 1914–1918, p. 62; LR 1915/16, No. 158 (T).

Wrecksite

The wreck – believed to be the *Talisman* – is orientated in a NW to SE direction and sits in a 0.75-m scour. It lies on a seabed of fine sand, mud and shell in a general depth of 47 m (LAT) with the bows facing NW. The wreck is fairly intact, standing around 2.5 m high and lying on its starboard side. The upper structures have collapsed exposing the engine and boiler. Soft corals encrust the highest sections and various fish shoal over the wreck.

RAVNANGER (?)

Date of loss: 11 November 1940
Wreck: ★★★★★
Depth: 42 m
Reference: 54 43'.691 N 001 03'.065 W
Location: 4.63 nm NE from The Heugh, Hartlepool

The Ravnanger, *a 3371-ton Norwegian steam cargo ship bombed and sunk off Hartlepool on 11 November 1940 (Author's collection)*

The *Ravnanger* was a steel-hulled 3371-ton (2004 tons net) Norwegian steam cargo ship measuring 102.26 m in length, with a 14.68-m beam and a 6.93-m draught. C.van der Giessen and Zonen's Scheepswerven NV, Krimpen a/d Yssel, in the Netherlands built and completed her as Yard No. 478 in June 1919. In January 1920 the ship was delivered to H. Westfal-Larsen and Company Aktieselskapet, Bergen. They were also the owners and manager at the time of loss. The single steel screw was powered by a 257-nhp three-cylinder triple expansion steam engine that, due to the size of the ship, probably used three boilers and gave 9 knots. The cylinders measured 58.42 cm, 69.85 cm and 172.72 cm with a 119.38-cm stroke (23 in., 37.5 in. and 68 in. with a 47-in. stroke). Rotterdamske Droogdok Maatschappij at Rotterdam manufactured the engine and ancillary machinery. She had one deck, water ballast, a 98-ton (277.50-cu.m) poop deck, 139-ton (393.60-cubic.m) housedeck and 21-ton (59.46-cu.m) forecastle. The designated code recognition signal letters were: LDGJ.

1940 was a bad year altogether for the *Ravnanger*. On 16 January the tip of one of her screw blades broke off while in the lock pit of Alexandra Dock, Hull. In February she was discharging coal in Drammen, Norway and had problems with ice. On 24 May, on leaving port, she grounded at Charlottetown, Prince Edward Island, Canada; however, was re-floated and, after the balance of her cargo of fertiliser was discharged, declared seaworthy following a survey. In August problems with the crew held up her departure from New York. The

Ravnanger eventually sailed on 4 September arriving at Sydney, Nova Scotia on the 10th. Nine days later she departed Sydney and reached the Clyde on 4 October before leaving again on the 15th. She arrived at Methil Roads on the 20th and two days later sailed for Middlesbrough which she reached on the 23rd.

Final voyage

On 11 November 1940 the *Ravnanger* (Captain Johan Edvard Grung) was bombed and sunk by German aircraft about one to one and a half miles NE off buoy no. 20 off Middlesbrough. The aircraft was almost certainly a German twin-engine Heinkel He-115 of the 3rd squadron (*staffel*) of the Coastal Flyers (*Kustenfliegergruppen*). The ship had left Middlesbrough, in ballast, on 10 November at 1415 hrs and proceeded at half speed while awaiting a convoy for the return trip to Sydney. She carried a crew of 37 and three passengers.

At about 0025 hrs on the 11th, an aircraft was heard closing in from seaward and passed astern of the vessel. A greenish light was observed underneath the plane as it passed over the moonlit sky. It cruised at an altitude of about 200–300 ft and was thought to be British. However, the aircraft came back a second time and dropped a bomb or a mine 700–900 ft (about two or three ship lengths) from the ship before turning back and out to sea. An explosion occurred under the front section of *Ravnanger* and she immediately began to sink by the bow. All hands were summoned and ordered to the lifeboats. One of the lifeboats was caught and pulled under as the ship sank, but the five men in it scrambled to get onto the rafts that drifted past. The third engineer was last seen on his way to his cabin, and most probably was lost with the ship. As the motor lifeboat with the survivors headed for land the ship's bow was already on the seabed with the stem still visible above water.

Twenty-six men (some boys) survived, but one was lost in the attack.

The maritime inquiry was held in London on 26 November 1940. Captain Grung, the first and second engineers, the first, second and third mates, stoker Holte and stoker Reklev appeared at the hearing. The following report was given by Captain Grung. The first mate, I.A. Thornquist, made a similar statement:

> SS RAVNANGER departed Middlesbrough at 1415 hrs 10 November 1940 and continued to anchorage off the Fairway buoy, at a spot decided by Naval Control, and that also the pilot directed me to upon leaving the vessel at the breakwater. We anchored about 1600 hrs and received an order from the guardboat (examination vessel) to join convoy at buoy no. 20 about 0000 hrs. As the initial order had been for 2200 hrs, we had already weighed anchor and were waiting, alternating between stop and slow ahead on engine. Continued to buoy no. 20 at 2300 hrs British day light saving time, and remained in vicinity of buoy no. 20 from 2300 hrs to 0015 hrs. When no convoy could be observed, vessel was turned around abt. 0030 hrs in order to return at half speed to anchorage. At this time, an aircraft was heard closing in from seaside and passed astern of vessel. A greenish light was seen underneath the plane that cruised at about 200–300ft altitude. The aircraft dropped a bomb or a mine in the sea 700–900ft from vessel, and then made a turn back to sea. A bomb or mine exploded in the front part of the vessel and she immediately started to sink. All hands were summoned and ordered to the lifeboats.
>
> The lifeboats were put out on both sides, but it was difficult to clear them from ship's side due to the fast increasing port list. As soon as I observed that the boats were ready to go on the water, I went from boat deck to midship deck with intention to go into saloon to pick up vessel's documents which had been prepared and put in my bag,

but sea was already above the midship deck and I therefore returned to boatdeck and entered one of the lifeboats. Both lifeboats were launched, but just as the ship rapidly keeled over and started sinking very fast, port side lifeboat was hooked by the davit and was dragged under. Five men were in this boat, myself included, and we all fell in the water. We grabbed hold of two liferafts that came drifting by and dragged ourselves onto these. The liferafts drifted past the stern of the ship, and the poop was now the only visible part of the ship. We drifted over towards the motor lifeboat where the rest of the crew were, with the exception of the Third Engineer, Ola Karlsen, who was missing. We tried to enter the vessel to search for the missing person, but as the sea was very rough and the motorboat took on water, we had to give it up.

After a while the motor stopped, and we started rowing toward shore. After several attempts, we managed to start the motor again and we continued towards examination anchorage in order to find the guardboat and notify about the accident. We could not locate the guardboat in the dark, and we started for the mouth of the Tees, and we landed at the pilot station about 4.45 a.m. We disembarked at the pilot station, and a bus took us to the Seamen's Mission in Middlesbrough where we were given dry clothes and food. The motor lifeboat was left in the pilot station's custody, as was some of the wet clothings of the crew. None of the crew was able to save any of their personal belongings. The only injury was to myself when I had a finger on my left hand squeezed between our lifeboat and a spare lifeboat drifting by Middlesbrough, 11 November 1940.

Ola Mikal Karlsen, the Norwegian 3rd Engineer, lost his life. (Above statement courtesy of Warsailors.com.)

LCWLR 1939–1945, p. 154; LR 1940/1, No. 82042 (R); Starke Schell Registers; Maritime Inquiry-26.11.1940

Four of the surviving crewmembers of the *Ravnanger*, 1st Engineer Herman Parelius Knutsen, Captain Johan Edvard Grung, 1st Mate Ingolf Arthur Thornquist and 2nd Mate/Radio Operator Anders Kaldefoss were killed when working on board the steamer *Christian Krohg*, which sank on 10 June 1941.

Wrecksite

The wreck – most likely that of the Ravnanger – sits in a 1.5-m scour and is orientated in a SE to NW direction. It lies on a seabed of sand, mud, gravel and shells in a general depth of 42 m (LAT). It is intact and upright with the highest section amidships standing 8.8 m tall (as of 1989) and covering an area 90 m in length and 10 m across. Great numbers of fish and crustaceans has taken up residence in the wreck, which is said to be an interesting one to explore, though the upper structures are collapsing.

CAIRNESS

Date of Loss: 8 November 1911
Wreck: ✯✯
Depth: 49 m
Reference: 54 44'.125 N 000 56'.050 W
Location: 9.75 nm N by W of Skinningrove and 8.73 nm ENE from The Heugh

The *Cairness* (Official No. 110853) was a steel-hulled 174-ton British steam trawler measuring 33.59 m in length, with a 6.42-m beam and 3.52-m draught. Hall Russell and Company,

Aberdeen built and completed her as Yard No. 322 in 1899 for Fraserburgh and North of Scotland Steam Trawling Company. The single steel screw was powered by a three-cylinder triple expansion steam engine that used one single-ended boiler. From 1909 until the time of loss, J. Graham at Hartlepool was the registered owner. The Hartlepool Port/Fishing registration number was HL.44.

Final voyage

On 8 November 1911 the trawler *Cairness* sank following a collision with the 2138-ton Spanish steamer *Santiago* (1888: Cia. Naviera La Blanca, Bilbao) about 12 miles off the village of Skinningrove near Redcar. The trawler was carrying a crew of nine on a return fishing trip. Little is known of the rescue, but it is recorded that two of her crew were lost.

The *Santiago* was holed and filled up with water, but managed to reach the shore and was beached on Coatham Sands. After examination she was written off as a total loss. The *Santiago* had been carrying a crew of 24 and a cargo of coal from Newcastle upon Tyne for Bordeaux and Pauillac in the Gironde Estuary. None of the crew was lost.

Board of Trade Wreck Return 1912, p. 104 (403); The Aberdeen Built Ships Project; *The Times*: Friday 10 November 1911, p. 22, Issue no. 39739.

Wrecksite

The wreck sits in a one-metre scour and is orientated in an almost N to S direction. It lies on a seabed of fine sand, mud and stones in a general depth of 49 m (LAT). The wreck, which has collapsed, stands about 3 m high around the boiler and engine amidships. It is intact and covers an area 36 m long and 6 m across. Lots of anemones are established on the highest parts and numerous species of fish have been reported.

AURORA

Date of Loss: 25 November 1885
Wreck: ✯✯
Depth: 36 m
Reference: 54 44'.924 N 001 07'.865 W
Location: 3.47 nm NNE from The Heugh, Hartlepool

The *Aurora* (Official No. 86969) was an iron-hulled 1717-ton steam powered brigantine measuring 79.24 m in length, with a 10.97-m beam and 5.54-m draught. Messrs Raylton Dixon and Company, Middlesbrough built and completed her as Yard No. 219 in October 1883. She was launched on 2 August 1883 for Ebdy, Blacklin and Company at West Hartlepool where she was registered as a brigantine. Ebdy, Blacklin and Company owned her at the time of loss. The single screw was powered by a two-cylinder compound direct acting, surface condensing steam engine producing 180 hp and nine knots service speed.

Final voyage

The *Aurora* was commanded by Captain J.F. Ormandy and carried a crew of 23 hands with two stowaways on board. She left London on 22 November 1885 at 0100 hrs – high water

– with a 1500-ton cargo of phosphate shipped by Messrs Gibbs and Company of London. At this time she was in good seaworthy condition and bound for Savannah via Hartlepool. She reached Hartlepool at 1400 hrs on the 23rd where she took on 621 tons of coal for the voyage to Savannah.

At about 1645 hrs on the 25th she left Hartlepool Dock with the Hartlepool pilot, Mr George Davidson in charge, under her own steam but with a tug ahead of her that had an 8-inch (20.32-cm) four-strand Manila towrope to keep her straight in the Channel. The wind was ESE and blowing a gale. A high sea was running across the flats off the entrance to the harbour. She proceeded out of the harbour. The pilot left her at Middleton Pier, refusing to travel further on the grounds that the weather would prevent him from getting back in his coble. At the time of leaving it was stated that she had a free board of 3 ft (0.91 m) and was marked by Lloyd's Rules at 2 ft 4 in. (0.71 m). The pilot on leaving the ship gave various instructions on the pilotage out of the harbour and told the master to follow the tug as the tug master knew the Channel as well as he himself did.

About five minutes after the pilot left, the ship arrived at the entrance of the harbour where she was met with an easterly current setting across the mouth of the harbour. The tug master was not prepared to meet the resistance of the current with port helm. The *Aurora* proceeded at full speed, which left the tug slightly over to the starboard bow. The east current (stated in the Board of Trade wreck report) appears to have swept the *Aurora* towards the east bank. The towrope parted as the tug came perpendicular to the starboard bow of the *Aurora*, which continued on ahead at full speed, passing on the port side of the black buoys marking the east side of the channel.

The chief mate reported that the *Aurora* had struck ground, but the master had not perceived it. The second mate confirmed the report of the chief mate. The master then steered for the Coatham light, still going at full speed. The sea was flooding the upper deck and orders were given to sound the holds to check for flooding. Some time appears to have been lost before they were able to do it. At about 1800 hrs the engine was eased and, on sounding, 7 ft (2.13 m) of water was found in the forehold, so all the pumps were turned on. A consultation was held by the master and principal officers and it was decided to make for the Tyne. Ten minutes later the vessel began to settle by the head, rolling heavily. The chief engineer reported that the water was coming into the engine room and the fires would be out within a few minutes. The master steered for the beach but the water in the engine room put out the fires and directions were given to clear away the boats. The starboard lifeboat was manned by eleven hands and ordered to remain alongside in charge of the boatswain. The port lifeboat was then put out, manned by eight hands. The second mate fell overboard but saved himself by catching hold of the log line and was hauled into the boat. The gig was then got out at about 1945 hrs and all that was necessary, such as signals, were put into her. It was clear that the ship was sinking, the water being level with the forecastle, and the captain considered it necessary to leave the ship in his gig with six hands. At 2100 hrs, a squall with rain came on obscuring the ship. When it had passed away the ship was not to be seen. Some wreckage identified as having been stowed on the upper deck was seen floating near the spot.

From this point the boats were kept head to sea all night. At daylight the lifeboats were nowhere to be seen. The master advised keeping clear of the land for the better chance of being picked up, but the majority of the crew preferred making for the beach while they had the strength left in them to swim. At about 1030 hrs the master gave way to the opinion of the crew and decided to head for shore. They were making for the coast when a wave caught the boat, swamping her and knocking the crew out of the boat. The chief engineer, the chief mate and two seamen drowned.

The master and Edward Lawrence AB were saved by two men from the beach named George Harrison and John Chilton who very gallantly rushed into the water and dragged them through the surf to the shore. The eleven men in the starboard lifeboat landed safely at Old Seaham.

The second boat with eight men came on shore about three miles from the same spot. The steward died from presumed exhaustion after landing in spite of assistance given to him by the coastguard men.

Starke Schell Registers; Board of Trade Wreck Report: Aurora, 1885.

Wrecksite

The wreck – which was identified by Yorkshire diver Gordon Wadsworth after he located the bell – is orientated in a SSE to NNW direction and sits in a one metre scour. It lies on a seabed of sand, stone and gravel in a general depth of 36 m (LAT). The remains are now partially buried and cover an area of about 70 m in length by 30 m across with the bow and stern sections both collapsed. The highest part of 5 m is around the compound steam engine and single boiler, which lie over on their starboard side. A shoal of pout whiting hovered around the engine area and a few crustaceans were observed under the plates.

SUAVITY

Date of loss: 27 October 1940
Wreck: ★★★★
Depth: 38 m
Reference: 54 44'.174 N 001 05'.832 W
Location: 3.61 nm NE from The Heugh, Hartlepool

The *Suavity* (Official No. 165417) was a steel-hulled 634-ton British motor cargo vessel measuring 53.34 m in length, with an 8.45-m beam and 2.94-m draught. George Brown and Company (Marine), Greenock built and completed her as Yard No. 198 in March 1937. She was launched on 29 December 1936 for F.T. Everard and Sons, London which registered her in London and was the owner at the time of loss. A 167-nhp six-cylinder, two-stroke single-acting diesel oil engine powered the single screw. Newbury Diesel Company manufactured the aft-positioned machinery. She had one steel deck, a cruiser stern and three bulkheads part cemented and an aft superstructure consisting of a 34.3-m quarterdeck and 3.9-m forecastle. She also had some cellular double bottom and a fore peak and aft peak tank. Lloyd's classed her as 100 A1. Her designated code recognition signal letters were: MMDZ.

Final voyage

The *Suavity* left Sunderland as part of the south-bound 52 ship convoy FS.321 (Methil–Southend) and carrying 760 tons of wheat for passage to London. On 27 October 940, one mile north of buoy no. 20 off Hartlepool, she detonated a mine and sank. The mine had been dropped by German aircraft. All nine of her crew survived.

LCWLR 1939–1945, p. 146; BVLS 1939–1945, p. 12; LR 1940/1, No. 84044 (S); Starke Schell Registers.

Wrecksite

The wreck is orientated in a N to S direction and lies on a seabed of mud and fine sand in a general depth of 38 m (LAT). In the late 1980s it was reported to be virtually intact, sitting upright with part of the superstructure in place and the lower sections of one mast still secured and standing upright. The screw is still in place and the stern end has numerous species of fish shoaling around it. The wreck sits in a one-metre scour and soft corals lighten up the superstructure on what is a rather dark dive site. This ought to be an excellent boat-angling venue.

PITWINES, EX WANDLE

Date of loss: 19 November 1941
Wreck: ✭✭✭✭✭
Depth: 46 m
Reference: 54 44'.624 N 001 01'.282 W
Location: 6.06 nm NE from The Heugh, Hartlepool

The *Pitwines* (Official No. 146694) was a steel-hulled 889-ton British steam cargo vessel measuring 63.78 m in length, with a 9.55-m beam and a 4.03-m draught. Burntisland Shipbuilding Company built and completed her as Yard No. 119 in January 1923. She was launched as the *Wandle* on 20 December 1922 for Wandsworth, Wimbledon and Epsom District Gas Company, London (which later simply became the Wandsworth and District Gas Company). Her single screw was powered by a 121 hp three-cylinder triple expansion steam engine that used one single-ended boiler working at 180 pressure psi, with three corrugated furnaces, 5.29 sq.m (57 sq.ft) of grate surface and 197.88 sq.m (2130 sq.ft) of heating surface. North East Engineering Company, Newcastle upon Tyne, manufactured the aft machinery. She had one steel deck, a well deck, four bulkheads part cemented and an aft superstructure consisting of a 35-m quarterdeck, 4.6-m bridge deck and a 7.3-m forecastle. She also had some cellular double bottom and a fore peak and aft peak tank. Lloyd's classed her 100 A1. Her code signal recognition letters were: MLJT.

In 1932 she was renamed *Pitwines* by new owner Stephenson Clarke and Associated Companies Ltd., London which owned her at the time of loss.

Final voyage

On 19 November 1941 the *Pitwines* sank off the 19D Buoy, about seven miles NE of The Heugh, west Hartlepool, following a collision with the 754-ton steamer *Gateshead* (1919: Tyne-Tees Steam Shipping Company, Newcastle). The *Pitwines* was part of the south-bound, 69-ship convoy FS.650 (Methil–Southend) and was transporting coal from Middlesbrough to London. Hermann Alfred Pettersen, a donkeyman aged 61, died in the incident.

CWGC; LCR 1941, p. 8 (f); LR 1941/2 No. 30142 (P); Starke Schell Registers.

Wrecksite

The wreck is orientated in a NNE to SSW direction and sits in a one-metre scour. It lies on a seabed of fine sand, shell and mud in a general depth of 46 m (LAT). The wreck is very substantial and stands 6.5 m high, is fairly intact and lying on its port side with the bows facing ENE. The hull and superstructure are now starting to collapse in on itself. This wreck also attracts numerous varieties of fish, including cod, ling, conger, anglerfish and pout whiting, so the site should make a good boat-angling venue. The upper structures are coated in an array of soft corals, a sure sign of the very strong tidal streams that sweep around and over the wreck.

ABBOTSFORD (?)

Date of loss: 22 October 1906
Wreck: ✯✯✯✯
Depth: 71 m
Reference: 54 55'.073 N 000 55'.034 W
Location: 17.66 nm SE of the Tyne

The *Abbotsford* (Official No. 62287) was an iron-hulled British steam cargo vessel measuring 69.31 m in length, with an 8.94-m beam and a 6.88-m draught. Blackwood and Gordon at Port Glasgow built and completed her as Yard No. 103 in 1870 as a 1035-ton brig-rigged steamer. She was launched on 21 April 1870 for M.C. Gibson and Company Leith, which owned her at the time of loss and registered her at Leith. The single iron screw was powered by a 100-nhp two-cylinder compound steam engine that used one single-ended boiler. The cylinders measured 66.04 cm and 116.84 cm, with a 91.44-cm stroke (26 in. and 46 in. with a 36-in. stroke). Blackwood and Gordon also manufactured the engine and auxiliary machinery. She had a spar deck and five bulkheads. In 1888 the tonnage was altered to 1068 tons.

The designated code recognition signal letters were: JNHQ.

Final voyage

On 22 October 1906 the *Abbotsford*, under the command of Captain A.G. Bridges, sank following a collision with the 156-ton Hull-registered steam trawler *Helen McGregor* (H.94), about 14 miles SE of the river Tyne. The *Abbotsford* was carrying a crew of 18 and a general cargo from Ghent to Leith. There is no mention of any crew being lost so the trawler presumably saved them.

Board of Trade Wreck Return 1906, p. 139 (607); Miramar Ship Index; American Lloyd's Register of American and Foreign Shipping, 1857–1900; LR 1870–1900.

Wrecksite

The wreck, which is most likely the *Abbotsford* due to its depth and position, is orientated in a SE to NW direction with the highest point at the NW end. It sits in a small scour and lies on a seabed of mud, fine sand and black shells in a general depth of 71 m (LAT). The wreck is intact but appears to be on its side, standing over 8 m high and 8 m across. Little else is known about the wreck, but it will be an exciting one to explore for those with the expertise to do so. It will also be an excellent boat-angling venue.

OTTOLAND, EX SARKANI, EX SINT JANSLAND (?)

Date of loss: 5 October 1940
Wreck: ✯✯✯✯✯
Depth: 70 m
Reference: 54 54'.640 N 000 53'.201 W
Location: 16.03 nm E by S of Roker light, Sunderland

SS Ottoland *detonated a mine off Hartlepool during the Second World War*

The *Ottoland* was a steel-hulled 2202-ton Dutch steam cargo ship measuring 82.90 m in length, with a 12.19-m beam and 5.53-m draught. Schpw. V. Jan Smit, Czn., Alblasserdam, Netherlands built and completed her as Yard No. 478 in August 1916. She was launched as the *Sint Jansland* in 1916 for The Shipping and Coal Company (NV Scheepvaart en Steenkolen Maatschappij) in Rotterdam. The single screw was powered by a 208-nhp three-cylinder triple expansion steam engine that used two single-ended boilers working at 180 psi, with six corrugated furnaces, 9.38 sq.m (101 sq.ft) of grate surface and 344.67 sq.m (3710 sq.ft) of heating surface. The cylinders measured 50.8 cm, 81.28 cm and 134.62 cm with a 90.06-cm stroke (20 in., 32 in. and 53 in. with a 39-in. stroke). Schelde in Flushing manufactured the engine and ancillary machinery. She had one steel deck, a well deck, five bulkheads cemented and an aft superstructure consisting of a 20.9-m poop deck, a 26.2-m quarterdeck and a 7.6-m forecastle. She also had cellular double bottom up front and a fore peak and aft peak tank. In 1940 the engine was increased to 212 nhp. She was equipped with wireless direction finder.

In 1936, N. V. Stoomschip Willem van Driel, sr., Rotterdam purchased the ship and renamed her *Sarkani*. Nederl. Bevrachtingskantoor, N. V. was the manager. N. V. Europeesche Vrachtvaart Mij., was the registered owner in 1937 and they used the same manager. From 1939, N. V. Scheepvaart en Steenkolen Mij. Rotterdam was the registered owner and renamed her *Ottoland*. In 1940 the engine was 212nhp. The designated code recognition signal letters were: PSFT.

Final voyage

On 5 October 1940 the *Ottoland* sank after detonating a magnetic mine off Hartlepool, four miles south of the 20A Buoy. The Luftwaffe had dropped the mine.

As part of convoy CS.3 (Sidney Cape Breton Island, Nova Scotia - Liverpool) consisting of 48 ships and eight escorts, the *Ottoland* left the harbour of Buctouche, New Brunswick, Canada on 2 September 1940 for passage to Immingham with a cargo of mining studs (pit props) and timber. Altogether there were 1192 m of pit props and timber stowed in the holds and stacked on the deck. The convoy was only lightly protected and during this voyage across the Atlantic at least four of the ships were sunk after they separated from the convoy: the 4343-ton Greek *Alexandros*, the 5319-ton British SS *Empire Volunteer*, the 1780-ton Greek *Kalliopis* and the 5152-ton British SS *Kenordoc*. The *Ottoland* reached Methil Roads on 2 October. She departed Methil for Immingham on the 4th as part of the south-bound convoy FS 300 (Methil–Southend) which was comprised of 50 ships and *en route* to Southend. Early in the morning of the 5th, just off Hartlepool, the ship was rocked by an enormous explosion. The crew assumed this was caused by a magnetic mine or a torpedo because no enemy aircraft was seen or heard. The bow was heavily damaged and the blast caused much of the cargo on deck to fall overboard. The ship began sinking slowly by the head and the stern steadily rose until the ship was at an angle of 45° with its bows under water and the screw still turning. Just before noon there was a huge bang as the hatch of No. 2 hold blew off and the rest of the cargo spilled overboard. With so much timber floating about, a stiff wind blowing and large waves, the men had great difficulty in getting clear of the sinking vessel. A message was relayed from an aircraft and a minesweeper steamed out rescuing all of the crew. On board the warship the men watched as their ship plunged vertically beneath the surface at 1300 hrs.

LCWLR 1939–1945, p. 134; LR 1940/1, No. 80946 (O); Starke Schell Registers.

Wrecksite

The wreck – most likely that of the *Ottoland* – is orientated in a general W to E direction. It lies on a dirty seabed of mud, fine sand and broken shells in a general depth of 60 m (LAT). The wreck is broken into two large sections, each over 30 m in length and standing over 6.3 m high and 8 m wide. The western part is orientated 052/232° while the other section is 140/320°. There is also a separate piece of wreckage lying about 60 m to the south-west of the main wreck, but this is not very tall. The ship's bell – when, or if, located – will be inscribed: *Sint Jansland 1916*. There are reported to be large shoals of fish of numerous species all around the site and should make a good boat-angling venue.

2

HARTLEPOOL TO THE RIVER WEAR

EUCLID (?)

Date of loss: 17 April 1890
Wreck: ✯✯
Depth: 34 m
Reference: 54 45'.825 N 001 09'.045 W
Location: 4.12 nm NNE from The Heugh, Hartlepool

The *Euclid* was an iron-hulled 686-ton British schooner-rigged steam cargo vessel measuring 59.84 metres length, with an 8.86-m beam and a 5.02-m draught. T.R. Oswald at Pallion, Sunderland built and launched her in September 1866. The single iron screw was powered by a 90-nhp two-cylinder compound inverted steam engine that used one simple boiler. George Clark and Company, Sunderland manufactured the engine and ancillary machinery. She had one deck, four bulkheads. Lloyd's classed her as 100A1. At the time of loss, E.J. Weatherly of Sunderland was the registered owner.

Final voyage

In the early hours of 17 April 1890 the *Euclid* sank following a collision with the 1.041-ton steamer *Altyre* (1878 – Adam and Co., Aberdeen). The *Altyre* had left Middlesbrough in water ballast for the Tyne at 0030 hrs, while the *Euclid* sailed from Sunderland at 0230 hrs, bound for Rochester with a cargo of coal. During south-east force 5 wind conditions, the two vessels were between Seaham and Hartlepool when the *Euclid* was struck on the starboard side, amidships, and penetrated about 6 ft (1.82 m). She immediately began to settle.

Captain Anderson of the *Altyre* ordered the lifeboat to be lowered and boats on the *Euclid* were also made ready. At the time of the collision, many of the men were in their berths. After the shock of the impact they rushed up on deck to help lower the boats. The crew of the *Euclid* boarded the boats safely, just before the bows of the ship rose upright and disappeared beneath the surface, stern first. One of the boats from the *Euclid*, however, capsized and its occupants were thrown into the sea. The lifeboat from the *Altyre* and another boat from the *Euclid* rescued ten crewmen from the sea. Captain Anderson stood by, hoping to save the others, but four men, including the master, drowned:

Beck, Thomas, 2nd Mate, from Rochester
Brass, Michael, Able Seaman, from Sunderland
Eden, Joseph, Donkeyman, from Sunderland
Knott, Charles, Master, from Sunderland.

Several of the survivors were picked up from the water, clinging to floating wreckage. They were all were taken on board the *Altyre* and landed at South Shields at 0800 hrs. The only observable damage to the *Altyre* was a piece of the stem above the waterline had been carried away and some of the plates were bent.

LR 1887/8, No. 767 (E); BoT Wreck Return 1890, p. 141 (653); *The Times*: Friday, 18 April 1890, p. 11, Issue no. 32989.

Wrecksite

The remains – which are understood to be that of the *Euclid* – lie on a seabed of sand, pebbles, gravel and mud in a general depth of 34 m (LAT). It is partially buried, collapsed, badly decayed and well broken up, standing no more than 3-m tall amidships where the boiler and engine are located. The wreck sits in a small scour, orientated in a N to S direction. It is rather dispersed covering an area about 50 m by 10 m. The iron plates, engine, boiler and broken machinery are covered in hard, white, marine worm casings and are fairly concreted together. There are also signs of non-ferrous metal pipes and brass flanges lying among the jumbled pile of debris. A few decent-size fish were observed on the fishfinder.

BUTE (?)

Date of loss: 14 July 1916
Wreck: ✯✯
Depth: 57 m
Reference: 54 46'.641 N 000 45'.368 W
Location: 15.28 nm ENE from The Heugh, Hartlepool

The *Bute* was a steel-hulled 176-ton British steam trawler registered in Hull and measuring 33.02 m in length, with a 6.55-m beam and 3.5-m draught. Earle's Shipbuilding and Engineering Company Ltd. Hull built and completed her as Yard No. 498 in June 1905. She was launched on 9th June for Hull Steam Fishing and Ice Company Ltd. which owned her at the time of loss. The single steel screw was powered by a 39-nhp three-cylinder triple expansion steam engine that used one boiler. The *Bute* had one deck, four bulkheads and was ketch-rigged as a back-up to the auxiliary engine.

Final voyage

On 14 July 1916 the *Bute* was on a voyage to the fishing grounds in the North Sea from her temporary base in Tynemouth when the KDM submarine SMU *UB 39*, commanded by Oblt.z.S. Werner Fürbringer, captured her. The crew were ordered to abandon ship and it was disposed of using explosive scuttling charges.

LCWLR 1914–1918, p. 47; BVLS 1914–1918, p. 109; Miramar Ship Index.

Wrecksite

The wreck – possibly that of the *Bute* – is orientated in a NNE to SSW direction. It sits in a one-metre scour and lies on a seabed of sand, mud and shells in a general depth of 57 m (LAT). The wreck stands 4.3 m at the south end and covers an area 30 m by 5 m. It is intact and in quite good condition, but nets cover much of it. A shoal of pout whiting were observed swimming over the wreck. Cod have also been observed among the wreckage.

Kptlt Fürbringer ('Fips') later commanded *UB 110* and was captured 4.5 nm NE from Huntcliff, Saltburn-by-Sea. His autobiography *Alarm! Tauchen!!: U-boot in Kampf und Sturm* was published in 1933 and republished in 1999 by Pen and Sword Books as *FIPS: Legendary U-boat Commander 1915–1918*. It is a classic First World War maritime account and provides a compelling insight into the life (and death) of this KDM U-boat commander.

NORTHUMBRIA

Date of Loss: 9 January 1919
Wreck: ✭✭✭
Depth: 55 m
Reference: 54 46'.224 N 000 53'.633 W
Location: 10.3 nm NE from The Heugh, Hartlepool

The *Northumbria* (Official No. 129652) was a 4215-ton cargo steamship measuring 109.72 m in length, with a 14.63-m beam and an 8.53-m draught. Northumberland Shipbuilding Company at Howdon near North Shields built and completed her as Yard No. 127 in January 1906. She was launched on 16 October 1905 for Westminster Shipping Company, London, with Sir John Jackson Ltd. the manager. The single screw was powered by a 327-nhp three-cylinder triple expansion steam engine that used three single-ended boilers, nine corrugated furnaces, 13.93 m (150 sq.ft) grate surface and (551.84 m (5940 sq.ft) of heating-surface, giving ten knots. The cylinders measured 63.5 cm, 104.14 cm and 175.26 cm, with a 121.92-cm stroke (25 in., 41 in. and 69 in. with a 48-in. stroke). Richardsons, Westgarth and Company manufactured the engine and ancillary machinery at Sunderland. She had one steel deck, a steel spar deck and deep framing.

Final voyage

On the morning of Thursday, 9 January 1919, the *Northumbria* was on passage from Baltimore, USA to Sunderland when she detonated two mines off the Tees during a storm. She was under the command of Captain Harry Thomsom, carrying a crew of 39 and a cargo of wheat.

After the ship had left Yarmouth Roads, it picked up a pilot on Wednesday January 8th and continued its journey to Sunderland. The *Northumbria* was estimated to be about seven nm off Middlesbrough and steering NW when, at about 0300 hrs on the 9th, there was an explosion near the bows. Heavy seas were running and there was a strong southeasterly wind blowing. Those on deck got to the boats first and 17 men climbed into the starboard lifeboat which drifted away in the wind. Unfortunately, because the hostilities of the First World War were over and there was less chance of being sunk, the company – 'in their wisdom'– had removed most of the rowlocks and locked the life jackets away in a cupboard. No lifeboat drills had been carried out over the previous weeks. There were just three rowlocks in the lifeboat and eight oars, so it was impossible to row the thing. Within minutes the ship had disappeared beneath the waves. The lifeboat did have biscuits, fresh water and sweets on board.

One of the men – who later died – had been hit by a block of wood. When dawn broke at about 0800 hrs, they were still drifting in the boat. A small sail was put up so they were able to steer using a compass on board.

A survivor who was witness at the inquiry, Mr Michael Boyd of Barra, in the Western Isles of Scotland, said: 'We kept running before the wind, or the boat would have been swamped in such a heavy sea. We sighted no ships at all. We ran before the wind all day, then about 1700 hrs we saw a light and, at first we thought it was a vessel. We started putting up torch flares, but there was no response, the light was in sight for about an hour, but we drifted past. At about 1900 hrs in the moonlight, we noticed a light what we first took to be that of a vessel, but now know to have been Dunstanburgh Castle. We heard the surf and knew that we were near the coast.'

Three of the men in the boat, Edmund, Ogilvie and Muir, were already dead from exposure. Edmund had been ill three times during the voyage. Muir and Ogilvie had had influenza. Mr Boyd said they could not prevent the boat going ashore and when it struck the rocks, all those that could do jumped out. Only William Paterson and Michael Boyd were able to reach shore safely, the others were dashed against the rocks and drowned.

The two exhausted men remained on the beach for a quarter of an hour before they had enough strength to move on and reach a cottage for help.

Mr Paterson, a steward from Glasgow, said: 'I was the last one to get into the lifeboat. I was in my bed when the ship struck the mine and sleeping with my lifejacket as a pillow. About seven or eight men in the boat had no right to be in there, but that was due to there being only one lifeboat being swung out after the ship struck the mine. There were two large lifeboats on the ship, but only one was swung out, even though the pilot had ordered two swung out at Yarmouth Roads. I thought the *Northumbria* had struck three mines in quick succession. The mines seemed to be anchored. By order, the lifeboats had been swung in since Armistice Day and not used since.'

It appears that most of the crew survived the sinking and managed to take to the boats. However, there was a failure in lifeboat drill and most of the boats overturned – a common occurrence. Unfortunately, the ones that remained upright had had the rowlocks removed by the 'penny-pinching' owners, this resulted in the men not being able to steer the lifeboats and they simply drifted north in the strong wind and currents. One boat load of bodies and one live, naked and raving man beached at Embleton a week later. There was an inquiry and the owners were heavily criticised, but weren't even fined. Those men are buried at Embleton village in CWGC graves, alongside dead from a Norwegian ship, which was torpedoed off Aberdeen.

The crewmen that died were:

Adams, Edwin Richard Phillpott, Able Seaman MM
Allen, Thomas, Foster 1st Engineer MM
Brown, Thomas, Donkeyman MM
Bruhn, Charles Allan, Plt MM
Burnie, William Cummings, second mate MM
Cresswell, William Alfred, 2 Steward MM

Currie, James Herbert, third Engineer MM
Dean, Alfred Neal, Fireman and Trimmer MM
Edmond, Thomas Moncur, Sailor MM
Ferguson, Donald, John 2nd Cook MM
Hart, John Alexander, Carpenter MM
Henderson, J., Fireman and Trimmer MM
Inouye, S., fourth engineer MM
Laing, James, 1st Engineer MM
MacDonald, Joseph, MI MM
Mackie, John James, 2nd Engineer MM
McIntosh, James Donald, WO MM
McIntyre, Peter, Ordinary Seaman MM
McKinnon, Neil, Able Seaman MM
McLean, John, Able Seaman MM
McLennon, J. M., Able Seaman MM
McLennon, John, Able Seaman MM
Meehan, John, Fireman and Trimmer MM
Mitchell, James, Fireman and Trimmer MM
Mizzi, Carmelo Akoysius Jose George, Fireman MM
Molloy, Charles, Fireman and Trimmer MM
Ogilvie, J. McF, Fireman and Trimmer MM
Owen, Albert Edward, Chief Officer MM
Paterson, John, Boatswain (Bosun) MM SS
Paterson, John, Scollick WO MM
Rangasami, William, Chief Cook MM
Reed, Alfred Ernest, third Mate MM
Robertson, Hugh, Sailor MM
Scott, R., Fireman MM
Smart, James, Fireman and Trimmer MM
Thompson, Harry, Master MM

Wrecksite

The wreck – which is probably that of the *Northumbria* – is orientated in a NW to SE direction and lies on a seabed of mud, fine sand and black shells in a general depth of 55 m (LAT) with no scour. The wreck is very substantial, although the hull and superstructure have all totally collapsed, leaving what appears to be the three boilers and the engine exposed. The highest point is reported to be the north-west end of the wreck, which is probably the bow section. Though substantial the wreck is very broken up and scattered over an area of 105 m by 30 m, but stands only about 6 m high.

STANGATE, EX DRAKEDENE, EX EMSWORTH MANOR, EX RIVIT, EX ELVET

Date of loss: 7 December 1942
Wreck: ★★★★★
Depth: 45 m
Reference: 54 46'.391 N 001 03'.649 W
Location: 6.06 nm NE from The Heugh, Hartlepool

The *Stangate* (Official No. 129797) was a steel-hulled 1289-ton British steam cargo ship measuring 73.15 m in length, with a 10.18-mbeam and a 4.67-m draught. William Dobson and Company at Low Walker, Newcastle upon Tyne built and completed her as Yard No. 177 in April 1912. She was launched as the *Elvet* on 5 February 1912 for Sharp Steam Ship Co., Ltd., Newcastle. Sharp and Company was the manager. The single screw was powered by a 201-nhp three-cylinder triple expansion steam engine that used two single-ended boilers with a working pressure of 180 psi, with six furnaces to give nine knots. The cylinders measured 48.26 cm, 78.74 cm and 129.54 cm, with a 91.44-cm stroke (19 in., 31 in. and 51 in. with a 36-in. stroke). North Eastern Marine Engineering Co., Ltd., at Newcastle manufactured the engine and ancillary machinery. She had one deck, a well deck, four bulkheads cemented and a 38.6–m quarterdeck, a 3.9-m bridge deck and 7.62-m forecastle.

According to *Lloyd's Register*, sometime in 1912 she was renamed *Rivet* by the same owners.

In 1925 Manor Line (London) Ltd. London purchased and renamed her *Emsworth Manor* and C. Angel and Company, Cardiff became manager. In 1930 Henley Steam Ship Co., Ltd., London took over ownership and in 1934 Drakelow Steam Ship Co., Ltd., London purchased her. Angel, Bethell & Co., Ltd., Cardiff was the manager. In 1935 P.E. Bethell and Co., Ltd., became the manager.

In 1936 the same owners renamed her *Drakedene*. In 1937 Stanhope Steam Ship Co., Ltd., London, the new registered owner, renamed her Stangate; the manager became J.A. Billmeir and Company Ltd.

Final voyage

On 7 December 1942 the *Stangate* foundered seven miles off The Heugh, following a collision with the 4255-ton Greek steamship *Agios Georgios* (1911: D. Pantaleon Sons, Piraeus). The *Stangate* sailed as part of the south-bound 40-ship convoy FS.979 (Methil–Southend) and was *en route* from Newcastle upon Tyne to Portsmouth with a cargo of coal.

Starke Schell Registers; Lloyds Register 1941/42 No. 32599 (S); LCR 1942, p. 8 (f).

Wrecksite

The wreck sits in a one and a half metre scour and is orientated in a NNW to SSE direction. It lies on a seabed of fine sand and mud in a general depth of 45 m (LAT). Referred to as the Coal Wreck, it is 7.9 m high, upright and virtually intact.

This is a large and very interesting wreck, which requires more than a couple of dives to have a full look round. Soft corals adorn the hull and superstructure, illuminating the wreck in the dim light. The vessel was equipped with a brass pedestal-mounted telegraph and steering helm. Her bell, if or when recovered, will almost certainly be inscribed: *Elvet 1912*. Large ling and cod can be seen as well as large conger, so the site should make a good boat-angling venue.

H.A. BRIGHTMAN

Date of Loss: 17 January 1879
Wreck: ★★
Depth: 22 m
Reference: 54 46'.424 N 001 14'.481 W
Location: 5 nm NNW from The Heugh, Hartlepool

The *H.A. Brightman* (Official No. 60528) was an iron-hulled 1121-ton three-masted British steam cargo vessel measuring 76.2 m in length, with an 8.86-m beam and 5.28-m draught. Schlesinger, Davis and Company built and completed her as Yard No. 19 at Wallsend. She was 808 gross tons when launched on 24 July 1869 for H.A. Brightman and Company, Newcastle. The single iron screw was powered by a 99-nhp two-cylinder compound inverted steam engine that used one boiler. T. Clark and Company manufactured the machinery at Newcastle. She had five bulkheads, a 9.1-m forecastle, 18.2-m bridge deck and a reinforced

10-m fore deck. The ballast consisted entirely of water contained in tanks lying along the bottom of the vessel. She was classed as 90 A1 and valued at £23,000 when built. In 1873 the *H.A. Brightman* was lengthened by 12.19 m (40 ft) amidships by Messrs Fellon and Company, Howdon.

In early June of 1871 the owners were taken to court because the *H.A. Brightman* had been involved in a collision with the barque *Prudoe* in the river Tyne; the court decided that the Prudhoe was to blame. On 1 August 1871 the *H. A. Brightman* was on passage from Sunderland for Constantinople but had to call in at Weymouth because of damage to machinery.

In 1877 Thomas Sutton, of New Quay, North Shields became the new owner and was also managing owner with Henry Anson Brightman

Commanded by Captain White, the *H.A. Brightman* sailed from Galați in eastern Romania for Rotterdam with a cargo of grain. Having discharged her cargo, she set off in ballast from Rotterdam for Cardiff on 30 December 1876, where she was to load up with coal. She carried a crew of 22 hands and a Mr Boyer, who was the superintending engineer of the owners of the vessel.

On 1 January 1877 the ship encountered a terrible gale in the English Channel – the same gale that destroyed the Admiralty Pier at Dover. The ship became unmanageable when the throat halyards of the fore trysail gave way and the sail came down. According to the second mate, they had hardly 'picked up the shreds' before the main trysail also blew away. Their efforts to bring the vessel to the wind were unsuccessful. The crew then tried to wear her, and got her before the wind. A forestay sail was set and the engines were put full speed ahead, the helm, being kept hard-a-port. But, all efforts proved useless as the huge seas battered the ship.

Seeing that it was impossible to clear Dungeness, Captain White decided the only means of saving the lives of those on board was to run the ship onto the beach. Orders were given to set the engines to full speed and she was beached within a ship's length of the Lydd coastguard station. The coastguards immediately brought down the rocket apparatus and on the second attempt a rope was thrown over the vessel, thus allowing communication with the shore. All the crew were brought safely to land. On the following tide the vessel was driven over a bank into a natural creek formed by the sea. There she remained until 3 January 1877 when she came off with her own engines and steamed to Dover before going on to the Victoria Docks for repairs.

Lloyd's reports of Arrivals and Departures listed in *The Times* confirm that the *H.A. Brightman* visited many countries around the world during her service career, including India, Egypt, Romania, Malta and Greece, to name but a few.

Final voyage

On 17 January 1879 the *H.A. Brightman* left Newcastle for a voyage to Lisbon with a cargo of coal and a crew of 21. At around 1700 hrs that day she ran agound in thick fog – near Staithes according to a telegraph from Middlesbrough to the *The Times*. Seven of the crew were said to have left the ship in a boat to look for a tug, however, she managed to refloat at high tide next morning. The captain must have decided to return to the Tyne to have the ship inspected because it then foundered five miles NNW of Hartlepool. The remaining crew, including the captain, took to a boat. They were picked up by the 280-ton steamer *Glencairn* and landed at Middlesbrough.

The Times: Saturday, 18 January 1879, p. 12, Issue no. 29468; BoT Wreck Report: H.A. Brightman, 1877; LR 187809 No 1 (H); BoT Wreck Return 1879, p.105.

Wrecksite

The wreck – or what remains of it – is orientated in a SE to NW direction. It lies on a seabed of sand and stones in a general depth of 22 m (LAT). The wreck is well broken up, decayed and dispersed, with much of it lying under a thick layer of colliery waste. Only the boiler and engine and a two-metre section of the hull stand proud of the seabed. After about 10 m in any direction, nothing else remains visible. Although they only cover a small area, the boiler and engine are worth looking at because they are covered in a myriad of soft corals, with shoals of small coleys and pout whiting swimming around. It is very photogenic. Gordon Wadsworth identified the wreck in 1989 after recovering the bell.

VESTRA

Date of loss: 6 February 1917
Wreck: ✯✯✯
Depth: 45 m
Reference: 54 47'.607 N 001 05'.699 W
Location: 6.43 nm NNE from The Heugh, Hartlepool

The *Vestra* (Official No. 90916) was a steel-hulled 1021-ton British steam cargo ship measuring 65.73 m in length, with a 9.75-m beam and a 4.29-m draught. Ramage and Ferguson Ltd. Leith built and completed her as Yard No. 147 in February 1897. She was launched on 18 January 1897 for J.T. Salveson and Company, Grangemouth, which registered her at Grangemouth and was the owner at the time of loss. The single iron screw was powered by a 99-nhp three-cylinder triple expansion steam engine that used one single-ended boiler and gave a service speed of ten knots. She had one deck, four bulkheads cemented, an 8.2-m poop deck, 11.5-m quarter deck, a 17.6-m bridge deck and 9.1- m forecastle. In 1916 the ship was armed for defence.

Final voyage

On 6 February 1917 the *Vestra* (Captain G. Ross) was torpedoed and sunk without warning by the KDM submarine SMU *UB 35*, commanded by Oblt.z.S. Rudolf Gebeschus. The steamer was on passage from the Tyne for Rouen with coal. Two crewmen – I. Brady, Able Seaman MM and Claude Erik Patrick, Ordinary Seaman MM – were killed.

CWGC; Starke Schell Registers; BVLS 1914–18, p. 205; LCWLR 1914–18, p. 91; Lloyds Register 1915/16 No. 305 (V); Jarvis (2000), Vol. 5.

Wrecksite

The wreck sits in a half-metre scour and is orientated in a NE to SW direction. It lies on a seabed of dirty mud and fine sand in a general depth of 44.6 m (LAT). The wreck is intact but collapsed. The remains cover an area of 75 m in length by 15 m wide, with the highest point standing 7 m from the seabed. Monofilament fishing lines, rusting hooks and trawl nets are draped over the wreck. Soft corals adorn the upper structures. The ship's bell, which identified the ship, was recovered in the late 1990's. The vessel was supposed to be carrying a cargo of coal but nothing can be seen of it.

FAWN

Date of loss: 24 August 1919
Wreck: ★★★
Depth: 42 m
Reference: 54 47'.324 N 001 06'.549 W
Location: 5.94 nm NNE from The Heugh, Hartlepool.

The *Fawn* (Official No. 109842) was an iron-hulled 191-ton British steam trawler measuring 32.7 m in length, with a 6.4-m beam. Cook, Welton and Gemmell at Hull built and completed her as Yard No. 219 on 22 December 1898. She was registered as GY.1008 on 4 October 1898 for Thomas E. Fisher and Henry Morris Company, Grimsby, and launched as the *Fawn* on 26 November 1898. The single iron screw was powered by a 50-nhp three-cylinder triple expansion steam engine that used one single-ended boiler and gave a speed of 10 knots. Amos and Smith Ltd. manufactured the machinery at Hull.

Henry Croft Baker, Grimsby purchased the boat on 11 June 1916. On 26 April 1917 John Green of Grimsby became the registered owner. The Admiralty requisitioned the vessel for the Fishery Reserve Service in 1918 until her return to John Green in 1919.

Final voyage

On 24 August 1919 the *Fawn* was on a fishing trip from Grimsby, but never returned to port. She was posted as missing, presumed mined and lost, off Hartlepool with all ten hands:

Barker, George, Deckhand MM
Brown, Hany, Cook MM
Chester, Fred, 1st Engineer MM
Christiansen, Henry Nicolie, Deckhand MM
Cooney, Patrick, Trimmer MM
Hillam, John Philip, 2nd Hand MM
Nudd, Charles Henry, 3rd Hand MM
Stevenson, Ben, Deckhand MM
Swainston, Abraham, Trimmer MM
Taylor, Thomas, 2nd Engineer MM

CWGC; Thompson (1999); *Lloyd's War Losses*: World War I, p. 378; Jarvis (2000), Vol. 5.

Wrecksite

The wreck – understood to be that of the *Fawn* – is orientated in a SSE to NNW direction. It lies on a seabed of mud and fine sand in a general depth of 42 m (LAT). It is totally collapsed, partially buried and well broken up with the largest part just 1.5 m high. The remains are coated in colourful soft corals. A section of the bows is recognisable but most of the wreck is a mound of twisted broken machinery and steel plates. Tidal streams are quite strong.

THE STEWART'S COURT

Date of loss: 21 August 1918
Wreck: ★★
Depth: 19 m
Reference: 54 47'.763 N 001 15'.182 W
Location: 3.42 nm SSE of Seaham Harbour piers

The *Stewart's Court* (Official No. 123959) was a steel-hulled 813-ton British steam cargo vessel measuring 60.96 m in length, with a 9.14-m beam and a 3.68-m draught. S.P. Austin and Son in Sunderland built and completed her as Yard No. 248 in April 1909. Registered in Sunderland, she was launched on 28 March 1909 for the Marquis of Londonderry (Charles Stewart Henry Vane-Tempest-Stewart, 7th Marquess of Londonderry) who was the owner at the time of loss. S.J. Ditchfield was the manager. The single steel screw was powered by a 138-hp, three-cylinder triple expansion steam engine that used one boiler. North Eastern Marine Engineering Company Ltd. manufactured the engine and ancillary machinery. She had one deck, four bulkheads, a 6.4-m poop deck, 13.4-m quarter deck, a 14-m bridge deck and a 6.4-m forecastle. D.N. Grimes was the manager in 1912 and until the ship was lost. In 1916 the steamer was armed for defence.

Final voyage

At 1445 hrs on 21 August 1918 the *Stewart's Court* (Captain Hardy) was torpedoed and sunk by the KDM submarine SMU *UB 112*, commanded by Oblt.z.S. Wilhelm Rhein. The ship was on passage from Seaham for London with 1000 tons of coal and carrying a crew of 16. The first mate, Joseph Watson, was killed and the captain's leg broken when the torpedo, which was fired without warning, detonated amidships. The steamer sank in five minutes, but the 15 survivors abandoned ship in their own boat. The Seaham lifeboat, *Elliot Galer*, was launched at 1510 hrs, took the men on board and landed them at Seaham Harbour. The submarine remained submerged and unseen. Information about who fired the torpedo eventually came to light when German records were released after the First World War.

ADM 137/2964; Starke Schell Registers; LR 1914–18, No. 542 (T); BVLS 1914–18, p. 95; LCWLR 1914–18, p. 231; Morris (1988).

Wrecksite

The Seaham Sub Aqua Club were first to discover the wreck of *Stewart's Court* and dive the remains regularly during the summer months. It lies on a seabed of rock and sand in a general depth of 19 m (LAT). The wreck is totally collapsed, well broken up and decayed, with a mound of broken machinery and twisted metal surrounding the engine and boiler, said to be lying on their sides. There are still bits of non-ferrous metal to be seen amongst the jumble of debris and the occasional large cod and lobsters can be found under the steel plates.

CAMARGO, EX BENHEAD

Date of loss: 18 October 1912
Wreck: ☆☆☆☆
Depth: 58 m
Reference: 54 47'.124 N 000 50'.517 W
Location: 13.02 nm ENE from The Heugh, Hartlepool

The *Camargo* (Official No. 105320) was a steel-hulled 1725-ton Spanish steam cargo ship measuring 76.2 m in length, with an 11.61-m beam. John Scott and Company of Kinghorn, Fife in Scotland built and completed her as Yard No. 90 in July 1895. She was launched as the schooner-rigged *Benhead* on 27 June 1895 for S.S. Benhead Company Ltd. at Liverpool. J. Hoult was the manager. The single steel screw was powered by a 189-hp, three-cylinder triple expansion steam engine that used two boilers. The cylinders measured 45.72 cm, 76.2 cm and 127 cm, with a 91.44-cm stroke (18 in., 30 in. and 50 in. with a 36-in. stroke). She had four bulkheads and water ballast. (Code letters: JGLM.)

In 1899 she was renamed *Camargo* by the new owners, Cia. Montañesa de Nav., Santander; M. Piñeiro y Cia., was the manager. In 1903 M. Piñeiro Bezanilla became manager although she remained under the same ownership. At the time of loss Cia. Montañesa de Nav., Santander was the registered owner (M. Piñeiro Bezanilla remained manager).

Final voyage

On 18 October 1912 the *Camargo* sank following a collision with the 2513-ton British steamer *Etona* (1890: Clydesdale Navigation Company Ltd., London (Glasgow) 16 miles ENE from Hartlepool. The Spanish ship was voyaging from Rotterdam to the Tyne in ballast.

The *Camargo* was struck on the starboard bow and sank in three minutes. There was no time to board the lifeboats so the men were forced to leap into the sea, grabbing hold of any floating wreckage they could find. Five of the crew drowned. Eighteen survivors were picked up and taken to Hartlepool by the steam trawler *Loch Garry*, though one, the second mate, died on the way to port. All crewmembers were foreign nationals. After effecting temporary repairs, the *Etona* was able to proceed to London.

BoT Wreck Return 1890; Starke Schell Registers; *The Times*: Saturday, 19 October 1912, p. 8, Issue no. 40034; American Lloyd's Register of American and Foreign Shipping 1857–1900.

Wrecksite

The wreck – most likely that of the *Camargo* – is orientated in a SW to NE direction. It lies on a seabed of mud, sand and shell in a general depth of 58 m (LAT). The wreck is intact with what appears to be the stern to the SW and the bows at the NE end, mostly buried. It stands about 5.3 m high and covers an area 75 m long and 13 m across. The upper structures are covered in soft corals. A lot of large fish have been observed on the fishfinder so this ought to make an excellent boat angling venue.

SCANDIA, ex EASTERN STAR

Sate of loss: 23 December 1899
Wreck: ★★★★
Depth 44 m
Reference: 54 48'.923 N 001 06'.064 W
Location: 7.76 nm ESE of Seaham Harbour piers

The *Scandia* (Official No. 86966) was an iron-hulled 1158-ton Swedish steam cargo ship measuring 70.25 m in length, with a 9.9-m beam and a 4.16-m draught. Robert Thompson and Sons, at Southwick, Sunderland built and completed her as Yard No. 136 in August 1883. She was launched as *Eastern Star* on 7 August 1883 for Johnson Bros. and Company, West Hartlepool. The single iron screw was powered by a 120-hp, two-cylinder compound steam engine that used one boiler. J. Dickinson and Company Ltd. at Sunderland manufactured the engine and ancillary machinery. She had one deck, four bulkheads, a 27-m quarterdeck, 17.3-m bridge deck and a 7-m forecastle.

F. Richardson of West Hartlepool purchased the ship in 1885. V.T. Thompson and Company West Hartlepool became the owner in 1888. In 1891 the registered owner was Thompson Steam Shipping Company Ltd. West Hartlepool.

In 1896 she was renamed *Scandia* (Official No. 2900) by Ångfartygs A/B Scandia of Helsingborg, Sweden, who was the new registered owner and H.V. Horndahl was the manager until the time of loss.

Final voyage

On 23 December 1899 the *Scandia* (Captain F.P. Moller) was in ballast steaming north on passage from London for Sunderland when she was involved in a collision with the 2988-ton steamship *Headland* (1892: R. Hardy and Company, West Hartlepool). The *Scandia* foundered 9.5 miles east of Hartlepool. The crew of 17 were rescued by the *Headland.*

Starke Schell Registers; LR 1898/99, no. 384 (S); BoT Wreck Return 1899, p. 140 (656).

Wrecksite

The wreck of the *Scandi*a was discovered in 1998 when divers from Dawdon Sub Aqua Club located the bell, which was inscribed: *Eastern Star 1883*. It wasn't until some months later that the author saw the bell at a local dive centre. He traced it through his wreck database and identified it as the *Scandia.* The wreck lies on a seabed of fine sand, mud and black shells in a general depth of 44 m (LAT). It stands quite tall at the stern end for about 15 m and from there, forward, it is collapsed down with the boiler and engine exposed. The rest of the wreck is collapsed, well smashed up and decayed. Pipes, bollards, frames, ribs, and pieces of broken derricks and hollow masts are intermingled and spread across the seabed. Dead-man's fingers cover and lights up, illuminating the stern end where its iron screw is still attached, but the wreck is largely draped in a series of trawl nets. A number of large cod have been observed in the vicinity of the wrecksite.

THAMES

Date of loss: 26 May 1918
Wreck: ✯✯✯✯
Depth: 38 m
Reference: 54 48'.557 N 001 09'.632 W
Location: 5.83 nm SE of Seaham Harbour piers

The *Thames* (Official No. 90903) was a steel-hulled 930-ton British steam passenger cargo vessel measuring 70 m in length with a 9.49-m beam. A. & J. Inglis built her at their Pointhouse yard on the Clyde, Glasgow. She was completed as Yard No. 197 in April 1887 and launched on 25 January 1887 for Carron Company of Grangemouth, the owner at the time of loss. A single steel screw was powered by a 316-hp, three-cylinder triple expansion steam engine that used two boilers. She had two decks, five bulkheads, a 15.2-m poop deck, 32.3-m bridge deck and a 15.5-m forecastle.

In 1907 the ship was lengthened amidships by the shipbuilders, A. & J. Inglis to 85.16 m in length, a 9.49-m beam and 4.67-m draught. Her tonnage was increased to 1327 gross tons. A bronze screw was also fitted. Around 1916 the *Thames* was equipped for defence with a 406-kilo (8-cwt) stern-mounted 12-pounder (5.44-kilos) deck gun.

Final voyage

On 26 May 1918 the KDM minelaying submarine SMU *UC 17*, commanded by Oblt.z.S. Nikolause Freiherr von Lyncker, torpedoed the *Thames* (Captain W.A. McPhail) without warning. The *Thames* was transporting a general cargo from London to Leith. Two explosions, occuring almost simultaneously, ripped through the aft section at 1045 hrs and blew the entire stern end completely off, killing the chief officer, a fireman and one able seaman who was a DAMS gunner. The master was attempting to destroy the codebook and confidential papers he had on board, and is believed to have gone down with the ship. The *Thames* was abandoned within four minutes and sank at 1052 hrs. Royal Navy patrol vessels picked up 24 survivors soon afterwards. The crewmen that died were:

McKinnon, John 41yrs Chief Officer MM
McPhail, W.A. Master MM
Ogg, Hamilton 36 yrs Fireman MM
Winser, Richard Lane AB RNVR (DAMS gunner)

ADM 137/2964; CWGC; Starke Schell Registers; LCWLR 1914–18, p. 218; BVLS 1914–18, p. 90; Jarvis & Jarvis (1993) Vol. 2; Jarvis (2000) Vol. 5.

Wrecksite

The wreck sits in a slight scour and is orientated in a NNE to SSW direction. It lies on a seabed of fine sand, stones and mud in a general depth of 38 m (LAT). The hull and superstructure have collapsed down but it is almost intact and very substantial, standing around 6 m high with the bow section to the east where there is a colourful array of soft corals. The wreck used to be full of live shell cases but someone has removed most of them fairly recently. Most of the non-ferrous has also been removed. Trawl nets and monofilament fishing lines are snagged on the upper structures. Shoals of pollack and large cod have adopted the wreck, along with a few large crustaceans.

AZIRA

Date of loss: 4 September 1917
Wreck: ✭✭✭✭
Depth: 38 m
Reference: 54 48'.399 N 001 09'.715 W
Location: 5.84 nm ENE of Seaham Harbour piers

The *Azira* (Official No. 140683) was a steel-hulled 1144-ton British steam cargo ship measuring 70.4 m in length, with a 10.38-m beam and a 4.11-m draught. Trondhjems Mekaniske Verksted (TMV), Trondheim built and completed her as Yard No. 130 in December 1907. She was launched on 20 November 1907 for H. Grønsdal, Bergen. The single screw was powered by a 106-nhp three-cylinder triple expansion steam engine that used one single-ended boiler. TMV also manufactured the engine and ancillary machinery.

In 1916 Rasmus F. Olsen, Bergen became the owner.

In 1917 the Admiralty requisitioned the ship and Pelton S. S. Co., Ltd., Newcastle was the Crown nominee manager.

Final voyage

On 4 September 1917 the *Azira* (Captain J. Traasdahl) was torpedoed and sunk off Seaham Harbour by SMU *UB 22*, a KDM submarine commanded by Oblt.z.S. Karl Wacker. The steamer was on passage from Newcastle for Cherbourg, carrying a cargo of coal and a crew of 18. The *Azira* was about six miles SE of Seaham Harbour when the first mate on watch saw the periscope of the submarine about 550 metres off the port bow, but he thought it was a DAN buoy marking the safe channel. The ship had only travelled a short distance further when an exploding torpedo rocked her amidships. It killed Andrew Lehtman, the ship's carpenter.

The crew of the steam tug *Bureacrat*, which was only 100 metres away at the time, had already sighted the torpedo heading towards the *Azira* and wasted no time in reaching the stricken vessel. Twelve of the *Azira*'s crew got away in a lifeboat, but the rope snapped leaving five of the men stranded. The SS *Aberline*, which was also close by, launched its lifeboat and successfully rescued four of the men. The master was the last man off the ship. He was taken on board the tug only minutes before the *Azira* foundered.

All that was ever seen of the submarine was her periscope and it wasn't until German records were released after the war that SM *UB 22* was found to be the U-boat responsible.

ADM 137/2962; BVLS 1914–18, p. 62; Lloyds's Register 1915–16, No. 1961 (A); LCWLR 1914–18, p. 181.

Wrecksite

The wreck is orientated in a N to S direction, with the bows to the north. It lies on a seabed of pebbles, mud and sand in a general depth of 38 m (LAT). The wreck is lying to port with a slight collapse in the structure of the first hold. The port side stands 2–3 m clear of the seabed, while the starboard side is collapsed down to the seabed for the full length of the wreck. There is a slight break to the stern section, which used to stand 6–7 m clear of seabed, but recently (2005/6) has suffered partial collapse leaving it about 3 m clear. The bronze propeller used to be totally exposed, which allowed the removal of one of the blades, but three others are still in position, now covered in wreckage and hard to find.

ATLAS

Date of loss: 14 February 1918
Wreck: ★★★★★
Depth: 54 m
Reference: 54 48'.174 N 000 55'.150 W
Location: 10.92 nm NE from The Heugh, Hartlepool

The 3090-ton steamer Atlas, *c.1908*
(Author's collection)

The *Atlas* (Official No. 106964) was a steel-hulled 3090-ton British steam cargo ship registered in West Hartlepool and measuring 99.6-m in length, with a 14.35-m beam and a 6.7-m draught. William Gray & Co., Ltd., West Hartlepool built and completed her as Yard No. 541 in June 1897. She was launched on 17 May 1897 for Rickinson, Sons and Company, West Hartlepool, which owned her at the time of loss. The single screw was powered by a 260-nhp three-cylinder triple expansion steam engine that used six ribbed furnaces and two single-ended boilers operating at 160 pressure psi, with 7.89 sq.m (85 sq.ft) of grate surface and 354.88 sq.m (3820 sq.ft) of heating surface. The cylinders measured 60.96 cm, 96.52 cm and 162.56 cm, with a 106.68-cm stroke (24 in., 38 in. and 64 in., with a 42-in. stroke).

Central Marine Engineering Works, West Hartlepool manufactured the engine and ancillary machinery at West Hartlepool. She had one iron deck, an 8.22-m poop deck, a 24.99-m bridge deck and 9.75-m forecastle. She also had two tiers of beams, web frames, five bulkheads cemented, cellular double bottom aft and under the engine, and an aft peak tank. She was classed as 100 A1. The designated code recognition signal letters were: PSFC. In 1916 the *Atlas* was armed for defence with a stern mounted deck gun.

Final voyage

On 14 February 1918 the *Atlas* was torpedoed eight miles east (magnetic) of the Fairway Buoy, by the KDM mine-laying submarine SMU *UC 71*, commanded by Oblt.z.S. Walter

Warzecher. The *Atlas* was on passage from Murmansk for Middlesbrough with a cargo of iron ore and was sunk without warning.

Lloyd's War Losses 1914–18, p. 201; American Lloyd's Register of American and Foreign Shipping 1857–1900; Starke Schell Registers.

Wrecksite

The wreck sits in a 0.75-metre scour and lies on a seabed of mud, fine sand and black shells in a general depth of 54 m (LAT). It is in intact and orientated in a NNW to SSE direction. The wreckage stands 4.8 m proud of the seabed from amidships to the stern section, which remains reasonably intact up to the bridge superstructure. However the bridge section up to the bows has now totally collapsed and exposed the boilers. From the bows to the midships area there is reported to be a large mound of collapsed steel debris as well as her winches, pieces of broken mast, twisted handrails and her anchors and other debris all lying intermingled. Soft corals decorate the decaying remains and it should make an excellent boat-angling venue.

MEREDITH (?)

Date of loss: 31 March 1891
Wreck: ★★
Depth: 23 m
Reference: 54 48'.854 N 001 13'.750 W
Location: 3.51 nm SE of Seaham Harbour piers

The *Meredith* (Official No. 65589) was an iron-hulled 976-ton British steam cargo vessel measuring 67.18 m in length, with an 8.89-m beam and a 5.18-m draught. Iliff, Mounsey & Co., at South Dock, Sunderland built and completed her as Yard No. 50 in February 1871; she was launched in February 1871 for J. W. Mounsey & others, London. The single iron screw was powered by a 99-nhp two-cylinder inverted compound steam engine that used one boiler. T. Bates & Company manufactured the engine and ancillary machinery at Sowerby Bridge, West Yorkshire. She had four bulkheads, a 27.73-m quarterdeck, 12.49-m bridge deck and 5.79-m forecastle. She was surveyed in September 1871 and classed as 18. In 1874 Wilkinson & Watt, London wa the registered owner. John White of London was the registered owner in 1875. In 1876 she was purchased by R. Fletcher, London. John Chapman in London bought the vessel in 1877. Large damage repairs were carried out in 1878, but the reason in unknown. In 1879 the ship was bought by G. N. Wilkinson, London. S. Ditchfield in London became the registered owner in 1879. A new boiler was fitted by J. T. Eltringham, S. Sheilds in 1881 and in June of that year she was surveyed and classed A1 by Liverpool. In 1881 R. Thorman & Co., London (Seaham Harbour) was the registered owner. R. Thorman, London became the registered owner in 1886. From 1884.85, R. Thorman at the port of Seaham Harbour was the registered owner. The signal code letters were: LRNV.

Final voyage

On 31 March 1891 the *Meredith*, commanded by Captain R.T. Humble, foundered following a collision with the 1878-ton steamer *Longnewton* (1884: Marquis of Londonderry, Sunderland).

The *Meredith* was in ballast and on passage from London for Sunderland carrying a crew of 17. Wind conditions were a NE force 4 at the time of the incident and the sea was choppy. The fate of the crew is unknown.

BoT Wreck Return 1890/91, p. 146 (672); LR 1883/84 No. 760 (M); LCR 1891, p. 6 (d); American Lloyd's Register of American and Foreign Shipping 1857–1900; *The Times*: Wednesday, 1 April 1891, p. 5, Issue 33287.

Wrecksite

The wreck – possibly that of the *Meredith* – is orientated in a NW to SE direction. It lies on a seabed of fine sand and mud in a general depth of 23 m (LAT). The wreck is badly decayed, well broken up and completely collapsed with the highest section of 4 m being amidships, where the two-cylinder compound engine and boiler are located and exposed. A large mound of iron debris surrounds the amidships section. A large shoal of pout whiting usually swim around the boiler and engine area.

TEAL

Date of loss: 29 April 1916
Wreck: ✯✯✯
Depth: 23 m
Reference: 54 49'.523 N 001 14'.217 W
Location: 3.01 nm ESE of Seaham Harbour piers

The *Teal* (Official No. 73660) was a steel-hulled 766-ton British schooner-rigged steam cargo vessel measuring 67.08 m in length, with a 8.66-m beam and a 4.47-m draught. M. Pearse and Company, Stockton-on-Tees built and completed her as Yard No. 147. She was launched on 25 April 1876 for General Steam Navigation Company Ltd. which also owned her at the time of loss. The single screw was powered by a 174-hp two-cylinder compound steam engine that used one boiler. Blair and Co., Ltd., Stockton manufactured the engine and ancillary machinery. She had two decks, a 23.4-m poop deck and 13.7-m forecastle.

Final voyage

On 29 April 1916 the *Teal*, with Captain W.A.W. Hove in charge, was south of Seaham Harbour when the KDM submarine SMU *UB 27*, commanded by Oblt.z.S. Viktor Dieckmann, suddenly appeared through a fog bank and attacked her with a torpedo. The steamer was *en route* from Leith to London with a general cargo and carrying a crew of 19. Captain Hove saw the track of the torpedo on the starboard beam and immediately put the helm hard over to port. The torpedo missed the ship by a few feet but the U-boat began shelling the steamer with its deck gun. Realising they had little chance of escape, the master stopped the vessel and ordered his crew into the boats. *UB 27* then went alongside and the German submariners placed explosive timing devices below the decks at 0820 hrs.

The U-boat left the area in pursuit of another merchant ship. From a distance the *Teal*'s crew watched as the scuttling charges all detonated. Amazingly the little vessel refused to sink. Fifty minutes later, however, the U-boat reappeared and fired a second torpedo, which scored a direct hit and the *Teal* went up in a huge explosion. The submarine then headed seawards in an easterly direction and the survivors were picked up from their small boats by the 107-ton steam trawler *Rugby* (1889) and taken to Hartlepool.

ADM 137/2960; LCWLR 1914–18, p. 41; BVLS 1914–18, p. 18; Miramar Ship Index; LR 1914–18, No. 319 (T); American Lloyd's Register of American and Foreign Shipping 1857–1900.

Wrecksite

The wreck lies on a seabed of coarse sand and pebbles in a general depth of 23 m (LAT). Keith Lawrence from Seaham informed the author that it is well broken up, having totally collapsed down on top of itself, except for the stern section which is relatively intact with the iron screw still attached. The boiler, condenser and engine are now exposed amongst the jumble of steel debris, which is (or was) intermingled with long twisted copper pipes and brass flanges. The highest point of the wreck is the boiler and both this and the stern end are ablaze with soft corals. It also has at least one trawl net draped over it. Quite a few large lobsters have been spotted and a shoal of pout whiting were seen swarming over the wreck near the engine.

ADA

Date of Loss: 22 February 1894
Wreck: ✯✯✯
Depth: 43 m
Reference: 54 49'.294 N 001 09'.486 W
Location: 5.91 nm ESE of Seaham Harbour piers

The *Ada* (Official No. 84992) was an iron-hulled 876-ton schooner-rigged steam cargo vessel measuring 67.05 m in length, with a 9.14-m beam and 4.19-m draught. Robert Thompson and Sons, at Southwick, Sunderland built and completed her as Yard No. 113 in September 1881. She was launched as the *Ada* on the 26th of that month for Turner, Edwards and Company, Bristol.

A 99-hp two-cylinder compound steam engine that used one boiler powered the single iron screw. The cylinders measured 66.04 cm and 121.92 cm, with a 91.44-cm stroke (26 in. and 48 in., with a 36-in. stroke). She had four bulkheads, one deck and water ballast.

In 1886 the *Ada* was sold to Alfred Suart, Bristol and registered in London. In 1888 Dansey and Robinson, London became registered owner.

From 1891 until the time of loss Green, Holland and Sons, in London was the registered owner. The designated code recognition signal letters were: WDCS.

Final voyage

At 0800 hrs on 22 February 1894 the *Ada* was transporting coal from Seaham and Sunderland to Devonport, Devon when she sank following a collision with the 169-ton steam tug *Englishman* (1889: Thomas Gray and Company, Hull), eight miles ESE of Seaham Harbour. The *Englishman*, which rescued the *Ada*'s crew, arrived at the Tyne in a seriously damaged condition.

The Times: Friday, 23 February 1894, p. 8, Issue 34195; Starke Schell Registers; BoT Wreck Return 1894, p. 151.

Wrecksite

The wreck – which is likely that of the *Ada* – sits in a slight scour and is orientated in a SSE to NNW direction. It lies on a seabed of mud and sand in a general depth of 43 m (LAT). The wreck stands around 4 m high, is partially buried in parts and covers an area 74 m long and 10 m across. Lots of broken pipes and various items of machinery can be observed. Some fair-sized cod have also been spotted.

ACHIEVEMENT

Date of Loss: 23 March 1884
Wreck: ☆☆
Depth: 43 m
Reference: 54 49'.570 N 000 09'.322 W
Location: 5.71 nm ESE of Seaham Harbour piers

The *Achievement* (Official No. 53479) was an iron-hulled 125-ton British steam powered paddle tug measuring 31.27 m in length, with a 5.71-m-beam and 3.17-m depth. It was registered at North Shields as SN.1352. Thomas Hepple and Company, at Low Walker, Newcastle upon Tyne built and completed her in August 1866 for G. Sutton and Others at North Shields.

A one-half-beam 50-nhp two-cylinder compound steam engine that used one boiler powered her two side paddles. The cylinders measured 76.2 cm by 76.2 cm, with a 142.24-cm stroke (30 in. and 30 in. with a 56-in. stroke). Thomas Hepple and Company Ltd. also manufactured the machinery.

(The book "Beyond the Piers" by Ron Wright – 'history of the North Shields trawlers/liners/drifters', suggests that the *ACHIEVEMENT* was a steam powered paddle sloop, built in 1868.)

The *Achievement* was probably used as a fish carrier for a box fleet. In 1884 the registered owner was J.M. Scott of North Shields. At the time of loss she was registered to Scott Brothers, Sunderland., Port Reg: No. SN.1352.

Final voyage

On the evening of Tuesday, 23 March 1884 the *Achievement*, under the command of Skipper J. Brown, was on a return voyage in ballast from Hartlepool to Sunderland, when she sank following a collision with the 826-ton steam *Dunelm* (1877: W.A. Watson, Sunderland) about eight miles off Seaham Harbour. All of her crew of seven were picked up by the *Dunelm*. The steamship was on passage from Rochester to Sunderland, where she arrived with the survivors on the Wednesday morning.

The Times: Friday, 28 March 1884, p. 3, Issue 31093; British Parliamentary Papers 1868-1871; BoT Wreck Return 1884, p. 133; NLR Underwriters ; Liverpool Underwriters` Registry for Iron Vessels, 1871/2; Liverpool Underwriters` Registry for Iron Vessels, 1874/5; Liverpool Underwriters` Registry for Iron Vessels, 1884/5.

The *Dunelm* became a total loss when she drove ashore onto the Sow and Pig Rocks at Blyth on 11 January 1913 while voyaging from Cowes to Blyth in ballast.

Wrecksite

The wreck – most likely that of the tug – sits in a slight scour and is orientated in a NE to SW (040/220) direction. It lies on a seabed of sediment, mud and dirty sand in a general depth of 43 m (LAT). The wreck stands just 2.4 m high, is very collapsed, broken partially buried and in a very decayed condition. It covers an area of about 28 m by 10 m. Bent and broken rib sections, battered iron plates and pieces of machinery protrude from the seabed. A number of crustaceans can also be found under the wreckage but there are not many fish around.

GOTHIA, ex NINIAN STUART

Date of loss: 11 May 1918
Wreck: ★★★★
Depth: 61 m
Reference: 54 49'.334 N 000 46'.118 W
Location: 15.86 nm NE from The Heugh, Hartlepool

The *Gothia* (Official No. 89164) was an iron-hulled 1880-ton Swedish steam cargo ship measuring 82.4 m in length, with a 12.3-m beam and a 5.6-m draught. William Pickersgill & Sons Ltd., at Southwick, Sunderland built and completed her as Yard No. 64 in September 1883. She was launched as the *Ninian Stuart* on the 1st of that month for Morel Bros. Shipping Company, Cardiff (later Morel Ltd. Cardiff). The single iron screw was powered by a 150-nhp two-cylinder compound steam engine that used one boiler. The cylinders measured 83.82 cm and 157.48 cm with a 106.68-cm stroke (33 in. and 62 in. with a 42-in. stroke). She had one deck and five bulkheads.

The registered owner in 1888 was Morel, Ltd. Cardiff.

In 1891, Ebbwvale S.S. Co., Ltd., Cardiff was the registered owner and Morel Bros. & Co., was the manager. In 1894 the master was Captain J. Tippett.

In 1895, she had the same owner but Morel, Ltd. was the manager.

From 1898 to at least 1900, the master was Captain D.S. Roberts.

In 1912 Rederi A/B Trelleborg, Trelleborg, Sweden purchased and renamed her *Gothia*; G. Österberg was the manager; Official No. 5374

From 1918 R. Göhle, Norrköping was the registered owner. The designated code recognition signal letters were: JFHN.

Final voyage

On 11 May 1918 the *Gothia* was torpedoed and sunk by SMU *UB 21* a KDM submarine, commanded by Oblt.z.S. Bruno Mahn. The steamer was understood to be eight miles north-east of Hartlepool, in ballast and on passage from Hull for Blyth. At the moment of explosion, the messroom boy, Birger Mauritz Eriksson, had just arrived on the bridge with coffee for the second mate and was injured in the face and shoulder by flying debris. He still managed to get himself into one of the lifeboats. His injuries were not serious and he soon recovered fully.

Starke Schell Registers; Swedish Official WWI Losses; LWL 1914–18, p. 216; American Lloyd's Register of American and Foreign Shipping 1857–1900.

Wrecksite

The wreck of the *Gothia* is orientated in a SSE to NNW direction and lies on a seabed of mud, fine sand, broken black shells and pebbles in a general depth of 61 m (LAT). The wreck stands on an even keel in a one-metre scour and is intact with the highest point being 5.5 m high at the SE end, which is covered in trawl nets. It covers an area of about 65 m in length by 7 m in width. Plenty of marine life has been observed, including some large cod. The bell, if located, will be inscribed: *Ninian Stuart 1883*. The wrecksite should make an excellent boat-angling venue.

TATIANA, EX CLAUDIUS (?)

Date of loss: 31 July 1916
Wreck: ☆☆
Depth: 61 m
Reference: 54 50'.085 N 00 56'.980 W
Location: 12.84 nm E of Seaham Harbour piers

The *Tatiana* was a steel-hulled 285-ton British steam trawler measuring 41.63 m in length, a 7.01 m-beam and a 3.68 m-draught. Cochrane and Sons Ltd. built and completed her as Yard No. 448 in April 1909. She was launched as the *Claudius* at Selby on 6 February 1909. An 87-hp three-cylinder triple expansion steam engine that used one boiler powered her single steel screw. Amos and Smith Ltd. at Hull manufactured the amidships-positioned machinery. She had one deck, four bulkheads, a 21.9-m quarterdeck and 6.7-mforecastle. A. Bannister of Grimsby owned her at the time of loss and renamed her *Tatiana*.

Final voyage

On 31 July 1916 the *Tatiana* (Captain W.F. Jenner) was captured by SMU *UB 39*, a KDM submarine commanded by Oblt.z.S. Fürbringer (see page 87). The crew was ordered to abandon ship and attempts were made by the Germans to sink her with gunfire, before they sank her using explosive scuttling charges.

The *Tatiana* was on a return voyage to Grimsby fully laden with fish from an area around the Faroe Islands when she was captured. The Germans attempted to sink her with gunfire before she was sunk using explosive scuttling charges. Before this, though, the Germans – according to allegations reported by *The Times* – allegedly plundered the vessel for food and every bit of brass they could find. The crew, along with the crew from the trawler *Braconash* (see page 112), was picked up by the Lowestoft herring drifter *Diadem*.

BVLS 1914–18, p. 110 ; LCWLR 1914–18, p. 49; LR 1914/15, No. 274 (T) ; *The Times*: Wednesday, 2 August 1916, p. 3, Issue 41235.

Wrecksite

The wreck – possibly that of the *Tatiana* – is orientated in an ENE to WSW direction. It lies on a seabed of fine sand, broken shells and mud in a general depth of 61 m (LAT). The wreckage is partially buried, totally collapsed, decayed and well broken up, standing just over 2 m high amidships, where the boiler and engine are exposed. Surrounding the boiler and engine is a small mound of debris covering an area of about 10 m by 5 m. It is possible that her instruments and other interesting machinery are still around, but they are likely buried beneath the silt and debris.

LLWYNGWAIR

Date of loss: 26 April 1918
Wreck: ✯✯✯✯
Depth: 36 m
Reference: 54 50'.123 N 001 11'.265 W
Location: 4.66 nm E by S of Seaham Harbour piers

The *Llwyngwair* (Official No. 128947) was a steel-hulled 1304-ton British steam cargo ship measuring 69.85 m in length, with a 10.84-m beam and 4.4-mdraught. Antwerp Engineering Company Ltd. in Hoboken, Belgium built and completed her as Yard No. 66 in November 1913. She was launched on 15 October 1913 for Harries Brothers and Company, Swansea, who owned her at the time of loss. The single steel screw was powered by a 156 hp, three-cylinder triple expansion steam engine that used two boilers and gave 9.5 knots. The engine and ancillary was manufactured at Sunderland by MacColl and Pollack Ltd. She had one deck, four bulkheads, a 4.2-m poop deck, 22.2-m quarterdeck, 14-m bridge deck and 7.3-m forecastle. In 1915/16 the ship was armed for defence with one stern mounted 18-pounder deck gun.

Final voyage

On 26 April 1918 the *Llwyngwair*, under the command of Captain James Stevenson, was in ballast and on passage from Dunkerque for Newcastle upon Tyne when, at 0010 hrs, the KDM submarine SMU *UC 64*, commanded by Oblt.z.S. Ferdinand Schwartz, torpedoed her amidships. The *Abbas* (1911: Stephenson Clarke and Company, London), a 1430-ton steamer, had already sighted the U-boat on the surface and fired at it with the deck gun. The U-boat was forcedto submerge, but the *Abbas* was too late to save the *Llwyngwair*, which went down to the bottom soon after the engagement. Eight of her crew of 18 were drowned. The *Abbas* picked up the remaining ten survivors and landed them at Sunderland. Eight of the crewmen who died:

Bergstrom, Otto, 23 yrs, Boatswain (Bosun) MM
Coull, Robert, Leading Seaman RNR (DAMS gunner)
Harris, John George Edward, 26 yrs, 2nd Engineer MM
MacLeay, John, Leading Seaman RNR (DAMS gunner)
Shepherd, William John, 38 yrs, Steward MM
Stevenson, James, Master MM
Whorlow, Alfred John, 28 yrs, 2nd Mate MM
Williams, Joseph Alexded, 34 yrs, 1st Engineer MM

ADM 137/2964; CWGC; Starke Schell Registers; BMS 1914–18 p. 87; Tennent (1990), p. 118; LCWLR 1914–18, p. 213.

Wrecksite

The wreck – probably that of the *Llwyngwair* – is orientated in a NNE to SSW direction. It lies on a seabed of sand, gravel and mud in a general depth of 36 m (LAT). The wreck is very substantial, intact, but mostly collapsed. The bows, also fairly intact, are probably the highest section. The rest of the wreck is rather flattened except for the two boilers and the engine. The wreck stands 6 m high in parts and covers an area 70 m by 10 m. The steering binnacle, recovered in the 1990s, was manufactured by Donkins at Newcastle.

EIDENT

Date of loss: 24 October 1902
Wreck: ✯✯
Depth 44 m
Reference: 54 50'.838 N 001 08'.485 W
Location: 6.19 nm E by N of Seaham Harbour piers

The *Eident* (Official No. 81464) was an iron-hulled 1558-ton steam cargo ship measuring 79.37 m in length, with a 10.36-m beam and 5.66-m draught. Short Brothers at Pallion, Sunderland built and completed her as Yard No. 103 in January 1880. She was launched on the 28th of that month for James Westoll of Sunderland, who registered her in Sunderland and was owner at the time of loss. A 178-hp two-cylinder compound steam engine that used one boiler powered the single iron screw. The engine and ancillary machinery was manufactured at Hartlepool by T. Richardson and Sons. She had one deck, five bulkheads and a 30.5-m quarterdeck, an 18.8-m bridge deck and 9.1-m forecastle.

Final voyage

On 24 October 1902 the *Eident*, commanded by Captain J. Martin, foundered following a collision with the 579-ton Norwegian steamer *G.M.B.* (1878 – A/S G. M. B., Christiania). The *Eident*, which was uninsured, was in ballast on passage from London for South Shields and carrying a crew of 18. None of the crew was lost.

LR 1902/3, No. 161 (E); BoW Return 1902, p. 143; LCR 1902, p. 7 (d); Starke Schell Registers; *The Times*: Tuesday, 28 October 1902, p. 2, Issue 36910.

Wrecksite

The wreck is orientated in a NW to SE direction with the bows to the NW. It lies on a seabed of dirty sand, mud, broken shells and gravel in a general depth of 44 m (LAT). The remains are partially buried, totally collapsed, well broken up and badly decayed, with the highest 3 m section being around her boiler and engine – both of which are exposed to the strong tidal streams and covered in an array of dead-man's fingers. Masses of iron debris and broken, decayed machinery surround the boiler and engine. Little else is recognisable.

CRANFORD (?)

Date of loss: 12 October 1910
Wreck: ★★★★
Depth: 41 m
Reference: 54 50'.407 N 001 10'.631 W
Location: 5.02 nm E of Seaham Harbour piers

The *Cranford* (Official No. 95459) was a steel-hulled 2293-ton schooner-rigged British steam cargo ship measuring 89.30 m in length, with an 11.36-m beam and draught of 5.65 m. William Gray and Company, West Hartlepool built and completed her as Yard No. 341 in September 1888. She was launched on 10 August 1988 for Pyman Bros., London. The single steel screw was powered by a 240-nhp three-cylinder triple expansion steam engine that used two Scotch boilers with three furnaces all positioned amidships and gave nine knots. The cylinders measured 58.42 cm, 92.71 cm and 157.48 cm with a 99.06-cm stroke (23 in., 36.5 in. and 62 in., with a 39-in. stroke). She had two masts, a 25.60-m raised quarterdeck, an 8.53-m bridge deck, one deck, five bulkheads and web frames.

From 1898 London & Northern S.S. Co., Ltd., of Bishopsgate Street, London was the registered owner. Pyman Bros. was the manager. The designated code recognition signal letters were: KTQN.

Final voyage

The SS *Cranford*, with Captain Fettes in command, sailed from the Tyne on the evening of Wednesday, 12 October 1910 for passage to Pozzuoli, Naples with gun mountings, machinery, steel billets, lead ingots and general cargo. Weather conditions were very bad and during the night a violent storm was blowing. Distress signals were seen off Hartlepool, but soon after no more were sighted. Over the following few days, wreckage including that from a sailing vessel, and six bodies were washed up along the coast near Blackhall Rocks, Company Durham. The bodies had on lifebelts identifying them as being crew of the *Cranford*. Two of the ship's boats, a lifeboat and a jolly boat, were also washed ashore, one bearing her name and the other marked: *London*. Twenty-three crewmen died:

Banister, A., Boatswain MM from South Shields
Buglass, S., third Engineer MM from South Shields
Campbell, M., MM from Newcastle
Carruthers, N., MM
Edward, J., Mess-room Steward MM
Fettes, Master, MM from Montrose
Gillings, John Albert, first mate from Robin Hood's Bay
Gredin, G., second mate MM from Bridgend Staffs
Hall, J., Steward MM from Liverpool
Heatley, G., 2nd Engineer MM from Blyth
Hogg, John, Fireman MM from Pelaw on Tyne
Horsfall, J.E., Mess-room Steward MM from Leeds
Jayne, Frederick, 1st Engineer MM from Bristol
Kennedy, T., Seaman MM
Marning, J., Fireman MM from South Shields
Mclean, D., MM from South Shields
Murray, P., MM
O'Neill, W., MM from Aberdeen
Ramsey, R., MM from Waterford
Ramus, Manuel, MM a Cook from Coventry
Robinson, George, Donkeyman MM from South Shields
Spence, A., MM
Whitman, F., MM

The body of George Robinson, the donkeyman, showed signs of scalding, which pointed to the vessel being involved in a collision according to the inquest at Blackhall.

Starke Schell Registers; Hocking (1969); Miramar Ship Index; American Lloyd's Register of American and Foreign Shipping 1857–1900; BoT Wreck Return 1910; *The Times*: Saturday, 15 October 1910, p. 8, Issue 39404.

Wrecksite

The wreck – which is possibly that of the *Cranford* – sits in a small scour and is orientated in an ENE to WSW direction. It lies on a seabed of coarse sand, broken shells and pebbles in a general depth of 41 m (LAT). The wreck covers a general area of 68 m by 11 m and appears to be broken into two sections, with the bows to the west. The engine and boilers stand about 4 m high and the stern is quite intact, but most of the wreck is no more than one or two metres high. The bow section is broken off and lies north of the starboard side. Various pieces of cargo are scattered around the wreck, including earthenware jars, an assortment of bottles, lead-based ingots and a 2–3 m mound of steel pipes. However, the latter may be abandoned drilling equipment left by a construction company. A lot of crustaceans and shoals of fish can be observed on and around the wreck.

CARMARTHEN COAST, EX NOVA, EX LANGFJORD

Date of loss: 9 November 1939
Wreck: ★★★
Depth: 26 m
Reference: 54 50 '.879 N 001 15'.400 W
Location: 2.32 nm ENE of Seaham Harbour piers

The *Carmarthen Coast* (Official No. 147175) was a steel-hulled 964-ton British steam cargo ship measuring 64.74 m in length, with a 10.23-m beam and 3.78-m draught.

Ardrossan Dry Dock and Shipbuilding Company, Ardrossan built and completed her as Yard No. 316 in December 1921. The keel was laid down as the *Svanfos*, but she was launched as the *Langfjord* on 23 March 1921 for Aktieselskapet Den Norske Amerikalinje, Kristiania (Oslo). Plenty and Son Ltd. Newbury manufactured the machinery, as well as the engine and ancillary machinery. The single steel screw was powered by a 142-nhp three-cylinder triple expansion steam engine that used two single-ended boilers working at 180 psi pressure, with four corrugated furnaces, 7.61 sq.m (82 sq.ft) of grate surface, 237.64 sq.m (2558 sq.m) of heating surface and giving 9.5 knots. The cylinders measured 41.91 cm, 68.58 cm and 111.76 cm with a 76.2-cm stroke (16.5 in., 27 in. and 44 in. with a 30-in. stroke). She had one steel deck, a steel shelter deck with freeboard and a 10.36-m forecastle on the shelter deck, some cellular double bottom and a fore peak and aft peak tank. She was also equipped with wireless direction finder. She was classed as 100 A1. The designated code recognition letters were: MLGT.

In 1921 Det Bergenske Dampskibsselskab, Bergen became the registered owner and renamed her *Nova*. From 1922, Coast Lines Ltd. Liverpool was registered owner and renamed her *Carmarthen Coast*.

Final voyage

On 9 November 1939 the *Carmarthen Coast* detonated a mine which has been laid on 27 October 1939 by the Kriegsmarine Type IIB submarine, *U 24*, commanded by Kplt Harald Jeppener-Haltenhoff. Five men were injured in the explosion and two men lost when the steamer foundered within minutes. The 14 survivors took to the boats and were rescued by the RNLI motorised lifeboat from Seaham. The ship was on passage from Methil for London with a 1000-ton general cargo, which included granite kerb stones and rolls of linoleum. John Kerr (38 yrs, donkeyman MM) and Henry G. King (46 yrs, second engineer officer) died.

BVLS 1939–45, p. 2; LCWLR 1939–45, p. 19; LR 1938/9, No. 71815 (C); CWGC.

Wrecksite

The wreck is orientated in an ESE to WNW direction with the bows to the WNW. It lies on a seabed of sand, pebble, gravel and shells in a general depth of 26 m (LAT). Keith Lawrence from Seaham Sub Aqua Club identified the wreck from the radio he recovered about 20 years ago. The remains have collapsed and the wreck is well broken up. In the first hold are the granite kerb stones. Then there is a two- to three-metre pile of linoleum up to the boilers. The starboard hull stands one metre clear back to the boilers, but the rest of the hull is broken. The forecastle on the port side is about two or three metres clear. One boiler used to stand against the other and the stern used to be relatively intact, however, a few years ago a large crane vessel was launched on the river Wear; during its sea trials it anchored off Seaham for a few days immediately over the wreck. It would seem that its anchor pulled the wreck to pieces.

There is no report of her bell having been recovered, but it would most likely be inscribed:

Langfjord 1921.

HASLINGDEN

Date of loss: 12 May 1918
Wreck: ✯✯✯✯
Depth: 46 m
Reference: 54 51'.701 N 001 07'.836 W
Location: 6.76 nm ENE of Seaham Harbour piers

The *Haslingden* (Official No. 102725) was a steel-hulled 1934-ton schooner-rigged British steam cargo ship measuring 82.39 m in length, with an 11.3-m beam and a 5.68-m draught. William Gray & Co., Ltd., West Hartlepool built and completed her as Yard No. 490 in March 1895. She was launched on 26 February 1895 for Murrell and Yeoman at West Hartlepool.

The single screw was powered by a 169-hp three-cylinder triple expansion steam engine that used two boilers and gave a service speed of 11.5 knots. The cylinders measured 50.8 cm, 80.01 cm and 142.24 cm, with a 91.34-cm stroke (20 in., 31.5 in. and 56 in. with a 36-in. stroke). Central Marine Engineering Works, West Hartlepool manufactured the engine and ancillary machinery. She had one deck, four bulkheads, water ballast, web frames, an 8.8-m poop deck, a 21.4-m quarterdeck and a 35.3-m bridge deck.

F. Yeoman, West Hartlepool was the registered owner in 1901. From 1915, F. Yeoman & Sons, West Hartlepool was the registered owner. The vessel was armed for defence in 1916 with one 12cwt (610-kilo) stern mounted 12-pounder deck gun.

Final voyage

At 0524 hrs on 12 May 1918 the *Haslingden* was torpedoed without warning by the submerged KDM submarine SMU *UB 21*, commanded by Oblt.z.S. Bruno Mahn. The ship was in ballast and *en route* from Rouen to Newcastle upon Tyne when one of the crew observed the track of a torpedo heading towards their ship. The master, Captain H. Johns, tried taking evasive action but within one minute of being sighted the torpedo had slammed home, striking the steamer amidships on her port side. The explosion that followed destroyed the wireless room, the bridge and all of the ship's upper controls, including the wheelhouse; even the funnel was blown into the air and landed in the sea. Captain Johns died instantly, along with the radio operator, second officer and the helmsman. The *Haslingden* heeled over to port and sank almost immediately. Another seven of the crewmen were either trapped in the ship when it went down or died in the sea. A patrol vessel picked up the remaining 15 survivors and landed them at the Tyne.

The submarine was never actually sighted and it was only after the war that records revealed the U-boat that sank the *Haslingden*. Eleven crewmen died:

Bell, John Lenney, 17 yrs, Sailor MM
Carroll, Edward, 28 yrs, 2nd Engineer MM
Crawshaw, James, 17 yrs, Wireless Operator MM
Heugh, Robert, 26 yrs, Fireman and Trimmer MM
Hunt, Cyril Reynolds, 22 yrs, Cook MM
Johns, H., (DSC) 60 yrs, Master MM
Lyth, Harry, 21 yrs, 2nd mate MM
Tucker, William, AB RNVR
Whitehurst, 19 yrs, Mess Room Steward MM
Whitfield, William, 17 yrs, Sailor MM
Wiles, William Thomas, 65 yrs, first mate MM

ADM 137/2964; CWGC; Starke Schell Registers; BVLS 1914–18, p. 89; LR 1915/16, No. 323 (H); Jarvis & Jarvis (1993), Vol. 1; Jarvis (2000), Vol. 5; LCWLR 1914–18, p. 216; BMS 1914–18, p. 240.

Wrecksite

The wreck lies on a seabed of broken black shells, pebbles, mud and fine sand in a general depth of 46 m (LAT). The Dawdon Sub Aqua Club, which reported it as being very substantial, first discovered the wreck. The bows to forecastle section of the wreck is lying on its side and is still intact up to about the two boilers, which stand next to each other, across the wreck. To the rear of the boilers stands the exposed huge engine block, surrounded by broken machinery, pieces of derricks, lifeboat davits, steel frames, ribs and plating, and intermingled with twisted girders where the wreck has collapsed in on its self. The stern section rises up again, however, it too is lying on its side. The highest points such as the forecastle, bows and stern are coated in a colourful array of soft corals where the strong current sweeps past in both directions of the tidal run. Unfortunately a number of trawl nets get caught up in the structures from time to time. Cod and large pollack frequent the wrecksite, which makes a good boat angling venue.

BRACONASH, ex CASPIANA (?)

Date of Loss: 31 July 1916
Wreck: ★★★
Depth: 63 m
Reference: 54 51'.773 N 001 00'.433 W
Location: 10.97 nm ENE from Seaham Harbour

The *Braconash* (Official No. 15558) was a steel-hulled 192-ton British steam trawler measuring 35.2 m in length, with a 6.5-m beam and a 3.5-m draught. Mackie and Thomas at (old) Govan, Glasgow built and completed her as Yard No. 267 in December 1901. She was launched as the *Caspiana* on Saturday, 14 December 1901 for Grimsby owners Ross and Duncan manufactured the machinery in Glasgow. A 65-nhp three-cylinder triple expansion steam engine that used one boiler powered her single steel screw.

Ocean Trawling Company, Aberdeen became the registered owner in 1915.

Don Fishing Company, Aberdeen renamed her *Braconash* and owned her at the time of loss.

Final voyage

On 31 July 1916 the *Braconash* was fully laden with fish from her voyage from an area around the Faroe Islands and was returning to port when she was captured 18 miles SE of the Tyne by the KDM submarine SMU *UB 39*, commanded by Oblt.z.S. Werner Fürbringer. The crew were ordered to abandon their vessel. According to the report in *The Times*, as with the steam trawler, *Tatiana* – captured and sunk on the same day (see page 105) – the *Braconash* too was plundered for food and brass. The Germans also attempted to sink the *Braconash* with gunfire, but it too was eventually sunk with explosive scuttling charges. The *Braconash*'s crew along with the crew from the *Tatiana* was later picked up by the Lowestoft herring drifter, *Diadem*.

LCWLR 1914–18, p. 49; Starke Schell Registers; *The Times*: Wednesday, 2 August 1916, p. 3, Issue 41235.

Wrecksite

The wreck – possibly that of the *Braconash* – is orientated in an ESE to WNW direction. It lies on a seabed of mud, pebbles and fine sand in a general depth of 63 m (LAT). The wreck is upright, intact and stands 5.8 m high, with the highest point being at the south-eastern end. A lot of fish has been observed around the wreck on the echo sounder and the wreck should make an interesting boat angling venue.

HILDAWELL (?)

Date of Loss: 20 December 1916
Wreck: ★★★★
Depth: 63 m
Reference: 54 51'.607 N 000 50 '.118 W
Location: 8.25 nm ENE from Seaham Harbour piers

The *Hildawell* (Official No. 98530) was a steel-hulled 2494-ton steam cargo ship measuring 88.40 m in length, with an 11.88-m beam and a 6.17--m draught. William Gray and Company, West Hartlepool built and completed her as Yard No. 452 in September 1892. They also manufactured the engine and ancillary machinery. The *Hildawell* was launched on 22 August 1892 for G.B. Harland and Company, West Hartlepool. The single screw was powered by a 224-hp three-cylinder triple expansion steam engine that used two boilers. The cylinders measured 55.88 cm, 88.9 cm and 149.86 cm, with a 99.06-cm stroke (22 in., 35 in. and 59 in., with a 39-in. stroke). William Gray and Company She had one deck, five bulkheads cemented, water ballast and web frames.

From 1903 T.W. Willis, West Hartlepool was the registered owner. The designated code recognition signal letters were: MSRF.

Final voyage

On 20 December 1916 the *Hildawell* detonated a mine in the North Sea off Sunderland and foundered with all 22 hands, while transporting iron ore from Bilbao to Middlesbrough. The mine had been laid on the 14th of that month by SMU *UC 32*, commanded by Oblt.z.S. Herbert Breyer. The crew lost were:

Capsey, J., Able Seaman MM
Clarke, John Stephen Lloyd, Donkeyman MM
Hansell, Robert Ernest, 1st Mate MM
Helland, M., Able Seaman MM
Henderson, Benjamin, Fireman MM
Ingram, Heniy, Master MM
Kaju, Joseph, Sailor MM
Kohn, Ole, Fireman and Trimmer MM
Lee, Thomas Wallis, Steward MM
Parkin, Richard Jefferson, Fireman MM
Patterson, Robert, Masters Ship's Cook MM
Peterson, Alexander, Able Seaman MM
Prentice, Robert, 2nd Engineer MM
Pulli, Jacob, Sailor MM
Rowlands, Harold, Boatswain (Bosun) MM
Screeton, George Robert, 2nd Mate MM
Small, F., Fireman MM
Stubbernd, H.C., Sailor MM
Warren, David Stewart, Mess Steward MM
Wheeler, George William, Fireman MM
Wilmhurst, Walter, 3rd Engineer MM
Witten, Richard Arthur, 1st Engineer MM

Wrecksite

The wreck – which is possibly that of the *Hildawell* – is orientated in an E to W direction. It lies on a seabed of mud and fine sand in a general depth of 63 m (LAT). The wreck is upright and intact, covering an area 83 m long, with the highest 5 m sections being the bows and stern. Lots of fish have been observed on the echo sounder so the site should make an interesting boat angling venue.

JAMES CAMERON, EX PRINZ ALBRECHT

Date of loss: 27 January 1910
Wreck: ☆☆☆
Depth: 60 m
Reference: 54 51'.883 N 001 01'.756 W
Location: 10.23 nm ENE of Seaham Harbour piers

The *James Cameron* (Official No. 90343) was an iron-hulled 1805-ton British steam cargo ship measuring 79.24 m in length, with an 11.63-m beam and a 5.40-m draught. Short Brothers at Pallion, Sunderland built and completed her as Yard No. 129 in August 1882. She was launched as the *Prinz Albrecht* on 31 August 1882 for Dampfs. Ges., 'Anglia', Hamburg. The single iron screw was powered by a 150-nhp two-cylinder compound steam engine that used two boilers, all positioned amidships. The cylinders measured 83.82 cm and 157.48 cm, with a 106.68-cm stroke (33 in. and 62 in. with a 42-in. stroke). She had one deck, six bulkheads and water ballast.

From 1905 until the time of loss James Westoll, Sunderland was the registered owner and renamed her *James Cameron*.

Final voyage

The *James Cameron* was in ballast and *en route* from Rouen for the Tyne with a crew of 18 when, on the evening of 27 January 1910, she sank following a collision with the 1166-ton steamer *Vanessa* (1872: Renwick, Wilton and Company). The entire crew abandoned ship 30 miles from the Tyne.

BoT Wreck Return 1910, p. 120 (168); Starke Schell Registers; *The Times*: Saturday, 29 January 1910, p. 12, Issue no. 39182; American Lloyd's Register of American and Foreign Shipping 1857–1900.

Wrecksite

The wreck – most likely that of the *James Cameron* – is orientated in a NW to SE direction. It lies on a dirty seabed of mud and broken shells in a general depth of 60 m (LAT). The wreck is quite substantial but appears to be inverted and standing some 6 m high amidships, where the hull has collapsed onto the boilers and engine, all of which are now exposed and covered in a myriad of soft corals. Very little is recognisable but most of the instruments of interest will be somewhere under the pile of iron debris. A large number of fish were picked up on the echo sounder so the site should be a decent boat-angling venue.

VIANNA

Date of loss: 31 March 1918
Wreck: ★★
Depth: 28 m
Reference: 54 51'.305 N 01 14'.862 W
Location: 2.75 nm ENE from Seaham Harbour piers

The *Vianna* (Official No. 136762) was a steel-hulled 401-ton British steam cargo vessel measuring 41.32 m in length, with a 7.05-m beam and 3.07-m draught. Schiffswerft von Henry Koch, Lübeck, Germany built and completed her as Yard No. 107 on 24 January 1899. She was launched on 20 December 1898 for "Vianna" Oldenburg-Portugiesische Dampfs. Rhed. A.G., Oldenburg. The single steel screw was powered by a two-cylinder compound steam engine that used one boiler and gave a service speed of eight knots. The cylinders measured 34.92 cm and 64.13 cm, with a 40-cm stroke (13¾ in. and 25¼ in. with a 15¾-in.

stroke). Ottenser Masch. Fab. J. F. Ahrens, Altona Werft (Shipyard) 11, manufactured the engine and ancillary machinery.

On 1 January 1907 she was registered to G. Kettler Ziegelei. Oldenburger Ziegelverkaufs-verein GmbH, Oldenburg became the registered owner on 7 January 1907. On 9 July 1907 Reederei and Kohlenkontor Oldenburg AG purchased her. The Admiralty seized the vessel at Granton on 4 August 1914 and appointed Everett and Newbiggin, London the Crown nominee manager, which registered her in London.

The *Vianna* was armed for defence with one Mk V stern mounted 3-pounder deck gun. The designated code recognition signal letters were: NGTP.

Final voyage

On 31 March 1918 the *Vianna* was torpedoed by the submerged and unseen SM *UC 64*, a KDM mine-laying submarine, commanded by Oblt.z.S. Ferdinand Schwartz. The steam collier was transporting 360 tons of coal from the Tyne to Ipswich and was reported to have been four miles east of Seaham when the torpedo detonated on the port side against the No. 2 hold. She sank within minutes. Four of her crew of 15, including the first mate, were lost with the ship. The 11 survivors were picked up by a patrol vessel within 15 minutes and landed back at the Tyne. The four crewmen that died were:

Brackenbury, Walter, 51 yrs, 1st Mate MM
Dunton, Herbert George, 36 yrs, Able Seaman MM
Howell, Joseph James, 49 yrs, Donkeyman MM
Rusher, Charles Bonnes, 42 yrs, Able Seaman MM

ADM 137/2964; CWGC; BVLS 1814–1918, p. 85; LCWLR 1914–1918, p. 209; Starke Schell Registers; Jarvis (2000).

Wrecksite

The wreck is orientated in a N to S direction and lies on a seabed of coarse sand, shells, gravel, stones and mud in a general depth of 28 m (LAT). It has totally collapsed onto the seabed except for the bows, which are reasonably intact but beginning to decay and strewn with fishing nets and wires. The engine and boiler stand upright but are visibly exposed and surrounded by a lot of battered steel framework intermingled with long, flattened and twisted pipes and other debris.

LOCH-NA-GAR

Date of Loss: 14 December 1901
Wreck: ✯
Depth: 26 m
Reference: 54 51'.350 N 001 15'.712 W
Location: 2.32 nm ENE from Seaham Harbour North Pier

The *Loch-Na-Gar* (Official No. 44001) was a 467-ton iron dumb barge measuring 49.14 m in length, with a 7.92-m beam and a 4.19-m draught. Pile, Spence and Company (1859–1865), built and launched her as an iron-hulled 464-ton barque at West Hartlepool in 1861 for Lenox Nephew and Company. She had one deck, a 14.63-m quarterdeck and one bulkhead.

In 1875 Park Bros. of London became the owner. Shaw Saville and Company, London became the registered owner in 1898. The designated code recognition signal letters were: TRHJ.

The vessel was converted to a dump barge of 467 tons in 1899/1900.

From 1901 the registered owner was Derwent, E. East Coast Tug Company Middlesbrough-

Final voyage

On 14 December 1901 – one month after the Great Storm of 1901 – the *Loch-Na-Gar* foundered off Seaham Harbour during easterly force 9 winds. All of her crew of six were lost. She had been under tow and carrying burnt ore from King's Lynn to Newcastle.

BoT Wreck Return 1901, p. 110; Lloyds Register 1901/02 No. 433 (L); American Lloyd's Register of American and Foreign Shipping 1857–1900.

Wrecksite

The wreck is orientated in a SSE to NNW direction and lies on a seabed of sand, pebbles, mud and black shells in a general depth of 26 m (LAT). It is generally well broken up, with the highest point being a single-cylinder steam donkey engine standing 2.2 m from the seabed. The wreckage covers an area of 25 m by 20 m. A large strand of trawl net is also floating up to about 10 m above wreck.

MONICA

Date of loss: 14 September 1883
Wreck: ★★★
Depth: 63 m
Reference: 54 52'.184 N 000 53'.906 W
Location: 14.73 nm E by N of Seaham Harbour piers

The *Monica* (Official No. 79621) was an iron-hulled 854-ton British steam cargo vessel measuring 71.73 m in length, with a 9.88-m beam and 5.41-m draught. Austin and Hunter and Company, Wear Dock, Sunderland built and completed her as Yard No. 124 in June 1878. She was launched on 17 June 1878 for Messrs F. Gordon and Stamp of Sunderland, who owned her at the time of loss. The master was Captain Gordon, one of the owners. The single iron screw was powered by a 120-hp two-cylinder compound inverted steam engine that used one boiler. The cylinders measured 73.66 cm and 139.7 cm, with a 91.44-cm stroke (29 in. and 55 in., with a 36-in. stroke). Black, Hawthorn and Company, Sunderland manufactured the machinery. The ship had one deck, five bulkheads, an 18.5-m reinforced quarterdeck, a 12.8m bridge deck and 7.3-m forecastle.

Captain E. Andrews became the master in 1881, Captain Milne in 1882 and 1883, and Captain W. Thacker at the time of loss. She was classed as 100A1. The designated code recognition signal letters were: SHRF.

Final voyage

On 14 September 1883 the *Monica* foundered and was lost following a collision with the 985-ton London-registered steamer *John McIntyre* (1863), which was sailing from London in ballast. The *Monica* was carrying a crew of 17 and a cargo of coal from South Shields to Hamburg via London. At the time of the incident the force 2 wind was blowing easterly and conditions were fine, except for it being dark. The *John McIntyre* rescued the crew. It was found to have had her bows stove in and stern damaged when she arrived at the Tyne on Friday.

Miramar Ship Index; BoT Wreck Return 1883, p. 130 (572); Starke Schell Registers; LR 1881/2, No. 1184 (M); American Lloyd's Register of American and Foreign Shipping, 1857–1900; *The Times*: Monday, 17 September 1883, p. 6, Issue no. 30927.

Wrecksite

The wreck lies on a dirty seabed of fine sand and mud in a general depth of 63 m (LAT). It is partially buried but stands about 3 m high amidships where the boiler, condenser and engine block lie visibly exposed, surrounded by a mass of collapsed, decayed and badly broken up iron plates and flattened machinery. The vessel's bridge equipment is most likely still among the jumble of decayed iron debris and the flattened and bent lead pipes. A few very large fish were picked up on the fishfinder so this wreck should make an excellent boat angling venue.

CREOSOL, Royal Fleet Auxiliary

Date of loss: 7 February 1918
Wreck: ✩✩✩✩✩
Depth: 44 m
Reference: 54 52'.240 N 001 11'.915 W
Location: 4.71 nm NE of Seaham Harbour piers

The RFA Elderol, *sister ship to the 1179-ton RFA OL class tanker* Creosol *which was torpedoed and sunk off Seaham by SM* UC 17 *(Courtesy World Ship Society)*

The RFA *Creosol* (Pennant No. N11; Official No. 139147) was a steel-hulled 1179-ton OL class tanker measuring 64.0 m in length, with a 10.60m beam and a 3.6-m draught. She was one of 18 of this class of Admiralty-designed 1000-ton harbour tankers registered in London. Short Brothers Ltd. Sunderland built and completed her as Yard No. 405. She was launched on 5 February 1916, fitted out at Laing's on the Tyne and completed on 22 August 1916 for the Royal Fleet Auxiliary service. The single screw was driven by an aft-positioned 700 ihp oil powered steam engine with cylindrical boilers and giving 12 knots. She carried 40 tons of fuel oil and used 12 tons per day. The ship also had two masts and one funnel positioned at the stern.

Final voyage

On 7 February 1918 the *Creosol* was torpedoed and sunk off Seaham by the KDM mine-laying submarine SMU *UC 17*, commanded by Oblt.z.S. Ulrich Pilzecker. There is very little information available about the vessel's crew and cargo as information about the ship is rather vague. It is known, however, that two of her 19 crew were lost:

William Brocklehirst, 19 yrs, scullion Merchant Marine Reserve
Michael Walsh, 37 yrs, leading fireman MMR.

CWGC; Starke Schell Registers; Miramar Ship Index; *Jane's Fighting Ships of WWI*; Jarvis & Jarvis (1996).

Wrecksite

Apparently the wreck of *Creosol* is also registered under the Protection of Military Remains Act 1986, meaning there is a look-but-don't-touch policy in force. Divers may visit but not enter this wreck, interfere or remove items without permission. Anyone knowingly allowing or assisting a diver in committing any such illegal activity will be committing an offence. The law does apply to dive boat skippers and dive schools or clubs.

The wreck is lying on a seabed of fine sand, gravel, black shells and mud in a general depth of 41 m (LAT). It is very substantial and intact, standing up to 8 m in height, with the bows and stern facing N to S. It would seem no expense was spared in the building of the vessel as most of the machinery, fittings and instruments are made of copper or brass. The bridge structure is gone from the bows and the accommodation has collapsed, but much of the vessel is still largely intact with a walkway down the centre and lots of pipe work showing. Looking into the wheelhouse divers report it as an Aladdin's cave, with brass instruments, including clocks and gauges, everywhere. The wheelhouse navigational equipment is still there, including the ornate solid brass pedestal-mounted telegraph, the compass binnacle and the brass pedestal-mounted steering helm – complete with the remains of half of the wooden wheel.

In the bow section a cabin can be seen which contains dozens of beautiful three-sided, glass hand-held brass oil lamps, all complete with the glass still intact. The lamps were probably used to inspect the various gloomy parts of the ship.

The bronze screw and hydraulic steering is still in place. The wreck, which is awesome in its size, is covered in an array of colourful anemones and soft corals. Two trawl nets are entangled on it. Large cod and ling have been observed around the wreck.

INTENT (?)

Date of loss: 7 March 1918
Wreck: ★★★★
Depth: 40 m
Reference: 54 52'.332 N 001 12'.901 W
Location: 4.19 nm NE of Seaham Harbour piers

The *Intent* (Official No. 132057) was a steel-hulled 1564-ton British steam cargo ship measuring 74.37 m in length, with an 11.45-m beam and a 4.9–m draught. William Pickersgill and Sons Ltd. at Southwick, Sunderland built and completed her as Yard No. 170 in February 1911. She was launched on 31 January 1911 for James Westoll, Sunderland who owned her at the time of loss. The single steel screw was powered by a 197 nhp three-cylinder triple expansion steam engine that used two boilers. G. Clark Ltd. at Sunderland manufactured the engine and ancillary machinery. She had one deck, four bulkheads, a 6.1-mpoop deck, 19.8-m quarterdeck, 15.2-m bridge deck and a 7.6 m forecastle.

On 8 September 1917 the *Intent* was involved in a collision with the 1472-ton steamer *Hockwold* (1911: Cory Colliers Ltd. London), which sank 6.5 miles west by south of the Lizard. The *Hockwold* had been voyaging from Penarth to Dover with Admiralty coal.

Final voyage

On 7 March 1918 the *Intent* (Captain W.H. Wood) was torpedoed and sunk by the submerged KDM mine-laying submarine SMU *UC 40*, commanded by Oblt.z.S. Hermann Menzel. The steamer was in ballast and on passage from Sheerness for the Tyne. The crewmen had sighted the U-boat's periscope just before the torpedo detonated in the engine room at 0730 hrs, killing the second engineer, Thomas William Morgan, who was on duty at the time. The 21 survivors mustered on deck and abandoned the vessel in their boats.

Captain Wood disposed of confidential papers and a wartime codebook by sinking them in order to prevent them falling into the hands of the enemy. The crew watched from the boats as the ship sank beneath the surface just 15 minutes after being attacked.

ADM 137/2964; LCWLR 1914–1918, p. 208; Starke Schell Registers; BVLS 1914–1918, p. 83; LR 1915/16, No. 286 (I); Jarvis (2000); CWGC.

Wrecksite

The wreck – possibly that of the *Intent* – lies on a seabed of fine sand, broken shell, mud and gravel in a general depth of 40 m (LAT). It is very substantial, standing upright, reasonably intact and 7 m high around the area of the partially collapsed bridge structure. Its two boilers and engine are rather exposed. The main outline of the wreck can still be made out. The bow section seems reasonably intact and is adorned with soft corals, however, the rest of the vessel is totally collapsed and lying in a large mound of debris. Masses of rusting anchor chain, the large anchor and windlass are lying close to a huge winch just aft of the bows. A lot of fish frequent the wreck which ought to make a good boat angling venue.

ELFI, EX JOHANNA

Date of loss: 7 February 1918
Wreck: ★★★
Depth: 36 m
Reference: 54 52'.666 N 001 14'.136 W
Location: 4.8 nm SE of Roker light

The *Elfi* was a steel-hulled 1128-ton Norwegian steam cargo vessel measuring 70.2 m in length, with a 10.41-m beam and a 4.16-m draught. Rotterdam Droogdok Maats., built and completed her as Yard No. 12 in February 1908. She was launched as the *Johanna* on 16 January 1908 and registered in Rotterdam for N.V. Mij. S.S. Johanna Rotterdam, with J. de Poorter the manager. The single steel screw was powered by an aft-positioned 147 nhp three-cylinder triple expansion steam engine that used one boiler. She had one deck, a well deck, four bulkheads and an aft superstructure, comprised of a 39-m quarterdeck, a 3.9 m-bridge deck and 7.6-m forecastle.

In 1915 she was renamed *Elfi* by new owners Hannevig Brothers, Kristiania (Oslo) Norway and registered in Kristiania.

From 1916 A/S Thor O. Hannevigs D/S, Kristiania was the registered owner and T.O. Hannevig and Company was the manager. The designated code recognition signal letters were: MPLH.

Final voyage

The KDM mine-laying submarine SMU *UC 17*, commanded by Oblt.z.S. Erich Stephan, torpedoed the *Elfi* (Captain Thorbjørn Thorbjørnsen) on 7 February1918. The *Elfi* was reported as being 2.5 miles SE of Sunderland. She was carrying crew of 16 and a cargo of coal from Jarrow to Rouen. The torpedo detonated in the engine room and she sank quickly. Six men were rescued by means of the lifefloat. Four men jumped into the sea. They were were all rescued by a British patrol boat and landed at Sunderland. Six men were killed, most likely in the explosion:

Carlsen, Anders, 24 yrs, Stoker, Copenhagen, Denmark
Christiansen, Hartvig, 41 yrs, 1st Engineer, Kristiania (Oslo), Norway
Johanson, Jens, 27 yrs, Stoker, Luleå, Sweden
Martinsen, Harald, 21 yrs, Donkeyman, Kristiania
Pedersen, Peder, 51 yrs, Cook, Odense, Denmark (lived in Cardiff)
Sæthre, Mads, 63 yrs, 2nd Engineer, from Bergen, Norway

The *Elfi* was covered under war risk insurance for 1,900,000 Norwegian kroner (NOK) and was sailing on the owners' account. However, only 950,000 NOK was paid out by the insurance company.

Maritime Accident Statements for Norwegian Ships Sunk in Wartime: 1814–1918; Starke Schell Registers; LCWLR 1914–1918, p. 200; ANCL 1914–1918, p. 81.

Wrecksite

The *Elfi* was alleged to have been sunk 2.5 miles SE of Sunderland but no wreck can be found anywhere near this position. This wreck is much further out to sea but it could be that of the Norwegian steamer. It is orientated in a NNE to SSW direction and lies on a seabed of sand, mud, stones and shell in a general depth of 36 m (LAT). The wreck is partially collapsed and covers an area 70 by 19 m, with the highest sections being at the bow and stern. The stern stands about 7 m high. A lot of fish have been observed over the bows and stern end, so this should make an interesting boat angling venue.

KING JAMES (?)

Date of Loss: 31 July 1916
Wreck: ✯✯✯
Depth: 68 m
Reference: 54 53'.244 N 000 58'.901 W
Location: 12.93 nm ESE of the Roker light

The *King James* (Official No. 13213) was a steel-hulled 163-ton British steam trawler measuring 43.13 m in length, with a 6.42-m beam and a 3.22-m draught. Schofield, Hagerup and Doughty Ltd. at Grimsby built and completed her as Yard No. 13 in November 1900. She was launched on 11 August 1900 for Consolidated Steam Fishing and Ice Company Grimsby. The single screw was powered by a 40 hp, three-cylinder triple expansion steam engine that used one boiler. Muir and Houston at Glasgow manufactured the machinery. The *King James* had one deck, three bulkheads, a 5.48-m quarterdeck and 6.40 m forecastle. She was classed as 100 A1.

Final voyage

On 31 July 1916 the *King James* was on a return fishing voyage from the Faroe Islands to her home port of Grimsby when she was captured by SMU *UB 39*, a KDM submarine commanded by Obl.t.z.S.Fürbringer (see page 87). The crew was ordered to abandon ship. The Germans sank her using explosive scuttling charges.

That same day *UB 39* also captured and sank the steam trawlers *Tatiana* (see page 105) and *Braconash* (see page 112) off coast of Durham. The crew of the *King James* – unlike the crews of the *Tatiana* and the *Braconash* – was allowed to get away in their boat. They landed at a north-east port.

BVLS 1914–1918, p. 110; LGWLR 1914–1918, p. 49; LR 1914/15, No. 516 (K); *The Times*: Wednesday, 2 August 1916, p. 3, Issue no. 41235.

Wrecksite

The wreck – possibly that of the *King James* – is orientated in a SE to NW direction. It sits in a 0.5 m scour and lies on a seabed of mud, fine sand and black shells in a general depth of 68 m (LAT). It is partially buried, well broken up, stands over 3 m high and covers an area of 32 m by 19 m. The outline of the wreck is still clearly defined, though most of it is a mass of broken machinery, with the boiler and engine exposed. Very little marine life can be seen.

GATESHEAD, ex WILHELMINAPOLDER, ex GOUWZEE

Date of loss: 21 December 1932
Wreck: ✯✯✯✯
Depth: 57 m
Reference: 54 53'.673 N 001 05'.349 W
Location: 9.24 nm ESE of Roker light, Sunderland

Far left: Capt Hall as a young seaman on the yacht owned by Mr Tree with one of the Russian bears (Courtesy of John King)

Left: Captain Hall of the SS Gateshead *with his wife Florence and daughter Edith, aged four, c.1919 (Courtesy John King)*

Left: Captain Hall's grave in the churchyard at Reighton, East Yorkshire. Apparently his wife tried to have the body exhumed and returned to North Shields but this was refused (Courtesy of John King)

Right: New engine being lowered into the Gateshead (Courtesy of John King)

The *Gateshead* (Official No. 149486) was a steel-hulled 731-ton British steam cargo vessel measuring 55.32 m in length, with an 8.58-m beam and a 3.73-m draught. Gebr. Bodewes Bros at Lobith, the Netherlands built and completed her as Yard No. 183 in March 1917 and launched her as the *Gouwzee* for N.V. S.S Gouwzee, Rotterdam where she was registered. N.V. W. van Driel's Stoomboot and Transport Ond was the manager. The single steel screw was powered by an 82 rhp, three-cylinder triple expansion steam engine that used one boiler and gave nine knots. The cylinders measured 38.1 cm, 60.96 cm and 99.06 cm with a 66.04 cm stroke (15 in., 24 in. and 39 in. with a 26-in. stroke). Verschure and Company, Amsterdam manufactured the engine and ancillary machinery. The *Gateshead* had one deck, three steel masts and a very small superstructure.

In 1918 N.V. Algemeene Nederlandsche Scheepvaart Mij,. in Rotterdam, purchased and renamed her *Wilhelminapolder*. Cornelder's Scheepv. Mij. N.V. was the manager.

She was sold to N.V. Stoomv. Mij. "Westpolder", Rotterdam in 1923, using the same manager.

From 1928 Tyne-Tees Steam Shipping Co., Ltd., Newcastle upon Tyne was the registered owner and renamed her *Gateshead*.

Final voyage

Just before 0300 hrs on 21 December 1932 the *Gateshead* foundered and was lost following a collision with the 1328-ton Norwegian SS *Miranda* (1920: D/S A/S Miranda, Bergen) in dense fog eight miles north-east of Seaham Harbour. The *Gateshead* had left Pelaw in Gateshead just after midnight on a voyage from Newcastle upon Tyne to Amsterdam with coal and a general cargo. The *Gateshead* was struck amidships on the port side and she sank two minutes after the collision. Several men were in their bunks. When they heard the captain shout 'lower the boats', they ran on deck. Most of the crew plunged into the sea from the bridge and, although a lifeboat was lowered from the *Miranda*, only five survivors were picked up by the *Miranda*, which was *en route* for the Tyne. After taking the rescuees on board, the *Miranda*'s lifeboat cruised around for about three hours trying to find the *Gateshead*'s missing crew, but without success. The survivors were landed at South Shields. Eight crewmen perished, including the captain.

Gray, R. 2nd Engineer MM, Newcastle
Hall, M.W. Master MM, North Shields
Longstaffe, H. Able Seaman MM, Newcastle
McCan, A. 2nd Mate MM, Felling
Pattinson, E. Chief Engineer MM, Low Fell
Scorer, C. Fireman MM, South Shields
Towns, E.T. Able Seaman MM, Gateshead
Turnbull, N. Fireman MM, Newcastle

Mr T.H. Hewitt of Wallsend said: 'I was at the wheel when it happened. I saw the ship move towards us out of the fog, but before anything could be done, it struck us in the stokehold. Our captain gave orders for the lifeboats to be lowered, but the sea was rushing along the deck and the ship was already sinking stern first. She went down in two minutes ... The thick fog and a swell on the sea made it very difficult for the rescuers to locate the Gateshead's crew, while they were struggling in the water. The survivors lost all their gear and money and all the Christmas fare which they had taken with them.'

Able Seaman John Bell reported: 'In recent weeks the mate had been particularly strict about the men keeping their lifebelts in their bunks. It was lucky he was so strict, otherwise none of us would have been saved.' One of the seaman was without his lifejacket so Captain Hall apparently gave him his own. That was the last time he was seen. His body was washed up at Flamborough Head in February 1933. The body was wearing an officer's uniform, and from his clothing he was later identified by laundry marks on his underwear and a pair of cuff links which had been a present from his wife.

LR 1931/2, No. 21565 (G); Starke Schell Registers; LCR 1932, p. 9 (f); BoT Wreck Return 1933; The Times: Thursday, 22 December 1932, p. 14, Issue no. 46323.

Born on 9 November 1888 Captain Matthew William Hall was in command of the 1134-ton steamer *Teesider* (1909: Tyne-Tees Steam Shipping Company, Stockton) when he was involved in a dramatic rescue in November 1927. He rescued the crew from the schooner *Gauntlet* off Flamborough Head. His skill and courage attracted the attention of the shipping community.

The *Gauntlet* had been on passage from Charlestown, Cornwall for Kirkaldy with a cargo of clay and got into difficulties during a heavy storm off Flamborough Head. Water was flooding into the vessel and her crew manned the pumps for 28 hours, but she was foundering. Distress signals were sent out and the *Teessider* responded and stood by for three hours. Captain Hall twice manoeuvered his ship to within a few feet of the schooner to enable his men to throw lines aboard, however the *Gauntlet's* crew were too exhausted to catch them. Eventually, after a tremendous struggle, Captain Hall managed to transfer the men to his own ship via a lifeboat. A long line attached the boat and it was floated over to the schooner. Only one of the four men on board the *Gauntlet* had enough strength left to jump into the boat. He dragged his comrades in, after which the lifeboat was hauled back to the steamer. Captain Hall was awarded the Royal Humane Society's bronze medal and certificate – signed by the Prince of Wales – and an inscribed silver cup from the Board of Trade.

On another occasion, in Antwerp, Captain Hall's ship was boarded at night by a group of men. They pumped some type of narcotic gas into the ship's ventilation system and the whole crew were put to sleep. The intruders raided the ship but only got away with its papers. The Belgian port police arrested them and everything was recovered.

Even before he was 20 years old Matthew William Hall had saved several people from drowning.

Wrecksite

The wreck – most likely that of the *Gateshead* – is orientated in a SE to NW direction. It sits in a half-metre scour and lies on a seabed of dirty fine sand, mud and broken shells in a general depth of 57 m (LAT). The wreck is intact and covers an area of 54 m by 7 m but much of it is covered in sediment. The highest part stands almost 10 m but the UK Hydrographic report states that it could be part of a mast. This should make quite an interesting boat-angling venue.

STAG (5), ex WELLINGTON

Date of loss: 11 February 1950
Wreck: ★★★★
Depth: 50 m
Reference: 54 56'.261 N 001 10'.879 W
Location: 5.89 nm ENE of Roker light

The *Stag (5)* (Official No. 106863) was a steel-hulled 148-ton British steam tug measuring 28 m in length, with a 6.1-m beam and a draught of 3.2 m. B. Cummings and Ellis, at Inverkeithing built and completed her in 1897. She was launched as the *Wellington* for the Alexandra Towing Company. The single screw was powered by an 84 rhp two-cylinder compound steam engine that used one boiler. The cylinders measured 53.34 cm and 106.68 cm, with a 68.58-cm stroke (21 in. and 42 in., with a 27-inch stroke). J. Cran and Company at Leith manufactured the machinery. She had one steel deck.

R.L. Cook Towage Company, Sunderland purchased the tug in 1924 and renamed it *Stag*, R.L.G. Baister was the manager.

The 148-ton France, Fenwick Tyne and Wear Company tug Stag (5) *towing a full-rigged sailing ship down the river Wear, in the early 1900s (Courtesy Joseph Coatsworth)*

During the last months of the Second World War, *STAG (5)* was on charter to France, Fenwick Tyne and Wear Company and operated on the river Tyne. She retained her white funnel with red star colour scheme of the previous company.

In November 1947 R.L. Cook Towage Company Ltd. was taken over by France, Fenwick Tyne and Wear Company Ltd and the *Stag (5)* was transferred with the business of R.L Cook Towage Co. Ltd., along with another tug, *Snowdon*.

Final voyage

On 11 February 1950 *Stag (5)* was assisting six other tugs with the towing of a newly built 7585-ton steamship, *City Of Manchester*, which had just had her new turbines fitted at Wallsend and was being returned to her shipbuilder's yard on the river Wear. The *Stag (5)* and the steam tug *Fulwell* (Skipper Tommy Tim) were towing at the bows of the 'dead' steamer – meaning her own engine was not operating. A strong force 8 westerly gale was blowing and it was reported that by the time the vessels had reached the halfway stage of the voyage, the tow was yawing from side to side, making the tow extremely difficult to manage. As the wind whipped up the sea the steamer was driven sideways and the *Stag (5)* was pulled over and sank.

Four of her crew of six drowned. They were all from Sunderland:

William Brown, 40 yrs, mate, from Harold Street, Hendon
Allex Mollinson, 48 yrs, engineman, George Street
John William Noble, 23 yrs, deckhand, Havelock Street
Ronald Wigham, 17 yrs, deckhand, Waterworks Road.

Some local people alleged that the tow ropes parted in the strong wind and the *City Of Manchester* was quickly blown out to sea, with the tugs trying desperately to make contact. The Volunteer Life Brigade (VLB) were called, but were helpless as the vessels disappeared out of view. At 1430 hrs, the VLB was informed that the *Stag (5)* had been pulled under and was lost with four men.

The tug skipper Ernest Theodore Cook Baister and fireman George Brown were rescued and after treatment for shock at Sunderland Royal Infirmary were allowed to go home. A Sunderland lifeboat spent five hours searching unsuccessfully for the missing men before returning to her berth that night.

Exactly one year after the event, a memorial service was held over the site of the tragedy on board the company's steel 166-ton steam paddle tug *Eppleton Hall.*

In October 1950 France, Fenwick Tyne and Wear Company Ltd. introduced the first diesel-powered tugs when they purchased two ex-American army tugs, powered by 8-cylinder General Motors engines delivering 700 bhp and capable of 14 knots.

The iron 106-ton steam paddle tug *Snowdon* went to the breakers yard in 1950. The steam paddle tug *Eppleton Hall* was sold to Seaham Harbour Dock Company, which kept her until November 1967, after which she was sold to Clayton and Davie Ltd. at Dunston for demolition. After having most of her wood burnt out she was purchased from the breakers by Scott Newhall – the editor of the *San Francisco Chronicle* – and the trustees of the San Francisco Maritime Museum for £2,500 in May 1969. She was rebuilt to her original 1914 appearance, registered in San Francisco and sent to the USA via Dover, Lisbon, Madeira, St Vincent in the Cape Verde Islands and on across the south Atlantic, where she arrived in Georgetown in Guyana. After spending Christmas in Trinidad she went on through the Panama Canal to San Diego and eventually reached her destination on 23 March. The tug was put on display at the San Francisco Maritime Museum where she remains to this day.

During that epic six-month voyage the boat was manned by a volunteer crew of eleven, including three young girls.

In 1977 – with the severe decline in shipbuilding and like most of the other tug companies on the rivers Tyne, Wear and Tees – France, Fenwick Tyne and Wear Company Ltd. ceased to exist after 59 years of service.

BoT Wreck Return 1950; Hydrographic Wk No. 5679; *The Times*, Monday, 13 February 1950, p. 6, Issue no. 51614.

Wrecksite

The wreck of the tug *Stag (5)* was thought to be the tug wreck at 54 53' .873 N 001 08' .215 W, but in September 2010, divers from Allan Lopez's Charter boat Spellbinder, found the *Stag (5)* a little futher north. This wreck is upright, clean, totally intact and in excellent condition. It stands 8-metres high and is 34-metres in length by 5-metres across. All of the bridge machinery and instruments were intact and appear to have just sunk recently.

DAFNI, EX VAZIRIANDJIKIS, EX BERYL

Date of loss: 16 December 1917
Wreck: ✯✯✯✯
Depth: 38 m
Reference: 54 54'.124 N 001 14'.819 W
Location: 3.82 nm SE from Roker light

The *Dafni* was an iron-hulled 1190-ton Greek steam cargo ship measuring 71.32 m in length, with a 9.75-m beam and a 4.57-m draught. W.B. Thompson, Dundee built and completed her as Yard No. 35 in 1881. She was launched as the schooner-rigged *Beryl* (Official No. 82740) on 16 February 1881 for P.M. Duncan of Dundee. Captain J. Campbell was the master. The single iron screw was powered by a two-cylinder compound steam engine that used one boiler. The cylinders measured 68.58 cm and 137.16 cm, with a 91.44-cm stroke (27 in. and 54 in. with a 36-in. stroke). She had one deck, five bulkheads and water ballast.

In 1884 Dundee Gem Line S.S. Company Ltd. Dundee became registered owner; P.M. Duncan and Son was manager. In 1910 she was renamed *Vaziriandjikis* by the new owner S. Perris, of Piraeus, Greece. In 1913 C. Bataki of Galatz in Roumania purchased her and C. Vaziryandjikis and Company was appointed the manager. In 1915 she was sold again, this time being purchased by Pandelis Brothers in Piraeus and renamed *Dafni*. Pandelis Brothers owner her at the time of loss.

Final voyage

On 16 December 1917 the *Dafni* (Captain C. Vldstaris), three miles NNE from The Heugh, Hartlepool, was torpedoed without warning and sunk by Oblt.z.S. Hellmuth von Ruckteschell in the KDM submarine *UB 34*. The *Dafni* had been on passage from Rouen for Sunderland in ballast.

LCWLR 1914–1918, p. 190; ANCL 1914–1918, p. 26; LR 1914/15, No. 21 (D).

Wrecksite

The wreck – probably that of the *Dafni* – is orientated in an E to W direction. It lies on a seabed of gravel, mud, sand and shells in a general depth of 38 m (LAT). The wreck is fairly intact, probably on its side, with the highest points about 5.8 m at the bow and stern ends. The remains cover an area of about 77 m by 20 m. A large shoal of small pout whiting has adopted the upper sections of the wreck and soft corals are everywhere.

SAMSÖ, EX DRONNINGEN

Date of loss: 1 May 1918
Wreck: ✯✯
Depth: 35 m
Reference: 54 54'.492 N 001 15'.598 W
Location: 3.26 nm ESE of Roker light

The *Samsö* was an iron-hulled 371-ton Danish motor vessel measuring 54.62 m in length, with a 6.79-m beam and 3.13-m draught. Sir Raylton Dixon and Company, Middlesbrough built and completed her as Yard No. 125. She was launched on 4 April 1876 as the passenger paddle steamer *Dronningen* for I/S Dampsk. Selsk. Dronningen, Kristiansand, Norway. Hans G. Kirsebom was manager. The two side paddles were powered by a diagonal, two-cylinder compound steam engine that used one boiler.

In June 1888 Det Forenede Dampskibs Selskab, Aarhus purchased the vessel. From September 1916 the registered owner was Aktieselskabet Dansk Gemyse- and Kartoffele-ksport, Copenhagen and E. Holm was the manager. She was converted to a twin screw aft-positioned diesel motor cargo vessel of 324 gross tons and renamed *Samsö* (*Samsoe*). She had a stern bridge superstructure and foreward hold.

On 21 July 1916 the *Samsö* was transporting timber from Halmstad, Sweden to Hull. She was attacked with gunfire from *UB 37*, 30 miles ENE from the Tyne. The *Samsö* remained afloat and was towed to the Tyne on the 22nd. She had been. The designated code recognition signal letters were: NWPQ.

Final voyage

On 1 May 1918 the *Samsö* (Captain Marius Niels Svarre) detonated a mine laid by the KDM submarine SMU *UC 49*, commanded by Oblt.z.S. Hans Kükenthal.

The *Samsö* had been waiting to join a convoy at the Tyne, having left Aarhus for London with a crew of 12 and a cargo of 180 tons of mechanical parts. The master had asked for a pilot and one was agreed but he didn't show up for the convoy's departure time of 0215 hrs. At around 1600 hrs the ship steamed out of the Tyne and caught up with the convoy, which started moving south. At about 1700 hrs there was a massive explosion and by the time the third engineer had rushed up from the engine room aft, the stern end of the ship was the only part above water. Captain Svarre (born 10 June 1878) later confirmed in court that the ship was part of a great convoy, and that those on the bridge had been speaking about a big ship outside of the convoy, that had given several warnings with her whistle. In response, three or four aeroplanes were directed towards that ship, but in that same moment the explosion occurred on the *Samsö*.

Shortly after the explosion a patrol boat arrived rescuing three of the men: the captain, third engineer, K. Billing, and ordinary seaman, E. Rasmussen.

The captain explained in court that the ship didn't have the word *DANMARK* written on it, or the Danish national flag' painted on her sides, as they had been to France on their last voyage. The French Authorities, for their own reasons, would not allow these to be painted on the ship's hull. However, no one had bothered to paint them on after leaving France.

Information extracted from the official hearings at Newcastle upon Tyne and Copenhagen in 1918; Starke Schell Registers; LCWLR 1914–1918, p. 247; American Lloyd's Register of American and Foreign Shipping, 1857–1900.

Wrecksite

The wreck, most likely that of the *Samsö*, lies on a seabed of mud, fine sand, gravel and broken shells in a general depth of 35 m (LAT). It covers an area of 68 m by 40 m and is broken up in two main sections, the highest part standing 2.7 m from the seabed. The wreck looks like a motorised barge with two shafts, and matches the specifications of the *Samsö*. If the bell is recovered it should be inscribed: *Dronningen 1876*. There is very little marine life around the wreck, which is covered in sediment.

GRAN

Date of loss: 23 May 1917
Wreck: ✭✭
Depth: 11 m and 13 m
Reference: 54 53'.871 N 001 19'.512 W
Location: 1.5 miles SE of river Wear

On 23 May 1917 the 1153-ton Norwegian Gran *detonated a mine off Ryhope, Sunderland (Courtesy Rolf Kristensen and Stein-Erik Dagsland)*

The *Gran* was a steel-hulled 1153-ton Norwegian steam cargo ship measuring 69.82 m in length, a 10.69-m beam and 4.8-m draught. Bergens Mekaniske Verksteder, Bergen built and completed her as Yard No. 144 in July 1907. They also manufactured the engine and ancillary machinery. She was owned by Aktieselskapet "Gran", Lyngør and registered in Lyngør. B.A. Olsen and Søn was the manager. The single steel screw was powered by a 106--nhp three-cylinder triple expansion steam engine that used one boiler. The cylinders measured 41.91 cm, 66.04 cm and 111.76 cm, with a 76.2 cm (16½ in., 26 in. and 44 in. with a 30-in. stroke). She had one deck, deep framing and a 43-ton (121.78-cubic.m) poop deck, a 23-ton (65.12-cubic.m) deck house and 34-ton (96.27-cubic.m) forecastle.

Wm. Kallevig, Arendal became purchased her in 1916. The designated code recognition signal letters were: MDLG.

Later that yeat, Aktieselskapet Dampskipsselskapet "Gran", Bergen became the registered owner; Alme and Christie was the manager.

From 1916, Agdesidens Rederi Aktieselskapet, Arendal was the registered owner; Wilson and Mørland was the manager.

Final voyage

On 23 May 1917 the *Gran*, with 28-year-old Captain Finn Larsen in charge, detonated a mine one mile off Ryhope, Sunderland. The KDM submarine SMU *UC 40*, commanded by Oblt.z.S.Gustav Deuerlich, had laid the mine on 3 April 1917. The steamer was blown in two by the explosion. The halves sank about 200 metres apart, just off the northern end of the White Stones Rocks and about half a mile from shore.

The ship was in ballast and carrying a crew of 16 on passage from Rouen for Newcastle. One man was killed in the explosion. A patrol boat rescued one man, while the rest were picked up by various other vessels.

This ship was insured against war risks on the London market for a total sum of 960,000 Danish kroners (DKK). The man who died was Ernst Nielsen, a sailor from Verløse in Denmark.

Maritime Accident Statements for Norwegian Ships Sunk in Wartime: 1814–1918; Starke Schell Registers; LCWLR, p. 136.

Wrecksite

The stern section of the wreck, with the boiler, a steel screw, two large winches and the remains of the engine, lies to the southern end in a general depth of 13 m. The remains are scattered and well concreted into the seabed with hard, white marine worm casings covering the few remaining pipes and plates. The surrounding rocks and seabed appear to be rather void of visible forms of marine life. During the summer, pollack shoals can be seen all around this area and it is popular with local angling boats. The stern section of the wreck was professionally salvaged, so there are very few, if any, items of interest.

The rest of the wreck – the bow section and decking – accounts for two thirds of the ship and lies approximately 200 m NW of the boiler/engine, in a general depth of 11 m to 13 m (LAT). There are some huge boulder-type reefs, just to the SE of it, which gives misleading information on the echosounder. The wreck lies up against the base of the reef on flat rocky ground and is orientated in a south-west to north-east direction. The flat steel decking makes up 70% of the wreck and lies more or less flush with the seabed. There are still a few large brass valves still bolted onto the decking. At the head of the flat decking is what appears to have been the wheelhouse, which is the highest structure left. There are no visible signs of any brass artefacts around, but the author did find the clapper of the ship's bell, which must lie under the surrounding pile of debris. You can see into the 'wheelhouse', but it would be impossible to enter due to the twisted steel plates and girders, and the very narrow entrance. The most interesting spot to explore is between the two sections, though there is still nothing to get too excited about.

DENHAM

Date of loss; 22 February 1894
Wreck: ★★
Depth: 48 m
Reference: 54 53'.423 N 001 08'.649 W
Location: 6.9 nm NE of Seaham Harbour piers

The *Denham* (Official No. 76234) was an iron-hulled 869-ton British steam cargo vessel measuring 64 m in length, with a 9.19-m-beam and a 4.87-m draught. Wigham, Richardson Ltd. at Newcastle built and completed as Yard No. 107 in 1878 for Burradon and Coxlodge Coal Company, Newcastle. John H. Reah, Newcastle was the manager. The single iron screw was powered by a 98-nhp two-cylinder compound steam engine that used one single-ended boiler. J. Shaw and Company, Newcastle manufactured the engine and ancillary machinery. The cylinders measured 68.58 cm and 127 cm, with an 83.82-cm stroke (27 in. and 50 in. with a 33 in stroke). She had one deck, four bulkheads, a 6.7-m poop deck, 11.9-m bridge deck and 7.9-m forecastle. In 1879 John He. Reah and nine other people became owners.

Under the command of John William Lambert the *Denham* sailed from Riga, Latvia on 19 August 1880, bound for South Alloa, Falkirk with a cargo of railway sleepers and carrying a crew of 17. The captain was called by his wife (who was onboard the ship) at 1645hrs When he got on to the bridge he found his vessel aground with the engines going full speed astern. Salfer Ort light was plainly visible, bearing NNE at a distance of about 5.5 miles.

The after tank was emptied and the deck cargo removed from the fore of aft. The fore deck cargo was also jettisoned and the fore hatch emptied until it was flush with the deck. A small sailing craft assisted in getting a bower anchor out on each quarter. When the wind gained strength, the crew of the *Denham* pulled on the cable chains and kedges and sent the engines full speed astern. The vessel came off at 2130 hrs on the 20th. The vessel was then taken to a safe anchorage before going on to South Alloa where it discharged the cargo and continued on the Tyne for repairs.

From 1886 the registered owner was John H. Reah of Newcastle.

Final voyage

Early in the morning of 22 February 1894 the *Denham*, commanded by Captain John William Lambert left the Tyne for Rochester. It foundered following a collision with the 1103-ton Danish steamer *Rolf* (1870 – Dampsk. Selsk. Danmark, Copenhagen) – which was bound for Blyth – and was lost six miles NE of Seaham Harbour. The *Denham* was carrying a cargo of coal and a crew of 17. The crew were taken on board the *Rolf* and landed at North Shields.

American Lloyd's Register of American and Foreign Shipping, 1857–1900; LR 1887/8, No. 157 (D); BoT Wreck Return 1894, p. 152; Starke Schell Registers; BoT Wreck Return: Denham, 1881; *The Times*: Friday, 23 February 1894, p. 8, Issue no. 34195.

Wrecksite

The wreck – most likely that of the *Denham* – lies on a seabed of fine sand, mud, gravel and broken shell in a general depth of 48 m (LAT). It is partially buried and covers an area of 64 m by 20 m, standing 2 m high. What remains is covered in a layer of marine worm casings. Items of interest ought to be somewhere in the wreck, but much is now concreted debris.

LONCLARA, EX PORT OF LONDON AUTHORITY

Date of loss: 4 January 1917
Wreck: ★★★
Depth: 16 m
Reference: 54 54'.027 N 001 19'.395 W
Location: 1.5 nm SSE of Wear South Pier light and 1 nm ESE of old South Dock entrance

The *Lonclara* (Official No. 132641) was a steel-hulled 1126-ton steam powered mud hopper measuring 65.53 m in length, with a 10.82-m beam. Ropner and Sons, Ltd. Middlesbrough built and completed her as Yard No. 463 in November 1911. She was launched as *Port Of*

London Authority Hoppper No. 20 on 20 October 1911 for the Port of London Authority. The single screw was powered by a 1500-ihp three-cylinder triple expansion steam engine that used one boiler. In 1916 she was renamed *Lonclara* and temporarily fitted out for cargo service.

Final voyage

The *Lonclara* detonated a mine off the river Wear on 4 January 1917 and sank with the loss of four crewmen:

William John Kennedy, 50 yrs, 1st Engineer MM
John Palmer, Able Seaman MM
George William Wells, 56 yrs, 1st Mate MM
William Robert Young, 28 yrs, Steward MM. T

The KDM submarine SMU UC 31, commanded by Kapitanleutnant Otto von Schrader, had laid the mine on 30 December 1916.

Starke Schell Registers; CWGC; Jarvis & Jarvis (1993); LCWLR 1914–1918, p. 83.

Wrecksite

The wreck was located during a survey in 1999. It is orientated in a SE to NW direction and lies on a seabed of silty sand and rocks, in a general depth of 16 m (LAT). It is upright, broken into three main sections and stands 5 m high. When divers first visited it, in 2002, huge heavy copper pipes were all over the wreck site. The following year the wreck was identified when a diver located the bell. During the summer months, shoals of pollock gather around the wreckage.

BALZAC

Date of loss: 26 July 1940
Wreck: ★★★
Depth: 16–17 m
Reference: 54 54'.521 N 001 19'.320 W
Second half: 54 54'.510 N 001 19'.621 W
Location: 1.2 nm SE of Roker light

The *Balzac* (Official No. 143619) was a steel-hulled 962-ton Norwegian motor cargo vessel, registered in Oslo. It measured 65.53-m in length, a 10.5-m beam and a 3.88-m draught. Odense Staalskibsvaerft, Odense built and completed her as Yard No. 9 in December 1921; she was launched on 30 August 1921 for Aktieselskapet Granger Rolf, Kristiania and Fred Olsen and Company was the manager. The single steel screw was powered by a 225-hp, 4-stroke single acting 6-cylinder oil/diesel engine. Akt Burmeistr and Wain of Copenhagen manufactured the aft machinery. She had one steel deck, water ballast, a 42-m poop deck and 9.4-m forecastle. She was also fitted with electric lighting and wireless. The designated code recognition signal letters were: LOKG.

Left: The 962-ton motor vessel Balzac *mined and sunk off Sunderland during the Second World War (Courtesy Thorbjørn Andersen, Norwegian Seamen's Association, Lillesand, Norway)*

Right: Balzac *(Courtesy Norwegian Maritime Museum)*

On 18 January 1940, the *Balzac* rescued four survivors from a raft belonging to the 1193-ton Swedish *Flandria* (1898 – Förnyade Ångfartygs A/B Gotha, Götebor), which had been sunk by the Kriegsmarine submarine *U 9* (Oblt.z.S. Wolfgang Lüth (Knight's Cross), 95 miles off Ymuiden at position 54° 00'N 03° 40'E. The men had been on the raft for about 48 hours before they were picked up.

On another voyage, the *Balzac* ran aground in the Minches when part of convoy NS 2 (Clyde – Narvik) bound for Narvik in northwest Norway on the night leading up to 6 May 1940. She pulled free, however, and was directed to Stornoway, where the cargo of anti-aircraft equipment was transferred to a British vessel which then proceeded to Narvik.

Final voyage

The *Balzac* left Sunderland on 26 July 1940 with 1350 tons of coal for Cowes, Isle of Wight, this being her third such voyage. While anchored about one mile SE of Roker pier light and waiting for the convoy, just north of Hendon Rock, the ship was rocked by an explosion underneath her and a little aft of amidships, towards the port side. Degaussing cables were installed, but according to the boatswain's statement at the subsequent Maritime Inquiry, it was understood that the mine, which was German, had exploded just as the engine was stopped. The ship broke in two and sank within minutes, the bow first, while listing to port, and the stern 70 m away. Most of the survivors jumped overboard and a pilot vessel rescued them. Eight crewmen, including the two British DEMS gunners, had been on a raft while three were picked up from the water by the pilot boat. One man sank below the water half way between the raft and the ship, while Ordinary Seaman Hø and the Messboy were observed standing on board; both were believed to have gone down with the ship. The captain and the British pilot had been in the saloon at the time of the explosion. The steward and Able Seaman Kristoffersen were taken to a hospital and were still there at the time of the inquiries that were held in London on 13 August 1940; Boatswain Einar Johannesen, Deck Boy Thore Grini and Able Seaman Hans Wold all attended.

Those that died were:

Johansen, Knut Captain
Sutherland, Leif, 1st Mate
Gundersen, Sverre, 2nd Mate

The men that survived were:

Johannesen, Einar, Boatswain
Kristoffersen, Knut, Able Seaman
Wold, Hans, Able Seaman

Høe, Thor, Able Seaman
Kvalvik, Einar, Able Seaman
Grorud, Kristian Hansen, 1st Engineer
Hansen, Hans Ingvald, 2nd Engineer
Olsen, Ove Breno, Mess Boy
Hall, George, Sunderland Pilot
Grini, Thor, Deck Boy
Eriksen, Leif, Mechanic
Blickfeldt, Jakob, Mechanic
Danielsen, Arne, Engine Boy
Juliussen, Sigurd, Steward
Dahl, Gunnar, Cook

DEMS Gunners:

Baxter, A. of the British 1st London Irish Rifles
Carlisle, S. of the British 1st London Irish Rifles

CWGC; Starke Schell Registers; LCWLR 1939–45, p. 105; LR 1939–40 No. 70464 (B).

Wrecksite

Stern section

The stern section lies upside down in a N to S direction at a depth of 16 m. When she was first discovered in 1978, the upside-down stern section of the hull stood some 8 m off the seabed, with just a short shaft protruding out of the rear where the screw had been. It was later discovered that two divers using explosives in the 1960s had salvaged the bronze screw. From the stern end, the hull sloped down to the seabed over a distance of about 20 m and was more or less sealed, except for a very small hole at the base, which could be penetrated with some careful manoeuvring; once inside, though, a powerful torch revealed masses of machinery and large pipes hanging down from the top. Thirty five years later, the sea has taken its toll on the hull, which has thousands of pinprick-sized rust holes all over it, and there is now a huge gaping hole right through the centre, almost from top to bottom, making it very easy to swim through from one side to the other. Next to the hole is a great jumble of iron pipes and machinery, while at the base on the western side there is a gap, making it possible to swim along the inside of the hull from N to S. There used to be a row of eight brass portholes complete with their steel flanges bolted from the inside of the hull, but in very recent years someone has removed most of the most easily accessible ones. There is a 1.5 m scour around this part of the hull and a sand bank has built up inside the wreck, making it rather restricted in the centre and southern end. Shoals of various kinds of fish, including large cod and pout whiting can usually be found inside the hull, along with the occasional lobster.

Bow section

The bow and middle parts lie some 70 m or so to the northeast of the stern section. They consist of a large number of steel pipes, collapsed plates and framework, parts of the section where the bridge once stood resembling large open boxes; there is no sign of any brass or copper. Just to the northeast of the wreck, giant boulder reefs rise from the seabed, so there is the possibility that other parts of the wreck may be found further out, amongst the boulders.

POVENA

Date of loss: 3 June 1899
Wreck: ☆☆
Depth: 16 m
Reference: 54 53'.965 N 001 19'.112 W
Location: 1.76 nm SSE of Roker pier light

The *Povena* was a Spanish steel-hulled 2104-ton schooner-rigged steam cargo ship measuring 83.9-m in length, with a 12.7-m beam and a 5.3-m draught. William Gray and Company built and completed her as Yard No. 553 at West Hartlepool in May 1898; she was launched on March 9th 1898 for Ramón de la Sota of Bilbao, who registered here there and owned her at the time of loss. The single steel screw was powered by an 188 hp, three-cylinder triple expansion steam engine that used one boiler. The cylinders measured 50.8 cm, 80.01 cm and 134.62 cm with a 91.44-cm stroke (20 in., 31½ in. and 53 in. with a 36-in. stroke). Central Marine Engine Works Ltd. at Sunderland manufactured the engine and ancillary machinery. She had one deck, four bulkheads, water ballast, web frames and was a well deck steamer.

Final voyage

On the afternoon of 3 June 1899, this fairly new steamer struck the White Stones Rocks, 1.88 nm SSE of the Roker pier light at Sunderland, while on passage from Bilbao for the Tyne with a cargo of iron ore. She was refloated on the following tide and an attempt was made to tow her, but she foundered and was lost soon after. All of the crew were rescued.

Miramar Ship Index; Starke Schell Registers; *The Times*: Tuesday, 6 June 1899, p. 10, Issue no. 35848.

Wrecksite

The wreck lies on a rocky seabed, in a general depth of 16 m, just north and outside of the White Stones Rocks off Sunderland. It was salvaged almost 20 years ago when the wreck was found untouched since the day she sank. The boiler stands upright next to the engine that lies on its side and the brass/copper condenser lies beneath the engine. The bell, stern equipment, screw, shaft, anchor, chains and most non-ferrous items have now been salvaged, but it is still worth a good rummage dive. There are a number of small reefs about one metre high at the stern end of the remains.

UC 32, Seiner Majestät Unterseeboot

Date of Loss: 23 February 1917
Wreck: ☆☆
Depth 11 m
Reference: 54 54'.451 N 001 20'.544 W
Location: 0.39 nm ENE from Roker light, Sunderland

During the Great War, KDM submarines regularly mined the busy roadsteads of Tyne, Wear and Tees. The soluble chemical plugs within the mine mechanism designed to give the UC

Oberleutnant zur See Herbert Breyer's SMU UC 32 *(Author's collection)*

submarines time to clear the area were frequently unstable. The UC crews were thus under threat not just from British anti-submarine forces, but from their own deadly cargoes.

UC 32 was a double-hulled UCII coastal mine-laying boat measuring 49.45 m in length and 7.46 m in height, with a 5.22-m beam and a 3.68-m draught. She had a 400-ton surface displacement and a 480-ton underwater displacement. She was ordered on 29 August 1915 as part of the batch UC 25–UC 33, and built by Vulcan AG for KDM who laid her keel as yard number 71. She was launched on 12 August 1916 and Oberlt.z.S. Herbert Breyer commissioned her on 13 September 1916. She was combat ready on 27 November 1916.

The machinery consisted of two 250-hp diesel oil engines manufactured by Maschinenfabrik Augsburg Nürnberg (MAN) and powered by two bronze screws that gave a surface speed of 11.6 knots carrying 41 tons plus 14 tons of diesel oil. Her surface operational range was 10 040 nm at 7 knots and submerged range was 55 nm at 4 knots. For underwater, she was equipped with two 230-hp electric motors using lead-acid batteries and giving 6.6 knots.

Armament consisted of a maximum of seven 50.04-cm (19.7 in.) torpedoes, with two external 50.04-cm (19.7 in.) torpedo tubes at the bow - one on either side of the mine chutes and one stern internal tube. Her torpedo load was designed to allow for a torpedo in each tube plus a reload for the stern tube. Internally storing an additional torpedo in pieces for the stern tube later augmented this, although this was optional. A total of two extra torpedoes for the external bow tubes could be carried as well, lashed to the deck, making a total of seven torpedoes, although not all boats sailed with that many. *UC 32* was also armed with one 88-mm deck gun at the fore and carried 133 rounds of ammunition for the gun. Other weapons on board were 18 Type UC 200 mines with six mine chutes for laying the mines. She was capable of diving to a maximum operational depth of 50 m (164 ft), accomplished in 33 seconds on a crash dive, and was usually manned by three officers and 23 ratings.

Final patrol

On 17 February 1917, on her third patrol, *UC 32* left Heligoland to operate and lay mines off the English east coast, with Oblt.z.S. Herbert Breyer in command. The Heligoland U-boat base intercepted radio messages from British merchantmen, which showed that Breyer was attacking Allied shipping five days after he left port. Breyer's instructions were to block the Tyne estuary with six mines, which he achieved on 21 February. On the 23rd, a further barrier was to be laid just off the piers at Sunderland. At 1830 hrs and in darkness, Breyer was on the surface at the entrance to the River Wear and had just laid his first mine when there was a violent explosion under the hull of the U-boat. (It is believed that a plug holding the mine to the sinker had dissolved prematurely, releasing the mine under her stern end; the mine was the one at the bottom of the fifth chute.) Oblt.z.S. Breyer and Oberstauermansmaat Skau, who were in the conning tower when the vessel blew up, quickly found themselves in the water. As *UC 32* sank, an inrush of air pushed the only other survivor Oberheizer Schirm, to the surface. An examination vessel, which happened to be close to the scene, rescued the three men.

Extract from PRO records:

> UC 32 was 328 yards from the breakwater, according to navigating officer, Oberstauermansmaat Skau. Breyer had ordered the laying of the last mine when the boat suddenly keeled over, the stern seemed to break away from the rest of the boat.

This account of the sinking was found in a letter addressed to the mother of survivor Reinhard Schirm:

> *Friday 6.15*
> I was in the Control Room. The explosion extinguished the lights immediately and I was hurled forward owing to the pressure of the water flooding in *(for the boat had been torn in half)*.
>
> I was driven upward. I held my breath. At the same moment the bottles containing compressed air burst and I was thrown into the conning tower. As for the moment the pressure was greater from inside than outside, I could take breath again. The boat in the meantime had sunk to the bottom. I let go and was at last thrown out. I swam on the surface 200 metres from the boat. I shouted for help and found my strength failing me (I had not slept for some 28 hours) and had swallowed a good deal of oil. I also had my heavy leather clothing and sea boots on. I took my boots off and managed to pull one leg out of my leather breeches but swallowed a great quantity of oil in the process; now for the other leg. Because my hands were quite numb I could not get my knife out, but somehow I managed to get my remaining leg out of the leather breeches with great difficulty. I felt my limbs stiffening with the cold. I shouted for help again. At last I saw a light and soon after a second one. The first was the Sunderland (sic) lighthouse, the second the light of an English patrol boat. I swam towards it and when I was about 20 yards off someone threw me a lifebelt. An English sailor handed me an oar and pulled me into his boat. I heard a voice "Hullo Schirm, you here too?" I recognised the captain. There were only three of us.
>
> We were very well looked after on the steamer and the English sailors were kind to us. They must have felt sorry for us because they kept giving us their cigarettes. My English helped a bit. We were given dry clothes and in the evening taken off to hospital. Again we were kindly treated and well fed, but we were strictly guarded. On Sunday we

> were taken to the station. We were not exactly looking at our best, but you should have seen the curiosity of the crowd, particularly the women.

The following day (24 February) the wreck was located by a chain sweep and divers were sent down, but 'soup-like' visibility from the River Wear prevented them from examining the U-boat. On the 27th, iron gratings covering the mine chutes were found by a diver and he managed to retrieve a fraction of the shattered pressure hull. The 88-mm forward deck gun and its mountings were also reported as intact. Next day the divers found the conning tower and two intact periscopes and noticed that the conning tower hatch was open, although the entrance was too small to accommodate a fully-suited diver. Although the forward section of the U-boat was undamaged, the hull near the engine room was severely shattered and about 30 feet of the stern, with the screws and rudders attached, was missing; divers came across this portion on 1 March.. "Small trawling nets were towed continuously round the wreck for books, loose gear, etc.," however nothing was found. Over the next few days all operations were halted when gale force winds and heavy seas developed and the wreck markers/buoys were torn free and lost. Lt. Cdr. Guybon C.C. Damant, who was previously Inspector of Diving and primarily responsible for salvaging gold from the sunken liner Laurentic off Lough Swilly for the 1917 dive season, was called away to Sunderland to oversee the diving on *UC 32*.

On 18 March a diver located the rear door of the starboard bow tube and twelve hours later Lt. Cdr. Damant had one of the torpedoes, complete with its warhead and pistol intact, retrieved for examination. By the end of March it was decided to end further salvage operations because they did not expect to find anything new and because the wreck still harboured fourteen unexploded mines in the fore section, posing a serious hazard to both vessels and salvage crews. It was at first proposed that the mines be detonated by charge, but in the end the Admiralty decided not to blow the wreck up. The crewmen who died in *UC 32*:

Adler, Wilhelm, U-Oberheizer
Beyes, Adolf, U-Maschinistenmaat
Dreyer, A., U-Maschinistenmaat
Ebenkamp, Heinrich, U-Heizer
Eckloff, Franz, U-Bootsmannsmaat
Eissler, Wilhelm, U-Heizer
Falcke, Franz, Leutnant zur.See.der Reserve
Gabriel, Otto, U-Heizer
Handreck, Max, U-Obermaschinistenmaat
Hansen, Heinrich, Marine Ingenieur Asp
Hein, Peter, U-Heizer
Hoffmann, Edwin, U-Matrose
Kasch, Max, U-Obermatrose
Klöden, Kurt, U-Obermatrose
Lachmund, P., U-F.T.Gast
Reidhardt, Fr., U-Matrose
Schmidt, Otto, U-Maschinistenmaat
Schulzke, Max, U-Heizer
Ungenannt, E., U-Maschinistenmaat
Vollert, Karl, Marine Ingenieur
Wind, Paul, U-Matrose
Zahn, Michael, U-Oberbootsmannsmaat der Reserve

ADM 137/3897, 137/3918, 137/3875; NARA: T-1022, Roll 85, PG61944; Möltenort U-boat Memorial Foundation; NARA: Roll T-102, Roll 81 Abschriften aus Fragebogen series.

Mr Rolf Mitchinson, a resident of Hendon, Sunderland at the time, recalled: 'As a young boy of nine years old, I can remember living in a house that overlooked the quayside and docks and I remember watching as three U-boat sailors, one of whom was the commander or captain, were brought ashore under armed escort. I can still see the hatred against the

Germans on the faces of those local Hendon people who lined the quay, they must have really despised them. The three men were jeered and spat on when they were helped ashore from the boat and onto the quayside, before some armed policemen led them away.' Smiling slightly, he continued, 'The captain, however, did show his gratitude at being rescued because he gave one of his rescuers a memento from his pocket, I think it may have been a cigarette lighter or case, they certainly seemed happy to still be alive, because the North Sea around here is very cold at the best of times.'

Wrecksite

Up until about 1980, a substantial amount of the U-boat's wreck was still intact, including the twin bronze screws, which were inscribed 'Vulcanwerke, Volcad Werke, Rubel Bronze, 29/7/1916' and 'Durchmess, Steigung'. When it was found, the complete periscope and about five whole telegraphs were also there, as well as the two screws. They, though, are now long gone, plundered when the wreck was first discovered by chance.

In the early 1990s, a diver from a Sunderland Sub Aqua Club rediscovered the wreck and told the media about what he had found. Officialdom, including the German Embassy, immediately became involved and it was designated as a war grave. As it was close to the shipping channel and because there were still live mines and torpedoes on board, the Royal Navy brought in divers to examine the remains and decided to disperse it. Nowadays, the police launch from the River Wear usually appears to warn off any diving boats moored anywhere near the wrecksite. It lies approximately 400 metres ENE of the Roker light at Sunderland, in 12–13 m of water, depending on the tide. There is still a substantial amount of it left, in three main sections, and plenty of copper and brass can be seen, along with dozens of giant lead batteries standing in rows. One torpedo tube still contains a live torpedo, too, just ready for firing.

CLEMATIS (?)

Date of loss: 18 April 1894
Wreck: ✯✯
Depth: 40 m
Reference: 54 55'.437 N 001 15'.169 W
Location: 4.01 nm ESE of Souter Point

The *Clematis* (Official No. 89462) was a 1234-ton iron-hulled British steam cargo ship measuring 70.15 m in length, with a 9.75-m beam and a 4.67-m draught. R. Cragg and Sons, Middlesbrough built and completed her as Yard No. 36 in March 1884; she was launched as *Clematis* in March 1884 for Lilly, Wilson and Company, West Hartlepool.

The single iron screw was powered by a 99-hp, two-cylinder compound steam engine that used one boiler. Westgarth, English and Company, Middlesbrough manufactured the engine and ancillary machinery.

The registered owner in 1891 was J. Lilly and Company, West Hartlepool. From 1894, North Eastern Shipping Company Ltd. West Hartlepool was the registered owner and J. H. Buck was the manager.

Final voyage

At 0540 hrs on 18 April 1894, during a light southerly wind and thick fog, the *Clematis*, commanded by Captain T. Batty, foundered following a collision with the 1270-ton British steamer *Beamish* (1883, J. Fenwick and Son, London), 1½-miles south of Sunderland. The *Beamish*, which was bound for Rotterdam and laden with coals shipped at Dunstan, struck the *Clematis* broadside on and stove in many of her plates. The *Clematis*, which was carrying a crew of sixteen and a pilot, was in ballast and on passage from Stockton-on-Tees for Blyth. No lives were lost and the 16 hands of the *Clemantis*, scrambled onto the deck of the *Beamish*, however it was not accomplished without a lot of danger and difficulty. When all the crew had been rescued, the *Beamish* freed herself of the *Clematis*, which rapidly filled up and sank in about ten minutes. The *Beamish*, with her bows stove in, then sailed back to the Tyne with the rescued crewmen.

BoT Wreck Return 1894, p 152; LR No. 906 (C); Starke Schell Registers; American Lloyd's Register of American and Foreign Shipping, 1857–1900; *The Times*: Thursday, 19 April 1894, p. 10, Issue 34242.

Wrecksite

The wreck, possibly that of the *Clematis*, is orientated in a N to S direction. It lies on a seabed of dirty sand, broken shells, mud and gravel, in a general depth of 40 m (LAT). The wreck stands 5.2 m high at amidships and covers an area of 77 m by 25 m, but is well decayed, broken up and partially buried, with soft corals adorning the engine area. It is covered in silt, but most of the interesting equipment should still be around, along, hopefully, with the bell. Quite a number of cod have been observed amongst the wreckage and shoals of pout whiting have adopted it.

ZEELAND, ex SILVERSPRAY

Date of loss: 1 August 1916
Wreck: ✭✭✭✭
Depth: 51 m
Reference: 54 56'.223 N 001 09'.782 W
Location: 6.61 nm E by N of Roker Lighthouse

On August 1st 1916, UB 39 *captured and sunk the Zeeland, ex Silverspray, 7-miles east of Sunderland (Author's collection)*

The *Zeeland* was a steel-hulled 1293-ton Netherlands steam cargo ship measuring 70.46 m in length, with a 10.46-m beam and a 4.47-m draught. N.V.Werf Voorhen Rijkee and Company, Rotterdam built and completed her as Yard No. 125 in September 1907. She was launched as *Silverspray* for Tyzack and Branfoot, but acquired by N.V. Scheepvaart en Steenkolen Mij., Rotterdam, who renamed her *Zeeland.* The single screw was powered by a 147-nhp three-cylinder triple expansion steam engine that used two single-ended boilers with four corrugated furnaces and 229.28 sq.m (2468 sq.ft) of heating surface, which gave 10.25 knots. The cylinders measured 44.45 cm, 71.12 cm and 114.3 cm with a 91.44-cm stroke (17½ in., 28 in. and 45 in. with a 36-in. stroke). Wilton, E. and Slipway manufactured the machinery at Rotterdam. She had one deck and a well deck.

Final voyage

On 1 August 1916, the KDM submarine SMU *UB 39*, commanded by Oblt.z.S. Werner Fürbringer captured the *Zeeland* seven miles east of Sunderland. The crew was forced to take to the boats, after which their ship was sunk by gunfire. The *Zeeland* was commanded by Captain J.J. Schutt and had been transporting a cargo of coal from Methil to Rouen in France.

LCWLR 1914–18, p. 50; LR 1915/16 No. 199 (Z); ANCL 1914–18, p.71;Starke Schell Registers.

Wrecksite

The wreck is orientated in a north to south direction and lies on a seabed of firm sand, mud and broken black shells, in a general depth of 51m (LAT). It is still very substantial and stands about 9.5m high and covers an area of 92m in length by 10m wide. The wreck also appears to be lying on it's side.

PRESTO

Date of loss: 6 April 1917
Wreck: ✯✯
Depth: 9.3 m
Reference: 54 55'.397 N 01 20'.298 W
Location: 0.5 nm E of Roker pier light, Sunderland

The *Presto* (Official No. 118652) was a steel-hulled 1143-ton British steam cargo ship measuring 69.59 m in length, with a 9.8-m beam and a 4.31-m draught. John Crown and Sons Ltd. built and completed her at Sunderland in March 1905 as Yard No. 115. She was launched on 29 April 1907 for Pelton Steam Ship Company Ltd. who owned her at the time of loss; R.S. Gardiner and J. Reay was the manager. The single steel screw was powered by a 135- hp, three-cylinder triple expansion steam engine that used one boiler. G. Clark Ltd. Sunderland manufactured the engine and ancillary machinery. She had one deck, a well deck, four bulkheads and a 5.8-m poop deck, an 18.5-m quarterdeck, a 14.6-m bridge deck and 8.5-m forecastle. The vessel was also armed for defence in 1916 with a stern-mounted six-pounder (2.72-kilo shells) deck gun.

Final voyage

At 0940 hrs on 6 April 1917, the *Presto*, with Captain Lowery in charge, detonated a mine under the No. 1 hold; she was making about 9.5 knots and was in ballast, on passage from London for Newcastle upon Tyne. SMU *UC 40*, a KDM submarine under the command of Kapitänleutnant Gustav Deuerlich, had laid the mine on 3 April 1917, four miles east of Roker Point, Sunderland. The violent explosion killed six of the crew and the ship immediately began to sink by the head. The survivors abandoned ship in the boats and were picked up by the examination vessel that happened to be close by at the time, taking the *Presto* in tow by the stern. Two tugs then came out from the Wear and assisted in the tow, but by 1100 hrs the *Presto* had taken in so much water that the fore part actually struck the seabed, about 1.5 miles from Roker light, where she was abandoned, settling on the bottom in 17 m. The men who died were:

Calvey, Victor, 46yrs, Fireman MM
Lagois, Jean, 52yrs, Able Seaman MM
Somerville, Thomas, Prentice 37yrs, Able Seaman MM
Strandel, John, 43yrs, Steward MM
Wynn, John, 32yrs, Fireman MM
Briggs, George, 72yrs, Able Seaman MM

CWGC; LCWLR 1914–18, p. 114; BVLS 1914–18, p. 41; LR 1915/16 No. 995 (P); Jarvis (2000), Vol. 5; Tennent (1990), p. 181.

Wrecksite

The wreck is orientated in a N to S direction and lies on a seabed of fine sand, mud and rock, in a general depth of 9.3 m (LAT). The wreck is in line with the main shipping channels for the river and appears to have been dispersed with explosives at some time or other, because it is reported as being totally collapsed, badly broken up, rather flattened and concreting into the seabed. The highest section stands about 3.4 m and covers an area of 60 m in length by 25 m wide. Shoals of pout whiting have adopted the remains and a number of crustaceans can be found, but Lion's Mane jellyfish can be a real nuisance during the months of July and August, in the brisk tidal streams and over the wreck.

HEBBLE

Date of loss: 6 May 1917
Wreck: ★★★
Depth: 18 m
Reference: 54 55'.473 N 001 18'.892 W
Location: 1.28 nm E of Roker light, Sunderland

The *Hebble* (Official No. 98385) was a steel-hulled 904-ton British steam cargo ship measuring 68.58 m in length, with a 9.6-m beam and a 4.69-m draught. William Dobson and Company, Newcastle upon Tyne built and completed her as Yard No. 47 in August 1891; on 24 August she was launched at Low Walker Yard, Newcastle for Goole Steam Shipping

The 904 ton steamer Hebble *was on government service as Ammunition Stores Carrier No.3 when she detonated a German laid mine on May 6th 1917 and foundered almost at once. (Courtesy of Rolf Kristensen and Stein-Erik Dagsland, Norway)*

Company Ltd. Goole. The single screw was powered by an 181-hp, three-cylinder triple expansion steam engine that used two single-ended boilers and gave 12 knots. Wallsend Slipway Company Ltd. Newcastle upon Tyne manufactured the engine and ancillary machinery. She had one deck, five bulkheads and a 9.1-m poop deck, a 16.4-m bridge deck and a 10-m forecastle.

From 1905, Lancashire and Yorkshire Railway Company was the registered owner.

Final voyage

The *Hebble* (Captain Flower) detonated a German-laid mine at 1150 hrs on 6 May 1917 and foundered almost at once. The KDM submarine SMU *UC 42*, commanded by Kapitänleutnant Otto Heinrich Tornow had laid the mine just the previous day. The steamer was on passage from Scapa Flow to Sunderland. The *Hebble* was on government service as Ammunition Stores Carrier No. 3. Out of her complement of 16 crew, the chief engineer and four able seamen died in the explosion, while 11 survivors were rescued by a motor launch and landed at Sunderland. The crewmen that died were:

Cutter, Thomas, 49 yrs, Able Seaman MM
Ford, Charles Johnathan, 56 yrs, Able Seaman MM
Howard, Archibald, 36 yrs, Fireman MM
Jackson, Abraham, 41 yrs, Fireman MM
Laycock, Emanuel, 62 yrs, Chief Engineer MM

PRO ADM 137/2962; CWGC; Jarvis & Jarvis (1993); LR 1915/16 No. 406 (H); Starke Schell Registers; LCWLR 1914–18, p. 130; BVLS 1914–18, p. 49.

Wrecksite

The *Hebble*, or what remains of it, is orientated in a N to S direction. It lies on a hard flat stony seabed, in a general depth of around 18 m (LAT). The wreck is very difficult to locate because of its size. The boilers, condensers and engine stand upright, but are concreted together, amid a mass of huge copper pipes and steel framework. The whole area of wreckage is only about 20 m in diameter but is absolutely carpeted in a colourful array of beautiful anemones and soft corals. Huge shoals of pout whiting, pollack and saithe swarm over the top, while cod and large conger, crab and lobsters can be found hiding under the twisted mass of metal. There are no interesting artefacts to be found, and the large lumps of copper and brass that can be seen sticking out across its entire surface are well concreted into the debris. This is a really fabulous dive, if only for the amount of marine life to be seen. The surrounding seabed is just hard flat stony ground, so if the tide is running and the anchor does not quickly catch onto something, you will soon drift away from the wreck.

RAVENSBOURNE

Date of loss: 31 January 1917
Wreck: ★★★★
Depth: 42 m
Reference: 54 55'.815 N 001 14'.582 W
Location: 3.81 nm E by N of Roker light, Sunderland

The *Ravensbourne* (Official No. 139132) was a steel-hulled 1226-ton British steam cargo ship measuring 70.1 m in length, with a 10.87-m beam and a 4.72-m draught. Campbeltown Shipbuilding Company Ltd. built and completed her as Yard No. 102 at Campbeltown in July 1916; she was launched on 2 June 1916 for the South Metropolitan Gas Company Ltd. London, who also owned her at the time of loss. The single steel screw was powered by a three-cylinder triple expansion steam engine that used two single-ended boilers. D. Rowan and Company, Glasgow manufactured the engine and ancillary machinery. She had one deck, a 24-m quarterdeck, a 12.6-m bridge deck and 7.9-m forecastle. After completion, the vessel was armed for defence with one stern-mounted six-pounder (2.72-kilo) deck gun.

Final voyage

At 0040 hrs on 31 January 1917, the *Ravensbourne* detonated a mine laid on 27 January 1917 by the KDM submarine SMU *UC 31*, which was commanded by Kapitänleutnant Otto von Schrader. The steamer was making 9.5 knots, on passage from Newcastle for London and transporting a cargo of coal. A violent explosion rocked the ship on the port side amidships, blowing a massive hole in the engine room, killing the chief engineer, the second engineer and a donkeyman. The survivors abandoned ship in the starboard boat as the vessel immediately began to sink; the port boat had been smashed up in the explosion. The men had just got clear from the ship when it went down, just eight minutes after striking the mine. The Danish steamer *Ajax* picked up the survivors soon after and landed them at the Tyne quay at 1700 hrs. The crewmen that died were:

Carter, George William, 36 yrs, Donkeyman MM
Gilfoyle, Thomas, 29 yrs, 2nd Engineer MM
Harrowar, Harry, 39 yrs, Chief Engineer MM

LCWLR 1914–18, p. 88 ; CWGC ; BVLS 1914–18, p. 31 ; LR 1915/16 No. 53 (R) (supplement) ; Tennent (1990) p. 211: Jarvis (2000), Vol. 5.

Wrecksite

The wreck, believed to be that of the *Ravensbourne*, is orientated in a NNE to SSW direction. It is quite substantial and lies on a seabed of sand and stone in a general depth of 42 m (LAT). The remains cover an area of 85 m in length by 30 m across and stand about 5.3 m high. The wreck is partially intact with a lot of damage at the southern end, which is rather flattened and leads into the seabed. Lots of trawl nets and trammel nets cover the wreck, but shoals of fish, mostly large cod and pout whiting have also adopted it, so it should be a good boat-angling venue.

TRIDENT

Date of loss: 1 August 1941
Wreck: ✯✯✯✯✯
Depth: 46 m
Reference: 54 55'.946 N 001 13'.325 W
Location: 4.53 nm E by N of Roker light, Sunderland
Also given: 55 00'.849 N 001 14'.065 W
Location: 7.63 nm ESE from South Shields light

The *Trident* (Official No. 140687) was a steel-hulled 4317-ton British steam cargo ship measuring 114.3 m in length, with a 15.57-m beam and a 7.69-m draught. Sunderland Shipbuilding Company Ltd. Sunderland built and completed her as Yard No. 293 in September 1917 for Hall Bros. S.S. Company Ltd, Newcastle, and Hall Bros. was the manager. The single steel screw was powered by a 371-nhp three-cylinder triple expansion steam engine that used two single-ended boilers working at 180 psi pressure with six corrugated furnaces, 13.09sq.m (141sq.ft) of grate-surface and 547.38sq.m (5892sq.ft) of heating surface gave nine knots. The cylinders measured 63.5 cm, 106.68 cm and 175.26 cm with a 121.92-cm stroke (25 in., 42 in. and 69 in. with a 48-in. stroke). North East Marine Engineering Company Ltd. Sunderland manufactured the engine and ancillary machinery. She had one deck, six bulkheads cemented, an 8.8-m poop deck, a 32.3-m bridge deck and an 11.6-m forecastle; she also had some cellular double bottom, a forepeak and an aft peak tank. She was classed as 100A1.

From 1937, Quayside Shipping Company Ltd. Newcastle was the registered owner and Connell and Grace Ltd. was the manager.

Final voyage

At 2350 hrs on 1 August 1941, the *Trident* was lying at anchor off the 20C buoy, waiting to enter the River Tyne, when German aircraft bombed her. The ship was seriously damaged and the crew abandoned ship in the boats, but the *Trident* remained afloat for almost another two more hours, sinking at 0140 hrs the following morning. She was part of the southbound 41-ship convoy FS.557 (Methil–Southend) and had just arrived from Montreal, heading for London via the Tyne with a 6000-ton cargo of bagged grain and beans. All of her crew of 43, including seven DEMS gunners, were rescued.

LCWLR 1939–45, p. 281 ; BVLS 1939–45, p. 25 ; LR 1941/2 No. 33827 (T).

Wrecksite

No positive identification has yet been made for this substantial vessel, but two sets of co-ordinates have been supplied, both of which are very large wrecks and will be well worth investigating.

The first co-ordinates place the wreck 4.53 nm east by north of Roker lighthouse. The latitude and longitude position said to have been given when the vessel sank was 54° 55 30'N 01° 14 00'W, but survey vessels searching the area in 1952 and 1957 failed to find it and the wreck was deleted from the charts. A very substantial wreck is, however, positioned very close to those co-ordinates and is in fact shown on modern Admiralty charts. It lies orientated in a NNW to SSE direction on a seabed of mud, sand and black shells, in a general depth of 46 m (LAT). The wreck stands upright some 9 m high amidships, with much of the upper bridge structures, handrails and decking still completely intact, but showing signs of damage and partial collapse. Probably all of the ship's interesting bridge equipment will still be in place, including the bell. This will make an excellent boat-angling venue.

The second co-ordinates are for a wreck which is 5.25 miles SE of the River Tyne, in a general depth of 52 m (LAT). It is orientated in a northeast to southwest direction on a seabed of hard sand, and is very substantial, lying side by side in two large sections, with the highest part standing around 6 m in height, with some superstructure, decking, handrails and walkways visible. The wreck has been dived on a number of occasions and while large portholes have been recovered, nothing has been found to positively prove her identity. Most of her interesting bridge equipment should still be around, but the solid brass pedestal-mounted steering helm, which bears the words 'John Hastie and Coy Ltd. Greenock, Patent 2464', has already been recovered. All efforts to trace the numbers have been fruitless.

3

THE RIVER WEAR TO THE TYNE

ATLANTIC, EX HORACE (?)

Date of loss: 17 September 1902
Wreck: ★★
Depth: 29 m
Reference: 54 57'.735 N 001 18'.705 W
Location: 2.79 nm NNE from Roker light, Sunderland

The *Atlantic* (Official No. 749) was an iron-hulled 1558-ton Russian steam cargo ship measuring 79.09 m in length, with a 10.49-m beam and 5.89-m draught. Weighing 1634 tons gross, John Redhead and Co. Ltd. South Shields built and completed her as Yard No. 145. She was launched as the *Horace* (Official No. 78418) in October 1878 for Groves, MacLean and Co. West Hartlepool. Captain J. Payne was the master in 1880. The single iron screw was powered by a 164-nhp two-cylinder compound steam engine that used two boilers. The cylinders measured 78.74 cm and 149.86 cm, with an 86.36-cm stroke (31 in. and 59 in. with a 34-in. stroke). She had one deck, four bulkheads, water ballast, a 29-m quarterdeck, 18.2-m bridge deck and 9.1-m forecastle.

James Groves of West Hartlepool became the registered owner in 1880 and J. Payne the master. In 1888, Maclean, Doughty and Co. West Hartlepool was the registered owner.

The tonnage was altered from 1634 tons gross to 1558 tons gross in 1892. In 1898, she was renamed *Atlantic* by her new owners Rederi A/B Ocean, Wiborg, Russia and the manager was N.O. Gulbrandsen.

Final voyage

On 17 September 1902 the *Atlantic*, commanded by Captain P.G. Lindroos, foundered three miles SSE 0.25 E of Souter light, following a collision with the 1717-ton steamer *Twizell* (1901: J. Thompson, Newcastle). The *Atlantic* was *en route* from Sunderland to Kronstadt, Russia with a cargo of coal and a crew of 21.

On 20 November 1903 the *Twizell* was wrecked in the Elbe Estuary.

LCR 1902, p. 6 (d); LR 1902/3, No. 1291 (H); American Lloyd's Register of American and Foreign Shipping, 1857–1900; Board of Trade Wreck Return 1902, p. 142 (782).

Wrecksite

The wreck, possibly that of the *Atlantic*, is orientated in a NNE to SSW direction and lies on a seabed of dirty sand, gravel, black shells and rock in a general depth of 31 m (LAT). It is now partially buried and totally collapsed into a pile of decayed, twisted plates and broken machinery. The tallest point is 3.8 m. The wreckage covers an area 63 m by 26 m, with a few crustaceans sheltering among it. The ship's bell will almost certainly be inscribed: *Horace 1878.*

FOLMINA

Date of loss: 25 January 1918
Wreck: *
Depth: 27 m
Reference: 54 56'.232 N 001 18'.149 W
Location: 1.96 nm NE from Roker light

The *Folmina* was a steel-hulled 1158-ton Dutch steam cargo ship measuring 70.15 m in length, with a 10.36-m beam and a 4.01-m draught. N.V.Wilton's Machinefabriek en Scheepswerf, Rotterdam (Wilton's Engineering and Slipway Co.) built and completed her as Yarc No. 274 in November 1915. She was launched on 11 October 1915 for N.V. Holland-Gulf Stoomv. Mij., Rotterdam and Jos. de Poorter was the manager. The single steel propeller was powered by a 120-hp, three-cylinder triple expansion steam engine that used one boiler. The builders also manufactured the aft-positioned machinery. She had one deck, four watertight bulkheads, an aft-positioned 39.9-m quarterdeck and a 7.3-m forecastle. She was classed as 100 A1.

Final voyage

On 25 January 1918 the SS *Folmina* (Captain H.A. Prins) was torpedoed and sunk two miles east of Sunderland at 54° 56'N 01° 18'W, by the KDM submarine SMU *UB 34*, which was commanded by Oblt.z.S. Hellmuth von Ruckteschell. The steamer was in ballast and on passage from Rotterdam for Leith; eight of her crew were killed, their names are unknown._

Starke Schell Registers; LCWLR 1914–18, p. 97; ANCL 1914–18, p. 66; LR 1915–16 No. 430 (F).

Wrecksite

The wreck of the *Folmina* lies on a seabed of gravel, mud and boulders in a general depth of 27 m (LAT), very close to that of the *Mayoress Pelican* barge. The wreck is totally collapsed and well broken up, with much of it partially buried and covering an area about 60 m long and 20 m across. The highest parts stand at no more than 1.5 m, with very little of interest.

MAYORESS PELICAN

Date of loss: 1998
Wreck: ★★
Depth: 27 m
Reference: 54 56'.280 N 001 18'.192 W
Location: 1.96 nm NE of Roker light, Sunderland

The *Mayoress Pelican* was a flat steel barge measuring approximately: 39.6 m in length with a 9.1-m beam. It was fitted with a compressor, crane and a moon pool for the purposes of drilling. M. Devlin, owner of the Tyne Towage Co. based at the River Tyne.

Final voyage

On 27 March 1996, the vessel was under tow of the motor tug *Pengarth* with a cargo of steel pipes and drilling equipment when they encountered heavy weather. The barge capsized and sank south of the rifle range buoy off Whitburn. The barge had been drilling for soil samples in the River Tees and was being returned to its owner. Jeff Maine of Tyne Wear Marine Co. based at Tyne Dock, Jarrow-on-Tyne, dived on and surveyed the wreck for the owners in 1999.

Jeff Maine, Tyne Wear Marine Company; UK Hydrographic Department.

Wrecksite

The wreck is close to the remains of the *Folmina* and is orientated in an almost N to S (010/190-degrees) direction. It lies on a seabed of sand and gravel in a general depth of 27 m (LAT). The barge is upside down, with the crane sticking out on one side and about 1 m of space beneath the vessel; it would be possible, but not advisable, to crawl underneath. Visible on top of the hull is the moon pool, through which it would also be possible to drop down onto the seabed. A number of large cod and lobsters are said to have taken refuge under the wreck.

MAINDY BRIDGE, EX BEGONIA

Date of loss: 8 December 1917
Wreck: ★★★★
Depth: 39 m
Reference: 54 56'.414 N 001 16'.051 W
Location: 3.11 nm ENE from Roker Lighthouse, Sunderland

The *Maindy Bridge* (Official No. 109908) was an iron-hulled 3653-ton British steam cargo ship measuring 84.8 m in length, with a 12.5-m beam and 5.5-m draught. Tyne Iron Shipbuilding Co. Ltd. Newcastle built and completed her as Yard No. 126 in December 1899; she was launched as the *Begonia* for Stag Line Ltd. North Shields; J. Robinson and Sons was the manager. The single iron screw was powered by a 287-nhp three-cylinder triple expansion steam engine that used two single-ended boilers working at a pressure of 180 psi, with six corrugated furnaces, 10.77 sq.m (116 sq.ft) of grate surface and 408.77 sq.m (4400 sq.ft) of heating surface. The cylinders measured 58.42 cm, 97.79 cm and 162.56 cm with a 106.68 cm stroke (23 in., 38½ in. and 64 in. with a 42-in.stroke). N. E. Marine manufactured the engine and ancillary machinery at Newcastle. She had one deck and a spar deck.

From 1916, Maindy Shipping Co. Ltd. North Shields was the registered owner and renamed her *Maindy Bridge*; Jenkins, Richards and Evans Ltd. at Cardiff was the manager.

Final voyage

On 8 December 1917, four miles ENE of Sunderland, the *Maindy Bridge* was torpedoed and sunk without warning by the KDM mine-laying submarine SMU *UC 49*, commanded by Oblt.z.S. Karl Petri. The steamer was in ballast, on passage from Middlesbrough for the Tyne and the following two crewmen were lost:

John Perry (Mess Steward MM)
Peter Cunningham (Foreman Runner MM).

CWGC; Starke Schell Registers; LCWLR 1914–18, p. 188; Jarvis (2000), Vol. V.

Wrecksite

The wreck, probably that of the *Maindy Bridge*, is orientated in a SSE to NNW direction. It lies on a seabed of dirty sand and stone in a general depth of 39 m (LAT). The wreck is broken into two sections, the larger being the stern and midships part, which stands 8.6 m high and is heavily netted. The rear-mounted deck gun points downwards because the decking beneath it is sloping and damaged. The second section is the bow and lies 60 m to the south. Lots of soft corals enhance the highest and most exposed parts of the wreck and a large shoal of pout whiting has adopted the stern end, where nets float upwards like curtains. High numbers of large cod have been observed so it should make an excellent boat-angling venue.

DOREEN, ex BRACONHILL

Date of Loss: 22 August 1921
Wreck: ★★★
Depth: 45 m
Reference: 54 56'.145 N 001 13'.551 W
Location: 4.43 nm ENE of Roker lighthouse

The *Doreen* (Official No. 118176) was a steel-hulled 194-ton British steam trawler measuring 34.26 m in length with a 6.57-m beam and a 3.7-m draught. J. T. Eltringham and Co. at Stone Quay, South Shields built and completed her as Yard No. 248 in October 1903; she was launched that same month as the *Braconhill* for Don Fishing Co. Ltd. of Commercial Road, Aberdeen, with John S. Doeg the manager. The single steel screw was powered by a 50-rhp, three-cylinder triple expansion steam engine that used one boiler. George T. Grey and Co. Ltd. at South Shields manufactured the machinery. She had one deck and one bulkhead. In 1914 she was sold to Wear Steam Fishing Co. Ltd. of Fish Quay, South Dock at Sunderland and renamed *Doreen*, Port Reg: SD.130.

The Admiralty requisitioned the trawler in May 1916 and converted it to a Boom Defence Vessel; in 1917 she was converted to a training ship and in 1919, was returned to Wear Steam Fishing Co. Ltd. who owned her at the time of loss.

Final voyage

On the morning of 22 August 1921, the *Doreen* set out for the fishing grounds in dense fog but sank off Sunderland, following a collision with the 4937-ton steamship *Wyncote* (1907 – Furness, Withy and Co. Ltd. Liverpool). The trawler was cut in two and sank almost immediately with five of her crew of nine being drowned, including:

Bone, Robert, Chief Engineer MM
Boscrock, George, Cook MM
Webb, William, Mate MM

LR 1920/1 No. 56410 (D); LCR 1921, p. 7 (f); Miramar Ship Index; Toghill (2004); *The Times*: Tuesday, 23 August 1921, p. 8, Issue 42806.

Wrecksite

The wreck, probably that of the *Doreen*, is orientated in a SSE to NNW direction. It sits in a half- metre scour on a seabed of mud and sand in a general depth of 45 m (LAT). The wreck is upright and intact, with lots of nets enveloping the upper structures, which also have a nice covering of soft corals. It stands about 3.3 m high and covers an area of 35 m in length by 13 m across. The bell, if located, will almost certainly be inscribed: *Braconhill 1903*.

SAGA

Date of loss: 1 August 1915
Wreck: ✯✯✯✯
Depth: 44 m
Reference: 54 56'.302 N 001 15'.045 W
Location: 3.63 nm ENE of Roker lighthouse, Sunderland

The *Saga* (Official No. 140447) was a steel-hulled 1130-ton British steam cargo vessel measuring 70.47 m in length with a 10.43-m beam. Burmeister and Wain, Copenhagen built and completed her as Yard No. 216 in July 1901; she was launched on 22 July 1901 for Aktieselskapet Saga, Kristiania; Hagb. Waage was the manager. The single screw was powered by an 111-nhp three-cylinder triple expansion steam engine that used one boiler and gave 8.5-knots. The cylinders measured 40.64 cm, 66.04 cm and 114.3 cm with a 76.2-cm stroke (16 in., 26 in. and 45 in. with a 30-in. stroke). Burmeister and Wain manufactured the machinery in Copenhagen. She had one deck.

In 1917, the Shipping Controller in London requisitioned her and Robinson, Brown and Co. at Newcastle was appointed as the Crown nominee manager; she was also registered in Newcastle.

Final voyage

On 14 February 1918, the *Saga*, on passage from Sunderland for Rouen with a cargo of coal, was torpedoed and sunk off Sunderland by Oblt.z.S. Woldemar Petri, in the KDM submarine SMU *UB 64*.

Starke Schell Registers; LWCLR 1914–18, p. 201.

Wrecksite

The wreck, probably that of the *Saga*, is orientated in an ESE to WNW direction. It lies on a seabed of fine sand and mud in a general depth of 44 m (LAT). It is quite substantial, but most of the vessel has now collapsed and is well broken up and partially buried. It covers an area of 74 m in length by 22 m across with the highest part standing 3.5 m high around the engine. Lots of broken machinery, bollards, winches, anchors, large sections of hollow mast and various pipes lie scattered amongst the collapsed steel debris. Large numbers of cod have been sighted under the wreckage, so it should be a good boat-angling venue.

SUNNIVA

Date of loss: 28 June 1918
Wreck: ✯✯✯✯
Depth 41 m
Reference: 54 56'.757 N 001 15'.907 W
Location: 3.34 nm NE of Roker Lighthouse, Sunderland

The *Sunniva* (Official No. 140704) was a steel-hulled 1913-ton British steam cargo ship measuring 81.4 m in length, with an 11.6-m beam and 5.4-m draught. John Crown and Co. Ltd. at Monkwearmouth, Sunderland, built and completed her as Yard No. 165 in December 1917; she was launched on 16 October 1917 for Newbigin Steam Shipping Co. Ltd. E. R. Newbigin Ltd. at Newcastle was the manager. The single screw was powered by a 199-nhp three-cylinder triple expansion steam engine that used two single-ended boilers working at 180 psi pressure, with four furnaces, 7.15 sq.m (77 sq.ft) of grate surface and 287.25 sq.m (3092 sq.ft) of heating surface. The cylinders measured 52.07 cm, 83.82 cm and 137.16 cm with a 99.06-cm stroke (20½ in., 33 in. and 54 in. with a 39-in. stroke). North Eastern Marine Engineering Co. Ltd. manufactured the engine and ancillary machinery at Sunderland. She also had one deck and a well deck.

Final voyage

On 28 June 1918, the *Sunniva* was torpedoed and sunk without warning by the KDM mine-laying submarine SMU *UC 17*, commanded by Oblt.z.S. Nikolaus Freiherr von Lyncker. The steamer was armed for defence and in ballast, on passage from London for the Tyne; two men were lost, including able seaman Victor Benedictus Olssen.

Starke Schell Registers; CWGC; LWCLR 1914–18, p. 223; Jarvis (2000), Vol. V.

Wrecksite

The wreck, most probably that of the *Sunniva*, sits in a one-metre scour and is orientated in a SE to NW direction, with the bows to the SE. It lies on a seabed of dirty sand and stone in a general depth of 41 m (LAT). The wreck is very substantial, standing upright with the rear third of the ship's hull still intact. The screw and a large stern-mounted deck gun are still in place, but the wreck has collapsed just before the boilers and engines. These are surrounded by broken steel framework, plates and masses of copper pipes before the wreck goes level with the seabed and disappears. The ship's telegraph and a number of portholes are clearly visible amongst the collapsed debris, but would take a lot to dislodge. This wreck will make an excellent boat-angling venue because shoals of fish, especially pout whiting and cod, are often present around, and over the top of the wreck.

MONKSEATON

Date of loss: 8 December 1877
Wreck: ★★★
Depth: 44 m
Reference: 54 56'.334 N 001 14'.030 W
Location: 4.18 nm ENE from Roker Lighthouse

The *Monkseaton* was a steel-hulled 964-ton British schooner-rigged steam cargo vessel measuring 68.19 m in length, with a 9.27-m beam and a 5.28-m draught. T. and W. Smith Co. at North Shields built and completed her in June 1870 as Yard No. 41 and launched for Elliot, Lowrey & Dunford, Newcastle. The single four-blade iron screw was powered by a 110-hp, two-cylinder inverted compound steam engine that used one boiler. R. and W. Hawthorn at Newcastle upon Tyne manufactured the amidships-positioned engine and ancillary machinery. She had one deck, four bulkheads and was classed as A1.

J. Elliott and Co. of Newcastle upon Tyne was the registered owner at the time of loss.

Final voyage

Between 0500 hrs and 0600 hrs on 8 December 1877, the *Monkseaton*, with Captain W. Weightman in command, foundered and was lost following a collision with the 1451-ton steamship *Jenny Otto* (1877 – George Otto, Newcastle). The *Jenny Otto*, which was registered at North Shields, had left the Tyne at around 0400 hrs for passage to Bombay with a cargo of coal when she struck the Elliott steamer. The *Monkseaton* was in ballast and *en route* from Rotterdam to the Tyne. The crew quickly scrambled onto the deck of the *Jenny Otto*, all except the donkey-engineman Loren Larsen, who was down at the fires and was presumed to have been killed in the collision. The *Jenny Otto* returned safely to the Tyne with the survivors, although the bows were somewhat stove in.

LR 1877/8 No. 1259 (M); Board of Trade Wreck Return 1877, p. 111; *The Times*: Monday, 10 December 1877, p. 6, Issue 29121.

Wrecksite

The wreck, probably that of the old steamer, is orientated in a more or less SE to NW (115/295°) direction. It lies on a dirty seabed of sand and rock in a general depth of 44 m (LAT). It is completely collapsed, well broken up and decayed, with the highest section of 3 m being around the boiler and engine. It covers an area 75 m long and 22 m across, but the outline of the wreck can be clearly made out.

JYTTE, ex HADSUND, ex ØSTEN, ex EAST, ex DEMETRIOS, ex BEN LEDI

Date of Loss: 19 December 1939
Wreck: ★★★★★
Depth: 68 m
Reference: 54 56'.673 N 000 49'.268 W
Location: 18.33 nm E of Souter Point

The *Jytte* (Official No. 89791) was an iron-hulled 1916-ton Netherlands steam cargo ship measuring 86.29 m in length, with an 11.07-m beam and a 6.40-m draught. James Laing Engineering at Deptford, Sunderland built and completed her as Yard No. 291 in March 1884; she was launched on 29 March 1884 as the schooner-rigged *Ben Ledi* for J. Morrison and Son at North Shields. The single screw was powered by a 173-nhp two-cylinder compound steam engine that used two single-ended boilers working at a pressure of 80 psi, with four plain furnaces, 6.68 sq.m (72 sq.ft) of grate surface and 259.57 sq.m (2794 sq.ft) of heating surface. The cylinders measured 81.28 cm and 157.48 cm with a 99.06-cm stroke (32 in. and 62 in. with a 39-in. stroke). G. Clark manufactured the engine and ancillary machinery at Sunderland. She had four bulkheads cemented, one iron deck, a well deck, a 29.87 m quarterdeck, a 17.06 m bridge deck and 10.36 m forecastle and was later fitted with wireless direction finder. She was classed as 100 A1. The designated code recognition signal letters were: JLHP.

Captain W. H. Oram was the master until 1887 and again from 1894 until at least 1900.

Morrison Shipping Co. Ltd. of North Shields was the registered owner in 1901 and S. A. Morrison the manager.

She was renamed *Demetrios* in 1902 by the new owner Vagliano Bros, Cephalonia in Greece.

In 1908 she was registered to P. Ambatielos, Argostoli in Greece. G. Vergottis, at Piraeus in Greece became the owners in 1911. In 1915, Otto Dalman, Göteborg, in Sweden purchased and renamed her *East*. In 1916, she was renamed Østen by her new owner Nordisk Fjerfabrik AS, of Copenhagen. AS DS Rollo, Copenhagen was the registered owner in 1916 and Th. Just was the manager. In 1920, she had the same owners but J. L. Didrichsen was the manager. In 1921, AS DS Gylfe was the owner using the same manager, but T.C. Christensen became the manager in 1922. She was renamed *Hadsund* in 1925 by the same owners. In 1927, DS AS Halla purchased her using the same manager. DS Hafnia AS became the registered owner in 1927, with the same manager. From 1935, DS Ove Skou AS, Copenhagen was the registered owner and renamed her *Jytte*. Ove Skou was the manager.

Final voyage

On 19 December 1939, the *Jytte* was voyaging independently while transporting a cargo of coal from Immingham to Göteborg when she detonated a mine and was lost with ten of her crew (names unknown), 18 miles east of Souter Point. The mine had been laid by Bronte's Kriegsmarine destroyers: *Z 4* (Richard Beitzen), *Z 8* (Bruno Heinemann), *Z 14* (Friedrich Ihn) and *Z 15* (Erich Steibrick) during the night of 12–13 December 1939, under the cover of *Z 19* (Hermann Künne).

LCWLR 1939–45, p. 30; American Lloyd's Register of American and Foreign Shipping, 1857–1900; Starke Schell Registers.

Wrecksite

The wreck, which is probably that of the *Jytte*, sits in a one-metre scour and is orientated in a SSE to NNW direction. It lies on a seabed of sand, mud and shells in a general depth of 68 m (LAT). The wreck is standing upright some 9.2 m high and is generally intact, but broken about a third of the way along from the southeastern end. Soft corals adorn the upper sections and numerous large fish can be found all around and above the wreck, so it will make an excellent boat-angling venue. If the ship's bell is located, it should be inscribed: *Ben Ledi 1884.*

BLAIRHALL, EX HEROS

Date of loss: 26 July 1918
Wreck: ✯✯✯✯
Depth: 40 m
Reference: 54 57'.879 N 001 16'.538 W
Location: 3.72 nm NE of Roker Lighthouse, Sunderland

The *Blairhall* (Official No. 137783) was an iron-hulled 2549-ton schooner-rigged British steam cargo ship measuring 91.45 m in length, with a 12.25 m-beam and a 6.36-m draught. A. Rodger and Co. Port Glasgow built and completed her as Yard No. 343 in November 1899 at 2520 tons; she was launched as the *Heros* on 23 October 1899 for AB Navigator, Kristinestad, Russia; G. W. Snellman and Co. was the manager. The single screw was powered by a 249-nhp three-cylinder triple expansion steam engine that used two ingle-ended boilers. Hall-Brown and Buttery and Co. in Glasgow manufactured the engine and ancillary machinery. She had a steel spar deck, five bulkheads cemented, two transverse bulkheads, deep framing, an 8.83-m poop deck, a 24.38-m boat deck and an 8.83-m foredeck. She also had a flat keel, cellular double-bottom aft, under engine and forward; 635 tons of ballast and a 34-ton aft peak tank.

In 1903, A. Carlström was the manager. G. W. Snellman was manager in 1906.

In 1913 she had the same owner, but was based at Helsingfors and reduced by 339-tons.

From 1915, Clydesdale Navigation Co. Ltd. Glasgow was the registered owner and renamed her *Blairhall*; G. Nisbet and Co. was the manager. In 1916, she was armed for defence with one 75- mm deck gun, which was actually a four-inch field piece, adopted for marine use.

Final voyage

The KDM mine-laying submarine SMU *UC 40* commanded by Oblt.z.S. Hermann Menzel torpedoed the *Blairhall* without warning on 26 July 1918; the ship was in ballast and on passage from Middlesbrough for the Tyne. The steamer managed to move closer inshore, but on the following day, the 27th, she foundered within five minutes of passing inside the South Buoy, 3.5 miles ENE of Sunderland. Leading Seaman William McDonald (DSM), who was an RNR DAMS gunner, was lost with the ship.

LCWLR 1914–18, p. 226; Starke Schell Registers; CWGC; Jarvis & Jarvis (1996), Vol. IV.

Wrecksite

The wreck is orientated in an almost E to W direction and lies on a hard seabed of dirty fine sand, mud and broken shell in a general depth of 40 m (LAT). It is very substantial, standing upright and at least 7.5 m high from the stern for a third of its length and is completely intact, but damaged, with her deck gun and bronze screw still attached. The amidships part has collapsed in on itself and onto the boilers and engine block, while the bow section is just a flattened pile of debris; much of the decking and deck fittings, though, are still in place at the stern, all quite heavily coated with soft corals, with a couple of old trawl nets draped over the ends. Large copper pipes and brass/bronze valves are everywhere. It is possible that the bridge equipment and navigation are still around. The ship was fitted with a brass pedestal-mounted telegraph and brass pedestal-mounted steering helm. If the bell is recovered, it will almost certainly be inscribed: *Heros 1899*.

There seems to be an abundance of different varieties of fish so the wrecksite should make a good boat-angling venue.

POLTAVA, EX GEORGE-R, EX GEORG

Date of loss: 19 April 1917
Wreck: ★★★
Depth: 42 m
Reference: 54 58'.239 N 001 16'.400 W
Location: 2.88 nm ENE of Souter Point

The *Poltava* (Official No. 139078) was an iron-hulled 938-ton British steam cargo vessel measuring 65.36 m in length, with a 9.61-m beam and a 4.02-m draught. Rostocker A.G. für Schiffs- and Maschinenbau, of Rostock in Germany built and completed her as Yard No. 102 on 1 April 1889; she was launched as the *Georg* on 26 January 1889 for 'Georg' Heinrich Schuldt, Flensburg, Germany. The designated code recognition signal letters were: LMDP. The single iron screw was powered by a 145-hp, two-cylinder compound steam engine that used one boiler and gave 8.5 knots.

In May 1905, the registered owner was AG "Neptun" of Rostock. On 6 August 1914 she was captured by HMS *Cormorant* and taken to Gibraltar. In 1915 she was renamed *George-R*, registered in London and Tyzack, and Branfoot, Newcastle was appointed as the Crown nominee manager. Later in 1915, she was renamed *Poltava* by the Shipping Controller and Kaye, Son and Co. Ltd. London was appointed as the Crown nominee manager; she was also registered in London.

Final voyage

On 19 April 1917, the *Poltava* had set out with a cargo of coal on a voyage from the Tyne to an unknown destination, but detonated a mine three miles ENE of Souter Point; she foundered within minutes, but none of her crew was lost. The KDM submarine SMU *UC 44*, commanded by Kapitänleutnant Kurt Tebbenjohanns, had laid the mine on 18 April 1917.

American Lloyd's Register of American and Foreign Shipping, 1857–1900; BVLS 1914–18; Starke Schell Registers; LCWLR 1914–18, p. 120.

Wrecksite

The wreck is orientated in a SE to NW direction and lies on a seabed of dirty fine sand and mud in a general depth of 42 m (LAT). It is upright, standing 3.8 m high amidships and is partially buried, but the top upper structures and most of the hull has now collapsed in on itself. There are lots of jumbled iron plates and debris, along with some iron bollards, pieces of lifeboat davit, and broken hatch covers to be seen. The wreck covers an area of 70 m in length by 18 m across. Myriads of soft corals have taken hold at the most exposed ends, but monofilament trammel nets used in cod fishing also hang like spiders' webs all over one end of the wreck. Cod and pout whiting are in abundance, making this an excellent boat-angling venue, and a number of crustaceans could clearly be seen amongst the wreckage. The bell, if located, will most probably be inscribed: *Georg 1889*.

GRIT

Dat of loss: 5 November 1943
Wreck: ✯✯✯✯✯
Depth: 55 m
Reference: 54 57'.939 N 001 10'.482 W
Location: 6.53 nm E by S of Souter Lighthouse

The *Grit* (Official No. 163519) was a steel-hulled 501-ton British motor vessel measuring 48.89 m in length, with an 8.1-m beam and a 2.84-m draught. George Brown and Co. of Greenock built and completed her as Yard No. 188 in September 1934; she was launched on 11 August 1934 for F. T. Everard and Sons Ltd. London, who registered her in London and was the owner at the time of loss. The single screw was powered by 2S.C.SA, 140-nhp five-cylinder diesel oil engines; Newbury Diesel Co. Newbury, built the aft-positioned machinery. She had a cruiser stern, one deck, three bulkheads, a 94-ton (266.17-cubic.m) forepeak tank, a 56-ton (158.57-cubic.m) aft peak tank and an aft superstructure consisting of a 31.1-m quarterdeck and 5.79-m forecastle. The designated code recognition signal letters were: MBYG.

Final voyage

On 5 November 1943, the *Grit* sank about one mile south by east of buoy no. 20C off the River Tyne, following a collision with the 7225-ton US steamer *Thomas Sully* (1943 – US Government). The *Grit* was sailing as part of a convoy and was transporting a cargo of wheat from King's Lynn to the Tyne. None of her crew was lost.

LR 1943/4 No. 25148 (G); LCR 1943, p. 8 (f); Starke Schell Registers.

Wrecksite

The wreck sits in a 0.75 m scour and is orientated in an E to W direction, just outside the local spoil ground. It lies on a seabed of dirty sand, mud and silt in a general depth of 55 m (LAT). The wreck, including the bridge superstructure at the western end, is completely intact and stands almost 7 m high, but at least two trawl nets have become entangled with the stern end, making things very eerie in the dim green light as they sway in the tide like huge shrouds.

Large numbers of fish, cod in particular, have taken up residence in the wreck and some very large lobsters have also been observed, while the top and most exposed structures are a myriad of soft corals and magnificent plumose anemones. This wreck will make an excellent boat-angling venue.

ILIOS

Date of Loss: 16 December 1898
Wreck: ✯✯
Depth: 22 m
Reference: 54 58'.725 N 001 20'.764 686 W
Location: 0.79 nm NE of Souter Point

The *Ilios* (Official No. 85017) was an iron-hulled 2020-ton British steam cargo ship measuring 83.68 m in length, with an 11.27-m beam and an 8.25-m draught. Short Brothers at Pallion, Sunderland built and completed her as Yard No. 130 in July 1882; she was launched on 29 July 1882 for Lumsden, Byers and Co. at Sunderland, who owned her at the time of loss. The single screw was powered by a 162-nhp two-cylinder compound steam engine that used two boilers. The cylinders measured 73.66 cm, 139.7 cm with an 83.82-cm stroke (29 in., 55 in. with a 33-in. stroke). The first master was Captain A. Wilson.

Final voyage

Twenty people were drowned on the evening of Friday, 16 December 1898, when the *Ilios* sank off Souter Point, following a collision with the 892-ton British steamer *Pierremont* (1877 – Sir W. Gray, West Hartlepool). Commanded by Captain R. W. Clarkson, the *Ilios* was *en route* from the Tyne to Genoa with a crew of 23 and a cargo of coal, under the charter of Messrs James Joicey and Co. She had signed articles at South Shields on Thursday for a voyage to Genoa and the *Pierremont* had left Dunstan Staithes on Friday afternoon with coals for Bilbao. Although badly damaged, the *Pierremont* cruised around the area of the sunken *Ilios* for quite a considerable time, searching for survivors, but found none, so it returned to the Tyne that evening.

William Owen, boatswain of the *Pierremont* said: "I was in the forecastle at the time and suddenly heard the cry, 'All hands on deck!' – a collision! I rushed out and just then heard a loud crash, as if the vessel was being broken in. On going to the forecastle head, I saw men scrambling in all directions, both on the *Pierremont* and on the *Ilios*. Thinking that our ship was going down, I jumped from the *Pierremont* forecastle head and caught the fore rigging of the *Ilios* and flung myself on board that vessel. There I found all the men in a state of panic to that which prevailed on my own ship. All hands were making for the boats and I assisted with releasing the boats from the grips, but considerable time was lost getting the boats from the chocks. I cut two of the chocks myself, but before the boat could be got out of the chocks, a number of men clambered into it. An officer shouted, 'For God's sake, get out of the boat and get it hoisted out!', but they would not leave and the boat could not be freed. The *Ilios* at this time began to heel over to one side. Half an hour after the collision the vessel gradually settled down and only 15 minutes after I went on board, it went down head first. The crew were thrown into the sea. I fortunately caught hold of a life buoy that had washed off the sinking steam and pulled it over my head. Half an hour later, the 153-ton steam paddle-tug *Challenger,* from South Shields, owned by Charles Evan Walton and Robert Stewart at South Shields, came on the scene, attracted by the cries of drowning men. Lines were thrown to me and two other men, Joseph Kirtley, of 43 Frost Street, Tyne Dock and Martin Flinkman, a native of Finland, who were beside me in the water, and we were taken on board the tug."

Another man was seen floating in the sea, but after being hauled on board the *Challenger*, he was found to be dead. A note in his pocket identified him as Robert Stove from Cardiff, the second mate on the *Ilios*. The tug cruised around for some time, but found no one else, it then landed the shipwrecked men at South Shields, where they were given dry clothes and attended by the river police. Late on Friday night, the steamer *Zanetta* arrived at Tyne Dock, where the master reported having rescued George B. Nicholson, the second engineer, who had been found floating on an empty oil drum.

The *Pierremont*'s starboard bow was stove in from the waterline to the forecastle head and it was probably also damaged below the waterline, but none of her crew was missing.

The crewmen who died were:

Ballard, Byron, Cook MM from London
Bristow, William, Fireman MM from Sunderland
Clarkson, R.W., Master MM of Sunderland
Cogle, Thomas, Able Seaman MM from South Shields
Davidson, John, Steward MM from Sunderland
Fairbairn, T.W., Third Engineer MM from Sunderland
Harkwell, W., Able Seaman MM from South Shields
Heary, Charles, Able Seaman MM from South Shields
Jamieson, J.D., Boatswain MM from South Shields
Johns, F., Messroom Steward MM from Bristol
Kirtley, Anty, Fireman MM from Tyne Dock
Lewis, A, Fireman MM from Aberdovey
Lillico, Thomas, Fireman MM from South Shields
Page, Ernest, Able Seaman MM from Darlington
Rumcie, W.J., Carpenter MM from Sunderland
Stove, R., Second Mate MM from Cardiff
Strong, Robert, Chief Mate MM from Sunderland
Thompson, J, Fireman MM from South Shields
Wade, Henry W., Able Seaman MM from South Shields
Wardle, William James, Chief Engineer MM from Sunderland

American Lloyd's Register of American and Foreign Shipping, 1857–1900; Starke Schell Registers; Board of Trade Wreck Return: Ilios, 1898; *The Times*: Monday, 19 December 1898, p. 10, Issue 35703.

Wrecksite

The wreck is orientated in a NW to SE direction and lies on a firm sandy seabed in a general depth of 22 m (LAT). It is now broken up and rather dispersed, but the bows are reasonably intact and have a covering of soft corals. Jeff Maine informed the author that the boilers are standing upright next to the engine block, which is rather smashed open and lying on its side, showing all of the large bronze bearings.

The wreck has been well salvaged over the years. The anchor chain and prop shaft were removed some time ago, along with the ship's bell and many of the other interesting items, but it still makes an nice rummage dive. Bits of brass and copper pipe can still be found, as well as the occasional porthole under the piles of iron debris. Large cod are not uncommon and local angling boats regularly make good catches while fishing over the top of the wreck.

SEDGEFLY, HM TRAWLER EX NORMAN

Date of loss: 16 December 1939
Wreck: ✯✯✯✯
Depth: 50 m
Reference: 54 58'.895 N 001 13'.589 W
Location: 6.28 nm ESE of South Shields Lighthouse

The *Sedgefly* (Official No. 167051) was a steel-hulled 520-ton British steam trawler which measured approximately 53.6 m in length, with an 8.7-m beam and a 2.80-m draught. Smith's Dock Co. Ltd. at South Bank-on-Tees, Middlesbrough built and completed her as Yard No. 1059 in February 1939; she was launched as the *Norman* on 20 January 1939 for Hull Northern Fishing Co. Ltd. Hull (H. 28); Hellyer Bros. Ltd. was the manager. The single screw powered a 169-nhp three-cylinder triple expansion steam engine that used one single-ended boiler with a working pressure of 225 psi, with three corrugated furnaces, 5.10 sq.m (55 sq.ft) of grate surface and 248.05 sq.m (2670 sq.m) of heating surface. The cylinders measured 36.83 cm, 60.96 cm and 105.41 cm with a 68.58 cm stroke (14.5 in., 24 in. and 41.5 in. with a 27-in. stroke). Smith's Dock Co. Ltd. manufactured the machinery. She had four bulkheads cemented, a 26.51-m quarter deck and an 8.75-m forecastle; side tanks in 0.74 sq.m (8 sq.ft) deep tanks of 25 tons, 11 tons and an aft peak tank of 15 tons; she was also equipped with wireless direction finder and echo sounding device.

In September 1939, the trawler was requisitioned by the Admiralty and renamed *Sedgefly*; she was then converted to Anti-Submarine Trawler No. FY.122, equipped with one 4-in. (102 mm) gun.

Final patrol

On 16 December 1939, just three months after being requisitioned, HMT *Sedgefly* was under the command of Chief Skipper Royce William Stocks RNR and on patrol duties about six miles off the Tyne when she detonated a German-laid mine and sank with all 16 hands. It is believed that Bronte's Kriegsmarine destroyers: *Z 4* (Richard Beitzen), *Z 8* (Bruno Heinemann), *Z 14* (Friedrich Ihn) and *Z 15* (Erich Steinbrick) had laid the mines during the night of 12/13 December 1939, under the cover of *Z 19* (Hermann Künne).

The crewmen who died were:

Dyball, Edward, 2nd Hand, RNR (PS)
Elliott, Charles, Able Seaman
Greening, Alfred, Seaman
Hare, Albert, Stoker, RNR (PS)
Higgins, Joseph, Stoker, RNR (PS)
Innes, John, Leading Seaman, RNR (PS)
Jenkinson, George, 1st Engineman, RNPS
Ladgefoged, Thane, Ordinary Signalman

Pool, Charles, Seaman Steward, RNPS
Pratt, Harry, Seaman Cook, RNPS
Rilatt, Eric, Able Seaman, RNR (PS)
Smith, Alexander, Engineman, RNPS
Stocks, Royce, Chief Skipper, RNR
Thames, Samuel, Seaman, RNPS
Wilson, George, Seaman, RNPS
Worrell, William, Seaman, RNPS

BVLS 1939–45, p. 3 ; SRN Vol. 2, p. 326 ; CWGC.

Wrecksite

The wreck, which is possibly that of the *Sedgefly*, is orientated in an ENE to WSW direction and lies in a general depth of 50 m (LAT). It is intact and upright and standing 5.4 m high with damage at the bows. The wreckage covers an area of 55 m in length by 18 m across and soft corals cover the upper sections. Lots of fish have been observed, so this should be an interesting boat-angling venue. If the wreck is the trawler, the bell will be inscribed: *Norman 1939.*

HUMBER

Date of loss: 25 January 1918
Wreck: ✯✯✯
Depth: 29 m
Reference north end: 54 57'.174 N 001 18' .809 W
Reference south end: 54 57'. 154 N 001 18' .799 W
Location: 2.79 nm NNE from Roker Lighthouse, Sunderland

The *Humber* was an iron-hulled 280-ton British steam cargo vessel measuring 39.5 m in length, a 6.7-m beam and a 3-m draught. The vessel was originally subcontracted to Grangemouth Dock Yard as Yard No. 205, but Ardrossan Dry Dock Co. Ltd. Ardrossan built and completed her as yard number 179 in 1899; she was launched on 21 October 1899 for E.P. Hutcheson. The single iron screw was powered by a 35-rhp two-cylinder triple expansion steam engine that used one single-ended boiler working at a pressure of 130 psi with two corrugated furnaces, 2.78 sq.m (30 sq.ft) of grate surface and 65.49 sq.m (705 sq.ft) of heating surface, giving eight knots. The cylinders measured 35.56 cm and 73.66 cm with a 53.34 cm stroke (14 in. and 29 in. with a 21-in. stroke). Walker, Henderson and Co. manufactured the engine and ancillary machinery at Glasgow. She also had one deck.

J. B. Knapton was the registered owner at the time of loss.

Final voyage

On 25 January 1918, the *Humber* sank two miles east of Sunderland, following a torpedo attack by SMU *UB 34*, a KDM submarine commanded by Kapitänleutnant Hellmuth von Ruckteschell. The steamer, which was armed for defence, was sunk without warning while transporting a cargo of wheat from King's Lynn to Dunston. The following seven crewmen, including the master were killed:

Brasnett, Lewis Robert, 36 yrs, Mate MM
Cook, David, Master MM
Halliday, William, 27 yrs, Able Seaman MM
Legood, Thomas James, 53 yrs, 1st Engineer MM

Legood, Thomas William, 23 yrs, 2nd Engineer MM
Wann, Joseph Oliver, 32 yrs, Fireman MM
Welberry, Albert Joseph, 31 yrs, Cook and Steward MM

LWCLR 1914–18, p. 196; CWGC; Jarvis (2000)

Wrecksite

The wreck was positively identified as the collier *Humber* in 2009 by divers from Allan Lopez's Tyne-based charter boat *Spellbinder* who found the bell. It is orientated in a NNE to SSW direction and lies on a seabed of dirty sand, gravel, black shells and rock, in a general depth of 29 m (LAT). It is now partially buried and totally collapsed into a pile of decayed, twisted plates and broken machinery. The highest point being 3.8 m. The wreckage covers an area 63 m long and 26 m across, with a few crustaceans sheltering amungst it.

EAGLE III, ex DARGLE, ex SCHOKLAND, ex ENERGIE

Date of loss: 17 November 1977
Wreck: ★★★★★
Depth: 55 m
Reference: 54 58'.806 N 001 10'.515 W
Location: 6.54 nm E of Souter Lighthouse

The *Eagle III* (Official No. 16651) was a steel-hulled 399-ton Panamanian-registered motor vessel measuring 51.23 m in length, with an 8.13-m beam and 3.04-m draught. Van der Werff's Scheepsbouw Mij, Westerbroek, Netherlands built and completed her as Yard No. 276 in 1956; she was launched as the *Energie* on 14 March 1956 for Rederij "Energie", Amsterdam, The Netherlands; W. F. Kampman's Bevr. and Controlbedrijf was the manager. The single screw, possibly bronze, was powered by an aft-positioned 375-hp, five-cylinder 4.SA diesel oil engine with a 305 mm x 460 mm stroke and gave 9.5 knots. D. and J. Boot "De Industrie", Alphen manufactured the machinery. She also had a small aft-positioned bridge structure.

In 1965–75 she was renamed *Schokland* by G. Dekker, Kampen, Netherlands, who acquired her; Wagenborg Scheepvaart BV was the manager. She was renamed *Dargle* in 1975 when Vartry Shipping Ltd. Dublin, purchased her. In 1975 she was renamed *Eagle III* by Eagle Shipping Co. Ltd. Panama who bought her.

Final voyage

On 16 November 1977, the *Eagle III* was transporting a cargo of stone from Tayport to Bergen-op-Zoom in the southwest Netherlands, but developed a serious leak about ten miles east of the Tyne. A heavy list developed and her master radioed for assistance; the coaster was abandoned by her crew and was taken in tow by the MFV *Nova Spero,* but sank the following morning,. when the vessels were eight nm SE of the Tyne entrance.

LCR 1977, p. 49; Starke Schell Registers.

Wrecksite

The wreck is orientated in a NW to SE direction and lies on a seabed of dirty muddy sand and silt in a general depth of 55 m (LAT). It is completely intact, sitting upright some 7.5 m high at the southeastern end, which is the highest point, where the bridge structure is located. The wreck is covered in an array of soft corals and some beautiful plumose anemones. There is also a strong possibility that trawl nets will have become entangled with the wreck. The engine maker's plate on this wreck will be written in Dutch.

CRATER

Date of loss: 2 June 1926
Wreck: ★★★
Depth: 54 m
Reference: 54 58'.917 N 001 10'.900 W
Location: 7.74 nm ESE of South Shields Lighthouse

The *Crater* (Official No. 106669) was a steel-hulled 132-ton yawl-rigged steam trawler measuring 30.25 m in length, with a 6.57 m beam and a 3.7 m draught. Mackie and Thomson at Old Govan near Glasgow built and completed her as Yard No. 117 in 1896; she was launched on 19 September 1896 for Grimsby and North Sea Steam Fishing Co. Ltd. Grimsby; GY.111. The single steel screw was powered by a 47-hp, three-cylinder triple expansion steam engine that used one boiler. Muir and Houston Ltd. at Glasgow manufactured the machinery. She had one deck, a 5.18 m quarterdeck and 5.79 m forecastle.

On 29 May 1917, the *Crater* was requisitioned as a Fishery Reserve Vessel (Port Reg: SN.135) and in 1919 was returned to her Grimsby owner. In July 1919, Ashford and Taylor Ltd. at Fleetwood was the registered owner and New Docks Steam Trawling Co. Ltd. Fleetwood was the manager. On 20 July 1919, she was registered at Fleetwood as FD.330. However, on 29 November 1923 the Fleetwood registry closed. From 1923, the *Crater* was owned by Richard Irvin and Sons Ltd. North Shields and on 29 November 1923, she was registered as SN.135. The North Shields registry closed in 1926.

Final voyage

On 2 June 1926, the *Crater* was fishing off the Tyne when she sprang a serious leak after striking a submerged object, which was believed to have been floating wreckage. The frantic efforts to keep the water down were futile and the trawler had to be abandoned; she then sank almost at once. The crew of eight men, including the skipper, Albert Annan, were picked up by a herring boat and landed at the Tyne.

LCR 1926, p. 7 (g); *The Times*: Thursday, 3 June 1926, p. 10, Issue 44288.

Wrecksite

The wreck, which is probably that of the *Crater,* is orientated in a SE to NW direction. It lies on a seabed of fine sand, mud and black shells in a general depth of 54 m (LAT). The wreck covers an area 29 m long and 10 m across and stands just over 5 m high amidships. It appears intact and upright, with a large shoal of fish swimming over the top of it. A large trawl net is also caught up on the wreck and floats up over it.

ADAM'S BECK

Date of loss: 29 July 1941
Wreck: ★★★★★
Depth: 52 m
Reference: 54 58'.472 N 001 11'.421 W
Location: 7.58 nm ESE of South Shields Lighthouse

The *Adam's Beck* (Official No. 168193) was a steel-hulled 2816-ton British steam cargo ship measuring 96.01 m in length, with a 13.53-m beam and a 6.01-m draught. Burntisland Shipbuilding Co. Ltd. Burntisland built and completed her as Yard No. 235 in June 1941; she was launched on 24 April1941 for Gas, Light and Coke Co. Ltd. who owned her at the time of loss; Stephenson Clarke and Associated Co. Ltd. were the managers. The single steel screw was powered by an aft-positioned 240-nhp three-cylinder triple expansion steam engine that used two single-ended boilers working at a pressure of 200 psi, with six corrugated furnaces, 9.38 sq.m (101 sq.ft) of grate surface and 319.02 sq.m (3434 sq.ft) of heating surface. The cylinders measured 46.99 cm, 78.74 cm and 132.8 cm with a 99.06 cm stroke (18.5 in., 31 in. and 52 in. with a 39-in. stroke). D. Rowan and Co. Ltd. Glasgow manufactured the machinery. She had a cruiser stern, one deck, five bulkheads partly cemented and an aft superstructure that consisted of a 58.6-m quarterdeck and 8.8-m forecastle; she also had some cellular double bottom and a fore-peak and aft peak tank. Lloyd's classed her 100 A1. The designated code recognition signal letters were: BCJT.

Final voyage

On 29 July 1941, the *Adam's Beck* was sailing as a part of the southbound 56-ship convoy FS.554 (Methil–Southend) when she was bombed by an aircraft of the Luftwaffe, 235° and one nautical mile from Buoy no. 20C off the River Tyne. She was voyaging from the Tyne to London with 4181 tons of coal. One man was lost and the ship was so badly damaged that the surviving crewmen abandoned ship, but she remained afloat until the early hours of the following morning, foundering at 0030 hrs. The man who died was a 66-year-old donkeyman, Kristian Theodor Nicolas Kristofferson.

BVLS 1939–45, p. 25 ; CWGC ; LCWLR 1939–45, p. 280.

Wrecksite

The wreck, probably that of the *Adam's Beck*, is orientated in a NE to SW direction. It lies on a seabed of dirty fine sand, mud and black shells in a general depth of 52 m (LAT). It is very broken up, stands 5.6 m high and covers an area 99 m long and 42 m wide. Large copper pipes protrude from the broken debris and lots of fishing tackle and nets cover some of the wreck; soft corals are also well established on the highest sections.

ROTHA

Date of loss: 23 February 1902
Wreck: ★★★
Depth: 39 m
Reference: 54 57'.472 N 001 17'.295 W
Location: 2.15 nm E of Souter Point

The *Rotha* (Official No. 101839) was a steel-hulled 1008-ton British steam cargo vessel measuring 67.05 m in length, with a 9.49-m beam and a 4.69-m draught. James Laing at Deptford Yard, Sunderland built and completed her as Yard No. 529 in September 1893; she was launched on 12 August 1893 for Sharp and Co. Newcastle upon Tyne, who was the owner at the time of loss. The single, four-blade 13.81-m (12½ ft) screw was powered by a 156-nhp three-cylinder triple expansion steam engine that used one single-ended boiler. The cylinders measured 48.26 cm, 80.01 cm and 130.81 cm with an 83.82 cm stroke (19 in., 31½ in. and 51½ in. with a 33-in.stroke). North East Marine Engineering Co. Ltd. Sunderland manufactured the engine and ancillary machinery. She had one deck, four bulkheads cemented, a well deck and a superstructure consisting of a 28.04-m poop deck, a 28.04-m quarter-deck, a 13.41-m bridge deck and a 6.7-m forecastle; a mast adjacent to the quarter deck and one adjacent to the poop deck, four hatches and three deck winches. She also had web frames, a flat keel, some cellular double bottom and a forepeak and aft peak tank. She was classed as 100 A1.

Final voyage

Less than an hour after leaving the River Tyne early on the morning of 23 February 1902, the *Rotha* (Captain J. Hay) sank, following a collision with the 1548-ton Danish steamer *Skjold* (1881 – DS Skjold, Copenhagen), three miles east of Souter lighthouse. The *Rotha* was on passage from the Tyne for Devonport with a crew of 14 and a cargo of coal. With a light southwesterly wind blowing, weather conditions were very good, but it was dark. The *Skjold*, which was on passage from Rouen for Newcastle, was left badly damaged, but managed to rescue all of the *Rotha*'s crew and land them back at the Tyne.

LR 1900/1 No. 550 (R); Board of Trade Wreck Return 1902, p. 145; *The Times*: Monday, 24 February 1902, p. 10, Issue 36699.

Wrecksite

The wreck, believed to be that of the *Rotha*, lies on a seabed of dirty sand, mud and broken shells in a general depth of 39 m (LAT). It is still rather substantial but totally collapsed and well broken up, with the bows fairly intact and lying at an angle of about 60°. The section where the hold is located has still got its shape and it is possible to swim into it, but the wreck is generally a jumbled pile of twisted girders, steel plates, big lengths of loose, bent and flattened copper pipe and broken machinery. The boiler/engine is openly visible amidships and close by is a huge and complete iron steering wheel, lodged solid; everything is covered in a heavy coating of sediment. A number of small cod, pout whiting and a medium-sized conger eel have been observed and the whole wreck is covered in an abundance of urchins and dead man's fingers.

BEN ARDNA, HM TRAWLER, ex DORILEEN, ex HMT JOHN BRADFORD

Date of loss: 12 May 1942
Wreck: ✯✯
Depth: 20 m
Reference: 54 58'.813 N 001 21'.221 W
Location: 0.66 nm NE of Souter Lighthouse

The *Ben Ardna* (Official No. 144415) was a steel-hulled 237-ton British steam trawler measuring 36 m in length, with a 6.7-m beam and 3.48-m draught. Hall Russell and Co. Ltd. at Aberdeen built and completed her as Yard No. 607 on 16 June 1917; she was launched as the *John Bradford* for the Admiralty on 25 April 1917. The single steel screw was powered by a 74-nhp three-cylinder triple expansion steam engine that used one boiler and gave ten knots. The cylinders measured 30.48 cm, 50.8 cm and 86.36 cm with a 60.96-cm stroke (12 in., 20 in. and 34 in. with a 24-in. stroke). Hall Russell and Co. Ltd. manufactured the machinery at Aberdeen. She had one deck and water ballast.

In July 1920 the Admiralty sold the boat to Richard Irvin and Sons, Aberdeen, who renamed her *Dorileen*, Port Registration: A.417. She was renamed *Ben Ardna* by Richard Irvin and Sons, Aberdeen in 1923. In August 1939 the Admiralty requisitioned and employed her in the Tyne area for the Examination Service, as Admiralty Trawler no. 3647; she was then equipped with one 12-pounder deck gun and fitted with listening hydrophones.

Final patrol

On 12 May 1942, HMT *Ben Ardna* was escorting the southbound eleven-ship convoy FN.41 (Methil– Southend) when she foundered off Souter Point, following a collision with the 1887-ton steamship *Bruce M* (1927 – Mooringwell S.S. Co. Ltd. Cardiff); none of her crew was lost.

SRN Vol. 2, p. 43; Miramar Ship Index; Toghill (1994), p. 41.

Wrecksite

The wreck is orientated in an E to W direction and lies on a seabed of hard dirty, silty sand in a general depth of 20 m (LAT). It is totally collapsed and well broken up, but still reasonably substantial. It stands 4 m high, with the boiler positioned close to the large engine block, in the middle of a pile of twisted steel frames, ribs and plates where it has collapsed in on itself.

HEKLA

Date of loss: 23 April 1902
Wreck: ✯✯
Depth: 25 m
Reference: 54 59'.526 N 001 21'.038 W
Location: 1.37 nm NNE of Souter Lighthouse

The *Hekla* (Official No. 67559) was a steel-hulled 1185-tons gross cargo steamer measuring 71.65 m in length, with a 9.46 m beam and a 5.10 m draught. William Gray and Co. at West

Hartlepool built and completed her as Yard No. 143 and launched her as the schooner-rigged *Hecla* for Fritz Herskind, West Hartlepool in November 1874. The single iron screw was powered by a two-cylinder compound steam engine that used one boiler. Blair and Co. Ltd. in Stockton manufactured the engine and ancillary machinery. She had one deck, two tiers of beams, four bulkheads, water ballast and an 81-ton (229.36-cubic.m) quarterdeck, a 109-ton (308.65-cubic.m) bridge deck, a 16-ton (45.30-cubic.m) housedeck and 33-ton (93.44-cubic.m) forecastle. The designated code recognition signal letters were: HKGT.

Herskind and Woods, West Hartlepool was the registered owner in 1885. In 1887, an 110-nhp three-cylinder triple expansion steam engine that used one boiler manufactured by Blair and Co. Ltd. replaced the compound engine. The cylinders measured 43.18 cm, 71.12 cm and 118.11 cm with an 83.82-cm stroke (17 in., 28 in. and 46½ in. with a 33-in.stroke). In 1892 she was renamed *Hekla* by new owners AS Hekla of Christiania, Norway and W. M. Holby was the manager. From 1894 Hekla S.S. Co. Christiania was the registered owner and C. Andersen was the master.

Final voyage

On 23 April 1902, the *Hekla* was two miles south of the Tyne on a voyage from Bilbao to Tyne Dock with a cargo of iron ore, when she sank following a collision with the new 2667-ton steamer *Dilkera* (May 1902 – Adelaide Steamship Co. Ltd. Adelaide). As soon as the vessels struck the hull was seen to have a huge hole in it and water immediately flooded the ship; within minutes she settled, going down by the stern. The crew rushed to the bows and the mate succeeded in getting hold of the anchor stock of the *Dilkera* and clung onto it. He was immediately followed by the *Hekler*'s master, Captain Jespersen. However, a trimmer had grabbed the master's feet and he would have been pulled down but for the fact that the trimmer slipped his hold and fell back into the gash in the side of the *Hekla* and was not seen again. The captain and second mate were drawn aboard the new steamer by means of ropes and several more men were rescued in this manner. There were 17 crewmen on the *Hekla*, but seven of them lost their lives.

Mr Hills, the chief engineer, was last seen alive standing near a lifeboat on the deck; his body was later picked up from the sea. Another body which was seen floating in the water was supposed to be that of Mr Larsen, the second engineer, who had been in his bunk. Among the other men who drowned were: Seaman Niels Merenssen, the steward called Ditriksen and a trimmer and boy, who was the stepson of the chief engineer. The rescued men were landed at North Shields and taken to the Sailors' Home. It was later stated that Captain Jespersen left his vessel only when there was no hope.

The *Dilkera* was a newly-built ship and was out on her first sea trial from Tyne Iron Shipbuilding Co at Newcastle; having been laid as yard number 138 and launched on 25 March 1902 for Adelaide Steamship Co. Ltd. Adelaide. In 1931 she was renamed *Mary Moller* by E. Moller of Shanghai. In 1935 she was owned by the Moller Line, Ltd. Shanghai. She was seized by the Japanese on 8 December 1941 in the Whangpoo River and renamed *Kaiko Maru* for the Japanese Government. The ship was bombed and sunk by USAAF aircraft on 26 October 1944, NE of Hainan.

The Times: Thursday, 24 April 1902, p. 10, Issue 36750; LCR 1902, p. 6 (d); Board of Trade Wreck Return 1902 p. 146; Starke Schell Registers; Miramar Ship Index; American Lloyd's Register of American and Foreign Shipping 1857–1900.

Wrecksite

The wreck is orientated in a more or less NW to SE direction. It lies on a dirty seabed of mud and sand in a general depth of 25 m (LAT). It is completely collapsed, well broken up and decayed, with the highest section of 3 m being around the boiler and engine. Between amidships and the stern, lumps of copper pipe have been seen, but everything is coated in hard white marine- worms casings. Higher parts of the wreck have soft corals attached to them. A number of crustaceans have been sighted and the occasional cod can be seen hiding amongst the debris, but there are much better wrecks than this one to spend any time fishing over.

NUBIA

Date of loss: 17 October 1941
Wreck: ✯✯
Depth: 40 m
Reference: 54 59'.026 N 001 17'.281 W
Location: 2.74 nm ENE of Souter Lighthouse

The *Nubia* (Official No. 113246) was a steel-hulled 196-ton steam trawler measuring 34.56 m in length, with a 6.29-m beam and a 3.4-m draught. Cook, Welton and Gemmell built and completed her as Yard No. 352 at Hull on 28 August 1903; she was launched on 25 August for Great Grimsby and East Coast Steam Fishing Co. Ltd. Grimsby, who registered her as GY.1275 on 28 August. The single steel screw was powered by a 59-rhp three-cylinder triple expansion steam engine that used one single-ended boiler working at a pressure of 180 psi, with two plain furnaces, 3.06 sq.m (33 sq.ft) grate surface and 97.54 sq.m (1050 sq.ft) of heating surface, giving ten knots. The cylinders measured 29.845 cm, 50.8 cm and 83.82 cm with a 60.96-cm stroke (11¾ in., 20 in. and 33 in. with a 24-in. stroke). Amos and Smith Ltd. manufactured the machinery at Hull. She had one deck, three bulkheads cemented, a 14.9-m quarterdeck and 5.8-m forecastle.

In 1917 the Admiralty requisitioned her into the Fishery Reserve and in 1919 she was returned to the owner. Henry G. Hopwood and Charles Taylor of Grimsby purchased her in February 1937.

Japan Fishing Co. Ltd. acquired the boat on 20 May 1937. In November 1939, she was requisitioned by the Admiralty, renamed *Weazel,* converted to an Auxiliary Patrol Vessel (APV) and equipped with an echo sounding device. In 1940 she was returned to the owners. From 1940, Japan Fishing Co. Ltd. was the registered owner and C. Taylor was the manager. The designated code recognition signal letters were: MGQW.

Final voyage

On 17 October 1941 the *Nubia* foundered with six of her crew, following a collision with an unnamed vessel, six miles off the River Tyne. The crewmen that died were:

Hornby, William 52 yrs, Deck Hand MM
Johnson, Robert Henry William 41 yrs, Deck Hand MM
Ross, Thomas Horne 52 yrs, Chief Engineer MM

Stanforth, John, 52 yrs, Third Hand MM
Walker, John, Charles Henry 34 yrs, Trimmer MM
Ward, Richard, 60 yrs, Skipper MM

LCR 1941, p. 8 (f); LR 1941/2 No. 61924 (N); Thompson (1999); CWGC.

Wrecksite

This wreck, believed to be that of the *Nubia*, is orientated in an ESE to WNW direction. It lies on a seabed of sand and gravel in a general depth of 40 m (LAT). The wreck is upright, intact and about 3 m high, with its bridge structure broken down almost to deck level and the bottom of the hull partially buried in the sand. There is an open hold on the deck into which it would be possible to swim. A broken jib or derrick lies over the top of the hull and a long steel hawser leads away from the stern end for about 25 metres.

MOTOR MINE SWEEPER-180

Date of loss: 13 February 1942
Wreck: ☆☆☆
Depth: 39 m
Reference: 54 59'.930 N 001 17'.335 W
Location: 3.11 nm SE of Souter Lighthouse

HMS MS 34, *sister ship to the wooden-hulled 226 ton Admiralty* motor mine-sweeper 180 *(Author's collection)*

The HMS *MMS-180* was a wooden-hulled 226-ton Admiralty motor minesweeper measuring 36.2 m in length, with a 7-m beam and a 2.8-m draught. She was completed on 29 January 1942. The single bronze screw was powered by a 500-bhp diesel engine that gave a top speed of 11 knots. The vessel was armed with two 20-mm AA guns and two machine guns and carried a complement of twenty.

Final voyage

On 13 February 1942, only two weeks after she was completed, *MMS-180* was rammed in a convoy and sunk near the T.2 Buoy off the mouth of the River Tyne, but none of the crew was lost.

Wrecksite

The wreck is orientated in an ESE to WNW direction and lies on a well-swept seabed of hard sand and stone in a general depth of 39 m (LAT). It is broken into two sections, with its bows and stern end still fairly intact and covered in a myriad of soft corals, but it has collapsed down amidships into a pile of twisted broken machinery. The bronze screw is reported to be still in place at the stern end and is half-buried in the seabed. The wreck now stands about 6 m from the seabed at its highest point. There is very little non-ferrous metal among the remains, but the ship's bell should still be around, although this was a Royal Navy vessel.

JÖNKÖPING I, ELIZABETH, ex ELIZABETH ALLEN

Date of loss: 13 August 1918
Wreck: ★
Depth: 46 m
Reference: 55 00'.372 N 001 16'.140 W
Location: 4.52 nm E of South Shields Lighthouse

The *Jönköping I* (Official No. 82894) was a steel-hulled 1570-ton Swedish schooner-rigged steam cargo ship measuring 79 m in length, with a 10.5-m beam and a 5.80-m draught. Bartram, Haswell and Co. at South Dock, Sunderland built and completed her as Yard No. 114 in May 1881; she was launched as the *Elizabeth Allen* on 25 May 1881 for J. Allen and Co. Ltd. London; the master was Captain J. Bates. The single steel screw was powered by a 193-nhp two-cylinder compound steam engine that used one boiler. The cylinder diameters measured 81.28 cm and 152.4 cm with a 99.06-cm stroke (32 in. and 60 in. with a 39-in.stroke). She had one deck, five bulkheads and used water ballast. The designated code recognition signal letters were: VWBS.

In 1887 the master was Captain J. Allen. In March 1898, she was sold to Rederi A.B. Amphitrite Helsingborg, Sweden and renamed *Elizabeth*; P. L Påhlsson was the manager. From June 1917, Rederi AB Nordstjernan, Stockholm in Sweden was the registered owner and renamed her *Jönköping I*; Axel Axson Johnson was the manager.

Final voyage

On 13 August 1918, the *Jönköping I* was transporting a cargo of rough wood pulp from Gothenburg to Hull when the KDM submarine SMU *UB 104*, commanded by Oblt.z.S. Thomas Bieber, torpedoed her without any warning. The steamer broke in two and the fore-section sank immediately, but the stern part was towed ashore and beached at Herd Sands. From her crew of 19, five crewmen died in the incident and two were injured. Those that died were:

Dahlström, Arthur Thodor, 24 yrs, second mate
Tuvesson, Carl, 40 yrs, 1st Engineer

Jansson, David Gottfrid, 28 yrs, 2nd Engineer
Karlsson, Konrad Ludvig, 27 yrs, Donkeyman
Berggren, Per Gösta Magnus, 17 yrs, Messroom boy

The two men injured were H. Larsson (Ordinary Sailor) and David Vilhelm Almgren (Cook).

ANCL 1914–18, p. 118; American Lloyd's Register of American and Foreign Shipping, 1857–1900 – Register of American and Foreign Shipping 1857–1900; LCWLR 1914–18, p. 229.

Wrecksite

This small wreck is possibly all that is left of the *Jönköping I*. It lies on a seabed of mud and fine sand in a general depth of 46 m (LAT). The remains stand just over 4 m high and cover an area 25 m long and 14 m wide, but most of it is collapsed and broken up.

PROTECTOR

Date of loss: 31 December 1916
Wreck: ✯
Depth: 23 m
Reference: 55 00'.024 N 001 22'.881 W
Also given: 55 01'.054 N 001 22'.170 W
Location: 1.60 nm ENE of South Shields Lighthouse

Pilot Cutter Protector, *sank by a mine laid by* UC 31 *off the Tyne mouth in 1916 (Author's collection)*

The *Protector* was a steel-hulled 200-ton steam-powered pilot cutter that was sail-rigged and measured 33.52 m in length, with a 6.73-m beam and a 3.22-m draught. J. P. Rennoldson and Sons at South Shields built and completed her as Yard No. 251 in October 1907; she was launched on 9 September for the Tyne Pilotage Commissioners, who owned her at the time of loss. The single bronze screw was powered by a 50-hp, three-cylinder triple expansion steam engine that used one boiler, positioned amidships.

Final voyage

On 31 December 1916, the *Protector*, with Captain Thomas Reed in charge, was lying off the Tyne entrance awaiting pilotage duties when she was seen to suddenly blow up and sink. The explosion lifted the vessel clean out of the water and she sank almost immediately, taking down with her 19 people, including the captain. It was believed that she had detonated a German mine, laid early that same morning. After WWI, it was discovered that the KDM submarine SMU *UC 31*, commanded by Kapitänleutnant Otto von Schrader, had laid the mine.

Losing virtually all of the Tyne pilots paralysed the Tyne for nearly two weeks. There was a national coal shortage as a result and this hit the London power stations hard. The navy had to draft in local reservists, tug-boat skippers and retired pilots in order to get river trade moving again. For two weeks there was a build up of large vessels off the mouth of the Tyne.

Inside St. Stephen's Church, Tynemouth is a plaque, which is inscribed:

> 'To the Glory of God and in Memory of the Pilots, Pilot's Assistants and Crew of the Tyne Pilot Cutter "*Protector*" who died in the service of their Country when their vessel was destroyed by enemy action off the Tyne on 30 December 1916:
>
> 1st Class Pilots: John Y. Bone, Charles Burn, Robert Chambers, Thomas Heron, Thomas H. Marshall, Robert Philips, William H. Tinmouth, Matthew Young and William Young.
>
> 2nd Class Pilot, John H. Burn. Pilot's Assistants: John H. Crane, Alexander Leslie, William Leslie, Ralph Philips. And the Crew: Thomas Reed Master, William R. Forster Chief Engineer, John W. Nicholson Steward, Benjamin Rumney Cabin Boy, James Macconnachie Fireman.
>
> Also in Memory of Pilot's Assistants Septimus Sloanee SS Phare. Hylton Young SS Spennymoor, who lost their lives at sea through enemy action.
>
> This Tablet is erected by the Tyne Pilots' Authority'

ADM 137/2960 ; LCWLR 1914–18, p. 80 ; BVLS 1914–18, p. 29 ; CWGC ; Jarvis (2000), Vol. V.

Wrecksite

The wreck has not been positively identified, but two positions have been suggested:

The first two sets of co-ordinates are for someone's 'secret wreck', which he claims is that of the *Protector*. There is a screw that has one blade missing and a couple of badly corroded Admiralty pattern anchors, while on the port side at the bows, a rusting winch can be found. In between, steel ribs run the full length of the wreck. Off the starboard side, other wreckage and debris can be seen, partially buried in the seabed a few metres away.

The second co-ordinates have the wreck orientated in a SSE to NNW direction; lying on a seabed of dark dirty sand and stone in a general depth of 21 m (LAT). It is totally collapsed onto the seabed in a one metre pile of twisted steel plates, frames and broken machinery, with the remains of the steam engine in the midst of it all, typical of a small wreck of this period. There are a few copper pipes and brass valves and flanges to be seen, but much of it is partially buried. The wreck covers an area of around 35 m in length and is 3 m high.

STAINSACRE

Date of loss: 30 November 1885
Wreck: ✯✯
Depth: 15 m
Reference: 55 00'.744 N 001 23'.526
Location: 0.40 nm ESE from Tynemouth light

The *Stainsacre* (Official No. 72135) was an iron-hulled 1108-ton British steam cargo vessel measuring 67.8 m in length and with a 9.2 m beam. Thomas Turnbull and Sons, Whitby built and completed her as Yard No. 47 in June 1876; she was launched for the ship builders on 24 June 1876. The single iron screw was powered by a 99-nhp two-cylinder compound inverted steam engine that used one boiler. The cylinders measured 68.58 cm and 139.7 cm with a 83.82- cm stroke (27 in. and 55 in. with a 33-in. stroke). Blair and Co. Ltd. manufactured the engine and ancillary machinery at Stockton. She had a 26.51-m quarterdeck, a 26.21-m bridge deck and 8.22-m forecastle.

Final voyage

The *Stainsacre* sank following a collision with the 1380-ton steamer *Harvest* (1881 – English and Co. West Hartlepool), at 2300 hrs on the night of 30 November 1885, just off the Tyne mouth, while on passage from the Tyne to Copenhagen with a cargo of coal. The *Stainsacre* had dropped her pilot off abreast of the Herd Buoy and was proceeding down the River Tyne and approaching the pier ends, keeping well to the south of the mid-channel. She was making about five to six knots when the red light of the *Harvest* was seen about one mile distant. It was bearing about three points on the starboard bow, but because no masthead light was visible, she was taken to be a sailing ship and the *Stainsacre* was kept on her course until she passed the end of the South Pier, at which time the two ships were about half a mile apart. The helm of the *Stainsacre* was then put hard-a-port, but when the ship was around a point, the *Harvest* blew two blasts on its whistle, showing that she was a steamer and was starboarding her helm. The *Stainsacre* immediately put her helm hard-a-starboard and the engines were put in full reverse. However the *Harvest* came on with only her red light visible and with her stem and starboard bow, struck the *Stainsacre* on the starboard side at right angles; so much damage was inflicted that she sank soon after.

The master of the *Harvest* later claimed that he had been coming up the coast from the south and was approaching the Tyne on a NW ¾ W course, steering for Tynemouth light. According to his account, she then starboarded her helm to steer W ¾ N and when the masthead and red lights of the *Stainsacre* were seen a little on the port bow and about a mile off coming out of the river, the helm was ported a little and the whistle sounded one short blast. The two ships, he said, were in a position to pass clear portside to portside, but as they approached the *Stainsacre*, it starboarded her helm and opened her green light at a distance of about 200 yards. The helm of the *Harvest* was immediately put hard-a-port and the engines made full speed astern, but the collision occurred nevertheless.

At the Court of Inquiry on 11 January 1886, Mr Justice Butt found that:

> the *Harvest* was to blame, because Article 20 of the Tyne Rules states that vessels coming from southward should keep so far out to sea till they struck the line of the leading lights, as to give vessels plenty of room to come out clear of the pier head on the south side. This Mr Justice Butt had found that the *Harvest* had not done, but had approached the river in such a way as to cut across a great deal too close to the South Pier and had therefore infringed the rule in question and caused the collision.

The *Harvest* suffered a similar fate when she sank following a collision with the 528-ton steamer *Regent*, on 12 September 1889, in the entrance to the River Tees, while voyaging from Middlesbrough to Stettin with 1750-tons of pig iron. The following was a report that appeared in the North Eastern Daily Gazette on Friday, 13 September 1889:

> A MIDDLESBROUGH VESSEL SUNK IN THE TEES
>
> THE CREW SAVED
>
> Early yesterday morning a serious collision occurred at the mouth of the Tees. The screw steamer Harvest owned by Messrs English and Co. of Middlesbrough, commanded by Captain Moorson, having loaded a cargo of 1750 tons of pig-iron, sailed from Middlesbrough to Stettin on the morning tide, the crew of 18 hands, all told, when just at the mouth of the river, she was struck on her port side just behind her foremast, by the screw steamer *Regent*, and sank. The weather was fine and clear. The *Regent* is a vessel of 1000 tons burthen and owned by Messrs Edward Harris and Co. of Middlesbrough. Her Master was Captain Britton and she was making for the Tees Light from Portland, with a crew of 14 hands.
>
> The *Harvest* was so considerably damaged that she sank almost directly after the catastrophe. The crew were picked up by the steam-tug *Ryhope* and conveyed back to Middlesbrough.
>
> Serious damage was also done to the *Regent* about the bows, but she was able to proceed to Middlesbrough, where she was laid up by the shipyard of Messrs Raylton Dixon and Co. Ltd. Attempts are being made to raise the sunken vessel, and with the present favourable weather, the efforts will probably be successful.

Those efforts, though, were not successful, and the wreck remains there to this day.

The Times: Tuesday, 22 December 1885, p. 4, Issue 31636; Starke Schell Registers; Board of Trade Wreck Report 1885; Court of Inquiry in London on 11 January 1886, before Mr Justice Butt and Trinity Masters.

Wrecksite

The wreck of the *Stainsacre* is orientated in a NE to SW direction. It lies on a firm seabed of dirty sand and stones in a general depth of 15 m (LAT). The wreck is very broken, well collapsed and partially buried, with a wide debris field. It stands just 1.5 m high and covers an area 68 m long and 23 m across. The remains were thought to be that of the 1441-ton steamer *Sargasso*, which sank following a collision with the 3605-ton steamer *Mary Ada Short* (1896

– James Westoll, Sunderland), on 18 April 1912, but that wreck was raised and disposed of by the Tyne Commissioners soon after it sank.

OSLOFJORD

Date of loss: 1 December 1940
Wreck: ★★★
Depth: 12 m
Reference: 55 00'.161 N 001 23'.917 W
55 00'.108 N 001 23'.435 W
Engines: 55 00'.147 N 001 23'.359 W
Location: 0.5.4 nm S by E of South Shields Lighthouse

The 18,673-ton Norwegian passenger liner Oslofjord *during happier times (World Ship Society)*

The *Oslofjord* was a steel-hulled 18 673-ton Norwegian passenger liner measuring 171.68 m in length, with a 22.35 m beam and 10.38 m draught. Deutsche Schiff-und Maschinenbau AG, Weser, Bremen in Germany built and completed her as Yard No. 932 in May 1938; she was launched by Lisken Henriksen, the wife of company director Gustav Henriksen, on 29 December 1937 for Aktieselskapet Den Norske-Amerikalinje (NAL), Oslo.

The two huge bronze screws were powered by four 4400-bhp MAN double-acting two-stroke seven-cylinder engines, arranged in pairs and hydraulically coupled to twin shafts. The combined horsepower was 17,600 bhp driving twin bronze screws at 90 rpm for a cruising speed of 18.75 knots. Maschinenfabrik Augsburg-Nürnberg A.G., Augsburg manufactured the machinery.

The ship had a cruiser stern, ten bulkheads, twelve 88-person capacity lifeboats and two 48-person motorboats carried in the davits, a 92.1-m bridge-deck and 13.4-m forecastle. She had six passenger decks, a sports and upper promenade, shelter A and B, with a swimming pool and sauna on C deck. She could accommodate 152 cabin, 307 tourist and 401 third class passengers. In all she was designed to carry 310 crew and 860 passengers. Truly a magnificent ship by any standard, but sadly one with an extremely short career, ending up as the largest merchant ship wrecked off the east coast of Britain. The designated code recognition signal letters were: LJFX.

The *Oslofjord* sailed on 5 May 1938 for sea trials and made over 20 knots on the measured mile on the 9th. The swastika flew from her foremast, but at the mainmast (at half mast until she was delivered) were the Norwegian ensign and NAL house flag. She was handed over on 10 May. The beautiful liner made her maiden progress up the fjord for which she was named on 16 May, the day before Norwegian Independence Day, slicing a wide white wake through the dark waters, bedecked with waving flags and escorted by a flotilla of small boats.

Germany invaded Poland on 30 August 1939 and the *Oslofjord* arrived at Oslo the following day. From that date forth she ferried stranded Americans to the USA while operating under the neutral flag line.

The ship's first cruise was to Haiti, Panama and Cuba between 20 December and 2 January 1940, but it was to be her last commercial voyage. NAL. declared that she was to be laid up in New York harbour on 30 January, alongside another beautiful NAL. liner and future troop transport, the 10 709-ton *Bergensfjord.*

On 26 October 1940 the *Oslofjord*, under Captain Ole Bornemann Bull, left Bayonne, N.J. for Halifax, Nova Scotia for conversion to a troopship, arriving there on the 28th. While in Halifax, she was fitted with degaussing and bridge protection and armed for defence with one four-inch gun, a 12-pounder AA gun, eight Colt Marlin machine guns and four Lewis guns. The ship left Halifax on 21 November 1940 and sailed alone across the Atlantic for the UK, carrying a general cargo of 3374 tons, 13 734 bags of mail, 1775 tons of diesel oil, 299 tons of various other oils, 1350 tons of drinking water, a crew of 188 and 150 troops, plus enough provisions for 350 people over 18 days. She arrived at Gourock with a destroyer escort on 28 November, and the troops disembarked. The following day, still with her cargo on board, the Admiralty gave orders that the ship leave for the Tyne that same afternoon, with the destroyer HMS *Vimy* as escort. Captain Bull protested that when his ship was requisitioned as a troopship, one of the conditions was that it would go only to west coast ports and not to the east coast; he objected several times to the orders from the Admiralty, but was overruled.

Final voyage

On 1 December 1940 the *Oslofjord* was approaching the Tyne and was about two ship lengths behind the destroyer. At 0820 hrs, when approximately two nm ESE of the River Tyne entrance and 220°, half a mile from buoy no. T2, she detonated either an acoustic or magnetic mine on the starboard side, directly beneath the engine room. Apart from the chief officer Thorbjørn Thorsen, all those on the bridge - Captain Bull, the third mate Anton Øvre, the fourth mate Roaldkvam and helmsman Yngvar Halvorsen, were thrown down by the explosion. The chief officer was still standing and ordered the engines stopped; he then discovered that the captain and helmsman were both unconscious, although the captain, injured and bleeding, soon came round. The lifeboats were all launched and the two injured men were helped into one of them. Helmsman Halvorsen was transferred to a minesweeper, but died from his injuries later that morning.

A crewman called Kristen Hauan who lived at Agricola Gardens, Hadrian Park, Wallsend and was one of six quartermasters on board, said: 'At around 9.30 am there was one hell of a bang. After having got off the rest of the crew, eight or ten of us were left aboard to try and save the vessel.'

As the ship began to heel over, Mr Hauan and a 4th Officer bravely checked all the cabins to ensure everyone was safely out and in the boats, even though the ship was barely afloat.

The big liner was listing heavily to starboard, but was not in immediate danger of sinking, so the chief mate, using a megaphone, decided to call for assistance from nearby vessels. Several tugs responded and towing commenced at around 0845 hrs. Captain Bull came back on board the ship, as did the deck crew. A pilot called Duncan also turned up, but, after consulting with the Admiralty, declined to take her into port; the reason given was that if she did sink, she would obstruct the Tyne entrance, one of the busiest ports in the UK.

Cullercoats lifeboat *Westmorland* was launched and rescued 40 of the crew and then stood by.

With the *Oslofjord*'s engine room filling up rapidly, it was agreed to beach the ship on the south side of South Shields pier.

Later that afternoon, Tynemouth 's Watson class motor lifeboat *John Pyemont* was called out to the *Oslofjord* and took off another 17 crewmen, landing them at 1820 hrs; the captain had been admitted to hospital with a crushed vertebra.

Over the next few days, volunteers unloaded about 9000 bags of mail and work went on to try to refloat the vessel. However, on 7 December, a NNE gale sprang up and at 0005 hrs on the 8th, distress signals were fired by the skeleton crew of 33, still on board the stranded ship.

Mr Selby E. Davidson, secretary of the RNLI at Tynemouth, assembled the crew of the *John Pyemont* at their station. Within 25 minutes the boat was launched and on its way, in a howling wind and dark stormy conditions. By the time they reached the *Oslofjord* she was already beginning to break up, as huge waves crashed over her, dislodging lifeboats from their davits. Coxswain George Lisle decided to take the lifeboat into the ship's starboard side, the only place where they could get any shelter from the heavy seas. The surrounding water was littered with debris from the stricken, once beautiful ship, yet in extremely hazardous conditions Coxswain Lisle manoeuvred his boat between the lifeboats that were hanging from their davits and held her there with the engine and rudder, while ropes were thrown down to her. The crew managed to rescue the 21 men in an hour. Unfortunately, when they got back to Tynemouth, it was discovered that the chief officer was still on board and they had to make another perilous journey later that morning to bring him off. The aft end was stripped, but salvage attempts were abandoned after the ship broke in two and the forepart capsized in gale on the 21 and 22 January 1941.

On 18 December 1940, the Chief Officer Thorbjørn Thorsen, first mate Harald Kotler, third Mate Anton Øvre, 4th Mate Olav Roaldkvam, Able Seaman Rolf Antonsen, a lookout, the second engineer Gudmund Eide, fourth engineer Knut Aarseth and fourth engineer Leif Lerstad, all attended an inquiry at Newcastle upon Tyne, the captain still being in hospital at that time.

Following the mine detonation, access to the Tyne harbour had been denied by the Commanding Admiral of the Fleet in the Tyne area, even though the captain would have preferred to have taken the ship into port. However he understood the problem of blocking important British fighting units in the harbour, if she had sunk. The Germans in Norway however, took full advantage of their radio propaganda broadcasts, trying to convince sailors that this proved how pointless it was to sail for the UK.

On 13 February 1941, Mr Davidson and Coxswain George Lisle were both awarded the RNLI's bronze medal. The man who died, Halvorsen, Yngvar, a quartermaster, is commemorated at the memorial for seamen at Stavern, in Norway.

The wreck remained in place for almost two years, the top sections well clear of the surface, until the elements took their toll and it eventually broke up.

Morris (1994 & 1995); LCWLR 1939–45, p. 165; LR 1940/1 No. 80891 (O); Starke Schell Registers.

Wrecksite

The bow end of the wreck is situated approximately 600 metres out from about the centre of Herd Sands, the long beach at South Shields. The wreck is now mostly collapsed, except for part of the bow section. There are large overhanging steel plates and box sections which allow access underneath and where lobsters and cod often hide, although usually well out of reach. A little bit further lies the area where the ship's bridge used to be and where as many as 360 large intact brass portholes were once to be found along the hull sides, but they are few and far between now. Moving seaward along the wreck, it gradually becomes flatter and is almost level with the seabed, with most of the wreck disappearing under the sand. About another 100 m on are the huge impressive engines, towering some 6 m up towards the surface. Looking down between the copper pipes and engine frames, deep holes and hollows some 5 m deep can be seen, where much of the engine's base has gradually sunk into the sand. Everything around the engines – pipes, wheels, cogs, framework and so on – is slowly concreting into one large mass, but you can still see parts of cooking utensils, like pans, knives and forks, sticking out of it all. Thirty years ago, the wreck was absolutely brilliant, with rows of complete toilets and wash bowls, their wash tap system still attached to them and from where steel ladders led up from one deck to the next, while thousands of kitchen utensils lay in heaps. Unfortunately, winter storms and thousands of foraging divers over many years have taken their toll and it is now only a shell of what it once was, although still an interesting dive site. The ship's compass binnacle was found, albeit rather bruised and battered, in the late 1990s, but each year the winter storms shift the giant sheets of steel plating and wash away the sand, exposing lots of other objects of interest. The stern of the *Oslofjord* overlaps and intermingles with the remains of another wreck, the 5300-ton *Evgenia Chandris*.

The depth to the seabed around the Oslofjord varies between about 11 m and 12.5 m at low tide. Mooring over the wrecks can sometimes be a problem at weekends during the summer months, when hoards of diving boats gather together and dozens of divers stir up the silt.

EVGENIA CHANDRIS, ex STADSDIJK, ex ROCKY MARU

Date of loss: 15 March 1943
Wreck: ✯✯✯
Depth: 15 m
Reference: 55 00'.132 N 001 23'.869 W
Location: 0.5 nm S by E of South Shields Lighthouse

The *Evgenia Chandris* (Official No. 744) was a steel-hulled 6786-ton Greek steam cargo ship measuring 130.45 m in length, with a 16.33 m-beam and an 8.1-m draught. Harima (Aioi) Dockyard Co. Harima, Japan built and completed her as Yard No. 17 in March 1920 and launched her as the *Rocky Maru* for Teikoku Kisen K.K., at Kobe, in Japan.

The single steel screw was powered by a 552-nhp three-cylinder triple expansion steam engine that used two single-ended boilers working at a pressure of 200 psi, plus one auxiliary boiler and 11 corrugated furnaces, 17.83 sq.m (192 sq.ft) of grate surface and 761.41 sq.m (7227 sq.ft) of heating surface, which gave 12 knots. The cylinders measured 68.58 cm, 119.38 cm and 200.66 cm with a 129.54-cm stroke (27 in., 47 in. and 79 in. with a 51-in.stroke). Kobe Steel Works Ltd. Kobe, Japan manufactured the engine and ancillary machinery. The ship had six bulkheads cemented, two steel decks and a steel shelter deck with freeboard, 1139 tons of cellular double bottom and a forepeak and aft peak tank.

In 1920 Nederl.-Amerik. Stoomv. Mij., Rotterdam, Netherland renamed her *Stadsdijk.*

John D. Chandris, Panama, renamed her *Evgenia Chandris* and registered her in Panama in 1932. The designated code recognition signal letters were: SVKN. From 1934, John D. Chandris was still the owner, but she was registered in Piraeus, Greece.

Final voyage

On 15 March 1943, the *Evgenia Chandris* was sailing as a part of the southbound 26-ship convoy FS.1063 (Methil – Southend) and the captain was bringing his ship into the Tyne when he mistook the buoys marking the safe-channel entrance and collided with the 760-ton Dutch steamer *Export* (1918 – N.V. Rotterdam-London Stoomv. Mij., Rotterdam). The Greek vessel was to be beached on Outer Herd Sand, but she struck the stern-end of the wrecked *Oslofjord* and settled on the seabed off Outer Herd Sands; she was then written off as a total loss. The *Evgenia Chandris* was on passage from St John, New Brunswick for the Tyne, via Halifax, Loch Ewe and Methil with a general cargo, which included foodstuffs, tinned fish, flour, sheets of steel of varying sizes, timber, 300 drums of trichloroethylene, 4874 drums of carbide, 437 cases of ordnance stores, 9000 cases of ammunition, including thousands of empty brass pom-pom shell cases, hundreds of large empty brass shell cases and millions of live 303 rifle bullets, truck radiators and large lead batteries, to name just a selection. She also carried thousands of 14-kilo aluminium ingots and tons of 15-kilo copper ingots. It was rumoured that the copper ingots were transferred from another vessel while she was at sea.

Between 23 and 26 September 1970, the no.1 and no.2 holds were inspected by a professional NE diving team and were found to be full of sand. It was impossible to ascertain whether any ammunition remained and no further attempts were made to check her out.

LCR 1943, p. 9 (f); LR 1941/2 No. 23588 (E); Starke Schell Registers.

Wrecksite

Local divers know the wreck as the *Chandris.* The two wrecks, *Chandris* and *Oslo* lie end to end in a southwest to northeast direction, with the Oslo closer inshore. It is rather difficult to observe where one wreck ends and the other begins, as the two more or less overlap each other and both hulls are well buried in the sandy seabed. However, moving northeast, it soon becomes apparent which are the remains of the *Chandris,* because the seabed around the protruding hull plates and ribs is carpeted with thousands of rounds of live 303 rifle bullets.

There were at one time so many that you could, if you so wished, shovel them up by the bucketful. Many were in fact collected and the bullet ends removed, with the brass/lead bullet then drilled out to put onto key rings. Moving further along this part of the wreck, dozens of giant sheets of steel plate, which were part of her cargo, are stacked up on top and overlap each other, providing a convenient home for lobsters and shelter for large cod and wrasse. Lots of aluminium ingots still protrude from the seabed, although most are well concreted in. Moving about another 100 m further seaward, you eventually arrive at the boilers and then the engines and winches. On the western side, pom-pom shells can still be found in the silty concretion of wreckage on the seabed, just three metres away from the boilers. Moving past the boilers, there is a huge pile of twisted steel frames, pipes, chains and machinery and then more signs of aluminium ingots, buried beneath the silty rubble: many ingots, both copper and aluminium, are still being recovered today. A huge brass and copper condenser lies loose on its side, half buried in the seabed and surrounded by more wreckage. From here, a giant screw shaft is raised about one metre off the seabed and slopes out to the northeast, towards the stern end of the ship, where shoals of pout whiting hover, and cod and wrasse intermingle beneath the high towering box-like structure of the stern end. From here the seabed is flat and stony and there is little more of interest.

The depth at the stern end is around 16 m and the tidal flow usually a little stronger, but you can still dive at any state of the tide. More care should be taken when the visibility is down because of the possibility of gillnets getting caught up in the steel structures. Both wrecks are worth a visit and it is possible to swim the whole length of the two ships, unless you stop to look at things in between. During the summer, some divers leave marker buoys or dans over both wrecks, usually near to the engines, so neither wreck is difficult to find, but trailing an anchor will soon locate one of them.

DILIGENT

Date of loss: 30 August 1878
Wreck: ⋆⋆
Depth: 15 m
Reference: 55 00'.041 N 001 22'.883 W
Location: 0.93 nm SE from South Shields Lighthouse

The *Diligent* (Official No. 68977) was an iron-hulled 1414-ton steam cargo vessel measuring 73.27 m in length and 10.13 m in beam. Bartram, Haswell and Co. built and completed her as Yard No. 97 at South Dock, Sunderland in April 1878; she was launched on 18 April 1878 for James Westoll of Sunderland. The single iron screw was powered by a two-cylinder compound steam engine that used one boiler.

Final voyage

At 0500 hrs on 30 August 1878, the *Diligent* left the Tyne for Alexandria on just her second voyage, with a £30,000 cargo of coal. She steamed SE with a new compass adjuster on board, swinging the equipment for the first time. About a mile after rounding the pier head at South Shields, however, the 1221-ton steamer *Filey* (1870- H. Clapham and Co. Newcastle), ran into her abaft the mainmast. The stern of the *Diligent* was almost cut off and she sank in a few minutes; the crew of 24 and one passenger immediately took to the boats and tugs from the Tyne picked them up. The men, who had lost everything when the ship sank, were returned to the Tyne and taken to the Sailors' Home, just over an hour after they had sailed. The *Filey* was seriously damaged, but with help from three powerful Shields tugs, arrived back at the Tyne during the course of the day.

The Times: Saturday, 31 August 1878, p. 10 and 12, Issue 29348; Starke Schell Registers; Board of Trade Wreck Return 1878, p. 115.

Wrecksite

The wreck, which is possibly that of the *Diligent*, is orientated in an ENE to WSW direction. It lies on a seabed of sand in a general depth of 15 m (LAT). The wreck is mostly buried with just the upper parts of the engine and boiler and some iron ribs showing above the seabed; it covers an area 53 m long and 16 m across. Following big heavy seas, the remains are more exposed.

RENEN, EX PROSPERO, EX PRIMA

Date of loss: 26 January 1920
Wreck: ✯✯✯
Depth: 16 m
Reference: 55 00'.263 N 001 22'.879 W
Location: 0.8 nm SE of South Shields Lighthouse

Prospero *(Courtesy Norwegian Maritime Museum)*

The Renen *during earlier times as the steamer* Prospero *in Baltic port for repairs – circa 1906 (Courtesy Norwegian Maritime Museum)*

The *Renen* was an old iron-hulled 656-ton Norwegian steam cargo vessel measuring 54.71 m in length, with an 8.54-m beam and 4.42-m draught. Denton, Gray and Co. West Hartlepool built and completed her as Yard No. 89 in 1869; she was launched as the *Prima* on 16 September 1869 for Flensburger Dampfschiffahrts Ges., at Flensburg, in Germany.

The single iron screw was powered by an 85-nhp two-cylinder compound steam engine that used one boiler. T.Richardson and Sons, Hartlepool manufactured the machinery. She had one deck, a well deck and small amidships-positioned bridge superstructure. The designated code recognition signal letters were: HFGR.

In 1879, Flensburger Schiffb. Ges., Flensburg in Germany was the registered owner. Flensburger had begun building ships themselves on the Baltic Coast close to the Kiel Canal, in 1872.

On 24 July 1882, "Prospero" Østlandske, Lloyd, Kristiania purchased and renamed her *Prospero* on 28 August 1882; R. Andvord was the manager.

In 1884 the ship was rebuilt with enough cabins for 80 passengers.

On 23 May 1906, she was sold to Aktieselskapet Ganger Rolf; F. Olsen was the manager.

On 22 June 1906, the owner was Aktieselskapet Otto Wathnes 'arvinger' (herring) and T. Wathne was the manager.

Aktieselskapet Stavanger Privatbank, Stavanger was the registered owner from 13 July 1910.

From 16 December 1911 she was registered at the port of Bergen.

A.S. Prospero purchased her on 12 February 1912 and Erik Rusten, Bergen was the manager.

On 25 November 1915, O. Langerud m. fl., Drammen was the registered owner.

"Renen" ACES Rusten, Thomas J. Wiborg and Søn of Kristiania (Oslo), Norway acquired her and renamed her *Renen* in February 1916.

The Admiralty requisitioned the vessel in 1917 for the Shipping Controller, London, with R.A. Constantine and Donking Ltd. the Crown nominee managers.

She was returned to the owner and from 1919, "Renen" ACES Rusten, Thomas J. Wiborg & Sön, in Kristiania was the registered owner.

Final voyage

On the evening of 26 January 1920, the *Renen* had just left the Tyne with a cargo of coke for Tonsberg when she foundered and was lost, following a collision with the 522-ton Swedish SS *Fermia* (1906 – Ångbåts AB Ferm, Kristinehamn) near the mouth of the Tyne. All of the *Renen*'s crew were picked up by the pilot steamer *Queen o' the May* and landed at North Shields. The *Fermia* had just arrived from Gothenburg; damage to her is unknown.

LR 1919–20, No. 24398 (R); LCR 1920, p. 7 (f); Starke Schell Registers; *The Times*: Wednesday, 28 January 1920, p. 17, Issue 42319.

Wrecksite

The wreck is orientated in a SE to NW direction and lies on a seabed of dirty coarse sand in a general depth of 16 m (LAT). It is now totally collapsed and well broken up, with her boiler and engine exposed and surrounded by lots of broken iron spars, plates and bits of machinery. The highest section is around the boiler/engine area, but is no higher than 3 m. It covers an area of about 50 m in length by 14 m wide. A couple of large monkfish have been observed amongst the wreckage and the occasional cod and lobster have been seen, but the wreck is hardly worth spending any time fishing over.

HERCULES

Date of loss: 22 November 1940
Wreck: ✯✯
Depth: 18 m
Reference: 55 00'.545 N 001 23'.109 W
Also given: 55 00'.602 N 001 22'.933 W
Location: 0.75 mile E of Tyne, north pier

The *Hercules* (Official No. 99594) was a steel-hulled 82-ton British steam tug measuring 24.56 m in length, with a 5.51-m beam and a 2.86-m draught. Cook, Welton and Gemmell, Hull built and completed her as Yard No. 99; she was launched on 4 May 1893 for Hull Dock Co. Hull. The single steel screw was powered by a 45-nhp three-cylinder triple expansion steam engine that used one boiler and gave ten knots. Earles and Co. at Hull manufactured the machinery.

Later in 1893 she was sold to North Eastern Railway Company, York. London and North Eastern Railway Co. of London was the registered owner in 1922. South Stockton Shipbreaking Co. Ltd. Stockton-on-Tees purchased her in 1936. From late 1936, William Pace Robson of St Anthony's, Newcastle upon Tyne was the registered owner.

Hercules *(Courtesy Norwegian Maritime Museum)*

Final voyage

On 22 November 1940, the *Hercules*, commanded by Captain James Robson, foundered after detonating a mine laid by a German aircraft at position: 55° 00 33'N 01° 22 45'W, about three-quarters of a mile east of the Tyne entrance. The tug had been towing hopper barge no.116 full of rubbish to the spoil ground, when she blew up and sank almost immediately; four crewmen were missing and one man was found dead. The barge was only slightly damaged and was later recovered by another vessel and towed back into the Tyne. The four crewmen lost were:

Clayton, James Henry Young Thomas, 36yrs, Fireman
Robson, Harold, 27yrs, Mate
Robson, James, 66yrs, Master
Robson, Ralph, 43yrs, Engineer Officer

CWGC; Thompson (1999); Jarvis & Jarvis (1993), Vol. II.

Wrecksite

Some confusion surrounds this vessel's position, because two precise wreck positions have been given. The first co-ordinates report her as being orientated in a more or less E to W direction, straight out from the mouth of the River Tyne, in a general depth of 18 m (LAT). The wreck is partially buried and stands 2.5 m at the highest point, around the boiler/engine area, and the wreckage covers an area 32 m long and 17 m wide.

The second co-ordinates report her as: the hull is completely intact, standing 3.5 m high, but all of the deck and superstructure has gone, except for a few cross girders and ribs strengthening the hull sides. The boiler/engine is still in place and the wreck covers an area of about 25 m in length by 10 m across. The wreckage is absolutely covered in a myriad of soft corals and makes an excellent photographic subject. Shoals of small saithe and pollack have adopted the wreck and the occasional crustacean can be found sheltering inside the hull.

KALUA, EX DECAPO

Date of loss: 29 April 1941
Wreck: ✯✯✯
Depth: 39 m
Reference: 55 00'.460 N 001 17'.585 W
Location: 3.68 nm, 10° S of E. of Tyne north pier

The *Kalua* (Official No. 142408) was a steel-hulled 724-ton British steam cargo vessel measuring 59.43 m in length, with a 9.16-m beam and 3.35-m draught. John Crown and Sons Ltd. at Monkwearmouth, Sunderland built and completed her as Yard No, 127 in May 1908; she was launched as the *Decapo* on 30 March 1908 for Aktieselskapet Decapo, Trondheim, Norway and registered in Trondeim; A. Gjersøe was the manager. The single steel screw was powered by a 75-rhp three-cylinder triple expansion steam engine that used one single-ended boiler working at a pressure of 180 psi, with two corrugated furnaces, 5.94 sq.m (64 sq.ft) of grate surface and 143.62 sq.m (1546 sq.ft) of heating surface. The cylinders measured 35.56 cm, 59.69 cm and 96.52 cm with a 68.58-cm stroke (14 in., 23½ in. and 38 in. with a 27-in. stroke). North East Marine Engineering Co. Ltd. Sunderland manufactured the engine and ancillary machinery. She had one steel deck, a well deck, four bulkheads cemented, a 28-m quarterdeck, a 4.6-m bridge deck and 6.7-m forecastle; she also had some cellular double bottom and a 198-ton aft peak tank. Lloyd's classed her 100 A1. The designated code recognition signal letters were: MLRW.

In 1911, she had the same owners, but Bachke and Co. was the manager. The Shipping Controller, London requisitioned the vessel in 1918 and Alexander Bros. was appointed as the Crown nominee manager. She was returned to the owner in 1919. From 1923, Hook S.S. Co. Ltd. Goole was the registered owner and renamed her *Kalua*; Goole and Hull Steam Towing Co. Ltd. was the manager.

Final voyage

On 29 April 1941, the *Kalua* was half a mile NNE of the T.2 Buoy, off the River Tyne, when she was hit by a bomb from a German aircraft during an air raid on Tynemouth. The *Kalua* was sailing as part of the southbound 43-ship convoy FS.476 (Methil–Southend) and was transporting a cargo of coal from the Tyne to London; all of the crew of 14 were saved.

Starke Schell Registers; LCWLR 1939–45, p. 235; BVLS 1939–45, p. 21.

Wrecksite

The wreck, which is known locally as the 'South Aquastar', is orientated in a NNW to SSE direction. It lies on a seabed of hard sand and broken shell in a general depth of 39 m (LAT). It is very substantial, partially intact and sitting upright, 4 m high, but with a list to port. The wreck is complete except for the bridge structure; there is a large hole where it used to be. The winches, bollards and windlass are still in place on the bow section and there are handrails all round the rear part of her decks. The cargo hold is a large black hole and it is possible to swim into it and through the hatches on the bow section. At the stern end, the screw stands about 2 m high and is still attached to the shaft, with two trawl boards lying one on each side of the screw and behind a large intact steel rudder. Above the stern, floats a large trawl net which waves about in the tide. The wreck is infested with fishing lures and monofilament fishing lines, making it a very dangerous place to be in the gloomy green light. There is also a debris field of wreckage close to the eastern side of the wreck.

FIRELIGHT, ex ROOKWOOD

Date of loss: 1 May 1917
Wreck: ★★★
Depth: 27 m
Reference: 55 00'.496 N 001 22'.118 W
Location: 1.43 nm ESE of South Shields Lighthouse

The *Firelight* (Official No. 105860) was a steel-hulled 1143-ton British steam cargo ship measuring 71.93 m in length, with a 9.73-m beam and a 4.49-m draught. J. Blumer and Co. Ltd. at North Dock, Sunderland built and completed her as Yard No. 137 in August 1896; she was launched as the *Rookwood* on 24 July 1896 for Steam Colliers Ltd. London, who registered her there; H. C. Pelly and Co. was the manager. The single screw was powered by an 180-nhp three-cylinder triple expansion steam engine that used two single-ended boilers. J. Dickinson and Sons Ltd. manufactured the engine and ancillary machinery at Sunderland. The cylinders measured 50.8 cm, 82.55 cm and 134.62 cm with a 91.44-cm stroke (20 in., 32.5 in. and 53 in. with a 36-in. stroke). She had one deck, four bulkheads and a 5.5-m quarterdeck, a 22.6-m bridge deck and 7.9-m forecastle.

Wm. France, Fenwick and Co. Ltd. London purchased her in 1901. From 1916, Gas Light and Coke Co. London was the registered owner and renamed it *Firelight*; S. Clarke and Co. was the manager.

Final voyage

On 1 May 1917, the KDM mine-laying submarine SMU *UC 29*, commanded by Oblt.z.S. Ernst Rosenow torpedoed the *Firelight* without any warning, 1.75 miles east of Tynemouth pier. The steamer had just left the River Tyne for passage to London with a cargo of coal. The track of the torpedo was observed by some of the crew, just prior to it detonating amidships on the port side at 0825 hrs. The crew abandoned ship immediately, but the sea was washing over the upper decks even before they had got clear of the vessel. The survivors, who could see the U-boat's periscope for a short time after the ship went down, were picked up soon after by the 1278-ton steamer *Collingwood* (1905 – Furness, Withy and Co. Ltd. Newcastle) and landed at North Shields.

LCWLR 1914–18, p. 127; BVLS 1914–18, p. 48; LR 1915/16, No. 771 (R).

Wrecksite

The wreck is orientated in an E to W direction and lies on a firm, dirty seabed of sand and stone in a general depth of 27 m (LAT). The wreck is very substantial, but totally collapsed and well broken up, covering an area of about 85 m long and 40 m across, with the engine and boilers, which are exposed, being the highest point at 5.5 m; plumose anemones are well established on the upper parts of the boiler. The mangled bow section has a large Admiralty anchor and two huge piles of rusting steel chains, while the rest of the wreck is one mass of twisted, broken steel plates, girders, framework, ribs and broken, unrecognisable machinery, all jumbled together; lots of broken pottery also litters the seabed. Quite a number of fish, especially cod and pout whiting, have taken up residence amongst the wreckage, so it should make an interesting boat-angling venue. If the bell is located, it should be inscribed: *Rookwood 1896*

RAGNI, EX EBCHESTER, EX HILLBROOK, EX FRITHJOF EIDE

Date of loss: 15 December 1939
Wreck: ★★★★★
Depth: 52 m
Reference: 55 00'.505 N 001 12'.813 W
Location: 6.5 miles ESE of Tyne north pier

The Norwegian steamer Ragni *as the* Fithjof Eide, *circa 1920 (Courtesy of Rolf Kristensen, Åsgårdstrand & Stein-Erik Dagsland, Heinavegen, Norway)*

The *Ragni* (Official No. 145734) was a steel-hulled 1264-ton Norwegian steam cargo ship measuring 69.9 m in length, with a 4.69-m beam and a 4-m draught. Campbeltown Shipbuilding Co. Ltd. Campbeltown built and completed her as Yard No. 113 in Decenber 1919; she was launched as the *Frithjof Eide* on 10 October 1919 for Aktieselskapet Dampskipsselskapet Frithjof Eide of Haugesund; Birger. Pedersen and Søn, Haugesund was the manager. The single screw was powered by a 142-nhp three-cylinder triple expansion steam engine that used two, boilers working at a pressure of 180 psi, with four corrugated furnaces, 7.33 sq.m (79 sq.ft) of grate surface and 221.66 sq.m (2386 sq.ft) of heating surface. The cylinders measured 45.72 cm, 69.85 cm and 114.3 cm with an 83.82-cm stroke (18 in., 27½ in. and 45 in. with a 33-in. stroke). Ross and Duncan Ltd. manufactured the engine and ancillary machinery at Glasgow. She had one steel deck, a well deck, four bulkheads cemented and a 24-m quarterdeck, a 14.6-m bridge deck and 8.2-m forecastle. She also had some cellular double bottom and an 85-ton aft peak tank. A wireless direction finder was also fitted. She was classed as 100 A1. The designated code recognition signal letters were: MLRC.

Portland S.S. Co. Ltd. Cardiff purchased her in 1923 and renamed her *Hillbrook*; R. McNeil and Sons was the manager. In 1925, the Portsmouth S.S. Co. Ltd. of Cardiff was the registered owner and McNeil and Jones the manager. W. Dickinson and Co. Ltd. of Newcastle bought and renamed her *Ebchester* in 1928. Rederi Aktieselskapet Ragnito in Oslo purchased the ship in October 1936 and renamed her *Ragni*; Erling Mortensen Aktieselskapet was the manager.

From 28 April 1939, Dampskipsselskapet Aktieselskapet Alf Lindøs Rederi of Haugesund was the registered owner and Alf Lindø was the manager.

Final voyage

On 15 December 1939, the *Ragni* detonated a German-laid mine, 6.5 miles ESE of the Tyne north pier. The explosion almost blew her bows off and she foundered immediately, taking six of her crew down with her. She was on passage from Hull for Malmö with a cargo of coal and coke. Out of a crew of 19, six men were lost; the rest were rescued and taken to Newcastle.

The mine was laid by Bronte's Kriegsmarine destroyers: *Z 4* (Richard Beitzen), *Z 8* (Bruno Heinemann), *Z 14* (Friedrich Ihn) and *Z 15* (Erich Steinbrick), which had laid mines in the area during the night of 12/13 December 1939, under the cover of *Z 19* (Hermann Künne).

The crewmen that died were:

Hansen, Ingvald Kristian, Able Seaman
Jakobsen, Jens Birger, Donkeyman
Johannessen, Johan Ingolf, Seaman
Kristensen, Birger Otto, Deck Boy
Lund, Petter Andreas, Ordinary Seaman
Olsen, Sigmund Arnold, Stoker

Starke Schell Registers; LWL 1939–45, p. 21; Norwegian War Losses 1939–45.

Wrecksite

This wreck, probably that of SS *Ragni*, is orientated in a SE to NW direction. It lies on hard sand seabed in a general depth of 52 m (LAT). The wreck is stands 9 m high, with the superstructure still fairly intact, but with quite a lot of damage in the amidships and bows areas. It is quite possible to fin through many of the open doors and various openings and all of the bridge and navigational equipment is still in place. The ship's bell, if or when located, will almost certainly be inscribed: *Frith of Eide 1919*. The sides of the wreck are covered in a myriad of soft corals and beautiful plumose anemones. Lots of pout whiting shoal around the area where the bridge structure lies protruding over the sand. Some very large cod have been observed around the perimeter of the wreck and amongst the bottom plates, so it will be an excellent boat-angling venue.

ROSA

Date of Loss: 15 December 1939
Wreck: ✯✯✯✯
Depth: 52 m
Reference: 55 00'.849 N 001 14'.065 W
Location: 5.7 nm E of South Shields Lighthouse

The *Rosa* was a steel-hulled 1146-ton Belgian steamship measuring 70.13 m in length, with a 10.36-m beam and a 4.01-m draught. Verschure and Co. Amsterdam built and completed her as Yard No. 37 in November 1919 for L. Hermans, Bruges, Belgium. The single steel screw was powered by an aft-positioned 120-nhp three-cylinder triple expansion steam engine that used one single-ended boiler working at a pressure of 180 psi, with three corrugated furnaces, 6.40 sq.m (69 sq.ft) of grate surface and 186.73 sq.m (2010 sq.ft) of heating surface, which gave ten knots. The cylinders measured 39.37 cm, 64.77 cm and 105.41 cm with a 91.44-cm stroke (15½ in., 25½ in. and 41½ in. with a 36-in. stroke). Verschure and Co manufactured the engine and ancillary machinery in Amsterdam. She had one steel deck, a well deck, four bulkheads cemented, a 42.1-m quarterdeck, 3.9-m bridge deck and 7-m forecastle, plus some cellular double bottom and a forepeak and aft peak tank. She was classed as 100 A1. The designated code recognition signal letters were: ONXC.

In 1933 Armement L. Hermans, Soc. Anon., Bruges was the registered owner.

Final voyage

On 13 December 1939, the *Rosa* was lost and one of her crew of 15 was killed after she detonated a German mine, 6.5 miles east of the River Tyne; she was on passage from the Tyne for Belgium with a cargo of coal. A patrol boat found the survivors in a boat and landed them at North Shields.

Bronte's Kriegsmarine destroyers: *Z 4* (Richard Beitzen), *Z 8* (Bruno Heinemann), *Z 14* (Friedrich Ihn) and *Z 15* (Erich Steinbrick) had laid the mines during the night of 12/13 December 1939, under the cover of *Z 19* (Hermann Künne).

LCWLR 1939–45, p. 28; LR 1938/9 No. 82459 (R); *The Times*: 16 December 1939, p. 10, Issue 48490.

Wrecksite

The wreck, probably that of the Belgian steamer, is orientated in a NE to SW direction. It lies on a firm seabed of fine sand in a general depth of 52 m (LAT). The wreck is broken into two sections which lie side by side, with some superstructure visible. It stands 5.1 m high and covers an area 38 m long and 29 m across. Lots of fish have been observed amongst the wreckage, including some large cod.

EVELINA, HM TRAWLER, ex JOHN HOWARD

Date of loss: 16 December 1939
Wreck: ✯✯✯
Depth: 79 m
Reference: 55 00'.522 N 001 04'.183 W
Location: 11.46 nm E from Tynemouth pier

The *Evelina* (Official No. 144362) was a steel-hulled 202-ton British steam trawler measuring 35.15 m by length, with a 6.73-m beam and 3.68-m draught. She was built and completed as Yard No. 1330 by Rennie Forrest Shipbuilding and Dry Dock Co. Ltd. Wivenhoe, completed as a fishing vessel late in 1919; she was delivered to the Royal Navy as the *John Howard* (Adm. No. 4203) on 22 July 1919. The boat was placed on the London register by the Admiralty to await disposal and on 3 February 1920 was registered as L.317. The single steel screw was powered by a 75-hp, three-cylinder triple expansion steam engine that used one single-ended boiler working at a pressure of 180 psi. with three furnaces and giving ten knots. The cylinders measured 30.48 cm, 50.8 cm and 86.36 cm with a 58.42-cm stroke (12 in., 20 in. and 34 in. with a 23-in. stroke). A.G. Mumford Ltd. at Colchester manufactured the machinery. She had one steel deck and three bulkheads cemented. Echo sounding device was also fitted.

In 1921 she was sold to Mercantile and on 12 December 1921, Consolidated Steam Fishing and Ice Co. Ltd. Grimsby bought and registered her at Grimsby as GY.1331. In February 1922 she was renamed *Evelina*. In September 1927, she was owned by Consolidated Fisheries Ltd. Grimsby and Sir John Denton Marsden, Baronet was the manager. In 1929 the Grimsby registry closed.

Rutherford Brothers at North Shields was the registered owner from December 1929.

On 17 January 1930 she was registered at North Shields as SN.62.

In 1935, J. Tomlinson and J. Tomlinson Jnr at North Shields acquired her.

In November 1939 the Admiralty requisitioned the boat as an Armed Patrol Vessel (Adm. No. 4203, Port Reg: WWII: SN.4)

Final patrol

On 16 December 1939, HMT *Evelina* (Skipper John William Cowling RNR) was patrolling offshore from the Tyne when she detonated a mine, laid by one of Bronte's Kriegsmarine destroyers: *Z 4* (Richard Beitzen), *Z 8* (Bruno Heinmann), *Z 14* (Friedrich Ihn) and *Z 15* (Erich Steibrick), which had laid mines during the night of 12/13 December 1939, under the cover of *Z 19* (Hermann Künne).

The wreck was never located and is a war grave. The men who died were:

Bailey, Richard, 2nd Engineman, Naval Auxiliary Patrol
Brunton, Robert, Fireman, Naval Auxiliary Patrol
Cowling, John, Skipper, RNR
Curtis, Matthew, 2nd Hand, Naval Auxiliary Patrol
Pearson, William, 3rd Hand, Naval Auxiliary Patrol
Reed, George, Deckhand, Naval Auxiliary Patrol
Robinson, Robert, Cook, Naval Auxiliary Patrol

Sutherland, David, 1st Engineman, Naval Auxiliary Patrol
Tripp, Jack, Deckhand, Naval Auxiliary Patrol

BVLS 1939–45, p. 3 ; SRN Vol. 2, p. 125 ; LCWLR 1939–45, p. 29.

Wrecksite

The wreck, possibly that of HMT *Evelina*, is orientated in an E to W direction. It sits in a slight scour, on a seabed of soft sand and mud in a general depth of 79 m (LAT). The wreck is intact, standing nearly 4 m high and covers an area of 36 m in length by 6 m across. If it is the trawler, the bell will be inscribed: *John Howard 1919*.

H. C. FLOOD

Date of loss: 15 December 1939
Wreck: ✭✭✭✭✭
Depth: 52 m
Reference: 55 00'.510 N001 13'.412 W
Location: 6.5 miles ESE of Tyne north pier

Norwegian steamer H.C. Flood, *circa 1930 (Courtesy: Stein-Erik Dagsland, Heinavegen & Rolf Kristensen, Åsgårdstrand, Norway)*

H. C. Flood was a steel-hulled 1902-ton Norwegian steam cargo ship measuring 81.3 m in length, with a 12.82-m beam and 5.48-m draught. Bergens Mekaniske Værksteder, Bergen built and completed it as Yard No. 193 in October 1917 for Dampskipsselskapet Aktieselskapet. H. C. Flood, Haugesund and Knut Knutsen, O.A.S. was the manager. The single screw was powered by a 208-nhp BMV, three-cylinder triple expansion steam engine that used two single-ended boilers. The cylinders measured 49.53 cm, 76.2 cm and 132.08 cm with a 91.44-cm stroke (19½ in., 30 in. and 52 in. with a 36-in.stroke). Bergens Mekaniske Værksteder, Bergen manufactured the engine and ancillary machinery. She had one deck, four masts and a 7.9-m poop deck, a 20.4-m bridge deck and 7-m forecastle. Direction Finding Equipment was also fitted. The designated code recognition signal letters were: LCNR.

From January 1936, Dampskipsselskapet Aktieselskapet Falkeid of Haugesund was the registered owner and Th. Nordbø, Jr. of Haugesund was the manager.

Final voyage

On 15 December 1939, the *H. C. Flood*, under Captain Conrad Johan Johannessen, detonated a German-laid mine and the ship foundered 6.75 miles ESE of the River Tyne. She was on passage from Hull for Oslo with a cargo of coke; four of her crew of 21 were killed. The mine had been laid by one of Bronte's Kriegsmarine destroyers: *Z 4* (Richard Beitzen), *Z 8* (Bruno Heinemann), *Z 14* (Friedrich Ihn) and *Z 15* (Erich Steinbrick), which had laid mines in that area during the night of 12/13 December 1939, under the cover of *Z 19* (Hermann Künne). The crewmen that died on *H. C. Flood* were:

Aanesen, Odin Kristian S., Donkeyman
Johannessen, Conrad Johan, Captain
Kristensen, Thorleif Martinius, Able Seaman
Salomonsen, Hans Ole, Ordinary Seaman

Starke Schell Registers; LWL 1939–45, p. 21; Norwegian War Losses 1939–45.

Wrecksite

The wreck, probably that of *H. C. Flood*, lies on a seabed of fine sand and mud in a general depth of 52 m (LAT). It is orientated in a northeast to southwest direction, is very substantial, sitting upright but in two pieces, with the bow section broken off and lying at a slight angle. The stern end is almost completely intact and standing almost 10 m high, with much of the superstructure still in place; it is possible to swim through many of the various openings and a number of portholes are visible. The wreck, which is covered in a profusion of soft corals, is possibly one of the most interesting wrecks off this part of the coast. Masses of fish, including cod, pollack, pout whiting and saithe surround the wreck so it will make an excellent boat-angling venue.

ETHEL TAYLOR, ex CREMLYN, ex JAMES HUNNIFORD

Date of loss: 22 November 1940
Wreck: ★★★
Depth 18.8 m
Reference: 55 00'.597 N 001 22'.984 W
Location: 0.60 nm E (7.5 cables) of South Shields Lighthouse

The *Ethel Taylor* (Official No. 143786) was a steel-hulled 276-ton British steam trawler measuring 38.22 m in length, with a 7.11-m beam and a 3.86-m draught. Smith's Docks Co. Ltd. South Bank-on-Tees built and completed her as Yard No. 665; she was launched as *James Hunniford* on 24 January 1917 for Clifton Steam Trawlers Ltd. Fleetwood (Fleetwood Port Registration FD.363).

The single screw was powered by an 87-nhp three-cylinder triple expansion steam engine that used one single-ended boiler working at a pressure of 180 psi with three plain furnaces, 4.64sq.m (50sq.ft) of grate surface and 150.13 sq.m (1616 sq.ft) of heating surface. The cylinders measured 31.75 cm, 53.34 cm and 88.9 cm with a 66.04-cm stroke (12½ in., 21 in. and 35 in. with a 26-in. stroke). Smith's Docks Co. Ltd. manufactured the machinery. She had one deck, three bulkheads cemented and a 21.9-m quarterdeck and 6.4-m forecastle; she was also equipped with a wireless direction finder and echo sounding device. She was classed as 100 A1. The designated code recognition signal letters were: GTCJ.

On 16 January 1920, Cygnet Steam Fishing Co. Fleetwood purchased and renamed her *Cremlyn* (FD.363). New Docks Steam Trawling Co. Ltd. Fleetwood purchased and renamed her *Ethel Taylor* in 1934.

On 15 March 1936, *Ethel Taylor* was fishing off the west coast of Scotland when she was in collision with the 331-ton Fleetwood steam trawler *Winooka*, (ex *Seaward Ho*), owned by Boston Deep Sea Fishing Co. Ltd. Fleetwood, which resulted in the sinking of the *Winooka.*

In 1939 the registered owner was Clifton Steam Trawlers Ltd. Fleetwood. In 1939 *Ethel Taylor* was requisitioned by the Admiralty and converted to Auxiliary Patrol Vessel no. 3504; she was then armed with a 12-pounder deck gun (5.44-kilo shells).

Final patrol

On 22 November 1940, *Ethel Taylor*, commanded by Skipper Richard Cowling, foundered after detonating a German mine laid off the mouth of the Tyne. The Cullercoats lifeboat *Westmorland* was launched at 1758 hrs and rescued the last man from the sinking trawler; two men were lost, but the survivors were taken off by a Royal Navy drifter and put on shore at the Tyne quay. The crewmen that died were:

Hardman, John A., Stoker 2nd Class RNPS, LT/KX 108570, MPK
Pearson, John W., Engineman, RNPS, LT/KX 124600, MPK

LCWLR 1939–45, p. 158; LR 1940 No. 57465 (E); SRN Vol. 2, p. 124; Toghill (2004), p. 155; Morris (1994).

Wrecksite

The wreck is orientated in a WNW to ESE direction and lies on a dirty hard seabed of sand and stone in a general depth of 18.8 m (LAT). It is upright, quite intact, standing some 3.5 m high and is very impressive; an ideal site for taking underwater photographs. Pout whiting can often be found shoaling over the top of the wreck during the summer months and some large cod have been observed.

ALBIA, EX MONMOUTH

Date of loss: 5 February 1915
Wreck: ✯✯
Depth: 15 m
Reference: 54 00'.452 N 001 23'.050 W
Location: 0.62 nm ESE from South Shields Lighthouse

The *Albia* (Official No. 95770), was a steel-hulled 2506-ton steam cargo ship measuring 91.44 m in length with a 12.03-m beam. Tyne Iron Engineering Shipbuilding Co. Ltd. at

Willington Quay near Wallsend built and completed her as Yard No. 82 in October 1890; she was launched as the schooner-rigged *Monmouth* on 1 September 1890 for Great Western S.S. Co. Ltd. who registered her in Bristol; Mark Whitwill and Son was the manager. The single screw was powered by a 232-hp, three-cylinder triple expansion steam engine that used two single-ended boilers. Her cylinders measured 57.15 cm, 92.71 cm and 152.4 cm with a 99.06-cm stroke (22½ in., 36½ in. and 60 in. with a 39-in. stroke). The shipbuilders manufactured the engine and ancillary machinery. She had six bulkheads, web frames and water ballast. The designated code recognition signal letters were: LWJG.

In 1895 she was sold to Ramón de la Sota, renamed *Albia* and registered in Bilbao, with Captain Goicocchea as the master. Captain T. De Urrestizal was the master from 1897. Sota y Aznar, Bilbao was the registered owner in 1900. In 1904 the registered owner was Cia Anon del Vapor Albia, Bilbao and Sota y Aznar was the manager. From 1906, she was owned by Cia Nav Sota y Aznar, using the same manager.

Final voyage

On 5 February 1915 the *Albia* stranded on the Whitestones Reef, one mile SE of Roker lighthouse, Sunderland, while on a voyage from Sagunto to Jarrow; she was carrying a crew of 24, eight passengers and a cargo of iron ore. The crew managed to refloat the vessel, which had a badly damaged hull; the master then decided to make full speed for his destination in the Tyne. However, as she reached the mouth of the Tyne, so much water had flooded in that the vessel was in immediate danger of sinking. A skipper of a Tyne pilot cutter, who saw the predicament, rushed to aid the *Albia* and took off 21 people in all. Those remaining must have taken to the boats just minutes before she sank, just outside the river mouth and close to the main shipping lane. All 24 people were rescued.

LCR 1915, p. 8 (g); Starke Schell Registers; Board of Trade Wreck Return 1915, p. 16; American Lloyd's Register of American and Foreign Shipping, 1857–1900.

Wrecksite

The wreck lies in a general depth of 15 m (LAT). It is very substantial with some large box sections, but it is well broken up and covered in many fishing lures and monofilament fishing lines. The boilers are standing upright, along with the engine, and these are surrounded by jumbled mounds of steel debris, masses of broken pipes and broken machinery that are covered in heavy sediment. It has been extensively salvaged over the years but is still worth a visit. Shoals of pout whiting and lots of small saithe, pollack and cod can be seen around the wreck during the summer months.

CRYSTAL

Date of loss: 7 January 1892
Wreck: ★★
Depth: 15 m
Reference: 55 00'.742 N 001 23'.728 W
Location: 0.23 nm E of South Shields Lighthouse

The *Crystal* (Official No. 83916) was an iron-hulled 2613-ton British steam cargo ship measuring 100.54 m in length, with a 14.68-m beam. J.L. Thompson and Sons at North Sands Yard, Sunderland built and completed her as Yard No. 167 in 1881; she was launched on 8 September 1881 for J. Dent and Co. of Newcastle, who was the owner at the time of loss; Captain R.A. Darling was the first master. The single iron screw was powered by a 300-hp, two-cylinder compound steam engine that used two boilers. The cylinders measured 101.6 cm and 193.04 cm with a 121.92-cm stroke (40 in. and 76 in. with a 48-in. stroke). Wallsend Slipway Co. Ltd. manufactured the engine and ancillary machinery at Wallsend. She had two decks, an awning deck, seven bulkheads and water ballast.

From 1887, she was registered to Arrow Shipping Co. Ltd. Newcastle upon Tyne, and Dent and Co. was the manager; the master was Captain R. B. Stannard. Code letters: WFLK.

Final voyage

On the night of Thursday, 7 January 1892, the *Crystal*, a well-known vessel that had been employed in the American trade for many years and commanded by Captain R. B. Stannard, was partly loaded and proceeding from the Tyne to Dundee, *en route* for New York, when a collision occurred just off the piers with the steamship *Elder* (1856 – Blaydon and London Steam Shipping Co. Blaydon). The *Elder* was in ballast, on passage from London for the Tyne. The *Crystal* was struck amidships on the starboard side and cut down to the water line. She began to fill up at once and although the crew immediately tried to keep the ship clear enough to enable the master to return the ship to harbour, their most strenuous efforts were futile. The *Crystal* was about to founder and the assistance of a steam tug was engaged, but she sank before she reached the piers. The crew saved themselves by taking to the boats, from which they were taken on board the tug and landed at North Shields. The *Elder* sustained considerable damage to her bows but reached the harbour safely and was taken to Wallsend for repairs.

LCR 1892, p. 6 (d); LR 1890/1 No. 1035 (C); Board of Trade Wreck Return: *Crystal*, 1892; American Lloyd's Register of American and Foreign Shipping, 1857–1900; Starke Schell Registers; *The Times*: Saturday, 9 January 1892, p. 7, Issue 33530.

Wrecksite

The wreck is located about 500 metres seaward and east of the lighthouse at South Shields. It lies on a seabed of dirty sand and stone in a general depth of 15 metres. It is sitting almost in the direct shipping lane for the mouth of the river, so great care should be taken when diving at the wrecksite. Huge ships pass very close by this wreck and the noise created by their enormous engines and screws, is very nerve-racking. There is a substantial amount of the wreck left, but it is totally collapsed and well broken up. Bronze valves and copper pipes still attached to battered machinery can be found, while rusting steel plates, bent framework and girders lie in flattened heaps on top of each other. The ship engine is just a broken heap and there is no sign of the two boilers. The ship was carrying a general cargo, which must have included large stone mill-grinding wheels, because dozens of these lie stacked up in one section of the wreck.

RIO COLORADO, EX SHEILA

Date of loss: 22 March 1917
Wreck: ★★
Depth: 15 m
Reference: 55 00'.960 N 001 22'.710 W
Location: 0.82 nm ENE of Tynemouth Lighthouse

The *Rio Colorado* (Official No. 118356) was a steel-hulled 3565-ton British turret-decked steam cargo ship measuring 103.65 m in length, with a 15.29-m beam and a 6.85-m draught.

William Doxford and Sons Ltd. at Sunderland built and completed her as Yard No. 312 in November 1903; she was launched as the *Sheila* on 23 October 1903 for Lion Line, Ltd. London and registered in London; Weddel, Turner and Co. was the manager.

The single screw was powered by a 300-nhp three-cylinder triple expansion engine that used three boilers and gave 9.5 knots. The cylinders measured 66.04 cm, 106.68 cm and 172.72 cm with a 106.68-cm stroke (26 in., 42 in. and 68 in. with a 42-in. stroke). The shipbuilders manufactured the engine and ancillary machinery. She was classed Bureau Veritas (BV).

Turner, Davidson and Co. was the manager in 1911.

In 1913 she was renamed *Rio Colorado* when purchased by European and Brazilian Shipping Co. Ltd. London; Petersen and Co. Ltd. was the manager. From 1915, London-American Maritime Trading Co. Ltd. was the registered owner, with the same manager.

Final voyage

At 0545 hrs on 22 March 1917, the *Rio Colorado*, with Captain Arthur Garbutt Cromach in charge, detonated a mine laid by the KDM submarine SMU *UC 50*, commanded by Kapitänleutnant Rudolf Seuffer, on 18 March 1917. The steamer had just reached the Tyne having made the perilous voyage across the Atlantic, on passage from Montevideo for Newcastle and had been approaching the examination vessel just off the mouth of the Tyne with her valuable and very much-needed cargo of wheat, when she struck the mine amidships, blasting a massive hole in the side of the hull. Sea conditions were extremely rough at the time and she foundered in just 40 minutes. The chief officer, boatswain and two seamen drowned, while three firemen and the second engineer were lost and also presumed drowned. The unfortunate captain drowned while attempting to swim the short distance to the examination vessel, but the remaining 19 crewmen and the pilot were picked up by it and taken to the New Quay at North Shields. Those crewmen who died were:

Aylasen, John, Able Seaman MM
Bowie, C.M., 46 yrs, Mate MM
Codde, Joseph, 46 yrs, Fireman MM
Cromack, Arthur Garbutt, 45 yrs, Master Mariner MM
Jessop, George, 32 yrs, Second Engineer MM
Nilsen, Oaubak, 27 yrs, Fireman MM
Quesada, Jose, 27 yrs, Donkeyman MM
Svensson, Karl Raganr, 24 yrs, Able Seaman MM

ADM 137/2961; CWGC; BVLS 1914–18, p. 38 ; LCWLR 1914–18, p. 108.

Wrecksite

The wreck is orientated in an E to W direction and lies on a seabed of dirty hard sand and stone in a general depth of 15 m (LAT). Because of the location in relation to the shipping channel, the wreck was dispersed with explosives soon after it sank. Although it is totally collapsed and well flattened, the debris is spread over a wide area, covering 105 m by 50 m, with lots of twisted steel plates, ribs, pipes and framework all jumbled together. The three upright boilers and the battered remains of the steam engine lie in the midst of it all. Shoals of small saithe and large pollack often swarm around the wreck during the summer months

HORTENSE LEA, EX SKJOLD

Date of loss: 21 September 1919
Wreck: ★★★
Depth: 36 m
Reference: 55 01'.213 N 001 19'.155 W
Location: 2.86 miles ENE of South Shields Lighthouse

Skjold *(Courtesy Norwegian Maritime Museum)*

The 1,125 ton Norwegian steamer Skjold *circa 1910, later to become the* Hortense Lea, *which foundered off the Tyne in 1919. (Courtesy of Rolf Kristensen and Stein-Erik Dagsland, in Norway)*

The *Hortense Lea* was a steel-hulled 1125-ton Norwegian steam cargo ship measuring 69.72 m in length, with a 10.71-m beam and a 4.87-m draught. Laxevaags Maskin and Jernskibsbyg Værksted, Bergen built and completed her as Yard No. 90 in September 1908; she was launched as the *Skjold* on 15 August 1908 for Johs. Sundfør, Haugesund. The single screw was powered by a 101-nhp three-cylinder triple expansion steam engine that used one boiler. The cylinders measured 40.64 cm, 64.77 cm and 109.22 cm with a 76.2-cm stroke (16 in., 25.5 in. and 43 in. with a 30-in. stroke). The shipbuilders manufactured the engine and ancillary machinery. She had one deck, a 64-ton (181.22-cubic.m) housedeck and 31-ton (87.78-cubic.m) forecastle. She was classed NV. Code letters: MFHW.

In 1916, Aktieselskapet Dampskipsselskapet 'Hortense Lea', Bergen purchased and renamed the ship *Hortense Lea*; Erik Grant Lea in Bergen was the manager. From 1917, Bergen Lloyd Aktierederi, Bergen was the registered owner and Bjørnstad and Brækhus was the manager.

Final voyage

At 0500 hrs on 21 September 1919, the *Hortense Lea*, commanded by Captain A. Nielsen, was on passage from Arundel for the Tyne with a cargo of rough wood pulp, when she foundered off the Tyne with the loss of nine lives. She carried a crew of 19 and two passengers. Heavy seas were raging, smashing open the hatches, and she quickly began to sink. Rockets were sent up and the 563-ton Swedish steamer *Wargon* (1919 – Wargöns AB, Wargön) went to her assistance, but the *Hortense Lea* foundered before the steamer could reach her. The *Wargon* rescued fifteen people and took them to Sunderland. Three of them, including one female passenger, died from exposure, the weather being bitterly cold, and six of the crew were lost with the vessel.

LCR 1919, p. 5 (b); LR 1919/20 No. 15936 (H); Starke Schell Registers; *The Times*: Monday, 22 September 1919, p. 12, Issue 42211.

Wrecksite

This wreck is orientated in a NE to SW direction and lies on a seabed of dirty sand, stone and colliery waste in a general depth of 36 m (LAT). It is sitting upright, fairly intact and standing up to 7 m high, but with quite a bit of damage to the bow section at the southwestern end. The highest part is the stern section, where much of the bridge structure is understood still to be in reasonable condition, with a number of portholes visible, all covered in soft corals. The author is not aware of the bell having been recovered, which should be inscribed: *Skjold 1908*, but the wreck has been well visited by local divers. Lots of fish of various species shoal over and around the wreck, especially cod and pout whiting, so it will make an interesting boat-angling venue.

LYNG, EX LIVONIA, EX AMBLESIDE, EX MAINDY TRANSPORT

Date of loss: 9 December 1942
Wreck: ✯✯✯✯✯
Depth: 39 m
Reference: 55 01'.516 N 001 18'.943 W
Location: 3.05 nm ESE of South Shields Lighthouse

The *Lyng* (Official No. 143513) was a steel-hulled 969-ton Norwegian steam cargo ship measuring 63.22 m in length, with a 10.21-m beam and a draught of 4.08 m. Rennie, Ritchie and Newport Ship Building Co. Ltd. Wivenhoe built and completed her as Yard No. 1309 in July 1920 and launched her as the *Maindy Transport* for Maindy Transport Co. Ltd. Cardiff; Jenkins, Richards and Evans Ltd. was the manager. The single screw was powered by a 106-nhp three-cylinder triple expansion steam engine that used one single-ended boiler. The cylinders measured 31.75 cm, 68.58 cm and 111.76 cm with a 76.2-cm stroke (16½ in., 27 in. and 44 in. with a 30-in.stroke). Plenty and Son Ltd. Newbury manufactured the aft engine and ancillary machinery. The vessel had one steel deck, water ballast and an aft superstructure, two forward holds, two masts (one forward and one in front of the bridge) and a control wheelhouse on top of the bridge. She was also fitted with wireless direction finder. The designated code recognition signal letters were: LJHP.

Sir David R. Llewellyn, Bart., Cardiff purchased her in 1922, while D.R. Llewellyn, Merrett Brothers and Price managed her. She was registered in Cardiff. Merrett Bros., Ltd. managed her in 1923. In 1924, D.R. Llewellyn, Merrett and Price, Ltd. was the manager. Quayside Shipping Co. Ltd. Newcastle, who was the registered owner in 1925, renamed her *Ambleside*; Connell and Grace, Ltd. was the manager. In 1933 she was renamed *Livonia* with the same owners, but was registered in Riga, Latvia; J. Zalcmanis, K. Jansons and J. Freyman was the manager. In 1936, she was renamed *Lyng* by new owner AR Jotun, Bergen, Norway; Paul Jebsen was the manager.

Final voyage

On 9 December 1942, the *Lyng*, under the command of Captain Oskar Monsen, sank following a collision with the 1142-ton British steamer *Greyfriars* (1923 – Newbigin Steam Shipping Co. Ltd. Newcastle) about three miles east of Tynemouth lighthouse. The *Lyng* was sailing as part of a northbound 39-ship convoy FN.886 (Southend–Methil) and had left Southampton for the Tyne on 7 December. She reached Barrow Deep on the 8th, where she received her sailing orders from the boarding officer, including orders to follow a northbound convoy (Station 60). On the following day they met some southbound vessels, and lit some of the lamps. According to the captain's statement, they had passed buoy no. 20C about ten minutes earlier when he noticed three red lights on the starboard bow, about one mile off. Two of the vessels passed by safely, but the third one, *Greyfriars,* ran into *Lyng* on the port side, near no.1 hatch, despite evasive manoeuvres and signals by Captain Monsen. The *Lyng* quickly began listing to port and was going down by the bow. Orders were immediately issued to make the lifeboats ready. Captain Monsen, however, decided to make an attempt to reach the Tyne, but her bow was deep in the water and the list was worsening. After about 30 minutes the crew abandoned ship in the starboard lifeboat, just before the *Lyng* foundered; the port boat was already lost, due to the severe list. The examination vessel picked up all the crew and landed them safely at North Shields quay.

The crew consisted of:

Monsen, Oskar, Captain
Berg, Harald, First Mate
Nilsen, Olof, Second Mate
Brandal, Leif, Able Seaman
Pedersen, Leif G., Able Seaman
Olsen, Arthur, Able Seaman
Kristoffersen, Torleif, Able Seaman
Dyrkom, Odd, Ordinary Seaman
Ellingsen, Øivin, 1st Engineer
Hansen, Bruno, Stoker
Sørensen, Sigard, Stoker
McCue, Thomas, Stoker
Miller, Jacob, Stoker
Gulbrandsen, Anders, Steward
Ask, Thorvald, Cook
Lunde, Magnus, 2nd Cook
Whinter, William, Mess Boy

Plus three more seamen whose names are not known.

LR 1941/2 No. 27790 (L); LCR 1942, p. 8 (f); Starke Schell Registers.

Wrecksite

The wreck is orientated in an E to W direction and lies on a seabed of dirty sand and stone in a general depth of 39 m (LAT). It stands over 7 m high around the stern section, but the bridge deck structure has collapsed down, exposing the boiler and engine. Amidships, where the two holds were positioned, is now collapsed and badly broken up, but the bows and stern are still reasonably intact. The wreckage covers an area of 76 m in length by 26 m across and has many fish swarming around it, so this should make a good boat-angling venue. The stern end is adorned with plumose anemones and lost fishing gear.

After a great deal of detective work by Glasgow University staff, the wreck was eventually identified by the numbers and other detail on the brass pedestal-mounted steering helm. When recovered, it still had the complete mahogany steering wheel attached, although that has now unfortunately fallen to pieces.

POLLEON, ex LEONORA

Date of loss: 22 March 1918
Wreck: ★★★★
Depth: 39 m
Reference: 55 01'.683 N 001 18'.968 W
Location: 3.10 nm ENE of South Shields Lighthouse

The *Polleon* (Official No. 140433) was a steel-hulled 1155-ton British steam cargo ship measuring 70.1 m in length, with an 8.83-m beam and a 4.78-m draught. Wilton's Engineering and Slipway Co. at Rotterdam in the Netherlands built and completed her as Yard No. 269 in August 1915; she was launched as the *Leonora* on 14 June 1915 for N.V. Stoomvaart Mij. Leonora in Rotterdam, Netherlands and Jos. de Poorter was the manager. The single steel screw was powered by an 180-nhp three-cylinder triple expansion steam engine (no. 390) that used one single-ended boiler (no. 650) working at a pressure of 180 psi pressure and three corrugated furnaces, 5.57 sq.m (60 sq.ft) of grate surface and 184.22 sq.m (1983 sq.ft) of heating surface. The cylinders measured 39.37 cm, 64.77 cm and 104.14 cm with a 91.44-cm stroke (15½ in., 25½ in. and 41-in.with a 36-in. stroke). Wilton's Engineering and Slipway Co also manufactured the machinery at Rotterdam. She also had one steel deck and a well deck.

The *Leonora* was captured in the North Sea by the newly built Yarrow class destroyer HMS *Sybille* on 16 August 1917, while on a voyage from Rotterdam to Stockholm with coal; she was taken into Harwich and condemned by a prize court. In 1917, she was renamed *Polleon* when taken over by the Shipping Controller, London; Everett and Newbigin was appointed as the Crown nominee manager.

Final voyage

On 22 March 1918, the KDM submarine SMU *UB 78*, which was commanded by Oblt.z.S. Arthur Stoßberg, torpedoed the *Polleon*; the steamer was on passage from Blyth for the Tyne with a cargo of coal. No prior warning was given of the attack and the *Polleon* foundered with the loss with four of her crew, three miles ENE of the Tyne entrance. The four crewmen that died were:

Amans, Gustav Albion, 49 yrs, Able Seaman
Anderson, Carl Erik, 56 yrs, Able Seaman
Kasaki, Y. 25 yrs, Able Seaman
Larsen, Kudvig Mattias, 57 yrs, Able Seaman

BVLS 1914–18, p. 84; LCWLR 1914–18, p. 208; CWGC; Jarvis (2000), Vol. V.

Wrecksite

The wreck, believed to be the *Polleon*, is orientated in a SSE to NNW direction. It lies on a seabed of mud, sand and black shells in a general depth of 39 m (LAT). The wreck is upright, broken and rather decayed and covers an area 60 m in length by 25 m across. It stands just over 5 m high, with some of the superstructure visible, covered in soft corals. Quite a number of large cod and pollack have been observed, so the wreck should make an interesting boat-angling venue.

PINK ROSE

Date of loss: 10 March 1936
Depth: 76 m
Reference: 55 01'.322 N 001 07'.799 W
Location: 9.39 nm E of the South Shields pier

The *Pink Rose* (Official No. 161148) was a steel 739-ton British steam cargo vessel measuring 54.86 m in length, with an 8.55-m beam and 3.81-m draught. N. V. Scheepsbouwwerf de Merwede, Hardinxveld-Giessendam built and completed her as Yard No. 207 on 19 March 1930; she was launched on 23 January 1930 for R. Hughes and Co. Ltd. The single screw was powered by an aft-positioned 89-rhp, three-cylinder triple expansion steam engine that used two single-ended boilers working at a pressure of 180 psi, using four plain furnaces, 5.75 sq.m (62 sq.ft) of grate surface and 195.09 sq.m (2100 sq.ft) of heating surface, giving 10.5 knots. The cylinders measured 38.2 cm, 63.5 cm and 101.6 cm with a 68.58-cm stroke (15 in., 25 in. and 40 in. with a 27-in. stroke). Earle's Co. Ltd. manufactured the machinery at Hull. She had one steel deck, a well deck, three bulkheads cemented and an aft superstructure consisting of a 32-m quarterdeck, a 3.9-m bridge deck and 7.3-m forecastle, along with some cellular double bottom and a forepeak and aft peak tank. Lloyd's classed her 100 A1. Code letters: LFRS.

From 1934, Richard Hughes and Co. Ltd. Liverpool was the registered owner.

Final voyage

Early on the morning of 10 March 1936, the *Pink Rose* foundered following a collision with the 659-ton steamer *George Frusher* (1901 – Consolidated Fisheries Ltd. Lowestoft), 11 miles SE of the Tyne piers. She was bound from Dunston-on-Tyne to Shoreham with a cargo of coke. All the crew were saved by the *George Frusher*, which sustained considerable damage to the bows. The hull of the *Pink Rose* was valued at £7,000.

LCR 1937, p. 9; LR 1935/6 No. 3182 (P); Board of Trade Wreck Return: *Pink Rose*, 1936; *The Times*: Wednesday, 11 March 1936, p. 27, Issue 47320.

Wrecksite

There is no wreck with the same proportions as the *Pink Rose* anywhere near the area suggested for the wreck. Her position was estimated in the dark and at a time of panic,though, so it may be that this wreck is that of the steamer. It is orientated in a SE to NW direction and sits in a small scour, lying on a seabed of sand, mud and broken shells, in a general depth of 76 m (LAT). The wreck appears to be either inverted or lying on its side. It stands 10 m high and covers an area 60 m long and 6 m across, so the wreck should make an interesting boat-angling venue.

4

THE RIVER TYNE TO BLYTH

MARIE

Date of loss: 5 July 1907
Wreck: ★★★
Depth: 33 m
Reference: 55 02'.936 N 001 22'.251 W
Location: 2.3 nm NE from Tynemouth light

The *Marie* was a steel-hulled 865-ton German steam cargo vessel measuring 61.89 m in length, with a 9.16-m beam and a 4.29-m draught. Howaldtswerke at Kiel built and completed her as Yard No. 214 in August 1890; she was launched in July 1890 for H. Diederichsen at Kiel, who was the owner at the time of loss. The single steel screw was powered by a 65-nhp triple expansion steam engine that used one single-ended boiler and gave nine knots. Howaldtswerke at Kiel also manufactured the engine and ancillary machinery. She had one deck, a 17.98-m quarterdeck, a 24.38-m bridge deck and 8.83-m forecastle.

Final voyage

At 0240 hrs on 5 July 1907, the *Marie* was transporting coal from Dunston-on-Tyne to Hamburg when she sank off the mouth of the River Tyne, following a collision with the 9600-ton destroyer-tender HMS *Assistance*. Unfortunately the master's wife drowned, but the rest of the crew was picked up by one of His Majesty's warship. The *Marie* was valued at £8200.

Starke Schell Registers; American Lloyd's Register of American and Foreign Shipping, 1857–1900; Miramar Ship Index; *The Times*: Tuesday, 9 July 1907, p. 13, Issue 38380.

Wrecksite

The wreck, which is probably that of the German steamer, is orientated in a SSE to NNW direction with the bows to the NNW. It lies on a seabed of fine sand and mud in a general depth of 33 m (LAT), with a field of debris stretching E to W. The amidships section of the wreck is collapsed, well broken up and decayed, but the whole outline can be made out. The bow section is fairly intact, and close by are the anchor, chain and winches. The boiler and remains of the engine are still there, but there is no sign of any non-ferrous metal. The wreck covers an area 60 m long and 15 m across and stands over 3 m at the two highest points.

JAMES LUDFORD, HM TRAWLER

Date of loss: 14 December 1939
Wreck: ★★★★
Depth: 50 m
Reference: 55 02'.483 N 001 16'.297 W
Location: 4.78 nm NE by E of Tynemouth light

The *James Ludford* was a steel-hulled 438-ton Mersey class steam trawler measuring 45.11 m in length, with a 7.23-m beam and a 3.96-m draught. Cochrane, at Selby built and delivered her for the Royal Navy on 1 May 1919 as Admiralty Trawler No. 4232. The single screw, using one shaft, was powered by an 87-rhp three-cylinder triple expansion steam engine that used one single-ended boiler working at a pressure of 180-lb psi, with three plain furnaces, 4.45 sq.m (48 sq.ft) of grate surface and 133.78 sq.m (1440 sq.ft) of heating surface, which gave 11 knots. The cylinders measured 33.02 cm, 58.42 cm and 93.98 cm with a 66.04-cm stroke (13 in., 23 in. and 37 in. with a 26-in. stroke). C.D. Holmes and Co. Ltd. manufactured the machinery at Hull. She had one steel deck, four bulkheads cemented and a 23.77-m quarterdeck and 5.78-m forecastle.

Normal armament consisted of two three-inch single guns, but this varied.

Once the hostilities of the First World War had ceased, *James Ludford* was laid up in reserve in 1921 and brought back into commission in 1930, employed as a Marker Buoy Vessel. In 1939 she was converted to minesweeper Port No. T.16.

Final patrol

On 14 December 1939 *James Ludford*, commanded by Lt. Cdr. Harry Richard John Lewis, retired, RN, was on patrol some five miles east of Tynemouth when she detonated a mine and foundered; one man died, Seaman William A, Gilmour, RNR (PS), LT/X 19248.

Bronte's Kriegsmarine destroyers: *Z 4* (Richard Beitzen), *Z 8* (Bruno Heinemann), *Z 14* (Friedrich Ihn) and *Z 15* (Erich Steinbrick) had laid the mines during the night of 12/13 December 1939, under the cover of *Z 19* (Hermann Künne).

BVLS 1939–45, Pt 1, p. 3 ; SRN, Vol. 2, p. 181 ; CWGC ; *The Times*: Saturday, 16 December 1939, p. 10, Issue 48490.

Wrecksite

The wreck is orientated in a SE to NW direction and lies on a seabed of hard sand and shells in a general depth of 50 m (LAT). It is fairly substantial, standing upright with the highest point at 6.7 m, but the bridge structure and decks have partially collapsed. The boiler/machinery is visible, along with her winches and lots of flattened copper pipes protrude through the mound of wreckage. Large fish of different species have also been observed.

STRINDHEIM, EX GUERMOR, EX ARBEIT

Date of loss: 15 December 1939
Wreck: ★★★★
Depth: 46 m
Reference: 55 02'.604 N 001 17'.2649 W
Location: 4.10 nm NE by E of Tynemouth light

Norwegian SS Strindheim
(Author's collection)

The *Strindheim* was a steel-hulled 327-ton Norwegian steam coaster measuring 43 m in length, with a 6.9-m beam and 3.8-m draught. Gebr. E. and M. Coops, Hoogezand built and completed her in October 1923 on a canal in the northern Netherlands, a fair distance from the sea. She was launched as the *Arbeit* for Seeschiffahrts AG, Danzig, Danzig Free State. The single screw was powered by a 31-nhp three-cylinder triple expansion steam engine that used one single-ended boiler. The cylinders measured 26.03 cm, 40 cm and 67.94 cm with a 50.038-cm stroke (10¼ in., 15¾ in. and 26¾ in. with a 19 7/10-in. stroke). Botje, Ensing and Co. manufactured the engine and ancillary machinery at Groningen. She had one deck, water ballast and a 12.49-m poop deck and 7.01-m forecastle.

In 1925, Cie Nantaise de Navigation à Vapeur, Nantes, in France purchased and renamed her *Guermor*; Services des Messageries de l'Ouest was the manager.

From 1938, Aktieselskapet Strindheims Rederi, at Trondheim, Norway was the registered owner and renamed her *Strindheim*; Bjarne Isaksen was the manager. The designated code recognition signal letters were: LJXP.

Final voyage

On 15 December 1939, the *Strindheim* was on passage from Murvik for Hull with a cargo of ferrochrome, when she detonated a mine and sank almost at once, five miles northeast of Tynemouth pier. Nine of her crew of thirteen were lost, but the 1614-ton Norwegian ship *Finse* (1916 – WW II – Hjemmeflåte) rescued four survivors.

Bronte's Kriegsmarine destroyers: Z 4 (Richard Beitzen), Z 8 (Bruno Heinemann), Z 14 (Friedrich Ihn) and *Z 15* (Erich Steinbrick) had laid mines during the night of 12/13 December 1939, under the cover of *Z 19* (Hermann Künne), but German aircraft also dropped mines around the same time. The nine crewmen lost were:

Andersen, Fredrik, Able Seaman
Grøtting, Kristian Alfred, Able Seaman
Krangnes Olaf Sefenias, 2nd Engineer
Lian, Martin Nikolai, Stoker
Løvø, Paul, Mate
Olsen, Ingvald Kristian, Engineer
Refsnæs, Karl Nikolay, Captain
Stenn, Gustav, Able Seaman
Støbak, Ingbert,.Steward

LCWLR 1939–45, p. 28; LR 1938–40, No. 82044 (R)

Wrecksite

This wreck is orientated in a SSE to NNW direction. It lies on a seabed of dirty coarse sand, stone, shale and colliery waste in a general depth of 46 m (LAT). The wreck stands up to 8 m high and is relatively intact from the stern to just forward of the bridge. Everything forward of the winches to the bows section is totally collapsed and spread out in a jumble of large pieces of steel debris, extending some 30 m or more to the north, due probably to the exploding mine. Her bows lie to the SE and the highest sections and bows are now supporting a large colony of dead man's fingers. The ship's bell and telegraph are no longer present and most other items of interest are also long gone, but the wreck still makes an excellent dive. It must be treated with the utmost caution – poor visibility and a curtain of nets often hang over it like a shroud.

CLEADON

Date of loss: 31 August 1904
Wreck: ★★★
Depth: 39 m
Reference: 55 03'.333 N 001 20'.009 W
Other section: 55 03'.357 N 001 20'.036 W
Location: 3.39 nm NE from Tynemouth Pier

The *Cleadon* was an iron-hulled 760-ton steam passenger/cargo vessel measuring 51.28 m in length, with an 8.83-m beam and a 5.79-m draught. William Watson built and completed her at the Pallion's yard in Sunderland as Yard No. 406. She was launched on 7 January 1871 for H. T. Morton & Co., Sunderland. The single iron four-bladed screw was powered by a two-cylinder compound steam engine which used one boiler and gave eight knots. In 1895 the registered owner became the Earl of Durham at Sunderland and T. Nicholson was the manager. Lambton Collieries Ltd., at Sunderland was the owner from 1896 until the time of loss and T. Nicholson remained the manager.

Final voyage

On the morning of Wednesday, 31 August 1904, the *Cleadon* was in ballast and en route from Aberdeen to Sunderland when she sank after a collision with the Norwegian-registered steamer *Dagne* (1902 – A/S Dagny, Kristiania) Fourteen members of the *Cleadon*'s crew and passengers, including her master, Captain Atkins, scrambled over the bows of the *Dagne* to safety. The chief engineer and chief mate went into the water and it was 15 minutes before they were picked up, in a very exhausted condition. The *Dagne*, though its bows were seriously damaged, returned to the river Tyne to land the people she had rescued.

Board of Trade Wreck Return: *Cleadon*, 1904; Starke Schell Registers; American Lloyd's Register of American and Foreign Shipping, 1857–1900; *The Times*: Thursday, 1 September 1904, p. 4, Issue 37488.

Wrecksite

These two wrecks – most likely that of the *Cleadon* - lies on a seabed of fine sand, mud and gravel in a general depth of 39 m (LAT). It is orientated in a SSE to NNW direction. The wreck is broken into two sections, with the first part being the inverted bow section, standing about 4 m high and covering an area approximately 15 m long and 13 m wide. What appears to be a spare four-bladed screw can be observed inside the wreck, while what looks to be the second section of the wreck is also orientated in a SSE to NNW direction and stands about 5 m high. This part is about 10 m long and 8 m wide. Both parts are likely to attract a variety of fish.

ESTON

Date of loss: 28 January 1940
Wreck: ✯✯
Depth: 22 m
Reference: 55 03'.475 N 001 24'.646 W
Location: 1.57 nm SSE of St Mary's light

The *Eston* (Official No. 143913) was a steel-hulled 1487-ton British steam cargo ship measuring 73.15 m in length, with a 10.97-m beam and a draught of 4.80 m. Goole Shipbuilding

The 1,487-ton P & O steamer Eston, *was lost off Blyth with all hands on January 28th 1940 (Author's collection)*

and Repairing Co. Ltd. built and completed her as Yard No. 250 on 8 December 1919. She was launched on 13 September 1919 for Peninsular and Oriental Steam Navigation Co. Ltd. (P&O) and registered in London. (She was actually laid down for The Shipping Controller.) The single steel screw was powered by a 172-nhp three-cylinder triple expansion steam engine that gave ten knots. The cylinders measured 45.72 cm, 76.2 cm and 127 cm, with an 83.82-cm stroke (18 in., 30 in. and 50 in. with a 33-in. stroke). Steam was supplied by two single-ended coal fired boilers operating at 180 psi pressure and used six corrugated furnaces, 9.01 sq. m (97 sq. ft) of grate surface and 268.11 sq. m (2886 sq. ft) of heating surface. Earles and Co. at Hull manufactured the machinery. The *Eston* was a single deck vessel with a raised 7.01-m forecastle and the 15.84-m bridge deck and engine room positioned amidships. Cargo was carried in four holds, two forward and two aft with 2914.99 cubic m (102 942 cubic ft) and a deadweight of 1950 tons on a 5.66-m draught. A derrick was provided at each hatchway for cargo work. These were rigged on the fore- and mainmasts, which were between no. 1, 2, 3 and 4 hatchways. The *Eston* had one steel deck and accommodation for 12 passengers in the midships deck-house. She had some cellular double bottom, a fore-peak and an aft-peak tank. The designated code recognition signal letters were: MJTD.

Eston was one of a pair of coasters bought by P & O from the Government before they were completed; the other, *Redcar Eston,* could carry 2915 cubic metres of cargo at ten knots.

When the *Eston* was launched, she slid down the slip so fast that she ran onto the opposite bank of the river Ouse and it was quite possible to walk under the hull at low tide. On 5 December 1919 sea trials were run and she was delivered to P&O on the eighth.

Final voyage

The steamer departed Hull in ballast on 26 January 1940 on passage for Blyth, Northumberland. The crew consisted of 21 men – three officers, six seamen, two petty officers, one cook, one boy, one steward, two engineers and five firemen. She was sailing as part of the northbound convoy FN.81, 11 ships in all, but the *Eston* had been straggling behind the convoy and was last reported off the coast near Blyth on 28 January 1940 before disappearing. Several days later a man's body and one of the ship's lifeboats were found washed ashore near Tynemouth. It was suspected that the *Eston* had detonated a German mine and sunk. It was later discovered that the Kriegsmarine submarine *U 22*, commanded by Kptlt Karl-Heinrich Jenisch, had, on 20 December 1939, laid a barrier of nine mines in Kriegsmarine quadrant AN5461 off Blyth, the first mine having been dropped at 0207 hrs (CT), at position 55°05.7'N.

From the KTB of *U 22*:

> *20.12.39 AN 5461 0207–0250 9 Minen vor Blyth/Hafen uW gelegt. 55°07,7' – 55°08,8N/01°26,8' – 01°27,7W*

The 16 men that died on the *Eston* were:

Bathgate, William, 43 yrs, 2nd Engineer Officer MM
Edwards, Edward John, 38 yrs, Fireman MM
Elphick, Willian, 44 yrs, Fireman MM
Harris, Herbert Roser, 48 yrs, Master MM
Hellens, John Millar, 47 yrs, Able Seaman MM
Hole, Larry Charles, 23 yrs, Able Seaman MM

Kent, Frederick, 44 yrs, Able Seaman MM
Liddle, George, 63 yrs, Donkeyman MM
Millar, David, 59 yrs, Chief Engineer Officer MM
Mitchell, Laurence, Porter 40 yrs, Chief Officer MM
Robinson, Robert, 14 yrs, Mess Room Boy MM
Robinson, Robert, 40 yrs, Steward MM
Sproates, George, Fireman MM
Stiff, William Henry Neville, 66 yrs, 2nd Engineer Officer
Ward, Thomas Edward, 29 yrs, second mate MM
Williams, John, 29 yrs, Boatswain (Bosun) MM

At least three of the men are buried in Commonwealth War Graves Commission (CWGC) graves at Blyth Beach Cemetery. The graves are marked: Unknown.

CWGC; LCR 1940, p. 7 (c); KTB of *U 22*.

Wrecksite

The wreck is orientated in a more or less ESE to WSW direction and lies on a seabed of rocks and stone in a general depth of 22 m (LAT). The location is about one mile straight out from the site of the old Spanish City amusement park at Whitley Bay. It was positively identified in 1978 when someone recovered the ship's bell on the bow section of the wreck. The wreck was fairly substantial in the 1980s and stood about 4 m high, but the elements have now taken their toll. It is totally collapsed and well broken up, lying in three sections, with her bows to the north and her boilers and engine about 50 m to the south; the stern end is some 60 m to the southwest of the boilers/engine. The wreck is well dispersed, but in jumbled heaps of steel frames, plates and pipes. There seems to be very little marine life around the wreck and quite a lot of sediment, but it still makes an interesting rummage dive.

WILLIAM HALLETT, HM TRAWLER

Date of loss: 13 December 1939
Wreck: ★★★
Depth: 38 m
Reference: 55 03'.753 N 001 21'.400 W
Location: 3.22 nm ESE of from St Mary's Lighthouse

The *William Hallett* was a steel-hulled 210-ton Strath class steam trawler that measured 37.49 m in length overall, with a 6.70-m beam and a 3.65-m draught (depth of hold). Forest, Rennie of Wivenhoe built her in 1918 and delivered her to the Admiralty on 7 January 1919. The single steel screw was powered by a reciprocating (VTE) 56-rhp, three-cylinder triple expansion engine engine that used one single-ended boiler working at a pressure of 180-lb psi, with three plain furnaces, 3.90 sq.m (42 sq.ft) of grate surface and 125.14 sq.m (1347 sq.ft) of heating surface, giving 10.5 knots. The cylinders measured 30.48 cm, 50.8 cm and 86.36 cm with a 58.42-cm stroke (12 in., 20 in. and 34 in. with a 23-in.stroke. A. G. Mumford at Colchester manufactured the machinery. She had one steel deck, a 19.05-cm (7½-in) bar keel, three bulkheads cemented, a double bottom forward of 8.53 m (28 ft) and 19 tons of ballast. Lloyd's classed her 100 A1.

In 1921, Ivey Steam Trawling Co,. London was the registered owner and R. J. Williams was the manager.

In 1935–36, T. B. Bilton and Sons of North Shields was the registered owner, but the port of registration was London: Port Reg: LO.353.

In November 1939, she was requisitioned by the Admiralty and converted to Auxiliary Patrol Vessel no. 3776, Port Reg: FY.554

Armament consisted of one 12-pounder forward and possibly twin 0.5 in. aft with two Lewis or Vickers K machine guns on the bridge, plus wireless and echo sounding device.

Final patrol

On 13 December 1939, the *William Hallett* was on patrol off the River Tyne when she detonated a German mine, foundered and was lost with all her crew of eight.

Bronte's Kriegsmarine destroyers: *Z 4* (Richard Beitzen), *Z 8* (Bruno Heinemann), *Z 14* (Friedrich Ihn) and *Z 15* (Erich Steinbrick) had laid the mines during the night of 12/13 December 1939, under the cover of *Z 19* (Hermann Künne), but German aircraft also dropped mines around the same time.

The crewmen that died were:

Addison, James, Deck Hand, RNR
Cole, Albert, 2nd Mate, RNR
Hannant, Charles, Skipper, RNR
Holland, Norman, Fireman, RNR
Lindores, Gavin, 3rd Hand, RNR
Lindores, Robert, Deck Hand, RNR
Theodavakis, Andrew, 2nd Engineman, RNR
Young, John, Cook, RNR

BVLS 1939–45 Vol. 1 , p. 3; Toghill (2003), p. 192; SRN, Vol. 2, p. 391; CWGC.

Wrecksite

The wreck, probably that of the *William Hallett*, is orientated in a NNE to SSW direction and lies on a seabed of hard sand and stone in a general depth of 38 m (LAT). It stands about 4 m high around the engine/boiler area and is broken in two. Aft of the boiler, the stern is fairly smashed up and buried, but the screw can be seen sticking out of the seabed. Forward of the boiler is reasonably intact, but it lists over to starboard. There is wooden decking still in place, but it is gradually rotting away. Soft corals and plumose anemones have established themselves in fair numbers on the upper structures.

MARS, ex IDA

Date of loss: 20 December 1939
Wreck: ★★★
Depth: 27 m
Reference: 55 03'.819 N 001 24'.192 W
Location: 1.64 nm ESE from St Mary's Lighthouse

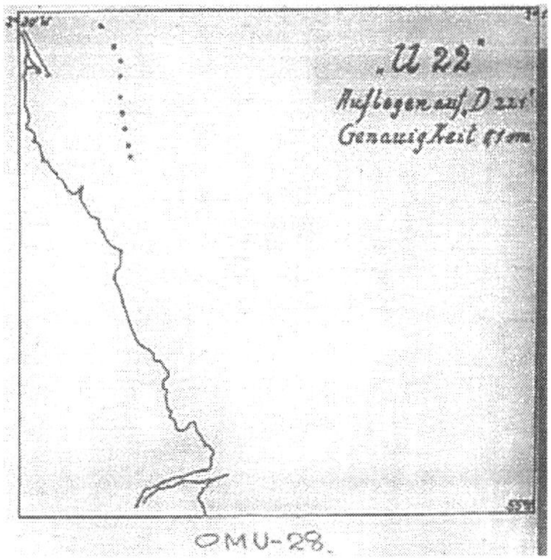

Above: On December 20th 1939, the Mars, *ex* Ida *detonated a mine laid by the Kriegsmarine submarine* U 22 *(Courtesy of Rolf Kristensen and Stein-Erik Dagsland, in Norway)*

Right: Position of mines laid by U 22 *off Blyth (Author's collection)*

The *Mars* (Official No. 8054) was a steel-hulled 1912-ton Swedish steam cargo ship that measured 81.30 m in length, with a 12.85-m beam and 5.38-m draught. AS Bergens Mek.Verksteder, Bergen built and completed her as Yard No. 204 in January 1924; she was launched as the *Ida* on 26 December 1923 for Aktieselskapet Dampskipsselskapet Jeanette Skinner at Haugesund in Norway; K. Knutsen, O.A.S. was the manager. The single steel screw was powered by a 162-hp, three-cylinder triple expansion steam engine that used two single- ended boilers. The cylinders measured 49.53 cm, 76.2 cm and 132.08 cm with a 91.44-cm stroke (19½ in, 30 in and 52 in with a 36-in. stroke). Bergens Mek Værks, Bergen manufactured the engine and ancillary machinery. She had one deck, water ballast and a 77-ton (218.03-cubic m) poop deck, a 96-ton (271.84-cubic.m) deck house and an eight-ton (22.65-cubic.m) forecastle.

From 1936, Rederi AB Iris, Stockholm in Sweden was the registered owner and renamed her *Mars*; C. Abrahamsen became the manager. The designated code recognition signal letters were: SEFN.

Final voyage

On 20 December 1939, the *Mars* detonated a mine laid by the Kriegsmarine submarine *U 22*, commanded by Kapitänleutnant Karl-Heinrich Jenisch. The steamer was on passage from Kopmanholmen/Helsingborg for London with a cargo of rough wood pulp. After the explosion the *Mars* foundered almost immediately and all of her crew of seven were lost.

U 22 had laid a barrier of nine mines off Blyth on 20 December 1939 in Kriegsmarine quadrant AN5461; the first mine having been dropped at 0207 hrs (CT), in position 55°05.7'N.

From the KTB of *U 22*:

20.12.39 AN 5461 0207–0250 9 Minen vor Blyth/Hafen uW gelegt. 55°07,7' – 55°08,8N/01°26,8' – 01°27,7W

LCWLR 1939–45, p. 30; LR 1938/9 No. 79247 (M); KTB of *U 22*.

Wrecksite

The wreck is orientated in an ENE to WSW direction and lies on a seabed of hard sand, stone and shingle in a general depth of 27 m (LAT). It is quite substantial, but totally collapsed and well broken up, with the highest point being over 4 m around the boilers/engine amidships. The wreckage, which includes lots of pieces of non-ferrous metal, large lengths of copper pipe of varying diameters and thicknesses, bronze valves, cog wheels and broken sections of hollow masts, as well as the odd porthole, covers an area 90 m long and 30 m wide. The two boilers are standing upright and exposed, close to the remains of the steam engine and a brass condenser, and the bows and stern end, are, or were, both still recognisable.

DIANA

Date of loss: 5 June 1897
Wreck: ★★
Depth: 51 m
Reference: 55 04'.189 N 001 16'.118 W
Location: 6 nm NE from Tynemouth

The *Diana* was an iron-hulled 382-ton steam collier that measured 48.48 m in length and 6.45 m across the beam. Coulson, Cooke and Co. at Wallsend, Newcastle built and completed her as Yard No. 4 in April 1873 for B. Sars and Co. Bergen, Norway. The single iron screw was powered by an inverted-compound 50-nhp two-cylinder steam engine that used two boilers working at a pressure of 90-lb psi and giving eight knots; she also had a surface condenser, and the boilers had two horizontal returning tubes, a shell with a diameter of 3.65 m (12 ft) and a length of 3.01 m (9.9 ft) with two furnaces in each, measuring 1.09 m (43.3 in.). The cylinders each measured 45.72cm & 91.44cm with a stroke (18in & 36 in with a 24-in stroke.). Pattison and Atkinson manufactured the machinery at Newcastle.

In 1876, Johan Troye and Co. Bergen was the registered owner. In 1895 she was owned by W. Hansen, Bergen.

Final voyage

On the night of Saturday, 5 June 1897, the *Diana* had left the Tyne with a cargo of coal on a voyage to Stornoway when, during darkness and thick fog, she was in collision with the 2213-ton SS *Ganges* (1880 – SS. Jacona Co. Ltd. Dundee) reportedly about ten miles NE of Tynemouth. The *Diana* received a terrific blow on the port side and immediately began to settle. Captain Sars from the *Diana* and his crew all saved themselves by scrambling over the bows of the *Ganges*, which returned them to the Tyne.

The Times: Monday, 7 June 1897, p. 6, Issue 35223; Starke Schell Registers; Miramar Ship Index; Norwegian Veritas.

Wrecksite

The wreckage is orientated in a N to S (000/180) direction and lies on a hard dirty seabed in a general depth of 51 m (LAT). It is totally collapsed, well broken up and dispersed over an area 32 m long and 17 m across, with the highest pieces standing no more than 2 m from the seabed.

SPRAY, EX FIRSBY, EX DENABY

Date of loss: 14 April 1917
Wreck: ★★★★
Depth: 46 m
Reference: 55 04'.061 N 001 19'.015 W
Location: 4.55 nm E by S from St Mary's Lighthouse

The *Spray* (Official No. 99552) was a steel 1150-ton British steam cargo ship which measured 68.58 m in length, with a 10.16-m beam and a 4.31-m draught. S P. Austin and Son at Wear Dock, Sunderland built and completed her as Yard No. 174 in December 1891; she was launched as the *Denaby* on 17 November 1891 for Denaby Main Colliery Ltd. Hull. The single steel screw was powered by a 136-hp, three-cylinder triple expansion steam engine that used one boiler. The cylinders measured 46.99 cm, 76.2 cm and 124.46 cm with an 83.82-cm stroke (18½ in., 30 in. and 49 in. with a 33-in.stroke). J. Dickinson at Sunderland manufactured the engine and ancillary machinery. She had one deck, four bulkheads cemented and an 8.5-m poop deck, a 15.2-m quarterdeck and a 13.4-m bridge deck.

Denaby and Cadeby Main Collieries Ltd. Hull was the registered owner in 1895.

In 1900, she had the same owners but was renamed *Firsby*.

Ellis and McHardy, Aberdeen purchased her in 1904 and renamed her *Spray*.

Final voyage

On 14 April 1917, the KDM mine-laying submarine SMU *UC 31*, under the command of Kapitänleutnant Otto von Schrader, torpedoed and sank the *Spray* without any warning. The steamer, which was in ballast and *en route* from Aberdeen to Sunderland, was steaming south at a steady ten knots when a huge explosion rocked the ship close to the stern at 0615 hrs. The aft section was totally destroyed and as shattered steel plates and debris filled the air, she immediately began to fill up and go down by the stern. The master, Captain C. O. Lawrence, gave the order to stop the engine and abandon ship and she sank within 25 minutes. A torpedo-boat destroyer arrived shortly after, picked up all of the crew and landed them at North Shields.

LCWLR 1914–18, p. 117; BVLS 1914–18, p. 43; LR 1915/16 No. 1810 (S).

Wrecksite

The wreck is orientated in an E to W direction and lies in a general depth of 46 m (LAT). It is still fairly substantial, but is mostly well broken up and partially buried, with some superstructure visible. The wreck stands over seven metres high around midships and is spread over an area 86 m long and 20 m wide. The boiler, condenser and engine are all visibly exposed and soft corals have established themselves on the highest structures. Shoals of pout whiting have adopted the boiler area as a haven.

PRUNELLE, ex ASBJÖRN SELSBANE, ex SATURNUS, ex GÖTA

Date of loss: 22 August 1918
Wreck: ★★★★
Depth: 24 m
Reference: 55 05'.365 N 001 26'.410 W
Location: 1.06 nm NNE of St Mary's Lighthouse and 2.32 nm SSE of Blyth south pier

The *Prunelle* was an iron-hulled 572-ton British steamship that measured 47.47 m in length, with an 8.1-m beam and a 3.88-m draught. Bergsunds Mekaniska Verkstads AB, Stockholm built and completed her as Yard No. 114 in September 1874 and launched her as the *Göta* for Rederibolaget "Sverige", Stockholm. The single iron screw was powered by a 65-hp, two-cylinder compound steam engine that used one boiler and gave eight knots.

In 187? Ångbåtsaktiebolaget, Stockholm was the registered owner and C. H. Backert was the manager.

In 1878, she was sold to Det Bergenske Dampskibsselskab, Bergen and renamed *Saturnus*. The registered owner was Dampskipsselskapet Saturnus, Bergen in August 1910 and C. Daae-Olsen was the manager.

In January 1911, she was owned by part-owners Johnsen and Bergman, Kragerö in Norway.

Aktieselskapet Tore Hund, Harstad in Norway purchased her in February 1912 and renamed her *Asbjörn Selsbane*; L. H. Andreassen was the manager.

In August 1915, she was sold to Aktieselskapet Dampskipsselskapet 'Prunelle', Bergen in Norway; Aktieselskapet Erik Rusten was the manager.

In December 1915 she was renamed *Prunelle*.

On 27 August 1916, the vessel struck the seabed near Bergen, while *en route* to Lübeck in Germany.

In February 1918, Rederi Aktieselskapet Harald Grenske, Skien in Norway was the registered owner and H. Haraldsen was the manager.

From 1918, the Shipping Controller requisitioned the vessel and renamed her *Prunelle*. H. W. and C. M. Ezard was the Crown nominee manager. The designated code recognition signal letters were: JQSK.

The vessel was armed for defence with a 12-pounder (5.44-kilo) deck-mounted gun.

Early in August 1918, the *Prunelle* ran aground near Flamborough Head, while *en route* from Drammen to London.

Final voyage

At 1340 hrs on 22 August 1918 the *Prunelle* was torpedoed and sunk without warning by the KDM submarine SMU *UB 112*, commanded by Kapitänleutnant Wilhelm Rhein. The *Prunelle* was voyaging from Tilbury, Essex to Dundee, carrying a crew of 16 and a 500-ton cargo of jute. The torpedo detonated next to where the engine room was located on the port side. Twelve crewmen, including Captain Storm Thomas, were lost. The vessel sank almost immediately, but the remaining four crew, who were left clinging to floating wreckage, were picked up by the examination vessel and landed at Blyth. Two bodies were recovered and buried ashore, but the following ten were lost:

Bishop, John Arthur, 34 yrs, Able Seaman
Bliss, James, 19 yrs, Fireman
Cartwright, John, 38 yrs, Able Seaman
Cheetham, Alfred Buchanan, 51 yrs, 2nd Officer
Davis, William Wood, 23 yrs, Chief Engineer
Dix, Arthur Henry, 45 yrs, Fireman
Halls, William H, Leading Seaman, RNVR
Hampson, Henry, Able Seaman, RNVR
Howard, James, 41 yrs, 1st Officer
Jackson, George Edward, 33 yrs, 2nd Engineer
Lee, Charles, 17 yrs, Assistant Steward
Storm, Thomas, 51 yrs, Master

ADM 137/2964; LCWLR 1914–18, p. 231; LR 1915/16 No. 1577 (A); BMS 1914–18, p. 87; CWGC; Jarvis (2000), Vol. 5.

Wrecksite

The wreck is orientated in a SE to NW direction and lies on a seabed of rock and coarse shale in a general depth of 24 m (LAT). The bows are facing to the east and are 50 m to the south of the main wreck. It is broken into two large sections, with scattered bits of iron plate and broken machinery in between. A local diver recovered the ship's bell and engine maker's plate in recent years, but there are still items of interest, such as portholes, to be found under the iron frames and plates. This vessel had a large deck gun that was recently removed by local divers, along with many of the boxes of live 12-pounder shells that can be found amongst the wreckage. Long lengths of copper pipe with brass flanges and a few brass valves can still be seen protruding from the pile of twisted debris. Divers often refer to this wreck as *Elise*, but that is the name of another wreck lying very close by.

FERRYHILL

Date of loss: 21 January 1940
Wreck: ✯✯
Depth: 23 m
Reference: 55 05'.666 N 001 26'.932 W
Location: 1.3 nm N of St. Mary's Lighthouse and 1.9.n.m. SSE of Blyth south pier

The 1,086 ton Aberdeen Coal & Shipping Co. Ltd, Aberdeen. steamship Ferryhill, *circa 1925. (Author's collection)*

The *Ferryhill* (Official No. 139814) was a steel-hulled 1086-ton British steam cargo vessel that measured 67.38 m in length, with a 10.16-m beam and a 4.26-m draught. Hall, Russell and Co. Ltd. Aberdeen built and completed her in October 1919 as Yard No. 673 for Aberdeen Coal and Shipping Co. Ltd. Aberdeen. The single steel screw was powered by a 178-hp, three-cylinder triple expansion steam engine that used two single-ended boilers operating at a pressure of 180-lb psi, with six corrugated furnaces, 9.66 sq.m (104 sq.ft) of grate surface and 306.58 sq.m (3300 sq.ft) of heating surface.. The cylinders measured 44.45 cm, 73.66 cm and 119.38 cm with an 88.82-cm stroke (17.5 in., 29 in. and 47 in. with a 33-in. stroke). Hall, Russell and Co. Ltd. manufactured the engine and ancillary machinery at Aberdeen. She had one steel deck, a well deck, four bulkheads cemented and a 39.8-m quarterdeck, a 4.8-m bridge deck and an 8.2-m forecastle, along with some cellular double bottom, an aft-peak and forepeak tank. Lloyd's classed her 100 A1. The designated code recognition signal letters were: MGSJ.

Final voyage

At 2130 hrs (CT) on 21 January 1940, the *Ferryhill*, commanded by Captain Taylor, detonated a mine and sank, 1.5 miles north of St. Mary's Lighthouse; it was later discovered that the Kriegsmarine submarine *U 22* had laid the mine.

The steamer was sailing independently and was carrying a 1200-ton cargo of coal, on passage from Blyth for Aberdeen. The *Ferryhill* keeled over and foundered in minutes, taking eleven of her crew down with her. The 99-ton armed British drifter *Young Jacob* (FY.975 – Skipper Thomas Williamson) picked up two survivors, the first mate and second engineer, who were landed at North Shields and taken to Preston Hospital. The crewmen that died were:

Cracknell, William, 38 yrs, Donkeyman MM
Innes, James, 32 yrs, Able Seaman MM
Irvine, Robert, 57 yrs, Cook MM
Mennie, George Alexander, 16 yrs, Ordinary Seaman MM
Nolan, James, 55 yrs, Fireman MM
Pirie, Edward, 31 yrs, Fireman MM
Ross, Peter, 52 yrs, Chief Engineer Officer MM
Scarborough, William Ritchie, 30 yrs, 2nd Officer MM
Scott, Archibald James Howie, 37 yrs, Lamp Trimmer MM
Smith, William Nelson, 28 yrs, Able Seaman MM
Stephen, Williamson John Taylor, 35 yrs, Master MM

U 22, commanded by Kapitänleutnant Karl-Heinrich Jenisch, had laid a barrier of nine mines off Blyth on 20 December 1939, in Kriegsmarine quadrant AN5461, the first mine having been dropped at 0207 hrs (CT) in position 55°05.7'N.

From the KTB of *U 22*:

> *20.12.39 AN 5461 0207–0250 9 Minen vor Blyth/Hafen uW gelegt. 55°07,7' – 55°08,8N/01°26,8' – 01°27,7W*

CWGC; LCWLR 1939–45, p. 36; BVLS 1939–45, p. 3; LR 1938/9, No. 74410 (F).

Wrecksite

The Ministry of War Transport dispersed the wreck with explosives in 1955. It is orientated in a N to S direction and lies on a flat, firm seabed of sand and stone in a general depth of 20 m (LAT). The wreck was dispersed so the remains are now totally collapsed and well broken up, leaving a pile of steel and smashed or broken machinery, plates, frames and iron pipes. Hundreds of pout whiting shoal around the top of the wreck and during the summer months, lion's mane jellyfish can be a nuisance .The wreck still makes a nice rummage dive, although there is little non-ferrous metal remaining and most of the portholes have long since gone.

ELISE, HM TRAWLER

Date of loss: 22 September 1918
Wreck: ✯✯✯✯
Depth: 24 m
Reference: 55 05'.758 N 001 26'.305 W
Location: 1.45 nm NNE from St Mary's Lighthouse

The *Elise* (Official No. 124697) was a steel-hulled 239-ton British steam trawler that measured 38.53 m in length, with a 6.7-m beam and a 3.5-m draught. J. Duthie, Sons and Co. Ltd. Aberdeen built and completed her as Yard No. 272 in December 1907; she was launched on 9 November 1907 for Jackson and Dickenson at Fleetwood. The single steel screw was powered by a 68-hp, three-cylinder triple expansion engine that used one boiler. W. V. Lidgerwood, Glasgow manufactured the machinery. She also had one deck and three bulkheads.

In 1914, the *Elise* was sold to J. Marr and Sons Ltd. Fleetwood as Port Reg: FD.164.

On 23 December 1914, crewman David Robinson was killed in an accident on board the trawler.

In June 1915, she was requisitioned and converted to Admiralty minesweeper no.1622 and equipped with one bow-mounted six-pounder (2.72-kilo) gun. Port Reg: PD.164

The vessel was employed on convoy escort duties in northern waters and was part of the escort for a Scandinavian convoy sailing from Lerwick on 17 October 1917. The crew of *Elise* rescued the CO and 44 other survivors from the 900-ton British destroyer HMS *Strongbow*, which had been attacked and sunk by gunfire from KDM surface warships.

Final patrol

On 22 September 1918, HM Trawler *Elise* was torpedoed and sunk without warning by the KDM submarine SMU *UB 34*, commanded by Oblt.z.S. Hans Illing. Captain James Henry was the skipper in charge of the trawler on that ill-fated day; the boat was patrolling two miles SE of Blyth and she sank almost at once. The crewmen that died were:

Armitage, David, Trimmer RNR
Bagshaw, Septimus, Leading Deckhand RNR
Barne, Frederick, Deckhand RNR
Burnett, James Wallace, Deckhand RNR
Clarke, Charles William, 2nd Hand RNR
Fitzpatrick, Myles, Trimmer RNR
James, Henry, Skipper RNR
Low, James (DSM), Engineman RNR
Painter, Harry, Engineman RNR
Sharman, Cecil Robert, (MiD) Seaman RNR
Sheriff, Stephen, Deckhand RNR
Simpson, William George, Deckhand RNR

CWGC; Jarvis & Jarvis (1993); Jarvis & Jarvis (1996); LCWLR 1914–18, p. 235; LR 1915/16 No. 452 (E); BVLS 1914–18, p. 27; Aberdeen Built Ships Project at: http://www.aberdeenships.com/browse.asp.

Wrecksite

The wreck is orientated in a SE to NW direction and lies on a seabed of hard sand, small rocks and stones in a general depth of 24 m (LAT). This is a small wreck and not too easy to find because of its size. The engines and boiler are lying together amidst a pile of steel frames, plates and pipes where the vessel has collapsed in on itself. The bow section, which is connected to the wreck, still has its shape, but the top structure and deck part have also collapsed inside. There is a considerable amount of non-ferrous metal lying around under the jumbled heap of steel, but the 6-pounder gun has been removed, leaving only the base plate. The large winches lie about 50 m to the east of the main wrecksite, with bits of scattered wreckage in between. A large shoal of pout whiting that swim together in unison, have adopted the bows section.

CRATHIE, HM TRAWLER

Date of loss: 27 August 1914
Wreck: ★★★
Depth: 62 m
Reference: 55 05'.372 N 000 46'.252 W
Location: 22.16 nm ENE from the Tyne piers

The *Crathie* (Official No. 129352) was a steel-hulled 210-ton British steam trawler that measured 35.05 m in length, with a 6.85-m beam and a 3.70-m draught. J. Duthie Torry Shipbuilding Co. Aberdeen built and completed her as Yard No. 348 in February 1911; she was launched in January 1911 for Caledonian Steam Trawling Co. Ltd. Aberdeen. Port Registration: A.350.

The single steel screw was powered by a 56-rhp, three-cylinder triple expansion steam engine that used one boiler. James Abernethy and Co. manufactured the machinery at Aberdeen. She had one deck and machinery positioned amidships.

In August 1914, she was requisitioned for war service and converted for minesweeping duties as Admiralty minesweeper no. 106, based with the Tyne Auxiliary Patrol Division, Area VIII.

Final patrol

Between 25 and 26 August 1914, under the cover of darkness and in heavy mist, the Germans used their two quickest minesweepers to lay a barrier of mines, up to 30 miles off the Tyne.

The ships were the 2200-ton Imperial minelaying crusier SMS *Albatross*, which carried up to 600 mines, and the 3470-ton light cruiser SMS *Stuttgart*, capable of carrying 108 mines; however, the mines were laid five miles further seaward than had been calculated.

News of the mining reached the Admiralty and on 27 August, four RN minesweeping trawlers from the Tyne Auxiliary Patrol Division, Area VIII left Tynemouth at 0745 hrs and met up with torpedo boat No. 24 at 1030 hrs. The trawlers were: No. 61 (ex *Thomas W. Irvin*), No. 62, No. 105 and No. 106 (ex *Crathie*, with Skipper Herbert Henry Cook RNR in charge of No. 106).

Work began immediately on their reaching the minefield area off the Tyne, but trawler No. 62 fouled her screw, so T.B. No. 24 stood by to protect her. The second pair of trawlers, No. 105 and No. 106 (*Crathie*) had gone off to the south, but whilst rigging up in the heavy sea mist, two mines detonated in the sweep and then, at 1545 hrs, a third blew up, destroying No. 106 (ex *Crathie*). Trawler No. 105 sounded her siren and rescued eight survivors before rejoining the others, but two men died. At 1625 hrs, No. 61 (ex *Thomas W. Irvin*) with Skipper Henry Charles Thompson RNR in charge, was in company with No.105 when she too detonated a mine, blew up and sank, killing three crewmen. The torpedo-boat destroyer moved in and rescued those in the water before returning to the Tyne with all the survivors, including the men taken off No. 105 trawler. No. 62 was towed back to port by No. 105. The losses occurred because the trawlers were equipped with Skipjack pattern mine defences on the bows, which were deadly, tending to scoop up the mine then force it against the hull. They were not replaced by Otter gear until 1917, following the losses of HMS *Mignonette* and *Alyssium*.

Five men had been killed; two on No. 106 and three on No. 61 and seven were wounded on No. 106. The men that died on *Crathie* (No. 106) were:

Dunbar, Francis Grant, Deckhand RNR
Noble, Thomas, Trimmer RNR

According to The Times, the injured men, numbering eight in all, were:

Baxter, Arthur, of Aberdeen
Burford, Fred, Petty Officer of North Shields
Cook, Herbert, of Aberdeen
Cruikshank, Robert, of North Shields
Goodwin, Petty Officer of North Shields
Johnson, George, of North Shields
Munro, Fred, of Aberdeen
Waddell, Robert, of North Shields

The Times: Friday, 28 August 1914, p. 6, Issue 40618; LCWLR 1914–18, p. 2; ADM 137/1002; BVLS 1914–18, p. 10; CWGC; Jarvis & Jarvis (1996), Vol. IV; 'Trial and Error' The Royal Navy and Mine Countermeasures, 1904–1914.

Wrecksite

The wreck, possibly that of the *Crathie*, is orientated in a NE to SW direction. It lies on a seabed of sand, shell and mud in a general depth of 62 m (LAT). The wreck sits in a slight scour and appears to be intact and on its side, standing over 3 m high and covering an area 33 m long and 8 m across, with lots of fish over the top of it.

THOMAS W. IRVIN, HM TRAWLER

Date of loss: 27 August 1914
Wreck: ★★
Depth: 88.3 m
Reference: 55 05'.872 N 001 06'.633 W
Location: 12.25 nm NE from the Tynemouth light

The *Thomas W. Irvin* was a steel-hulled 201-ton British steam trawler that measured 35.12 m in length, with a 6.85-m beam and a 3.88-m draught. Hall Russell and Co. Ltd. at Aberdeen built and completed her as Yard No. 502 in December 1911 and launched her on 21 December 1911 for Richard Irvin and Sons Ltd. at North Shields, Port Reg: SN.265. An amidships-positioned 78-hp, three-cylinder triple expansion steam engine that used one boiler powered her single steel screw. Hall, Russell and Co. Ltd. also manufactured the machinery. She had one deck.

The vessel got her name from Thomas W. Irvin, who, along with Richard Irvin Junior and George Driver Irvin established Shields Engineering Co. for the purpose of building and repairing of trawlers. The men then acquired the firm of Young's Dock Co. which was amalgamated to form the Shields Engineering and Dry Dock Co. The business then became involved in the herring drifting fishery around the same time as steam-powered drifters came into use in northeast England and Scotland. The East Coast Herring Drifter Co. was established in 1900, followed shortly after by the Shields Ice and Cold Storage Co. Ltd.)

In August 1914 the vessel was hired by the Admiralty, converted to Admiralty minesweeper No. 61 (ex *Thomas W. Irvin*) and based with the Tyne Auxiliary Patrol Division, Area VIII, with Skipper Henry Charles Thompson RNR in charge of the boat.

Final patrol

See: ***CRATHIE***

The crewmen who died on the trawler were:

Millward, Henry Woodvine, Deck Hand RNR
Norris, George Crossley, Deck Hand RNR
Sadler, Robert Henry, Trimmer RNR, TS 92

Wrecksite

The wreck, probably that of the *Thomas W. Irvin*, sits in a 1.2 m scour. It lies on a seabed of soft mud and sediment in a general depth of 88.3 m (LAT). The wreck is partially buried, well broken up and covers an area of 34 m in length by 28 m across, with the highest part standing just over 3 m above the seabed.

DOLPHIN, EX HMS PANDORA, EX SETI

Date of loss: 23 December 1939
Wreck: ✯✯
Depth: 18 m
Reference: 55 06'.085 N 001 27'.282 W
Location: 1.74 nm N from St Mary's Lighthouse and 1.46 nm SE of Blyth south pier

The submarine depot ship HMS Dolphin *was de-commissioned and selected as a block-ship for the River Clyde, but on December 23rd 1939, she detonated a mine and sank off Blyth. (Author's collection)*

The *Dolphin* (Official No. 115319) was a steel-hulled 4530-ton British Submarine Depot steamship that measured 104.2 m in length, with a 13.1-m beam and an 8.2-m draught.

Sir Raylton Dixon and Co. Ltd. built and completed her at Cleveland Dockyard, Middlesbrough as Yard No. 490 in September 1902, for Moss Steamship Co. Ltd. Liverpool; James Moss and Co. was the manager. Miss Hilda Moss launched her as the *Seti* on 5 July 1902, for their company's Egyptian trade. She was moulded and built to the British Corporation's highest class spar rule, had a deadweight capacity of 3700 tons, with a steel main deck and the upper poop deck, bridge and forecastle deck of steel, but sheathed with wood. The accommodation for first class passengers was handsomely fitted at the forepart of the bridge, while the second class was situated under the aft end of the poop. The saloon framing was of beautiful satinwood with Hungarian ash panels, relieved by Maltese crosses with a house flag in the centre of each panel. The iron stanchions were covered in satinwood with elaborately carved capitals and Tynecastle panelling on the ceiling, all lighted by a fine-combed skylight. The smoke room, separately designed by Messrs Waring and Son of Liverpool, was framed in oak, with carved pillaster parquet flooring, carved grotesque beams and Tynecastle panels on the ceiling in rich relief. The vessel was installed throughout with electric lights, electric bells and steam heating throughout. She also had a freshwater condenser, five bulkheads, water ballast in all fore and aft and aft peaks, direct steam windlasses, five powerful steam winches and all the very latest equipment for rapid loading/reloading of her cargo.

The single fine-steel screw was powered by a three-cylinder triple expansion steam engine that used three large single-ended boilers that worked at a pressure of 180-lb psi, developing 2200-ihp and giving 11 knots. The cylinders measured 63.5 cm, 106.1 cm and 177.8 cm with a 126.9- cm stroke (25 in., 40 in. and 70 in. with a 48-in. stroke).

On 9 November 1914, the *Seti* was purchased by the Admiralty and renamed *Pandora*.

Between 1920 and 1921 the ship was converted at HM Dockyard, Devonport and commissioned as a Submarine Depot Repair/supply ship.

On 3 October 1924, the Admiralty renamed her *Dolphin*. She carried a complement of 255 and a fuel load of 590 tons of coal.

Final voyage

Being a rather elderly ship, *Dolphin* was decommissioned and selected as a blockship for the River Clyde, to which she was being towed, but during the voyage on 23 December 1939, she detonated a mine and sank, 1.75 miles SSE of Blyth, the mine having been laid by the German submarine *U 22*.

U 22, under the command of Kapitänleutnant Karl-Heinrich Jenisch, had laid a barrier of nine mines on 20 December 1939, in navy quadrant AN5461 off Blyth, the first mine having been dropped at 0207 hrs (CT) in position 55°05.7'N.

From the KTB of *U 22*:

> *20.12.39 AN 5461 0207–0250 9 Minen vor Blyth/Hafen uW gelegt. 55°07,7' – 55°08,8N/01°26,8' – 01°27,7W*

Starke Schell Registers; SRN, Vol. 1, p. 407.

Wrecksite

Divers know this wreck locally as the *Pandora* and some still believe the *Dolphin* is a separate wreck, but they are in fact one and the same.

The wreck is orientated almost N to S and lies on a seabed of sand and stone in a general depth of 18 m (LAT). It is now well broken up and dispersed over a wide area, as the wreck has been professionally salvaged at least a couple of times in recent years. Except for the engines and boilers, much of the wreck is partially buried with the hull sides going into the seabed, but the bow section is still fairly intact and stands some 6.7 m high, which makes a very impressive sight. Most of her non-ferrous metal has now been picked clean, as she has become a big attraction for a number of local diving clubs. A vast shoal of pout whiting and high numbers of saithe are always to be seen swimming around inside the semi-closed section of the high bow section and have adopted it as a home.

MOLLUSC, HM YACHT, ex MEDUSA, ex HMY MEDUSA II, ex MEDUSA

Date of loss: 17 March 1941
Wreck: ★★
Depth: 28 m
Reference: 55 06'.268 N 001 26'.174 W
Location: 1.94 nm NNE from St Mary's Lighthouse and 1.88 nm ESE of Blyth south pier

The *Mollusc* (Official No. 119744) was a steel-hulled 598-ton steam powered schooner, rigged with two masts and sails. She measured 60.65 m in length, with a 7.92-m beam and 4.57- m draught. Day Summers at Northam, Southampton built and completed her as Yard No. 136 in August 1906; she was launched as *Medusa* in 1906 for the Rt. Hon. Colonel J. Gretton CBE MP of Stapleford Park, Melton Mowbray near Leicester. She had a figurehead at the

The 598-ton schooner rigged steamer Medusa, *completed for the Rt. Hon. Colonel J. Gretton CBE MP of Stapleford Park, Melton Mowbray in 1906; she later became HMS* Mollusc *in 1939. (Author's painting)*

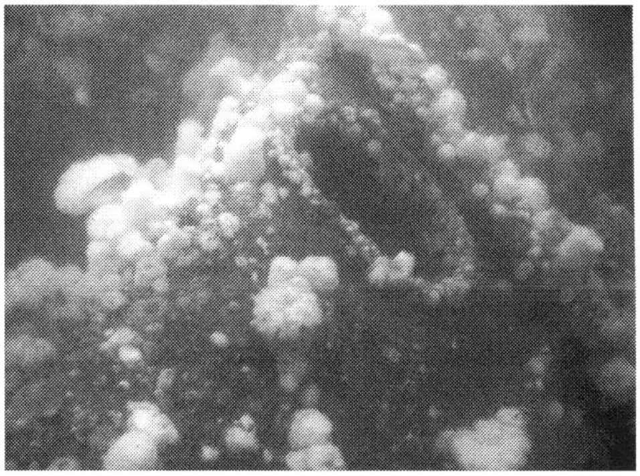

Underwater photos of the Mollusc *wreck. (Courtesy of Keith Birtle of Blyth)*

bows, about 22 portholes along each side, one deck and a three-tiered superstructure, with the funnel positioned just aft of the bridge/wheelhouse, amidships. *Medusa* was one of the most luxurious vessels afloat. Every fitting on her was made of high quality bronze, copper or brass and most of it shone like a new penny. The single bronze screw was powered by a three-cylinder triple expansion steam engine that used one boiler. Day Summers also manufactured the machinery at Southampton. Lloyd's: No. 4459. The designated code recognition signal letters were: GQXL.

From 12 January 1915, the *Medusa* was hired by the Admiralty as an Auxiliary Patrol Yacht, but in June 1915 was renamed *Medusa II*, because a new destroyer built on the Clyde in that year had taken the same name. Armament during WWI consisted of two guns, one 12-pounder and one 6-pounder AA gun. She served until 22 March 1919 when she was returned to the owner and then sold to the famous Irish Guinness family.

In September 1939 she was again requisitioned as *Medusa* (Pennant no. FY.018) as an Anti- Submarine Yacht, but in November 1939 was renamed *Mollusc*, because a hired 793-ton minesweeper was also named *Medusa*. Flag: R.Y.S.

Final voyage

On 17 March 1941, HM Yacht *Mollusc* was on active duties some two and a half miles off the submarine base at Blyth, Northumberland, when Luftwaffe aircraft attacked her. Two of the plane's bombs exploded so close to the *Mollusc* that they split her hull plates and she foundered soon after. Gun-layer Frank Herbert Weighill RNVR, a survivor of the attack, said that the *Mollusc* sank so slowly that he went back onto her for his best suit and belongings.

LCWLR 1939–45, p. 207 ; SRN, Vol. 2, p. 232.

Wrecksite

The wreck is orientated in a SSE to NNW direction and lies on a seabed of sand and stone in a general depth of 28 m (LAT). Thirty years ago, this wreck was upright and completely intact, but professional salvage work carried out over a number of years has left the remains well smashed and broken up. The highest 4.7 m section is situated around the engine/boiler area, which stands amidst a jumble of twisted plates and pipes, under which, the glint of a considerable amount of copper and brass can still be seen.

CHRISTIAN

Date of loss: 2 October 1895
Wreck: ☆
Depth: 48 m
Reference: 55 07'.135 N 001 20'.897 W
Location: 4.94 nm E from Blyth light

The *Christian* was an iron-hulled 854-ton German steam cargo vessel that measured 61.62 m in length, with an 8.42-m beam and a 4.76-m draught. Henry Koch, Lübeck in Germany built and completed her as Yard No. 2 in November 1883; she was launched in September 1883 for Zerssen and Co. Tönning. The single iron screw was powered by a 2-cylinder compound steam engine that used one boiler. The designated code recognition signal letters were: LRFM.

From 1884, "Christian" Zerssen and Co. Rendsburg was the registered owner.

Final voyage

On 2 October 1895, the *Christian* was under the command of Captain P. Plahn when she sank, following a collision with the 1325-ton British steamship *Albireo* (1878 – R.H. Penney and Co. Shoreham), five miles off Blyth. The *Christian* was on a return voyage from Blyth to

Neufahrwasser in Poland with a cargo of coal; the crew of 16 were all saved by the *Albireo*.

Board of Trade Wreck Return 1895, p. 141 (871); Starke Schell Registers.

Wrecksite

The wreck, probably that of the *Christian*, is orientated in a NNE to SSW direction. It lies within an area of spoil ground, on a seabed of fine sand, mud, shells and silt in a general depth of 48 m (LAT). The wreck is totally collapsed and well broken up, covering an area of 20 m in length by 12 m wide, with much of it buried under a heavy covering of fly ash, dumped from the Blyth power station. The highest section stands about 2 m high where the boiler and engine are located. Very little marine life can be found.

HANNE, EX C. BOM, EX OTSO, EX DAGRUN

Date of loss: 28 December 1939
Wreck: ★★★
Depth: 17 m
Reference: 55 07'.066 N 001 27'.398 W
Location: 0.94 nm E of Blyth light

The 1,085 ton Danish steamer C. Bom *circa 1930, later renamed* Hanne *and sank off Blyth on 28 December 1939. (Courtesy Thorbjørn Thaarup, cand. scient. Soc, Handels- og Søfartsmuseet på Kronborg)*

The *Hanne* (Official No. 615) was a steel-hulled 1085-ton Danish steam cargo vessel which measured 70.13 m in length, with a 10.69-m beam and a 4.39-m draught. Fredriksstad Mekaniske Verksteder, Fredrikstad in Norway built and completed her as Yard No. 100 in September 1905; she was launched as the *Dagrun* for Aktieselskapet Dagrun, at Kristiania, Norway; J. P. Pedersen and Søn was the manager. The single steel screw was powered by a 104nhp three-cylinder triple expansion steam engine that used one single-ended boiler and gave 9-knots. The cylinders measured 41.91 cm, 68.58 cm and 111.87 cm with an 81.28-cm stroke (16½ in., 27 in. and 44 in. with a 32-in.stroke). Fredriksstad Mekaniske Verksteder, Fredrikstad manufactured the engine and ancillary machinery. She had one steel deck, a ten-ton (28.31-cubic.m) poop deck, a 67-ton (189.72-cubic.m) house deck and a 34-ton (96.27-cubic.m) forecastle. The designated code recognition signal letters were: OYBD.

In 1909, she was sold to Aktieselskapet Ocean, who used the same manager Helsingin Lloyd OY, Helsingfors in Finland purchased and renamed *Otso* (Official No. 615) in 1927; Herbert Janhonen was the manager.

In 1930 she was renamed *C. Bom* when Aktieselskabet Rederiet Bom, Thurø in Denmark purchased her; Axel I. Jørgensen was the manager.

From 1937 she was registered to Dampskibsselsk. af 1937 Aktieselskabet, Copenhagen and she was renamed *Hanne*; Ove Skou was the manager.

Final voyage

At 0932 hrs (CT) on 28 December 1939, the *Hanne* struck a mine laid by the German submarine *U 22*. The steamer, which was in ballast and on passage from Copenhagen for Blyth, was approaching Blyth harbour entrance when the mine detonated and blew the ship in two; she sank almost at once with the loss of all 15 hands. The 16 men shown below may include some from another ship called *Hanne* (1903 – Near East Shipping Co. Ltd. London) that was bombed and sunk in the Eastern Mediterranean on 22 February, 1942:

Andersen, Sv., Aa. Fireman
Espersen, V., Ordinary Seaman
Holst, J., Chief Steward
Jacobsen, C. Bastland, Engineer
Jensen, M. M., Engineer
Johansen, H. P. J., Fireman
Jørgensen, K. Søndergaard, Ordinary Seaman
Kallesen, S. Nielsen, Mate
Larsen, H. C. L,. Engineer
Larsen, L. V,. Master
Mikkelsen, J., Mate
Nielsen, C. H., Fireman
Petersen, F.Agerlund, Able Seaman
Poulsen, O., Engineer
Tarby, Jac Rich., Ordinary Seaman
Woxnæs, K., Cook

U 22, commanded by Kapitänleutnant Karl-Heinrich Jenisch, had laid a barrier of nine mines on 20 December 1939, in Kriegsmarine quadrant AN5461 off Blyth, the first mine having been dropped at 0207 hrs (CT), in position 55°05.7'N.

From the KTB of *U 22*:

20.12.39 AN 5461 0207–0250 9 Minen vor Blyth/Hafen uW gelegt. 55°07,7' – 55°08,8N/01°26,8'– 01°27,7W

BVLS 1939–45, p. 33; LCWLR 1939–45, p. 31; Starke Schell Registers; Hjort (1946).

Wrecksite

The wreck lies on a seabed of sand and stones in a general depth of 17 m (LAT). The position given is for the main section of the wreck, which stands about 3 m high and is well collapsed, broken and scattered, and where a number of winches and bollards can be seen. The single boiler and engine are in the main section and a large conger eel has made the boiler and furnaces its permanent lair. Above and around the engine, a large shoal of pout whiting can usually be found. The bows lie a short distance away and are rather harder to locate, due to their standing only about one metre high. Local divers from Blyth are reported to have recovered the name plate in recent years, positively identifying the wreck.

MURISTAN, EX HAVRE

Date of loss: 19 November 1916
Wreck: ✯✯
Depth 6 m
Reference: 55 06'.316 N 001 29'.286 W
Location: 0.68 nm S of Blyth south pier

The *Muristan* (Official No. 128946) was a steel-hulled 2886-ton British steam cargo ship which measured 97.61 m in length, with a 14.19-m beam and a 6.42-m draught. William Gray and Co. Ltd. West Hartlepool built and completed her as Yard No. 831 on 26 September 1913; she was launched as *Havre* on 3 September 1913 for the London and Paris Steamship Co. Ltd. who owned her at the time of loss. Soon after the launch, she was renamed *Muristan*; F. C. Strick and Co. Ltd. was the manager. The single steel screw was powered by a 288-hp, three-cylinder triple expansion engine that used two boilers. Central Marine Engineering Works, West Hartlepool manufactured the engine and ancillary machinery. She had one deck, five bulkheads and a 7.6-m poop deck, a 29.8-m bridge deck and 10.3-m forecastle.

Final voyage

On 19 November 1916, the *Muristan*, commanded by Captain G. Pritchard, was on passage from the Tyne for Rouen, France with a cargo of coal and a crew of 24 when she encountered a severe easterly gale and heavy seas off Blyth. Her steering gear failed and she was driven into shallow water, just off a long stretch of sandy coastline. The vessel embedded itself firmly into the sand some 250 metres offshore, huge waves crashing clean over it. Conditions were so bad that at times, only the funnel and top of the masts were visible from the shore. Captain Pritchard and one of the crew were washed overboard and drowned, but three of the crew managed to reach shore safely. The Rocket Brigade arrived and tried repeatedly to fire lines over the stranded vessel, without success.

The pulling/sailing lifeboat stationed at Blyth was unable to launch because of the prevailing conditions and a message was eventually sent to Tynemouth asking for help. At 0730 hrs on 20 November, the Tynemouth self-righting motorised lifeboat *Henry Vernon,* under the command of Coxswain Robert Smith, one of the heroes in the *Rohilla* rescue off Whitby, slipped her moorings. Unfortunately the lifeboat had to wait inside the harbour until 0900 hrs for a lull in the storm to allow it to leave the harbour. When, late in the morning, the lifeboat did eventually reach the scene, conditions were so bad that only the *Muristan*'s bridge and chart house were visible. The lifeboat crew were unable to render any assistance, as huge seas still hurled over the wreck and vast quantities of wreckage floated all around it. There was no sign of life on board. Coxswain Smith decided to try to return to base at Tynemouth but after only half an hour, the lifeboat was hit by a massive wave, flooding the boat and causing the engine to fail. They dropped anchor until the sails could be set and tried desperately to restart the engine, succeeding eventually but only temporarily. Coxswain Smith decided to put into nearby Blyth using the auxiliary sails. With help from the local naval authorities, the engine was repaired during the night and at daybreak the following morning, 21 November, the *Henry Vernon* put back out to sea and, in horrendous conditions, rescued the remaining sixteen *Muristan* crew members, who were found huddled together in the remains of the chart house. The men were taken to Blyth and the lifeboat arrived back at her station at 1030 hrs.

On 8 December 1916, Coxswain Robert Smith and Second Coxswain James Brownlee were both awarded silver medals by the RNLI for their part in the rescue. Coxswain Robert Smith was also awarded the RNLI's Gold Medal for rescuing people from the wreck of the hospital ship *Rohilla* off Whitby in October 1914.

Altogether, five of the crew from the *Muristan* were lost and the ship soon broke up and became a total wreck. The ship was valued at £52 000.

Board of Trade Wreck Return 1916 Part II Table A Page 24 – LR 1915–16 No. 166 (M) – Starke Schell Registers - 'The History of Tynemouth Lifeboats', by Jeff Morris – *The Times* Tuesday, 21 November, 1916; Page 5; Issue

Wrecksite

This is a very substantial wreck that lies close inshore, about 250 m out from the beach and about three quarters of a mile south of Blyth light. It lies on a seabed of sand in a general depth of 6 m (LAT). The wreck has totally collapsed in on itself and is a huge jumbled pile of steel plates that surround and cover the two boilers and engine. Very little non-ferrous metal is visible. Winter storms usually dislodge the mass of steel plates and the wreck scene changes each year. Fair numbers of lobsters can be seen under the wreckage and cod are also much in evidence.

KAMMA, ex BLACK PRINCE, ex YORK MINSTER

Date of loss: 22 January 1917
Wreck: ✶✶
Depth: 15 m
Reference: 55 06'.588 N 001 27'.665 W (bows)
55 07'.000 N 001 27'.318 W (stern)
Location: 0.97 nm SE of Blyth Lighthouse

The *Kamma* (Official No. 4714) was a steel-hulled 1516-ton Swedish schooner-rigged steam cargo ship that measured 76.37 m length, with a 10.74-m beam and a 5.25-m draught. Palmers' Ship Building & Iron Co. Ltd. Newcastle built and completed her as Yard No. 510 in November 1883; she was launched as the *York Minster* (Official No. 84889) on 20 August 1883 for Thompson and Pattinson at Newcastle. The single iron screw was powered by a 142-hp, two-cylinder compound steam engine that used one boiler. The cylinders measured 76.2 cm and 147.32 cm, with a 91.44-cm stroke (30 in. and 58 in. with a 36-in. stroke). She had one deck, four bulkheads, water ballast and a 27.2-m quarterdeck, a 15.8-m bridge deck and 9.1-m forecastle. The designated code recognition signal letters were: JBTR.

In 1884 she was sold to J. Knott of North Shields and renamed *Black Prince*; she then weighed 1520 tons gross and Captain J. Harrison was the master.

Dampskibsselskabet Heimdal, Copenhagen renamed her *Kamma* when they purchased her in April 1896.

Rederi AB Henckel, Helsingborg in Sweden purchased her in April 1907, and her tonnage was altered to: 1489 gross, 690 net and 2700 tons dead weight; N. P. Swensson was the manager.

Oscar Thorstenson, Halmstad in Sweden was the registered owner on 7 June 1916. From 16 November 1916, Rederi AB Hallandia, Halmstad in southwest Sweden was the registered owner and Oscar Thorstenson was the manager.

Final voyage

The *Kamma* was under the command of Captain L. O. Norman when she detonated a mine and sank on 22 January 1917, one mile SE of Blyth harbour. The mine had been laid on 17 January 1917 by KDM submarine SMU *UC 40*, commanded by Kapitänleutnant Gustav Deuerlich. The steamer was manned by 18 crewmen and carrying a cargo of wood from Gefle to Rouen; 14 survivors were landed at Blyth, but four men were killed:

Eneroth, Thor Teofil, 35 yrs, 1st Engineer
Fagerström, Axel, 31 yrs, 2nd Engineer
Löf, Per Otto, 23 yrs, Stoker
Ström, Karl Ruben, 25 yrs, Trimmer

LCWLR 1914–18, p. 86; ANCL 1914–18, p. 118; Starke Schell Registers.

Wrecksite

The wreck lies on a seabed of sand, stones and rock in a general depth of 10 m (LAT). The stern end, where the engine and boiler are situated, stand upright, more or less concreted together and carpeted in a myriad of soft corals with a huge shoal of pout whiting swarming all over and around them, making a very picturesque sight. The midships and bow section are well broken up and dispersed over an area of about 50 m in length by 70 m wide, lying inshore and 200 metres southwest of the stern section. Lost monofilament cod trammel nets are interlaced around this wreckage and often still ensnare unwary fish and even the occasional crustacean. Copper pipes lie dispersed and mixed up amongst the half-buried steel debris.

LONGBIRD, EX NEWTON BAY, EX HMS KILMUCKRIDGE

Date of loss: 16 January 1943
Wreck: ✯✯✯✯✯
Depth: 66 m
Reference: 55 06'.599 N 001 13'.439 W
Location: 8.38 nm NE of Tyne north pier light

The *Longbird* (Official No. 145386) was a steel-hulled 636-ton British steam cargo vessel that measured 51.8 m in length, with a 9.1-m beam and a 4.8-m draught. Smith's Dock Co. Ltd. at South Bank, Middlesbrough built and completed her as Yard No. 755 in October 1919; she was launched for the Admiralty on 28 July 1919 as the patrol gunboat *Kilmuckridge.* The single steel screw was powered by a 94-rhp, three-cylinder triple expansion steam engine that used one boiler and gave 13 knots. The cylinders measured 40.64 cm, 66.04 cm and 111.76 cm with a 66.04-cm stroke (16 in., 26 in. and 44 in. with a 26-in. stroke). Smith's Dock Co. Ltd. manufactured the machinery. She had one deck and was equipped with wireless.

In 1920 she was sold to Allen Adams and Co. Ltd. Southampton and renamed *Newton Bay.*

J. S. White and Co. Ltd. at Cowes, Isle of Wight rebuilt her in 1920 and registered her at Southampton in 1922.

Grundwell, Thompson and Co. Ltd. Southampton was the registered owner in 1924.

Canada Traders, Ltd. Halifax, Newfoundland in Canada purchased her in 1925.

In 1927, Newton Bay Ltd. Halifax was the registered owner.

Acadia Shipping Co. (Quebec) Ltd. Halifax purchased her in 1927.

In 1929, J. F. O'Boyle, New York purchased the *Newton Bay*.

In 1930, she was renamed *Longbird* when Bermuda and West Indies S.S. Co. Ltd. Hamilton in Bermuda (British) bought her; Furness, Withy and Co. Ltd. was the manager. The designated code recognition signal letters were: KMRW.

In 1935 she was sold to Herbert F. Williams, Hamilton, Bermuda but was registered in New York.

Viking Marine Corp., Inc. in Nassau, N.P. purchased the *Longbird* in 1937. Code letters: VQJL.

In 1940, William A. Wilson, Nassau (registered in Southampton) purchased the ship.

From late in 1940, Daren't S.S. Co. Ltd. Newcastle was the registered owner and Anthony and Bainbridge, Ltd. was the manager.

Final voyage

The *Longbird* had sailed from the Clyde anchorage for passage to Hull with a cargo of vegetables and oilseed rape, travelling via Loch Ewe where she had joined the unescorted 23- ship convoy WN.379 for Methil; the convoy sailed, but for reasons unknown, the steamer put back to Loch Ewe. On 4 January 1943, she sailed again, but as part of the 11- ship convoy WN.380 for passage via Aberdeen to Methil, arriving there on the 6th. On 16 January 1943, the *Longbird* was voyaging independently on the final leg of her journey when she foundered following a collision with the 1544-ton steamship *Beltoy* (1915 – Shamrock Shipping Co. Ltd. London /Belfast), ten miles northeast of Tynemouth pier. It is not known if anyone was killed or lost.

LCR 1943, p. 9 (f); Starke Schell Registers; Convoy Web at: http://www.convoyweb.org.uk/

Wrecksite

The wreck is orientated in a NNE to SSW direction and lies on a seabed of silty sand and mud in a general depth of 66 m (LAT). It is reported to be relatively intact but on its side, standing 6.8 m high, with sections of the bridge structure visible. The bows, with a large winch attached, are intact, but from the hold to the bridge is also partially collapsed. The whole wreck, especially the upper part, is covered in soft corals. A variety of large fish, particularly cod and ling, have adopted it as a sanctuary. The bell, if located, will almost certainly be inscribed: *Kilmuckridge 1919*.

SAXON, EX SAXON II, EX SAXON

Date of Loss: 22 April 1931
Wreck: ✯✯✯
Depth: 87 m
Reference: 55 06'.805 N 001 06'.283 W
Location: 12.07 nm NE from Tynemouth pier

The *Saxon* (Official No. 104190) was an iron-hulled, 119-ton steam trawler that measured 26.94 m in length, with a 6.12-m beam and 3.22-m draught. Cook, Welton and Gemmell built and completed her as Yard No. 131 at Hull on 10 November 1894. She was launched as the *Saxon* on 20 October 1894 for Alfred Bannister of Grimsby, who registered her as GY.722 on 10 November 1894. A single iron screw was powered by a 43-rhp, two-cylinder compound steam engine that used one boiler and gave ten knots. The cylinders measured 40.64 cm and 81.28 cm with a 55.88 cm- stroke (16 in, and 32 in. with a 22-in. stroke). C.D. Holmes and Co manufactured the machinery at Hull. She had one deck and a 5.48-m quarterdeck amidships.

A new boiler was fitted in 1906.

On 22 January 1901, she was sold to Onward Steam Fishing Co. Ltd. Grimsby.

On 10 May 1904, the 23 year-old spare hand, Harry Lofthouse, of 9 West Dock Avenue, Hull was lost overboard, ten miles south of Reyaness, Iceland.

The Royal Navy requisitioned her in January 1915, as Admiralty minesweeper no. 732, equipped with one six-pounder, and renamed her *Saxon II*; in 1918 she was returned to the owners and the name reverted to *Saxon*.

W. Lilburn of North Shields purchased the boat on 8 March 1920 and registered her as SN.22.

From 1926, J. D. Irwin, North Shields was the registered owner.

Final voyage

On 22 April 1932, the *Saxon* was on a fishing voyage from North Shields when she foundered, 15 miles from Tynemouth. It is not known why she sank or if anyone was lost.

LCR 1931, p. 5 (b); LR 1931/2 No. 09690 (S); Toghill (2004).

Wrecksite

The wreck, probably that of the *Saxon*, is orientated in an ESE to WNW direction. It lies on a seabed of fine sand and mud in a general depth of 87 m (LAT). The wreck, which appears intact and is on its side, is about 3.5 m high and covers an area 32 m long and 6 m wide, with some separate bits of debris close by.

TURNERSONS, ex AGATE

Date of loss: 4 October 1931
Wreck: ★
Depth: 32 m
Reference: 55 07'.914 001 25'.357 W
Location: 2.39 nm ENE of Blyth north pier

The *Turnersons* (Official No. 99546) was an iron-hulled 156-ton two-masted ketch-rigged steam trawler that measured 30.78 m in length, with a 6.22-m beam and 3.35-m draught. Cochrane, Cooper and Schofield at Beverley built and completed her as Yard No. 66 in November 1891; she was launched as the *Agate* (Official No. 994) in 1891 for Kingston Steam Trawling Co. Ltd. Hull. The single iron screw was powered by a reciprocating 48-nhp two-cylinder compound steam engine that used one multi-tubular steel boiler working at a pressure of 110-lbs psi, with two corrugated furnaces, 3.90 sq.m (42 sq.ft) of grate surface and 133.87 sq.m (1441 sq.ft) of heating surface, giving nine knots. The cylinders measured 40.64 cm and 96.52 cm with a 55.88-cm stroke (16 in. and 38 in. with a 22-in. stroke). Amos and Smith Ltd. at Hull manufactured the machinery. She had one deck, three bulkheads cemented, a 5.8-m quarterdeck and a 5.8-m forecastle.

Boatswain Richard Wood was lost overboard on 2 March 1896, 130 miles off Spurn Point.

In 1913, she was sold to Pochet-Decroix in Boulogne.

On 24 January 1921, Robert Henry Turner of 2, Frobisher Terrace, in Plymouth purchased and renamed her *Turnersons* (Official No. 132767); Ernest Walter Jennings of Plymouth was the master.

Leonard Brown of Glenmore, Ashleigh Grove, Tynemouth was the sole registered owner from 18 September 1928.

From January 1931, Arthur Brown of Tynemouth (Port Reg: PH.204) was the registered owner.

The trawler had at least twelve skippers from 1921, but William Patterson was the master from 9 October 1930 until she foundered.

Final voyage

The *Turnersons* sank on 4 October 1931, presumably after developing a serious leak in heavy seas, while on a fishing voyage off Blyth. The Blyth pilot cutter rescued the crew of nine.

LCR 1931, p. 5; LR 1931/2 No. 10140 (T); *The Times*: Tuesday, 6 October 1931, p. 18, Issue 45946.

Wrecksite

This wreck, most probably that of the *Turnersons*, is orientated in a WNW to ESE direction and lies on a seabed of fine sand, silt and stone in a general depth of 32 m (LAT). The wreck is thought to be reasonably intact but is mostly buried, with just the bows and the top half of the boiler showing above the seabed.

ANDREA, EX ANTONIOS STATHATOS

Date of loss: 16 November 1914
Wreck: ☆☆☆☆
Depth: 75 m
Reference: 55 07'.506 N 000 25'.388 E
Location: 34.47 nm E by N from Tynemouth pier

The *Andrea* (Official No. 32) was an iron-hulled 1507-ton Swedish steam cargo ship that measured 75.89 m in length, with a 10.97-m beam and a 5.2-m draught. John Readhead and Co. South Shields built and completed her as Yard No. 196 in July 1883; she was launched as the *Antonios Stathatos* for Stathatos Bros., Ithaca in Greece on 21 July 1883. The single iron screw was powered by a 139-nhp two-cylinder compound steam engine. The gross tonnage when built was 1412 tons.

In 1897 she was sold to M. and A. Dall'Orso fu G., La Spezia, Greece who renamed her *Andrea*. The new owners fitted a three-cylinder triple expansion steam engine and the gross tonnage went up to 1507 tons.

In 1907, C. A. Banck and Co. Helsingborg, Sweden purchased the ship, Official No. 4701.

From 1909 Ångfartygs AB Libra in Sweden was the registered owner and C. A. Banck and Co. was the manager.

Final voyage

On 16 November 1914, the *Andrea* detonated a mine and sank, 30 miles ENE of Middlesbrough at 55° 07.30'N 00° 25.30'E, while *en route* from Törefors, Sweden to Hull with a cargo of timber. The crew took to the boats and were later rescued. It is believed that the 2200-ton *Kaiserlichen Marine minenkreuzer* SMS *Albatross* had laid the mine.

Starke Schell Registers; LCWLR 1914–18, p. 5.

Wrecksite

The wreck is orientated in a NE to SW direction, with the bows to the NE. It lies on a seabed of sand, mud and shells in a general depth of 75 m (LAT). The wreck is upright, intact and very substantial and stands around 5 m high, with the upper sections covered in soft corals, although the bridge structure has collapsed somewhat. If the bell is recovered, it should be inscribed: *Antonios Stathatos 1883*. Massive shoals of fish have also been observed on the fish finder, so this should make an excellent boat-angling venue.

5

BLYTH TO COQUET ISLAND, INCLUDING THE GRAVEYARD

HANS HOTH

Date of Loss: 10 February 1952
Wreck: ✯✯
Depth: 92 m
Reference: 55 07'.471 N 001 03'.417 W
Location: 13.72 nm ENE from the Tyne

The *Hans Hoth* was a steel-hulled 374-ton German motor cargo vessel that measured 43.05 m in length, with a 7.65-m beam and a 3.55-m draught. Stader Schiffswertf GmbH, Stade, in Lower-Saxony, Germany built her as Yard No. 143 and launched her in April 1945; however, she was not completed as *Hans Hoth* until September 1949 for "Hans Hoth" P.H. Ahrens in Hamburg. The single steel screw was powered by an aft-positioned, 420-hp, four-stroke single high pressure motor. Deutsche Werke Kiel AG, Kiel-F manufactured the engine and ancillary machinery. The designated code recognition signal letters were: DKTD-DGNT.

On 14 May 1951, the *Hans Hoth* was involved in a collision with the 1441-ton Dover steam ferry *Halladale* (1944 – Townsend Bros. Ferries Ltd.), just after the *Halladale* had passed through the eastern entrance at Dover, bound for France. The ferry suffered considerable damage and was taken to Tilbury for repairs; any damage to the *Hans Hoth* does not appear to have been recorded.

From 7 June 1951, Otto A. Müller was the registered owner and Otto A. Müller von Beginn the manager.

Final voyage

On 9 February 1952, the *Hans Hoth* was on passage from Borrowstounness (Bo'ness) in the Firth of Forth for Hamburg, but 56 miles ENE of the Tyne, her cargo shifted in heavy seas and she developed a substantial list. A radio message was transmitted and at 12.15 p.m. the Tynemouth motorised lifeboat *Tynesider* was launched, the tug *Hendon* also putting out to assist. The sea was rough and there was a steadily strengthening northerly wind. The lifeboat, guided by an aeroplane and then flares from the vessel itself, eventually reached the *Hans Hoth* at 12.38 a.m. on the 10th, in a position 88 miles ENE of the Tyne. The lifeboat stood by the vessel for two hours until the tug arrived on the scene. The lifeboat then headed back to the Tyne, which she safely reached at 9.55 p.m., having been at sea in very bad weather for nearly 34 hours. The *Hans Hoth* was taken in tow by the tug, but about 14 miles ENE of the Tyne, she sank, with no lives lost. The *Hendon* had spent almost 50 hours trying in vain to save the vessel and her master, Captain H. Steward of South Shields, had been on the bridge for the whole of that time.

The Times: Tuesday, 12 February 1952, p. 3, Issue 52233; Starke Schell Registers.

Wrecksite

The wreck, which is probably what remains of the *Hans Hoth*, is orientated in a more or less S to N direction. It sits in a 1.2 m scour and lies on a seabed of mud and shells in a general depth of 92 m (LAT). The wreck stands just over 3 m high, but is collapsed and well broken up, covering an area 48 m long and 20 m across.

PHALANE, EX STRATHERRICK

Date of Loss: 30 June 1939
Wreck: ✯✯✯✯
Depth: 64 m
Reference: 55 07'.255 N 000 45'.136 W
Location: 23.28 nm ENE of Tynemouth pier

The *Phalane* (Official No. 123373) was a steel-hulled 201-ton British steam trawler that measured 34.26 m in length, with a 6.62-m beam and 3.53-m draught. Hall, Russell and Co. Aberdeen built and completed her as Yard No. 415 in November 1906; she was launched as the *Stratherrick* on 15 November 1906, for Aberdeen Steam Trawling and Fishing Co. Ltd. Aberdeen and registered as A.105. The single steel screw was powered by a 67-hp, three-cylinder triple expansion steam engine that used one boiler. The cylinders measured 30.48 cm, 50.8 cm and 83.82 cm with a 53.34-cm stroke (12 in., 20 in. and 33 in. with a 21-in. stroke). Hall, Russell and Co. Aberdeen manufactured the machinery. She had one deck and was later equipped with wireless, a direction finder and an echo sounding device.

In September 1914 she was requisitioned and converted to Admiralty minesweeper No. 417 and equipped with one six-pounder AA gun, one 7.5 in. gun and an anti-submarine Howitzer bomb-thrower; in 1919, she was returned to Aberdeen Steam Trawling and Fishing Co. Ltd. Aberdeen.

R. Robson of Aberdeen was the registered owner in 1920.

Musgrave Co. Ltd. Aberdeen sold the trawler to unknown buyers in September 1921, possibly to W. Lyle, Aberdeen, because they owned her later. The designated code recognition signal letters were: GJJR.

In 1929, she was acquired by G. Gordon of Aberdeen.

Clarence Steam Trawling Co. Scarborough later acquired the vessel, according to Gerald Toghill in *Royal Navy Trawlers, Part Two: Requisitioned Trawlers.*

From 1938, J. W. Johnstone of Aberdeen, who renamed her *Phalane*, was the registered owner.

Final voyage

The *Phalane* had left Aberdeen on a fishing trip but for some unknown reason, sank on 29 June 1939, 23 miles NE of the Tyne. The North Shields trawler *Agnes H. Hastie* rescued all the crew and landed them at her home port.

LCR 1939, p. 6 (b); LR 1937/8 No. 14897 (S); *The Times*: Saturday, 1 July 1939, p. 25, Issue 48346.

Wrecksite

The wreck, probably that of the *Phalane,* is orientated in an almost S to N direction just south of the area known as the Graveyard. It lies on a seabed of sand, shell and mud in a general depth of 64 m (LAT). The wreck is intact, standing 4.3 m high at the north end and covering an area 35 m long and 10 m wide. If the bell is located, it should be inscribed: *Stratherrick 1906*. High numbers of fish were observed on the echo sounder, so it should make an interesting boat-angling venue.

NIKE, EX MARIO, EX CALEDONIA

Date of loss: 12 December 1917
Wreck: ✯✯✯✯
Depth 54 m
Reference: 55 08'.626 N 001 17'.497 W
Location: 6.87 nm ENE of Blyth Lighthouse

The *Nike* (Official No. 89173) was an iron-hulled 1834-ton Swedish steam cargo ship that measured 82.39 m in length, with an 11.58-m beam and 5.63-m draught. Oswald, Mordaunt and Co. at Southampton built and completed her as Yard No. 214 in December 1883, and she was launched as the *Caledonia* on 15 December 1883 for United Kingdom S.S. Co. Cardiff and registered there.

The single iron screw was powered by an 184-hp, two-cylinder compound steam engine that used two boilers. She had one deck, a well deck, four bulkheads and a 28.6-m quarterdeck, an 18.8-m bridge deck and 9.1-m forecastle. She was classed as 100A1.

In 1893 she was sold to G. Pastorino fu P, Genova.

Figli Catrellino di G, Genova was the registered owner in 1896 and renamed her *Mario*; Gio Batta Catrellino was the manager.

Rederi A.B. Nike in Göteborg owned her in May 1900 and renamed her *Nike*; W.R. Lundgren was the manager.

Rederi AB Transatlantic, Göteborg was the registered owner in April 1908 and W.R. Lundgren was the manager.

In May 1912, she was sold to Erik A. Brodin, Gävle in Sweden.

Ångfartygs A.B. Nike, Gävle was the registered owner in August 1915 and Erik A. Brodin was the manager.

From May 1917, Erik Brodins Rederi A.B., Torö in Sweden was the registered owner and Erik Brodin was the manager. Certificate of Nationality issued November 1917.

Final voyage

On 12 December 1917, four high-speed German torpedo-boat destroyers attacked the *Nike* with torpedoes, one after the other, eight miles east of Blyth. They are believed to have been SMS *V.100*, *G.101*, *G.103* and *G.104*, although some sources contend that SMS *B.97* and *B.111* were involved. The steamer, under the command of Captain Anderson, was in convoy and carrying a general cargo including soft wood and deals on a voyage from Kramfors and Malmö to London. Huge explosions rocked the *Nike* from stem to stern, sending her down to the bottom within minutes; 16 crewmen died and two were injured. The crewmen who died were:

Eriksson, Karl Verner, 31 yrs, 1st Mate
Kristiansson, John Sigurd, 23 yrs, 2nd Mate
Olsson, Johan Olof Gottfrid, 23 yrs, 2nd Engineer
Berg, Karl Johan, 24 yrs, Ordinary Sailor
Fröbom, John Teodor, 22 yrs, Ordinary Sailor
Hedman, Per Johan, 23 yrs, Ordinary Sailor
Marklund, Knut Birger, 22 yrs, Ordinary Sailor
Hedblom, Gustaf, 17 yrs, Deck Boy
Hedlund, Axel Einar, 23 yrs, Deck Boy
Wiklund, Gustaf Einar, 31 yrs, Donkeyman
Andersson, David, 30 yrs, Stoker
Berg, Carl Adolf, 23 yrs, Stoker
Svensson, Frans Oskar Wilhelm, 23 yrs, Stoker
Fredriksson, Karl Edvin, 21 yrs, Trimmer
Holm, Gustaf Arnold, 22 yrs, Trimmer
Sandberg, Johan David, 17 yrs, Messroom Boy

The two injured men were:

Andersson, Anders Sigfrid, Master
Bonnevier, Alfred Valdemar, 1st Engineer

LCWLR 1914–18, p. 189; ANCL 1914–18, p. 119; LR 1915/16 No. 486 (N); Starke Schell Registers.

Wrecksite

The wreck is orientated in a NNE to SSW direction with a slight scour to the east. It lies on its side on a seabed of mud and sand in a general depth of 54 m (LAT). The wreck is covered in soft corals and is home to large shoals of fish. It is broken into two equal sections, covering an area of 86 m in length by 25 m wide and stands 8.4 m from the seabed. The bell, if recovered, will almost certainly be inscribed: *Caledonia 1883.*

PAUL SPOLIANSKY, EX PANAMA

Date of Loss: 26 September 1914
Wreck: ★★★
Depth: 88 m
Reference: 55 08'.877 N 001 05'.976 W
Location: 13.39 nm ENE from Blyth pier

The *Paul Spoliansky* was an iron-hulled 2018-ton schooner-rigged steam cargo ship that measured 85.34 m in length, with a 10.97-m beam and a 6.42-m draught. Osbourne, Graham and Co. at North Hylton, Sunderland built and completed her as Yard No. 47 in February 1881; she was launched as the brig-rigged *Panama* on 16 February 1881 for A. D'Orbigny and Faustin fils, La Rochelle, in France. The single iron screw was powered by an 180-hp, two-cylinder compound steam engine that used two single-ended boilers. The cylinders measured 86.36 cm and 162.56 cm with a 106.68-cm stroke (34 in. and 64 in. with a 42-in. stroke). She had one deck and five bulkheads. The designated code recognition signal letters were: KNBJ. The master until 1883 was Captain Magnaiet.

A. D'Orbigny, Faustin and Cie., La Rochelle was the registered owner in 1900.

From 1904, P. Spolyanskiy, Batum, Russia 78, was the registered owner and renamed her *Paul Spoliansky* – (*Pavel Shpolyanskiy*) – (*ПАВЕЛ ШПОЛЯНСКИЙ*).

Final voyage

On 26 September 1914, the ship sailed from Blyth for Arkhangelsk in Russia, but was never seen nor heard of again. However, maritime experts now strongly believe that she was most probably lost with all hands after detonating one, or possibly two of the mines in the barrier laid by the 2200-ton Kaiserlichen Marine minenkreuzer SMS *Albatross*, commanded by Korvettenkapitänleutnant West, along with the 3470-ton light cruiser SMS *Stuttgart* on 26 August 1914.

American Lloyd's Register of American and Foreign Shipping, 1857–1900; Starke Schell Registers; Michael Lowrey, *personal communication*.

Wrecksite

The wreck, which is probably that of the Russian steamer, is orientated in an ESE to WNW direction. It lies on a seabed of sand, mud and gravel in a general depth of 88 m (LAT). A long deep scour surrounds the wreck on each side and the scour runs north – south, evidence of the strong currents; there is also a 50 m-long field of debris. The wreck is upright and in line, but is collapsed and broken in two around amidships; it covers an area 80 m long and 25 m across and stands over 3.5 m on the highest sections. If this is the Russian steamer, the bell will almost certainly be inscribed: *Panama 1881*. Plenty of marine life has been observed over the wreck on the fish finder, so it should make a good boat-angling venue.

JOHAN, ex PALMDENE, ex MOORGATE

Date of loss: 27 October 1905
Wreck: ★★★
Depth: 88 m
Reference: 55 08'.877 N 001 05'.976 W
Location: 13.39 nm ENE from Blyth pier

The *Johan* (Official No. 98941) was a steel-hulled 2363-ton Swedish steam cargo ship that measured 88.39 m in length, with an 11.75-m beam. J. L. Thompson and Sons, at North Sands, Sunderland built and completed her as Yard No. 275 in May 1891; she was launched as the schooner-rigged *Moorgate* (Official No. 1122) on 27 April 1891 for Moorgate S.S. Co. Ltd. London and H.W. Dillon was the manager. The single screw was powered by a 233-hp, three-cylinder triple expansion steam engine that used two boilers. The cylinders measured 55.88 cm, 93.98 cm and 152.4 cm with a 99.06-cm stroke (22 in., 37 in. and 60 in. with a 39-in. stroke.) J. L. Thompson and Sons manufactured the engine and ancillary machinery. The *Moorgate* had one deck, web frames, six bulkheads and water ballast. The designated code recognition signal letters were: MDWP.

The master in 1891 was Captain T. Görvin.

London Gate S.S. Co. Ltd. was the registered owner in 1898 using the same manager.

In 1898 she was renamed *Palmdene* by the new owners: J. T. Lunn and Co. of Newcastle.

From 1899, Rederi AB Luleå, Ofoten, Stockholm, Sweden was the registered owner and she was renamed *Johan* (Official No. 3361).

Final voyage

On 27 October 1905, the *Johan* sank following a collision with the Russian schooner *Antares,* which also sank in the North Sea, due east of Blyth. The *Johan* was on passage from Narvik to Middlesbrough with a cargo of iron ore and most of her crew was lost, the master and a carpenter being the only survivors. The schooner *Antares*, which was transporting a full cargo of coal from the Tyne to Reval (now Tallin) in Estonia, sank with most of her crew; although a carpenter was picked up by the 1517-ton German steamer *Brietzig* (1891 – Heinrich F. C. Arp, Hamburg) and landed at Helsingborg, while the master and cook were rescued by another vessel and landed at Stromness.

American Lloyd's Register of American and Foreign Shipping, 1857–1900
Starke Schell Registers; American Lloyd's Register of American and Foreign Shipping, 1857–1900; Miramar Ship Index; *The Times*: Wednesday, 1 November 1905, p. 14, Issue 37853.

Wrecksite

The wreck, most probably that of the *Johan*, is orientated in an ESE to WNW direction. It lies on a seabed of sand, mud and gravel, in a general depth of 88 m (LAT). A long deep scour surrounds the wreck on each side and the scour runs north – south, a sure sign of strong currents; there is also a 50 m long field of debris. The wreck is upright and in line, but is collapsed and broken in two around amidships; it covers an area 80 m long and 25 m across and stands over 3.5 m on the highest parts. If this is the Swedish steamer, the bell will almost certainly be inscribed: *Moorgate 1891.* Lots of marine life has been observed on the sounder, so it should make a good boat-angling venue.

EIDSFOS

Date of loss: 17 December 1918
Wreck: ★★★★
Depth: 82 m
Reference: 55 08'.105 N 000 57'.667 W
Location: 17.01 nm ENE from Tynemouth

The *Eidsfos* was a steel-hulled 1350-ton Norwegian steam cargo ship that measured 67.38 m in length with a beam of 10.41 m. Nylands Verksted, Kristiania built and completed her as

Yard No. 170 on 18 January 1907; she was launched on 11 December 1906 for AS Manchester in Kristiania, who owned her at the time of loss; Winge and Co. was the manager. The single screw was powered by a 106-nhp three-cylinder triple expansion steam engine that used one boiler working at a pressure of 175-lb psi. The cylinders measured 41.91 cm, 68.58 cm and 111.76 cm with a 76.2-cm stroke (16½ in., 27 in. and 44 in. with a 30-in. stroke). Nylands Verksted, Kristiania manufactured the engine and ancillary machinery. She had two decks. The designated code recognition signal letters were: MDCQ.

In 1908, Thor Thoresen Jr. was the manager.

Final voyage

On 17 December 1918, after hostilities had supposedly ceased, the *Eidsfos* was transporting iron ore and coke from Newcastle to Kristiania when she detonated a mine and sank in the North Sea, 18 miles ENE from Tynemouth. The following six crewmen were lost:

Aasrum, H,. 2nd Engineer
Holden, Johannes, 1st Engineer
Karlsen, Guldebrand, Stoker
Karlsen, Kristian, Master
Østby, J. A., Sailor
Paulsen, Henry, Donkeyman

Maritime Accident Statements for Norwegian Ships Sunk in Wartime: 1814–1918; Starke Schell Registers; Miramar Ship Index.

Wrecksite

The wreck, which is probably that of the *Eidsfos*, is orientated in an ESE to WNW direction and sits in a half-metre scour. It lies on a seabed of sand, mud and shells, in a general depth of 82 m (LAT). The wreck appears intact, but probably lies on its side, and stands eight metres high, covering an area 64 m long and 7 m across. This wrecksite should make an excellent boat-angling venue, as plenty of big fish were observed over the wreck on the echo-sounder.

LOCH DOON, HM TRAWLER

Date of loss: 25 December 1939
Wreck: ★★★
Depth: 49 m
Reference: 55 09'.613 N 001 21'.920 W
Location: 4.93 nm NE of Blyth Lighthouse

The *Loch Doon* (Official No. 165659) was a steel-hulled 534-ton British steam trawler that measured 52.9 m in length, with an 8.7-m beam and 8.68-m draught. Smith's Dock Co. Ltd. at Southbank, Middlesbrough built and completed her as Yard No. 1027 in 1937; she was launched on 12 April 1937 for Loch Fishing Co. Hull, Port Reg: H.435, and Harry Wight Ltd. was the manager. The single steel screw was powered by a 99-rhp, three-cylinder triple expansion steam engine that used one single-ended boiler working at a pressure of 225-lb psi, three corrugated furnaces, 5.75 sq.m (62 sq.ft) of grate surface and 249.72 sq.m (2688 sq.ft) of heating surface, which gave 12 knots. The cylinders measured 36.83 cm, 60.96 cm and 105.41 cm with a 68.58-cm stroke (14.5 in., 24 in. and 41.5 in. with a 27-in. stroke). Smith's Dock Co. Ltd. manufactured the engine and ancillary machinery. She had one deck, a cruiser stern, four bulkheads cemented, a 26.51-m quarterdeck and 9.75-m forecastle; she was also equipped with wireless, direction finder and an echo sounding device.

In August 1939 the Admiralty requisitioned and converted her to an Anti-Submarine Trawler, armed with one four-inch gun (10.2 cm). The designated code recognition signal letters were: GZRC.

On 24 December 1939, Seaman Edward Story (PS), LT/X 21069RNR, died on HMT *Loch Doon*.

Final patrol

On 25 December 1939, HMT *Loch Doon* was under the command of her skipper, G.H.A. Thomson RNR, patrolling off Blyth, but failed to return to base; it was presumed that the boat had detonated a German-laid mine and had been lost with all 15 hands:

Altass, Fred, 39yrs, Engineman, RNPS
Cressey, Arthur Thomas, 24yrs, Seaman, RNPS
Hunter, James F., Stoker, RNPS
Johnson, Eric Menzies, 19yrs, Seaman, RNPS
Kaveney, James William, 29yrs, Seaman, RNPS
Mercer, John, Seaman, RNPS
Savage, John, Stoker, RNR (Patrol Service)
Seymour, William, 26yrs, Seaman, RNR (PS)
Spice, Leonard Victor, Leading Seaman, RNR (PS)
Teasdel, Leonard Percy, Seaman Cook, RNPS
Thompson, George Henry Alexander, Skipper, RNR
Wadsworth, Frederick, Able Seaman, RN
Walker, George Thomas Edwin, 18yrs, Ordinary Signalman RN
West, Richard, 33yrs, Engineman, RNR (PS)
Winpenny, Christopher, 2nd Hand, RNR (PS)

It was later discovered that *U 22*, commanded by Kapitänleutnant Karl-Heinrich Jenisch, had laid a barrier of nine mines off Blyth on 20 December 1939, in Kriegsmarine quadrant AN5461, the first mine having been dropped at 0207 hrs (CT) in position 55°05.7'N.

From the KTB of *U 22*:

20.12.39 AN 5461 0207–0250 9 Minen vor Blyth/Hafen uW gelegt. 55°07,7' – 55°08,8N/01°26,8' – 01°27,7W

BVLS 1939–45, p. 3; SRN, Vol. 2, p. 213; KTB of *U 22*.

Wrecksite

The wreck, possibly that of the *Loch Doon*, is orientated in an E to W direction. It lies on a seabed of sand and mud in a general depth of 49 m (LAT). It is partially buried and badly broken up, but stands 4.8 m high and covers an area 45 m long and 19 m wide. Immediately west of the wreck is also a field of debris, probably from this wreck.

PRINCESS MAUD

Date of loss: 10 June 1918
Wreck: ★★★★
Depth: 41 m
Reference: 55 12'.125 N 001 26'.403 W
Location: 2.15 nm E by N of Beacon Point, Newbiggin-by-the-Sea

The *Princess Maud* (Official No. 114008) was a steel-hulled 1566-ton British steam passenger/cargo ship that measured 78.15 m in length, with an 11.15-m beam and 4.97-m draught. Napier and Miller Ltd. at Yoker Yard, Glasgow built and completed her as Yard No. 121 in January 1902; she was launched on 14 November 1901 for M. Langlands and Sons, Glasgow. The single steel screw was powered by a 202-hp, three-cylinder triple expansion steam engine that used two boilers and gave 12 knots. The cylinders measured 53.34 cm, 86.36 cm and 142.24 cm with a 106.68-cm stroke (21 in., 34 in. and 56 in. with a 42-in.stroke). Dunsmuir and Jackson Ltd. manufactured the engine and ancillary machinery at Glasgow.

In 1916 the ship was also armed for defence with one 12-pounder (5.44-kilo) gun.

From May 1916 to February 1918, she was requisitioned as a commissioned Fleet Messenger.

Final voyage

On 7 June 1918, the *Princess Maud*, under the command of Captain W. E. Taylor, sailed from London in convoy for passage to Leith, carrying a 690-ton general cargo and a crew of 26. At 1246 hrs on the 10th, the KDM submarine SMU *UB 88*, commanded by Oblt.z.S. Reinhard von Rabenau, torpedoed the ship without warning in a position given as five miles NE by N from Blyth. The chief engineer, a donkeyman and one fireman were killed instantly when the torpedo detonated in the engine room on the starboard side. The War Time code books and confidential papers were destroyed by the master before the 23 men abandoned ship. A British trawler which picked up the crew also rescued 11 men who had jumped into the sea from the 1526-ton Swedish steamer *Dora*, which had been torpedoed close by at 1240 hrs. The *Dora* and *Princess Maud* were the two foremost steamers in the convoy. Two escort trawlers took the *Princess Maud* in tow, but she foundered 25 minutes later, just 45 minutes after being hit. All the survivors were landed at North Shields quay. The three men who died were:

Howard, William, Centennial Donkeyman MM
Jackson, Charles, Fireman MM
Nicholson, Frederick Stanley, Chief Engineer MM

ADM 137/2964; LCWLR 1914–18, p. 221; CWGC; BVLS 1914–18, p. 91; KTB of *UB 88*.

Wrecksite

The wreck of the *Princess Maud* is orientated in an E to W direction. It lies on a seabed of mud, fine sand, gravel and rocks in a general depth of 41 m (LAT). The wreck is upright and intact and covers an area 81 m long and 19 m across; it also stands over seven metres high with some superstructure visible, but is covered in nets. Lots of big fish have been observed all around the wreckage and the highest parts are covered in soft corals.

DORA, EX VARUS, EX WESTWOOD

Date of loss: 10 June 1918
Wreck: *****
Depth: 44 m
Reference: 55 12'.063 N 001 25'.290 W
Location: 2.75 nm E by N of Beacon Point, Newbiggin-by-the-Sea

The *Dora* (Official No. 82508) was an iron-hulled 1526-ton Swedish steam cargo ship that measured 82.67 m in length, with a 10.38-m beam and a 5.1-m draught. Robert Thompson and Son at Southwick, Sunderland built and completed her as Yard No. 114 in September 1881; she was launched on 10 September 1881 as the schooner-rigged *Westwood* (Official No. 5263) for R. Jameson of Hull. She was 1336 tons and measured 73.15 m in length, with a 10.36- m beam and holds that were 5.10 m in depth. The single iron screw was powered by a two-cylinder compound steam engine. She had one deck, two tiers of beams and four bulkheads cemented, double bottom, aft 16.76 m (55 ft), forward 9.14 m (30 ft), 260 tons and fore peak tank of 40 tons.

In 1882 she was registered to R. Jameson at Hull

G. R. Sanderson and Co. Hull was the registered owner in 1885.

In 1887, the vessel was lengthened by R. Thompson and Son in Sunderland and she then weighed 1502 gross tons.

The registered owner in 1893 was Bryson, Jameson and Co. Hull.

A new 175-nhp three-cylinder triple-expansion steam engine that used two single-ended boilers operating at a pressure of 180-lb psi.was fitted in 1894. The cylinders measured 43.81 cm, 77.47 cm and 139.7 cm with a 91.44-cm stroke (17.25 in., 30.5 in. and 55 in., with a 36-in. stroke). She had four plain furnaces, 6.03 sq.m (65 sq.ft) of grate surface and 224.63 sq.m (2418 sq.ft) of heating surface. Reihest. Maschinenf. in Hamburg manufactured the machinery. She had one deck, a 29.5-m quarterdeck, a 26.5-m bridge deck and 8.5-m forecastle. The designated code recognition signal letters were: JSMB.

In 1898, she was sold to Gebrüder Andersen in Kiel, Germany, who renamed her *Varus*.

Dampskibsselskabet Spero, Copenhagen, Denmark purchased and renamed her *Dora* in 1906; R Christensen was the manager.

On 14 October 1911 the *Dora* ran aground at Västra Finngrunden, off Gävle, Sweden, while transporting pit props from Brahestad to West Hartlepool. The Swedish salvage company Neptun salvaged her and their two salvage vessels, *Neptun* and *Belos*, towed her to Gävle.

In 1912 the *Dora* was sold as a wreck to Erik Axel Brodin, Gävle for 32 000 Swedish Krona. Reg. No. 5263.

From 1917, Erik Brodins Rederi AB, home port Torö was the registered owner and E. Brodin was the manager. The master was Captain H. J. Cronberg.

Final voyage

On 10 June 1918 the KDM submarine SMU *UB 88*, commanded by Oblt.z.S. Reinhard von Rabenau, torpedoed and sunk the SS *Dora*, 16 nm north of the Tyne. The steamer had left Hull the day before on passage to Methil and joined a convoy near Bull light vessel. At 1550 hrs the convoy left the rallying area and proceeded peacefully until after the Tyne. At 1200 hrs on the 10th they were continuing on a northern heading, but at 1240 hrs the crew sighted a periscope from a distance of about 300 metres. Shortly after that, a torpedo exploded against the ship and destroyed the lifeboats. The 11 survivors were picked by a trawler, which had also picked up the survivors from the steamer *Princess Maud.* The crewmen from the *Dora* said they were picked up soon after jumping into the sea and also that *Princess Maud* was torpedoed while they were still in the water, so the two attacks must have been made very close to each other.

According to the KTB of *UB 88,* the attack took place at 1340 hrs, and the name *Dora* was seen on one of the two targets, the two foremost steamers in the convoy. The U-boat dived deep and only one explosion was heard by the U-boat crew.

Nine of *Dora*'s crew of 20 were killed:

Andersson, Erik Gustaf, 19 yrs, Stoker (Linköping)
Andersson, Evald Mander, 17 yrs, Coal Trimmer (Laholm)
Bonnevier, Johan Gottfrid, 44 yrs, Engine Man (Gävle)
Ekelund, Gustaf Adolf, 57 yrs, Engine Man (Stockholm)
Johansson, Axel Manfred, 28 yrs, Cook (Stockholm)
Karlsson, Karl Oskar, 22 yrs, Stoker (Sundsvall)
Österling, Karl Helge, 29 yrs, Stoker (Göteborg)
Rydberg, Fredrik Wilhelm, 34 yrs, Seaman (Torsö)
Westergren, Jonas Emil, 49 yrs, Donkeyman (Söderhamn)

LCWLR 1914–18, p. 12; BVLS 1914–18, p. 6; Tennent (1990), p. 148; LR 1915/16 No. 571 (D); KTB of *UB 88*; American Lloyd's Register of American and Foreign Shipping, 1857–1900.

Wrecksite

The wreck is orientated in a NNE to SSW direction and has debris scattered to the south and east. It lies on a seabed of fine sand, mud, shells, gravel and rock, in a general depth of 44 m (LAT). The wreck, which was identified by the bell inscribed: *Westwood 1881*, stands 6.3 m high and covers an area 75 m long and 21 m across. It is upright, somewhat collapsed, but with some superstructure visible and the bows broken off. Lots of fish have adopted the wreck so it will make an excellent boat-angling venue; it is also covered in a profusion of soft corals and is home to some large crustaceans.

GUDBRAND, ex ULLER

Date of loss: 16 March 1917
Wreck: ★★★★
Depth: 48 m
Reference: 55 12'.093 N 001 57'.160 W
Location: 3.98 nm E by N of Beacon Point, Newbiggin-by-the-Sea.

The *Gudbrand* was an iron-hulled 1860-ton Norwegian steam cargo ship that measured 82.65 m in length, with a 12.03-m beam and a 4.97-m draught. John Priestman and Co.

Uller *(Courtesy Norwegian Maritime Museum)*

at Southwick, Sunderland built and completed her as Yard No. 67 in August 1897; she was launched as the *Uller* on 4 June 1897 for Aktieselskapet Uller, Tønsberg in Norway; Hjalmar Røed was the manager. The single iron screw was powered by a 196-hp, three-cylinder triple expansion steam engine that used two boilers and gave 11 knots. The cylinders measured 50.07 cm, 86.36 cm and 142.24 cm with a 99.06-cm stroke (20½ in., 34 in. and 56 in. with a 39-in. stroke). North East Marine Engineering Co. Ltd. at Wallsend manufactured the engine and ancillary machinery. She had one deck, four bulkheads and water ballast. The designated code recognition signal letters were: HMGK.

Captain O. Svendsen was the master in 1900.

In 1906, Hjalmar Røed and Co. was the manager

AS Import, Skien was the registered owner in 1915 and Einer Stensrud was the manager.

Later in 1915, AS DS Uller, Bergen was the owner and S. Hansen AS the manager.

In 1916, Aktieselskapet "Uller", Bergen was the owner and Sverre Hansen AS was the manager.

From 1916, Dampskipsselskapet Aktieselskapet "Gudbrand", Sverre Hansen Aktieselskapet, Bergen was the registered owner and she was renamed *Gudbrand*; Sverre Hansen AS was the manager.

Final voyage

On 16 March 1917, the KDM mine-laying submarine SMU *UC 50*, commanded by Kapitänleutnant Rudolf Seuffer, torpedoed and sunk the *Gudbrand* without any warning, seven miles NE ½ E of Blyth. The steamer, with Captain Hans Hjorth of Bergen in charge, was *en route* from the Tyne to Kristiania with a cargo of coal; her crew of twenty and six passengers were all rescued. The *Gudbrand* was hit on the starboard side, probably close to the bow. The crew and passengers were all picked up by the RN patrol boat *Faithful Friend* at 2130 hrs on 16 March, and taken to North Shields to be lodged at the Sailors' Home. The Court of Inquiry was set for 21 March at the Norwegian Consulate in Newcastle on Tyne.

Maritime Accident Statements for Norwegian Ships Sunk in Wartime: 1814–1918; LCWLR 1914–18, p. 105; ANCL 1914–18, p. 85; Starke Schell Registers; LR 1900.

Wrecksite

The wreck is orientated in an almost S to N (170/350 degrees) direction with the bows to the north. It lies on a seabed of sand and stone, in a general depth of 48 m (LAT). The wreck is very substantial and covers an area 88 m long and 20 m across. It stands six metres high, is intact and upright with some superstructure in place, although it is now gradually collapsing. The boilers and engine are now exposed to view and surrounded by masses of iron plates, pipes, broken lifeboat davits, shattered machinery and debris at the stern end, which is the highest point on the wreck. The upper, most exposed structures are impressive, where soft corals have established themselves in a profusion of colour. At least one trawl net is entangled on it.

RECORDER

Date of loss: 14 July 1916
Wreck: ✭✭
Depth: 84 m
Reference: 55 13'.195 N 001 11'.175 W
Location: 14.44 nm NNE by E of the Tyne

The *Recorder* (Official No. 13090) was a steel-hulled 149-ton British steam trawler that measured 31.69 m in length, with a 6.27-m beam and 3.27-m draught. Wood Skinner and Co. Ltd. at Bill Quay near Hebburn-on-Tyne built and completed her as Yard No. 97 in March 1901. She was launched on 20 February 1901 for Reaver Fishing Co. Ltd. at North Shields, who also owned her at the time of loss; Port Reg: SN.293. The single steel screw was powered by a 55-nhp three-cylinder triple expansion steam engine that used one boiler. She had one deck and the skipper was J. Warren.

Final voyage

On 14 July 1916, the *Recorder* was on a return fishing voyage from North Shields when she was captured by the KDM submarine SMU *UB 39*, commanded by Werner Fürbringer. The crew was forced to abandon their trawler and it was scuttled using explosive charges, 15 nm NNE ½ E from the Tyne; none of the crew was lost.

LCWLR 1914–18, p. 47; Miramar Ship Index.

Wrecksite

The wreck, which is probably that of the *Recorder*, is orientated roughly in an ENE to WSW direction and sits in a long one-metre scour that stretches over 6 m. It lies on a seabed of sand, mud and broken shells, in a general depth of 84 m (LAT). The wreck is intact, partially buried, but collapsed and well broken up.

BANGARTH

Date of loss: 13 December 1917
Wreck: ★★★★
Depth: 52 m
Reference: 55 13'.815 N 001 19'.007 W
Location: 6.66 nm ENE of Beacon Point, Newbiggin-by-the-Sea

The *Bangarth* (Official No. 124009) was a steel-hulled 1872-ton British steam cargo ship that measured 83.82 m in length, with a 12.19-m beam and a 6.4-m draught. Sir Raylton Dixon and Co. Ltd. Middlesbrough built and completed her as Yard No. 526 in November 1906; she was launched on 19 September 1906 for Rea Shipping Co. Ltd. London, who owned her at the time of loss; A.L Rea was the manager. The single screw was powered by a 217-hp, three-cylinder triple expansion steam engine that used two boilers. The cylinders measured 55.88 cm, 88.9 cm and 149.85 cm with a 99.06-cm stroke (22 in., 35 in. and 59 in. with a 39-in. stroke.). J. Dickenson and Sons Ltd. manufactured the engine and ancillary machinery at Sunderland. She had one deck and a 9.29-m forecastle. The designated code recognition signal letters were: HJNM.

R. and J. H. Rea was the manager from 1910.

In 1916 the steamer was armed for defence.

Final voyage

On 13 December 1917, the KDM submarine SMU *UB* 34, commanded by Oblt.z.S. Hellmuth von Ruckteschell torpedoed and sunk the *Bangarth* (Captain T. Appleton) without any warning, 13 miles NNE of the Tyne. The steamer was engaged as an auxiliary collier for the Admiralty, carrying a cargo of coal from Methil to Dunkerque. Two men were lost:

Cook, Frank Alfred, 41 yrs, 1st Engineer MM
Jenkins, Taliesin, 42 yrs, 2nd Engineer MM

LCWLR 1914–18, p. 189; BVLS 1914–18, p. 75; CWGC; Tennent (1990), p. 192; Starke Schell Registers.

Wrecksite

The wreck is orientated in a SSE to NNW direction. In 1967 the wreck was said to be almost completely intact, sitting upright on a seabed of dirty sand and stone in a general depth of 52 m (LAT). Many years ago it was swept clear to 42 m and even though the superstructure and hull sides have crumpled up and collapsed in on themselves, it still stands some 5.5 m from the bottom and covers an area 54 m long and 16 m across. Myriads of soft corals adorn the highest structures and at least one trawl net is, or was tangled up and floating at the stern end. A sizeable number of fish of varying species gather over the top of the wreck during the summer months, so it should make a good boat-angling venue.

AMSTERDAM, EX AVON

Date of loss: 24 February 1918
Wreck: ★★★
Depth 50 m
Reference: 55 14'.473 N 001 22'.448 W
Location: 7.95 nm SE by E of Coquet light

The *Amsterdam* was an iron-hulled 806-ton British steam passenger cargo vessel that measured 66.75 m in length, with an 8.83-m beam and a 4.57-m draught. Cunliffe and Dunlop at Inch Yard, Port Glasgow built and completed her as Yard No. 129 in February 1878; she was launched as the schooner-rigged *Avon* (Official No. 105733) on a Saturday in December 1877 for William Sloan and Co. Glasgow. The single iron screw was powered by a 150-nhp two-cylinder compound steam engine that used one boiler. The shipbuilders manufactured the engine and ancillary machinery. She was capable of transporting 46 first class and 41 steerage passengers.

In July 1888 she was fitted with a new 169-nhp three-cylinder triple expansion engine which gave 11 knots. Cunliffe and Dunlop manufactured the machinery.

From 1903, the registered owner was Rankine Line, Glasgow and they renamed her *Amsterdam*; James Rankine and Son Ltd. was the manager.

Final voyage

On 24 February 1918, the *Amsterdam* was torpedoed and sunk without any warning by Oblt.z.S. Hans Kükenthal in the KDM submarine SMU *UC 49*, about six miles SE by E of Coquet light, according to *Lloyd's War Losses - WWI*. Two of the escorts, a small warship and a trawler picked up the survivors. The *Amsterdam* was in convoy and on a voyage from Leith to Rotterdam, carrying 87 passengers and a general cargo and coal. Escorts rescued all of the passengers and most of the crew, but the following four men were lost:

Craig, Norman Scott, 24 yrs, Wireless Operator MM
Daly, Peter, 18 yrs, Cabin Boy MM
McGregor, David Arthur, 26 yrs, 2nd Engineer MM
McMillan, Alexander 34 yrs, Mate MM

Oblt.z.S. Hans Kükenthal's logbook entry for 24 February 1918 reads:

'– convoy steering south, in sight consists of six steamers and is protected by destroyer and fishing boat
– Convoy steering zig zag course
– Fired from first tube
– Hit on laden steamer of 2500 tons
– Loud explosion – since destroyer is close behind stern of boat went to forty metres quickly'

CWGC; Jarvis (2000), Vol. V; LCWLR 1914–18, p. 202; BVLS 1914–18, p. 82; Tennent (1990), p. 192.

Wrecksite

This wreck, possibly that of the steamship *Amsterdam*, is orientated in an ESE to WNW direction, with the bows to the ESE. It lies on a seabed of mud, fine sand, broken shells and gravel in a general depth of 50 m (LAT). The wreck is upright and appears intact, standing nearly five metres high and covering an area 57 m long and 13 m across, with large quantities of fishing tackle snagged up on it. Plenty of marine life is to be seen, including some large fish and a number of crustaceans.

UB 115, Seiner Majestät Unterseeboot

Date of Loss: 29 September 1918
Location: position withheld

Aerial photo taken at 1,000 feet showing the attack on UB 115 *on 29 September 1918; one destroyer is off the photo listening in, while the RN trawlers are cutting off any line of escape for the U-boat. A second destroyer has just raced in to drop a depth charge over the contact.*

The photo is part of a unique montage taken from an East Fortune based RNAS balloon.

The other photos show a depth charge attack on UB 115 *by a destroyer. (Imperial War Museum)*

The UB 115 was a UBIII-type torpedo attack boat built by Blohm and Voss, Hamburg for the German navy. She was ordered on 23 September 1916 within the batch of UB 103 – UB 117 and her keel was laid as works no. 321. She was launched on 4 November 1917 and commissioned by Oblt.z.S. Reinhold Thomsen on 28 May 1918

The UB 115 had a double hull with a surface displacement of 519 tons and an underwater displacement of 651 tons. It measured 55.30 m in length, with a beam of 5.80 m, height of 8.25 m and draught of 3.68 m. The machinery consisted of 550-hp MAN/Vulcan diesel engines powered by two bronze screws that gave a surface speed of 13.3 knots. The surface operation range was 7420 nm at six knots and the submerged range was 55 nm at four knots. For underwater, the boats were equipped with 394-hp electric motors using lead-acid batteries and accumulators, giving 7.5 knots. Fuel capacity was 35 + 36-tons, and armament consisted of ten 50.04-cm (19.7 in.) torpedoes, with four tubes at the bow and one at the stern, along with one 105-mm forward-facing deck gun and 160 rounds of 105-mm ammunition. She carried no mines. The boat was capable of diving to a maximum operational depth of 50 m (164 ft), accomplished in 30 seconds on a crash dive, and was usually manned by three officers and 31 ratings.

UB 115 was formally assigned to Flandern I.U-Flottille, Zeebrugge on 3 September 1918, with Reinhold Thomsen the commander from 28 May 1918. *UB 115* left Hamburg on 31 August 1918 and transferred to Zeebrugge, where she arrived on 3 September.

Final patrol

UB 115 departed Zeebrugge, the last boat to do so, on 18 September 1918 for her first operational patrol. The boat arrived off Sunderland on 21 September and, one mile SSE from Roker lighthouse, Thomsen torpedoed and sank the 336-ton British steamer *Staithes* (1883 – Palmers' Ship Building and Iron Co. Ltd. Newcastle), which was *en route* from Port Mulgrave near Whitby for the Tyne with iron ore. The following four men died:

Jonson, Otto, 37 yrs, Mate
Radford, L.H, 48 yrs, Master
Worrell, A., 35 yrs, Able Seaman (Cook)
Wyatt, Charles Victor, 52 yrs, Engineer

But the tables were soon to be turned. Thomsen cruised off the Tyne and then moved up the Northumberland coast, reaching Newbiggin-by-the-Sea by 29 September. The crew must have been experiencing some problems with the tanks, because as she lay submerged 4.5 miles offshore, the crew of the British airship *R29*, fortuitously engaged on convoy protection duties nearby, observed oil bubbling to the surface. The convoy system had been introduced to the east coast just the month before, but the use of airships in convoy defence was an even more recent innovation. The East Fortune-based *R29*, proved her worth. The suspicious oil slick was reported and two 230-lb bombs and a calcium flare were released over the position. The destroyer HMS *Ouse* raced to the scene and was soon joined by the 1896 vintage destroyer HMS *Star*. The two warships then dropped seven depth charges, set at 50, 100 and 200 feet respectively. Three RN trawlers also joined in and ten more depth charges were dropped. The Royal Navy vessels were fitted with hydrophones and at 1400 hrs heard the U-boat start her engines, resulting in a further twelve depth charges being sent down. An hour later the engine noises were heard again, resulting in two more depth charges being dropped. From 1600 hrs the sound became intermittent but continued until 1825 hrs, by which time it was assumed that the U-boat crew must, mercifully, have died. Oil continued to pour up to the surface all night and for the following two days and minesweepers reported that an obstruction was the source of the oil. *UB 115* was lost with her entire crew of 39. The odds had tipped decisively against the Flanders U-boats.

The following extract is from the log of HMS *Star:*

> Sunday Sept. 29th – Berthed alongside collier Ryhope at Jarrow (am)
> 12.00 – Cruising stations starboard quarter of convoy escorting TM convoy. Proceeding up war channel – zig-zagging.
> 1.50 – Rigid airship observed to drop bomb to eastward.
> 1.51 – Full speed closed spot.
> 1.54 – Commenced dropping depth charge – dropped 5 in. quick succession
> 2.32 – Full speed. Dropped 6th depth charge on spot indicated by airship. Oil seen coming to surface, also air bubbles.
> 2.50 – Full speed.
> 2.51 – Dropped 7th depth charge on oil patch. Stopped to collect oil and examine vicinity
> 4.50 – Rejoined convoy

The crewmen that died in *UB 115*:

Bansemer, R., U-Matrose
Becker, Richard, U-Maschinistenmaat
Benz, Georg, U-Matrose
Bonn, Artur, Leutnant zur.See.d.Res
Bonningsen, H., U-Heizer
Buddenhagen, ?, U-Obermatrose
Börner, Max, U-Maschinistenmaat d.Res
Dmock, Willy, U-Oberheizer
Eckert, G., U-Obermaschinistenmaat
Eisermann, R., U-Obermaschinistenmaat
Grünau, Fritz, U-Maschinistenmaat
Hansel, Kurt F.T., Maat
Hausich, Karl, U-Matrose
Heinze, Johann, U-Heizer
Hösel, Ludwig, U-Matrose
Knörr, Christ, U-Maat
Kratzius, Richard, U-Steuermann
Krauthagen, C., U-Heizer
Köllmann, Alfred, Kapitänleutnant
Köppe, Otto, U-Matrose
Lob, Hermann, U-Matrose
Mebus, Erwin, U-Maschinistenmaat
Mehne, Richard, U-F.T.Gast
Moss, Hans, U-Heizer
Müller, Franz, U-Heizer
Nuss, Paul, U-Maschinistenmaat
Peters, Hans, U-Obermaat
Post, Arthur, U-Maschinistenmaat
Preising, Erich, U-Bootsmannsmaat
Ronkel, August, U-Heizer
Rosenbusch, Richard, U-Heizer
Rück, Waldemar, U-Obermatrose
Schauber, Michael, U-Oberheizer
Schieweg, R., U-Obermaschinist Anw
Schoth, R., U-Matrose
Tegge, K., U-Maschinist Anw
Thomsen, Reinhold, Oblt.z.S.
Trumpfheller, ?, U-Obermatrose
Wilkens, Ernst, Marine Ingenieur

The following are awards presented to members of the crews that helped to sink *UB 115*:

Stuart, Ronald N VC., DSO Lt. RNR 83P358 Star.
Vice Admiral East Coast of England 24.03.19 Gazetted
Action with enemy submarines Tyne Area 29.09.18 – UB.115 Mentioned in Despatches

Action with enemy submarine by H.M.S. Ouse, on 29 September 1918.
Captain (D) 7th Destroyer Flotilla, stated that H.M.S. "Star", *was handled in a most creditable and satisfactory manner".... "and co-operated with the Air Force in a most excellent and zealous manner.
Their Lordships' appreciation expressed.
The submarine in question was later ascertained to be UB.115, which was destroyed.
Lilley, William E N/E S/Lt. RNR 83P388 Star
Vice Admiral East Coast of England 24.03.19 Gazetted
Actions with enemy submarines 29.09.18 DSC
On the occasion of the destruction of the enemy submarine UB.115, on 29 September 1918, was Officer of the Watch, and showed an alertness to duty in the prompt alteration of helm and increasing of speed to clear the position over which Airship R.29 had released a bomb, and so enabling a successful depth charge attack to be made by "Star".
Peek, Arnold E DSC Lt. RNR 83P359 H.M.T. Bombardier
Vice Admiral East Coast of England 24.03.19 Gazetted
Action with enemy submarines Tyne Area 29.09.18 – UB.115 DSC – bar to
Action with enemy submarine by H.M.S. Ouse, on 29 September 1918.
H.M.T. "Bombardier" – Captain and Senior Naval Officer Tyne stated that he "displayed great ability and intelligence in organising the vessels of his group ... and contributed largely to the complete destruction of the enemy."
Their Lordships' appreciation expressed.
The submarine in question was later ascertained to be UB.115, which was destroyed.
Bird, Walter A.T DSC Lt. RN 83P358 Ouse
Vice Admiral East Coast of England 24.03.19 Gazetted
Action with enemy submarines Tyne Area 29.09.18 – UB.115 DSC – bar to
Action with enemy submarine by H.M.S. Ouse, on the 29th September, 1918.
Captain (D) 7th Destroyer Flotilla, described Lieutenant Bird as "indefatigable in his efforts and one of the most successful officers in anti-submarine warfare that I have ever had the honour to command."
Their Lordships' appreciation expressed. The submarine in question was later ascertained to be UB.115, which was destroyed.

ADM 53/61347; NARA: Series T-1022, Roll 42, PG61870; Möltenort U-boat Memorial Foundation; CWGC; Jarvis (2000), Vol. 5; Starke Schell Registers.

UPCERNE

Date of loss: 28 April 1918
Wreck: ★★★★
Depth: 40 m
Reference: 55 15'.520 N 001 27'.477 W
Location: 3.98 nm NNE of Beacon Point, Newbiggin-by-the-Sea

The *Upcerne* (Official No. 120694) was a steel-hulled 2984-ton British steam cargo ship that measured 100.89 m in length, with a 14.32-m beam and a 6.75-m draught. Ropner and Son, Middlesbrough built and completed her as Yard No. 425 in April 1906; she was launched on 12 March 1906 for Minterne S.S. Co. Ltd. London, who owned her at the time of loss; A. F. Hood was the manager. The single steel screw was powered by a 284-hp, three-cylinder triple expansion steam engine that used two boilers and gave 11.5 knots. Blair and Co. Ltd,

Stockton manufactured the engine and ancillary machinery. She had one deck, five bulkheads cemented, an 8.8-m poop deck, a 30.5-m bridge deck and 11-m forecastle.

Around 1916 the ship was armed for defence.

Final voyage

On 28 April 1918, the *Upcerne*, under Captain W.A. Milliken, was torpedoed and sunk without warning by the KDM mine-laying submarine SMU *UC 40*, commanded by Oblt.z.S. Hermann Menzel, four miles SE by S of Coquet Island, with the loss of 16 of her crew. The ship was carrying a cargo of iron ore and wood on a voyage from Narvik to Middlesbrough. The crewmen that died were:

Cockram, James Snell, 50 yrs, First Mate MM
Ellingsen, K., 49 yrs, Boatswain (Bosun) MM
Eriksen, E., 29 yrs, Able Seaman MM
Wvans, J., 42 yrs, Fireman and Trimmer MM
Gray, George, 35 yrs, second mate MM
Herapath, O., 33 yrs, 2nd Engineer MM
Hilden, William, 38 yrs, Able Seaman MM
Jones, David, 59 yrs, Fireman MM
Kinelato, Joseph, 44 yrs, Donkeyman MM
Larsen, C., 43 yrs, Carpenter MM
Marks, Daniel, 16 yrs, Pantry Boy MM
McCaffrey, Oswald Stanley, 16 yrs, Ordinary Seaman MM
McNab, James Henry, 27 yrs, Fireman and Trimmer MM
Smith, John, 56 yrs, Chief Engineer MM
Stroobants, Charles Louis, 44 yrs, Fireman and Trimmer MM
Theriault, Joseph Edward Edmund, 32 yrs, Able Seaman MM

Jarvis (2000), Vol. 5; CWGC; BVLS 1914–18, p. 88; LCWLR 1914–18, p. 213; LR 1915/16 No. 136 (U); Starke Schell Registers.

Wrecksite

The wreck is orientated in a SSE to NNW direction and lies on a seabed of fine sand, mud and black shells, in a general depth of 40 m (LAT). It is upright, very substantial but well broken up, with the engine lying to starboard and the boilers standing upright. Gordon Wadsworth identified the wreck by its bell in 1993. The wreck stands 6.2 m high and covers an area 116 m long and 26 m across. It makes a good boat-angling venue, because shoals of pout whiting can be seen over and around the wreck and large cod have been observed under the wreckage.

RIVER LEVEN, EX JOHN EDSWORTH

Date of Loss: 13 December 1953
Wreck: ✯✯✯✯
Depth: 79 m
Reference: 55 15'.137 N 000 44'.603 W
Location: 27 nm NE of the Tynemouth pier

The *River Leven* (Official No. 143841) was a steel-hulled 225-ton steam trawler that measured 35.15 m in length, with a 6.73-m beam and a 3.68-m draught. J. Fullerton and Co. at Paisley, Scotland built and completed her as Yard No. 252 in 1918; she was launched as the *John Eds-*

worth on 3 June 1918 for the Admiralty. The single steel screw was powered by a 57-nhp three-cylinder triple expansion steam engine that used one single-ended boiler working at a pressure of 180-lb psi, with three plain furnaces, 3.71 sq.m (40 sq.ft) of grate surface and 127.09 sq.m (1368 sq.ft) of heating surface. The cylinders measured 30.48 cm, 50.8 cm and 86.36 cm with a 58.42-cm stroke (12 in., 20 in. and 34 in. with a 23-in. stroke). W. H. Allen and Sons Co. Ltd. at Bedford manufactured the machinery, which gave ten knots. She had three bulkheads cemented and one deck. The bridge and forecastle was 8.83-m and weighed 19 tons.

In 1919, she was sold to the mercantile marine and renamed *River Leven*. Consolidated Fisheries of Grimsby then acquired the vessel, Port Reg: GY.293.

In August 1939, the *River Leven* was requisitioned, fitted out for the Examination Service and based at Grimsby as Admiralty Trawler No. 3744. She was also equipped with an echo sounding device and listening hydrophones.

In 1942 she was converted to an Escort Vessel and armed with one 12-pounder.

In April 1944, the vessel was converted to an Esso, which was an auxiliary oil tanker mainly used for bunkering but also carrying oil in drums to outlying stations.

In March 1945, she was returned to Consolidated Fisheries at Grimsby.

J. W. Tomlinson of North Shields later purchased her and was the registered owner at the time of loss.

Final voyage

On 13 December 1953, the *River Leven* was on a fishing trip from her home port of North Shields when she sprang a leak. The skipper sent out a call for help when the pumps seemed unable to cope. The 215-ton Hartlepool trawler *Friarage,* built in 1930, responded and took her in tow. She towed the *River Leven* for 19 miles, but the decision was taken to abandon her when she was on the verge of sinking; the *River Leven* then sank approximately 33 miles NE by E ½ E of Tynemouth. The *Friarage* landed all the crew at North Shields later that same day.

The Times: Monday, 14 December 1953, p. 4, Issue 52804; LCR 1953, p. 27; R 1951/2 No. 24368); Toghill (2003).

Wrecksite

The wreck, probably that of the *River Leven,* is located in an area ominously known as the Graveyard and is orientated in a SSE to NNW direction. It lies on a reasonably firm seabed of sand, mud and gravel in a general depth of 78.7 m (LAT). The wreck is upright, intact, stands just over 5 m high and covers an area 36 m long and 7 m across.

The six wrecks which follow are in that same Graveyard area.

RUNO

Date of loss: 5 September 1914
Wreck: ★★★★★
Depth 70 m
Reference: 55 10'.705 N 000 42'.103 E
Location: 26.09 nm NE of Tynemouth pier

The 1,654 ton Thomas Wilson Sons & Co. passenger/cargo steamer Runo *- circa 1908. (Author's collection)*

The *Runo* (Official No. 116074) was a steel-hulled 1654-ton British steam passenger/cargo ship that measured 85.34 m in length, with a 9.81-m beam and a 5.30-m draught. Caledon Shipbuilding and Engineering Co. Ltd. Dundee built and completed her as Yard No. 164 in July 1902; she was launched on 5 June 1902 for Thomas Wilson Sons and Co. Ltd. Hull, who owned her at the time of loss. The single steel screw was powered by a 196-nhp three-cylinder triple expansion steam engine that used two boilers and gave 12 knots. The cylinders measured 50.80 cm, 83.82 cm and 142.24 cm, with a 99.06-cm stroke (20 in., 33 in. and 56 in. with a 39-in. stroke). The *Runo* had accommodation for 12 first-class passengers and was fitted with refrigerating machinery.

Final voyage

At 1635 hrs on 5 September 1914, the *Runo* detonated a German-laid mine and sank. The steamer was on passage from Hull for Archangelsk, carrying a general cargo (although a large quantity, including £20 000-worth of raw rubber, was held back at the last moment), a crew of 33 and 237 passengers; most of them Russian reservists returning to Canada to rejoin the Russian forces. The explosion occurred amidships and her master immediately put the helm to starboard, with the intention of reaching land and beaching her. The vessel, though, began to settle by the head and many of the passengers rushed for the boats in panic. Six of the nine available lifeboats were quickly lowered down, but because of overcrowding, several of them capsized and twenty-nine persons were lost, including two crewmen and 27 Russian passengers. More panic ensued as the rope-falls of three of the boats were cut, preventing the remainder from being launched. The crew anticipated that, with the chains released, they would float off as the ship went down. At 1700 hrs the Grimsby steam trawlers *Silanion, Straton* and *Prince Victor,* came alongside and took off a large number of passengers and crew. Then, forty minutes later, another steam trawler, the 307-ton *Euripdcs* (1907 – City Steam Fishing Co. Hull) arrived at the scene, and took off the remaining people. The second officer and several of the crew re-boarded the *Runo* and she was taken in tow by the trawler *Euripdcs.* Unfortunately, however, the ship was settling and at 1825 hrs the tow was abandoned. The vessel went down five-minutes later.

It was later discovered that the *Runo* had in fact departed from her original sailing instructions, laid down by the Admiralty. At the subsequent Court of Inquiry, the loss of the vessel was attributed to the failure to keep close inshore after passing Whitby, contrary to Admiralty instructions. It was decided that, had the master observed his orders, the ship would have avoided the known minefield.

The casualties on the *Runo* were the very first recorded in a British merchant ship during the Great War and she was the first Wilson vessel to be sunk. The two crewmen killed were:

Hirst, Joseph Edward, Assistant Steward MM
McGuinness, John Patrick, Able Seaman MM

Incidentally, the *Runo* sank on the same afternoon that HMS *Pathfinder* was sunk with huge loss of life.

At a special presentation later, the skippers of the three Grimsby trawlers involved in the rescue - William Holt from *Silanion,* Henry Wicks from *Straton* and Mark Howard from the *Prince Victor,* were each awarded gold watches, complete with Alberts. The award was for 'succeeding, at great peril to themselves, in saving so many of the passengers and crew, which considerably minimised, what looked like being an appalling disaster.'

Between 0130 hrs and 0152 hrs on 26 August 1914 (continental time), the 2200-ton *Kaiserlichen Marine minenkreuzer* SMS *Albatross*, commanded by Korvettenkapitänleutnant West, along with the light cruiser SMS *Stuttgart,* had laid a barrier of 200 mines, 11 miles long on a SSE course from five miles NE to five miles SE of the Tyne estuary at approximately: 55° 07'N 01° 18'W to 54° 58'N 01° 10'W. The mines were 100 metres apart and laid at a depth setting of two metres under middle low ebb tide.

CWGC; Jarvis (2000), Vol. V; LCWLR 1914–18, p. 2; Groos (1922); *The Times*: Monday, 7 September 1914, pp. 5, 8–9, Issue 40628.

Wrecksite

The wreck of the *Runo,* which is located within the area known as the Graveyard, is orientated in a SE to NW direction and lies on a seabed of mud, fine sand and broken shells in a general depth of 70 m (LAT). It lies on its port side, is mostly intact and very substantial, standing over 8 m high in places, but the amidships section forward is heavily damaged. A Wilson Line plate led to the positive identification of the wreck by sport divers in July 2007. It should make an excellent boat-angling venue, because high numbers of fish have been observed.

ADELAIDE

Date of Loss: 6 February 1917
Wreck: ★★★
Depth: 71 m
Reference: 55 11'.538 N 000 36'.837 W
Location: 29.32 nm ENE from Tynemouth pier

The *Adelaide* (Official No. 102938) was an iron-hulled 139-ton steam trawler that measured 30.17 m in length, with a 6.22-m beam and a 3.35-m draught. Cook, Welton and Gemmell built and completed her as Yard No. 117 on 10 April 1894; she was launched and registered as H.239 on 10 April for Hull Steam Fishing and Ice Co. Ltd. Hull. A single iron screw was powered by a 34-nhp three-cylinder triple expansion steam engine that used one boiler and gave 9.5 knots. Amos and Smith Ltd. manufactured the engine and ancillary machinery at Hull. She had one deck and three bulkheads.

On 10 January 1912, the *Adelaide* was sold to William Robbens and Sons, Lowestoft and registered as LT.1164.

From 1915, the registered owner was H. Smethhurst of Grimsby, Port Reg: GY.604.

Final voyage

On 6 February 1917, the *Adelaide*, with Captain W. Corrick as the skipper, was stopped 30 miles ENE of Tynemouth by SM *UB 22*, a KDM submarine, commanded by Bernhard Putzier. The trawler's crew was forced to abandon ship and it was sunk using explosive charges.

SM UB 22 herself went on to detonate a mine on 19 January 1918 in the Heligoland Bight and was lost with all 22 hands, including her new commander, Oblt.z.S. Karl Wacker.)

LCWLR 1914–18, p. 91; BVLS 1914–18, p. 114; LR 1915/16 No.174 (A); Thompson (1999).

Wrecksite

The wreck, most probably that of the *Adelaide*, is located within the area known as the Graveyard and is orientated in an ENE to WSW direction. It lies on a seabed of sand, mud, shells and gravel in a general depth of 71 m (LAT). The wreck is intact, but partially buried, with lots of nets and fishing gear strewn over the eastern end. It stands some 4.2 m high and covers an area 30 m long and 7 m across, with lots of soft corals on the upper sections. A number of large crustaceans have been observed amongst the wreckage and a fair-sized shoal of pout whiting swarm over the top of it.

YSELHAVEN

Date of Loss: 14 March 1919
Wreck: ✯✯✯✯✯
Depth: 72 m
Reference: 55 11'.421 N 000 40'.037 W
Location: 28.42 nm ENE from Blyth North pier

The *Yselhaven* (Official No. 5604097) was a steel-hulled 3558-ton steam cargo ship that measured 110.13 m in length, with a 15.16-m beam and a 6.73-m draught. Rotterdamsche Droogdok Maats B.V., Rotterdam, the Netherlands built and completed her as Yard No. 55 in June 1916; she was launched on 15 April 1916 for Gebr. van Uden in Rotterdam. The single screw was powered by a 301-nhp three-cylinder triple expansion steam engine that used three boilers. The cylinders measured 63.5 cm, 104.14 cm and 170.18 cm with a 114.3-cm stroke (25 in., 41 in. and 67 in. with a 45-in. stroke). Rotterdamsche Droogdok Maats B.V., manufactured the engine and ancillary machinery at Rotterdam, She had one deck.

In March 1918 she was requisitioned from the Netherlands by the U.S. Government and operated by the U.S. Shipping Board under the U.S. flag.

Final voyage

On 14 March 1919, the *Yselhaven* was some 20 miles off Coquet Island, at about 55° 12.45N 00° 30W, on passage from Baltimore, USA to Copenhagen, when she detonated a mine at 0145 hrs and sank with the loss of ten crewmen. Ten hours later, the 407-ton British steamer *Taycraig* (1901 – Wraith Steam Shipping Co. Ltd. London) rescued 35 members of the crew and landed them at Hartlepool.

An inquest was held on 18 March 1919 at Hartlepool by Mr Coroner Newby, regarding the circumstances of the death of Richard E. Welsh, a 29-year old cadet engineer from Baltimore, who was one of the crew of the *Yselhaven*. The master of the steamer, Captain Lawrence Bell Adams, also of Brooklyn, said, "I received instructions as to the North Sea route, and these were closely followed. At about 0145 hrs on Friday, during a northeast gale, the ship was struck by a mine amidships; this occurring about 35 miles from Hartlepool. The second officer, who was on the bridge at the time, gave the general alarm. The engines were stopped and wireless calls were sent out. The crew were ordered to the boats, and, having an answer to the wireless calls, the wireless operator also left the ship".

The master was last to leave the vessel and said, "We were lucky to get clear; the boilers exploded and the smoke stack collapsed within three feet of the boat. The deceased, who was dressed but had no great-coat, was in the boat. He was asked to assist in bailing out the boat and thus keep himself warm. Heavy hail squalls were coming across at the time. Those in the second boat were picked up about 1230 noon, the chief officer's boat being picked up an hour earlier. Mr Welsh died in the boat. He was huddled up with six or seven others, all of whom were in a state of collapse. Everything possible under the circumstances was done".

The captain expressed the opinion that Welsh's death was due to exposure and shock. He also said they were not in a minefield. The second officer of the *Yselhaven* said that whilst Mr Welsh was getting into the boat, he fell into the sea, but was helped aboard by the witness. He was soaking wet and had died by the time he was carried aboard the *Taycraig*. Everything possible was done by the captain and crew of the vessel, who treated them with the greatest consideration. The captain asserted that "nine of the crew were missing, six of whom were seen to jump overboard, in the belief that the vessel was going to blow up and they would be taken down by the suction". The chief officer interposed, "They trusted to their chances of being picked up and they would have been if it had not been for the dense smoke". A verdict of death by misadventure was returned by the coroner.

According to the Boston Daily Globe on 18 March 1919, the casualties were:

Barlier, Preston, fireman, from Hamptonville, N. Carolina
Berglund, Ivor, boatswain, from Belgium
Colwell, Frank, coal passer, from Rome, NY
Gimenz, F., coal passer, from Ageath, Spain
Lippacher, W.E., fireman, from New Berlin, NY
Lopez, Manuel, oiler, no address given
Miller, R.E., supercargo, from Cleveland

Sawtell, W.R., 2nd cook, from Providence
Welch, Richard E., cadet engineer, from Baltimore

Starke Schell Registers; Miramar Ship Index; *The Times*: Tuesday, 18 March 1919, p. 6, Issue 42051; *Northern Daily Mail* (Hartlepool): Monday, 17 March 1919

Wrecksite

The wreck, which is probably that of the *Yselhaven*, is orientated in a SSE to NNW direction. It lies in a slight scour, on a seabed of mud, sand and shells in a general depth of 72 m (LAT). The wreck lists to the NE, stands over 8 m high and covers an area 70 m long and 12 m across; the highest section being at the SSE end. High numbers of fish can be seen over the top of the wreck on the echo sounder, so this should make an excellent boat-angling venue.

It is also possible that the wreck close by, at 55 11'.088 N 000 40'.420 W, is part of the *Yselhaven*. It lies in a general depth of 71 m (LAT) and covers an area measuring 35 m long and 12 m across and stands nearly 5 m high.

GJESØ

Date of Loss: 29 June 1915
Wreck: ✯✯✯
Depth: 70 m
Reference: 55 11'.538 N 000 42'.220 W
Location: 26.65 nm ENE from Tynemouth pier

The *Gjesø* was a steel-hulled 1094-ton Norwegian steam cargo vessel that measured 68.96 m in length, with an 11.07-m beam and 4.44-m draught. AS Trondhjems Mek Verksted, Trondheim built and completed her as Yard No. 152 in November 1912; she was launched on 24 September 1912 for AS Sørlandet, Arendal, with Engelbrethsen and Henriksen as the manager. The single steel screw was powered by an 116-nhp three-cylinder triple-expansion steam engine that used one boiler. The cylinders measured 43.18 cm, 69.85 cm and 116.84 cm with a 76.2-cm stroke (17 in., 27½ in. and 46 in. with a 30-in. stroke). The shipbuilders manufactured the machinery. She had one deck, a 3.65-m poop deck, a 15.84-m bridge deck and 7.62-m forecastle. Captain T. Toltefsen was the master. The designated code recognition signal letters were: MHWB.

Final voyage

On 29 June 1915, the *Gjesø* was on passage from Newcastle upon Tyne for Kristiania with a cargo of coal when, at 0800 hrs, she detonated a mine. She did not sink, however, until about an hour and a half later. The crew disembarked in the lifeboats and, at 0300 hrs the following morning, the 127-ton Aberdeen-built steam trawler *Sarah* (1885) picked them up, landing them four hours later at North Shields. The master, Captain Tarald Tollefsen, was 39 years old and resided in Arendal. The mine was taken to be a drifting one, as there was no reported minefield in that area, either German or British.

Maritime Accident Statements for Norwegian Ships Sunk in Wartime: 1814–1918; Starke Schell Registers; Groos (1922).

Wrecksite

The wreck, most probably that of the *Gjesø*, is orientated in a S to N direction. It sits in a slight scour and lies on a seabed of mud, sand and shells in a general depth of 70 m (LAT). The wreck is generally intact but broken in two, with the other section lying about 75 m to the east. Divers report it to be upright, but with the superstructure collapsed and standing around 6 m high. This section covers an area 32 m long and 10 m across. Plenty of marine life can be found, so this site will make an excellent boat-angling venue.

GOTTFRIED

Date of loss: 27 August 1914
Wreck: ★★★
Depth: 70 m
Reference: 55 11'.071 N 000 41'.670 W
Location: 26.21 nm NE from the Tynemouth pier

The SS Gottfried *circa 1913 Courtesy: Stein-Erik Dagsland, Heinavegen & Rolf Kristensen, Åsgårdstrand, Norway*

The *Gottfried* (Official No. 2568) was a 425-ton steel-hulled Norwegian steam cargo vessel that measured 42.59 m in length, with a 7.54-m beam. Bergsunds Mekaniske Verkstader, Stockholm built and completed her as Yard No. 202 in August 1889 for F. G. Althainz in Stockholm, Sweden. The single screw was powered by a 58-nhp, two-cylinder compound steam engine that used one boiler working at a pressure of 80 lb psi. The cylinders measured 49.53 cm and 96.52 cm with a 59.18-cm stroke (19½ in. and 38 in. with a 23⅜-in. stroke). Bergsunds Mekaniske Verkstader, Stockholm manufactured the engine and ancillary machinery.

In 1901 she was registered to Rederi AB Gottfried and F. G. Althainz was the manager. From 1904, K. J. Knudsen, in Haugesund, Norway was the registered owner.

Final voyage

On 27 August 1914, the *Gottfried* was travelling in ballast from Egersund in southern Norway to Blyth, when she detonated a mine and sank, 27 miles E ½ N from the Tyne; four of her crew, the master, chief mate, a fireman and a sailor, were saved, but eight other men were lost. The survivors were picked up by the North Shields drifter *Noreen* and landed at the Tyne. *Noreen*'s crew said that at about 2000 hrs on the 26th, a loud distant explosion alarmed them; another loud bang was heard at midnight and then two more followed at around 0300 hrs and 0400 hrs in the morning. At 0600 hrs they found a man floating on a plank of wood, who stated that he was from the *Gottfried*, which had blown up three hours earlier. The master was found some time later, floating on a lifebelt, and two other men were also found. At the time of the explosion, the survivors reported that five of the crew of 12 had been lying in their bunks, while three were in the forecastle and two amidships. The mine detonated in the forward section and the ship went down in two minutes; the master stated that the men in that area had no chance of surviving.

Between 0130 hrs and 0152 hrs on 26 August 1914, the 2200-ton, the German mine layer SMS *Albatross* and the light cruiser SMS *Stuttgart* had laid an 11-mile barrier of 200 mines on a SSE course from five miles NE to five miles SE of the Tyne estuary at approximately: 55° 07'N 01° 18'W to 54° 58'N 01° 10'W.)

Starke Schell Registers; American Lloyd's Register of American and Foreign Shipping, 1857–1900; Miramar Ship Index; *Maritime Accident Statements for Norwegian Ships Sunk in Wartime: 1814–1918*; *The* Times: Friday, 28 August 1914, p. 6, Issue 40618; Groos (1922).

Wrecksite

The wreck, most probably that of the *Gottfried*, is orientated in an NNE by SSW direction. It lies on a fairly firm seabed of mud, sand and broken shells in a general depth of 70 m (LAT). The wreck is reasonably intact and appears to be upright, standing 4.9 m high at the bows and stern and covering an area 40 m long and 8 m across. Lots of large fish have been observed on the echo sounder, so it should make a decent boat-angling venue.

AJAX

Date of Loss: 19 October 1895
Wreck: ✯✯✯
Depth: 72 m
Reference: 55 12'.105 N 000 38'.354 W
Location: 28.7 nm ENE from the Tyne

The *Ajax* was an iron-hulled 892-ton barque-rigged German steam paddle cargo vessel that measured 63.09 m in length, with a 9.14-m beam and 5.79-m draught. Messrs James Laing at the Deptford shipyard, Sunderland built and completed her as Yard No. 37 in 1862; she was launched on 18 November 1861 for Fenwick and Co. at Sunderland. The single iron screw was powered by a two-cylinder vertical direct-drive steam engine using one boiler, the cylinders each measuring 101.6 cm (40 inches). She had two decks, five bulkheads and was classed as A1✯.

In 1863, J. G. Dale was the registered owner and Captain Beard the master.

In 1869, Fenwick and Co. Sunderland was the registered owner and Captain Beard the master.

W. Cassop became the master in 1870, followed by Captain Beard in 1871. The two cylinders then measured 116.84 cm and 55.88 cm (46 in. and 22 in.).

In 1875, the registered owner was E. T. Gerley and Co. Liverpool. The tonnage was altered to 862 tons and she was fitted with a compound steam engine with two V-boilers.

In 1875, she was sold to F. Schichan and registered in Elbing, Germany and the master was Captain L. F. Tetzluff. The tonnage was altered to 852 gross tons.

From 1895, F. Dultz of Pillau, Germany was the registered owner.

Final voyage

Early on the morning of 19 October 1895, the *Ajax*, commanded by Captain R. Kaellander, was in ballast and on passage from Saardam (Zaardam) in the Netherlands to Burntisland when she sank, following a collision with the 1126-ton steamer *Diamond* (1881 – P.M. Duncan, Dundee), reportedly 17 miles east by north of Souter Point at 55.05N 00.54W. It was dark and wind conditions were westerly force one. Matilda Erickson, a German stewardess who was asleep in her berth, was the only fatality: the *Diamond*, which was towed into the Tyne in a seriously damaged condition, rescued the 16 survivors.

Starke Schell Registers; *The Times*: Monday 21 October 1895, p. 6, Issue 34713.

Wrecksite

There is no wreck of a similar size anywhere near the position given by the master for the position where his ship sank. However, the wreck of the *Ajax* could possibly be these remains, which are very old and well decayed. It is orientated in an ENE to WSW direction and lies on a seabed of sand, mud and gravel in a general depth of 72 m (LAT). The wreck covers an area of 58 m in length by 25 m across with the highest part of 7 m being at the eastern end. This should make a good boat-angling venue, with many more wrecks in the area to choose from.

UNITY, HM SUBMARINE

Date of Loss: 29 April 1940
Location: position withheld

This vessel was the prototype of the British Unity class (U-Class) Small Patrol Submarine. Built for the Royal Navy by: Vickers-Armstrong at Barrow-in-Furness, her pennant number was 66C (66D in 1939). The keel was laid on 19 February 1937, she was launched on 16 February 1938 and commissioned on 15 October 1938.

She had a double hull and displaced 540 tons on the surface and 740 tons under water. She measured 58.22 m in length, with a 4.88-m beam and a 4.22-m draught. The machinery consisted of two 400-hp Paxman diesel engines with a diesel-electric drive, powering two bronze screws and running at a maximum of 600 rpm. The constant rating was 380 hp at

HM S/M Unity. *(Author's collection)*

Above: Watercolour painting by submariner ERA William Fry DSM, of HM S/M Unity *sinking in accordance to the description of events given by his friend, Rob Roy McCurrach. William Fry died in HM S/M* Trooper *in 1943. (Courtesy Rob Roy McCurrach & Pamela Armstrong)*

Left: The engine room artificer's mess and some crewmen, in the closing stages of Unity's *penultimate patrol. (Courtesy Rob Roy McCurrach)*

Gus Britton, a crewman on HMS Unity *and Tribune (Courtesy Imperial War Museum)*

530 rpm. Her surface speed was 11.25 knots and her operational range was 4010 nm at 10 knots. While travelling submerged her range was 120 nm at two knots. Underwater, she used two 412-hp General Electric motors that gave nine knots. Her batteries were lead/acid and her fuel capacity was 41 tons. She was armed with six 53.34-cm (21 in.) torpedo tubes, four internal and two external, ten 53.34-cm (21-in.) torpedoes, one 105-mm (4.13-in.) forward deck gun, 160 rounds of 105-mm ammunition and no mines. Her maximum operational depth was 60.96 m (200 ft) and her peacetime complement was four officers and 23 ratings, with four more ratings during wartime.

Commanders:

15 November 1937 - Lieutenant-Commander S. H. Pinchin
7 January 1939 - Lt. Norris Edwin Cutler
15 June 1939 - Lt. J. F. B. Brown. Lt. Brown served in the boat for two months when WWII commenced and took her on eight active service patrols.
April 20th 1940 - Lt. Francis J. Brooks assumed command, but his command was short-lived, as his boat was lost after just eight days.

The U-Class boat was a simply-designed training submarine built to replace the H-Class. Rather than for the training of submariners, the boats were built to train operators of ASDIC who were based on surface warships and learning the art of submarine detection. *Unity*, *Undine* and *Ursula* were designed to carry no armaments whatsoever. After 1933 and the rise of Hitler, though, tubes were added. In order to bring them in line with the firepower of the S-class, two extra tubes were fitted as a bulbous addition to the bow. The original design of the U-Class boat had six bow torpedo-tubes (four internal and two external) but the external tubes were removed on all but the first three vessels built.

A second generation of boats, *Upholder*, *Upright, Usk* and *Utmost* also had the raised bow but did not have external torpedo tubes, as their construction was too advanced to allow for any change. *Una* and *Umpire* were built at Chatham and all the rest were built by Vickers at Barrow. The majority of U-Class boats were deployed in the North Sea and Mediterranean. All together, nineteen of these boats were lost during WWII.

Unity served in the sixth Flotilla based at Blyth, Northumberland. She did not sink any enemy vessels but her eight wartime patrols were carried out mainly in the shallow, mine-strewn waters of the Heligoland Bight and Kattegat at a time when the enemy had total superiority. During this phase, the Submarine Service suffered the worst losses in its history and the 6th lost more boats than any other flotilla. In the course of one patrol, on 5 April 1940 during the German invasion of Norway, *Unity* made an attack on *U 2*. On 9 April, a Q-ship pinned down *Unity* for several hours.

Final voyage

On 29 April 1940 a thick fog descended on the northeast coast. The commanding officer of the 6th Flotilla was in London; although a staff officer (Ops.) was on hand to advise a skipper in case he had any queries prior to sailing, no one at Blyth would take the responsibility of postponing the patrol, despite impossible conditions. In the hope that the weather might improve, *Unity*'s departure was delayed until 1730 hrs, but in fact by then visibility had deteriorated further. As usual, the Signals Distribution Office was buzzing with activity. Teleprinters rattled out minefield information updates and last-minute communications relayed from Horton's HQ. Each boat had its own pigeon hole; should a message arrive late, a WRNS messenger (Women's Royal Navy Service) sat poised on a motorbike ready to take it down to the harbour before the boat sailed.

The duty Petty Officer was usually given the responsibility of letting go a submarine, giving it permission to leave harbour. On the 29th this duty fell to Petty Officer Telegraphist Norman Drury of *Sturgeon*. Unable to see from one side of the harbour to the other, Norman was appalled to learn that the boat was to sail as planned. With visibility down to a matter of yards, this decision smacked of official madness. *Unity* cleared the wall and disappeared into the murk beyond.

Lieutenant Brooks had been ordered to Proceed with Dispatch, which was generally taken to mean that the submarine must travel on the surface to take advantage of the greater speed offered by the engines.

Lt. Trickey:

"At 1750 hrs, *Unity* rounded the fairway buoy and a course of 070 was set to make a position in the centre of the main swept channel By 1830 hrs the marker coded 20R was located, signifying the boat had now entered the main east-coast swept channel and a course of 345 degrees was set".

Despite the dreadful visibility, Brooks did not see fit to use the boat's siren to warn other vessels of his presence; after all, he did not expect to encounter any. Estimating that it would take another four hours before the boat reached Gap B through the minefield, the skipper was keen to maintain a steady eight knots. At 1900 hrs, Third Hand Lt. George Hunt stepped onto the bridge to relieve Lt. Trickey as Officer of the Watch (O.O.W.). He found the skipper, Lt. Trickey and the lookouts straining their eyes, trying to spot the next buoy, 20F. At 1907 hrs, the silence was pierced by a loud, mournful wail and the men on the bridge knew its significance only too well.

"Christ, a ship and she's close!"

More wails signified that *Unity* was sharing the channel with a convoy. Should that convoy happen to be steaming south, there was every possibility of a collision. Lt. Brooks acted quickly, ordering the helm to be put hard over, sounding *Unity*'s own feeble siren in the process. The lookouts stared through the mist to locate the ship, then another wail boomed out, this time so near, it was deafening. At 1909 hrs, looming out of the fog like some monstrous apparition, were the huge bows of a merchantman. The men on the bridge were momentarily transfixed with disbelief but collected enough to call out: 'Collision Stations, prepare to abandon ship!'

Lt Trickey:

"At 1909 I saw a merchant ship about 25 degrees on the port bow about 30 yards distant which seemed to be steering across the bow. The engines were put full astern and three short blasts were made. At 1910 the merchant struck the port bow about the bulkhead in the fore ends. The speed of the other ship appeared to be about four knots. The impact was gentle. I estimate our position to have been 55° 13.5N, 1° 19W"

Engine room artificer Rob Roy McCurrach was enjoying a cigarette down in the mess when the order to abandon ship came. Concluding it was an exercise, a collective groan broke out, for the sailors resented any interruptions of their otherwise ordered lives.

Rob Roy:

"I felt a bump up for'rard, no worse than coming alongside with an inexperienced boat handler. Telegraphs clanged 'Full Astern'. Chiefy Potter was galvanised into action. He shot through the Control Room to grab the Engine Room bulkhead just before a young seaman was about to shut it"

Had the door been shut against them, the Engine Room staff would have been asphyxiated by the diesels before they had the opportunity of shutting them down.

'Abandon ship' came the command.

The submarine went astern on her motors. Already taking on a bows-down angle, Brooks realised it was now a case of keeping her afloat for as long as possible to allow the crew to escape. Rob Roy slowly became aware that the emergency was for real:

... "Still sitting in the Mess, watching all this activity and fearful of being in someone's way, I heard Nat ask, 'You staying, Bob?'

I heard the engines being stopped and shut down. Charlie Foster and Dusty Miller came into the Control Room from aft. The First Lt. stood at the foot of the ladder.

'Can we take a D.S.E.A set?'

'Take anything you like', replied First Lt. John Low.

'Anything?' I looked round quickly. 'I'd like a sextant, a pair of binoculars and a telescope. And I wouldn't mind the Engine Room clock.' After all it had governed my life, night and day, awake or asleep."

The crew made their way up the ladder and crowded onto the bridge. As they climbed, Lieutenant Low called out reassuringly: 'No hurry lads, there's only three feet on the depth gauge.'

As Rob Roy dithered over his choice of souvenirs, he became aware of the Wardroom Steward urging him up the ladder:

"Up you go, Bob!'

'Oh no, up you go. You were here first.'

'Six feet of water showing on the gauge!' called out John Low.

I glanced round quickly. Nothing looked wrong. All lights on, the Mess neat and tidy. Curtains a bit off-centre and we were slightly bows-down. I went up to the bridge and heard the Captain shout, 'Some of you, down to the casing!'

With the submarine assuming an angle of 25 degrees, it dawned on the crew that Unity was finished. A short distance away, they could just discern the bulk of *Atle Jarl*, the Norwegian freighter, which had accidentally rammed them and was now hove to with its lifeboat lowered. Already submariners were entering the freezing water swimming towards it. Catching sight of the heads bobbing about in the swell, Lt. Brooks ordered: 'I must have the main motors stopped!'

Rob Roy knew why immediately:

"Of course, those screws would mince us. Knowing how to stop them, I shouted, 'Right Sir, I'll go', and turned to re-enter the boat, nearly treading on Dusty Miller's head. Having heard the last order, he said, 'I'll go, Bob, I'm better placed."

As Dusty clambered back down the ladder to join First Lt. Low, Rob Roy made his way down from the bridge to the casing.

"Water filled my shoes so I kicked them off. Through stockinged feet I felt the screw vibrations stop. I knew I could now swim away to safety. The sea was bitterly cold – so cold it took my breath away. Silly thoughts ran through my head, such as 'I bet I catch a chill' or, 'what I really need is a piece of my mother's blackberry and apple pie'. I wanted company. I didn't want to die alone. On spotting a head at the top of a wave I swam in that direction. 'Pusser' Hill was lying on his back, ears underwater, so I reached out and pulled his hair. "Pusser, have you a lifebelt?"

'No.'

'A D.S.E.A set?'

'No, not a thing, You okay?'

We trod water and saved our breath. The bow was well underwater now and lacking the restraining force of the motors on Full Astern."

At 1929 hrs and without warning, the stern swung up to a near vertical position, hung motionless for a few seconds: then, with her ensign still flying proudly, H.M.S/M *Unity* plunged to the bottom of the North Sea, taking John Low and Dusty Miller with her. Rob Roy and 'Pusser' had no time to dwell on it

"There was no break in the waves, just a strong oily swell. At the top of one I saw a lifeboat and a good dozen swimmers. I grabbed 'Pusser' and gasped 'Come on... swim!' We headed in the direction of the lifeboat and were making progress when it altered course. This was quite demoralising."

Rob Roy and 'Pusser' had drifted away from the main knot of swimmers. All around them miniature acts of courage and endurance were being played out. A man was drowning, his hands raised in a final gesture of resignation when Stoker Burville swam over to support him, risking his own life in the process. As the last man jumped from the bridge, the submarine had lurched over, trapping Charlie Foster against the bridge telegraphs. 'Chiefy' Potter spotted his predicament, refusing to leave him even though *Unity* was really gathering speed in her plunge to the bottom. Potter pulled Foster's D.S.E.A. set over his head as he frantically set about freeing him. Both were dragged down some distance when the formation of an air bubble allowed Potter to unhook Charlie from the repeater bar.

The two men surfaced together but Charlie had not followed D.S.E.A, drill, having failed to open the exhaust valve on his set. Potter turned to find his lifeless body, but still he refused to abandon his 'sprog' to the deep. Meanwhile Stoker Burville and the drowning man had reached the lifeboat when Alf spotted another swimmer in difficulty. Without hesitation, Burville turned his back on safety to return to the perishing water. He swam over to the man and hauled him to safety. Lieutenants Hunt and Trickey chose to remain in the water, a particularly courageous decision on the part of Trickey who could not swim. Eventually Rob Roy and 'Pusser' caught up with the rest:

"At last we made it and hung from the gunwales, whacked. To my right, in an equally sorry state, bobbed the Captain. 'Give us a hand!' shouted 'Pusser', as loud as he could. The men in the lifeboat just sat like numbed, frozen effigies. 'I can't hang on much 1onger, Mac. Can you pull me up?' I shook my head. 'No.' 'Look, push my left foot up and hook my heel over the gunwale.' 'Pusser' did this and with a great effort, I managed to scramble into the boat, then I turned and pulled him up. Between us we did the same for the captain"

They found themselves opposite Alf Potter and Charlie Foster, who although not dead, appeared to be in a very bad way.

"Charlie Foster lay in front of me, slumped in a heap, out cold, a flat D.S.E.A. set strapped to his chest. A green slime was oozing from his open mouth. He looked near to death. Suddenly a brand new tin of Grey's cigarettes was thrust under my nose and someone asked me 'Smoke?' I took one gratefully. Now that was clever. How did he keep them dry? The matches too! I puffed away luxuriously."

The submariners were helped onboard *Atle Jarl* by the anxious Norwegian crew. The ship had left Methil in Fife earlier that day in convoy, bound for the Tyne with a cargo of coal and coke. It had been estimated that the FS convoy should have been off Blyth by 1930. Tragically, Lt. Brooks was unaware of this and *Unity* had blundered directly into the course of the oncoming ships. . Each survivor was treated to a large glass of whisky while a scratch roll-call was made. The drink was enough to revive Charlie Foster who was now observed to be 'full of beans and grinning sheepishly'.

Apart from Low and Miller, two other men were missing: Stoker Shelton and A.B. Hare, last seen in the water making their way towards the lifeboat. Much earlier these men were known to have purchased some heavy boots sold off by Blyth Fire Station at a bargain price. They were known to have been wearing them at the time of the collision. The survivors solemnly concluded that these boots must have dragged them to their deaths. Indeed, Chief Engine Room Artificer Potter declared that his decision to kick them off before he entered the water had saved his life. When *Atle Jarl* anchored off the mouth of the Tyne, Rob Roy volunteered for lookout duties, wrapped in the Norwegian skipper's greatcoat. Next morning a motor launch picked up the survivors, landing them at North Shields Fish Quay.

Transport arrived in the form of some ancient fish lorries. For Lt. Brooks, already at the end of his tether, this was all a little too much. He telephoned HMS *Elfin* to demand more suitable transport. A short time afterwards, a brand new coach arrived to take the weary sailors back to Blyth, but Alf Potter did not remain with the rest. He left in a fast, hydrophone-equipped launch for the last known position of *Unity*. The launch stopped off Cresswell, where, more in hope than expectation, Potter listened in for any sounds which might indicate that Lt. Low and Miller were alive but trapped. There was just the chance that they had been able to shut the hatch before *Unity* sank. In these circumstances, they would have reverted to their D.S.E.A. sets and attempted to escape but in his heart, Potter knew that even if they had been able to escape and reach the surface, they would not have survived for very long. Chief E.R.A. Potter remained at sea until darkness and intense cold forced him to abandon his vigil.

Lt. Francis Brooks personally broke the bad news to Mrs Marjorie Low, then serving as a Wren Officer at *Elfin*. Simultaneously a telegram was sent to the home of Mrs Miller, informing her that the Submarine Service had claimed yet another of her sons, his caul having failed to protect him. The next day Rob Roy attended a compulsory medical with the base doctor.

"The M.O. asked me, 'How do you feel?' I was tempted to say, tired, jubilant, sad, cross...that 1 had become enormously attached to that little boat, that I had lost a significant part of that which made me tick. That I had a brush with death and there's nothing like it for making you realise how good it feels to be alive. As it was, knowing that survivors automatically get fourteen days leave, I replied, 'Fine, sir.' I was in two minds to add, 'Ask me when I get back.'

As experienced submariners, both Lt. Low and Henry Miller would have been aware of the risks when they volunteered to go back inside the boat. In so doing, they sacrificed their own lives to save those of their mates. Their courage was initially recognised with the award of the British Empire Medal, but this was later exchanged for the George Cross.

On 23 May, an Admiralty Inquiry was held at *Elfin* into the loss *of Unity*. Each witness was carefully examined and cross-examined and it rapidly became obvious that Lt. Brooks had been totally unaware of the southbound convoy. This was odd because there was little doubt that an Admiralty signal warning of its approach had been received at the Signals Distribution Office (S.D.) in *Elfin*, well before *Unity* was due to sail. The key questions were why Brooks had not been informed of Signal 1428/29/4, and, if the skipper had not known about its contents, had anyone else?

Chief Yeoman of Signals Christopher Reading remembered seeing the message come tapping through the teleprinter, and he had made sure he placed it in the appropriate pigeon hole ready for collection by Tom Moon, *Unity*'s signalman. Signalman Walter Warren corroborated this evidence. He too had seen the signal still awaiting collection when he came off duty at 1600 hrs but, interestingly, his relief, Tel. Percy Marks, had no recollection whatsoever of this message. It was a submarine signalman's responsibility to collect all available information from the S.D. Office before handing it over to the first lieutenant prior to sailing. The evidence of Thomas Moon was therefore of crucial importance. Moon's career to date had been exemplary. 'Shiner' Moon was insistent he had no knowledge whatsoever of Signal 1428/29/4. He was certain it had not been among the bundle of Q.7 messages he had collected from the S.D. Office. Moon assured the inquiry that, in keeping with routine practice, everything in the *Unity* pigeonhole had been handed to Lt Low. Obviously the inquiry was at a major disadvantage in that virtually all hard evidence had gone down with the boat, as had Lt. Low. Without his evidence, Moon's account could neither be disproved nor corroborated. Yet not all the available evidence was considered; only officers and selected ratings were called to give evidence. The court did not hear the disturbing tales of signals regularly ending up in the wrong pigeonholes, or of messages spasmodically appearing on the wrong submarines. In fact the inquiry was remarkably selective with regard to the material it wished to consider. A civil court would have doubtless reached an open verdict but this was not a civil court. Admiral Sir Max Kennedy Horton added the following conclusion:

"It appears most probable that the signal was in fact read by Leading Signalman Moon, who failed to show it to the Commanding Officer. I consider however that the probability of obtaining sufficient evidence to secure conviction of this rating for the offence is remote and that the assembly of a court martial is not justified under present conditions".

Max Horton 567/SM172

Francis Brooks was censured for his failure to discuss last minute developments with the Intelligence Officer. It was also noted that *Unity* had been travelling at high speed in bad visibility. The court did not see fit to question why the boat had ever been allowed to sail in such adverse conditions in the first place. While there was glowing praise for the way in which the crew of *Unity* had conducted themselves, the proceedings did little to dispel a lingering suspicion that the verdict was a whitewash. By deflecting the lion's share of the blame onto a rating, Admiralty had deftly sidestepped some embarrassing questions.

Submarine ace Cdr. 'Dead Eye Dick' Cayley demonstrated his view of the proceedings by selecting 'Shiner' Moon for his signalman, first on the crack submarine *Utmost*, then on *P311*. Both men died when *P311* sunk in early January 1943. As for Rob Roy, he was handed a draft-chit for Blockhouse. Blyth had been his home for the past six traumatic months; now it was time to say farewell to the people who had shown him such kindness:

"I packed my kit, then joined Cookem for one last run ashore in Blyth. We went to Seghini's for coffee and then, just like the old days, took all six girls to the cinema, walked them back home and then stepped out to the Watsons for a very special supper. Mr and Mrs. Watson were in tears when I left. They admonished me to be careful and come back soon'. This, to my eternal regret, I never managed to do."

Extracts from 'In Fear and Affection' reproduced by kind permission of Rob Roy McCurrach DSM **

First Lieutenant John Low and Able Seaman Henry Miller were posthumously awarded the Empire Gallantry Medal, which was later exchanged for the George Cross.

The crew of *Unity* was broken up and the submariners given a choice between joining two of the new U-class boats under construction at the time, *Upright* and *Utmost*. Lt. Commander Francis J. Brooks transferred to the Admiralty's Operations Division Staff and was later killed in an air crash.

The crewmen who died on *UNITY* were:

Hare, James, Able Seaman (25 years)
Low, John, Lieutenant GC (29 years)
Miller, Henry GC (39 years)
Shelton, Cecil, Stoker (21 years)

Friendly fire incidents were common during WWII and convoys opened fire and frequently tried, unwittingly, to run down the British submarines. Coastal command also often attempted to bomb the boats, particularly, for some unknown reason, when they were off Sunderland.

Wrecksite

The author has been requested not to divulge the location of the wreck of HM S/M Unity to save it from the same fate as all of the German U-boat wrecks lost off the English northeast and east coast; those boats have all been looted for artefacts and non-ferrous metal and explosives have even been used on some of them, even though the majority are war-graves.

HEROS, EX HERO

Date of loss: 23 August 1918
Wreck: ★★
Depth: 48 m
Reference: 55 13'.850 N 001 24'.337 W
Location: 3.91 nm NE of Beacon Point, Newbiggin-by-the-Sea

The *Heros* (Official No. 71) was a steel-hulled 354-ton Swedish steam cargo vessel that measured 39.11 m in length, with a 6.85-m beam and 3.96-m draught. William Lindbergs Mekaniske Verkstader, Stockholm, who also manufactured the machinery, built and completed her as Yard No. 171; she was launched her as the schooner-rigged *Hero* in 1884 for Ångfartygs AB Hero, Göteborg. The single screw was powered by a 37-nhp two-cylinder compound steam engine that used one boiler. She had one deck and a small bridge structure.

From 1904 to 1908, she had the same owner but was managed by A. F. Magnusson. In March 1915, the *Hero* was sold to Trawl AB Sill, Göteborg, and K. Engström was the manager.

In 1917, the manager was A. Quirist.

From December 1917, Rederi AB Vala, Helsingborg was the registered owner and she was renamed *Heros*; Otto Hillerström was the manager.

Final voyage

At 1445 hrs on 23 August 1918, the *Heros* was sighted eight miles SSE of Coquet Island by SMU *UB 112*, which was a KDM submarine commanded by Oblt.z.S. Wilhelm Rhein. *UB 112* then pursued the steamer before sinking it with a torpedo without any warning at 1505 hrs (CT). The little coaster was on passage from Göteborg for the Tyne with a cargo of rough wood pulp and carrying a crew of ten men and two women; two men were killed in the explosion and another man was injured. The crewmen who died were:

Adolfsson-Adén, Oskar Gustaf, 36 years, Able Seaman
Probst, Johan Herman. 25 years, Stoker

The injured man, who was left permanently disabled, was an ordinary sailor called Sven Olof Smedberg.

LCWLR 1914–18, p. 231; American Lloyd's Register of American and Foreign Shipping, 1857–1900; Starke Schell Registers; ANCL 1914–18, p. 117.

Wrecksite

The wreck, which is probably that of the *Heros*, is orientated in an ESE to WNW direction. It lies on a seabed of sand, mud, rock and stones in a general depth of 48 m (LAT). The wreck is totally collapsed and well broken up, with its boiler and engine exposed and surrounded by a mass of twisted steel plates and broken machinery. The wreck stands 3.6 m high and covers an area 24 m long and 7 m across, with little of interest to see, although a number of crustaceans have taken up residence.

RAGNHILD, EX BIANCA

Date of loss: 27 April 1917
Wreck: ★★★★
Depth: 46 m
Reference: 55 13'.900 N 001 25'.093 W
Location: 3.58 nm NE of Beacon Point, Newbiggin-by-the-Sea

The Ragnhild *in earlier times as Adolph Halvorsen's steamer* Bianca.
(Courtesy of the Norwegian Maritime Museum)

The *Ragnhild* was a steel-hulled 1117-ton Norwegian steam cargo ship that measured 69.79 m in length, with a 10.66-m beam and a 4.57-m draught. Bergen Mekaniske Verksteder, Bergen, in Norway built and completed her as Yard No. 157 in May 1909 and launched her as the *Bianca* for Adolph Halvorsen, Bergen. The single screw was powered by a three-cylinder triple expansion steam engine that used one boiler. The cylinders measured 41.91 cm, 66.04 cm and 111.76 cm with a 76.2-cm stroke (16½ in., 26 in. and 44 in. with a 30-in. stroke). Bergen Mekaniske Verksteder, Bergen manufactured the engine and ancillary machinery. She had one deck. The designated code recognition signal letters were: MFPW.

In 1915, Aktieselskapet Dampskipsselskapet Bianca was the registered owner and Adolph Halvorsen the manager.

From June 1916, Dampskipsselskapet Aktieselskapet Ragnhild of Haugesund renamed her *Ragnhild* and they were the registered owners at the time of loss; Haakon Christensen, Haugesland was the manager.

N. H. Hartmark of Kristiania managed her in 1917.

Final voyage

On 27 April 1917, the KDM mine-laying submarine SMU *UC 29*, commanded by Oblt.z.S. Ernst Rosenow, torpedoed and sank the *Ragnhild* without any warning, ten nm NNE of St. Mary's Island. Captain H. E. Gynther was in charge of the steamer, which was *en route* from the Tyne to Skien in Norway with a general cargo, including furnace fuel-oil and coke; a crewman and a passenger were lost:

De Silva, Bernardo, Donkeyman from Lisabon
Larsen, Torbjørn, passenger from Kristiania

Accident Statements for Norwegian Ships Sunk in Wartime: 1814–1918; LCWLR 1914–18, p. 125; Starke Schell Registers; ANCL 1914–18, p. 96.

Wrecksite

The wreck, probably that of the *Ragnhild,* is orientated in an almost S to N direction. It lies on a firm seabed of mud, sand and shells in a general depth of 46 m (LAT). The wreck is very substantial, standing up to 8 m high and covering an area 84 m long and 25 m across. It is, however, collapsed and well broken up with lots of scattered debris all around. Large pollack and shoals of the pout whiting can usually be observed, especially around the higher points, so the wreck should make an interesting boat-angling venue.

SVAVA, ex BJØRN

Date of loss: 10 March 1944
Wreck: ★★★★★
Depth: 52 m
Reference: 55 14'.582 N 001 18'.952 W
Location: 6.95 nm ENE of Beacon Point. Newbiggin-by-the-Sea

The *Svava* (Official No. 167614) was a steel-hulled 1163-ton British steam cargo ship that measured 71.12 m in length, with a 10.46-m beam and a 4.97-m draught. Kjøbenhavns Flydedok and Skibsverft, Copenhagen built and completed her as Yard No. 44 on 9 February 1904; she was launched as the *Bjørn* on 16 December 1903 for Dampsk. Selsk. Viking, Copenhagen, Denmark; A.O. Andersen and Co. was the manager. The single screw was powered by a 131-nhp three-cylinder triple expansion steam engine that used two single-ended boilers working at a pressure of 165-lb psi, with four corrugated furnaces, 4.45 sq.m (48 sq.ft) of grate surface and 177.63 sq.m (1912 sq.ft) of heating surface, giving ten knots. The cylinders measured 45.72 cm, 73.66 cm and 121.92 cm with an 83.82-cm stroke (18 in., 29 in. and 48 in. with a 33-in. stroke). Kibjnhavns Flydk and Skbsv manufactured the engine and ancillary machinery. She had one steel deck and deep framing, four bulkheads cemented, a 6.7-m poop deck, an 18.2-m bridge deck and 7.9-m forecastle. She was classed as 100 A1. The designated code recognition signal letters were: MJKZ.

In 1914, she was renamed *Svava* by Dampsk. Selsk. Valkyrien, who purchased her. They used the same manager.

Det Forenede Dampskibs Selskab, Copenhagen was the owner in 1926 and she was registered in Elsinore, Denmark. From 1931 to 1939 she was registered in Middelfart, Denmark.

The Belgian government requisitioned the ship at Antwerp on 9 April 1940, and on 10 May 1940, she reached England with a Dutch crew. The Ministry of War Transport (MoWT), London became the owners and S. Marshall and Co. was appointed Crown nominee manager.

Final voyage

On 10 March 1944, the *Svava* was under the command of Captain Niels Hansen Christensen when she sank following a collision with the 7130-ton cargo steamer *Fort Beausejour* (1943 – Ministry of War Transport (MoWT), London), east of Cresswell, Northumberland. She was sailing independently and without escort on a voyage from Warkworth, Northumberland to the Thames with a cargo of coal; six of her crew were lost:

Christensen, Niels Hansen, 61 years, Master MM
Clausen, Harry Simmel Kjaer, 27 years, 2nd Eng. Officer MM
Gavin, James, 42 years, Fireman and Trimmer MM
Hammershof, Sofus, 43 years, Fireman and Trimmer MM
Sorensen, Christian, 37 years, Chief Engineer Officer MM
Theoodosen, Hans Nikolai, 37 years, Third Eng. Officer

CWGC; LCR 1944, p. 8 (f); Starke Schell Registers

Wrecksite

The wreck is orientated in an E to W direction and lies on a seabed of mud, fine sand and shells in a general depth of 52 m (LAT). It is sitting upright and completely intact. The top of the bridge structure, which is roofed in a type of concrete mixture as a protection against bombs, is half-collapsed onto the deck. The walkways are intact, as are the handrails around them. The wreck is reported to be very photogenic. Unfortunately, much of the navigational and steering aids have been removed from the site, even though this wreck is the grave of six crewmen. It has a fair number of soft corals on it and lots of big fish can be found all around the wrecksite, so it should be an excellent boat-angling venue.

ALBANO

Date of loss: 2 March 1940
Wreck: ★★★★★
Depth 49 m
Reference: 55 15'.387 N 001 22'.068 W
Location: 5.82 nm NE of Beacon Point, Newbiggin-by-the-Sea

The *Albano* (Official No. 133420) was a steel-hulled 1176-ton British steam cargo ship that measured 76.25 m in length, with an 11.32-m beam and 4.44-m draught. Earle's Ship Building and Engineering Co. Ltd. at Hull built and completed her as Yard No. 593 on 13 January 1913; she was launched on 28 November 1912 for Thomas Wilson, Sons and Co. Ltd. at Hull.

The single screw was powered by a 168-nhp three-cylinder triple expansion steam engine that used one single-ended boiler and gave 10.75 knots. The cylinders measured 48.26 cm, 78.74 cm and 134.62 cm with a 91.44-cm stroke (19 in., 31 in. and 53 in. with a 36-in. stroke). Earle's Ship Building and Engineering Co. Ltd. manufactured the engine and ancillary machinery. She had a cruiser stern, one steel deck, water ballast and was later equipped with electric lighting. The *Albano* was fitted with one Brine Carb. Anhy. refrigerating appliance manufactured by Haslam Foundry and Engineering Co. Ltd. in 1912; it used a silicate cotton for insulating the two cargo chambers that had a combined capacity of 465.81 cubic.m (16 450 cubic.ft). The designated code recognition signal letters were: MDWB.

From 1917, Ellerman's Wilson Line, Ltd. Hull was the registered owner.

Final voyage

On 2 March 1940, the *Albano* was under the command of Captain Hutton when she detonated a German-laid mine and foundered in two minutes, 128.5° and 7.6 miles from the Coquet lighthouse. Ten of her crew were rescued by the Hull steam trawler *Stella Corino* and landed at an east coast port, while a warship picked up the other survivors. Amongst those rescued was the first mate, Mr H. J. Arnotte of Hull, who said he had been torpedoed six times in the Great War. The *Albano* was on passage from Hull for Bergen, carrying a general cargo which included 986 tons of coal and 268 tons of tar. The following nine crewmen were lost:

Anderson, Emil, Boatswain (Bosun) MM
Cherry, M.B., 23 years, Radio Officer MM
Hickey, R.P., 37 years, Able Seaman MM
Holland, Guy Ernest, 36 years, 2nd Officer MM
Hutton, Sydney, 51 years, Master MM
Mason, Alfred, 53 years, Chief Engineer Officer MM
Shepherd, Conrad, 48 years, Fireman and Trimmer MM
Short, Albert Reginald, 38 years, Able Seaman MM
Smith, W., 38 years, Sailor MM

LCWLR 1939–45, p. 47; BVLS 1939–45, p. 4; CWGC; LR 1939–40; No. 69320 (A).

Wrecksite

The wreck is orientated in a SE to NW direction and lies on a seabed of fine sand, mud, gravel and black shells in a general depth of 49 m (LAT). It is intact, standing about 8 m high, covering an area of 82 m in length by 21 m across, but is collapsed and well broken up. Lots of big cod and pollack have been reported all around this wreck and it is a popular venue for the angling charter boats from Blyth. Some large crustaceans have also been observed amongst the wreckage. The wreck is also the grave of the nine crewmen who went down with their ship, so it should be treated with respect.

BULLGER, EX CARTMEL

Date of Loss: 13 March 1941
Wreck: ✯✯
Depth: 8 m
Reference: 55 15'.182 N 001 32'.410 W
Location: In Druridge Bay, 4.86 nm S of Coquet Lighthouse

The *Bullger* (Official No. 125902) was a steel-hulled 304-ton steam tug that measured 39 m in length, with a 7.9-m beam and 3.65-m draught. Vickers Sons and Maxim Ltd. at Barrow-on-Furness built and completed her as Yard No. 358 in October 1907; she was launched as the tug *Cartmel* on 13 August 1907 for Furness Railway Co. Barrow. A pair of two-cylinder compound steam engines that developed 184 nhp and used two boilers powered the two screws, using two separate shafts. The cylinders measured 53.34 cm and 106.68 cm with a 60.96-cm stroke (21 in. and 42 in. with a 24-in. stroke). Vickers Sons and Maxim Ltd. also manufactured the engine and ancillary machinery. She had one deck, water ballast and was later equipped with wireless. The designated code recognition signal letters were: MDGN.

On 24 January 1919, the *Cartmel* had the 4076-ton British steamer *Domingo de Larrinaga* in tow close to Dingle Bay Harbour. Naval authorities sent out a six-inch pump to assist and the steamer was later anchored up in Ventry Harbour.

In 1922, London, Midland and Scottish Railway Co. London purchased her.

Redhead and Dry's Tugs Ltd. Newcastle was the registered owner early in 1934, but sold her soon after to Leith, Towage and Salvage Co. Leith, who renamed her *Bullger (2)* and Charles George (Gus) Bonner DSC, VC became the Skipper/Chief Salvage Officer.

In the summer of 1919, Gus Bonner, DSC and VC, was appointed assistant salvage officer with the Leith Towage and Salvage Company, Leith and later promoted to Chief Salvage Officer; he remained with them until he left in August 1940 to begin salvaging metal for the war effort with the British Iron & Steel Corporation (BISCO). Gus died at his home in Edinburgh at the age of 67 on 8 February 1951. He had won both the DSC and VC. On 7 June 1917, when HMS *Pargust* sank an enemy submarine, Gus Bonner had been in charge of two guns which, according to the citation, 'he worked most efficiently'. He was awarded a DSC for action with enemy submarines on 20 July 1917.

VC, 2 November 1917

And, on 2 November 1917, he was awarded a VC 'for magnificent discipline and gallantry displayed ... on the Q-Ship HMS *Dunraven* on 8th August, 1917, in an action with an enemy submarine. H.M. the King has been pleased to state that "greater bravery than was shown by all officers and men on this occasion can hardly be conceived". Lieutenant Bonner, having been blown out of his control station by the first explosion of a depth charge due to shell fire, crawled back into the four-inch gun hatch with the gun's crew of six men, well aware that it was only a matter of time before the magazine and depth charges below them would explode. They remained there until it happened. The gun was shifted bodily, and the gun's crew were blown up in the air, one man blown overboard, but fortunately none of them were killed, and only four wounded.

Gus Bonner's most dramatic incident occurred in November 1934, when the *Bullger (2)* and her crew were involved in the salvage of the Icelandic trawler *Geysir*, which had run onto the rocks at Torness Point. The Longhope lifeboat rescued the crew of 17 men and one woman. Gus Bonner and his salvage crew of 14 worked for 36 hours in terrible weather and mountainous seas until the trawler was refloated. Six members of the crew went on board the *Geysir* to man the pumps, while Gus and the rest of his men were towing from the *Bullger*. Without warning, after being towed for two and a half hours, the wooden hull of the *Geysir* started to break up and she began to sink. With the trawler going down rapidly, the 80 fathoms (73 m) of steel tow-rope between the two boats were slipped off and the *Bullger* raced back to the trawler. With just seconds to spare and despite the heavy seas, the men aboard made a hasty retreat from the sinking wreck and jumped across the space between the two boats. Within three minutes of the first sign of danger, she had disappeared beneath the water.

On 30 November 1935, during a howling gale, the *Bullger*, with the help of tide and wind, succeeded in refloating the 1600-ton Marius Nielson steamer *Elisabeth of Copenhagen*, which had run aground in a southwesterly gale on Johnstone's Point at Campbeltown and had been on the rocks for over a month; her crew had been rescued by local people who had braved the dreadful weather. When the ship's captain and chief engineer managed to board the vessel two days later, they had found her firmly lodged on the reef. Gus Bonner in *Bullger* towed the ship into Campbeltown harbour.

On 26 January 1936, the *Bullger* was in attendance four miles north of Whitby when the 316-ton Icelandic steam trawler *Andri* grounded on Kelder Steel; she later refloated. At 1323 hrs on 27 August 1938, Wick radio station received a wireless message from the German steamer *Helios* requesting help; the *Bullger* with Gus Bonner, now the Chief Salvage Officer, responded and assisted the ship, taking her in tow to Aberdeen Roads. They arrived at Aberdeen Bay at 0900 hrs on the 28th and the *Helios* berthed in the harbour later that day to allow divers to inspect the hull for damage.

There were in fact two different salvage vessels called *Bullger* with which Gus Bonner was involved during his time spent working with Leith Towage and Salvage Company. The first salvage tug was the iron-hulled 364-ton *Bullger* (Official No. 99990), which was built and completed by H. McIntyre and Co. Paisley as yard number 103 in February 1883 and launched as the salvage tug *Storm Cock* (Official No. 87932) on 7 December 1883 for W. B. Hill, Liverpool. She measured 49.07 m in length and had a 7.46-m beam and a pair of two-cylinder compound steam engines with two screws. The first master was W. Williamson.

On 22 April 1885 she was purchased by the Admiralty as a Fleet tug, equipped with four three-pounders and renamed *Traveller*. On 27 June 1903, the tug sank following a collision with the 12 000-ton HMS *Euryalus*, but was raised on 7 January 1904.

On 1 May 1920 she was purchased by Crichton Thompson.

In 1921, Leith, Towage and Salvage Co purchased and renamed her *Bullger*; Gus Bonner (DSC and VC) joined the company in the summer of 1919.

The following are some of the jobs Gus Bonner and *Bullger* were involved in:

On 7 January 1929, the 4887-ton liner *Idaho* (1903 – Ellerman's Wilson Line, Ltd. Hull) had attempted to enter Aberdeen harbour during a dense fog and heavy seas, but local tugs lost control of the ship and she ended up stuck firmly on the beach about one and a half miles north of the town. The ship had been transporting flour and oil from Hull and Aberdeen to New York. A local salvage company, followed by a team from Newcastle, made a number of unsuccessful attempts to refloat her. Huge crowds would gather and the local newspapers had a field day, It was not until May, however, that Gus Bonner, with his salvage crew and tug *Bullger* were called upon to have a go. After 11 weeks of hard work and skill, deliberately flooding parts of the ship while pumping other parts out and gradually manoeuvring the ship into the best position in conjunction with the tide, she was at last refloated on 16 July and towed into Aberdeen harbour. Gus and his team made the salvage company more than £10 000 for that job.

In June 1930, Gus and *Bullger* were involved in the salvage of the 739-ton steam collier *Beauport* (1920 – Sea Transport Co. Ltd. Guernsey) which had been wrecked on Little Russell Rocks off St Peter Port, Guernsey on 16 February. Crowds lined the foreshore and pleasure craft looked on as Gus and his team, using two submarines to act as pontoons, lifted the ship in what one newspaper described as 'an underwater trapeze.'

In 1932, Gus Bonner in *Bullger* tried unsuccessfully to salvage the Grimsby steam trawler *Marz* (GY.182), which had stranded in dense fog on Langaton Point, Stroma while homeward-bound from Iceland. Stroma L.S.A. fired a rocket line aboard her and connected up the breeches buoy while Longhope and Thurso lifeboats stood by, but they could not get alongside the vessel until the tide eased up. Some of the crew from the *Marz* were taken to Thurso by lifeboat. The trawler was later swept off the ledge by heavy seas and sank in deep water.

On 1 June 1932, *Bullger* arrived at Aberdeen with the 490-ton steamer *Pentland Firth* (Pentland S.S. Co. Ltd. Newcastle) in tow. The vessel had stranded at Burnside near Scrabster on 11 April 1932, while voyaging from Middlesbrough to Dublin with a cargo of sulphate of ammonia. She refloated and beached at Scrabster on 14 May and was later sold for scrap.

On 18 August 1932, the *Bullger* arrived at Aberdeen from Scrabster with the steam trawler *River Avon* in tow, after the latter had gone ashore.

On their last assignment, the *Bullger* was despatched to assist the Granton Trawler *Roseberry*, which had run aground between Crail and Fife Ness in January 1934. While entering Anstruther Harbour at low tide, the *Bullger* hit rocks and became a total wreck, sinking at the end of the East Pier on 20 January 1934 and becoming a hazzard to the fishing fleet.

It was then that Leith Towage and Salvage Company had to purchase another salvage vessel, the *Cartmel*, from Redhead and Dry's Tugs Ltd. Newcastle.

Final voyage

The *Bullger* left Warkworth harbour on 13 March 1941 and was steaming south towards Blyth when she detonated a mine dropped by aircraft of the Luftwaffe. The tug sank fairly quickly, but all her crew of 12 were safely picked up in Druridge Bay.

LCWLR 1939–45, p. 202 ; IDNS, p. 29; BVLS 1939–45, p. 18 ; *The Times*: Thursday, 2 June 1932, p. 22, Issue 46149; *The Times*: Saturday, 30 November 1935, p. 18, Issue 47235; *The Times*: Monday, 29 August 1938, p. 21, Issue 48085; *The Times*: Monday, 29 August 1938, p. 21, Issue 48085; *The Times*: Friday, 31January 1936, p. 8, Issue 47286.

Wrecksite

The wreck lies on a seabed of silty sand and mud in a general depth of 8 m (LAT). It was reported as having been heavily salvaged many years ago and to be missing its two boilers, but visiting BSAC divers from Tyneside gave a different opinion in August 2006. They first located the two boilers and, after swimming forward, found the intact bow section of the tug, absolutely covered in a profusion of beautiful plumose anemones. Other pieces of wreckage can often be found after winter storms. The wreck is a spectacular sight during the summer months, when a large shoal of pout whiting gathers around the bows.

CUPAR, HMS, ex ROSSLARE

Date of loss: 15 May 1919
Wreck: ✯✯✯✯✯
Depth: 79 m
Reference: 55 16'.754 N 000 42'.437 W
Location: 28.5 nm ENE of Blyth north pier

Cupar was a steel-hulled 710-ton Aberdare class minesweeper that measured 70.4 m in length, with an 8.53-m beam and a 2.43-m draught. Archibald McMillan and Son Ltd. at Dumbarton built and completed her as Yard No. 472 in 1916; she was launched as the *Rosslare* for the Admiralty on 27 March 1918, but later that year was renamed and commissioned as HMS *Cupar*. Her two bronze screws were powered by two vertical, three-cylinder triple expansion steam engines that produced 2200-ihp using two Yarrow-type boilers and gave 16 knots. She also carried 140 tons of coal and was armed with one QF four-inch gun forward, one QF 12-pounder gun aft and two twin 0.303 in. machine guns. Her normal complement was 73.

Final voyage

Six months after the end of the First World War, HMS *Cupar* had been commissioned just 48 hours before commencing minesweeping operations on 3 May 1919. Her crew was a mixture of experienced and very inexperienced men, 40% having transferred from HMS *Penarth,* 30% being raw Mercantile Marine Reserves and 10% having transferred from HMS Haythop. Before this operation, there had been no time in port to practice action stations and even at the time of her loss, on 5 May 1919, the crew was still finding their way around their new home. The Royal Navy flotilla, comprising HMS *Sherbourne, Burslem, Cupar, Sligo, Clonmel* and *ML 318,* left Alnmouth Bay at 0300 hrs BST, with the intention of clearing the WP19 line of mines in the Yorkshire minefield.

Cupar formed the second pair of a D formation with *Sligo* and commenced operations. After the *Sherbourne* pair had brought up several mines, an explosion was heard that parted their sweep. HMS *Cupar* and *Sligo* commenced a turn to take them onto the line. At 0845 hrs, having nearly completed the turn, a violent explosion at position: 55° 18 30'N 00° 36 50'W lifted the *Cupar,* and her engines stopped. Apparently, a mine had detonated aft of, but not, apparently, against *Cupar. Sherbourne* and *ML 318* immediately closed with *Cupar* and all ships in the vicinity sent boats across to assist. The injured were removed, as were most of her crew, but a number stayed on board to try and keep the ship afloat. Engine room stokers reported severe vibration from the shaft, indicating a probable loss of screws. A survey by Lieutenant Chilcott RNVR showed that the engines, telegraphs and steering gear were crippled and that the ship was settling by the stern. The damage report described the ship's starboard side and deck as being badly buckled, with lots of rivets sheared, allowing water much access into the ship from about amidships and as far aft as the eye could see. The pumps were started and by 0920 hrs, HMS *Sherbourne* took *Cupar* in tow, heading slowly for the Tyne at four knots. The tow was going well, but she was taking take in a lot of water; by 1110 hrs, *Cupar* was in danger of sinking and the Commanding Officer signalled that the engine room was filling up rapidly. When it was clear that she was going down, the tow-wires were cut and at 1120 hrs she went down stern first, at the approximate position: 55° 17 00'N 00° 44 00'W (0GB). All boats were immediately sent over from HMS *Sherbourne,* the 96-ton RN drifter *Sea Fog* and Admiralty *ML.318* and the survivors were picked up from the water.

There was no loss of life in the incidents, but six men sustained serious, but not life threatening injuries, while another three men received slight injuries. Several of the crew were commended for their coolness and assistance during this incident, including Chief Artificer Engineer E.L. Galloway, who, although injured and shaken by the explosion, went back into the dark, steam-filled engine room to make damage assessments and to get the pumps running. Despite his injuries, he remained on board and left the ship only as she foundered, being picked up from the sea in a state of exhaustion. by HM Drifter *Sea Fog.* The survivors and injured were taken on board *Sherbourne* and *Burslem* and landed at North Shields.

Report of SNO Tyne, 18 June 1919

In trying to locate witnesses for the Courts Martial, it is clear that the injured were dispersed and cared for locally, and hard to track down. Repeated enquiries about the whereabouts of Mr E. L. Galloway, Chief Artificer Engineer RN, finally led to a note saying, 'Mr Galloway was admitted to Miss Mallet's Nursing Home, Whitley Bay on 6th May'. Mr Galloway was obviously found there, as his statement to the Court, written on 20 May, is headed: 'The Nursing Home, Promontory Terrace, Whitley Bay'.

The finding of the Court of Inquiry was that no blame was attached to the officers and crew for the loss of HMS *Cupar.* However, it was found that no provision had been made for this class of vessel to carry spars and wedges for propping up bulkheads. It was thought possible that if the bulkhead could have been supported, the ship could have been saved. An order was therefore issued to allow these stores to be carried in all other vessels in future.

ADM.1/8560/152–9/9/22; SRN Vol. 1, p. 147; *JANE's Fighting Ships of World War I.*

Wrecksite

The wreck is orientated in a more or less N to S direction and lies within the Graveyard on a seabed of sand and gravel, in a general depth of 79 m (LAT). It is completely intact and appears to be on its side, standing five metres high and covering an area 75 m in length by 12 m across, with the bridge structure still in a reasonable condition. The wreck, which is covered in soft corals, is an interesting one to explore and is not classed as a war grave. In 2005 the wreck was identified by the ship's bell. Tidal streams are very strong, but underwater visibility is usually excellent this far from shore.

ST. PAUL

Date of loss: 2 September 1914
Wreck: ★★★★★
Depth: 84 m
Reference: 55 16'.021 N 000 46'.086 W
Location: 26.2 nm ENE from Blyth piers

The S*t. Paul* (Official No. 4599) was a 2534-ton steel-hulled Swedish steam cargo ship that measured 94.48 m in length, with a 13.41-m beam and a 6.32-m draught. John Blumer and Co. at North Dock, Sunderland built and completed her as Yard No. 190 in May 1907; she was launched on 10 March 1906 for Ångfartygs AB St. George, Göteborg, who was the owner at the time of loss; W. O. Wilson was the manager. The single screw was powered by a 271-nhp three-cylinder triple expansion steam engine that used two boilers and gave 10.5 knots.

In 1913, Th. Willerding was the manager.

Final voyage

The S*t. Paul* was travelling in ballast and *en route* from Göteborg to Sunderland when she detonated a German-laid mine and sank on 2 September 1914, reported as in a position 28 miles ENE from the Tyne. The 2200-ton SMS *Albatross* and light cruiser SMS *Stuttgart* had laid the barrier of 200 mines. No lives were lost and the crew was rescued by the 1711-ton Norwegian steamer *Bruse* (1911 – AS Bonheur, Kristiania), which was *en route* from the Tyne to Stockholm with coal but returned to the Tyne and landed the men at North Shields.

Starke Schell Registers; Miramar Ship Index; Groos (1922); *Maritime Accident Statements for Norwegian Ships Sunk in Wartime: 1814–1918.*

The wreck, lying within the Graveyard, was identified after the bell was located by divers from the charter boat *Spellbinder* (skipper/owner Allan Lopez) in 2006. The S*t. Paul* is orientated in a NE to SW direction and lies on a seabed of mud, sand and shells in a general depth of 84 m (LAT). The wreck is very intact and upright, with some derricks fore and aft, but the superstructure is now collapsing. Lots of big fish and shoals of pout whiting have been observed, so this should be an excellent boat-angling venue.

WEARSIDER

Date of loss: 19 December 1925
Wreck: ★★★★
Depth: 79 m
Reference: 55 17'.752 N 001 10'.407 W
Location: 12.78 nm NE of Beacon Point, Northumberland

The *Wearsider* (Official No. 133579) was a steel-hulled 373-ton steam cargo vessel that measured 41.2 m in length, with a 7.7-m beam and a 3.12-m draught. Messrs Charles Rennoldson and Co. Ltd. South Shields built and completed her as Yard No. 171 in October 1915; she was launched on 2 July 1915 for T Steam Coasters Ltd. at Newcastle and Robinson, Brown and Co. was the manager. The single steel screw was powered by an aft-positioned 80-rhp, two-cylinder compound steam engine that used one single-ended boiler. The cylinders measured 43.18 cm and 91.44 cm with a 68.58-cm stroke (17 in. and 36 in. with a 27-in. stroke). Shields Engineering Co. Ltd. manufactured the machinery at North Shields. She had one deck, a 10.05-m quarterdeck, a 3.36-m bridge deck and 5.79-m forecastle.

Final voyage

The *Wearsider* left Perth in Scotland with a cargo of potatoes on passage to Lynn, but disappeared and was declared missing on 19 December 1925. Nothing more was ever seen of the ship and her crew until the wreck was located by sport divers from Allan Lopez's Tyne-based charter boat *Spellbinder* in 2007.

Starke Schell Registers; LR 1916–1917.

Wrecksite

The wreck, which was identified when the ship's bell was recovered, is orientated within the Graveyard in a SE to NW direction. It lies on a seabed of fine sand and mud in a general depth of 79 m (LAT). The wreck stands 6.6 m high, is upright, reasonably intact and covers an area 59 m long and 19 m across. Fair amounts of marine life, including some large fish, have adopted this wreck.

TROMØ

Date of loss: 3 October 1914
Wreck: ✯✯✯
Depth: 88 m
Reference: 55 17'.788 N 001 06'.490 W
Location: 14.86 nm ESE from Coquet Lighthouse

The *Tromø* was a steel-hulled 694-ton Norwegian steam cargo vessel that measured 53.72 m in length, with a 9.01-m beam and a 3.81-m draught. Nylands Verksted, Kristiania built and completed her as Yard No. 194 on 16 December 1908; she was launched on 25 November 1908 for Aktieselskapet Sørlandet at Arendal; Engelbrethsen and Henriksen was the manager. The single screw was powered by an aft-positioned 67-nhp three-cylinder triple expansion steam engine that used one boiler. The cylinders measured 32.02 cm, 55.34 cm and 91.44 cm with a 68.58-cm stroke (13 in., 21 in. and 36 in. with a 27-in. stroke). Nylands Verksted manufactured the engine and ancillary machinery. She had one deck. The designated code recognition signal letters were: MFLG.

Final voyage

At 0600 hrs on 3 October 1914, the Norwegian steamer detonated a mine close to the bows on the starboard side and is thought to have sunk 12 miles NE of Coquet Island. The vessel was on a voyage from Porsgrunn to Hull with a cargo of pit props and poles. Out of her crew of fourteen, two men were lost; the survivors took to a ship's boat and were picked up at 1230 hrs by the British drifter *Lerita* (SN37) of North Shields and landed there. The 2200-

ton German minesweeper SMS *Albatross* and light cruiser SMS *Stuttgart* had laid the barrier of 200 mines.

The two crewmen lost were:

Pedersen, Peder Andreas Pedersen, First Mate, from Borøen, Norway
Staubo, Nils Olsen, Cook, from Norway

Maritime Accident Statements for Norwegian Ships Sunk in Wartime: 1814–1918; LCWLR 1914–18, p. 4; Starke Schell Registers; ANCL 1914–18, p. 103; LR 1913–14, No. 1138 (T); Groos (1922).

The wreck, possibly that of the Norwegian *Tromø*, lies within the Graveyard and is orientated in a SE to NW direction. It lies on a seabed of mud, fine sand and shells in a general depth of 88 m (LAT). The wreck is upright and intact, with the upper parts collapsed, and echo soundings suggest lots of big fish shoaling over the top of it. It stands nearly five metres high and covers an area 51 m in length by 31 m wide. A large amount of sediment has built up all around the remains.

GRANGE

Date of loss: 31 December 1908
Wreck: ★★★★
Depth: 81 m
Reference: 55 17'.337 N 000 45'.570 W
Location: 27.76 nm NE of Tynemouth light

The *Grange* (Official No. 90908) was a steel-hulled 1518-ton British steam passenger/cargo ship that measured 85.34 m in length, with an 11.02-m beam and a 5.35-m draught. Wigham Richardson and Co. at Low Walker, Newcastle built and completed her as Yard No. 274 in August 1892; she was launched on 12 May 1892 for Carron Co. Grangemouth. The single screw was powered by a 622-nhp three-cylinder triple expansion steam engine that used two donkey boilers and one single-ended boiler working at a pressure of 170-lb psi, with 15 corrugated furnaces, 31.77 sq.m (342 sq.ft) of grate surface and 875.23 sq.m (9421 sq.ft) of heating surface giving 15 knots. The cylinders measured 78.74 cm, 121.92 cm and 203.2 cm with a 121.92-cm stroke (31 in., 48 in. and 80 in. with a 48-in. stroke). Wigham Richardson and Co manufactured the engine and ancillary machinery. The ship had accommodation for 40 passengers.

Final-voyage

At 0600 hrs on 31 December 1908, the *Grange* foundered in the North Sea, 35 miles NE of the Tyne, while transporting 17 passengers, the same number of crew and general cargo from Grangemouth to London. The passengers on board included sixteen shipyard workers on an excursion to London. The ship had left Grangemouth at 1900 hrs on the previous evening, under the command of Captain Ison. Soon after leaving harbour, though, she encountered heavy weather and during the early hours, the hatches were washed off and the holds gradually filled up with water, destroying the cargo. The engineers, waist-deep in water, were forced to leave their posts. At 1000 hrs lifebelts were distributed and the master gave the order to abandon ship. The lifeboats were launched and the stewardess, the only woman on board, was first to be lowered. When three lifeboats had been filled, the master left his sinking vessel and everyone got safely away. After being tossed about in the small boats for about two hours, they sighted a trawler. To make sure they were spotted, the second officer, Mr Johnson, boarded the sinking ship again and gave the distress signals. The trawler was the West Hartlepool steam trawler *Eleazer*, which picked them all up and took them into the Tyne that same afternoon. On being landed at North Shields the men were taken to the Tyne Sailor's Home for dry clothing and food.

Board of Trade Wreck Return 1908; Starke Schell Registers; American Lloyd's Register of American and Foreign Shipping, 1857–1900; Miramar Ship Index; *The Times*: Friday, 1 January 1909, p. 6, Issue 38845.

Wrecksite

The wreck, which is most probably that of the *Grange*, is orientated in a more or less N to S direction and sits in a small scour on a seabed of sand and mud in a general depth of 81 m (LAT). The wreck is still quite substantial, but is broken into two main sections, with the southern end collapsed and broken. It stands almost 7 m high at the northern end and covers an area 80 m long and 12 m across.

QUEEN WILHELMINA

Date of loss: 8 May 1915
Wreck: ✯✯
Depth: 9 m
Reference: 55 17'.332 N 001 32'.000 W
Location: 1.32-n.m SSE of Bondicarr Bush and S of Coquet light

The *Queen Wilhelmina* (Official No. 109695) was a 3590-ton steam cargo ship that measured 110.77 m in length, with a 14.07-m beam and 5.68-m draught. Sir James Laing at Deptford shipyard, Sunderland built and completed her as Yard No. 566 in October 1898; she was launched on 31 August 1898 for Neptune Steam Navigation Co. Ltd. at Sunderland; W. and T. W. Pinkney was the manager. The single screw was powered by a 387-hp, three-cylinder triple expansion steam engine that used two single-ended boilers and gave 12 knots. G. Clark Ltd. manufactured the engine and auxiliary machinery at Sunderland. She had one deck, six bulkheads cemented, a 3.04-m poop deck, a 26.21-m bridge deck and 12.49-m forecastle.

In 1903, Bolham and Swinhoe was the manager.

Furness, Withy and Co. Ltd. Sunderland was the registered owner from 1906.

Final voyage

The *Queen Wilhelmina* was in ballast and voyaging from Leith to Fowey when she was captured by SMU *U 9* on 8 May 1915, 20 miles S by E of Longstone; the ship was then torpedoed but stayed afloat and the master managed to beach her at Bondicarr Bush, just south of Coquet Island. No lives were lost, but she was to be written off as a total loss. *U 9* was a KDM U-boat commanded by Johannes Spieß, who was assigned to the Germany-based I.U-

Flottille. During the First World War, *U 9* sank twelve merchant ships totalling 7696 tons and four warships totalling 43 350 tons, before she surrendered on 26 November 1918 and was broken up at Morecambe in 1919.

Wrecksite

The wreck is orientated in an ENE to WSW direction. It lies on a seabed of sand, stones and rocks in a general depth of 9 m (LAT). What remains of the wreck is well broken up and scattered over an area 27 m long and 20 m across, with the highest parts standing no more than a couple of metres. It still makes an excellent rummage dive where anything could turn up.

INVERGYLE

Date of loss: 12 March 1915
Wreck: ★★★★
Depth: 47 m
Reference: 55 18'.748 N 001 25'.610 W
Location: 4.02 nm ESE of Coquet light

The *Invergyle* (Official No. 124159) was a steel-hulled 1794-ton British steam cargo ship that measured 84.25 m in length with a 12.31-m beam. Grangemouth and Greenock Dockyard Co. Grangemouth built and completed her as Yard No. 288 in January 1907; she was launched on 21 December 1906 for Invergyle S.S. Co. Ltd. Glasgow, who was the owner at the time of loss; Stewart and Gray was the manager. The single steel screw was powered by a 197-nhp three-cylinder triple expansion steam engine that used two single-ended boilers working at a pressure of 180-lb psi with six plain furnaces, 8.54 sq.m (92 sq.ft) of grate surface and 290.60 sq.m (3128 sq.ft) of heating surface. The cylinders measured 50.8 cm, 82.55 cm and 137.16 cm with a 91.44-cm stroke (20 in., 32½ in. and 54 in. with a 36-in. stroke). Cooper and Greig manufactured the machinery at Dundee. She had one deck and deep framing.

Final voyage

On 12 March 1915, the *Invergyle* was in ballast and on passage from Scapa Flow for Hartlepool when she was torpedoed, 12 miles NNE of the Tyne, by the KDM submarine SMU *U 23*, commanded by Oblt.z.S. Hans Schultheß. No prior warning of the attack was given but all of her crew survived.

BVLS 1914–18, p. 5; LCWLR 1914–18, p. 9; Tennent (1990), p. 215; Starke Schell Registers.

Wrecksite

The wreck lies on a seabed of sand and small stone in a general depth of 47 m (LAT). In 1970 it was reported as intact and standing 9.5 m high, with a massive hole in the side where the torpedo detonated. However, the latest information is that she has now collapsed onto the seabed, with the two boilers and engine exposed, surrounded by a huge jumbled heap of twisted steel plates, wheels, cogs and broken machinery, with copper pipes protruding out of it all. Soft corals embellish the upper structures, especially around the bow and stern areas.

Large ling and cod are to be observed amongst the wreckage and a shoal of pout whiting, usually hovers over the top of the engine area.

LAFONIA, EX SOUTHERN COAST, EX DOROTHY HOUGH

Date of loss: 26 March 1943
Wreck: ✭✭✭✭✭
Depth 49 m
Reference: 55 18'.527 N 001 24'.772 W
Location: 4.55 nm ESE of Coquet Lighthouse

The Falkland Islands company steamship Lafonia, *which sank following a collision with the 1,246 ton steamer Como, on March 26th 1943. (Author's collection: a copy of the Falkland Islands 5 pence stamp)*

The *Lafonia* (Official No. 131348) was a steel-hulled 1961-ton British steam passenger/cargo ship that measured 86.33 m in length, with a 10.99-m beam and a draught of 5.79 m. Greenock and Grangemouth Dockyard Co. Grangemouth built and completed her as Yard No. 330 in June 1911; she was launched as the *Dorothy Hough* on 29 April 1911 for Samuel Hough Ltd. Liverpool. The single screw was powered by a 249-nhp three-cylinder triple expansion steam engine that used two single-ended boilers working at a pressure of 189-lb psi, with six corrugated furnaces, 10.03 sq.m (108 sq.ft) of grate surface and 393.54 sq.m (4236 sq.ft) of heating surface, giving 12 knots. The cylinders measured 21 3/16 in., 35 in. and 57 in. with a 39-inch stroke. J. G. Kincaid and Co. Ltd. Greenock manufactured the engine and ancillary machinery. She had one steel deck, a 20.42-m poop deck, a 19.56-m bridge deck and a 9.75-m forecastle. The ship was later fitted with an echo-sounding device. She was classed as 100 A1. The designated code recognition signal letters were: GRQY.

She was renamed *Southern Coast* by Powell, Bacon and Hough Lines Ltd. Liverpool, who purchased her in 1913.

Coast Lines, Ltd. Liverpool was the registered owner from 1917 to 1936.

From 1936, Falkland Islands Co. Ltd. Liverpool (London) who was the registered owner, renamed her *Lafonia*.

Final voyage

On 26 March 1943, the *Lafonia* was sailing independently and in ballast, on passage from London for Greenock, when she sank following a collision with the 1246-ton steamer *Como* (1910 – Ellerman's Wilson Line Ltd. Hull), reported as being at position: 55° 21'N 01° 22'W.

LCR 1943, p. 9 (f) ; Starke Schell Registers.

Wrecksite

The wreck is orientated in a NE to SW direction and lies on a seabed of fine sand and mud in a general depth of 49 m (LAT). It is reasonably intact and covers an area 91 m long and 20 m wide, with the highest parts standing at 10.2 m. Soft corals are now well established on the upper parts and lots of fish shoal over the top of it, so the wreck should also make an excellent boat-angling venue. The ship's bell will almost certainly be inscribed: *Dorothy Hough 1911*.

HERRING, HM TRAWLER

Date of loss: 22 April 1943
Wreck: ★★★
Depth: 55 m
Reference: 55 19'.353 N 001 21'.724 W
Location: 6.06 nm ESE of Coquet Lighthouse

The *Herring* was a steel-hulled 358-ton (670-tons) British Fish Class steam trawler that measured 49.37 m in length, with a 7.69-m beam and a 3.81-m draught. She was ordered on 17 April 1942; the keel was laid by Cochrane and Sons Ltd. at Selby, Yorkshire on 1 September 1942 and completed as Yard No. 1250 on 15 April1943. She was launched as the *Herring*

(T 307) for the Royal Navy on 24 December 1942. The single screw was powered by a reciprocating (VTE) 700-ihp, three-cylinder triple expansion steam engine that used one boiler and gave 11 knots. Amos and Smith Ltd. manufactured the machinery at Hull.

The *Herring* was an Anti Submarine trawler, armed with one four-inch (10.2-cm) gun and three single 20-mm AA guns. She carried a complement of 35.

Final patrol

On 22 April 1943, HMT *Herring* was escorting convoy FN 108 when she sank following a collision with the 1596-ton British steamer *Cassard* (1920 – Ministry of War Transport, Plymouth), two nm north of the 20E buoy, northeast of Blyth. The full complement of the *Herring* was picked up by the *Cassard*, which was in the same convoy. After *Cassard* had secured her leak, she headed for the Tyne and discharged the survivors.

Cassard had previously been owned by Compagnie Nantaise des Chargeurs de l'Ouest, Nantes, but was seized at Weymouth in July 1940, after which she was allocated to Crown nominee manager, Harries Brothers and Co. Ltd. until 1945.

Official Home Command Report; BVLS 1939–45, p. 28; SRN Vol. 2, p. 167, IDNS, p. 76.

Wrecksite

The wreck, which has been identified as the *Herring* by sport divers from Allan Lopez' Tyne-based charter boat *Spellbinder*, is orientated in an E to W direction. It lies on a seabed of fine sand and mud in a general depth of 55 m (LAT). The wreck is upright and intact, stands six m high and covers an area of 44 m in length by 13 m across. Fair quantities of marine life can be found, so it should make a decent boat-angling venue.

MOTO (?)

Date of loss: 10 December 1918
Wreck: ✯✯✯✯
Depth: 55 m
Reference: 55 19'.766 N 001 22'.128 W
Location: 5.88 nm E of Coquet Island

The *Moto* (Official No. 133536) was a 1941 British steam cargo ship that measured 81.38 m in length, with an 11.58-m beam and a 5.33-m draught. S. P. Austin and Son Ltd. at Wear Dock, Sunderland built and completed her as Yard No. 268 in July 1913; she was launched on 19 June 1913 for Pelton S.S. Co. Ltd. at Newcastle. The single steel screw was powered by a 221-nhp three-cylinder triple expansion steam engine that used two single-ended boilers. G. Clark Ltd. at Sunderland manufactured the engine and ancillary machinery. She had one deck, a well-deck, four bulkheads, a 32.7-m quarterdeck, a 3.6-m bridge deck and an 8.5-m forecastle.

Final voyage

At 0540 hrs on 10 December 1918, the *Moto* sank following a collision with the 3500-ton Arethusa-class light cruiser, HMS *Galatea*, about 20 miles north of the Tyne. The *Moto* was under the command of Captain T.W. Purvis and on passage from Methil Roads for the Tyne with a cargo of coal. All of her crew were saved by Royal Navy personnel.

LR 1915/16 No. 1586 (M); Board of Trade Wreck Return 1918, p. 40; SRN Vol. 1, p. 226.

Wrecksite

The wreck, possibly that of the *Moto*, is orientated in an ENE to WSW direction. It lies on a seabed of fine sand, mud, broken shells and gravel in a general depth of 55 m (LAT). The wreck is upright, partially buried, well broken up and stands over 9 m high. It covers an area 120 m long and 30 m across and is covered in various kinds of marine life. Lots of fish have been observed, so this should make an excellent boat-angling venue.

DON (?)

Date of loss: 8 May 1915
Wreck: ✯✯✯
Depth: 56 m
Reference: 55 19'.985 N 001 21'.117 W
Location: 6.40 nm E of Coquet Island

The *Don* (Official No. 98389) was a steel-hulled 939-ton British steam cargo vessel that measured 68.7 m in length, with a 10.13-m beam and a 4.74-m draught. William Dobson and Co. Ltd. at Low Walker, Newcastle upon Tyne built and completed her as Yard No. 54 in August 1892; she was launched on 11 July 1892 for Goole Steam Shipping Co. Ltd. at Goole. The single screw was powered by a 179-hp, three-cylinder triple expansion steam engine that used two single-ended boilers and gave 12.5 knots service speed. Wallsend Slipway and Engineering Co. Ltd. near Newcastle manufactured the engine and ancillary machinery. She had one deck, five bulkheads, a 9.14-m poop deck, an 18.89-m bridge deck and a 10.05-m forecastle.

From 1905, Lancashire and Yorkshire Railway Co. at Goole was the registered owner.

Final voyage

Kapitänleutnant Johannes Spieß, who commanded the KDM submarine SMU *U 9*, torpedoed and sunk the *Don* on 8 May 1915, seven miles east of Coquet Island. The steamer was in ballast and on passage from Cromarty for Blyth. None of the crew was lost.

LCWLR 1914–18, p. 12; BVLS 1914–18, p. 6; BMS 1914–18, p. 148; LR 1915/16 No. 571 (D); Starke Schell Registers.

Wrecksite

There is no wreck of the same proportions as the *Don* anywhere near the location in which it was reportedly sunk in 1915. The author, however, does think these could be the remains. The wreck is orientated in an almost E to W direction and lies on a seabed of fine sand, mud, broken shells and gravel in a general depth of 56 m (LAT). The wreck is reasonably intact, stands 4.5 m high and covers an area 40 m long and 8 m across. A fair amount of marine life has adopted the wreck, including some large fish, so it should make a worthwhile boat-angling venue.

GEM (?)

Date of loss: 27 May 1906
Wreck: ⭑⭑
Depth: 42 m
Reference: 55 20'.160 N 001 28'.268 W
Location: 2.32 nm E of Coquet Island

The *Gem* was an iron-hulled 180-ton steam cargo vessel that measured 36.57 m in length, with a 5.79-m beam and a 2.74-m draught. John Fullerton and Co. at Paisley built and completed her as Yard No. 39 in October 1878 and launched her for Mitchell and Rae at Newburgh, Aberdeenshire. The single iron screw was powered by an aft-positioned 45-rhp, two-cylinder compound steam engine that used one boiler. Lees, Anderson and Co. manufactured the machinery at Glasgow. She had one deck and a forward hold.

Rae, J., of Ellon, Aberdeenshire owned her at the time of loss and the master was Captain A.C. Myle.

Final voyage

The *Gem* sank following a collision with the 1041-ton steamer *Altyre* (1878 – Adam and Co. Aberdeen), 4.5 miles off Coquet Island on 27 May 1906. The *Gem* was carrying a crew of seven and was in ballast, on passage from Peterhead for Seaham Harbour.

Board of Trade Wreck Report 1906.

Wrecksite

The wreck, which is probably that of the little steamer *Gem*, is orientated in an ESE to WNW direction. It lies on a seabed of mud, fine sand and stones in a general depth of 42 m (LAT). The wreck is now totally collapsed and broken up, with the highest point standing about 2 m high, and it covers an area 17 m long and 10 m across. The site consists of two cylinders and scattered broken debris, with little or nothing of any interest.

FINGAL

Date of loss: 15 March 1915
Wreck: ★★★★
Depth: 56 m
Reference: 55 20'.720 N 001 20'.562 W
Location: 6.62 nm ENE of Coquet Island

The *Fingal* (Official No. 99246) was a steel-hulled 1548-ton British passenger/cargo steamer that measured 85.34 m in length, with a 10.66-m beam, a 5.48-m draught and a moulded depth of 5.86 m. W. B. Thompson and Co. Ltd. Dundee built and completed her as Yard No. 121 in May 1894; she was launched on 22 March 1894 for the London and Edinburgh Shipping Co. Leith, who was also the owner at the time of loss. The single screw was powered by a 616-nhp three-cylinder triple expansion steam engine that used two double-ended boilers and gave 17 knots. The cylinders measured 81.28 cm, 124.46 cm and 203.2 cm with a 121.92-cm stroke (32 in., 49 in. and 80 in. with a 48-in. stroke). W.B. Thompson and Co. Ltd. also manufactured the engine and ancillary machinery at Dundee. She had a 21.03-m poop deck, a 21.03-m bridge deck and a 22.25-m forecastle.

Final voyage

The *Fingal* was torpedoed and sunk at 1050 hrs on 15 March 1915, six miles east by south of Coquet Island, by SMU *U 23*, a KDM submarine commanded by Oblt.z.S Hans Schultheß. The steamer was on passage from London for Leith with a general cargo. Twenty one of her crewmen were picked up by the fishing vessel *Ayacanora* and landed at North Shields, but six others, including a stewardess from Leith, were lost:

Gray, Thomas, 19 yrs, Ordinary Seaman MM
Hogg, Walter Lumsden, 31 yrs, Able Seaman MM
Laurenson, John, 48 yrs, Able Seaman MM
McPherson, Nellie, 26 yrs, Stewardess MM
Reibelt, Walter, 28 yrs, Fireman MM
Smith, John Harper, 54 yrs, First Mate MM

On 20 July 1915, *U 23* was herself torpedoed and sunk by the British submarine HM S/M *C27*, at position: 58.55N, 00.14E. The British boat was working in conjunction with decoy trawler HMT *Princess Louise*; 24 of the U-boat's crew were killed, but ten survived.

LCWLR 1914–18, p. 9; BVLS 1914–18, p. 5; CWGC; Jarvis (2000), Vol. V; Starke Schell Registers; Tennent (1900), p. 156.

Wrecksite

The wreck is orientated in a SSE to NNW direction. It lies on a seabed of sand and shingle in a general depth of 56 m (LAT). The wreck is upright and intact, but well collapsed with lots of nets covering much of it. Large cod have been observed all around the wreck and a shoal of pout whiting have adopted the engine area. The ship's bell identified the wreck in May 2005 and items of crockery bearing the company's motif have also been recovered. Sadly, one of the divers who identified the wreck was lost on it soon after; his body has never been found, despite rigorous searches by friends and the police.

COQUET MOUTH

Date of loss: 4 July 1940
Wreck: ★★
Depth: 7 m
Reference: 55 20'.416 N 001 33'.900 W
Location: 200 metres ENE of Amble south pier

The *Coquet Mouth* was a steel-hulled 477-ton steam-powered bucket dredger that was registered at Newcastle upon Tyne. Fleming and Ferguson at Paisley, Port Glasgow built and completed her as Yard No. 487 in 1927 and she was launched in December 1926. The single screw was powered by a three-cylinder triple expansion steam engine that used one boiler. Amble Harbour Commissioners was the owner at the time of loss.

Final voyage

On 4 July 1940, the *Coquet Mouth* was returning to port in ballast when she struck a mine, just 200 metres out from the north breakwater light at Warkworth, and three crewmen were lost. Aircraft of the Luftwaffe had laid the mine.

The following two bodies were recovered and buried ashore, in Amble West Cemetery, Northumberland:

Brown, James, 66 yrs, Deck Hand of Linthorpe, Middlesbrough, Yorkshire – Sec F 96.Grave
English, Robert Forster., 45 yrs, Mate – Sec. A. Grave 10

Tower Hill Panel 130:

The body of 35 year old Sydney Lockey, Deck Hand of Amble, Northumberland was never found.

In 1978, it was proposed to dredge a new deep-water channel up to Warkworth harbour and the wreck was discovered just to the north of it. The authorities took the decision to buoy the wreck, with the intention of dispersing it completely at a later date, but this was never done.

BVLS 1939–45, p. 7; LCWLR 1939–45, p. 96; CWGC.

Wrecksite

Just a few years ago the wreck was reported as being intact, but upside down and orientated in a northeast to southwest direction. However the latest information is that it is now breaking up, with fair amounts of copper piping and pieces of brass to be seen near the boiler. It lies on a seabed of sand, in a general depth of 7 m (LAT). Lots of coley and pollack shoal around the wreck during the summer months.

OLYMPIA (?)

Date of loss: 3 August 1916
Wreck: ☆☆
Depth: 47 m
Reference: 55 20'.702 N 001 26'.032 W
Location: 3.70 nm E by N of Coquet Lighthouse

The *Olympia* (Official No. 122687) was a steel-hulled 221-ton steam trawler that measured 36.57 m in length, with a 6.55-m-beam and a 3.5-m draught. Cook, Welton and Gemmell at Beverley in Yorkshire built and completed her as Yard No. 71 on 26 May 1905; she was launched on 23 January 1905 for Great Grimsby and East Coast Fishing Co. Ltd. Grimsby and registered as GY 62 on 26 May 1905. The single screw was powered by a 66-nhp three-cylinder triple expansion steam engine that used one single-ended boiler and gave 10.5 knots. Amos and Smith Ltd. at Hull manufactured the engine and ancillary machinery.

Final voyage

On 3 August 1916, the *Olympia*, under Skipper A. Smith, was on a return fishing trip from Grimsby when the KDM submarine SMU *UB 39*, commanded by Oblt.z.S. Werner Fürbringer captured her without loss of life, three miles east of Coquet lighthouse. The crew was ordered to abandon ship, after which Fürbringer sank the trawler by gunfire.

LCWLR 1914–18, p. 50; BVLS 1914–18, p. 110; LR 1915/16 No. 218 (O).

Wrecksite

The wreck, probably that of the *Olympia*, sits in a half-metre scour and is orientated in an ESE to WNW direction, with the bows lying at 102°. It lies on a seabed of sand and stonein a general depth of 47 m (LAT). The wreck is upright, intact, standing 5 m high, with the decking missing and covering an area 21 m long and 6 m across. Lots of small fish shoal over the wreck during the summer months.

MORLAIX, EX EDMOND TROPPEY, EX FEDALAH, EX ORAN

Date of loss: 5 May 1942
Wreck: ☆☆☆☆
Depth 58 m
Reference: 55 22'.785 N 001 22'.095 W
Location: 8.48 nm NE from Coquet Lighthouse

The *Morlaix* (Official No. 167815) was a steel-hulled 419-ton British steam cargo vessel that measured 53.34 m in length, with an 8.55-m beam and a 2.8-m draught. Goole Shipbuilding and Repairing Co. Ltd. built and completed her at Goole as Yard No. 138 in May 1911; she was launched as the *Oran* on 18 March 1911 for M. Camuyrano, Buenos Aires. The single steel screw was powered by an aft-positioned 85-nhp three-cylinder triple expansion steam engine that used one single-ended boiler with three plain furnaces, 4.73 sq.m (51sq. ft) of grate surface and 148.64 sq.m (1600 sq.ft) of heating surface. The cylinders measured 34.29 cm, 53.34 cm and 88.9 cm with a 60.96-cm stroke (13½ in., 21 in. and 35 in. with a 24-in. stroke). Richardson, Westgarth and Co. Ltd. manufactured the engine and ancillary machinery. She had one steel deck, three bulkheads cemented, a 50-ton (141.58-cubic m) fore-peak tank, a 16-ton (45.30-cubic.m) aft-peak tank, a 5.48-m bridge deck and a 7.63-m forecastle. She was classed as 100 A1.

In 1917, she was renamed *Fedalah* by Cie. Chérifienne de Navigation, Casablanca, who purchased her.

L'Union Cie. Française de Commerce and de Transp. Maritime, Bordeaux, France, purchased and renamed her *Edmond Troppey* in 1921.

Soc. de Remorq. and de Transp. par Chalands et Allèges de Mer Remorqués, Le Havre, France, as the registered owner in 1923.

In 1925, she was renamed *Morlaix* by Soc. Havraise de Transp. and de Transit, Le Havre, France, who was then the registered owner. In 1934/1935 her code letters were: TSQO.

In June 1940, the Admiralty seized the vessel at Milford Haven and placed her under the control of the Ministry of War Transport (MoWT) at Cardiff; C. F. Cuthbert Brown and Co. Ltd. was appointed Crown nominee manager. The designated code recognition signal letters were: MKXS.

Final voyage

On 5 May 1942, the *Morlaix* sank following a collision with the 1344-ton, former French steam trawler *Finlande* (1937 – Ministry of War Transport), at 55° 25.30'N 01° 22.30'W. The *Morlaix* was in ballast and on passage from Macduff for Sunderland, was sailing independently and none of the crew was lost.

On 18 December 1944, the *Finlande* was wrecked off North Head, Peterhead, while voyaging from Iceland to Hull.

LCR 1942, p. 9 (f).

Wrecksite

The wreck is orientated in an ESE to WNW direction and lies on a seabed of hard sand and gravel in a general depth of 58 m (LAT). It is upright, intact and fairly substantial, standing 5.2 m high at the stern to midships section, with decking and some superstructure visible, but her bows to the east are reported to be broken off. The wrecksite covers an area of 55 m in length by 10 m across, with the upper structures coated in a beautiful array of soft corals and large plumose anemones. The ship's bell, which may still be around, will most probably be inscribed: *Oran 1911*. Shoals of various fish have adopted the wreck so it will make a reasonable boat-angling venue.

HORNCHURCH

Date of loss: 3 August 1917
Wreck: ✯✯✯
Depth: 42 m
Reference: 55 22'.132 N 001 28'.567 W
Location: 3 nm NE of Coquet Lighthouse

The *Hornchurch* (Official No. 139154) was a steel-hulled 2159-ton British steam cargo ship that measured 85.34 m in length, with a 12.31-m beam, a 5.61-m draught and a moulded depth of 8.45 m. Osbourne, Graham and Co. at North Hylton, Sunderland built and completed her as Yard No. 200 in September 1916; she was launched on 17 May 1916 for J. Hudson and Co. Ltd. London, who was also the owner at the time of loss. The single steel screw was powered by a 225-nhp three-cylinder triple expansion steam engine that used two single-ended boilers working at a pressure of 180-lb psi, with six corrugated furnaces, 9.75 sq.m (105 sq.ft) of grate surface and 308.43 sq.m (3320 sq.ft) of heating surface, which gave ten knots. Clyde Shipbuilding and Engineering Co. Ltd. Port Glasgow, manufactured the machinery. She had one deck, a well deck, a 28.65-m quarterdeck, a 7.01-m poop deck, a 15.84-m bridge deck and an 8.22-m forecastle.

The *Hornchurch* was also armed for defence on completion.

Final voyage

On 3 August 1917, the *Hornchurch*, *en route* from London to Methil with a cargo of coal and with Captain J. W. Gagen in charge, detonated a mine and sank 3.5 miles off Coquet Island. The KDM submarine SMU *UC 29*, commanded by Oblt.z.S. Ernst Rosenow, had laid the mine on 25 April 1917. The following two crewmen were lost.

Harrigan, Michael, 48 yrs, Lamp Trimmer
Nilsson, Oscar, 38 yrs, Fireman

On 7 June 1917, *UC 29* was south of Ireland at position: 51° 50'N 11° 50'W when the Q-Ship *Pargust* sank her by gunfire. Twenty three of the crew, including Oblt.z.S. Rosenow, were killed but two men, the watch officer and a seaman, survived.

LCWLR 1914–18, p. 161; CWGC; Jarvis (2000), Vol. V; BVLA 1914–18, p. 61.

Wrecksite

The wreck is orientated in a S by W to N by E direction. It lies on a firm seabed of sand, stone and shells in a general depth of 42 m (LAT). The wreck is broken into two main sections and is well smashed up and decayed, but still very substantial, with the highest parts standing over 8 m from the seabed. The wreck covers an area 90 m long and 23 m across and lots of flattened pipes, brass valves, iron/steel wheels and cogs, an anchor windlass, lengths of chain and two anchors lie intermingled with the mound of broken machinery and twisted steel plates. Soft corals adorn the highest sections around the boilers and shoaling fish, mainly pout whiting and pollack, are fairly common during the summer months,

THE TETRARCH (?)

Date of loss: 30 November 1941
Wreck: ★★★
Depth 58 m
Reference: 55 22'.785 N 001 22'.095 W
Location: 6.45-n.m ENE of Coquet Island

On November 30th 1941, the 225 ton steam trawler The Tetrarch *sank following a collision with the steamship Koolga near to the 20T buoy off Coquet Island (Author's collection)*

The Tetrarch (Official No. 135975) was a steel-hulled 225-ton British steam trawler that measured 35.7 m in length with a 6.7-m beam. Cook, Welton and Gemmell built and completed her on 12 October 1913 at Beverley as Yard No. 277; she was launched on 22 July 1913 for North Western Steam Fishing Co. Ltd. who registered her as GY 945 on 10 October. The single steel screw was powered by a 58-hp, three-cylinder triple expansion steam engine that used one single-ended boiler and gave ten knots. The cylinders measured 30.48 cm, 53.34 cm and 86.36 cm with a 60.96-cm stroke (12 in., 21 in. and 34 in. with a 24-in. stroke). Amos and Smith Ltd. manufactured the machinery at Hull. She had one deck, four bulkheads cemented, an 18.59-m quarterdeck and a 4.87-m forecastle. She was also equipped at a later date with DS and electric lights. The designated code recognition signal letters were: MDZS.

In August 1914, she was requisitioned by the Admiralty, converted to Admiralty minesweeper no. 254 and equipped with a three-pounder deck gun, DF and radio; the vessel was returned to the original owners in the early months of 1919.

On 11 October 1919, Thomas Baskcomb of Grimsby was the registered owner.

Dobson Ship Repairing Co. Ltd. Grimsby purchased her on 24 October 1935; C. Dobson was the manager.

From 24 December 1940, Perihelion Steam Fishing Co. Ltd. Grimsby was the registered owner and G.H. Grampin was the manager.

Final voyage

On 30 November 1941, *The Tetrarch* was on a return fishing voyage when she sank following a collision with the 1110-ton steamer *Koolga* (1910 – Aberdeen Steam Navigation Co. Ltd. Aberdeen), near to the 20T buoy off Coquet Island. The following nine crewmen were lost:

Carle, James, 43 yrs, First Engineman MM
Love, Edward Thomas Symonds, 38 yrs, Trimmer MM
Norris, Thomas Edward, 43 yrs, Skipper MM
Pearson, Jack, 35 yrs, Trimmer MM
Rendall, William, 55 yrs, Second Engineman MM
Revell, William, 43 yrs, Donkeyman MM
Shulver, Frederick Ernest, 46 yrs, Deck Hand MM
Singleton, George Lancelot, 34 yrs, Second Hand MM
Wareing, George, 40 yrs, Deck Hand MM

CWGC; LCR 1941, p. 8 (f).

Wrecksite

This wreck is very close to the position where *The Tetrarch* is recorded as having gone down in position: 55° 22.99'N 01° 21.42'W. The wreck, though, is 55 m in length and 10 m across, which is much larger than *The Tetrarch* was. There is a possibility that she may be the wreck of the steamship *Morlaix*, which was 419 tons and 53.34 m in length.

NETHERLANDSMAN, EX ZEELAND

Date of loss: 1 June 1924
Wreck: ✯
Depth: 46 m
Reference: 55 23'.936 N 001 27'.548 W
Location: 4.18 nm ESE of Boulmer

The *Netherlandsman* (Official No. 132727) was a steel none-propelled 86-ton British steam bucket dredger that measured 30.48 m in length, with a five metre beam and a 1.98-m draught. She was completed and launched as the *Zeeland* in the Netherlands in the early 1900s.

In 1912, she was owned by contractors William Robert Fasey and Charles Marcus Bles, at Leytonstone, Essex.

On 31 December 1920, she was registered in London and owned by William R. Fasey, Leytonstone, Essex, who renamed her *Netherlandsman*.

In 1922, The Jarrow Dredging and Salvage Co. Ltd. of Jarrow owned her through a mortgage.

She was nicknamed *The Dutchman*.

Final voyage

On 1 June 1924, the dredger was being towed by a tug, in heavy weather and foggy conditions, from Eyemouth to the Tyne when she capsized and sank about three miles off Boulmer, Northumberland. The crew was saved and landed at the Tyne. The dredger was valued in the London market at £1200.

The Times: Tuesday, 3 June 1924, p. 24, Issue 43668.

Wrecksite

The wreck is lying on its side, on a seabed of firm sand and shell in a general depth of 46 m (LAT). The highest part, which is actually the hull side, stands about 5.5 metres, while the other side on the seabed is slowly disintegrating. It had no screw or rudder, but was equipped with a three-cylinder triple expansion steam engine for operating the buckets. The first time divers found the wreck, the quantity of steel grab buckets at the site led them to believe that she had been a vessel carrying a cargo of steel buckets. Some large fish, including large pollack and cod, have been noticed around the perimeter of the wreck, and occasionally lobsters can be seen inside the steel structure.

6

COQUET ISLAND TO SEAHOUSES

DRIEBERGEN (?)

Date of loss: 28 August 1940
Wreck: ★★★★★
Depth: 54 m
Reference: 55 24'.142 N 001 24'.345 W
Location: 6.10 nm NE of Coquet Lighthouse

The Dutch steamer Driebergen *in port during happier days (Author's collection)*

The *Driebergen* was a steel-hulled 5231-ton Netherlands steam cargo ship that measured 122.53 m in length, with a 17.67-m beam and an 8.22-m draught. New Waterway Shipbuilding Co. of Schiedam built and completed her as Yard No. 116 in November 1923; she was launched on 25 August 1923 for N.V. Furness Scheepvaart and Agentuur Mij., Rotterdam. The single screw was powered by a 343-nhp DR-geared steam turbine that used three boilers and gave 12.5 knots. Metropolitan Vickers Electrical Co. Ltd. Manchester manufactured the engine and ancillary machinery. She had two decks, water ballast, an 11.37-m forecastle and was later equipped with wireless, DF and electric lights. The designated code recognition signal letters were: PDTD.

From 1926, N.V. Zuid Hollandsche Scheepv. Mij., Rotterdam was the registered owner and Furness, Rotterdam was the manager.

Final voyage

On 28 August 1940, the *Driebergen* sank near Alnmouth following a collision with the 10365-ton British motor vessel *Port Darwin* (1918 – Commonwealth and Dominion Line

Ltd. London). The *Driebergen* was sailing as a part of the southbound 47-ship convoy FS.265 (Methil – Southend) and was transporting wheat from Bahia Blanca via Methil to the Tyne. None of her crew was lost.

LCR 1940 Page 7 (f) – Starke Schell Registers

Wrecksite

The wreck, which is probably that of the *Driebergen*, is orientated in a SE to NW direction, with the bows detached. It lies on a seabed of sand, mud, black shells and rock in a general depth of 54 m (LAT). The wreck is upright and mostly intact, standing over 6.5 m high amidships around the partially collapsed superstructure. The bows lie to the SE, are broken off and lying intact close to the main wreckage. The wreck is very substantial and covers an area 81 m long and 19 m across, with lots of broken debris strewn around nearby. The upper and most exposed structures are covered in an array of soft corals that light up the dark green water when the sun's light is able to penetrate the eerie depths. Large cod, ling and conger have been observed and shoals of pout whiting swim over the wreck.

ELZIENA (?)

Date of loss: 2 March 1940
Wreck: ✯✯
Depth: 56 m
Reference: 55 24'.582 N 001 22'.907 W
Location: 7 nm NE of Coquet Lighthouse

The *Elziena* was a steel-hulled 197-ton motor cargo vessel that measured 33.07 m in length, with a 6.55-m beam and a 2.43-m draught. Scheepswerf Gideon, J. Koster Hzn. at Groningen in the Netherlands built and completed her in 1931 for J. Patje, Sappemeer in Groningen. The single steel screw was powered by a 4S.C.SA three-cylinder 36-nhp diesel oil engine. The cylinders measured 27.94 cm – 45.08 cm (11 in. – 17.75 in.). Motorenfbr "Deutz" AG Köln, Deutz manufactured the machinery. She had one deck and a 10.05-m quarterdeck.

Final voyage

On 2 March 1940, the *Elziena* was on passage from Antwerp for Leith with a cargo of onions and vegetables when German aircraft bombed her. Several of the bombs are reported to have hit the vessel, which sank with the loss of two of her crew.

LCWLR 1939–45 Page 47 – Lloyd's Registers, 1931–39 ELS-EMA.

Wrecksite

The wreck, possibly that of the *Elziena*, lies on a seabed of fine sand and mud in a general depth of 56 m (LAT). It is orientated in a N to S direction, is intact, upright and stands almost 5 m high. The wreck covers an area 26 m in length by 8 m across and has some superstructure still visible.

HOGARTH

Date of loss: 7 June 1918
Wreck: ★★★★
Depth: 49m
Reference: 54 55' .443' N 001 09' .942 W
Location: 6.46-n.m. east of Roker Lighthouse, Sunderland

The *Hogarth* (official no.99647) was a steel-hulled 1226-ton British steam passenger/cargo ship that measured 77.01m in length, with a 9.93-m beam and a 5.33-m draught. Hall, Russell & Co. of Aberdeen built and completed her as Yard No. .275 in January 1893; she was launched on 6 December 1892 for Aberdeen Steam Navigation Co. Aberdeen, who owned her at the time of loss. The single steel screw was powered by a 343-hp, three-cylinder triple expansion steam engine that used two double-ended boilers. The cylinders measured 55.04 cm, 109.22 cm and 177.8 cm with a 106.68 cm stroke (26 in., 43 in. and 70 in. with a 42-in. stroke). Hall, Russell and Co. manufactured the machinery at Aberdeen. She had two decks and a 21.64-m poop deck, a 19.81-m bridge deck and a 14.32-m forecastle.

On the night of 22 November 1905, *Hogarth* ran down the Banffshire fishing boat *Pomegranate* off Lowestoft. The stern of the little boat was cut nearly in two after the steamer ran into it almost amidships. She had nine men on board and only one of them was saved. Immediately following the collision, the steamer's engines were put in reverse and a boat was lowered, manned by the mate, Clarence Lowe, and five other men. A fresh breeze and choppy sea meant that it was some time before they could reach the drowning men, and by that time all but two had disappeared. The two were taken on board the *Hogarth*'s lifeboat, but one, 25 year old John MacKintosh, had died. The sole survivor, 58 year old John MacGregor, had saved his own life by securing a couple of floats around his arms as soon as the collision had occurred.

About 1915/1916, the *Hogarth* was armed for defence with one 13-pounder (5.90-kilos) deck gun.

For standing by one of their steamers that was torpedoed, Captain David Stephen was presented on 25 October 1916 with a gold watch by British Indian Steam Navigation Co.; he was also presented with Lloyd's Silver Medal in early June 1918 and with a cheque for saving another steamer in the same position.

Final voyage

The KDM submarine SMU *UB 107*, commanded by Kapitänleutnant Eberhard von Prittwitz und Gaffron, torpedoed the *Hogarth*, which was travelling alone off Sunderland, sinking her at 54°51'N, 1° 03'W at 0200hrs (CT) on 8 June 1918. The target was described in the U-boat log as a 2000-ton vessel. The steamer had left London for Aberdeen with a 650-ton general cargo, and when hit amidships at midnight sank almost at once. The master, Captain Stephen, and 25 crewmen, including one RNR DAMS gunner, were lost. The sole survivor was the senior DAMS gunner, who happened to be in his cabin at the time and who suddenly found himself in the freezing water, clinging to some of the ship's floating wreckage. It was two days before a passing patrol boat picked him up and took him to Newcastle upon Tyne, where he was treated for hypothermia. The 26 men who died were:

Adamson, Alexander, 19 yrs, Fireman MM
Anderson, Alexander, Second Engineer MM
Barnett, John, 33 yrs, Carpenter MM
Binnie, Alex, 43 yrs, Trimmer MM
Bodie, Alexander Ingram, 37 yrs, Cook MM
Bowles, Albert Edward, 18 yrs, Trimmer MM
Byres, Stephen Reynolds, 58 yrs, Able Seaman MM
Cheyne, George, 33 yrs, Greaser MM
Cooper, J., Greaser MM
Cormack, Peter, 33 yrs, Fireman MM
Dunlop, James Alexander, 31 yrs, Donkeyman MM
Gibb, Duncan Forbes, 33 yrs, Fireman MM
Main, Harry, 34 yrs, Fireman MM
Marr, George, Steward MM
McBrain, George, 61 yrs, Able Seaman MM
McDonald, John, 54 yrs, Boatswain (Bosun) MM
Niclasen, Niels Carl Sofus, 30 yrs, Able Seaman MM
Porter, David, 34 yrs, Able Seaman MM
Ritchie, Andrew, 45 yrs, Able Seaman MM
Robb, Alexander, 34 yrs, Able Seaman MM
Robertson, George, Seaman RNR (DAMS Gunner)
Robertson, James, First Engineer MM
Smart, Alexander, 45 yrs, Mate MM
Smith, Alexander Walker, 31 yrs, Fireman MM
Stephen, David, 55 yrs, Master MM
Steward, William, Second Mate MM

ADM 137/2964 - CWGC - The Cross of Sacrifice Vol V - LCWLR 1914-18 Page 220 - BVLS 1914-18 Page 91 - The Times Friday, 24 November 1905; Page 4; Issue 37873

Wrecksite

British reports always suggested that the *Hogarth* had been sunk ten miles south ½ east from the Longstone light, yet in the summer of 2009, divers on Allan Lopez's Tyne-based charter-boat *Spellbinder* discovered a wreck off Sunderland lying in 50 m (LAT). The wreck is well broken up and collapsed with little or no identifiable structure. Some of her cargo is still to be seen and appears to be general building materials. Amidships there is some wooden decking and what the divers described as parts "indicative of the superstructure". During the dive a broken compass and the ship's bell were recovered, which positively identified the wreck.

LADY ELEANOR (?)

Date of loss: 26 April 1895
Wreck: ★★★
Depth: 64 m
Reference: 55 25'.360 N 001 20'.658 W
Location: 8.32 nm NE of Coquet Island

The *Lady Eleanor* (Official No. 68929) was an iron-hulled 764-ton schooner-rigged steam cargo vessel that measured 60.96 m in length, with a 9.2 m beam. John G. Gulston of Sunderland built and completed her as Yard No. 3 in 1875 and launched her in September 1875 for the Earl of Durham, Sunderland; the ship was also registered at Sunderland. The single iron screw was powered by a two-cylinder compound steam engine that used one boiler.

From 1891, the registered owner was the Right Honourable Charles Grey, the Earl of Howick, at Sunderland.

Final voyage

During thick fog on 26 April 1895, the *Lady Eleanor*, a well-known Wear trader, sank following a collision with the 1242-ton passenger/cargo steamer *Iona* (1883 – London and Edinburgh Shipping Co. Leith), ten miles NE of Coquet Island. She had been on passage from Sunderland for Aberdeen with a cargo of coal when, at about 2215 hrs, she was struck in the port side by the bow stem of the *Iona*. From *Lady Eleanor*'s crew of 16, three men were lost: Mr Anderson, the chief engineer, William Todd, the steward and a fireman. The *Iona* did rescue the other 13 crewmen and took them back to Sunderland, where they arrived on the afternoon of the 27th. Captain J. Robinson from the stricken ship had a very narrow escape: as his vessel, which had been split almost in two by the force of the collision, went down; he seized hold of some wreckage and kept himself afloat for nearly half an hour before being picked up. The crewmen that drowned were last seen standing next to the rail of the sinking steamer. The *Iona*, which was carrying a crew of 28 and six passengers from Leith to London, was left badly damaged.

BoT Wreck Return 1895 Appendix C Table 1 Page 147 (669) – Miramar Ship Index – *The Times,* Monday, 29 April 1895; Page 6; Issue 34563 – Starke Schell Registers

Wrecksite

This wreck, probably that of the *Lady Eleanor*, is orientated in a SE to NW direction. It lies on a firm seabed of sand and gravel in a general depth of 64 m (LAT). The wreck is upright but totally collapsed and well broken up, standing just 2 m high and covering an area 61 m long and 17 m across. Quite a number of crustaceans but not many fish have been observed around the wrecksite.

SOPHIE ANNET, EX BELAIR (?)

Date of Loss: 25 September 1903
Wreck: ✭✭
Depth: 43 m
Reference: 55 26'.418 N 001 28'.263 W
Location: 4.24 nm NE from Seaton Point

The *Sophie Annet* was an iron-hulled 1369-ton schooner-rigged Dutch steam cargo ship that measured 74.62 m in length, with a 9.93-m beam and a 5.02-m draught. J. and G. Thomson at Clydebank, Glasgow built and completed her as Yard No. 175; she was launched as the 1419-ton *Belair* (Official No. 82273) on 16 October 1879 for D. Caw and Co. Glasgow. The single iron screw was powered by a 150-hp, two-cylinder compound steam engine that used one boiler. The cylinders measured 68.58 cm and 132.08 cm with a 91.44-cm stroke (27 in. and 52 in. with a 36-in.stroke). She had five bulkheads and water ballast. The designated code recognition signal letters were: SVDH.

In 1881 the master was Captain G. Boniface.

Caw, Prentice, Clapperton and Co. Glasgow was the registered owner in 1887.

In 1890 she was sold to Belair S.S. Co. Ltd. Cardiff with Jugo and Co. the managers; the master was Captain Broadfoot.

The Lloyd's registered tonnage was 1369 tons gross in 1891.

In early 1893, she was sold to William Stoker, Cardiff (South Shields).

Later in 1893, J. E. Guthe and Co. Cardiff (West Hartlepool) purchased her.

West Hartlepool Steam Navigation Co. Ltd. Cardiff was the registered owners in 1898.

Noord Nederl. Scheepvaart Maat at Harlingen in the Netherlands was the registered owner in 1900 and they renamed her *Sophie Annet*.

Final voyage

On the morning of 25 September 1903, the *Sophie Annet*, with Captain Khart in charge, was proceeding in ballast and on passage from Zaandam in the Netherlands for Grangemouth when, during dense fog, she struck some rocks at the south end of Longstone in the Outer Farne Islands. The ship was badly holed but managed to pull herself clear. Six of the crew put off in a boat, with instructions from the master to stand by, however the *Sophie Annet*, with ten feet of water in the holds, slipped off and set away in a southerly direction towards Alnmouth. Meanwhile, the Scottish steam trawler *Isabella* of Montrose found the six crewmen in the boat and took it in tow; the men were later landed at Berwick. As the *Sophie Annet* proceeded south she met the Leith steamer *Warsaw* sailing from Sunderland to Leith and, after a discussion between the two masters, it took her in tow. After travelling for some time, the *Sophie Annet* signalled to the Leith ship that she was sinking rapidly, so the remaining 14 crewmen were immediately taken on board the *Warsaw*. The wire hawser was let go and the *Sophie Annet* sank almost at once, going down bows first. The crew was landed at Leith but their luggage and personal effects went down with the ship. The Netherlands Consul at Leith, Mr Turnbull, then arranged the return journey home for all 20 Dutch seamen.

On the day the crew was landed at Leith, Lloyd's agent at Beadnell also telegraphed the London Times, alleging that 'the *Sophie Annet* has been involved in a collision with the Scottish herring boat *M.E. 606* off the Longstone' but this was a misunderstanding on the part of the agent.

The Times, Monday, 28 September 1903; Page 4; Issue 37197 – Starke Schell Registers
Register of American and Foreign Shipping 1857–1900

Wrecksite

The wreck, possibly that of the *Sophie Annet*, is orientated in a S to N direction and lies on a seabed of sand in a general depth of 43 m (LAT). It is now collapsed and well broken up, covering an area 43 m long and 15 m across, with the highest structures standing no more than 3 m from the seabed. A number of crustaceans but very few fish have been observed. If these are the remains of *Sophie Annet*, the bell, if located, will be inscribed: *Belair 1879*.

PEIK, EX REGULUS (?)

Date of loss: 21 April 1917
Wreck: ★★★★
Depth: 36 m
Reference: 55 27'.647 N 001 30'.132 W
Location: 3.56 nm SE from Dunstanburgh Castle Point

The *Peik* was a steel-hulled 701-ton Norwegian cargo steamship that was registered in Sandefjord and measured 62.5 m in length, with a 9.1-m beam and a 4.2-m draught. Porsgrund Mekaniske Verksteder, Porsgrunn built and completed her as Yard No. 56 in November 1910; she was launched as the *Regulus* on 10 October 1910 for Aktieselskapet "Regulus", Kragerø; A.O. Lindvig was the manager. The single screw was powered by a 91-nhp three-cylinder triple expansion steam engine that used one boiler and two furnaces. The cylinders measured 38.1 cm, 60.96 cm and 93.98 cm with a 66.04-cm stroke (15 in., 24 in. and 37 in. with a 26-in. stroke). Porsgrund Mekaniske Verksteder, Porsgrunn manufactured the engine and ancillary machinery. She was classed as 100 A1. The designated code recognition signal letters were: MGJB

In 1915, she was sold to Aktieselskapet "Peik", Kragerø and renamed *Peik*; the manager was E. Jüel.

From 1916, Dampskipsselskapet Aktieselskapet Asnæs, Sandefjord was the registered owner and she was renamed *Peik*; Ole Drolshammer was the manager.

Later in 1916, Håkon Rachlew was the manager.

Final voyage

On 21 April 1917, the KDM submarine SMU *UC 44*, commanded by Kapitänleutnant Kurt Tebbenjohanns, torpedoed and sunk the *Peik*. She had left the Tyne at 1130 hrs under the command of Captain Alfred Olsen for passage to Arendal in Norway with a general mixed cargo, including aluminium. At 1600 hrs she was reported as having passed Coquet Island and was four miles from land, when two of her crew, Thorvald Olsen (Second-in-Command of Pilots) who was on the gangway and Seaman Ivar Gabrielsen, on watch at the time, observed the white trail of a torpedo heading towards their ship on the starboard side. There was no time to take evasive action before it detonated against the machine-room at the stern end, causing a violent explosion that knocked the crew off their feet and fractured the pilot's leg in two places. The pilot and Seaman Gabrielsen both jumped into the sea. The port lifeboat, which was undamaged, was lowered down and the two men were picked up within ten minutes. All 15 crewmen were rescued by a British steam trawler and landed at the North Shields quay at 1930 hrs. The *Peik* went down by the bows and sank in between two and a half and three minutes, taking confidential papers with it. After the vessel had gone down, Captain Olsen, who was by this time in the lifeboat, noticed the submarine's periscope, identified later as belonging to *UC 44*, alongside the position of sinking. The submarine had given no prior warning of the attack, even though the vessel was clearly marked as Norwegian.

Sjøforklaringer over norske skibes krigsforlis 1914–1919 – ANCL 1914–18 Page 95 – LCWLR 1914–18 Page 121 – IDNS Page 119

Wrecksite

The wreck, which is probably that of the *Peik*, is orientated in an E to W direction. It lies on a seabed of fine sand, mud, broken shells and rock in a general depth of 36 m (LAT). The wreck – referred to by local divers as 'the upside down wreck' is reasonably intact but inverted and collapsed, with the highest part standing just over 3 m from the seabed. It covers an area 64 m long and 14 m across. Lying beneath the wreckage are large aluminium castings that appear to be part of a cargo.

ACCLIVITY

Date of loss: 20 January 1952
Wreck: ★★★
Depth: 26 m
Reference: 55 28'.118 N 001 32'.792 W
Location: 1.55 nm E of Craster and 2.06 nm SSE of Castle Point, Dunstanburgh

On January 20th 1952, the 389 ton motor tanker Acclivity *struck a submerged object and sank (Author's collection)*

The *Acclivity* (Official No. 162667) was a steel-hulled 389-ton British motor tanker that measured 49.98 m in length with a 7.46-m beam. George Brown and Co. at Greenock built and completed her over 12 months as Yard No. 182 in December 1931; she was launched on 29 October 1931 for F. T. Everard and Sons Ltd. London, who also owned her at the time of loss and registered her in London. The single bronze screw was powered by an aft-positioned 112-nhp two-stroke single acting 2S.C.S.A. four-cylinder diesel oil engine and a donkey boiler working at a pressure of 180 lb psi. Newbury Diesel Co. Ltd. Newbury manufactured the machinery. She had a flat keel, nine bulkheads cemented, one deck, a 13.10-m poop deck and a 6.09-m forecastle. The vessel also had 123 tons of cellular double bottom, a 46-ton deep-tank aft and a fore-peak and aft-peak tank. The designated code recognition signal letters were: MQDK.

The *Acclivity* was something of an innovation in her day as she was a low air draught tanker, designed to negotiate the bridges on the River Seine during her voyages with edible oil from Zwijndreche to Paris.

The tail shaft was inspected in May 1950 and fitted with an approved oil-retaining gland.

In January 1951 she was certified as 100A1 for carrying petroleum in bulk.

Final voyage

On 20 January 1952, the *Acclivity*, commanded by Captain C. Gould and transporting a cargo of linseed oil from Thames Haven to Newburgh, in Fife, struck a submerged object, which the master believed to be a wreck. When the vessel took on a heavy list to port, Captain Gould sent out a message saying his vessel was sinking and the crew took to the lifeboat. About one hour later, the 454-ton steam collier *Magrix* (1938 – R. Rix and Sons, Hull) picked them up, but the lifeboat broke up in the heavy swell just as they reached the collier's side. The *Acclivity* was then taken in tow by the *Magrix*, but after an hour the line parted and soon after that, at around dawn, the tanker foundered 1.55 nm east of Craster. The crew were all safely landed at Amble.

LCR 1952 Page 4 – Starke Schell Registers – Board of Trade Wreck Return 1952 – The Times, Monday, 21 January 1952; Page 6; Issue 52214

Wrecksite

The wreck is orientated in a N by E to S by W direction and lies on a seabed of hard sand and gravel in a general depth of 26 m (LAT). It is intact and leans over on its port side with the deck vertical against a small reef. The aft bridge structure has now fallen onto the stony seabed. There is a lot of debris lying in the small area between the decks and the reef. The bell has so far not been recovered and is very likely to have fallen into the silt and debris that have built up around the bow section.

The general layout is similar to any other small tanker, with few portholes and much of the forefront taken up with pipe-work. Steel railings still run the whole length of the vessel from the bridge to the small hatch at the bows. The stern section is well worth a visit, as the decking is now well deteriorated, making it reasonably easy to penetrate the open spaces below the decks. From this point, you can swim around to see the large rudder hanging from the pintles and the lovely bronze screw still attached to the shaft above it. Plumose anemones cover the entire wreck, making it very pretty.

BUKA, EX TIKA, EX HENJA, EX EBEN HAEZER

Date of loss: 7 April 1970
Wreck: ★★★
Depth: 36 m
Reference: 55 28'.782 N 001 30'.392 W
Location: 3.93 nm ESE from Castle Point, Dunstanburgh

The *Buka* was a steel-hulled 198-ton Netherlands Skute-type motor cargo vessel that measured 32.24 m in length, with a 6.31-m beam and a 2.47-m draught. She was specifically designed to navigate the shallow waters of the Netherlands. N.V. Noord Nederlandsche Scheepswerven, Groningen built and launched her as the *Eben Haezer* in 1930 for J. H. Timmer, Groningen; B. Oeseburg was the manager. A 44-nhp 4S.C.S.A four-cylinder diesel oil engine powered her single screw. The cylinders measured 26.99 cm & 34.61 cm (10⅝ in. & 13⅝ in). Appingedammer Bŕonz, Motorenfb. N.V., manufactured the engine and ancillary machinery. She had one deck, an 8.8-m quarterdeck and 3.3-m forecastle. The designated code recognition signal letters were: PDUE.

On 11 August 1942, the Kriegsmarine Office at Rotterdam requisitioned the *Eben Haezer* as a substitute for the coastal MV *Deni*, because the *Deni* didn't have enough horsepower and was given back to the owner. *Eben Haezer* was used as a transport in the Speer Flotilla-Wiking, Norway. In August 1943, she became a guard ship in the West Baltic Coastal Protection Flotilla. On 9 May 1945 she was seen at Salangsverket in Norway.

The *Eben Haezer* left Drontheim on 4 August 1945 and was taken over by representatives of the Netherlands Government at Kristiansand on 13 August.

Two days later, she left Kristiansand for Copenhagen, where she arrived on the 19th, before heading for Rotterdam where she arrived on 20 September 1945.

She was renamed *Henja* in 1958 when she was purchased by Henja. H. Prins at Groningen.

Fa. W.F. Kampman, Amsterdam purchased and renamed her *Tika* in 1962.

From 1963, H. Buitenwerf at Groningen was the registered owner and renamed her *Buka*.

Final voyage

On the evening of 7 April 1970, the *Buka* left St. David's in Fife, bound for London with a 238-ton cargo of roadstone. The following morning, however, she was reported to have sprung a serious leak while 3.5 miles east of Castle Point, Dunstanburgh, Northumberland. The four crewmen were said to have abandoned ship because the *Buka* immediately filled up with water. Within 30 seconds she had disappeared and a passing coaster, the *Eleanor Dawson*, picked up the four men and landed them at Craster, three miles away.

LCR 1970 Page 20 – LR 1969–70 No. 5415145 (B) – Starke Schell Registers

Wrecksite

The wreck is orientated in a SSE to NNW direction and lies on a seabed of firm sand, stone and rock in a general depth of 36 m (LAT). In 1997, this wreck was totally intact but the elements have taken their toll in recent times. Explosives were used on the wreck in around the year 1999 and it was reported to be lying partly on its side. It is now quite badly broken up, with the stern, which stands around 4.6 m from the seabed, listing about 45° to starboard. The bridge/wheelhouse is slowly collapsing and the hull sides of the hold have fallen over. The bows however, are still intact and upright and stand five metres high. The hold was supposed to have contained the 238 tons of roadstone but that area has always been largely empty, apart from some deposits of silt. It seems unlikely that such a heavy cargo should disappear, unless, of course, it was not there when the vessel sank.

NIDELVEN

Date of loss: 27 April 1917
Wreck: ★★★★
Depth: 39 m
Reference: 55 28'.647 N 001 29'.962 W
Location: 3.24-n.m ESE of Castle Point, Dunstanburgh

The *Nidelven* was a steel-hulled 1262-ton Norwegian steam passenger/cargo ship that measured 70.43 m in length, with a 10.13-m beam and a 4.11-m draught. Trondhjems Mekaniske Verksteder at Trondheim built and completed her as Yard No. 134 in November 1908; she was launched on 23 September 1908 for Det Nordenfjeldske Dampskibsselskap, Trondheim, who was the owner at the time of loss. The single screw was powered by a 132-nhp three-cylinder triple expansion steam engine that used one boiler. The cylinders measured 43.18 cm, 72.39 cm and 121.92 cm with an 83.82-cm stroke (17 in., 28½ in. and 48 in. with a 33-in. stroke). Trondhjems Mekaniske Verksteder, Trondheim manufactured the engine and ancillary machinery. She had one deck, an 84-ton (237.86-cubic.m) quarterdeck, a 41-ton (116.09-cubic.m) deck-house and a 29-ton (82.11-cubic.m) forecastle. The designated code recognition signal letters were: MFKR.

The 1,262-ton Norwegian steamer Nidelven *- circa 1910 (Courtesy: Rolf Kristensen, Åsgårdstrand & Stein-Erik Dagsland, Heinavegen, Norway)*

Final voyage

At 1145 hrs on 27 April 1917, the *Nidelven*, with Captain Agnar Bjarne Aas in charge, struck a mine on the starboard side and sank six miles northeast of Coquet Island, the mine having been laid the previous day by the KDM submarine SMU *UC 29*, commanded by Oblt.z.S. Ernst Rosenow. The steamer was on passage from the Tyne for Svolvær in Norway with a cargo of coal and passengers. Two of the crew were picked up from the sea by a steam trawler, the rest were rescued by the destroyer HMS *Test*. Later that evening, the whole crew were put on board the destroyer HMS *Penn* and taken to Leith, where they were put ashore the next morning. Eleven were taken to the naval hospital, with the rest of the crew going to the sailors' home. The three people who died were:

Handberg, Arne, Mess Boy from Trondheim
Lapaychuk, passenger from Russia
Svendsen, Gunnar, Sailor from Bod

Sjøforklaringer over norske skibes krigsforlis 1914–1919 – LCWLR 1914–18 Page 125 – ANCL 1914–18 Page 93 – LR 1915–16 No. 463 (N) – Starke Schell Registers

Wrecksite

The wreck is very substantial, sitting upright in a general depth of 39 m (LAT). The hull and outline is quite distinguishable all around and is intact up to about half way, to just below the deck, where it has collapsed down along with the superstructure and decking. These have collapsed down onto the boiler and engine, making access to anything rather difficult, but portholes and other artefacts are still recovered from time to time. Cod and other species of fish can sometimes be observed around the wreck, which should make an interesting boat-angling venue.

HESVIK, ex EDUARD GROTHMANN, ex NORDERNEY

Date of loss: 23 September 1914
Wreck: ✯✯✯
Depth: 34 m
Reference: 55 28'.182 N 001 29'.673 W
Location: 3.54 nm SE from Castle Point, Dunstanburgh

The *Hesvik* was a steel-hulled 1232-ton Norwegian steam cargo vessel that measured 71.09 m in length, with a 10.74-m beam and a 4.31-m draught. Act. Ges. "Neptun", Rostock in Germany built and completed her as Yard No. 164 in January 1898; she was launched as the *Norderney* at the end of 1897 for Nord-Ostsee Rhederei, Hamburg. Her steel propeller was powered by a three-cylinder, 93-hp triple expansion steam engine that used one boiler and gave ten knots. The shipbuilders manufactured the machinery. She had one deck, a 21.33-m quarter deck, an 18.28-m bridge deck and a 7.92-m forecastle.

In 1901 she was renamed *Eduard Grothmann* by her new owners Richard Grothmann, Hamburg in Germany.

In 1913 she was sold to AS Hesvik (Carl Bech and Co), Tvedestrand in Norway and renamed *Hesvik.*

Final voyage

On 23 September 1914, the SS *Hesvik* was in ballast and on passage from Arendal, Norway for Grimsby when she detonated a mine and sank at about 2300 hrs. The crew was picked up by the British motor torpedo-boat HMS *Itchen* at 1800 hrs the following day and were put ashore in North Shields. Two people were either killed in the explosion or drowned:

Andersen, Oscar, First Engineer from Kristiansand
Karlsen, Arnold, Donkeyman from Arendal.

Captain Sven Marcussen, master of the *Hesvik,* wrote in the ship's log book and said at the Maritine Declaration that he believed that his ship was 15-nm SSE of Longstone light when the mine detonated and it began to sink. Lloyd's, though, says that she was eight miles south.

LR 1915–16 No. 62 (1) – IDNS Page 79 – Starke Schell Registers

Wrecksite

The wreck, which is now believed to be the *Hesvik,* is orientated in a SSE to NNW direction. It lies on a seabed of dark sand, gravel and rocks in a general depth of 34 m (LAT). The hull is made from riveted iron and the remains are well and truly collapsed and broken up. Beginning at the iron screw, it is possible to swim along the prop shaft tunnel leading to the engine, which is still intact. All of the superstructure has fallen away and lies in a flattened tangle of rubble on either side, making it very low to the seabed. The engine and boiler, which stand upright, are still recognisable, with a donkey engine and boiler to the fore. Towards the bows, loose fittings, ribs and girders lie in a jumbled mass. Unlike many wrecks in this part of the sea, no nets have yet become entangled with the remains, making it a relatively safe dive, especially if the visibility is good. The wreck covers an area 80 m long and 22 m across and stands up about 3.2 m off the seabed. The bow itself has deteriorated, but still stands up about 3.5 m off the seabed. Off to the starboard of the bows there are a lot of jumbled steel plates and framework, which may be the remains of the superstructure. To date, no bridge instruments have been found and the bell appears never to have been salvaged, although divers have recovered a number of portholes.

If this is the wreck of the *Hesvik,* the bell will be inscribed *Norderney* and either *1897* or *1898*

This wreck has always been considered to be that of the *Hogarth*, but a bell was located about ten years ago inscribed *Gaelic 1898*. A lot of serious research by the author and by Andrew Anderson and Ian Wright from Bishop Auckland Diving Club has shown, however, that no ship of that name has been lost off the northeast coast.

One other interesting theory is that 3.15 nm NE of this wreck, at 55 30'.175 N 001 25'.317 W, there is a wreck called the *Igor*, which was owned by the Gaelic Steam Ship Company in 1898. Although they renamed the ship *Cairnbahn*, it is possible that when they acquired the ship in 1898, they also made a bell called *Gaelic* after the company. Could this be her wreck? The only problem with this theory is that she had two boilers while this wreck has only one.

BONHEUR (?)

Date of loss: 23 December 1918
Wreck: ★★★★★
Depth: 103 m
Reference: 55 28'.452 N 000 54'.586 W
Location: 23.04 nm ENE from Coquet light and 25.83 nm SE of Longstone Lighthouse

Bonheur *(Courtesy Norwegian Maritime Museum)*

The *Bonheur* was a steel-hulled 7133-ton Norwegian motor cargo vessel that measured 129.66 m in length, with a 16.84-m beam and an 8.40-m draught. AS Burmeister and Wain, Copenhagen, Denmark built and completed her as Yard No. 308 in June 1918; she was launched on 1 March 1918 for Aktieselskapet Dampskipsselskapet Bonheur, Kristiania and Fred. Olsen and Co was the manager. The twin steel screws were powered by two six-cylinder diesel engines that gave 11 knots. AS Burmeister and Wain, Copenhagen manufactured the machinery.

Final voyage

On 23 December 1918, this big new ship detonated a mine during a raging gale, 23 miles from Coquet Island, and very quickly began to founder. The *Bonheur* had left Kristiania on her maiden voyage carrying a crew of 37 and a general cargo to Hull and to South American ports. The master gave the order to abandon ship and twenty one of the crew got away in one boat, while the others were busy lowering another. The first boat was carried away from the stricken vessel by the heavy seas and the men in it, being scantily clad with very little food, spent a dreadful time from the Monday evening to Thursday afternoon. One of the men died from exposure on Christmas morning and another succumbed that afternoon. A donkeyman, a cook and the cabin boy were almost frozen to death by the time they were sighted by the 138-ton steam trawler *Ostero*, (built in 1897 by Edwards Bros., North Shields), which picked up the remaining ten men and took them to Grimsby. On arrival, several of the men were taken to hospital suffering from frostbite and exposure. The following 16 crewmen died in the sea:

Andersen, A.J.M., Boatswain, from Copenhagen
Andersen, Emil, Sailor, from Grandøse, Denmark
Andersen, Magnus, Cook, from Kristiania
Brunstrøm, O.A., Sailor, from Åbo, Finland
Drangseid, B, Assistant Engineer, from Flekkefjord
Haakonson, Nils, Sailor, from Sweden
Holther-Sørensen, R. Master, from Kristiania
Holm, Karl, Second Engineer, from Drammen
Knutsen, Sverre, First Engineer, from Hvidsten
Larsen, A.J.Fr., Oiler, from Denmark
Marthinsen, E., Fourth Engineer, from Kristiania
Petterson, Karl, Sailor, from Sweden
Pedersen Parkes, H.,Sailor, from Nakskov, Denmark
Schultz, Nils, Assistant Engineer, from Fredrikstad
Steen, Adolf, Oiler, from Kristiania
Teilman, Gunnar, Second Mate, from Kristiania

LCWLR 1914–18 Page 375 – Starke Schell Registers – The Times, Saturday, 28 December 1918; Page 3; Issue 41983

Wrecksite

The wreck, most probably that of the *Bonheur*, sits in a half-metre scour and is orientated in a SSE to NNW direction. It lies on a seabed of mud, sand and gravel in a general depth of 103 m (LAT). The wreck is intact, except that it is broken in two amidships. It stands almost 9 m high and covers an area of 90 m in length by 15 m across, with several areas of loose debris.

SPHYNX, ex ST. PHILIPPE, ex SPHYNX, ex SWANSEA (?)

Date of loss: 29 January 1919
Wreck: ★★★★
Depth: 63 m
Reference: 55 29'.690 N 001 24'.753 W
Location: 5.97 nm E of Castle Point, Dunstanburgh

The *Sphynx* was an iron-hulled 1698-gross ton Swedish steam cargo ship that measured 79.60 m in length, with an 11.09-m beam and holds 5.54 m deep. Blyth Shipbuilding and Dry Docks Co. Ltd. at Cowpen Quay, Blyth built and completed her as Yard No. 48 in September 1883; she was launched as the *Swansea* (Official No. 91226) in September 1883 for Mesnier and Cie, Le Havre, in France. The single screw was powered by a 168-hp, two-cylinder compound steam engine. The cylinders measured 81.28 cm and 157.48 cm with a 106.68-cm stroke (32 in. and 62 in. with a 42-in. stroke). R. and W. Hawthorn at Newcastle manufactured the engine and ancillary machinery. She had one deck, two tiers of beams, four cemented bulkheads, a 28.04-m quarterdeck, a 17.06-m bridge deck and a 10.05-m forecastle. The ship was originally 1493 tons, but was altered sometime later.

She was renamed *Sphynx* by Moss Steam Ship Co. Ltd. at Liverpool in 1885.

Soc. Navale de l'Ouest, Le Havre purchased and renamed her *St. Philippe* in 1896.

Welfare Shipping Co. Ltd. Sunderland purchased and renamed her *Sphynx* in 1909; C. J. Welch and Co was the manager.

In 1912, Ångfartygs A/B Sphynx, Helsingborg bought her and B. O. Börjesson was the manager. Her Official No. then became 5332.

She had the same owners in 1917, but F. Börjesson, became the manager.

In 1918 the ship was requisitioned by the Shipping Controller in London and H. Cail and Co. was appointed as the Crown nominee manager.

At the end of 1918 she was returned to the Swedish owners, Ångfartygs AB Sphynx. The designated code recognition signal letters were: JWNT.

Final voyage

On 29 January 1919, the *Sphynx* left Sunderland for Malmö, Sweden with a cargo of coal, but detonated a mine at 2200 hrs and sank in the North Sea, near Coquet Island. From her crew of eighteen men, only one survived; those that died were:

Andersson, Karl August Leonard, 37 yrs
Backe, Birger Pontus, 25 yrs
Bengtsson, Hugo Benjamin Palander, 19 yrs
Eriksson, Benjamin, 29 yrs
Gitkewitch, S., from Russia, 45 yrs
Ivanoff, Vladimir, from Poland, 21 yrs
Johansson, Axel Fredrik, 40 yrs
Johansson, O.V., from Finland, 28 yrs
Johansson, Ola, 46 yrs
Knutsson, Kristian, Master, 42 yrs
Lundgren, Johan Edvin, 32 yrs
Olsen, S., from Norway, 18 yrs
Pålsson, Emil Filip, 29 yrs
Roslund, Axel Wilhelm, 32 yrs
Sandgren, J.G., from Finland, 32 yrs
Stengård, Carl Emil, 34 yrs
Svensson, Karl Johan Ivan, 28 yrs

Starke Schell Registers – LCWLR 1914–18 Page 375

Wrecksite

The wreck, probably that of the *Sphynx*, is orientated in a NNE to SSW direction, with the bows to the NNE. It sits in a very long one-metre deep scour and lies on a seabed of mud, sand, black shells and gravel, in a general depth of 63 m (LAT). It is upright, appears intact, stands 6.7 m high and covers an area 62 m in length by 11 m across. 140 metres to the NE, however, there is also a large amount of wreck debris that could be from this wreck and is worth investigating. There are reported to be four holds that are still full of hundreds of tons of coal. If this is the *Sphynx* the bell if located will be inscribed: *Swansea 1883*.

BØR (?)

Date of loss: 21 February 1918
Wreck: ☆☆☆
Depth: 95 m
Reference: 55 29'.147 N 001 09'.585 W
Location: 15.66 nm NE of Coquet Island

Bør *(Courtesy Norwegian Maritime Museum)*

The *Bør* was a steel-hulled 1149-ton Norwegian steam cargo ship that measured 69.72 m in length, with an 11.02-m beam and a 4.77-m draught. Nylands Verksted built and completed her at Kristiania as Yard No. 239 on 27 July 1914; she was launched for Aktieselskapet "Ganger Rolf" (Bonheur), Kristiania, who was also the owner at the time of loss; Fred Olsen and Co. Kristiania was the manager. The single steel screw was powered by a 148-nhp three-cylinder triple expansion steam engine that used one boiler. Nylands Verksted also manufactured the engine and ancillary machinery at Kristiania. She had one deck, a 6.7-m poop deck, a 20.4-m bridge deck and an 8.2-m forecastle. The designated code recognition signal letters were: MKLT.

Final voyage

On 21 February 1918, the KDM submarine SMU *UC 49*, commanded by Oblt.z.S. Hans Kükenthal, torpedoed and sank the *Bør* off Coquet Island. The *Bør*, which had Captain John Sundby as the master, was on passage from the Tyne for Kristiania with 883 tons of coal and 520 tons of aluminium powder. Without any warning, she was struck at 1500 hrs in front of the no. 3 hatch and the First Engineer, Leif F. Dæhlin from Kristiania, was killed. The remaining 17 crew members were picked up by an armed escort trawler and landed at

Leith the following day. The position, according to the 'Maritime Declarations of Norwegian Ships', was at 55° 27'N 01° 09'W.

Sjøforklaringer over norske skibes krigsforlis 1914–1919 – LCWLR 1914–18 Page 202 – ANCL 1914–18 Page 76

Wrecksite

The wreck, which is probably that of the Norwegian steamer, is orientated in a SE to NW direction. It lies on a seabed of mud and fine sand in a general depth of 95 m (LAT). The wreck sits in a 1 m-deep scour that extends over 55 m in length, but the wreck itself covers an area 53 m long and 14 m across and stands 3.6 m high. It is probably intact, but appears to be inverted.

CALEDONIA, HM TRAWLER

Date of loss: 17 March 1917
Wreck: ★★★
Depth: 69 m
Reference: 55 30'.793 N 001 16'.458 W
Location: 10.86 nm ENE of Castle Point, Dunstanburg

The *Caledonia* was a steel-hulled 161-ton ketch-rigged steam trawler that measured 34.18 m in length, with a 6.42-m beam and a 3.37-m draught. Hall, Russell and Co. Ltd. Aberdeen built and completed her as Yard No. 409 in September 1906; she was launched on 22 August 1906 for Thomas L. Devlin at Granton. The single screw was powered by a 65-hp, three-cylinder triple expansion steam engine that used one boiler. She had one deck. Port reg: GN.34.

In 1915, the vessel was requisitioned and in March 1917 was designated for Special Service.

Final patrol

On 17 March 1917, HMT *Caledonia* was off Newton Point, Northumberland, on her way from Aberdeen to Lowestoft for fitting out as a Special Service vessel, when the KDM submarine SMU *UC 50*, commanded by Kapitänleutnant Rudolf Seuffer, captured her.

At 1500 hrs and 20 miles E by S of Longstone, *UC 50* had stopped and sunk the 181-ton British trawler *Kestrel*; the crew was ordered into the lifeboat, but her skipper was taken prisoner. Then at 1600 hrs, the *Caledonia* was sighted. *Caledonia* was flying the White Ensign, but quickly hauled it down and surrendered and the crew was taken on board the submarine. The circumstances probably did not allow for a closer inspection of the trawler. The *Caledonia* was then scuttled using explosive charges/grenades.

The 25-ton drifter, HMD *Gowan* which was also on her way from Aberdeen to Lowestoft for fitting out, was intercepted 15 miles SE of Longstone. The crew was ordered into the lifeboat and the drifter was sunk with an 88-mm shell hit. The skipper of the *Kestrel* joined the bulk of the crews of the *Caledonia* and *Gowan* in the lifeboats, where one of *Gowan*'s crew, George Holdsworth Moat, a deckhand in the RNR, later died of exposure.

Rudolf Seuffer took as prisoners of war the skipper of *Caledonia* (described as a warrant officer in the RNR) and a leading machinist. Initial interrogation by the U-boat's crew suggested that the purpose of the *Caledonia* was tending to the harbour defence minefields. Other sources claim that the *Gowan* was being towed by the *Caledonia.*

Lloyd's War Losses 1914–18 Page 106 – British Fishing Vessels Lost at Sea Due to Enemy Action, 1914–18 – ADM 137/339 – ADM 137/390

Wrecksite

The wreck, possibly that of the *Caledonia,* is orientated in a SE to NW direction, with the bows to the southeast. It lies on a seabed of fine sand, mud and black shells in a general depth of 69 m (LAT). The wreck is intact and stands over 4 m high with some debris close by. It covers an area of 32 m in length by about 6 m across, with large numbers of fish swimming over the wreck.

IGOR, ex CAIRNBAHN, ex TREVIDER (?)

Date of loss: 17 September 1918
Wreck: ★★★★
Depth: 58 m
Reference: 55 30'.175 N 001 25'.317 W
Location: 5.77 nm ENE from Castle Point, Dunstanburgh

The *Igor* (Official No. 81677) was an iron-hulled 1534-ton Swedish steam cargo ship that measured 79.07 m in length, with a 10.99-m beam and a 5.3-m draught. John Readhead and Co. at South Shields built and completed her as Yard No. 200 in October 1883; she was launched as the *Trevider* on 29 October 1883 for E. Hain and Son, St. Ives. The single steel screw was powered by a 161-nhp two-cylinder compound steam engine that used two single-ended boilers with four furnaces, 6.03 m (65 sq.ft) of grate surface and 251.39 m (2706 sq.ft) of heating surface. The cylinders measured 76.2 cm and 147.32 cm with a 91.44-cm stroke (30 in. and 58 in. with a 36-in. stroke). John Readhead and Company manufactured the engine and ancillary machinery at South Shields. She had one deck, a well deck, a 31.1-m quarterdeck, a 19.3-m bridge deck and an 8.5-m forecastle.

In 1885, Trevider SS. Co. Ltd. St. Ives was the registered owner and E. Hain and Son was the manager.

Gaelic S.S Co. Ltd. at Newcastle purchased the ship in 1898 and renamed her *Cairnbahn*; Cairns, Young and Noble was the manager. A new donkey boiler was fitted in 1900.

In 1904 she had the same owner but Cairns, Noble and Co. became the manager.

In 1912, Cairn Line of Steamships Ltd. was the registered owner using the same manager. She was renamed *Igor* in 1913 by Rederi AB Hebe, Helsingborg and G. W. von Liewen was the manager.

In February/March 1916, the registered owner was Rederi AB Igor, Sundsvall and L. Norström was the manager.

From July 1917, AB Svenska Amerika-Mexico-Linien, Göteborg in Sweden was the registered owner and Dan Broström became the manager.

Final voyage

At 1845 hrs on 17 September 1918, the *Igor*, commanded by Captain O. T. Christianson, reportedly developed a serious leak and sank ten miles south of the Longstone light. Lloyd's and a Swedish source stated that she was either torpedoed or struck by a mine. The steamer was part of a convoy and on passage from Göteborg for the Tyne with a general cargo, including wood. All of her crew safely abandoned ship in the boats and an escort vessel picked them up.

LR 1915–16 No. 62 (1) – IDNS Page 79 – Starke Schell Registers

Wrecksite

The wreck, probably that of the *Igor*, is orientated in an ESE to WNW direction. It lies on a firm seabed of dark sand and black shells in a general depth of 58 metres (LAT). The wreck is upright and intact, covering an area 63 m long and 15 m across and standing about 7 m high around the collapsed bridge superstructure. Plenty of marine life has been observed, including some very large cod, making this an excellent boat-angling venue. If the bell is recovered it will almost certainly be inscribed: *Trevider 1883*. Interestingly however, a ship's bell inscribed: *Gaelic 1898* was recovered from a wreck, thought to be the *Hesvik,* at 55 28'.188 N 001 29'.677 W. As mentioned above, the *Igor* was purchased by the Gaelic Steam Ship Company in 1898.

PATIA, HMS

Date of loss: 27 April 1941
Wreck: ★★★★★
Depth: 57 m
Reference: 55 31'.420 N 001 26'.098 W
Location: 6.54 nm SE of Beadnell Point

The Elders & Fyffes 5,355 ton steamer Patia – circa 1930, later to become HMS Patia in 1941. (Author's collection)

HMS *Patia* (Official No. 145920) was a steel-hulled 5355-ton British steam catapult ship that measured 123.05 m in length, with a 16-m beam and a 9.24-m draught. Camel Laird and Co. Ltd. Birkenhead built and completed her as Yard No. 885 in March 1922; she was launched on 14 January 1922 for Elders and Fyffes Ltd. Liverpool and registered there. The single screw was powered by a 447-nhp three-cylinder triple expansion steam engine that used three single-ended boilers and gave 13.5 knots. The cylinders measured 69.85 cm, 118.11 cm and 198.12 cm with a 137.16-cm stroke (47.5 in., 46.5 in. and 78 in. with a 54-in. stroke). Camel Laird and Co. Ltd. manufactured the engine and ancillary machinery at Birkenhead. She had two decks, two part decks, water ballast, a 12.89-m poop deck, a 47.85-m bridge deck and a 13.41-m forecastle. The *Patia* was fitted with a wireless direction finder. The designated code recognition signal letters were: GDCY from 1934.

The Admiralty requisitioned the ship as an Ocean Boarding Vessel in October 1940.

In March 1941, *Patia* was rebuilt to a Pegasus Class Auxiliary Fighter Catapult Ship, capable of launching Hurricane aeroplanes. She was armed with two six-inch guns, three H.A. quick-firing guns, two Hotchkiss, two pom-poms and three of the newly invented Harvey three-inch rocket-missile projectors, to use against enemy aircraft. This class, consisting of *Ariguani*, *Patia*, *Maplin*, *Springbank* and *Pegasus*, were converted from merchant cargo ships in an effort to combat the long-range German Focke Wulf 200 Condor reconnaissance aircraft that were exploiting the gap in the mid-Atlantic, beyond the range of Allied aircraft. The reconnaissance aircraft used this lack of air cover to guide their U-boat wolf packs towards Allied convoys. For a Hurricane Catapult pilot, it was a one-way journey once he had left the ship, with nowhere to land but the sea.

After her completion by Brigham and Cowan at South Shields, *Patia* was commissioned on 26 April as a Fighter Catapult Ship and the following day headed out of the Tyne for gun trials, returning at 1600 hrs.

Final voyage

At 1825 hrs on 27 April 1941, HMS *Patia* left her berth and sailed down the River Tyne for a voyage to Belfast, where she was to pick up Hurricane aircraft. Thousands of people lined the river to see her off on her maiden voyage. From South Shields she headed north, accompanied by a single Blenheim aircraft which left her when darkness set in. *Patia* was about four miles off Boulmer, Northumberland and the crew was looking for the 20F buoy when she was attacked by a Aalborg-based German Heinkel III, coming in from the eastward, bearing Green 130°. The ship was at cruising stations and her radar (RDF) set was faulty.

Lt. D.A. Chantler RNR, one of the survivors, stated at the Inquiry:

"We passed 20G Buoy at 2117 hrs and about three minutes later I spotted this attacking plane and we were taken by surprise, as it was flying at a height of 70 feet. On approaching, the aircraft dropped one bomb about one mile away; it was a bad miss. The plane then flew over the ship and dropped a second bomb, which was a near miss on the port side. Action Stations were sounded after the first bomb dropped. Unfortunately we were taken by surprise and no guns were brought into action on the first attack. She flew to the north and west and attacked again from the northward about five minutes later. At the time of the first assault, the commander put the helm hard to starboard.

In the second strike everyone held their fire until the plane was within range. All AA armament was brought to bear. In that attack, the aircraft opened fire with machine guns and dropped two more bombs, which fell well clear of the ship, slightly on port quarter, at masthead height. In that attack the starboard pom-pom and after port Hotchkiss jammed; Lieutenant Webb was on the gun. After flying over the ship she flew away to the southward and then attacked again from aft, this time raking us with machine gun fire. I think Lt Nicholls met his death on the Harvey Projector, amidships aft. The aircraft passed over the ship over port bow and flew out of sight and was again seen later to be flying east and south. We rested the gun crews; she made a final attack from port quarter. In that attack she opened fire with machine guns at a very low altitude and also dropped three bombs. All AA armament we could bring to bear opened fire. The first bomb was a near miss astern, the second hit the ship, holing either the after starboard side of the engine room, or forward side of no. 3 hold. The third dropped on the starboard side, a near miss that damaged the bridge. The plane dropped a flare and opened fire with after machine guns. Immediately flames burst from the tail of the plane and she seemed to disappear into the sea, close by. I went round the ship seeing boats away. I was with the captain just before I jumped overboard with the Carley float. The ship had righted herself after heeling over to port, but was beginning to founder. The sea came up on the boat deck and Lt Menhinick threw over the Carley float and Lt Cdr. Robbin jumped over together with Lt Menhinick, an AB and myself. We nearly went down with the ship, but fortunately her stern stuck in the mud and we drifted with the tide clear of her."

Temporary Lt. A. Menhinick RNVR was not part of the ship's company but was on passage with her to train the crews on the use of the Harvey Projector. He was rescued by the *Chassiron* at 0230 hrs.

Lt. Chantler also said that it was a fine twilight night at the time and he thought it was the Hotchkiss or pom-pom that had brought the plane down, as it was too short a range for the Harvey Projector. When asked if they had been able to take any avoiding action, Lt. Chandler said: "We could have, but we did not take it because Commander Baker said that he did not agree to the taking of avoiding action, we could bring more to bear when attacking from forward or aft." When asked about the aircraft being shot down, Mr S.V. Gibbs, a Commissioned Gunner RN, stated: "I saw it actually on fire which was caused by three-inch or by the Harvey Projector; firing was effective all round."

HM Trawler *Chassiron* picked Lt. Chandler up, along with the German flight crew and Chief Petty Officer Prior.

The following is an extract from an account written later by Chief Engineer Lt. Cdr. A. E. Robbin RNR, who was a survivor on *Patia* and was also a witness at the inquiry:

"During the action I was in the engine room with the 2nd, 4th, 6th and 7th engineers, electrical engineer, donkeyman, storekeeper and greasers. One bomb hit no. 3 hold, adjoining the engine room. The shock of the explosion fractured the main steam pipe, the engine room being filled with live steam and all the lights failing. The engine room had to be abandoned immediately. Of the engine room staff, the 2nd engineer was in hospital for more than four months, recovering from burns and shock. The 7th engineer and electrical engineer died in hospital. The 4th engineer's body was picked up on a Carley float, badly scalded. The donkeyman and storekeeper's bodies were never recovered.

After making our way to the upper-deck, the 6th engineer and myself assisted in shutting steam off the engine room, after which I reported to the commanding officer. By this time the ship was settling, the after deck being underwater. Some of the boats were badly damaged, the last being lowered away at this time. The C.O. and I decided that as this boat was overloaded, we could stay on board as long as possible, together with two officers, one seaman and a Carley float.

The C.O. left me to go to his cabin to destroy some confidential papers. This was the last time he was seen alive, his body being picked up on a float the following day, dead from exposure. A few minutes after the C.O. left me, at about 2150 hrs, the ship began to sink rapidly and the two officers, the seaman and myself jumped overboard with the Carley float.

Unfortunately, when the *Patia* sank, the last boat to be lowered capsized, throwing the occupants, including several wounded, into the water. We on the float paddled around and picked up about a dozen of these men. After being in the water for some time we found great difficulty in remaining conscious, the sea being so cold. Before being picked up by the French trawler HMT *Chassiron*, three of the men on the float had died from exposure. It picked us up at about 0230 hrs. We had then been in the water for approximately four and a half hours and were landed at North Shields at about 0800 hrs. After being there five days, I proceeded on survivor's leave."

(The report is thanks to Lt Cdr. (E) A.F. Robbin's daughter, Mrs Nena Murstad and Tel/Radar Officer William H. Pope).

Thirty-one of the bedraggled and exhausted crew, many with their clothes burnt off and suffering from terrible burns, broken bones and serious wounds, managed to drift and scramble the four miles to the shore in a lifeboat, where a policeman and soldiers directed them towards the little village of Boulmer. Some of the sailors, no more than boys who had lied about their ages to enlist in the navy, cried in despair. While the ship's crew was arriving on shore, the local lifeboat was called out with an armed escort to pick up three of the survivors from the German plane (one crewman had been killed in the attack) and it was only when they found themselves in the midst of a great deal of wreckage that the lifeboat crew realised that a British ship had gone down. Local people rallied round and gave the sailors dry clothes and towels and treated their wounds; then they were given wine and spirits set up in the Fishing Boat Inn. All the children at the village school were sent home a few hours early to allow them to see the ship's crew leave for North Shields in a bus. The men were given 14 days leave, after being shipwrecked, but sadly, and some would say disgracefully, their pay was stopped the moment the ship went down. A Board of Inquiry decided that, because the ship was at cruising stations when she was attacked, they were at fault for being taken by surprise. Following that tragedy, the whole of the British Fleet was reminded and instructed to stay on the alert while off the northeast coast.

Commander Baker had been Chief Officer with Elder and Fyffes during peacetime.

Rumours abounded about a German spy having been on board the *Patia*, but there was never any proof or evidence of this.

Commander David Marion Burton Baker RNR, seven officers and 31 ratings were reported missing or killed:

Baker, David M. B., Commander RNR, killed
Bartram, Norman, Petty Officer Steward NAP, killed
Cook, William Charles, Able Seaman RN, missing
Davis, Reginald, Acting Leading Signalman RN, missing
Day, Morris Nathanial, Fireman, NAP, missing
Doherty, John, Greaser NAP, killed
Downs, James Robert, Fireman NAP, killed
Ferguson, John, Donkeyman NAP, killed
Godley, Albert William, Ordinary Seaman RN, killed
Gray, William, Carpenter NAP, killed
Hengler, Sidney J., Storekeeper NAP, killed
Hughes, George, Butcher 2nd class NAP, killed
Huzzey, William Alfred, Assistant Storekeeper NAP, killed
James, John Edward, Ordinary Seaman RN
Jewers, William, Greaser NAP, missing
Jones, Alfred, Ordinary Seaman RN, killed
Lawence, Leonard, Greaser NAP, killed
Matcham, Arthur, Storekeeper NAP, missing
Minten, Leonard Alfred, Ordinary Seaman RN, missing
Neuling, Julius Peter, Greaser NAP, killed
Nicholls, Cyril Sydney, Temp. Lieutenant RNVR, killed
Orman, William Frank, Fireman NAP, killed
Owen, Frederick Joseph, Lieutenant RNR, missing
Owen, Royston William Henry, 2nd Writer NAP
Parish, Frederick Arthur, Able Seaman RN, missing
Pelling, Henry, Fireman NAP, missing
Phillips, Godfrey Sidney Philip, Ordinary Seaman RNVR
Prim, Benjamin K., Temp.Sub Lt. (E), RNVR, killed
Riley, Edward Lawrence, Lieutenant RNVR, missing
Rogers, Douglas, Fireman NAP, killed
Short, Cyril, Ordinary Seaman, killed
Smith, John, Ordinary Seaman RN, killed
Smith, Wilfred Stennentt, Ordinary Coder RN
Stafford, George, Fireman NAP, killed
Tompkins, Frederick E., Petty Officer Steward NAP Vowles, Raymond Hubert Ray, 1st Writer NAP, missing
Williams, Bertram Erskine Thomas, Py/Ty/Lt, RNR, missing

Died later from wounds:

Jennings, Neville, Electrician NAP, 28/4/41
Kirkham, W., Temp. Act. Sub Lt. (E) RNVR, 28/4/41

Wounded:

Connor, Walter, Telegraphist RNV (W) R
Cousins, Desmond A., Ordinary Coder RN
Downs, Robert, Fireman NAP
Edmond, John, Fireman NAP
Forster, Richard T., Fireman NAP
Gervause, Walter L., Fireman NAP
Gilbertstedt, Robert V., Able Seaman RN
Goodman, Alfred S., Assistant Steward NAP
Johnson, Raymond, Ordinary Seaman RN
Jones, Charles E., Assistant Steward NAP
Jones, E., Temporary Lt. Engineer RNR
Kilbride, John, Ordinary Seaman RN
Maddock, E. H., Temporary Sub.Lt. Engineer RNR
McDonald, J., Temporary Paymaster Sub. Lt. RNR
McDonald, Leslie, Fireman NAP
Moor, George, Ordinary Seaman
Pawley, Richard J., Able Seaman RN
Ryan, David J., Ordinary Seaman RN
Sadler, A., Ordinary Seaman RN
Shields, John R., Able Seaman RN
Swinney, Dixon, Ordinary Seaman RN
Wade, Stanley, Ordinary Seaman RN
Watt, A., Temporary Surgeon Lt. RNVR

ADM 1/11290 – N.L. 9782 – LCWLR 1939–45 Page 232 – BVLS 1939–45 Page 12 – SRN Vol 2 Page 271 – CWGC

Wrecksite

This large naval vessel is orientated almost N to S and lies on a seabed of firm sand in a general depth of 57 m (LAT), with her decks at 48 m and a least depth of 43 m. It sits upright all the way back to number three hold, where it was broken by the bomb's direct hit. From this point to the stern, it is twisted through 90°, leaving the decks lying nearly vertical. Starting near the bridge and swimming over to the bow on the port side, the diver can still see the railway track-like structure, which was used to launch the Hurricane fighter plane. Halfway back from this ramp stands the large derrick that was used to lift the Hurricane onto the tracks, still standing erect and pointing towards the surface, like some weird sentinel. The derrick is now festooned in masses of trawl net and is held aloft by dozens of floats. When descending down through the eerie gloom the net makes a strange but very spectacular sight. Moving back to the bridge, the main body is still recognisable, although there has been some collapse of the bridge roof, making the main bridge compartment only 1.5 m high. Inside are the remains of the bridge operating systems, with the wooden wheel, although badly worn, still intact and within arm's reach, while behind the wheel is the doorway leading into Captain Baker's cabin. The door has long since rotted off, leaving a black, cold and uninviting void. The bridge wings still have anti-aircraft guns defiantly pointing towards the surface with empty shells lying scattered around the base, testifying to the brave and heroic fight the crew put up against the Heinkel bomber. Moving away back from the bridge to the engine room, skylights allow the diver to see right down the stairwell to the engine room and further back still, revealing the gaping hole where the funnel once stood, flanked on four sides by ventilation shafts that supplied air to the engines. Close by are the davits that had been left outboard, providing the means of escape for the ship's crew. A little further back, the wreck is twisted and broken, with the decks changed from horizontal to vertical. Caution is required at this point, because a very large trawl net is suspended from the bottom of the deck and lies like a huge curtain, nearly parallel with the decks. The net is also suspended on floats and is a considerably danger to the diver in the very dim light and murky conditions. The ship's main bell lies someway off the wreck, left there when a lifting bag to which it was tied broke loose and fell back to the seabed. Large cod, pout whiting, pollack, ling and probably conger can be found all around the wreck, making it an excellent boat-angling venue.

Patia is one of the most spectacular wrecks off the northeast coast, but, because of her size and the depth involved, she presents the diver with much more of a challenge than do many other wrecks in similar depths. It should also be remembered that she is a war grave. As recently as September 1997, some of the ship's brave survivors visited the area to meet local people who helped them in their time of need.

STORFORS

Date of loss: 27 February 1940
Wreck: ✯✯✯✯✯
Depth: 75 m
Reference: 55 32'.075 N 001 19'.898 W
Location: 9.99 nm ESE of Beadnell Point

The *Storfors* (Official No. 5957) was a steel-hulled 550-ton Swedish steam cargo vessel that measured 50.08 m in length, with an 8.3-m beam and a 3.27-m draught. Göteborgs Mekaniske Verkstader AB, Göteborg, Sweden built and completed her as Yard No. 350 on 18 March 1918; she was launched on 19 December 1917 for Uddeholms AB, Uddeholm in Sweden, who was also the owner at the time of loss; A. Herlenius was the manager. The single steel screw was powered by an aft-positioned 68-nhp three-cylinder triple expansion steam engine that used one single-ended boiler and gave 8.5 knots. The cylinders measured 13⅜ in., 22¼ in. and 37⅜ in. with a 23⅝-in. stroke. Göteborgs MV.Altieb., Göteborg in Sweden manufactured the machinery. She had one deck, a 14.9-m poop deck, a 49-ton (138.75-cubic.m) house deck and a 7-m forecastle and was fitted with electric lighting. The designated code recognition signal letters were: SGOW.

In 1930, Fritiof Olsson was the manager.

Final voyage

On the night of 27 February 1940, the *Storfors* foundered following a collision with the 1690-ton destroyer HMS *Jackal*, 12 miles from Beadnell Point. The *Storfors* was sailing as part of the northbound 26-ship convoy TM.15 (Tyne to Methil) and was transporting a cargo of coal from Hull to Gothenburg. The crew of 14 abandoned the vessel, which was in danger of sinking, were picked up by the warship and landed at a northeast port the next day, although a local lifeboat had spent three hours searching for the men.

LCR 1940 Page 9 (f) – LR 1919–20 No. 27121 (S) – IDNS Page 144 – Starke Schell Registers – Miramar Ship Index.

Wrecksite

The wreck is orientated in a NE to SW direction and lies on a firm seabed of gravel and sand, in a general depth of 75 m (LAT). It is upright and intact and stands almost 7.5 m at the stern end, which faces to the southwest, where the bridge/wheelhouse superstructure is still almost complete and covered in a profusion of soft corals. All of the vessel's interesting bridge equipment, lifeboat davits, winches, doors and portholes are still in place. Lots of large fish, mostly cod, have been observed all over the wreck, so it will make an excellent boat-angling venue.

JAMES HARRIS

Date of loss: 14 April 1881
Wreck: ✯✯
Depth: 68 m
Reference: 55 32'.954 N 001 18'.247 W
Location: 10.76 nm E from Beadnell Point and 11.89 nm SE from Longstone Lighthouse

The *James Harris* (Official No. 68300) was an iron-hulled 902-ton schooner-rigged steam cargo vessel that measured 64 m in length, with an 8.99-m beam and a 5.18-m draught. Raylton Dixon and Co. of Middlesbrough built her as Yard No. 102 and launched her on 9

March 1874 for Hogg and Henderson at Middlesbrough. The single four-bladed screw was powered by a 99-hp, two-cylinder compound steam engine that used one boiler. Blair and Co. Ltd. Stockton and Henderson manufactured the engine and ancillary machinery at Middlesbrough. She had one deck, four bulkheads and was classed as 90 A1. The designated code recognition signal letters were: MRTQ. The first master was Captain W. Lynas.

Final voyage

At 0030 hrs on 14 April 1881, the *James Harris*, commanded by Captain Johnstone, foundered and was lost following a collision in thick fog with the 167-ton Glasgow-registered coaster *Andalusia*. The *James Harris* had sailed the previous afternoon from Middlesbrough with an 1150-ton cargo of pig-iron for Grangemouth, while the smaller Glasgow steamer was *en route* from Grangemouth to Calais with 280 tons of pig-iron. Survivors from the *James Harris* stated that the ship was travelling very slowly around midnight and was sounding the fog whistle constantly; they then heard a strange fog whistle off the port bow. Suddenly the masthead and port lights of another steamer were sighted just about a ship's length off the port bow and the helm was ordered hard-a-port. It was the *Andalusia* and within two minutes it had struck the *James Harris* on the port bow, abaft the fore rigging. The Middlesbrough steamer almost immediately began to fill up and went down by the head; her crew and only passenger left struggling in the sea. The *Andalusia* quickly lowered her boats and managed to pick up four men: the chief engineer John Bartley, the second engineer Thomas Rudd, Seaman William Hall and fireman Edward Bavington, but 13 other crewmen and the passenger all drowned.

James Scott, the chief mate on the *Andalusia* stated: "Our vessel had arrived at Leith yesterday afternoon and the weather was so thick and foggy that the steam and fog horns were constantly sounding and the two vessels came into sight with each other when they were just about six yards apart. The fog horn from the *James Harris* had been heard, although the whereabouts of the vessel could not be made out. As soon as it was seen, the engines on our vessel were put in reverse and the helm put hard-a-port. The *James Harris* was cut almost in half; her bow going almost immediately underwater, and as the water reached the boilers, they blew up and scattered wreckage all around". Mr Scott continued: "Lifebuoys were thrown out and a lifeboat was lowered from hour ship, so that four men were saved, although one or two were in the water for about half an hour. The stem of the *Andalusia* was shattered, but the forepart of the ship had a compartment and the vessel was kept afloat with the assistance of the steam engine."

The men who drowned were:

Anderson, Robert, Seaman MM
Boon, John, Seaman MM
Harrall, James, First Mate MM
Johnstone, James, Master MM
Masson, Robert, MM
Morgan, William, Seaman MM
Potkins, Peter, Cook MM
Scott, William, Second Mate MM
Thomson, Frederick, Seaman MM
Waters, Henry, Fireman MM
Whiffen, John, Fireman
A Steward, whose name is unknown
A Seaman from Edinburgh

The passenger had formerly been the Second Mate on the 595-ton steamer G.M.B. (1878 – William. A. Donaldson, Middlesbrough) and he was on his way to join a vessel at Grangemouth.

An inquiry into the incident was held at the Wreck Commissioners Court, Westminster. The four survivors from the sunken vessel were called, along with the master, mate and two other crewmen from the *Andalusia*, but the final outcome is not known. Captain Reid, the master of the *Andalusia*, and all his officers are known to have stated that they were keeping their course and that the accident was caused by the *James Harris* porting her helm when she heard the fog whistle and in so doing, brought herself into the path of the *Andalusia* and faster than represented.

Board of Trade Wreck Return 1881Appendix to Parts I-IV Page 138 (408) – LR 1875–6 No. 68 (J) – Wreck Commissioner's Court Report 1881: 'The James Harris and the Andalusia' – Record of American and Foreign Shipping 1885 – The Times, Friday, 15 April 1881; Page 3; Issue 30169

Wrecksite

The wreck is orientated in a S to N direction and lies on a seabed of fine sand, mud and gravel in a general depth of 68 m (LAT). The wreckage is partially buried, totally collapsed and well broken up, standing just 3.5 m high and covering an area 22 m in length and 15 m across.

LUNESDALE (?)

Date of loss: 12 March 1929
Wreck: ✯✯✯✯
Depth: 70 m
Reference: 55 32'.817 N 001 23'.397 W
Location: 7.81 nm E by S of Beadnell Point

The *Lunesdale* (Official No. 127934) was a steel-hulled 216-ton British steam cargo vessel that measured 35.07 m in length, with a 6.57-m beam and a 2.57-m draught. Thomas Dobson and Co. Ltd. at Hessle, Hull built and completed her as Yard No. 151 in October 1908; she was launched in the third quarter of 1908 for Lancaster and Liverpool S.S. Co. Ltd. at Liverpool. An aft-positioned 60-hp, two-cylinder compound steam engine that used one single-ended boiler powered the single steel screw. Shields Engineering Co. Ltd. manufactured the machinery at North Shields. She had one deck, three bulkheads, a 13.1-m quarterdeck, 2.7-m bridge deck and 5.8-m forecastle.

From 1919, she was registered in Wexford and owned by James J. Stafford of Paul Quay, Wexford until at least 1921.

Charlton, Oscar and Young owned her at the time of loss and Captain Daniel McLennan was the master.

Final voyage

At 0250 hrs on 12 March 1929, the *Lunesdale,* with Captain Daniel McLennon in charge, sank following a collision with the 1667-ton SS *Melrose* (1906 – George Gibson and Co. Leith) in thick fog, seven miles south by east of Longstone lighthouse. Four men were drowned, including the master, but the *Melrose* picked up three others. The *Lunesdale* was on passage from Sunderland for Banff with a cargo of coal. A number of boats, including the

Holy Island lifeboat, put to sea to search for the men, but after a fruitless search returned to base in the afternoon. The *Melrose* had a slight leak in the forepeak, but carried on with her voyage to Kirkpatrick. The crewmen lost were:

Lambert, G., MM of Hull
Mayne, H., MM of Avoch
McLennan, Daniel, Master MM of Avoch
Reid, W., MM of Avoch

The survivors were:

Reid, D., Mate MM
Sutherland, J., Seaman MM
Swanson, J., Chief Engineer MM

On 15 March 1940, the SS *Melrose* was mined and sunk near Ostend.

LCR 1929 Page 8 (f) – LR 1927–28 No. 27921 (L) – The Times, Wednesday, 13 March 1929; Page 18; Issue 45150

Wrecksite

The wreck, believed to be that of the *Lunesdale*, is orientated in a SSE to NNW direction with the bows to the NNW. It lies on a seabed of firm sand and gravel in a general depth of 70 m (LAT). It is upright, reasonably intact, with the aft superstructure 5.5 m high, but partially collapsed. The deck machinery, davits and jibs are completely intact, if a little bent, and a section of short broken mast, up forward towards the bows, is still in place, with the rest lying broken up across the deck. There is a large hole where the funnel once stood, giving access to the inside of the bridge structure and holds, which still contain part of the cargo of coal, although a section of hold is now split open.

BALTANGLIA, ex LANGFOND, ex LAATEFOS (?)

Date of loss: 23 January 1940
Wreck: ★★★★★
Depth: 59 m
Reference: 55 32'.925 N 001 28'.208 W
Location: 5.11 nm ESE of Beadnell Point

Norwegian steamship Baltanglia *was torpedoed by* U 19.

The *Baltanglia* (Official No. 165459) was a steel-hulled 1532-ton British steamship that was registered in London and measured 77.9 m in length, with a 12-m beam and 6-metre draught. Ardrossan Shipbuilding and Dry Dock Co. Ltd. Ardrossan built and completed her as Yard No. 319 in October 1921; she was launched as the *Laatefos* on 27 April 1921 for Thor Thoresens Linje Aktieselskapet, Kristiania, Norway; Thor Thoresen was the manager and she was registered in Kristiania. The single screw was powered by a 203-nhp three-cylinder triple expansion steam engine that used two single-ended boilers working at a pressure of 180 lb psi, with six corrugated furnaces, 9.75 sq.m (105 sq.ft) of grate surface and 326.83 sq.m (3518 sq.ft) of heating surface, which gave 9.5 knots. The cylinders measured 48.26 cm, 81.28 cm and 132.08 cm with a 91.44-cm stroke (19 in., 32 in. and 52 in. with a 36-in. stroke). J. G. Kincaid and Co. Ltd. Greenock manufactured the engine and ancillary machinery. She was equipped with wireless and had one deck, four bulkheads cemented, water ballast, a 7.31-m poop deck of 63 tons, a 106-ton (300.15-cubic.m) house deck and a 6.40-m forecastle of ten tons. She was classed as 100 A1.

In 1923, Svithun Linjen Aktieselskapet, Stavanger purchased her and renamed her *Langfond.* Sigval Bergesen was the manager.

She was sold to Rederi AB Fredrika, Stockholm, Sweden in 1937 and registered in Stockholm: Official No. 8132.

From 1937, Anglo-Lithuanian Shipping Co. Ltd. London was the registered owner and she was renamed *Baltanglia*; United Baltic Corp. Ltd. was the manager. The designated code recognition signal letters were: GZSJ.

Final voyage

The *Baltanglia* loaded her general cargo at Hommelvik and while still in Norwegian waters joined the 38-ship convoy HN.8 (Norwegian waters – Methil) on 19 January 1940, arriving at Methil without incident on 22 January. From Methil she sailed south, independently and unescorted behind the defensive minefields, for her destinations at the Tyne and Rochester. On 23 January 1940, however, the Kriegsmarine submarine *U 19*, commanded by Kapitänleutnant Joachim Schepke torpedoed and sank the steamer six miles east of Beadnell in Kriegsmarine quadrant AN5186. On the morning of 23 January 1940, *U 19* broke at high speed through the mine warning area off the Farne Islands and immediately found about 20 unescorted southbound ships, including *Baltanglia* and *Pluto*; both these ships had arrived in Methil with convoy HN.8. Schepke later observed minesweepers in that area and on 25 January, a similar group of northbound ships came into sight, of which *Everene* and *Gudveig* were torpedoed. These ships were *en route* to Methil to join a convoy bound for Norway

Captain G. Thomas of the *Baltanglia* said that they had left Methil at midnight and at 0710 hrs were abeam of the Longstone buoy. He stated that the Norwegian steamer *Pluto* was ahead of him by about a mile and that there were a number of other ships more or less in line. The captain said he heard an explosion and noticed the *Pluto* beginning to sink by the stern. He was making arrangements to rescue the crew when another ship, in a better position to pick up the lifeboats, dashed past him. Captain Thomas then told the man at the helm to go back on the course, full speed ahead, but just three minutes later, at 0843 hrs (CT) his ship 'detonated a mine'; the force of which knocked him unconscious for about half a minute. He asserted that the *Pluto* sank in six minutes, and that they were only about three quarters of a mile astern of her when she 'struck the mine'. He stated that his vessel was about 315° from her position where the *Pluto* struck a mine.

Baltanglia's crew abandoned their ship in two boats and local fishermen from nearby Seahouses towed them in, tidal conditions at Seahouses having prevented the RNLI lifeboat from launching.

Authorities later questioned the mine theory and records released after the war confirmed that torpedoes from Schepke's little *U 19* had sunk the two ships.

LCWLR 1939–45 Page 37 – IDNS Page 21 – Starke Schell Registers

Wrecksite

The wreck, probably that of *Baltanglia*, is orientated in an almost N to S direction. It lies on a seabed of muddy sand and black shells in a general depth of 59 m (LAT). The wreck is intact and upright with midships superstructure still in place and standing almost 8 m high, although much of it consists of steel girders and box-like structures. The cargo appears to consist of stacked tiles of a rubber-like material. Lots of fish have been observed so it will make an excellent boat angling venue. The wreck was identified in 2008 when the bell, inscribed *Laatefos*, was recovered.

PLUTO, EX RØVÆR (?)

Date of loss: 23 January 1940
Wreck: ★★★★
Depth: 67 m
Reference: 55 33'.963 N 001 26'.787 W
Location: 5.94 nm ENE from Beadnell Point

Norwegian steamer Pluto, ex Røvær, circa 1920 (Courtesy: Rolf Kristensen, Åsgårdstrand & Stein-Erik Dagsland, Heinavegen, Norway)

The *Pluto* was a steel-hulled 1598-ton Norwegian steam cargo ship that measured 74.98 m in length, with an 11.50-m beam and a 4.7-m draught. Laxevaags Maskin and Jernskibsbyg, Bergen in Norway built and completed her as Yard No. 126 in August 1918; she was launched as the *Røvær* on 6 July 1918 for Dampsk. Aktieselskapet John K. Haalands Rederi, Haugesund, Norway; John K. Haaland was the manager. The single steel screw was powered by a 138-nhp three-cylinder triple expansion steam engine that used two single-ended boilers, which gave nine knots. The cylinders measured 45.72 cm, 73.66 cm and 124.46 cm with an 83.83-cm stroke (18 in., 29 in. and 49 in. with a 33-in. stroke). Laxerags Mark and Jernskibs in Bergen manufactured the engine and ancillary machinery. She had one deck, four bulkheads cemented, a 40-ton (113.26-cubic.m) forecastle, a 12-ton (33.98-cubic.m) bridge deck, a 109-ton (308.65-cubic.m) quarterdeck, a 39-ton (110.43-cubic.m) poop deck and a 68-ton (192.55-cubic.m) house deck.

She was classed as 100 A1. The designated code recognition signal letters were: MSGW.

In 1923, she was renamed *Pluto* by Dampskipsselskapet Aktieselskapet "Pluto", Haugesund, who purchased her and B. Stolt-Nielsen and Co. was the manager.

She was later equipped with electric lights, wireless and direction finder.

From 1926, Dampskipsselskapet Aktieselskapet Facto was the registered owner and B. Stolt-Nielsen and Co. was the manager until 1927.

B. Stolt-Nielsen and Sønner Aktieselskapet became the manager from 1927. The designated code recognition signal letters were: LDEX.

Final voyage

The Kriegsmarine U-boat *U19*, commanded by Kapitänleutnant Joachim Schepke *Ritterkreuz* torpedoed and sank the *Pluto* in Kriegsmarine quadrant AN5186n 23 January 1940. The *Pluto* had sailed from Bergen as part of the 38-ship convoy HN.8 (Norwegian waters – Methil) and arrived at Methil on 22 January 1940. She then left Methil in ballast at midnight and was travelling south independently for Middlesbrough, although there were about twenty other vessels travelling south and unescorted not far away from her near the Farne Islands.

On 24 January 1940, Captain G. Thomas of *Baltanglia*, stated in an interview: "We sailed from Methil bound to the Tyne on 3 January (this should probably be the 23rd) with a general cargo of 1930 tons. Radio telephone was fitted and the ship was unarmed. The colour of my hull superstructure was grey. We were flying no ensign at the time of the explosion and our confidential books were all thrown over the side in a weighted canvas bag. The crew numbered 27 including myself and we carried no passengers.

We left Methil at midnight and at 10 minutes past 7 a.m. we were abeam of the Longstone Buoy. We then had to go two miles further south, then down on to the last true course and through the swept channel. There was a Norwegian steamer, the *Pluto*, ahead of me by about a mile, and ahead of him there were several other steamers more or less in line. I heard an explosion and then noticed the *Pluto* start to sink by the stern. I hauled over to port and came full astern, made a starboard cant to get a lee of his boats when I found another steamer dashing past me in a better position to pick his boats up. I then told the man at the wheel to go back on the course full speed ahead and three minutes afterwards, at 7.50 a.m., we struck a mine. The force of the explosion knocked me unconscious for perhaps half a minute.

The *Pluto* sank in six minutes, and we were only about three quarters of a mile astern of her when the mine hit her. We were about 315° from her position where she struck a mine."

Captain Thomas then described the damage to his own ship, adding that they abandoned her in two lifeboats which were towed in by local fishermen from Seahouses. They had tried to launch a lifeboat, but could not do so on account of the tide. Another unconfirmed report stated that a Finnish steamer picked up the crew and took them to Seahouses. Authorities later questioned the mine theory, and believed there was evidence the explosions had been caused by a torpedo. Records released after the war did indeed confirm that torpedoes from *U 19* had sunk both *Pluto* and *Baltanglia.* .

Norwegian Maritime Declarations 1914–1918 – LCWLR 1939–45 Page 37 – IDNS Page 119

Wrecksite

The wreck believed to be the *Pluto* is orientated in a NNE to SSW direction. It lies on a seabed of muddy sand and black shells in a general depth of 67 m (LAT). The wreck is mostly intact, but appears to be inverted and rather collapsed, covering an area 69 m long and 12 m across, with the highest structure about 8 m off the seabed; on both sides of the main wreckage are debris fields. There are also another three wrecks in fairly close proximity, so this should make an excellent boat-angling venue.

STAMFORDHAM (?)

Date of loss: 4 August 1916
Wreck: ★★★★
Depth: 65 m
Reference: 55 33'.885 N 001 26'.980 W
Location: 7.29 nm SW of Longstone Lighthouse

The *Stamfordham* (Official No. 106650) was a 921-ton steel-hulled cargo steam vessel that measured 64 m in length, with a 9.16-m beam and a 4.04-m registered depth and 4.87-m moulded depth. Wood, Skinner and Co. Ltd. at Bill Quay near Newcastle built and completed as Yard No. 78 in November 1898; she was launched on 27 October 1898 for T. and W. Smith at Newcastle. The single screw was powered by a 99-rhp, three-cylinder triple expansion steam engine that used one single-ended boiler. North East Marine Engineering Co. Ltd. at Newcastle manufactured the machinery. The cylinders measured 43.18 cm, 71.12 cm and 116.84 cm with a 76.2-cm stroke (17 in., 28 in. and 46 in. with a 30-in. stroke). She had one iron deck and web frames, four bulkheads and a 31.39-m quarterdeck, a 2.74-m bridge deck and 7.62-m forecastle.

In 1905, Stamfordham S.S. Co. Ltd. was the registered owner and T. and W. Smith was the manager.

From 1907, Harries Brothers and Co. Newcastle (Swansea) was the registered owner.

Final voyage

On 4 August 1916, the *Stamfordham*, with Captain T.J. Rees in charge, was captured by Commander Werner Fürbringer in the KDM submarine SMU *UB 39*, eight miles SW of Longstone light. The crew was forced to abandon ship before she was sunk by gunfire. The steamer was *en route* from Kirkwall to Seaham in ballast and none of the crew was lost.

Starke Schell Registers – LCWLR 1914–18 Page 50 – LR 1914–15 No. 1833 (S) – BVLS 1914–18 Page 21 – BMS 1914–18 Page 118.

Wrecksite

This wreck, probably that of the *Stamfordham*, is orientated in an ESE to WNW direction.

It lies on a firm seabed of gravel and sand in a general depth of 65 m (LAT). The wreck is quite substantial, upright and intact, with her bows to the ESE and standing almost 8 m high amidships. The partially collapsed bridge/wheelhouse superstructure is there, covered in a profusion of soft corals. Many of the vessel's decks, companionways, doors, air ducts and lifeboat davits are in good condition, making this an exciting wreck to explore. When weather conditions permit, this wreck will also make an excellent boat-angling venue.

AFRICAN PRINCE (?)

Date of loss: 10 June 1931
Wreck: ★★
Depth: 63 m
Reference: 55 33'.772 N 001 27'.105 W
Location: 5.73 nm E of Beadnell Point

The *African Prince* (Official No. 105215) was a steel-hulled 125-ton British steam trawler that measured 28.95 m in length, with a 5.84-m beam and a 3.22-m draught. J. T. Eltringham and Co. at Stone Quay, South Shields built and completed her as Yard No. 185 on 20 August 1896 and she was launched on 13 June 1896 for W. H. Storey at North Shields, registered as SN.224. The single steel screw was powered by an aft-positioned 45-nhp two-cylinder compound steam engine that used one single-ended boiler and gave ten knots. The cylinders measured 40.64 cm and 83.82 cm with a 55.88 cm stroke (16 in. and 33 in. with a 22-in. stroke). G. T. Grey at South Shields manufactured the machinery. She had one deck.

In 1901 the trawler was owned by Prince Steam Fishing Co. Ltd. at North Shields, with Richard Irvin the manager.

On 10 September 1914, the North Shields registry closed and she was owned by Walker Steam Trawling and Fishing Co. Ltd. Aberdeen and registered at Aberdeen as A.114.

From 1917 to 1919 she was requisitioned as a Fishery Reserve Vessel and returned to the owners in 1919.

From 1929, R. J. Balls at North Shields was the owner and she was registered as SN.111.

Final voyage

On 10 June 1931, the *African Prince* was on a fishing voyage when she developed a serious leak and foundered in heavy weather, approximately 35 miles north of the Tyne. The crew took to the boat and were picked up and landed at Leith on the 11th, after cruising around in the boat for eight hours.

LCR 1931 Page 5 – LR 1931–32 No. 06434 (A) – The Times, Friday, 12 January 1931; Page 13; Issue 45847

Wrecksite

This wreck could possibly be that of the *African Prince*, which sank around that latitude. It is orientated in a SE to NW direction and lies on a seabed of firm sand, gravel and shells in a general depth of 63 m (LAT). It is collapsed, well broken up and scattered, but standing some 8.5 m high and covering an area 24 m in length and 13 m across. A trawl net also floats upwards and over the wreckage.

KOPANES, HM TRAWLER, EX DARGLE, EX JERICHO, EX SIR JOHN JELLICOE

Date of loss: 19 April 1941
Wreck: ✯✯✯✯
Depth: 67 m
Reference: 55 33'.873 N 001 26'.681 W
Location: 6 nm E by N of Beadnell Point

The *Kopanes* (Official No. 136245) was a steel-hulled 351-ton British steam trawler that measured 43.9 m in length, with a 7.3-m beam. Cook, Welton and Gemmell at Beverley built and completed her as Yard No. 309 in March 1914; she was launched as *Sir John Jellicoe* on 22 September 1914 for the Imperial Steam Fishing Co. Ltd. Hull, who registered her in Hull as H.310 on 18 December 1914. The single steel screw was powered by a 100-nhp three-cylinder triple expansion steam engine that used one single-ended boiler working at a pressure of 200 lb psi, with three plain furnaces, 4.45 sq.m (48 sq.ft) of grate surface and 143.07 sq.m (1540 sq.ft) of heating surface, which gave 11 knots. The cylinders measured 33.02 cm, 57.15 cm and 93.98 cm with a 60.96-cm stroke (13 in., 22½ in. and 37 in. with a 24-in. stroke). Amos and Smith Ltd. at Hull manufactured the machinery. She had one deck and was classed as 100 A1. The designated code recognition signal letters were: MFZT.

In May 1915, the Admiralty requisitioned her as Minesweeper no. FY.1577 and renamed her *Jericho*; she was then equipped with two AC and employed on Anti- Zeppelin patrols in the North Sea.

On 20 November 1918, the boat was acquired by D Line Steam Fishing Co. Ltd. renamed *Dargle* and registered in Grimsby as GY.1170.

W. Garrat, Grimsby was the registered owner in 1928.

In 1932 she was sold to T. Fisher of Grimsby.

J. Little, Grimsby was the registered owner in 1933.

In December 1933 she was sold to the Kopanes Steam Fishing Co. Ltd. Grimsby and renamed *Kopanes*, with J. G. Little the manager.

When war broke out in 1939, she was requisitioned again and converted into an Admiralty Auxiliary Patrol Vessel (GY.1170) and equipped with one bow-mounted 12-pounder deck gun, wireless, direction finder and an echo-sounding device.

Final patrol

On 19 April 1941, HMT *Kopanes* was on patrol off Northumberland when German aircraft attacked and sank her with machine gun fire and bombs near to the 20G buoy, north of Coquet Island and six nm east of Beadnell. There were no casualties.

LCWLR 1939–45 Page 226 – SRN Vol 2 Page 200 – Cook, Welton and Gemmell 1883–1963

Wrecksite

The wreck, which has been identified by divers, is orientated in an E to W direction and lies on a seabed of sand, gravel and shells in a general depth of 67 m (LAT). It is standing upright, almost 7 m high, with some top structural damage to the bridge/wheelhouse area. There is a debris field all around the wreck and it is believed that part of the vessel may be missing. It is covered in a myriad of plumose anemones and masses of soft corals, but is also ensnared with monofilament and trawl nets. Numerous large fish have been reported around and over the wrecksite, including some very large cod, so she will make an excellent boat-angling venue.

SOMALI

Date of loss: 27 March 1941
Wreck: ✯✯✯
Depth: 28 m
Reference: 55 34'.134 N 001 36'.097 W
Location: 1.25 n.m NE of Beadnell

Left: The 6,890 ton Peninsular & Orient Steam Navigation Company steamer Somali, circa 1935. (Author's collection)

Right: The instant the Somali blew up (Courtesy of Selby Brown, Seahouses)

The *Somali* (Official No. 161938) was a steel-hulled 6890-ton British steam cargo ship that measured 139.9 m in length, with an 18.59-m beam and a 9.14-m draught. Harland and Wolff, Ltd. at Govan, Glasgow built and completed her as Yard No. 898 on 18 December 1930; she was launched on 9 October 1930 for Peninsular and Orient Steam Navigation Co. (P & O), Glasgow (London). The single screw was powered by a 1384-nhp four-cylinder quadruple expansion steam engine fitted with low pressure/exhaust turbines, with D.R. gearing and hydraulic cooling to a pressure of 230 lb psi that used five single-ended boilers and gave 15 knots. The cylinders measured 77.47 cm, 111.26 cm, 161.29 cm and 231.14 cm with a 152.4-cm stroke (30.5 in., 44 in., 63.5 in. and 91 in. with a 60-in. stroke). J. G. Kinnaird and Co. Ltd. manufactured the engine and ancillary machinery at Greenock. She had a cruiser stern, two decks and a shelter deck, seven bulkheads part-cemented and a 10.97-m forecastle, plus four insulated cargo chambers with a capacity of 1936.87-cubic.m (68 400-cubic.ft). She also had wireless, DF and electric lighting and one Carb Anhy refrigerating machine with two compressors manufactured by J. and E. Hall Ltd. The *Somali* also had a cellular double bottom covering 36.13 sq.m (389 sq.ft).

When war broke out, the ship was equipped for defence with one stern mounted 12-pounder (5.44-kilo shells) deck gun.

Final voyage

The *Somali* left London in the northbound convoy FN.442 (Southend – Methil) during March 1941, acting as the Commodore ship for a convoy that had assembled in the Pool of London. The convoy consisted of twenty three ships, mainly colliers, and travelled at seven knots. The *Somali* was on the first part of a voyage to Hong Kong, carrying two DEMS gunners, a crew of 77 and 9000 tons of general mixed cargo, including horses, fuses, cosmetics, ointments, medical supplies, canisters of celluloid films, shaving kits, salt cellars, bicycles, heavy lorry tyres, several 4×4s, shoes, large amounts of hay, straw and fodder, batteries, gas masks, fire extinguishers, coin for Hong Kong banks, paint, oil, explosives, drums of copper cable, mercury, hundreds of tons of white metal-bearing ingots and one hundred tons of toy lead soldiers. It was rumoured that part of the cargo of white metal ingots contained radioactive materials and were destined for India.

On the afternoon of 25 March, she was just north of Blyth in Northumberland when suddenly, out of the heavily cloud-laden sky, a squadron of German Heinkel III bombers came in for the attack, strafing the ship and scoring three direct bomb hits. At least one exploded in the hay-filled no. 3 hold, causing a raging inferno and leaving the ship very badly damaged. The two naval DEMS gunners put up a good effort with the old deck gun, but the Heinkels slipped back into the cloud cover, presumably untouched. A large sea-going tug, *Sea Giant*, was called to accompany the *Somali* on her voyage northwards while the crew fought desperately to get the fire under control, but by 2200 hrs on the following evening, when the vessels were seven miles SE of North Sunderland Point, the fire gained ground. With worsening weather, most of the crew were taken on board the escorting armed trawler HMT *Pelican*. In the early hours of 27 March, the flame and smoke from the fire had been observed from the shore and lifeboats from Holy Island, North Sunderland and Boulmer were launched and went to her aid, with the *W.R.A.* from North Sunderland being launched at 0155 hrs. On arrival, however, they discovered that the crew and passengers had already been taken on board the *Pelican*. The coxswains of the three lifeboats were each asked if they would put two crew members on board the steamer to help connect a tow line and this they did, returning to their lifeboats once the job had been carried out. The tow with the *Sea Giant* got underway at 0930 hrs and the two ships headed for the shelter of the Farne Islands, where they waited while the Holy Island lifeboat returned to her station.

The salvage vessel *Iron Axe* arrived on the scene and the salvage officer and two seamen were put on board the still-burning steamer by the Boulmer lifeboat *Clarissa Langdon* (a Liverpool class motorised lifeboat). The tug began to tow the damaged ship south with the intention of trying to save her by beaching her. At midday, the *Clarissa Langdon* took off the salvage vessel's officer and returned him to the *Iron Axe*, to which it was proposed to transfer the tow, while the two lifeboats remained on standby in case any assistance was required. They were at this stage some one and a half miles off Beadnell village. The *Clarissa Langdon* began to approach the *Somali* and begin the transfer, but when she was about 60 m from the steamer, an almighty explosion, thought to be the magazine going off, occurred in the bow section of the *Somali*. The force of the blast was so tremendous that it blew the bow section completely off and columns of smoke and pieces of debris were sent thousands of feet into the sky. The shock waves even caused structural damage in local houses and premises around the Beadnell area and many windows were shattered even in Seahouses, nearly five miles to the NW. The explosion lifted the lifeboat clear out of the water, knocking the boat's crew flat on the bottom, their caps were blown off, never to be seen again and it was reported that the blast even emptied some of their jacket pockets. Pieces of metal up to half a metre long then began to rain down on the two lifeboats and both were damaged in the fallout. Several of the lifeboat men were injured, with the bowman of the *Clarissa Langdon* receiving a severe gash to his head. The *Somali*'s stern end and centre section remained afloat with the two salvage men on board, but the bows went down to the bottom. Fearing for the men's safety, Coxswain Campbell on the *Clarissa Langdon* took his boat in through the mass of black smoke and fumes and rescued the two men, who slid down a rope into the sea before the lifeboat was brought clear at full speed, but the lifeboat's screw was fouled by some floating wreckage and the North Sunderland lifeboat *W.R.A.* had to come in and tow her out of the danger area. When the screw was cleared, the two lifeboats made for Seahouses, where the two seamen were landed at North Sunderland harbour at 1320 hrs.

The ship had a secret cargo compartment near to the bows and it was widely rumoured that she was carrying explosives, which may explain why the explosion was so great, ripping her in two at the bow section.

One person died on the *Somali*, possibly when the vessel was bombed.

For his excellent service, Coxswain James Campbell was awarded the RNLI's bronze medal on 17 April 1941, while his crew and Coxswain Dawson of the *W.R.A.* each received additional monetary awards.

LCWLR 1939–45 Page 210 – BVLS 1939–45 Page 19 – IDNS Page 140 – Starke Schell Registers 'The History of Seahouses and Holy Island Lifeboats' by Jeff Morris.

Wrecksite

The wreck of the *Somali* must rate as one of the most popular wreck dives off the northeast coast of England. Local dive charter-boat skippers usually buoy the wreck in three places: close to the boilers, near the starboard side of the hull remains and close to the stern end, although these are sometimes broken away by storms in the early months of spring. The wreck lies on a hard rocky seabed surrounded by numerous large reefs in a general depth of 28 m (LAT). When first discovered in the 1960s, she was fairly substantial, upright with most of her hull complete and standing 9 m high, her aft gun intact and deck fittings still in place. Unfortunately, although the remains of the ship still make an excellent dive, often with 15 m visibility, a considerable amount of salvage work has been carried out over the last twenty years and the wreck is just a shadow of its former self, being somewhat flattened now and dispersed around the seabed. The highest part is probably around 5 - 6 m. The remains of large drums of cement lie beneath the bulkheads near where the buoy is tied off at the starboard side of the three boilers, while at the port side is a gap and a further two boilers. Close by are the four huge cylinders, which are probably the highest part of the wreck, and the rest of its engine, pistons, rods and crankshaft, now exposed, where with a little care it is possible to swim through. Moving back towards the stern end, more cargo is visible, with large quantities of cement, piles of truck tyres with the cargo winch lying amongst them, empty rotting gas cylinders and even a large drum reel of heavy copper cable. The old 12-pounder deck gun and gun-mounting structure rests on the seabed next to a pair of bollards, with an anchor and spare screw not far away, although the screw has a section of broken mast lying across and slightly obscuring it. There are still large lumps of copper pipe and brass rods protruding out of the jumbled mass of iron, and steel and white metal ingots, looking like dirty white chocolate bars, can still be found. A word of warning, though: the shipwreck belongs to Stan Hall of Beadnell, who generally doesn't mind divers taking small trinkets, but the cargo belongs to someone else. Ocean Diving Services used to own the cargo until it was taken over by Novocastrian Diving Salvage Company who lost a valuable remote operated vehicle (ROV) from the site in 1991. The present owner of the cargo rights is unknown, and there has been no evidence to support rumours which circulated in 1998 that a large gold ingot had been found on the wreck.

The bow section remains a mystery, but there are plenty of reports of divers finding it by chance while on drift dives in the area. It is reputed to lie about 300 m away from the main wreck site, but whether to the north or south is unclear. Tales of unopened boxes strewn around the seabed are very unlikely to be true. Other reports, that the broken remains of the bow section are draped in steel cables or wires with lots of shoaling fish around them, sound more likely. Interestingly, the bow section was said to contain the ship's safe, either hidden in a secret compartment or in the forecastle, and the fact that it has never been located adds spice to the search for this section of the ship.

The tidal run is fairly strong and it is difficult to dive at anything but slack water. It is usually fairly easy to locate at weekends during the summer months because large numbers of diving boats, including the large charter boats from Seahouses, gather on the surface, the water teeming with divers. The best time to dive the wreck is on a neap tide and at low slack water, which is 1.5 – 1.75 of an hour after low water at Seahouses.

SAN BERNARDO, ex BELLASCO (?)

Date of Loss: 10 August 1916
Wreck: ★★★★
Depth: 72 m
Reference: 55 34'.660 N 001 14'.025 W
Location: 13.35 nm SE from Longstone and 13.25 nm ENE from Beadnell Point

The *San Bernardo* (Official No. 105992) was a steel-hulled 3803-ton steam cargo vessel that measured 106.8 m in length with a 13.84-m beam and a 7.82-m draught. David and William Henderson and Co. Ltd. Meadowside, Glasgow built and completed her as Yard No. 389 in May 1896; she was launched as the *Bellasco* on 2 March 1896 for Bellasco S.S. Co. Ltd. Glasgow, and Bell Brothers and McLelland was the manager. The single screw was powered by a 302-nhp three-cylinder triple expansion steam engine that used three boilers. The cylinders measured 60.96 cm, 101.6 cm and 167.64 cm with a 121.92-cm stroke (24 in., 40 in. and 66 in. with a 48-in. stroke). Shipbuilders D. and W. Henderson and Co. manufactured the machinery.

Bell Bros. and Co was the manager in 1908.

From 1916, Palmerston S.S. Co. Ltd. Glasgow (London) was the registered owner and that company renamed her *San Bernardo*; Edye and Co was the manager.

Final voyage

The *San Bernardo* left Norway on 8 August 1916 and was southeast of the Longstone at 1140 hrs on 10 August, when a submarine was sighted two miles distant, with two flags flying. The ship's master quickly turned and made off at full speed as soon as he realised it was an enemy boat. The submarine was in fact the KDM submarine SMU *UB 19*, commanded by Kapitänleutnant Walter Gustav Becker of the Flandern Flotilla. *UB 19* immediately opened fire with its deck gun and the fourth shell struck the ship's bridge. The steamer was then brought to a halt and her crew of 30 abandoned ship, but as they did so, the submarine approached one of the boats and captured its crew. Seven of the crew, including the master, were forced to accompany two German sailors back onboard the *San Bernardo* and the Germans placed explosive charges below her decks while the seven men were allowed to collect personal valuables and some food. All the men returned to the lifeboat and got clear of the ship before the explosives went off, but only two of them detonated. The U-boat commander questioned the men before allowing them to proceed on their way. They rowed in a westerly direction for a while before the 154-ton steam trawler *Magnus* (1896) picked them up at 0330 hrs on 11 August and landed them at North Shields quay at 0930 hrs. The *San Bernardo*, which had been in ballast and *en route* from Tyssedal, Norway to South Shields, sank about 17 miles SE of the Longstone.

ADM 137/2960 – Starke Schell Registers – LCWLR 1914–18 Page 52 – BVLS 1914–18 Page 21 – BMS 1914–18 Page 71 – LR 1915–16 No. 43 (B) and No. 137 (S) Supplement

Wrecksite

The wreck, which is probably that of the steamer, is orientated in a SE to NW direction. It lies on a rather firm seabed of fine sand, mud, black shells, stones and rock in a general depth of 72 m (LAT). The wreck is at least 6 m high, collapsed and well broken up and covers an area 87 m long and 25 m wide, with widely-scattered debris. The echo sounder showed an abundance of fish over the wrecksite, so it should make an excellent boat-angling venue.

JOHN G. WATSON (?)

Date of loss: 20 May 1930
Wreck: ✯✯✯✯
Depth: 77 m
Reference: 55 35'.810 N 001 20'.215 W
Location: 9.59 nm ESE of Longstone Lighthouse

The *John G. Watson* (Official No. 137384) was a 235-ton steam trawler that measured 37.33 m in length, with a 6.75-m beam and a 3.73-m draught. Hall, Russell and Sons Ltd. at Aberdeen built and completed her as Yard No. 588 in September 1916; she was launched on 30 August 1916 for Richard Irvin and Sons Ltd. at North Shields, who also owned her at the time of loss. Port reg: SN.305. The single steel screw was powered by a 78-rhp, three-cylinder triple expansion steam engine that used one single-ended boiler. The cylinders measured 30.38 cm, 50.8 cm and 86.36 cm with a 60.96-cm stroke (12 in., 20 in. and 34 in. with a 24-in.stroke). Hall, Russell and Sons Ltd. manufactured the machinery. The vessel had one deck and water ballast.

After she was completed, the boat was immediately requisitioned and converted to Admiralty Minesweeper No. 3322 and armed with one six-pounder AA gun. Later she was converted to an Armed Escort Vessel and in 1919 returned to the owners, R. Irvin and Sons Ltd. North Shields.

From May 1930, J.A. Doig was the registered owner.

Final voyage

On 20 May 1930, the trawler was being towed from Aberdeen to Grimsby for repairs when she sprang a leak and sank about five miles off Longstone lighthouse. No one was lost or injured.

LCR 1930 Page 5 (G) – LR 1929–30 No. 08267 (J) – The Times, Thursday, 22 May 1930; Page 13; Issue 45519

Wrecksite

The wreck, which is probably that of this trawler, is orientated in a roughly SE to NW direction. It lies on a firm seabed of broken shells, sand, gravel and stones in a general depth of 77 m (LAT). The remains appear intact and upright, but it is collapsed and broken, with the highest part standing about 4 m high. It covers an area 37 m long and 11 m wide.

TIOGA

Date of loss: 1 Nov 1943
Wreck: ★★★★
Depth: 63 m
Reference: 55 35'.903 N 001 25'.063 W
Location: 7.4 nm ENE of Beadnall Point

The *Tioga* (Official No. 132668) was a steel-hulled 742-ton British steam tanker that measured 54.78 m in length, with a 9.47-m beam and a 3.86-m draught. Greenock and Grangemouth Dockyard Co. Ltd. Grangemouth built and completed her as Yard No. 342 in February 1912; she was launched on 20 December 1911 for the Anglo-American Oil Co. Ltd. London, who owned her at the time of loss; R.A. Garder was the manager. The single screw was powered by an aft-positioned 110-nhp three-cylinder triple expansion steam engine that used one single-ended boiler working at a pressure of 180 lb psi, with three corrugated furnaces, 5.29 sq.m (57 sq.ft) of grate surface and 204.38 sq.m (2200 sq.ft) of heating surface. The cylinders measured 35.56 cm, 58.42 cm and 93.98 cm with a 60.96 cm stroke (14 in., 23 in. and 37 in. with a 24-in. stroke). Richardsons, Westgarth and Co. Ltd. at Middlesbrough manufactured the machinery. She had one part-steel deck and web frames, nine bulkheads cemented along with a 5.38-m cellular double base weighing 66 tons, a 3.35-m deep-tank fore of 35 tons, an eight-ton (22.65-cubic.m) fore-peak tank and a seven-ton (19.82-cubic.m) aft-peak tank. The superstructure consisted of: a 19.8-m poop deck, a 4.6-m bridge deck and an 8.53-m forecastle. Lloyd's classed her 100 A1. The designated code recognition signal letters were: MDRF.

Final voyage

The *Tioga* had joined the northbound 35-ship convoy FN.1165 (Southend – Methil) at Middlesbrough on 1 November 1943 and sailed in ballast, on passage for Grangemouth. Later that same day, she was seriously damaged following a collision with the 5305-ton steamer *Pundit* (1919 – Asiatic Steam Navigation Co. Ltd. London) at position 55° 40'N 01° 30'W. The *Tioga* was taken in tow but began listing badly and was in danger of sinking, so her crew were taken onboard an escort vessel. On 3 November, after she had continued to drift for many hours, Royal Navy warships escorting the convoy sank her with gunfire

LCR 1943 Page 8 (f) – Starke Schell Registers – Miramar Ship Index – LR No. 762 (T)

Wrecksite

The wreck is orientated in a N to S direction and lies on a seabed of hard sand and gravel in a general depth of 63 m (LAT). It is very substantial, standing upright and lying at a slight angle, but broken off into three sections, from just past the bows and to the fore of the bridge structure at the stern end, with the highest point of 8 m being at the stern. The wreck is rather broken up, but some of the bridge superstructure, decking, handrails, doors and deck machinery are still in reasonable condition and there are a number of places where access to the inside of the wreck would be possible. The ship's bell has been recovered, which identified the wreck. It is covered in silt and shoals of large fish swarm all around the superstructure, making the wreck a great boat-angling venue.

ATHELDUKE

Date of loss: 16 April 1945
Wreck: ✯✯✯✯✯
Depth: 55 m
Reference: 55 36'.384 N 001 27'.298 W
Other half: 55 36'.333 N001 28'.400 W
Location: 5.12 nm SE of Longstone light and 5.94 nm NE of Beadnell Point

The *Atheldu**ke*** (Official No. 161081) was a steel-hulled 8966-ton British motor tanker that measured 144.78 m in length, with a 19.26-m beam. Robert Duncan and Co. Ltd. Port Glasgow built and completed her as Yard No. 388 in January 1929; she was launched on 16 November 1928 for United Molasses Co. Ltd. Liverpool. Two aft-positioned 4S.C.S.A 12-cylinder oil engines that developed 709-nhp powered the two huge bronze screws and gave a service speed of 10.5 knots; she also used two donkey boilers working at a pressure of 180 lb psi. J. G. Kincaid and Co. Ltd. at Greenock manufactured the aft machinery. She had two steel decks, 16 bulkheads part-cemented, web frames with longitudinal framing, a 36.27-m poop deck, a 10.36- m bridge deck and a 14.63-m forecastle. She also had a 5.58-m deep-tank fore of 701 tons, a 219-ton (620.13-cubic.m) fore-peak tank and a 434-ton (1228.95-cubic.m) aft-peak tank. The ship was licensed for carrying molasses and petroleum in bulk. Lloyd's classed her 100 A1. The designated code recognition signal letters were: GSRP.

From 1940, Athel Line, Ltd. Liverpool was the registered owner.

On 17 January 1941, the *Atheldcuke* detonated a mine near Porthcawl at 51° 21'N 03° 20'W, and although the ship was only damaged, she was beached for repairs.

Final voyage

The *Athelduke* had sailed from Port Everglades, Florida with 12 600 tons of molasses for Salt End at Kingston-upon-Hull. The motor tanker first sailed from Port Everglades to Boston between 18 and 23 March 1945 and then joined the 21-ship convoy BX.152 to Halifax, Nova Scotia. From there she sailed across the Atlantic to Loch Ewe, leaving Halifax on 27 March 1945 as part of convoy CS.171 (Halifax – Liverpool), consisting of 22 ships and 15 escorts. From Loch Ewe she connected with the nine-ship convoy WN.685 to Methil, before joining the southbound 20-ship convoy FS.1784 (Methil – Southend) to make the final leg of her voyage to Hull. However at 1732 hrs (CT) on 16 April 1945, *U 1274*, commanded by Oberlt.z.S. Hans-Hermann Fitting attacked the *Athelduke* with two torpedoes within an interval of about three seconds, 5.75 miles SE of Longstone in the Outer Farne Islands. The first torpedo detonated on the port side of the cross bunker tank and the second one on the port side of no. 10 cargo tank. The bunkers took fire and clouds of smoke rose in the air. The vessel immediately began to settle at a very fast rate by the stern and by the time the members of the crew were making their way amidships, the poop was awash, the water extinguishing the bunker fire.

The master, Captain Joseph Errett, realising the immediate danger, gave the order to abandon ship in the two midship boats. The ship's complement embarked in the two boats, with the exception of William Alexander McKenzie, the senior fourth engineer, who was on watch at the time and had presumably been killed. No one had seen anything of Mr McKenzie, not even the senior second engineer, who had been in the engine room at the time, although he was on the middle platform and had managed to escape with scalds and burns. There was no panic amongst the crew and everybody abandoned ship in an orderly manner, although the chief officer, Mr G. W. Williams was left on board, floating off on a raft and picked up by one of the boats. The mess room boy, Thomas Wilson, had been trapped in his room below decks aft by the inrushing water and had attempted to escape via a porthole, but had become jammed in it. Mr H. Speed the senior third engineer, had been proceeding to the boat station when he heard the boy's cries. He immediately leant over the side whilst sitting in the waterway on the poop deck and, getting his feet on the boy's chest, took hold of his arms and hauled him out of the porthole and back on deck, undoubtedly saving his life. A few seconds more and the water would have reached the porthole, drowning him.

The ship sank stern first in three minutes and, owing to the reserve buoyancy contained in the forward ballast tanks, the forward hold up front, and the cofferdam and forepeak, remained for some time with her stern on the seabed and her forecastle above the surface. The forecastle eventually sank shortly before daylight the following morning, by which time she had remained afloat for about 12 hours. It is understood that the bulkheads in the after cargo

The 8,966 ton motor tanker Atheldukc *sank by* U 1274 *(Author's collection)*

tanks and in the cross bunker collapsed with two explosions, and divers later discovered that the ship broke in two and now lies in two separate sections on the seabed.

The 5224-ton British steamship *King Neptune* (1928 – Messrs Dodd, Thompson and Co. Ltd. Cardiff) rescued the master, 41 crew and four DEMS gunners and landed them at Grimsby at about 1800 hrs on 17 April. The master, Captain Errett, highly commended Mr Speed and on 16 April 1945 he was presented with the Lloyd's War Medal for Bravery at Sea.

Following the sinking, the aging 1325-ton destroyer HMS *Viceroy* relentlessly pursued *U 1274* and sank her with depth charges, 7.5 nm ESE of Longstone; all of the crew of 44 were lost.

ADM 199/232 – ADM 199/2148 – CWGC – LCWLR 1939–45 Page 804 – BVLS 1939–45 Page 71 – IDNS Page 19 – Report by Mr F.H. Formby, Marine Superintendant 20th April 1945, via Ms Pam Armstrong ADM 199/1047 – ADM 199/1046 – T1022 – roll 3900

Wrecksite

The wreck is orientated in a NW to SE direction and lies on a seabed of firm sand and stone in a general depth of 55 m (LAT). The wreck is in two huge sections, one 19 m high and the other 11 m high, with about 200 metres between them, and is now showing signs of collapsing in on itself. As would be expected of a tanker of such big proportions, the bulk of the wreck consists mainly of two huge steel plate hulks with the decks covered in dozens of metres of large steel pipes and tubes running the length of it. There are two bridge-type sections, one at the stern end and another about one quarter of the way forward from the stern, where the bridge/wheelhouse are located. The two sections of the wreck are absolutely enormous and would take literally dozens of dives to inspect properly. The giant 6 m bronze screws, weighing many tons, are still attached to the wreck, next to a massive rudder and surrounded by the overhanging steel structure of the ship's stern end, which is an awesome and eerie sight. Trawl nets draped over some of the huge superstructure hang like giant cobwebs. The wrecks will make excellent boat-angling venues too, thanks to an abundance of large fish, especially cod, ling, pollack and conger, sheltering in and around the remains.

7

SEAHOUSES TO THE FARNE ISLANDS

ASCOT, HMPMS

Date of loss: 10 November 1918
Wreck: ★★★★
Depth: 56 m
Reference: 55 37'.924 N 001 29'.860 W
Location: 6.34 nm NE of Beadnell Point and 3.83 nm ESE of Longstone Lighthouse

HMPS Ascot *was sunk by SM* UB 67 *on 10 November 1918, the day before the armistice was signed and all hostilities ceased. (Author's collection)*

The *Ascot* was a steel-hulled 810-ton Racecourse Class paddle steamer, designed and developed as a purpose-built minesweeper. Ailsa Shipbuilding Co. Ltd. Troon built and completed her as yard number 297 on 11 April 1916; she was launched for the Admiralty on 26 January 1916. Two inclined diagonal compound steam engines developing 1400 ihp (cylindrical return tube) that used four boilers powered her two 8.83-m (17.67-m at the paddles) side paddles and gave 14.5 knots. She carried 156 tons of coal and measured 74.86 m in length, with an 8.83-m beam and a 2.01-m draught. The *Ascot* was fitted with a derrick and winch to load and unload a small Sopwith Pup seaplane which she carried, plus an armament of one 7.6-cm (3-in.) bow gun and two aft-mounted 0.91-kilo guns (two-pounders) and one 2.72-kilo (six-pounder) gun, also mounted aft.

The *Ascot* was one of a flotilla of 32 Racecourse-design paddle vessels, laid down by the Admiralty in 1915. They served a useful purpose with their shallow draught, being able to venture into shallow water where other ships were unable to go. The danger of mines getting under the paddle wheels meant, though, that no more of this design were built, with those of the class that survived World War One being sold out of service.

Final voyage

On 10 November 1918, the KDM submarine SMU *UB 67*, commanded by Oblt.z.S. Hellmuth von Doemming, torpedoed and sank HMPMS *Ascot*. There were no survivors from her crew of fifty three (six officers, including three Mercantile Marine Officers and 47 other ranks). *UB 67* fired two torpedoes and one of them detonated in the boiler room, breaking her in two and apparently destroying the boats, leaving the crew with no chance of surviving the very rough sea. No attempt at rescue was made by the U-boat crew, because it was considered to be too close to land. The position given by *UB 67*'s KTB was 'the lower left corner of grid square 2247K', which is roughly 55° 37'N 01° 29'W.

Sadly, the following day the armistice was signed and all hostilities ceased. The crew became the last victims of submarine warfare in World War One.

The crewmen that perished on the *Ascot* were:

Bevan, William George, 205220, Leading Seaman RN
Boulton, Harry, 317TS, 21 yrs, Leading Trimmer RNR
Coneely, Peter, 8257A, 20 yrs, Seaman RNR
Connelly, Percy Janes, J/82042, 18 yrs, Ord. Seaman RNR
Cooper, William, 1345, 23 yrs, Seaman RNR
Coultas, William, 2367ST, 23 yrs, Leading Trimmer RNR
Cross, Cecil James Joseph, 18 yrs, K32192, Stoker 2nd Class RN
Dalton, Harry, 281TS, 26 yrs, Trimmer RNR
Davis, Patrick, 3693A, 27 yrs, Seaman RNR
Dobbs, George Henry, 209.TS, Trimmer RNR
Duggan, David Edward, Third Engineer, MMR
Edmunds, Samuel George, 13865DA, Deck Hand RNR
Gardner, Charles Edward Mafeking, Stoker, 2nd Class RN
Grubb, Wilfred Charles, J/33855, 19 yrs, Ord. Seaman RN
Hill, Charles, K/52369, Stoker 2nd Class RN
Horril, Edward Latham, 136091, 48 yrs, PO 1st Class RN
Irvine, James, 238L, Seaman RNR
Irwin, Robert Frederick, 37 yrs, Steward MMR
Jaffa, Leslie Charles Mersey, Z/1798, 29 yrs, Teleg. RN
Jones, Matthew George, 2677ST 21 yrs, Trimmer RNR
Judge, James, 2650ST Trimmer RNR
Juhle, Alexander Baxter, 3837TS 22 yrs, Ldg. Trimr RNR
Kersey, Robert, 10266DA, Deck Hand RNR
Keutenius, James William, 3034ST, Ldg Trimmer RNR
Kirman, George W., 20 yrs, Junior Engineer MMR
Kirton, Harold Ernest, Signalman RNVR
Lamb, David Bathie, 6881TS, 22 yrs, Trimmer RNR
Leabon. Archie Gordon, 18271DA, Second Hand RNR
Long, Arthur James, 20446DA, 18 yrs, Deck Hand RNR
MacDonald, Donald, 25 yrs, Lieutenant RNR
MacKay, Alexander, 15475DA, 20 yrs, Deck Hand RNR
McLean, Alexander Murray, 3082SD 21 yrs, Deck Hd. RNR
McLeod, James Fowler, Cook MMR
Munn, John William Clyde, Z/4540, 21 yrs, Teleg. RNVR
Osborne, James Walter, 7051TS, 32 yrs, Trimmer RNR

Parrott, Charles Fennell, 19906DA 35 yrs, Deck Hand RNR
Paterson, James Knox, 30 yrs, Engineer Lieutenant RNR
Paul, Thomas Samuel, 723TS, 36 yrs, Trimmer RNR
Pender, Patrick 2656ST, 28 yrs, Trimmer RNR
Postlethwaite, John Matthew, SS/325, 32 yrs, Able Sn. RN
Price, James 2678,.ST Trimmer RNR
Redding, Herbert, 858TS, 35 yrs, Trimmer RNR
Reynolds, Arthur, 7447TS, Trimmer RNR
Richards, Francis Arthur, 2232ST, 37 yrs, Leading Trimmer RNR
Robson, James, 6084TS, 27 yrs, Trimmer RNR
Smith, Baden, J/79220, 18 yrs, Ordinary Seaman RN
Tocher, John, 2776ST, Leading Trimmer RNR
Wallen, John William, 48 yrs, Lieutenant RNVR
Wheatland, Arthur, 35 yrs Lieutenant RNVR
Williamson, Robert, 120927 35 yrs, Able Seaman RN
Woolfe, George 6137TS, 21 yrs, Trimmer RNR
Youll, Alfred John, 33 yrs, Assistant Steward MMR

SRN Vol. 1, p. 53 ; Mine Warfare Vessels, pp. 71–72 ; p. 18 ; CWGC ; Jarvis & Jarvis (1993), Vol. II ; Jarvis & Jarvis (1996), Vol. IV; KTB of SM *UB 67*.

Wrecksite

The wreck lies on a firm seabed of stone, gravel and sand in a general depth of 56 m (LAT). The wreck of this once graceful ship is broken in two, has totally collapsed down on itself, is well broken up and rather decayed. The main section runs from the bows to just aft of the engine room. The starboard side is virtually collapsed into the sandy bottom, while the port side stands around four metres high. Forward of the decks have all gone and it is possible to see sections of the ribs and keelson. The forward sheerwater is still in place and the gun and searchlight lie (or did so) on their sides. The bridge is one of the highest parts of the wreck and is handy to anchor to. When the wreck was first dived, the radio room was still easily recognisable as an open box, and ladders and brass railings were all in place, but this area has been showing signs of collapse. The boiler room is well open just aft of the bridge with both boilers still in place. The area on either side of the paddle boxes is intact, and in good visibility it is possible to see right across the wreck at its widest point. Behind the paddle boxes the wreck peters out with the stern section nowhere to be seen. Most of the remains of both paddle wheels are still in place except for the wood, which has long gone, but the brass parts are still there. The upper bridge area of the ship has now collapsed in a huge pile, but is still recognisable. The ship's bell identified the wreck in the 1990s. Anyone contemplating diving on this wreck should remember that it was a Royal Navy vessel and is classed as a war grave in remembrance of those brave and unfortunate men who died with it.

U 1274

Date of loss: 16 April 1945
Wreck: ☆☆☆☆
Depth: 63 m
Reference: 55 37'.028 N 001 25'.672 W
Location: 6.32 nm ESE of Longstone Lighthouse and 7.58 nm NE of Beadnell Point

Clockwise from left: Guns on U 1274 *(Author's collection)*

Emblem of U 1274

Type VIIC/41 Kriegsmarine U-boat U 995, *similar to* U 1274. *(Courtesy Kevin Belcher)*

U 1274 was a VIIC/41 ocean-going attack boat built by Vulkan Vegesack Werft, Bremen for the German navy. She was ordered on 13 June 1942 within the batch of U 1271-U 1279, and her keel was laid as Yard No. 69 on 21 June 1943. She was launched on 25 January 1944 and commissioned by Oblt.z.S. Fedor Kuscher on 1 March 1944. *Feldpost*: M 50 816.

The VIIC boat became the 'workhorse' submarine of the German navy during World War Two. The official tonnage of the original design, as of 22 March 1941, was 761.89 tons on the surface and 864.69 tons submerged. These figures may change to a very small degree with later modifications: the standard official figures given throughout the war were usually 769 tons and 871 tons. Boats from different yards may also have differed to a certain degree due to small design variations. The overall general dimensions were 67.1 m in length overall, 6.22 m in beam, with a 4.8-m draught and a height of 9.60 m around the conning tower. Two diesel/oil engines powered the two screws, originally designed in bronze, but a shortage of non-ferrous metals led to the use of steel screws during the war. Boats already ordered before the war were fitted either with engines manufactured by Maschinefabrik-Augsburg-Nürnberg (MAN) or by the Germaniawerft (GW). After the start of the war, other companies or yards manufactured these two diesels types under licence. Frontline experience soon showed the more rigid GW construction to be superior and new constructions were gradually fitted with GW-type diesels only. Both types were fitted with super-chargers and each developed 1400 hp at 475 revolutions per minute continuous power, while 495 revolutions maximum power for 30 minutes developed 1600 hp, giving a maximum surface speed of 17 knots. The boat had a calculated operational range of 9700 nm at ten knots, or 6500 nm at 12 knots, and carried a maximum fuel/oil capacity of 113 tons. For running submerged, two 62-cell lead/acid batteries/accumulators, usually manufactured by Accumulatoren-Fabrik-Aktiengesellschaft

The aging destroyer HMS Viceroy
(Author's collection)

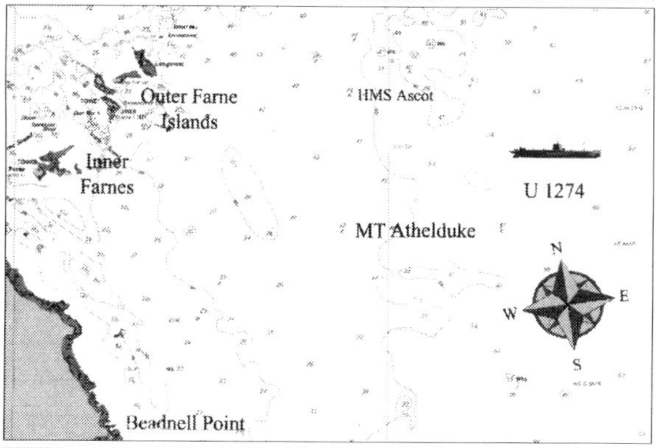

Diagram showing the positions of U 1274 *and* Atheldukе *(and HMS* Ascot*)*
(Author's collection)

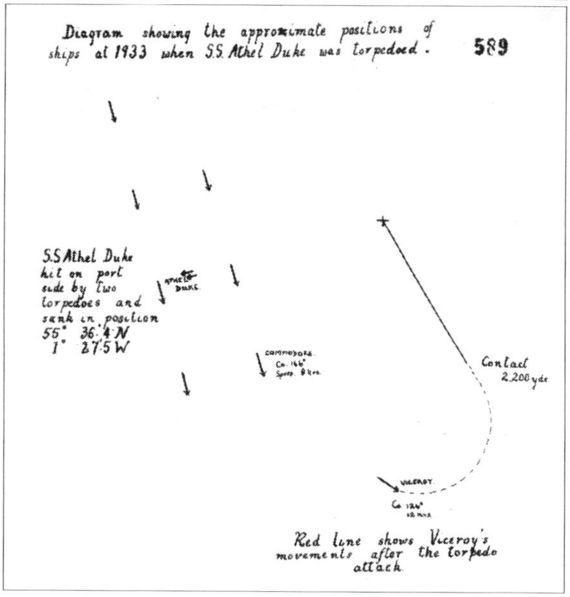

Original sketch drawn by HMS Viceroy's *commander showing the approximate positions of the ships at 1933hrs, when* Atheldukе *was torpedoed.*
(Crown copyright)

(AFA), powered the two electric motors which developed 375 hp at 295 revolutions and gave her a maximum speed of 7.6 knots. The four electric motor manufacturers were:

AEG (Allgemeine Elektrizitäts-Gesellschaft)
BBC (Brown, Boveri and Cie.)
GL u. Co (Garbe, Lohmeyer and Co)
SSW (Siemens-Schuckert-Werke)

These companies all produced motors of a very similar design, sometimes under licence (GL). Using battery power the boat had a calculated operational range underwater of 80 nm at a steady four knots.

The VIIC was designed with five torpedo tubes, four at the bow and one at the stern.

Fourteen torpedoes were carried until summer 1943, with two of them in the upper-deck reserve containers. These were subsequently removed to save weight and because it became too dangerous to reload them in North Atlantic waters. In 1944 the number was reduced to ten to increase living space in the bow room when the boats stayed submerged for long periods.

From autumn 1944 onward, on boats operating in the Atlantic or in British coastal waters, the ten torpedoes usually consisted of five T5 and five LuT, often stowed as follows:

T5 one in forward tube, three in forward bilges and one in aft tube. Five LuT stowed: three in forward tube, one in forward bilges and one in the aft bilges.

Mines were only carried on special order and,in exchange for torpedoes rather than in addition to them. The figures for mines offered in reference books are theoretical numbers and have little to do with operational realities. There were three different types of U-boat mines, delivered through the torpedo tubes:

TMA – moored floating mines, designed for, but never actually used on U-boats.

TMB – small ground mines with various fuses and an explosive charge of 1276 lbs (578.7 kg).

TMC – large ground mines with an explosive charge of 2200 lbs (997.9 kg).

The exchange ratios of mines / torpedoes were:

One torpedo – three TMB

One torpedo – two TMC

Initially, the VIIC gun specifications consisted of: one 88 mm (3.46 in.) deck gun, plus 220 rounds and one 20-mm (0.79-in.) AA flak gun, plus 4380 rounds of ammunition. On Atlantic boats the deck gun was removed in summer 1943. The single gun bandstand aft of the bridge (model 0) was modified in early 1943 by adding a second, lower bandstand with another single 20-mm gun (this was then called conning tower modification II). The Type I modification (two 13.2-mm twin machinegun mounts on the upper bandstand, a single 20-mm mount on the lower bandstand) was abandoned when test showed that the machine guns were not powerful enough. From May 1943, modification IV was introduced, showing at first two single 20-mm mounts on the widened upper bandstand and a quadruple 20-mm mount on the enlarged, lower bandstand. After 20-mm twin mounts became available in July 1943, they replaced the single mounts. From October 1943 onward, the 37-mm mount replaced the quadruple mounts. This represented the final variation of the Type IV conning tower modification. Later in the war, 37-mm twin mounts were tested experimentally on a few boats, but the snort had already reduced the threat from aircraft, by then. Apart from these standard AA-modifications on Atlantic boats, further experimental modifications were carried out on other boats but never became a standard form. Modifications were made to all frontline or working-up boats regardless of their date of commission and during yard layovers,. boats were continuously upgraded to the latest version.

The operational diving depth of a VIIC boat was 100 m (328 ft), with a maximum depth of 165 m (541.33 ft) and a crush depth of 200 m (656 ft). A crash dive to 20 m took an average of 30 seconds.

The VIIC/41 boat was the same in almost all respects as the VIIC, but was designed with a stronger pressure hull, which gave the boat an operational diving depth of 120 m (394 ft) and a crush depth of 250 m (820 ft). Both the VIIC and VIIC/41 boats carried between 44 and 52 crewmen. With increased AA-armament in 1943/1944, the crews were at their highest numbers. Following the introduction of the Schnorchel the crews were often reduced to 46–50 crewmen. Each Type VII U-boat carried 36 *Unteroffiziere* and ratings, generally two *Unteroffiziere* to every three ratings. Apart from the officers, the crew of a U-boat was divided between technical personnel and seamen. The technical division comprised specialist personnel; diesel machinists, electricians, radio operators and torpedo mechanics. There were four senior NCOs.

(The above technical details of the VIIC and VIIC/41 U-boats are the copyright and courtesy of Dr. Axel Niestlé of Dabendorf, Germany, who is a naval historian, author and a researcher).

U 1274 was assigned on 1 March 1944 to 8.U-Flotilla in Danzig as a training boat with Oblt.z.S. Fedor Kuscher as commander.

After having completed training in the Baltic Sea, *U 1274* formally joined 5.U-Flottille at Kiel for frontline operations on 1 March 1945. For her first voyage, *U 1274* left Kiel on 24 March 1945 and sailed to Horten (59° 22 29'N 10° 33 19'E) near Oslo in Norway, arriving there on the 27th.

Final patrol

U 1274 left Horten on 1 April 1945 bound for Kristiansand South, leaving there on 5 April. The next day, she was ordered to patrol off the east coast, the area from Fife Ness to Flamborough Head between grid squares AN 5110 and AN 5860. Passing through the east coast mine barrier would have presented no problem, as there were gaps, of which the Germans were aware, between Stonehaven abd Arbroath (Gap A), off Blyth (Gap B) and off Flamborough Head (Gap C). There were in any event no deep anti-submarine fields in the barrier for the length of *U 1274*'s patrol area and so she could have safely crossed at any point by diving beneath the mines.

At 1732 hrs (CT) on 16 April 1945, Fitting attacked the 8966-ton British motor tanker *Athelduke* (1928 – Athel Line Ltd. Liverpool) with two torpedoes, 5.75 miles SE of Longstone, in the Outer Farne Islands off Northumberland. The *Athelduke* was part of the 20-ship convoy FS.1784 (Methil – Southend) and was on passage

Fedor Kuscher was born in Trebus on 19 January 1919 and began his naval career in 1939. He served as Watch Officer with 34th Minesweeping Flotilla, 13th VP-Boat Flotilla and 22nd Minesweeping Flotilla before commencing U-boat training in March 1943. Kuscher was promoted to Oblt.z.S. (R) on January 1st 1944.

In early July 1944, Kuscher and the whole crew transferred onto the new Type XXI boat *U 3515* and *U 1274* was taken over by a fresh crew under Oblt.z.S. Hans-Hermann Fitting.

Fitting was born on 27 May 1920 in Stargard, Pomerania and began his naval career in 1939, doing his officer training between September 1939 and August 1940. He served with 23rd and 25th U-Flottille between May 1941 and March 1943 and was promoted to Oblt.z.S. on 1 October 1943.

from Port Everglades, Florida for Salt End (Kingston-upon-Hull) via Loch Ewe with 12 600 tons of molasses. The torpedoes detonated in the port-quarter, killing 23 year old William Alexander McKenzie, the fourth engineer officer. The 5224-ton British steamship *King Neptune* (1928 – King Line, Ltd. London) rescued the master, Captain Joseph Errett, forty-one crew and four DEMS gunners. Following the sinking, the ageing 1325-ton destroyer HMS *Viceroy* relentlessly pursued *U 1274*, the former First World War warship attacking the U-boat with depth charges 7.5 nm ESE of the Longstone.

Log of HMS *Viceroy*:

"Convoy FS.84 consisted of seven ships formed in two columns, three small ships being in the port column, and four larger ships in the starboard. Course: 1.66 degs. Speed: 8 knots.

Weather: wind light. Visibility good: 10 miles

HMS Viceroy was carrying out a broad zig-zag across the front of the convoy at twelve knots, and the other escort, HMS Woolston, was zig-zagging on the seaward quarter.

MT Athelduke, the second ship in the starboard column, was hit aft on the port side by two torpedoes. At this time, Viceroy was about one mile ahead of the Commodore and on his port bow, steering 126 degs.

Speed was increased to 18 knots and course altered to port. Three minutes later a good echo was picked up at 2200 yards, bearing 350 degs. Speed was reduced. The contact was classified as submarine with Moderate High Doppler and, at 1942½ hrs, an attack was carried out using 100- foot settings.

Range was opened and a second attack carried out ten minutes later using the same settings. This produced traces of oil.

The third attack was broken off during the later stages of the rim, the Operator picking up Hydrophone Effect from Woolston and losing contact and by this time the contact appeared to have no movement and was thought to have bottomed. The third attack was carried out at 2017, speed 15 knots, using 250 feet settings. The first charge of this pattern produced a distinctly prolonged explosion. The attack produced a smal, but steady flow of oil, a sample of which has been collected.

Viceroy's fourth and last attack was carried out at 2113 hrs.

SS Athelduke sank slowly in position 55° 36 04'N, 01° 27 05'W. The bows remained visible, bearing 249 degrees, 3200 yards from the contact. The bearing was checked each time the ship passed over the contact in the last three attacks.

The 30th Escort Group arrived in the area, and HMS Launceston Castle carried out a Squid attack on the contact at about 2157. Viceroy then set course to rejoin the convoy.

On returning to this wreck on 24 April, Viceroy again attacked and evidence including a bottle of brandy (made in Heilbron) was recovered.

Surface evidence 24 April:

German uniform, jacket trousers, pulped body parts, one crate German brandy, German currency notes, one German badge, leather wallet with German notes, leave passes, pages from German books.

Lt. Manners recommended for DSC. ASDIC op PO Mardin recommended for a decoration."

ADM 199/232; ADM 199/2148; AUD 810/45; NARA: Series T-1022, Roll 3900, PG31752; CWGC; IDNS, p. 151; Möltenort U-boat Memorial Foundation.

The bottle of brandy recovered was later presented to Winston Churchill.

The crewmen that died in *U 1274* were:

Balke, Hans Mash, Mt.
von Barlowen, Alexander, Leutnant zur See
Barnick, Klaus, Oblt.z.S.
Bellman, Werner, Masch.GFr.
Berek Ernst, Lt.Ing
Bier, Gerhardt, Mech.Gfr.
Blank, Harry, Masch.Mt.
Bojar Helmut, Bts.Mt.
Brehmer, Martin, Masch.Mt.
Briese, Otto, Ob.Masch.
Ebdorn, Friedrich, Flk.O.Gfr.
Ettinger, Jacob, Fk.Ogfr.
Fitting, Hans, Oblt.z.S. (Commander)
Fuchs, Werner, Mech.Mt.
Goldner, Erich, Masch.Gfr.
Grube, Ludwig, Mtr.Gfr.
Gurther, Heinrich, Masch.Gfr.
Holz, Bruno, Bts.Mt.
Kirchenhuber, Rdph, Flk.Ogfr.
Kirchmeier, Helmut, Flk.Ogfr.
Koppenhagen, Heinz, Masch.Gfr.
Langheinrich, Karl-Heinz, Masch Gfr
Lankamp, Heinz, Mtr.
Leschke, Walter, Mtr.
Ludwig, Fritz, Ob.Stm.
Lutjen, Heinrich, Masch.Gfr.
Miede, Heinrich, Leutnant zur See
Persicke, Reinhard, Fk.Ogfr.
Pillowski, Rudi, Mtr.
Potten, Hans, Masch.Gfr.
Schneider, Gottfried, Mtr.Gfr.
Schennegge, Heinz, Mtr.
Schwarzbach, Martin, Masch.Gfr.
Schweiselsen, Fritz, Flk.O.Gfr.
Stadele, Georg, Mt.Gfr.
Stenker, Gottfried, Masch.Gfr.
Stroble, Peter, Mtr.Gfr.
Tanzmann, Richard, Ob.Masch.
Tobe, Kurt, Masch.Gfr.
Warnicke, Karl, Masch.Mt.
Weiss, Richard, San.Mt.
Wende, Waldemar, Flk.Mt.
Zielke, Fritz, Mech.Gf

Wrecksite

The wreck of *U 1274* is reported to be standing upright on a clean, well-swept sand and stone seabed in a general depth of 63 m (LAT). It is still totally intact except for the stern end, which is very smashed up where it seems a number of the depth charges had exploded on, or close to the boat. The hatches are still sealed and the twin steel screws are there, with the marks of the maker embossed in them. The hull and conning tower have a covering of soft corals, but the conning tower is also draped with a trawl net. Anyone visiting this wreck should remember that it is a war grave and that entering the boat would not only be wrong but would also be a criminal offence.

GUDVEIG, EX ROBERT MÆRSK (?)

Date of loss: 25 January 1940
Wreck: ✯✯✯✯
Depth: 90 m
Reference: 55 37'.296 N 001 15'.580 W
Location: 11.92 nm ESE from Longstone Lighthouse

The *Gudveig* was a steel-hulled 1307-ton Norwegian steam cargo ship that measured 73.60 m in length, with an 11.04-m beam and a 4.95-m draught. Odense Staalskibsvft., Odense built and completed her as Yard No. 2 on 20 May 1920 and she was launched as *Robert Mærsk* on 20 December 1919 for Aktieselskabet Dampskibsselskabet Svendborg, in Svendborg, Denmark; P. M. Møller was the manager. A. P. Møller became the manager in 1925.

From 1935, Dampskipsselskapet Aktieselskapet Gudvin at Oslo in Norway was the registered owner and she was renamed *Gudveig*; H. Gjerpen was the manager.

The single steel screw was powered by a 106-nhp three-cylinder triple expansion steam engine that used one boiler and gave 9.5 knots. The cylinders measured 41.91 cm, 68.58 cm and 111.76 cm with a 76.2-cm stroke (16½ in., 27 in. and 44 in. with a 30-in. stroke). Flydk and Skbsv at Kjbnhavns in Norway manufactured the engine and ancillary machinery. She had one deck. The designated code recognition signal letters were: LJAR.

Final voyage

On 25 January 1940, the German submarine *U 19*, commanded by Kapitänleutnant Joachim Schepke, torpedoed and sank the *Gudveig* at 2130 hrs (CT). On the morning of 23 January, *U 19* had broken through the mine warning area off the Farne Islands at high speed and immediately found about 20 unescorted southbound ships from the Methil convoy HN.8. Of these, she sank the *Baltanglia* and the *Pluto*. After observing minesweepers in the area on 25 January, Schepke waited and later torpedoed the *Everene* and *Gudveig*, both of which were in another unescorted group, heading north for Methil to join a convoy bound for Norway.

The *Gudveig* had sailed from Bergen and on 9 January 1940 had joined the 38-ship convoy HN.7, sailing from Norwegian waters to Methil, arriving on 13 January. The *Gudveig* then travelled down to the Tyne where she loaded up with coal, intending to sail back to Bergen independently, but she sank in Kriegsmarine quadrant AN5186. Of her crew of eighteen, ten Norwegians and one Latvian were lost; three of the survivors being picked up by the 3782-ton Norwegian steamer *Dole* (1912 – Mrs. Z. Heinrichsons, Riga) and four by the 1114-ton Norwegian steamer *Vim* (1913 – AS Victor Müllers Rederi, Bergen); all the survivors were landed at Methil.

Six of the Norwegian crewmen that died on the *Gudveig* were:

Andriansen, Bredo, Steward
Andersen, Ellis, Able Seaman
Andersen, Rudolf, Chief Engineer
Beir, Augen, 2nd Engineer
Bjerke, Henry Olav, Seaman
Johannessen, Jens Aage, Mate

LCWLR 1939–45, p. 38; p. 72; LR 1938/9 No. 75344 (G).

Wrecksite

The wreck, possibly that of the Norwegian steamer, is orientated in a NE to SW direction. It lies on a seabed of fine sand in a general depth of 90 m (LAT). The wreck appears to be intact, is upright, with the superstructure still visible. It covers an area of 61 m in length by 16 m across and stands 6 m high. This should make an excellent boat-angling venue, as lots of fish can be detected on the echo sounder. If it is the *Gudveig*, the bell will be inscribed: *Robert Mærsk 1920.*

BRITANNIA

Date of Loss: 25 September 1915
Wreck: ★★
Depth: 6 m – 30 m
Reference: 55 37'.667 N 001 36'.219 W
Location: 3.05 nm NNE of Seahouses Harbour

Left: SS Britannia *circa 1910 (Author's collection)*

Right: The 717 ton Ipswich registered steam ship Helmsdale *the drove ashore at the NE corner of Crumstone Rock on 19 July 1939; she became a total loss and very little remains of the wreck today. (Author's collection)*

The *Britannia* (Official No. 91078) was an iron-hulled 727-ton steam passenger/cargo vessel that measured 64.10 m in length, with an 8.24-m beam and a 4.57-m draught. S. and H. Morton and Co. Leith built and completed her as Yard No. 46 in April 1885; she was launched on 28 February 1885 for the Leith, Hull and Hamburg Steam Packet Co. Ltd. Leith with J. Currie and Co. the manager. The single iron screw was powered by a 122-nhp two-cylinder compound steam engine that used two (OBS) single-ended boilers working at a pressure of 65 lb psi, with six corrugated furnaces, 6.50 sq.m (70 sq.ft) of grate surface and 197.88 sq.m (2130 sq.ft) of heating surface. The cylinders measured 76.2 cm and 132.08 cm with a 91.44-cm stroke (30 in. and 52 in. with a 36-in. stroke). S. and H. Morton and Co manufactured the machinery at Leith. She had two decks.

The *Britannia* left Leith for passage to Newcastle on the evening of 10 January 1891 with a general cargo and 43 passengers. At around 0330 hrs the next morning, she was involved in a collision off St Abb's Head with the steamer *Bear*; the incident happened in position 55 55'.360 N 002 07'.596 W and resulted in the loss of thirteen people. The *Bear* was a 593-ton cargo vessel built and completed by Raylton Dixon and Co. of Middlesbrough as yard number 137 in March 1877 for J. Watson and Co. of Middlesbrough; she was bound from Middlesbrough to Grangemouth with a dead-weight cargo of pig-iron. The *Britannia*, which had reversed her engines, struck the *Bear* amidships with her bow and the Middlesbrough vessel immediately began to founder. A boat was quickly lowered from the *Britannia* and while two men, the second mate A. J. Anderson and lamp trimmer A. Ireland, were rescued in an exhausted state, twelve other men went down with the ship. The weather was described as 'dark but clear', with a WSW force 5 wind blowing. David Wilson, the first mate on the *Britannia*, alleged that the helm of the *Bear* was put starboard to cross the bow of the Leith steamer, but two survivors from the *Bear* asserted that by blowing the whistle, they gave the *Britannia* warning that they were going starboard. By all accounts it appears that, on sighting each other, *Britannia* gave one single blast of her whistle to warn the *Bear* to port, while the latter gave two blasts indicating the *Britannia* to steer to starboard. The result was confusion between the crews and collision.

The *Britannia* had her bows stove in and water began to pour in, so the officers sent out distress signals, firing a number of rockets. Two vessels passed by without offering assistance, but the Carron Company steamer *Thames* of Grangemouth, which was *en route* to London, came to her aid. Given that the *Britannia* was in a poor condition, the 45 passengers were immediately transferred to the *Thames*, without a chance to gather together their belongings. A hawser was quickly passed beteen the two ships and the *Britannia* was towed slowly stern-foremost up the Firth, her crew remaining on board. Slowly, and with the utmost care, the towing proceeded until about 1500 hrs when the vessels were two miles to the west of Fidra Island. There, the hawser snapped and the *Britannia* foundered. Captain Robinson and the eight crewmen were thrown into the sea, but all, except for the captain, were wearing lifebelts. The Alloa tug *Yorkshire Lass* quickly arrived on the scene and succeeded in rescuing seven of the men including the captain, but sadly the chief engineer, David Ettershanks, was drowned.

The *Thames* and *Yorkshire Lass* returned to Leith Roads, where the 45 passengers were transferred from the *Thames* to the *Yorkshire Lass*, which, together with Captain Robinson, the two survivors from the *Bear* and the crew of the *Britannia*, sailed for Leith harbour. They arrived just after 1900 hrs and were taken to the Sailors' Home. It was later stated that when the vessels were opposite St Abb's Head, the officers of both vessels had observed the lights of the other ship and orders were given on each vessel in order to avoid a collision.

The *Britannia* was later salvaged, overhauled and put back into regular service.

Final voyage

On 25 September 1915, the *Britannia* was on passage from Newcastle upon Tyne for Leith with a general cargo when she ran aground in dense fog on the west side of one of the Farne Islands, the Callers Reef, and became a total loss. The *Forster Fawsett* from Seahouses, a self-righting 10.7-m oared lifeboat was launched at 0620 hrs and rescued seven of her crew of 19. Unfortunately, two men had already drowned, while the other ten had succeeded in getting ashore in one of the ship's boats.

Starke Schell Registers; Board of Trade Wreck Return World War I, p. 18; Morris (1995); *The History of Seahouses*. *The Times*: Monday, 27 September 1915, p. 12, Issue 40970; *The Times*: Monday, 12 January 1891, p. 7, p. 33219.

Wrecksite

The remains of the *Britannia* can be found on the sloping bank off the SW side of the third of the Callers islets, which is located just to the northwest of Crumstone. The wreck is now well broken up and dispersed on the steep, sloping reef, in depths ranging between 6 and 30 metres. The ship's engine lies partially buried in sand on the bottom, close to an upright boiler and condenser, in a gully at 6–10 m, while her iron screw and shaft is in an adjacent gully. The winch is further down in 23 m and the bows are some way out from the reef, ranging in depths of between 28 m and 30 m. The wreck itself is not much of a dive but the underwater scenery can be very interesting. The tidal streams are very strong on both flood and ebb, but a little worse on the ebb, especially near the bow section. Visibility varies greatly, but can be exceptional at times, reaching 15 m on neap tides during the summer months. The best time to dive this site is at low, slack water, (approx. 1½ to 1¾ hours after low slack water at Seahouses, depending on the size of tide) and when the Callers are showing above the surface.

ASSUAN, EX PTARMIGAN, EX GLANTON, EX GLANTON FIRTH

Date of loss: 17 October 1943
Wreck: ✯✯✯✯✯
Depth: 75 m
Reference: 55 38'.155 N 001 19'.810 W
Location: 9.48 nm E by S of Longstone Lighthouse

The *Assuan* (Official No. 142859) was a steel-hulled 499-ton Britsh steam cargo vessel that measured 49.17 m in length, with a 7.67-m beam and a 2.92-m draught. Ardrossan Dry Dock and Shipbuilding Co. Ltd. at Ardrossan built and completed her as Yard No. 307 in February 1920; she was launched as the *Glanton Firth* in January 1920 for Cheviot Coasters Ltd. Newcastle; G. T. Gillie and Co. was the manager. The single steel screw was powered by an aft-positioned 51-rhp, three-cylinder triple expansion steam engine that used one cylindrical multitubular steel boiler loaded to a pressure of 180 lbs psi and manufactured by Messrs. J. G. Kincaid and Co. Ltd. at Greenock in 1920, with three corrugated furnaces, 4.55 sq.m (49 sq.ft) of grate surface and 140.28 sq,m (1510 sq.ft) of heating surface. The cylinders measured 33.92 cm, 53.34 cm and 88.36 cm with a 60.96-cm stroke (13 in., 21 in. and 34 in. with a 24-inch stroke). Messrs Aitchison Blair Ltd. at Clydebank, Glasgow manufactured the engine and ancillary machinery. She had one deck, a well deck, three bulkheads cemented and a 29.98-m raised quarterdeck, a 2.7-m bridge deck and 6.4-m forecastle. She had some cellular double-bottom fore and the following main compartments: a forepeak, chain locker, crew space and a store room, a 26.21-m long cargo hold divided in the centre by a wooden bulkhead, the engine room, boiler room, a coal bunker and an after-peak. She was classed as 100 A1. The designated code recognition signal letters were: MJWC.

In 1920, she was renamed *Glanto*n by the same owners.

General Steam Navigation Co. Ltd. in London purchased and renamed her *Ptarmigan* in 1921.

From 16 January 1939, Gordonia Freighters Ltd. London was the registered owner and she was renamed *Assuan*; Mr. William Gillespie Gordon was the manager.

The normal crew was ten, including the master, but two DEMS gunners were carried in addition, making a total of twelve.

Final voyage

At about 1130 hrs on 17 October 1943, the *Assuan* left the loading berth at Lambton and Hetton Staiths at Sunderland for passage to Stromness with a cargo of coal and coke. The cargo included 426 tons and 10 cwt of Lambton house coal and 53 tons and 17 cwt of

Lambton large coke nuts. 283.9 tons of coal were stowed in No. 2 hold, 142.6 tons of coal were stowed in No. 1 hold, forward partly on top of the coke, which was stowed at the after end of No.1 hold. The coke was improperly loaded underneath the coal. However she sailed with a 5–6° list to port, with a considerable amount of water in one of the ballast tanks. As the vessel proceeded out to sea she had the wind, a fresh to strong breeze, about abeam on the starboard side. The list thereafter steadily increased and at about 1330 hrs water was entering the firemen's forecastle on the port side on the upper deck. The list continued to increase and at about 1400 hrs, several men left the forecastle and climbed aft along the starboard side of the ship towards the boats aft. The port lifeboat and rafts had been washed away and the men were unable to move the starboard boat, so they jumped into the water. According to the evidence, all the crew except the master were seen in the water at this time. After an interval, seven of the men swam back to the ship, which by this time had turned completely over, keel uppermost, and climbed on to the bottom. One of the boats then floated alongside and the four survivors scrambled on board. Shortly afterwards the vessel sank, east by south of Longstone lighthouse.

At around 1615 hrs (BST) the force of the wind had increased and by about 1700 hrs had reached its maximum force in a gust of a moderate gale at moderating and veering.

Her crew consisted of 12 men – the master, the mate, the two engineers, two able seamen, two deck hands, two firemen, one cook and one ordinary seaman. Eight of the men were lost, including the master, mate and both engineers.

LR 1942/3 No. 19752 (A); LCR 1943, p. 6; Starke Schell Registers; Board of Trade Wreck Report: *Assuan*, 1946 No. 7941.

Wrecksite

The wreck is orientated in an ESE to WNW direction and lies on a seabed of firm sand and gravel in a general depth of 75 m (LAT). It is upright, completely intact, standing 6.5 m high at the stern end, with the bows to the ESE and covered in a profusion of soft corals. The bridge structure at the stern is slightly collapsed, but apart from the mast, everything else is totally intact and in reasonable condition. The wreck covers an area 50 m long and by 11 m wide. If the bell is located, it should be inscribed: *Glanton Firth 1920.* This is an excellent if extremely deep wrecksite and will make a very good boat-angling venue.

AUCKLAND CASTLE

Date of loss: 24 August 1918
Wreck: ★★★
Depth: 53 m
Reference: 55 38'.777 N 001 30'.202 W
Location: 3.58 nm E of Longstone light, Outer Farne Islands

The *Auckland Castle* (Official No. 86358) was a 1,084-ton riveted iron-hulled steam cargo ship that measured: 68.58m in length, a 9.77m-beam and a 4.87m-draught. S. P. Austin & Son, at Wear Dock, Sunderland built and completed her as Yard No. 143 in August 1883; she

The 1,084-ton British steamer Auckland Castle *- circa 1910; built by S. P. Austin & Son, at Wear Dock, Sunderland in 1883; she was lost with 12 crewmen. (Courtesy of World Ship Society)*

was launched on August 21st 1883 for Mordey & Carney, at Newport. The single iron screw was powered by a 99hp, 2-cylinder compound steam engine that used one boiler. G. Clark of Sunderland manufactured the engine and ancillary machinery. She had one deck, a well deck, 4-bulkheads and a superstructure consisiting of a 26.8m-quarterdeck, a 14.6m-bridge-deck and a 7.9m-forecastle.

Mordey, Jones and Co. at Newport in Monmouthshire was the registered owner in 1890.

From 1910, Auckland Castle Steam Ship Co. Ltd. was the registered owner and Mordey, Jones and Co. was the manager.

Final voyage

On 24 August 1918, the defensively-armed *Auckland Castle* with D. Evans as captain was approaching the Farne Islands when she was hit by two torpedoes, fired without warning by the KDM minelaying submarine SMU *UC 59*, commanded by Oberlt.z.S.Walter Strasser. The steamer had left Hartlepool with 1133 tons of coal. on 23 August for a voyage to Moss in Norway. She sank in just three minutes, according to the chief officer, taking with her 12 of the crew, including the master, and confidential papers. The six survivors from her crew of 18 were picked up by an escort vessel and landed at Granton later that day.

The crewmen who died were:

Barker, Joseph, 28 yrs, Fireman and Trimmer MM
Chesney, Stephen, 22 yrs, Seaman MM
Evans, D., Master MM
Moore, Thomas McDonald, 25 yrs, Sailor MM
O'Donnell, M., 51 yrs, Able Seaman MM
Palmer, Sydney Harry, 23 yrs, Assistant Engineer MM
Poole, James, 70 yrs, Chief Engineer MM
Ryan, H., 29 yrs, Fireman and Trimmer MM
Reed, Sydney, 36 yrs, Fireman and Trimmer MM
Turner, William Thomas, 27 yrs, Steward MM
Upsan, Walter, 35 yrs, Able Seaman MM
Vaagbo, Johan, 17 yrs, Sailor MM

ADM 137/2964; CWLR 1914–18, p. 231; BVLS 1914–18, p. 96 ; p. 137 ; CWGC; Jarvis (2000), Vol. V.

Wrecksite

The wreck is orientated in a SSE to NNW direction. It sits in a half-metre scour, on a well-swept seabed of sand, gravel and shells in a general depth of 53 m (LAT). It stands 5.7 m high but is upside down, with the screw and rudder still attached and pointing skywards. The hull, which is covered in a myriad of soft corals, has now begun to crumble down and is showing signs of serious deterioration. Most of the bridge/wheelhouse structure is smashed up underneath the upturned hull, although broken sections of it are also strewn around on the brittle-starfish covered seabed. Further examination is required to ascertain whether the bow section is also upside down, because only the stern to amidships section has been dived on.

This, like many of the wrecks in this vicinity, has a good few trawl nets draped over it. Numerous large cod have been observed around the perimeter of the wreck, so she will make a useful addition to the boat-angling venues.

MERWEDE

Date of loss: 26 January 1918
Wreck: ★★★
Depth: 49 m
Reference: 55 38'.899 N 001 28'.891 W
Location: 4.31 nm E of Longstone Lighthouse and 7.44 nm NE of Beadnell Point

The *Merwede* was a steel-hulled 744-ton Netherlands steam cargo vessel that measured 54.86 m in length, with an 8.53-m beam and a 3.86-m draught. De Groot and Van Vliet, Slikkerveer built and completed her as Yard No. 67 in October 1917 for N.V. Scheepsexploitatie Mij. "Navis", Sliedrecht, in the Netherlands, who was the owner at the time of loss; H. K. Nederlof was the manager. The single steel screw was powered by an aft-positioned 83-nhp three-cylinder triple expansion steam engine that used one single-ended boiler and gave ten knots. The cylinders measured 38.1 cm, 63.5 cm and 101.6 cm with a 68.58-cm stroke (15 in., 25 in. and 40 in. with a 27-inch stroke). Y.V. van Capellen manufactured the engine and ancillary machinery at Bolnes in the Netherlands. She had one deck.

Final voyage

On 26 January 1918, the *Merwede*, on passage from Leith for Rotterdam with a cargo of coal, detonated a German-laid mine and sank in just six minutes, five miles east of Longstone lighthouse.

LCWLR 1914–18, p. 197; ANCL 1914–18, p. 68; Starke Schell Registers.

Wrecksite

The wreck, which is known locally as 'Gordon's Wreck', is orientated in a SSE to NNW direction and sits in a 2-metre scour with the bows to the north. It lies on a seabed of gravel and sand in a general depth of 49 m (LAT). The wreck appears intact, but is upside down and in two halves with a debris field between the two parts. It stands about 5 m high at the bow section and slopes down gradually into the seabed towards the stern. The superstructure has collapsed underneath the hull and there is a small section where access would probably be possible. A boiler was observed towards the stern and the whole wreck is a myriad of soft corals. Tidal streams are fairly strong and very few fish have been observed.

SAINT ANDRE

Date of loss: 28 October 1908
Wreck: ✯✯
Depth: 17–23 m
Reference: 55 37'.854 N 001 37'.258 W
Location: south side of Staple Island, Outer Farne Islands.

The *Saint André* (Official No. 1502) was a steel-hulled 1121-ton French steam cargo ship that measured 70.10 m in length, with a 9.06-m beam and a 4.19-m draught. Craig, Taylor and Co. of Stockton built and completed her as Yard No. 98 in November 1903; she was launched on 21 October 1903 for L. Larue, of Caen in France. The single steel screw was powered by a 900-ihp, three-cylinder triple expansion steam engine that used two Scotch-type boilers working at a pressure of 180 lb psi. North Eastern Marine Engineering Co. Ltd. manufactured the engine and ancillary machinery at Sunderland.

From 1908, Fernand Bouet of Caen was the registered owner.

Final voyage

On 28 October 1908, the *Saint André* stranded on Crumstone in dense fog. She was on passage from Caen for Grangemouth, carrying a crew of 16 and a cargo of iron ore. The vessel stood there for several days before being washed off and then drifted across to Staple Island, where she sank against the cliff face.

The Times: Friday, 30 October 1908, Page 19, Issue 38791; pp. 115–17; Starke Schell Registers; Board of Trade Wreck Return 1908, p. 109.

Wrecksite

The wreck lies at the base of the cliff face, half way along the southern end of Staple Island. It is orientated in an E to W direction and lies in depths of between 17 m and 23 m. It is totally collapsed, well broken up and rather decayed, with nothing but ribs, steel plates, framework and the boilers and broken engine remaining. There is very little to find in the way of artefacts but this is still a nice and very popular dive site during the summer months. The builder's nameplate, which was located in 1974, positively identified the wreck. It is sheltered from the main currents and it is possible to dive the site at most states of the tide, although the area is prone to a lot of backwash from the island during strong south and southeasterly winds.

CHRIS CHRISTENSEN

Date of loss: 16 February 1915
Wreck: ★★★
Depth 25–32 m
Reference: 55 38'.415 N 001 36'.210 W
Location: off S end of Longstone, Outer Farne Islands

The 1,461 ton Danish steamer Chris Christensen, *which was wrecked on the Longstone Rocks on 16 February 1915; photo circa 1910. (Courtesy of Selby Brown)*

The *Chris Christensen* was a steel-hulled 1461-ton Danish steam cargo ship that measured 76.25 m in length, with an 11.32-m beam and a 5.48-m draught. Flensburger Schiffbau Gesellschaft, Flensburg built and completed her as Yard No. 224 in June 1903 for Aktieselskab Dampskibsselskab Selsk. Vendila, Copenhagen; Svendsen and Christensen were the managers. The single steel screw was powered by a three-cylinder triple expansion steam engine that used two boilers and gave ten knots. Flensburger Schiffbau Ges., Flensburg, also manufactured the positioned engine and ancillary machinery. She had an amidships bridge, two holds forward and two holds aft.

Final voyage

On 16 February 1915, the *Chris Christensen* was in ballast, on passage from Aarhus via the Tyne for New York, when she stranded in heavy seas on Longstone Point in the Outer Farne Islands. The North Sunderland self-righting rowing lifeboat *Forster Fawsett* was launched at 0440 hrs and rescued the nineteen crewmen, completeing the mission and returning to Seahouses at 1830 hrs that evening. The stranding had torn a massive hole in the ship's bottom plates and she eventually slipped back and sank in deep water.

Board of Trade Wreck Return WW.1 1915 Page 16 (2) – 'The History of Seahouses Lifeboats' by Jeff Morris
Starke Schell Registers – IDNS Page 35

Wrecksite

The wreck is situated just off the southern corner of Longstone in the Outer Farne Islands. It is now well broken up and hardly recognisable as a ship these days, but still well worth a visit. Depths range between 27 m and 32 m depending on the tide, with the rudder and screw found at around 27 m, the latter being wedged upright in rocks and gravel. Not far away the decayed emergency steering helm still stands upright, or at least did so until recently. The shape of the wreck is easy to follow and it lies on a slope where many of the 'rocks' are in fact lumps of coal. It appears that the wreck broke in two, just forward of the wheelhouse, and that the starboard boiler rolled towards the centre. The port boiler stands upright, just a little forward of the starboard one, and the tubes are visible through a hole in the top where lobsters often shelter. The three-cylinder steam engine is reasonably intact but has fallen over to starboard and is located behind the starboard boiler. The lower section of the bow is standing upright from the seabed, while the rest of it, along with remnants of the forecastle, lie scattered to starboard. A couple of cargo winches, some pipes, a large and small anchor and an upside-down anchor winch are recognisable, although the winch is partially hidden beneath its mounting. A tightly-wound drum of cable can be seen.just behind the inverted port side of the bow section. Amazingly, an area of black-and-white tiled floor is also visible just inside the edge of the wreckage. The wreckage is covered in a colourful array of white and yellow dead man's fingers, a sure sign of very strong currents that sweep around the wrecksite.

ABESSINIA

Date of loss: 3 September 1921
Wreck: ★★★
Depth 10–17 m
Reference: 55 38'.947 N 001 36'.213 W
Location: SW side of Knivestone, Outer Farne Islands

The *Abessinia* was a steel-hulled 5753-ton four-masted German passenger-cargo steamer that measured 137.76 m in length, with a 15.89-m beam and an 8.53-m draught. Palmers' Ship Building and Iron Co. Ltd. Jarrow-on-Tyne built and completed her as Yard No. 746 in August 1900; she was launched on 16 June 1900 for the Hamburg-Amerika Line, Hamburg. The single screw was powered by a 642-hp, three-cylinder triple expansion steam engine that used three boilers and gave 11.5 knots. She also had two decks and seven bulkheads.

The *Abessinia*'s maiden voyage was spent acting as a troopship during the Boxer uprising in China. The ship also served as a supply collier to the KDM warship, SMS *Leipzig*.

In 1901, the steamer made her first merchant voyage from Hamburg to New Orleans.

When war broke out in 1914, the *Abessinia* was at anchor, sheltering in the Chilean port of Pisagua, and rather than return to Germany in 1918, the crew sabotaged the machinery.

In 1920, she was towed to Hamburg for repairs and delivery on reparations account.

Final voyage

On the morning of 3 September 1921, the *Abessinia*, commanded by Captain W. Schammert, was in ballast and *en route* from Hamburg to Leith for delivery when she stranded on the Knavestone Rock in the Outer Farne Islands, 0.39 nm NE of Longstone lighthouse. The weather conditions were fine and calm. Motor fishing boats from Seahouses went out to the scene, but assistance was refused and the ship soon became a total wreck. The crew abandoned the ship in their own boats.

LCR 1921, p. 7; LR 1920/1 No. 06328 (A); Starke Schell Registers.

Wrecksite

The wreck is orientated in a north to south direction, close to and parallel with the western side of the Knavestone Rocks in the Outer Farne Islands. The three battered broken boilers, two of which now lie on their sides, are almost up against the submerged western wall, on a sloping stony bank that eventually levels out at 18 m. The wreck is now totally collapsed in a jumble of large sections of double bottom plates, ribs, girders, lumps of hollow masts and broken machinery that extends all the way along to the giant submerged Seal Gut reef at the northwest end of Knavestone. If you look hard enough, there are still a few artefacts to be seen: brass valves, brass shell casings, the odd porthole and the huge winches, standing in about 15 m of water, still with heavy copper pipes attached to them. This is an excellent dive with lots of marine life to be seen, both swimming and crawling. There are strong tidal streams, with some nasty over-falls on a spring tide, making it quite dangerous for a small craft.

JAN VAN RYSWYCK, EX JOACHIM ZELCK, EX BALTIC SEA

Date of loss: 21 May 1924
Wreck: ★★★
Depth: 28 m
Reference: 55 39'.097 N 001 35'.965 W
Location: South side of the In Bus of Whirl Rocks, Outer Farne Islands

The *Jan van Ryswyck* (Official No. 125611) was a steel-hulled 2152-ton Belgian steam cargo ship that measured 87.47 m in length, with a 13.41-m beam and a 6.09-m draught. Craig, Taylor and Co. Ltd. at Stockton built and completed her as Yard No. 125 in August 1907; she was launched as the *Baltic Sea* on 25 July 1907 for Finland-London S.S. Co. Ltd. London; W. R. Medhurst was the manager. The single steel screw was powered by a 210-hp, three-cylinder triple expansion steam engine that used two single-ended boilers, giving 9.5 knots.

In 1911 she was sold to H. G. Harper and Co. London (Cardiff).

Dampfschiff Ges. "Joachim Zelck" m.b.H., Rostock in Germany purchased and renamed her *Joachim Zelck* in 1912; O. Zelck was the manager.

The Belgian Government, Régie de la Marine, Antwerp, Belgium owned her in 1919.

From 1922, La Maritime Belge, Antwerp, was the registered owner and she was renamed *Jan van Ryswyck*; F. Alexander fils et Cie was the manager.

Final voyage

During thick fog on 21 May 1924, the *Jan van Ryswyck* stranded on the treacherous In Bus reef, part of Whirl Rocks in the Outer Farne Islands. She was on passage from Antwerp for Grangemouth with a general cargo along with cast pig iron and steel ingots. The crew took to the boats and were eventually rescued and landed at Berwick later that day. The steamer broke its back and then broke into two halves, spilling her cargo all over the reef. The bow section soon disintegrated, but the stern half, which included the superstructure, engine and boilers, slipped back over the submerged cliff wall at the southern edge of the reef and down into deep water, where many of the remains can be seen today.

LCR 1924, p. 9 (g) ; IDNS, p. 85; *The Times*: Thursday, 22 May 1924, p. 28, Issue 43658.

Wrecksite

The ingots which were part of her cargo lie all over the top of the In Bus reef and fill many of the deep V-shaped gullies from top to bottom, along with the remains of the bow section, now shattered into a thousands pieces. Larger lumps of her hollow masts, steel plates, ribs and framework can be found at the base of a gully on the western side. The main stern section of the wreck lies at a depth of 28 m - 30 m and about 25 m away from the base of the cliff face, on the south side of high reef wall. Large lobsters can often be found sheltering in the boilers and various pieces of non-ferrous metal can be found lying around, while the site is made extremely interesting by the enormous diversity of marine life to be seen on the surrounding reefs and in deep gullies, along with the possibility of finding some long-hidden artefact from the many other vessels that have come to grief here. The reef walls on the south side also make a good boat-angling venue for large pollack during slack water and flood neap tides. The normal tidal streams are horrendous, on both flood and ebb, but especially so on Spring tides, when they can reach ten knots.

8

THE FARNE ISLANDS TO HOLY ISLAND

OTAGO, EX GERMANIA, EX IVANHOE, EX CARIB (?)

Date of loss: 10 June 1915
Wreck: ✯✯
Depth: 84 m
Reference: 55 40'.560 N 000 54'.816 W
Location: 23.69 nm E ¾ N of the Longstone Lighthouse

The *Otago* (Official No. 4344) was an iron-hulled 1437-ton Swedish steam cargo ship that measured 73.5 m in length, with a 10.23-m beam and a 4.97-m draught. Richardson, Duck and Co. at Thornaby, Stockton built and completed her as Yard No. 291 in October 1882; she was launched as the *Carib* (Official No. 84642) on 28 September 1882 for Anderson, Anderson and Co. at Stockton. The single iron screw was powered by a 145-nhp two-cylinder compound steam engine that used one double-ended boiler with four plain furnaces and 5.85 sq.m (63 sq.ft) of grate surface. The cylinders measured 73.66 cm and 139.7 cm with an 83.82-cm stroke (29 in. and 55 in. with a 33-in. stroke). T. Richardson and Sons manufactured the machinery at Hartlepool. She had one deck and a well deck.

In 1897, she was renamed *Ivanhoe* by new owners S.S. Ivanhoe Co. Ltd. Glasgow; Maclay and McIntyre was the manager.

In 1901, the new owners Memeler Dampfschiffs AG, Memel in Germany renamed her *Germania* and R. Schneider was the manager.

In 1904, she was renamed *Otago* (official number 4344) by her new registered owners, Handelsb. Sölvesborg Skeppsvarf Karlshamn, Sweden and J. Ingmansson was the manager.

From 1911, J. Ingmansson of Karlshamn, Sweden was the registered owner.

Final voyage

On 10 June 1915, the *Otago* was torpedoed and sunk without warning by Kapitänleutnant Constantin Kolbe in the KDM submarine SMU *U 19*, from the III.U-Bootflottille based at Wilhelmshaven. The steamer was voyaging from Hamsund, Sweden to Hull with a cargo of timber and sank about 20 miles E ¾ N of the Longstone light.

Starke Schell Registers; LCWLR 1914-1918, p. 16.

Wrecksite

The wreck, probably that of the *Otago*, is orientated in a NNE to SSW direction. It lies on a seabed of mud, fine sand and shells in a general depth of 84 m (LAT). The wreck appears to be intact but is collapsed, standing just over 2 m high and covering an area about 58 m long and 20 m wide. Lots of fish have been observed on the echo sounder over the top of her remains, which should make an excellent boat-angling venue. If this is the *Otago*, the bell will almost certainly be inscribed: *Carib 1882.*

EVERENE, EX LOUVAIN, EX LOUSIANA, EX BELLVIEW, EX STRATHYRE (?)

Date of loss: 25 January 1940
Wreck: ★★★★★
Depth: 83 m
Reference: 55 38'.838 N 000 50'.825 W
Location: 25.81 nm E of Longstone Lighthouse

The 4,434 ton Latvian steamer Everene, *which was torpedoed and sunk by Kapitänleutnant Joachim Schepke's Kriegsmarine submarine* U 19 *on 25 January 1940 (Courtesy of Rolf Kristensen and Stein-Erik Dagsland, Norway)*

The *Everene* (Official No. 121337) was a steel-hulled 4434-ton Latvian steam cargo ship that measured 112.77 m in length, with a 15.84-m beam and a 5.3-m draught. Grangemouth and Greenock Dockyard Co. at Cartsdyke built and completed her as Yard No. 273; she was launched as the *Strathyre* on 1 May 1906 for Strathyre S.S. Co. Ltd. Glasgow; Burrell and Son was the manager. The single steel screw was powered by a 353-nhp three-cylinder triple expansion steam engine that used three single-ended boilers working at a pressure of 180 lb psi, with nine corrugated furnaces, 18.48 sq.m (199 sq.ft) of grate surface and 511.89 sq.m (5510 sq,ft) of heating surface, which gave nine knots. The cylinders measured 63.5 cm, 104.14 cm and 172.72 cm with a 121.92-cm stroke (25 in., 41 in. and 68 in. with a 48-in. stroke). J. Kincaid and Co. of Greenock manufactured the engine and ancillary machinery. She had one steel deck, six bulkheads cemented, a spar deck and deep framing, a 7.6-m poop deck, a 28-m bridge deck and 12.5-m forecastle, plus some cellular double bottom, a 123-ton aft-peak tank and a deep tank of 610 tons fore.

Lloyd's classed her 100 A1. The designated code recognition signal letters were: YLFY.

The ship was seized at Emden in August 1914 and placed in the KDM Marine as a mine depot ship, based at Wilhelmshaven.

The title transferred from her owners to Newcastle War Risks Indemnity Associates Ltd. in 1915.

She was recovered in December 1918.

In 1919, she was renamed *Bellview* when sold to Hereford Shipping Co. Ltd. Hull; J. Bell and Co was the manager.

Late in 1919, she was renamed *Louisiana* by Fothergill and Nelson Ltd. Hull (London), who purchased her.

Fothergill and Co, Hull (London) became the registered owner in 1921

In 1921, she was sold to Cie. Transatlantique Belge, Antwerp, Belgium and Armement Deppe was the manager. The Belgian owners renamed her *Louvain* in 1923.

In 1926, Armement Deppe, S.A., Antwerp, Belgium became the registered owner.

From 1936, F. Grauds Shipping Co. Ltd. Riga, Latvia was the registered owner and she was renamed *Everene*.

Final voyage

At 2112 hrs on 25 January 1940, the *Everene* was hit aft with one G7a torpedo by the German submarine *U19*, commanded by Kapitänleutnant Joachim Schepke (Knight's Cross). She sank slowly by the stern in Kriegsmarine quadrant AN 5186. The steamer was sailing unescorted on passage from Blyth for Liepaja, but it is likely that she was intending to join a convoy at Methil before crossing the North Sea. Twelve people managed to get away in a lifeboat, while ten more had to cling to a life raft, but eight others were in the water with only lifejackets to help them stay afloat. One man was lost, but thirty survivors, all Latvian and including two women, were picked up by the *Everene*'s sister ship *Dole* (1912 – Mrs. Z. Heinrichsons, Riga) and the steam trawler *Evesham* and landed at a Scottish east coast port. During the rescue, some of the crew on the *Dole* distinctly saw a submarine, which quickly made off.

The *Everene* was the first Latvian ship to be lost during World War Two.

The *Dole* was requisitioned by the Germans in 1941 and renamed *Anke*. She was torpedoed and sunk by Norwegian Motor Torpedo Boats in Malangerfjord, Norway on 11 September 1943.

(See also the voyages of the *Baltanglia*, *Pluto*, and *Gudveig*)

LCWLR 1939–45, p. 38; Starke Schell Registers; LR 1930–1940.

Wrecksite

The wreck, which is possibly that of the Latvian ship, is orientated in a NNE to SSW direction. It lies on a seabed of mud, fine sand and shells in a general depth of 83 m (LAT). The ship was reported as having been sunk about five miles off the Longstone, but there is no wreck matching the size of the *Everene* anywhere near the Longstone. This is a massive wreck, which is reasonably intact and stands 13.5 m high. It covers an area 104 m long and 23 m across and has plenty of fish shoaling over the top of it, so it will make a very interesting boat-angling venue, although it is a fair way off shore.

JÆGERSBORG, EX HARROGATE (?)

Date of loss: 4 August 1916
Wreck: ★★★
Depth: 75 m
Reference: 55 41'.727 N 001 20'.966 W
Location: 10.02 nm NE of Longstone Lighthouse

The Danish steamer JÆGERSBORG *was scuttled using explosives by* UB 39, *12-miles NE of Longstone lighthouse. (Courtesy Thorbjørn Thaarup, cand. scient. Soc, Handels- og Søfartsmuseet på Kronborg)*

The *Jægersborg* (Official No. 86958) was an iron-hulled 1797-ton Danish steam cargo ship that measured 81.5 m in length, with a 10.79-m beam and a 5.96-m draught. E. Withy and Co. of West Hartlepool built and completed her as Yard No. 120 in August 1883; she was launched as the 1866-ton *Harrogate* on 6 June 1883 for T. S. Hudson of West Hartlepool. The single iron screw was powered by an 180-hp, two-cylinder compound steam engine that used one boiler. The cylinders measured 83.82 cm and 157.48 cm, with a 99.06-cm stroke (33 in. and 62 in. with a 39-in. stroke). She had one deck, four bulkheads and water ballast.

In 1886, F.I. Hudson was the registered owner and Surtees Jnr was the master.

Late in 1889 the registered owner was Gladstone and Cornforth, West Hartlepool and Captain Hasland was the master.

In 1896, she was renamed *Jægersborg* by new owners Dampsk. Selsk. af 1896, Copenhagen, Denmark, with C. K. Hansen the manager.

The registered owner was Dampsk. Selsk. Neptun from 1901 and C. K. Hansen was the manager.

Final voyage

On 4 August 1916, the KDM submarine SMU *UB 39*, commanded by Werner Fürbringer, captured the *Jægersborg* as she was voyaging, with Captain C.F. Matzen in command, from Narvik to Middlesbrough with magnetic iron ore. The crew was ordered to abandon ship and the steamer was scuttled using explosive charges, 12 miles NE of Longstone lighthouse;

Starke Schell Registers; LCWLR 1914–18, p. 51; LR 1914–15, No. 89 (J); ANCL 1914–18, p. 60; LR 1983–1900.

Wrecksite

The wreck, probably that of the Danish steamer, is orientated in an E to W direction. It lies on a seabed of fine sand, broken shells and gravel, in a general depth of 75 m (LAT). The wreck is very broken up and scattered but stands over 8 m high and covers an area 67 m in length and 29 m across. It has not been identified, but is in the same area where the ship sank. If it is the *Jægersborg*, the bell will be inscribed: *Harrogate 1883*.

AEPOS, ex TORKEL, ex UMAN (?)

Date of Loss: 25 December 1920
Wreck: ★★★★
Depth: 70 m
Reference: 55 42'.710 N 001 28'.731 W
Location: 5.97 nm NE from Longstone Lighthouse

The *Aepos* was an iron-hulled 630-ton steam cargo vessel that measured 51.86 m in length, with a 7.95-m beam and a 4.13-m draught. W. Lindbergs Warfs and Werkstads AB, Stockholm, Sweden built and completed her as Yard No. 89 in 1873 as a 493.75-ton schooner-rigged passenger/cargo steamer and she was launched as the *Uman* (Official No. 659) for Umans Ångbåtsbolag, Umeå, in northeast Sweden; E. Häggström, Umeå was the manager. The iron four-bladed screw was powered by a 100-nhp two-cylinder compound steam engine that used one boiler. W. Lindbergs manufactured the engine and ancillary machinery. The designated code recognition signal letters were: HKQG.

In 1876 she was registered to A. Grahn, Umeå.

In 1884 the owner was C. O. Scharins Söner, Umeå.

Umeå Nya Ångfartygs AB, Umeå was the registered owner in 1892.

On 6 June 1893 she was taken over by Umeå Nya Ångfartygs AB, Stockholm and a new boiler was fitted.

On 4 October 1900 the *Uman* ran aground on Renholmsgrundet, outside Umeå, and she was so badly damaged that she sank the following day.

In August 1901, the vessel was salvaged but at such high cost that the owners were forced to relinquish ownership of the vessel to the insurance company, who repaired and rebuilt her as a cargo ship.

On 29 August 1902, she was purchased by Johan Emil Löfgren of Umeå.

She was sold to Carl Georg Bayard of Stockholm on 27 July 1903.

In 1904 Ångfartygs AB Uman (Hjalmar Blomberg), Stockholm was the owner.

In 1905 she had the same owner but C. G. Bayard was the manager.

In 1916, the vessel was sold to Rederiaktiebolaget Uman in Stockholm

Nils Österman and Co. Stockholm was the registered owner in 1917.

Later in 1917 Claes Birger Below, Stockholm became the registered owner.

On 13 May 1918, Rederi AB Ivar, Stockholm purchased her.

Later that same day, 13 May 1918, she was taken over by Rederi AB Amazone, Stockholm and renamed *Torkel*. The company had tried to change the name to *Cerigo*, but the Swedish National Board of Trade would not allow it. T. Hillerström, Malmö was the manager.

On 27 March 1920, the *Torkel* was sold to Nicolas Pappalas and Collakis, Chios, Greece for £24 000 and renamed *Aepos*; Nicolas Pappalas was the owner at the time of loss.

Final voyage

On 25 December 1920, the *Aepos* was on passage with a cargo of iron from Rotterdam for Borrowstounness (Bo'ness) in the Firth of Forth, but sprang a leak 25 miles off the Longstone lighthouse in the Outer Farne Islands. The crew took to the lifeboat and abandoned their vessel, which was left drifting in a westerly direction, 15 miles east of Holy Island. The crew also reached Holy Island later that day.

The Times: Wednesday, 29 December 1920, p. 13 Issue 42604; Olsson (1996).

Wrecksite

The wreck, which is probably that of the *Aepos*, is orientated in a SSE to NNW direction with the bows to the NNW. It lies on a firm seabed of gravel, black shells, mud and fine sand in a general depth of 70 m (LAT). The wreck is upright and intact, standing over 6 m high and covering an area 51 m long and 7 m across. If the bell is located it should be inscribed: *Uman 1873*. Large numbers of fish have been observed over the top of the wreck.

SHADWAN

Date of Loss: 28 November 1888

Wreck: ✭✭

Depth: 14 m

Reference: 55 43'.212 N 000 51'.190 W

Location: 5.18 nm SE of Berwick Lighthouse and 1.96 nm NE of Goswick Tower

The *Shadwan* (Official No. 77013) was an iron-hulled 1538-ton schooner-rigged steam cargo ship that measured 78.02 m in length, with a 10.05-m beam and a 7.01-m draught. C. S. Swan and Co. at Wallsend built and completed her as Yard No. 31 in August 1877 for Watson and Pigg of London, with Captain Kennedy the master. The single iron screw was powered by a 150-nhp two-cylinder compound steam engine that used one boiler. The cylinders measured 78.74 cm and 147.32 cm, with a 76.2-cm stroke (31 in. and 58 in. with a 36-in. stroke). T. Clark manufactured the engine and ancillary machinery at Newcastle. She had one deck, five bulkheads, water ballast and an amidships bridge deck.

On 20 May 1879, the *Shadwan* had arrived at Plymouth with a cargo of maize from Sulina and at 0600 hrs on the 22nd was involved in an incident and grounded in the Channel outside the Great Western Docks, at what was supposedly high water. The ship was damaged, although no blame was attached to the steamer, but she was out of action for 45 days.

In 1880, Nelson, Donkin and Co. London was the owner and Captain Watson the master.

In 1881, she had the same owners with the Official No. 77012 and the designated code recognition signal letters were: RBNC.

At between 0100 hrs and 0200 hrs on 21 March 1881, the *Shadwan* was involved in a collision in the River Thames with the Russian schooner *Nora*. Both vessels were being towed by tugs; the *Shadwan* down the north side by the steam tugs *Contest* and *Lioness*. The owners of the Russian schooner took legal action against the steamer's owner Nelson, Donkin and Co. but the court found in favour of the *Shadwan*, because the tug towing the *Nora* had not taken proper precautions.

The bell off the 1,538 ton Duncan & Co steamer Shadwan, *built in 1877. (Author's collection)*

From 1886, the registered owner was Duncan and Co. and Captain John Willis was the master until she was wrecked.

The *Shadwan* crossed the Atlantic a number of times and also visited many European and Mediterranean ports on her voyages. On 27 July 1888, the *Shadwan* had arrived at Greenock following a voyage from Barcelona to Pretoria, according to Lloyd's Shipping Intelligence.

Final voyage

In mid November 1888, the *Shadwan* took on a full cargo of wheat, barley and flour at Fiume (later to become Rijeka, Yugoslavia's largest port) for passage to Leith. The weather remained pleasant until she was approaching Berwick when a violent northeasterly gale developed. Huge eight-metre breaking waves pounded the ship and Captain Willis must have known he would have trouble reaching the shelter of the Firth of Forth. On 28 November 1888, the red-funnelled steamer was driven into shallow water and was dismasted and lying beam-ends to the sea when her flag of distress was seen off Berwick. The steam trawler *Sir George Elliot* went to her assistance, along with a steamship which was travelling south. The crew of the stricken ship were observed on deck. It was intended, if possible to take her to the Tyne, but she foundered. Local newspapers claimed that the crew was rescued and the stricken ship then plundered.

American Lloyd's Register of American and Foreign Shipping, 1857–1900; Miramar Ship Index; *The Times*: Thursday, 29 November 1888, p. 8, Issue 32556; Starke Schell Registers.

Wrecksite

The wreck is orientated in an ENE to WSW direction, with the bow to the ENE. It is upright but totally broken up and largely buried, covering an area 31 m in length by 7 m across, with the highest part standing no more than 1.8 m and surrounded by large reefs. The starboard side is collapsed outwards, while the port side is collapsed inwards. The single boiler is well broken up on its side, next to the engine, which also lies over on its side. A four-bladed screw is also visible amongst the wreckage. In August 2003 the wreck was identified when the ship's bell was recovered, and soon after that came the discovery of the supporting legs of the steering binnacle: three beautiful bronze dolphins in an arched position.

ACANTHA

Date of Loss: 5 April 1915
Wreck: ★★★
Depth: 79 m
Reference: 55 46'.005 N 001 00'.208 W
Location: 21.79 nm ENE of Longstone Lighthouse

The *Acantha* (Official No. 137015) was a steel-hulled 322-ton British steam trawler that measured 42.72 m in length, with an 8.22-m beam and a 3.81-m draught. Cochrane and Sons Ltd. of Selby built and completed her as Yard No. 621 in December 1914 and launched her on 21 October 1914 for Equitable Steam Fishing Co. Ltd. at Grimsby. The single steel screw was powered by an 88-nhp three-cylinder triple expansion steam engine that used one single-ended boiler. The cylinders measured 33.02 cm, 57.15 cm and 83.98 cm with a 66.04-cm stroke (13 in., 22½ in. and 37 in. with a 26-in. stroke). She had one deck, a 23.46-m quarterdeck and 6.09- m forecastle.

Final voyage

On 5 April 1915, the *Acantha* was on a return fishing voyage from Grimsby when she was captured 25 miles E by N of the Longstone by the KDM submarine SMU *U 10*, commanded by Kapitänleutnant Fritz Stuhr. The crew was ordered to abandon ship and she was sunk by a torpedo fired on the surface.

However, the London Times states that 'the submarine had been firing at the trawler without warning. The *Acantha* was struck below the water line and began taking in water. The crew took to the boats, but while they were launching the craft on the weather side, several shots were fired, but no one was hit. After the crew had taken to the small boats, the submarine crew continued to fire at them with rifles and several shots hit the sides, making holes in the gunwales. Then the submarine fired a torpedo at the trawler, which sank immediately with a loud explosion. The submarine then went south. Two hours later the *Acantha*'s crew of thirteen hands were picked up by the Swedish steamer *Tord* and landed at Blyth. Captain Pederson, master of the *Acantha* had reason to believe that the submarine was SMU *U 20*; she was painted white with her number painted out.' German records later showed it, in fact, to have been SMU *U 10*.

LCWLR 1914–18, p. 10; Miramar Ship Index; *The Times*: Wednesday, 7 April 1915, p. 5, Issue 40822.

Wrecksite

The wreck is orientated in a NE to SW (052/232) direction and lies on a firm seabed of mud, fine sand and broken shells in a general depth of 79 m (LAT). It is fairly intact but collapsed, standing over 5 m high and covering an area 43 m long and 16 m wide. The wreck should make an interesting boat-angling venue, as there are few reefs nearby to offer shelter for fish.

FLORENCE DOMBEY, EX WYRE (?)

Date of loss: 5 May 1933
Wreck: ★★★★
Depth: 75 m
Reference: 55 44'.030 N 001 33'.026 W
Location: 5.77 nm NNE of Longstone Lighthouse

The *Florence Dombey* (Official No. 109673) was a 182-ton British steam trawler that measured 35.17 m in length, with a 6.42-m beam and a 3.47-m draught. Smith's Dock Co. Ltd. at North Shields built and completed her as Yard No. 629 in April 1900; she was launched as the *Wyre* on 17 March 1900 for Wyre Steam Trawling Co. Ltd. at Fleetwood (FD.196) and M. Hudson managed her. The single steel screw was powered by a 52-rhp, three-cylinder triple expansion steam engine that used one boiler. The cylinders measured 31.75 cm, 50.8 cm and 81.28 cm with a 57.15-cm stroke (12½ in., 20 in. and 32 in. with a 22½-in.stroke). NE Marine Engineering Co. Ltd. manufactured the machinery at Sunderland. She was equipped with wireless and had one deck and three bulkheads. The designated code recognition signal letters were: RQTN.

In 1911, she was sold to M. Hudson and renamed *Florence Dombey.*

The trawler served with the Royal Navy as a boom defence vessel from 1915 to 1917, when she was requisitioned into the Fishery Reserve, then returned to the owner in September 1918. No Admiralty number was issued.

In 1920, she was sold to Aberdeen owner R. Milne (Port Reg. A.264) who owned her at the time of loss.

T.T. Irvin Jr was the registered owner in 1930.

From 1933 Mrs E. Irvin was the registered owner and T.T. Irvin was the manager.

Final voyage

Carrying a crew of ten under skipper Jack Hague, the *Florence Dombey* sailed from Aberdeen and after a brief stop at Granton, set course for the North Sea fishing grounds via the Longstone Light. Unfortunately however, the boat foundered about six miles north of Longstone lighthouse on 5 May 1933.

Mr Hague later said that at about 1700 hrs on Friday the chief engineer reported an inrush of water from the main bunker. After opening the hatch to the fish room the crew discovered that sea water had flooded in and was just a few feet below the deck; the chief engineer then immediately started the pumps. Mr Hague signalled to the 193 ton Aberdeen trawler *Arora* (1903: A Robertson), which was close-by and asked her skipper to stop. He then manoeuvred his trawler in towards the *Arora*, getting virtually alongside her. The chief engineer reported that the pumps were not coping and the water was by that time almost level with the furnaces. The skipper was afraid his vessel would sink under their feet, so he gave the order to abandon ship and told the men to jump across to the *Arora.* There was a heavy swell running and they had to watch for their chance to leap at the exact moment. The second engineer, who had been in his bunk and was still in his underclothes, launched himself safely on board the other trawler. The other men were in a similar situation and scrambled onto the vessel the best what they could and in just the clothes they stood in. The *Arora* landed the eleven rescued crewmen at Anstruther and they all returned to Aberdeen by rail on Saturday.

LCR 1933, p. 5 (b); *The Times*: Monday, 8 May 1933, p. 11, Issue 46438; Navires à Vapeur et à Moteur de Moins de 300 TX Chaluties & LR 1832-1933.

Wrecksite

The wreck, most probably that of the *Florence Dombey*, is orientated in an ENE to WSW direction, with the bows to the southwest. It lies on a seabed of mud, sand and shell in a general depth of 75 m (LAT). The wreck is upright and intact and stands over 7 m high, with numerous fish observed over the top of it, which should make it a decent boat-angling venue. If the bell is located, it should be inscribed: *Wyre 1900.*

MAYSTONE, EX EMPIRE WAPPING (?)

Date of loss: 18 October 1949
Wreck: ★★★★★
Depth: 84 m
Reference: 55 43'.379 N 001 35'.844 W
Location: 4.74 nm N by E of Longstone Lighthouse, Outer Farne Islands

The *Maystone* (Official No. 180364) was a steel-hulled 2025-ton British Icemaid class Empire steam cargo ship that measured 82.9 m in length, with a 12.19-m beam and a 52.3-m draught. Grangemouth Dockyard Co. Ltd. at Grangemouth built and completed her as Yard No. 461 in May 1945; she was launched as the *Empire Wapping* on 15 March 1945 for the Ministry of War Transport (MoWT). Grangemouth and Stone and Rolfe Ltd. was the manager. The single screw was powered by an aft-positioned, three-cylinder triple expansion steam engine that used two single-ended boilers. The cylinders measured 43.18 cm, 68.58 cm and 121.92 cm with a 91.44-cm stroke (17 in., 27 in. and 48 in. with a 36-in. stroke). North East Marine Engineering Co. Ltd. Newcastle-upon-Tyne manufactured the engine and ancillary machinery. She had a cruiser stern, one deck and an aft superstructure consisting of a 49.5-m quarterdeck and 7.9-m forecastle. The designated code recognition signal letters were: GLKD.

The registered owner from 1947 was Thomas Stone Shipping Co. Ltd. of Swansea, who renamed her *Maystone.*

Final voyage

During a gale early on the morning of 18 October 1949, the *Maystone* sank four miles east of the Longstone lighthouse, following a collision with the new aircraft carrier HMS *Albion.*

Four crewmen, the only survivors from her crew of 23, were taken on board the *Albion*. The *Maystone*, which was valued at £105 000, had left Methil late on the previous night with a cargo of coal for Deptford. One of the three tugs towing the *Albion* from the Tyne sent out an SOS message and the Holy Island lifeboat was dispatched to the scene. Over a period of eight hours and in very rough seas, she searched an area of about 50 square miles, but returned to harbour without finding anyone else. Aircraft also made a fruitless search.

The men lost, were:

Buttlgice, C. M., Fireman MM from Cardiff
Camillieri, F., Fireman MM from Cardiff
Crombie, C., First Mate MM from Stirlingshire
David, J., Chief Engineer MM from Porthcawl
Davidson, J. B., Cook MM from Glasgow
Ethill, J. C., 2nd Engineer MM from Boldon, Co Durham
Gills, G. C., MM from Glasgow
Haywood, J., Able Seaman MM from Grays, Essex
Houston, W. J., Able Seaman MM from Belfast
Kirkwood, J., Boatswain MM from Grangemouth
Lodrenis, Second Mate MM from Cardiff
McGurk, A., Steward MM from Carrickfergus
Ross, J., Deckhand MM from Co Antrim
Snoddes, H., Catering Boy MM from Belfast
Thomason, J., Able Seaman MM from Gravesend
Vella, P. P., Fireman MM from Cardiff
Wahtris, M., Able Seaman MM
Williams, J. H., Master MM from Penarth
Wilson, J., Catering Boy MM from Belfast

HMS *Albion* was holed near the stern, but continued on her journey to Rosyth. Later, off Eyemouth, she was carried eastward by the strong gale-force wind, which had veered west. In case the big ship foundered, tugs tried to take her into shallow water. One of the tugs became disabled off St Abb's Head when some wire wrapped around its screw shaft and the *Albion* continued to drift out to sea. During the afternoon, another tug was sent out from Rosyth and the destroyer HMS *St James* was ordered by the Commander-in-Chief Home Fleet to render assistance. The *Albion* ended up ten miles off St Abb's Head before the wind eased and two tugs were able to tow her to the Firth of Forth, where they arrived the next morning.

The *Albion*, which was a sister ship to HMS *Centaur*, one of the 18 200-ton Hermes class light fleet aircraft carriers, capable of carrying 50 aeroplanes. She had been lying in a berth off Jarrow-on-Tyne for two months prior to the incident, with little work being done on her. In August the previous year, the Admiralty had decided that the job of fitting her out would be resumed; she was to be taken to Rosyth naval yard for dry-docking before returning to Wallsend for final completion.

LCR 1949, p. 9; LR 1948/9 No. 67945 (M); Board of Trade Wreck Report 1949; *The Times*: Wednesday, 19 October 1949, p. 4, Issue 51516.

Wrecksite

The original co-ordinates were kindly supplied by the late Ian Douglas, skipper/owner of Sovereign Divers at Seahouses in 1998. The wreck, believed to be the *Maystone*, is orientated in a S to N direction. It lies on a firm seabed of shell, sand and stone, in a general depth of 84 m (LAT). It is intact but on its side and stands 7 m high, with much of her bridge structures still intact and covered in a profusion of soft corals. Adjacent to the hull, there is a large debris field. Most of her navigational equipment should still be in place, along probably with the ship's bell, which to the author's knowledge has never been recovered but will be inscribed: *Empire Wapping 1945*. The wreck will most certainly make an excellent boat-angling venue.

ISABELLA FOWLIE (?)

Date of loss: 10 July 1941
Wreck: ★★★★
Depth: 71 m
Reference: 55 44'.694 N 001 31'.715 W
Location: 6.62 nm NNE of Longstone light

The *Isabella Fowlie* (Official No. 129371) was a steel-hulled 196-ton British steam trawler that measured 35.1 m in length, with a 6.73-m beam and a 3.58-m draught. Hall, Russell and Co. of Aberdeen built and completed as Yard No. 501 in November 1911; she was launched on 8 November 1911 for W. F. Dawson, Aberdeen and registered as A.418. The single steel screw was powered by a 78-rhp three-cylinder triple expansion steam engine that used one single-ended boiler. The cylinders measured 30.48 cm, 50.8 cm and 86.36 cm with an 86.36-cm stroke (12 in., 20 in. and 34 in. with a 34-in. stroke). Hall, Russell and Co. manufactured the machinery.

She had one deck. The designated code recognition signal letters were: GPGM.

In July 1915, the *Isabella Fowlie* was requisitioned and converted to Admiralty Minesweeper No. 473; she was then armed with one 12-pounder gun and one six-pounder AA gun.

While serving on *Isabella Fowlie*, Chief Petty Officer William Alexander McHardy (147548) died on 20 November 1916.

On 21 October 1918, HMT *Isabella Fowlie* rescued the entire crew of the 2100-ton American steamer *Lake Borgne* (1918 – Naval Overseas Transportation Service, USA), which sank after striking a rock close to Mathieu Point near Brest (48° 26'N 04°50.40'W); she was in convoy and transporting coal from Penzance to Roscanval in France. The ship was based at Cardiff and had been making runs from Cardiff and Belfast to French ports.

The trawler was returned to its owner in 1920. Later in 1920, J. Graham and Sons at Hartlepool was the registered owner.

The owner at the time of loss was Hartness Steam Fishing Co. Ltd. Hartlepool, Port Reg. D.677; J. Graham and Sons was the manager.

Final voyage

On 10 July 1941, the *Isabella Fowlie* had left Hartlepool for a fishing voyage when aircraft of the Luftwaffe bombed her, reportedly seven miles ENE from Longstone lighthouse; three of her crew of nine were lost, including:

Roders, Henry, 60 yrs, Cook MM
Smith, Thomas Richard, 54 yrs, Chief Engineer MM

LCWLR 1939–45, p. 277; BVLS 1939–45, p. 59; LR 1940/1 No. 59304 (I); CWGC.

Wrecksite

The wreck, probably that of the *Isabella Fowlie*, sits in a half-metre scour at the stern and bows and is orientated in an E to W direction. It lies on a seabed of sand, mud and shells in a general depth of 71 m (LAT). The wreck is upright and intact with the bows facing west. The highest section stands 4.5 m from the seabed and the wreck covers an area 41 m long and 9 m across. High numbers of fish were observed on the echo sounder, so the site should make a decent boat-angling venue.

AULTON, EX ARDENZA, EX MELFORD, EX GIPSY

Date of loss: 23 March 1918
Wreck: ★★★
Depth: 60 m
Reference: 55 44'.857 N 001 45'.339 W
Location: 3.77 nm NNE of Emanuel Head, Holy Island

The *Aulton* (Official No. 102003) was a steel-hulled 634-ton British steam cargo vessel that measured 55.67 m in length, with an 8.43-m beam and 3.37-m draught. Richard Williamson and Son, Workington built and completed her as Yard No. 162 in October 1899; she was launched as the *Gipsy* on 7 September 1899 for Waterford S.S. Co. Ltd. Limerick. The single screw was powered by an aft-positioned 85-nhp three-cylinder triple expansion steam engine that used one boiler. Ross and Duncan at Glasgow manufactured the engine and ancillary machinery. She had one deck, a well deck, three bulkheads, a 28.6-m quarterdeck, a 3.3-m bridge deck and a 6.7-m forecastle.

In 1901, she was sold to Limerick S.S. Co. Ltd. Limerick

J. Stewart and Co. Glasgow purchased her in 1911.

In 1912, she was renamed *Melford* by Ford Shipping Co. Ltd. Glasgow who purchased her. Mann, MacNeal and Co. was the manager.

T. C. Steven, Glasgow purchased and renamed her *Ardenza* in 1914.

From 1915, Adam Brothers Ltd. Aberdeen (Newcastle) was the registered owner and she was renamed *Aulton.*

The steamer was then armed for defence in 1915/1916 with a deck-mounted 12-pounder (5.44-kilo shells) gun.

Final voyage

At 0620 hrs on 23 March 1918, the submerged KDM submarine SMU *UB 83*, commanded by Kapitänleutnant Günther Krause, torpedoed and sank the *Aulton*, nine miles SE by E ½ E of Berwick Harbour. The steamer had left Seaham Harbour at 2203 hrs the night before, with Captain W. Wright in charge, for passage to Aberdeen with 650 tons of coal. The torpedo detonated in the no. 2 hold and two of her crew of 15 were killed instantly, the survivors quickly abandoning ship. The *Aulton* sank five minutes after the explosion and took the ship's confidential papers down with it. The surviving crew were picked up by a patrol vessel shortly afterwards and landed at Berwick. The two crewmen that died were:

Buyers, Alexander Bisset, 22 yrs, Fireman MM
Young, Alexander, 30 yrs, Cook MM

ADM 137/2964; LCWLR 1914–18, p. 208; BVLS 1914–18, p. 85; CWGC

Wrecksite

The wreck is orientated in a NE to SW direction, with the bows to the SW. It lies on a seabed of mud, sand and shells in a general depth of 60 m (LAT). The wreck is upright and almost intact, but with a trail of debris extending 10 m from the stern. The wreckage stands 7.1 m high and covers an area 46 m in length by 8 m wide. The bell, if and when it is located, will almost certainly be inscribed: *Gypsy 1899*. Quite a lot of fish have been observed on a depth sounder, so it should make a good boat-angling venue, although nets cover much of the upper sections.

BOWLING, EX CLYDEMHOR

Date of loss: missing since 19 November 1939
Wreck: ★★★★★
Depth: 67 m
Reference: 55 43'.644 N 001 29'.060 W
Location: 5.56 nm NE of Longstone Lighthouse

The *Bowling* (Official No. 129523) was a steel-hulled 793-ton British steam cargo vessel that measured 60.7 m in length, with a 9.2-m beam and a 3.4-m draught. John Fullerton and Co. at Paisley built and completed her as Yard No. 216 in October 1910; she was launched as the *Clydemhor* on 8 September 1910 for Clydeside S.S. Co. Ltd. Glasgow and J. B. Couper was the manager. A single screw was powered by an aft-positioned 150-nhp three-cylinder triple expansion steam engine that used two single-ended boilers working at a pressure of 170 lbs psi with four plain furnaces, 7.24 sq.m (78 sq.ft) of grate surface and 250.46 sq.m (2696 sq.ft) of heating surface, giving ten knots. The cylinders measured 43.18 cm, 69.85 cm and 114.3 cm with an 83.82-cm stroke (17 in., 27½ in. and 45 in. with a 33-in. stroke). Ross and Duncan in Glasgow manufactured the engine and ancillary machinery. She had water ballast, one steel deck, three bulkheads cemented, a 36.88-m quarterdeck and a 10.97-m forecastle. She also had some cellular double bottom fore of 186 tons and a 79-ton fore-peak tank. Lloyd's classed her 100 A1. The designated code recognition signal letters were: HRSJ.

In 1913, she was renamed *Bowling* by new owners Rankine Line Ltd. Glasgow.

From September 1914 to February 1919 the Admiralty requisitioned her as an ammunition carrier.

From 1920, George Gibson and Co. Ltd. Glasgow (Leith) was the registered owner and fitted her with electric lighting. The designated code recognition signal letters were: MDKN.

Final voyage

Under the command of Captain James Scott, the *Bowling* sailed from Leith on 19 November 1939 and was posted as missing while carrying a general cargo on a voyage from Bo'ness to Antwerp. However, at 2328 hrs (CT) that same day, the *Bowling* was torpedoed and sunk by the Kriegsmarine submarine *U 13*, commanded by Kapitänleutnant Heinz Scheringer, at Kriegsmarine quandrant: AN 5183, about six miles NE of Longstone in the Outer Farne Islands. None of the crew of 13 survived.

Kptlt. Scheringer reported hitting a 'darkened' tanker carrying a full cargo of about 2000 tons What he took to be a tanker was in fact the SS *Bowling*, which was hit with one torpedo, causing a massive explosion in the fore-section. The ship broke in two and sank within 40 seconds. The 13 crewmen lost were:

Cameron, Alexander, Second Officer MM
Gilfallan, Peter, Fireman MM
Hutchison, James, Second Engineer MM
McDiarmid, Alexander, Ordinary Seaman MM
McTaggart, Walter, Donkeyman MM
Moran, W., Ordinary Seaman MM
O'Brien, John, Able Seaman MM
Scott, James, Master MM
Short, James Ian Swanney, Ordinary Seaman MM
Stark, Donald, Chief Engineer MM
Watson, William, Chief Officer MM
Young, Alfred, Fireman MM
Young, Thomas Fisher, Steward MM

KTB of *U 13*; Starke Schell Registers; Miramar Ship Index; CWGC; LR 1930–39.

Wrecksite

The wreck is orientated in a S by E to N by W direction. It lies on a seabed of gravel, pebbles, fine sand, mud and shells in a general depth of 67 m (LAT). The wreck is upright and largely intact, but with about 9 m of the bow section separated from the hull. It stands 5.8 m high and covers an area 46 m in length by 7 m across. Shoals of pout whiting swarm over the wrecksite and large numbers of big cod have also been observed.

FORTUNA, HM TRAWLER

HM Trawler
Date of loss: 3 April 1941
Wreck: ✯✯✯✯
Depth: 44 m
Reference: 55 45'.957'N 001 48'.367'W
Location: 4.68 n.m. N from Snipe Point, Holy Island

The *Fortuna* (Official No. 123567) was a steel hulled 259 ton steam trawler completed as Yard No. 108 on 8 May 1906 by Cook, Welton and Gemmell at Beverley. She was launched on 14 March 1906 for Alec L. Black at Grimsby and registered as Grimsby trawler GY.140. She measured 39.85 m in length, had a 6.70 m beam and a 3.55 m draught. The single steel screw was powered by a 70 rhp (63 nhp) three cylinder triple expansion steam engine that used one single boiler, two corrugated furnaces, 33 square feet of ground surface and 115 square feet of heat surface that gave her 10.75 knots. The cylinders measured: 31.75 cm, 55.88 cm and 88.9 cm with a 60.96 cm stroke (12.5 in, 22 in and 35 in with a 24 in stroke). C.D. Holmes and Company manufactured the machinery at Hull. She had one deck, four bulkheads cemented and a 20.72 m quarterdeck. The boat was also fitted with wireless and an echo sounding device. The designated code recognition signal letters were: MCLD.

On 16 June 1909 she was sold to South Western Steam Fishing Company Ltd. Grimsby. On 5 may 1913 Thomas W. Baskcomb of Grimsby purchased the boat. Spurn Steam Trawling Company, Grimsby bought her on 27 September 1915. She was sold to George F. Sleight of Grimsby on 29 November 1916.

The Admiralty requisitioned her into the Fishery Reserve in 1917 with Port Registration GY.1048 and she was armed with one three pounder; she was returned to the owner in 1919. On 28 November 1933 Dobson Ship Repair Company Ltd. of Grimsby acquired the boat. On 11 June 1940 the Admiralty requisitioned her for a second time, but as an auxiliary patrol vessel (APV) and she was armed with one forward facing six-pounder; Port Registration GY.140.

Final patrol

On 3 April 1941 HM Trawler *Fortuna* was on patrol off Berwick when aircraft of the Luftwaffe bombed and sank her; all of her crew was lost with the boat.

The 15 crewmen lost were:

Bruce, Adam H. M. Seaman, RNPS
Charlton, William T. M. Temporary Skipper, RNR
Feeney, Edward V. Stoker, RNPS
Foote, Samuel E. 2nd Hand, RNPS
Glyde, Lawrence E. Seaman, RNPS
Hall, George O. Stoker, RNPS
Harris, Ernest E. Ordinary Seaman, RNPS
Jones, Henry, Ordinary Seaman, RNPS
Nicholson, William E, Engineman, RNPS
Phillips, Sidney, Stoker, RNPS
Robson, Edward, Engineman, RNR
Smith, William J. Seaman, RNPS
Whyte, Gilbert, Seaman, RNPS
Winsor, Stanley G. Seaman, RNPS
Wright, Josiah V. Seaman, RNPS

CWGC - Thompson M. 1999 - Toghill G. 2004 - Miramar Ship Index

Wrecksite

The wreck is orientated in a SE to NW (135/315-degrees) direction. It lies on a seabed of mud, fine sand and gravel, in a general depth of 44 m (LAT). The wreck is intact and upright, standing 5.8 m high and covers an area of 42 m by 7 m across. The ship's bell was recovered a few years ago by a diver from Seahouses, which identified the wreck as that of HMT *Fortuna*. Fifteen men of the Royal Naval Patrol Service (RNPS) and Royal Navy Reserve (RNR) died on the vessel so the wreck is a war grave and should be respected as such. Lots of fish are attracted to the remains, which should make an excellent boat angling venue.

VENUS, EX FRI, EX SIF, EX SERANTES

Date of loss: 14 April 1917
Wreck: ★★★
Depth: 52 m
Reference: 55 48'.101 N 001 51'.711 W
Location: 4.70-n.m NE from Berwick

The *Venus* was a steel-hulled 715-ton Norwegian steam cargo vessel that measured 63.72 m in length, with an 8.68-m beam and a 4.11-m draught. A. Simey and Co. (John and Luke Crown) at Monkwearmouth, Sunderland built and completed her as Yard No. 40; she was

Painting of the 715 ton Norwegian steam cargo vessel Sif, *which was built and launched by A. Simey & Co., at Monkwearmouth, Sunderland as the schooner-rigged Serentes, later renamed* Fri *and then* Venus. *(Courtesy of Rolf Kristensen, Norway)*

launched as the schooner-rigged *Serantes* on 17 October 1872 for Johnson and Co. Newcastle-upon-Tyne. The single screw was powered by an aft-positioned 95-nhp two-cylinder compound steam engine that used one boiler. The cylinders measured 63.5 cm and 121.92 cm with a 76.2-cm stroke (25 in. and 48 in. with a 30-in. stroke). John Stewart in London manufactured the engine and ancillary machinery. She had one calked deck and four bulkheads. The designated code recognition signal letters were: JVFB.

In 1876, C.L. Limpricht, Newcastle upon Tyne was the registered owner.

The registered owner in 1877 was T. W. Bulman, Newcastle.

In 1878, G. Northwanger & Partners, Newcastle was the owner.

Nelson, Donkin and Co. Newcastle owned her in 1879.

T.W. Bulman, Newcastle was the registered owner in 1886.

In 1887, H.C.F. Hartman, Goole, purchased her.

Jacob R. Olsen, Bergen, Norway, with others, renamed her *Sif* after acquiring the vessel in October 1889.

She was sold to Aktieselskapet B. Stolt-Nielsen, Haugesund, Norway in October 1898 and renamed *Fri.*

In 1899, B. Stolt-Nielsen with others, Haugesund, Norway, owned the *Sif* (official number 624).

In 1900, the *Sif* (The designated code recognition signal letters were: JVBF) was owned by J. R. Olsen of Bergen.

In 1905 she was purchased by E. B. Aaby and renamed *Fri.*

In March 1906 E. B. Aaby, Dramman, Norway renamed her *Venus.*

In 1912, Aktieselskapet Dampskipsselskapet "Venus", Porsgrunn, Norway owned the vessel; Nils Olsen was the manager. The engine was then changed to a 102-nhp three-cylinder triple expansion steam engine.

Aktieselskapet Dampskipsselskapet "Venus", Porsgrunn, Norway owned the *Venus* in 1913, but Fred. Th. Beergh was the manager.

In October 1915, Aktieselskapet Vigdis, Skien, Norway acquired her and C.B. Nilesen was the manager.

In December 1915, Aktieselskapet Prompt, Holmestrand, Norway was the registered owner and A.Steen and A. Rafen was the manager.

In 1916, Aktieselskapet "Prompt", Axel Steen and Niels Rafen, Holmestrand was the registered owner.

From June.1916, Aktieselskapet "Venus", Kristiania, Norway was the owner and Ole Sørensen was the manager.

Final voyage

On 14 April 1917, the *Venus*, with Captain Fr. Fredriksen in charge, was carrying a cargo of coal from Blyth to Drammen when she detonated a German mine. The mine had been laid on 15 March 1917 by the KDM submarine SMU *UC 50*, commanded by Kapitänleutnant Rudolf Seuffer. The steamer sank very quickly, sucking down a number of the crew that were attempting to launch the lifeboats. Some of the men managed to get back up to the surface and stayed afloat by clinging to bits of wreckage. Unfortunately, only two men of the crew of 16 were still alive by the time a fishing boat appeared. The survivors were taken back to hospital in Berwick. The 14 men who died were:

Abrahamsen, Jacob, Sailor from Harstad
Andersen, Martin, Cook from Tønsberg
Anderson, Axel, Stoker from Sweden
Fredriksen, Fr., Master from Hvaler, Fredrikstad
Friberg, Joh, Second Engineer from Kristiania
Hansen, Hans, M. Stoker from Kristiania
Hanssen, Peder, Stoker from Kristiania
Johannesen, Eugen, First Mate from Fredrikstad
Johannesen, Kristen, Sailor from Tjøme
Johannesen, Pefer, First Cook from Tønsberg
Johannesen, Rolf, Sailor from Drammen
Marthinsen, Sigurd, Sailor from Drammen
Reif, David, Stoker from Sweden
Wahlqvist, P., First.Engineer from Kristiania

Maritime Accident Statements for Norwegian Ships Sunk in Wartime: 1814–1918; ANCL 1914–18, p. 105; LCWLR 1914–18, p. 117; LR 1915/16 No. 227 (V); Starke Schell Registers; American Lloyd's Register of American and Foreign Shipping, 1857–1900.

Wrecksite

The wreck sits in a half metre scour and is orientated in a NNE to SSW (012/192- degrees) direction. It lies on a seabed of mud, fine sand and shells, in a general depth of 55 m (LAT). The wreck is upright and reasonably intact, with the bows to the NNE and stands 6.9 m high. It covers an area of 50 m in length by 8 m wide and there is a debris field extending 12 m from the bows. Soft corals are well established on the highest parts of wreck. Shoals of fish are attracted to the wreck, especially bib, cod and the occasional big ling, making this wreck a worthy boat-angling venue. In 2005, divers from Seahouses recovered the ship's bell, which identified the wreck.

HAVLIDE, ex FERRUM

Date of loss: 16 March 1916
Wreck: ★
Depth: 45 m
Reference: 55 47'.417 N 001 52'.013 W
Location: 4.57 nm ENE from Berwick Lighthouse

The *Havlide* (Official No. 98529) was a steel-hulled 425-ton Norwegian steam cargo vessel that measured 47.37 m in length, with a 7.34-m beam, a 3.50-m registered depth and a 3.81-m moulded depth. Helsingørs Jernskibsvft. and Maskinbyg., Helsingør built and completed her as Yard No. 39 in July 1892; she was launched as the *Ferrum* in 1892 for G. E. Casebourne and Co. at West Hartlepool, where she was registered. The single steel screw was powered by an aft-positioned 55-rhp, three-cylinder triple expansion steam engine that used one boiler, giving 9.75 knots. The cylinders measured 31.75 cm, 50.16 cm and 83.82 cm with a 45.72-cm stroke (12½ in., 19¾ in. and 33 in. with an 18-in. stroke). The ship builders manufactured the machinery. She had one iron deck, a well deck, a 5.18-m quarterdeck, an 11.27-m bridge deck and a 5.18-m forecastle.

From 1898, AS Havlide, Skien, in Norway was the registered owner and she was renamed *Havlide*; Blakstad, Holta and Co. was the manager.

Final voyage

The *Havlide* sank following a collision off Berwick with HMS *torpedo boat 94* on 16 March 1917, while voyaging from the Tyne to Skien with coal; the whole crew was rescued. Both vessels were part of a convoy traveling from the Tyne to Lerwick.

Starke Schell Registers; American Lloyd's Register of American and Foreign Shipping, 1857–1900; Miramar Ship Index; *Maritime Accident Statements for Norwegian Ships Sunk in Wartime: 1814–1918.*

Wrecksite

The wreck is orientated in a N to S direction, with the bows to the S. It lies on a seabed of mud, fine sand and shell, in a general depth of 45 m (LAT). The wreck, which was identified by the bell, inscribed *Ferrum 1892*, is partially buried and very flat, apart from the fairly small boiler. There is a small winch towards the bow and the bow is still quite visible. The whole wrecksite covers an area 28 m long and 8 m across and stands no more than 2 m high.

GENOA, ex CENTURION

Date of loss: after 15 January 1912
Wreck: ★★★★
Depth: 68 m
Reference: 55 49'.033 N 001 50'.783 W
Location: 5.62 nm ENE of Berwick Lighthouse

The *Genoa* (official number 97525) was a steel-hulled 1942-ton British spur-deck type steam cargo ship that measured 84.25 m in length, with an 11.58-m beam and 4.88-m depth, with a moulded depth of 7.21 m. John Blumer and Co. at North Dock, Sunderland built and completed her as Yard No. 100 on 22 April 1890; she was launched as the schooner-rigged *Centurion* on 8 February 1890 for A. Robson and J. Blumer at Sunderland. The single steel screw was powered by a 170-nhp three-cylinder triple expansion steam engine that used two single-ended boilers, six ribbed furnaces and gave 9.5 knots. The cylinders measured 53.34 cm, 83.82 cm and 134.16 cm with a 106.68-cm stroke (21 in., 33 in. and 54 in. with a 42-in. stroke). Alley and McLellan manufactured the engine and ancillary machinery in Glasgow. She had four bulkheads, water ballast and web frames. The designated code recognition signal letters were: LRBJ. The vessel was valued at £10 000.

From 1893 to 1896, the master was Captain R. Watson, with Captain G.F. Mauldon taking over.

In 1898, she was registered to Robson and Spencer at Sunderland.

In 1900, she was renamed *Genoa* when sold to Messrs Bailey and Leetham Ltd. at Hull.

Messrs Thomas Wilson, Sons and Co. Ltd. Hull became the registered owners in 1903.

The ship had been used for the Mediterranean trade, but her last two voyages had been to Baltic ports.

Final voyage

On 8 January 1912, the *Genoa*, under the command of Captain Westcott, sailed from Hull on passage to Blyth, where she took on a cargo of coal. Two Blyth men, Able Seamen H. Olsen and J. Dillon both left the ship at Blyth and were replaced by W. Allen and J. Marchland. With her cargo on board, the steamer left the port on 15 January for the six-day voyage to Riga. Nothing more was ever heard or seen of the vessel until, about two weeks later, lifebuoys marked '*Genoa*, Hull', lifebelts marked 'T.W.S. and Co. Ltd.' and some hatches were reported as being washed up along the coast between Berwick-upon-Tweed and Holy Island.. Just after the ship had sailed, a dense fog had enveloped the English and Scottish eastern coasts, followed soon after by southeast and then easterly gale-force winds. The company presumed that she had been overwhelmed in mountainous seas off Berwick and posted her as missing on 6 March 1912. The master, Captain Westcott, was an experienced mariner and had been in charge of the ship for six years. The crewmen lost were:

Allen, W., Able Seaman MM from Montserrat
Anderson, C., Carpenter MM from Gothenburg
Ankin, W., Boatswain MM from Croydon
Brameld, C., Assistant Steward MM from Hull
Cousins, L., Able Seaman MM from Hull
Daley, W., Fireman MM from Hull
Drury, T., Steward MM from Barton
Dunley, Second Officer MM
Fawcett, J.L., Third Engineer MM from Hull
Garner, T.G., Donkeyman MM from Sutton Bridge
Goodwin, A., Able Seaman MM from Hull
Haller, E., Fireman MM from Hull
Johnson, C., Cook MM from Hull
Marchland, J., Able Seaman MM from Blyth
Newman, J., Fireman MM from Wisbech
Rawson, F.R., Second Engineer MM from Liverpool
Shaw, W.J., Second Mate MM from Hull
Stark, R., First Engineer MM from Glasgow
Stevens, H., Sailor MM from Poole
Westcott, Master MM
Wilkinson, C., Fireman MM from Hull
Wrigley, J., Fireman MM

L. Cousins replaced a man who left the ship at Hull

Able Seaman H. Stevens was a former RN Sailor on HMS *Russell* and C. Johnson was a former RN Sailor on HMS *Enchantress*.

The Times: Tuesday, 30 January 1912, p. 6, Issue 39808; Starke Schell Registers; Board of Trade Wreck Return: *Genoa*, 1912.

The London Times: Monday, 29 April 1912, p. 22.

Wrecksite

The wreck is orientated in an ENE to WSW direction. It lies on a firm seabed of mud, fine sand and black shells in a general depth of 68 m (LAT). The wreck appears to be upright and intact, with the bows to the SW and covered in various nets, many of which float up over the top of it. Plenty of fish appear to shoal over the top of the wreck, but the risk of losing tackle will not endear it to the boat-angling fraternity. The bell, if or when located, should be inscribed: *Centurion 1890.*

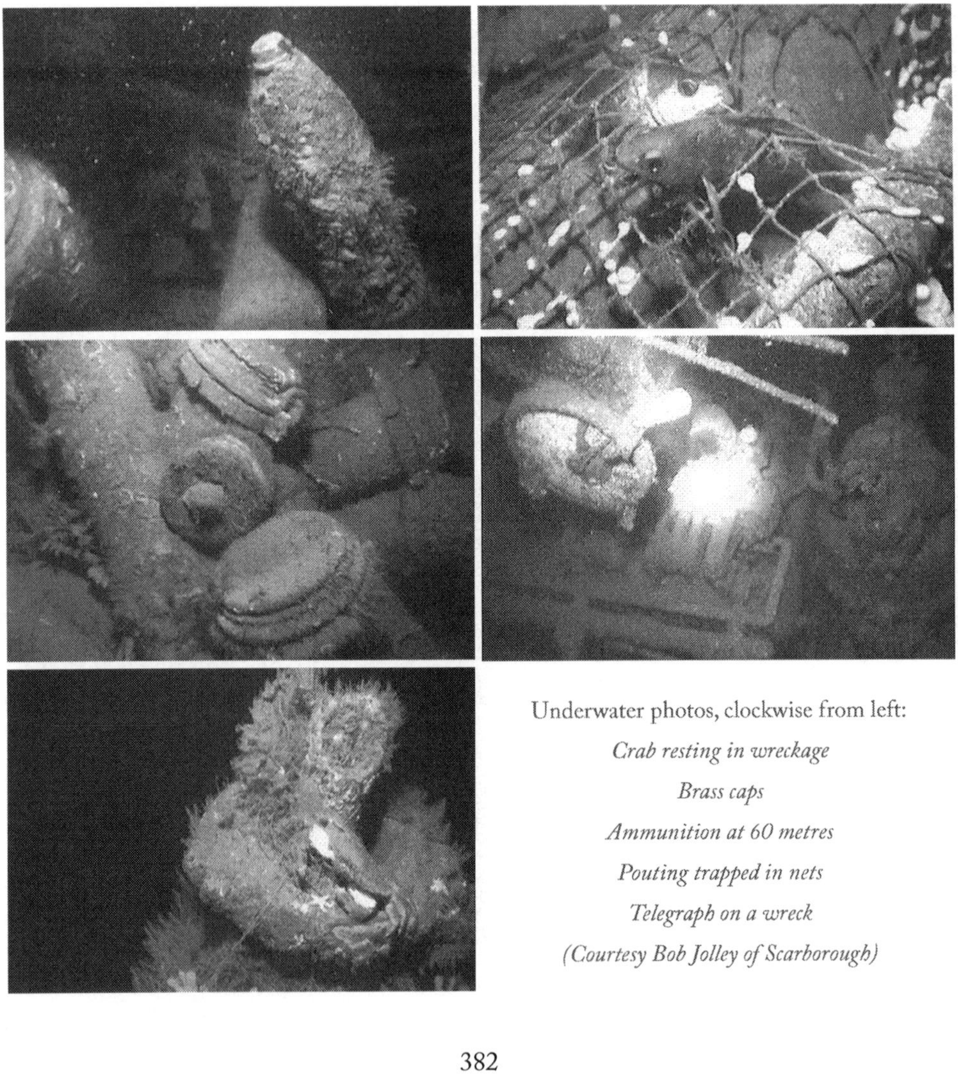

Underwater photos, clockwise from left:

Crab resting in wreckage

Brass caps

Ammunition at 60 metres

Pouting trapped in nets

Telegraph on a wreck

(Courtesy Bob Jolley of Scarborough)

BIBLIOGRAPHY AND SOURCES

American Lloyd's Register of American and Foreign Shipping, 1857–1900.
Lloyd's Confidential Index
Lloyd's Marine Collection

- Lloyd's Register of British and Foreign Shipping
- Lloyd's Register of Yachts
- Lloyd's List
- Lloyd's Shipping Index
- Lloyd's Weekly Casualty Reports
- Lloyd's Register Wreck Returns
- Lloyd's War Losses, First and Second World Wars
- Lloyd's Loss and Casualty Books
- Lloyd's Captains' Register

Lloyd's Register of Shipping
Lloyd's War Losses
The London *Times* archives.
Miramar Ship Index.
NLR Underwriters
Norwegian War Losses 1939–45:
(1) Sjøforklaringer for 2.verdenskrig - Maritime inquiries for the 2nd World War.
(2) Våre Falne - Our Fallen
Biographies of all Norwegians killed or lost at sea or land. Includes people that served on RNoN or allied vessels
(3) Krigsforliste Norske Skip 3 September 1939 - 8 Mai 1945 - published by Grondahl & Son for the Sjofartskontoret (Utgitt av Sjofartskontoret; Oslo 1 Kommisjon hos Grondahl & Son 1949).

Starke/Schell Registers 1873–1953.
Swedish Merchant Navy War Losses of the Years 1914-1920 (Report by the National Board. Stockholm 1921).
'Trial and Error' The Royal Navy and Mine Countermeasures, 1904–1914. Academic Papers on the Royal Navy by Len Barnett M.A.

Akermann, P. 2002. *Encyclopaedia of British Submarines*, Periscope Publishing Ltd. Penzance.
Baird, R. 1993. *Shipwrecks of the Forth*, Nekton Books, Glasgow.
Bendert, H. 2000. *Die UB-Boote der Kaiserlichen Marine 1914-1918*, - Verlag Mittler E.S. Mittler & Sohn GmbH. Hamburg, Berlin, Bonn.
Bendert, H. 2001. *Die UC-Boote der Kaiserlichen Marine 1914-1918*, Verlag Mittler E.S. Mittler & Sohn GmbH. Hamburg, Berlin, Bonn.
Busch, R & Röll, H.J. 1999. *German U-Boat Commanders of World War II*, Greenhill Books, London
Colledge, J.J. 1969. *Ships of the Royal Navy* (Vol. 1). David & Charles Ltd. Newton Abbot.
Colledge, J.J. 1987. *Ships of the Royal Navy* (Vol. 2). David & Charles Ltd. Newton Abbot.
Corbett & Newbolt, 1920. History of the Great War: Naval Operations 5-Volumes, Longmans.
Foynes, J.P. 1994. *The Battle of the East Coast (1939-1945)*, J. P. Foynes.
Godfrey, A. & Lassey, P.J. 1988 *Dive Yorkshire*, Underwater World Publications Ltd, Teddington.
Godfrey, A. & Lassey, P.J. 1974. *Shipwrecks of the Yorkshire Coast.* Dalesman Publishing Co. Ltd. Yorkshire.

Groner, E. *Die Deutschen Kriegsschiffe*, 2 Volumes, Lehmanns Verlag.
Groos, O. 1922. *Die Krieg in der NordZee*, Part of the *Der Krieg zur See, 1914–1918* series. E.S. Mittler, Berlin.
Hocking, C. 1969. *Dictionary of Disasters at Sea During the Age of Steam: Including Sailing Ships and Ships of War Lost in Action, 1824-1962*, Lloyd's Register, London.
Holt, S. 2004. *Shipwrecks of North East Norfolk*, Ayer Tikus Publications, West Walton.
Hool, J. & Nutter, K. 2003. *Damned Un-English Machines*, Tempus Publishing Ltd, Stroud.
Jarvis, S. & Jarvis D.B. 1993. *The Cross of Sacrifice Volume 1: Officers Who Died in the Service of British, Indian and East African Regiments and Corps 1914–1919*, Roberts Medals Ltd, Reading.
Jarvis, S & Jarvis, D.B. 1993. *The Cross of Sacrifice Volume 2: Officers Who Died in the Service of the Royal Navy, Royal Navy Reserve, Royal Navy Volunteer Reserve, Royal Marines, Royal Naval Air Service and Royal Air Force, 1914–1919*, Roberts Medals Ltd, Reading.
Jarvis, S & Jarvis, D.B. 1996. *The Cross of Sacrifice Volume 4: Non-commissioned Officers, Men and Women of the United Kingdom, Commonwealth and Empire Who Died in the Service of the Royal Navy, Royal Marines, Royal Naval Air Service, Royal Flying Corp and the Royal Air Force, 1914-1921, including the Commonwealth Navies and Air Forces*, Roberts Medals Ltd, Reading.
Jarvis, S. 2000. *The Cross of Sacrifice Volume 5: The Officers, Men and Women of the Merchant Navy and Mercantile Fleet Auxiliary 1914–1919*, The Naval & Military Press Ltd., Uckfield, East Sussex.
Jordan, R. 1999. *The World's Merchant Fleets 1939*, Naval Institute Press, Annapolis, Maryland.
Larn R. & B. 1997-2002. *Shipwreck Index of the British Isles*, 6 Volumes, Lloyd's Register, London.
Lloyd's of London. 1990. *Lloyd's War Losses: The First World War*, Lloyd's of London Press Ltd.
Lloyd's of London, 1989. *Lloyd's War Losses: The Second World War*, 2 Volumes, Lloyd's of London Press Ltd.
Magne, L. "Våre gamle skip" Sailing/Steamships from Haugesund area, Bjørkelund
McGee, B. 2008. *Ropner's Navy*, Cormorant Publishing, Hartlepool.
Moore, John, E. 2001 *Jane's Fighting Ships of World War 1*. Random House, London.
Morris, J. 1987. *The Story of the Staithes and Runswick Lifeboats*, Royal National Lifeboat Institution.
Morris, J. 1988 *The History of Seaham Lifeboats* (1856-1979) Royal National Lifeboat Institution.
Morris, J. 1994. *The History of the Cullercoats* Lifeboats, Royal National Lifeboat Institution.
Morris, J. 1995. *The History of the Seahouses Lifeboats*, Royal National Lifeboat Institution.
Morris, J. 1995. *The History of the Tynemouth Lifeboats*, Royal National Lifeboat Institution.
Office of Maritime Affairs, Oslo, Norway, Volume I-III 1917, Volume IV-V 1918 *Sjøforklaringer over Norske skibes Krigsforlis 1914-1918* (Maritime Accident Statements for Norwegian Ships Sunk in Wartime: 1914–1918, Kristiania)
Olsson, C.G. 1996. Svensk Kustsjöfart 1840-1940
Rohwer, J. 1999. *Axis Submarine Successes of World War Two*, Greenhill Books, London.
Rohwer, J. 1997. *Allied Submarine Attacks of World War Two*, Greenhill Books, London.
Rössler, E. 2001. *The U-Boat - Evolution and Technical History*, Cassell & Co. London.
Spindler, A. Konteradmiral, 1932-1966. *Der Krieg sur Zee: Der Handelskrieg mit U-booten* 5-Volumes. Mittler & Son.
Tarrant, V.E. 1989. *The U-Boat Offensive 1914-1945*, Arms and Armour Press, London.
Tennent, A.J. 1990. *British Merchant Ships Sunk by U-boats in the 1914–1918 War*, Starling Press, Newport.
Tennent, A.J. 2001. *British and Commonwealth Merchant Ship Losses to Axis Submarines 1939-1945*, Sutton Publishing Ltd, Stroud.
Ternström, John, Fritz 2001. *Memoirs of a Swedish Seafaring Family: A Narrative*, Ebor Press, York.
Thompson, M. 1999. *Cook, Welton and Gemmell: Shipbuilders of Hull and Beverley 1883–1963*, Hutton Press, Beverley.
Toghill, G. 2003. *Royal Navy Trawlers Part One: Admiralty Vessels*, Maritime Books, Cornwall.
Toghill, G. 2004. *Royal Navy Trawlers Part Two: Requisitioned Trawlers*, Maritime Books, Cornwall.
Young, J. 1988. *British Vessels Lost at Sea 1914–18*, Patrick Stephens Ltd, Wellingborough.
Young, J. 1988. *British Vessels Lost at Sea 1939–40*, Patrick Stephens Ltd, Wellingborough.
Young, R. 2003. *Shipwrecks of the East Coast*, 2 Volumes, Tempus Publishing Ltd, Stroud.
Young, R. 2002. *Shipwrecks of the North East Coast*, 2 Volumes, Tempus Publishing Ltd, Stroud.
Young, R. & Armstrong, P. 2006. *Silent Warriors, Submarine Wrecks of the United Kingdom*, Volume One, Tempus Publishing, Ltd, Stroud.

Websites used:

Aberdeen Built Ships Project:
http://www.aberdeenships.com

http://www.plimsoll.org/WrecksAndAccidents/wreckreports/default.asp
http://www.plimsollshipdata.org/
http://library.mysticseaport.org/initiative/VMSearch2.cfm
http://www.reach.net/~sc001198/Lloyds.htm
http://infotrac.london.galegroup.com/itweb/somelib

http://www.clydesite.co.uk/
http://www.ubootwaffe.net
http://www.warsailors.com
http://www.mariners-l.co.uk/WWI%20LOSSES%20INDEX.htm
http://www.battleships-cruisers.co.uk/naval_trawlers.htm
http://www.uboat.net
http://www.yorkshire-divers.co.uk/forums/
http://www.diverforum.co.uk
http://members.iinet.net.au/~eadej/homepage.html
http://www.multimap.com/index/NO1.htm
http://users.hunterlink.net.au/~maampo/militaer/glenn/marine/kaiserliche_marine_1914.htm
http://www.u-boot-net.de/
http://www.british-merchant-navy.co.uk/U-BOATS.htm
http://www.britsub.net/
http://web.ukonline.co.uk/chalcraft/sm/page6.html
http://www.dropbears.com/w/ww1subs/index.htm
http://www.usmm.org/ww1merchant.html
http://users.pandora.be/tree/wreck/wrecksite/wrecksite.html
http://www.gwpda.org/naval/sml00003.htm
http://www.dropbears.com/w/ww1subs/jclass.htm
http://www.rnsubmus.co.uk/losses.htm
http://www.cwgc.org/
http://www.gwpda.org/naval/n0000000.htm
http://www.royal-naval-reserve.co.uk/
http://www.cronab.demon.co.uk/wss.htm
http://www.harry-tates.org.uk/
http://www.world-war.co.uk/index.php3
http://www.hazegray.org/
http://www.feldgrau.com/
http://www.combinedfleet.com/ss.htm
http://www.usmm.org/ww1merchant.html
http://ubootwaffe.net/quadrant.cgi
http://tmg110.tripod.com/3reich1.htm
http://www.deutsche-marinesoldaten.de/lebenslaeufe/liste-ritterkreuztraeger-t-z.htm
http://www.ukdiving.co.uk/
http://www.2worldwar2.com/knights-cross.htm
www.uboat-memorial.org
http://www.aberdeenships.com/browse.asp
http://www.naval-history.net/xDKCas1914-08Aug.htm
http://www.grantontrawlers.com/
http://www.theshipslist.com/
http://www.mariners-l.co.uk/ON1.htm
http://www.southwestmafia.com/forumswm/forumdisplay.php?f=67
http://www.mariners-l.co.uk/WWI%20LOSSES%20INDEX.htm
http://www.battleships-cruisers.co.uk/naval_trawlers.htm
http://www.worldwar1atsea.net/WW1oFVLosses1914-16.htm

Möltenort U-boat Memorial Foundation

http://www.ubootehrenmal.de/en/index.htm

VESSEL INDEX

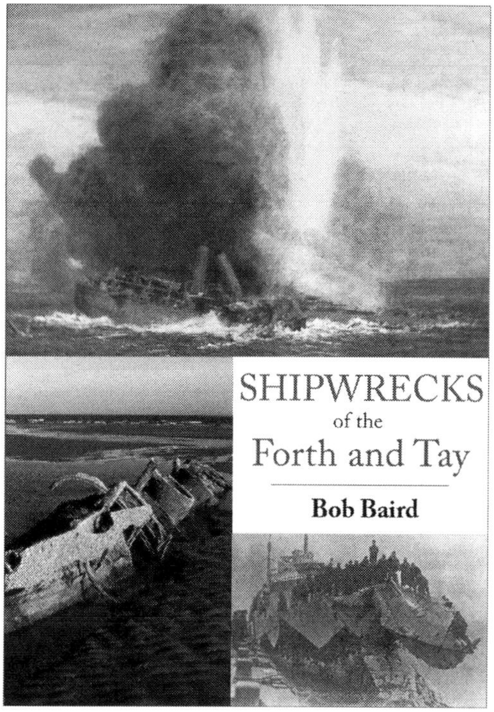

SHIPWRECKS OF THE FORTH AND TAY

Bob Baird

- ❖ **A wealth of detailed information without equal!**
- ❖ **Expanded and updated edition of a previous successful book**
- ❖ **Complemented with maps and charts, liberally illustrated with dramatic photographs**

This is a meticulously-researched reference guide to 300 shipping losses, and the events surrounding their sinking, off the coast of Scotland from Berwick-on-Tweed to the Forth and Tay, and northwards to Stonehaven.

It is a very much improved and updated edition of the successful previous edition, *Shipwrecks of the Forth*, and benefits hugely from the vast amount of vital new information gleaned by the author during 15 years of painstaking research.

- 'a triumph of research and dedication ... will prove to be an invaluable asset to all scuba divers and others who seek to learn more about these vessels and their history. ... I doubt a better book will ever be published and I congratulate the author on his attention to detail and painstaking research'. ***Sport Diver***
- '...will appeal to submarine buffs and all wreck divers ... contains masses of new information. ... Full of detail about the sinking, positions and what divers will see today, it is particularly strong on submarines'. ***DIVER***

ISBN 978-1904445-74-6 240 x 170mm 288pp liberally illustrated with b/w photos softback £18.99